Antarctic mineral exploitation

Studies in Polar Research
This series of publications reflects the growth of research activity in and about the polar regions, and provides a means of disseminating the results. Coverage is international and interdisciplinary: the books will be relatively short (about 200 pages), but fully illustrated. Most will be surveys of the present state of knowledge in a given subject rather than research reports, conference proceedings or collected papers. The scope of the series is wide and will include studies in all the biological, physical and social sciences.

Editorial Board
R. J. Adie, British Antarctic Survey, Cambridge
T. E. Armstrong (chairman), Scott Polar Research Institute, Cambridge
D. J. Drewry, Scott Polar Research Institute, Cambridge
B. Stonehouse, Scott Polar Research Institute, Cambridge
P. Wadhams, Scott Polar Research Institute, Cambridge
D. W. Walton, British Antarctic Survey, Cambridge
I. Whitaker, Department of Anthropology, Simon Fraser University, British Columbia

Antarctic mineral exploitation

the emerging legal framework

FRANCISCO ORREGO VICUÑA

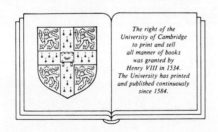

The right of the
University of Cambridge
to print and sell
all manner of books
was granted by
Henry VIII in 1534.
The University has printed
and published continuously
since 1584.

CAMBRIDGE UNIVERSITY PRESS

Cambridge

New York   New Rochelle   Melbourne   Sydney

Published by the Press Syndicate of the University of Cambridge
The Pitt Building, Trumpington Street, Cambridge CB2 1RP
32 East 57th Street, New York, NY 10022, USA
10 Stamford Road, Oakleigh, Melbourne 3166, Australia

First published 1988

Printed in Great Britain at the University Press, Cambridge

British Library cataloguing in publication data

Orrego Vicuña, Francisco
    Antarctic mineral exploitation: the emerging
    legal framework.
    1. Mineral industries – Antarctic Regions
    2. International Law   3. Mining Law
    I. Title
    341.7'62   K3486

Library of Congress cataloguing in publication data

Orrego Vicuña, Francisco.
    Antarctic mineral exploitation.
    Bibliography: p.
    1. Antarctic regions – International status.
    2. Mining law – Antarctic regions.   I. Title.
    JX4084.A5077   1988   341.2'09989   86-28392

ISBN 0 521 32383 5

Contents

Preface

Since the Antarctic Treaty was signed in 1959, co-operation in the Antarctic has been the subject of continuing evolution and rapid change. The negotiation and subsequent enactment of various regimes for the conservation and management of Antarctica's natural resources has been a particularly important cornerstone in this process of adaptation to, and regulation of, new activities in Antarctica. The aggregate of treaties, recommendations and other instruments and procedures which have come to be known as the Antarctic Treaty system, contribute today to an impressive body of emerging law which governs the activity of men in that continent and in the Southern Oceans.

The first part of this book examines the main characteristics of the international legal framework governing the co-operation of States in Antarctica, with particular reference to the problems of conservation of resources in the area, inquiring into the evolution of this process of co-operation at different stages of activity in Antarctica and the new problems and requirements which the system has had to address as a consequence of the changing conditions. The expansion of the system into new fields of co-operation has been a central feature of this evolutionary process, giving place not only to increased law-making by the Treaty parties but also to important institutional developments.

The key question which any Antarctic regime has had to face either directly or indirectly is that of the exercise of jurisdiction and the legal bases on which it could be founded. While the differing views existing on the issue of claims to sovereignty in the Antarctic continent and the relative uncertainty surrounding the exercise of jurisdiction in international law, whether on land or at sea, have made the answer to the above-mentioned question difficult, the system of Antarctic co-operation developed by the Treaty Parties has devised ingenious approaches to the matter. These approaches are also examined in the light of the existing law and the available practice, with particular reference to the existence of concurrent bases of jurisdiction and to the methods by which the system has managed to avoid potential conflicts in this context.

A new dimension of the jurisdictional problem has emerged with the development of the new Law of the Sea during and following the Third United Nations Conference on the Law of the Sea. The discussion about possible claims to a territorial sea in the Antarctic and the meaning of safeguarding rights in the high seas, which were paramount in the first years of co-operation under the 1959 Treaty, have today been supplemented by the question whether the concepts of the Exclusive Economic Zone, the Continental Shelf and other maritime zones are applicable to the Antarctic and if so what is their legal nature in the light of the legal and political realities of that continent. This set of problems is itself the subject of inquiry in relation to interpretation and application of the 1982 Convention on the Law of the Sea and the relevant developments of customary international law in the field.

Against the background of the legal framework of co-operation in the Antarctic, the regime for mineral resources is discussed in sufficient detail to identify the basic issues and interests which have to be accommodated in order to attain a convention which addresses this important area of potential Antarctic activity. The current negotiations and draft texts that have been prepared on the subject are examined in conjunction with the points of view of governments and authors in the context of their attempt to find solutions acceptable to the various interests represented in this effort. While the negotiating process has not yet been finalized, the essential elements of the regime and the position of the Consultative Parties on them have been made abundantly clear. This in turn has meant that to a large extent the range of options for a satisfactory settlement is already visible.

The specific rules and procedures which have been suggested for governing the activities of prospecting, exploring and developing mineral resources in the Antarctic are analysed in terms of their legal meaning and significance, together with such difficult questions as the criteria for access to the resources, the environmental standards, the granting of authorizations to initiate mining activities, the financial provisions, the area of application of the regime, the stability of contracts and the applicable law. In all of these matters the traditional approaches of international law are confronted with new challenges and the need in many cases to seek unprecedented solutions.

Given the different views on sovereignty and jurisdiction that have been mentioned above, the fundamental problem confronting the regime for mineral resources is who shall have the final authority for the granting of licences or approval of contracts and under what terms and conditions these could be issued. Various models and suggestions have been brought to the fore on this aspect, providing a wide range of options ranging from a territorial approach to a fully internationalized regime. It is on this point that the negotiators have had to make a particular effort to use their ingenuity to devise formulae which will satisfy the various interests at work. The careful distribution of competences that has been proposed to achieve this, the role of the proposed institutional machinery, the procedures for decision-making, the settlement of disputes and other factors central to this accommodation are discussed in successive sections of the book.

In view of the growing attention that Antarctica is attracting on the part of the world community at large, the accommodation of interests among the Consultative Parties is no longer the sole factor that will condition the achievement of a satisfactory settlement on the question of exploitation of mineral resources. The needs and interests of other parties to the Antarctic Treaty, of third States generally and of international organizations have become a consideration in the negotiation relevant to finalization of resource regimes in the area.

The important set of questions concerning these other interests is the subject of inquiry and research in the third part of the book, which discusses in particular the issue of expanded participation in the Antarctic Treaty system, the problems of international law posed by the eventual activity of third parties in the area and, most significantly, the meaning and prospects of the various initiatives that have taken place recently concerning the declaration of Antarctica as the common heritage of mankind and the more international organizational approaches that would ensue from adoption of a fully internationalized Antarctic regime.

 .The system of co-operation that applies today in Antarctica under the 1959 Treaty and related instruments has evolved a long way from the period of negative confrontation of competing claims and non-recognition of claims. The more positive approach of harmonizing interests within the framework of limited forms of internationalization has today become paramount in the Antarctic, the regime for mineral resources being the most recent and advanced example of this process. While sovereignty claims still have an important role to play in the context of this co-operation, it will be by means of their integration into the resources regimes in a way that will ensure their compatibility with other interests that have recently proved to be equally relevant. This important phenomenon is explored throughout the book.

The book covers the state of the law, State practice and developments in the negotiations, as well as in the relevant literature and documentation on the subject, up to September 1986, except where otherwise indicated.

Acknowledgement

The author wishes to express his gratitude to the staff of the following libraries where the research was conducted with their invaluable help and kind hospitality: Institute of Advanced Legal Studies of the University of London; Scott Polar Research Institute, Cambridge University; Royal Institute of International Affairs; London School of Economics and Political Science; Royal Geographical Society; British Library; Institute of International Studies of the University of Chile.

This book has developed from the PhD thesis researched by the author at the London School of Economics and Political Science, University of London; the author acknowledges with gratitude the useful suggestions received from Dr Patricia Birnie and Professor Rosalyn Higgins in the preparation of this work.

Abbreviations

A.F.A.R.   Australian Foreign Affairs Record
A.J.I.L.   American Journal of International Law
An. Fr. D.I.   Annuaire Francais de Droit International
Ann. Suisse D.I.   Annuaire Suisse de Droit International
Annals Air and S.L.   Annals of Air and Space Law
Ant. J.U.S.   Antarctic Journal of the United States
A.N.U.   Australian National University
A.S.I.L.   American Society of International Law
Aust. Quar.   The Australian Quarterly
Austr. L.J.   The Australian Law Journal
B.A.S.   British Antarctic Survey
B.I.I.C.L.   British Institute of International and Comparative Law
Bos. Coll. I.C.L.R.   Boston College International and Comparative Law
   Review
Bos. U.L.R.   Boston University Law Review
Brook. J.I.L.   Brooklyn Journal of International Law
B.Y.B.I.L.   British Yearbook of International Law
C.C.A.M.L.R.   Convention for the Conservation of Antarctic Marine Living
   Resources
C.I.A.   Central Intelligence Agency, U.S. Government
C.J.T.L.   Columbia Journal of Transnational Law
C.J.W.B.   The Columbia Journal of World Business
C.M.L.R.   Common Market Law Review
Cal. West. I.L.J.   California Western International Law Journal
Can. Y.B.I.L.   The Canadian Yearbook of International Law
Case W.R.J.I.L.   Case Western Reserve Journal of International Law
Comp. I.L.J. South Afr.   Comparative and International Law Journal of South-
   ern Africa
Conn. L. Rev.   Connecticut Law Review
Coop. and Confl.   Cooperation and Conflict

Corn. I.L.J.   Cornell International Law Journal
F.A.O.   Food and Agriculture Organization of the United Nations
For. Af.   Foreign Affairs
For. Pol.   Foreign Policy
G.A.T.T.   General Agreement on Tariffs and Trade
G.Y.I.L.   German Yearbook of International Law
Har. I.L.J.   Harvard International Law Journal
I.C.E.S.   International Council for the Exploration of the Sea
I.C.L.Q.   International and Comparative Law Quarterly
I.J.I.L.   The Indian Journal of International Law
I.L.M.   International Legal Materials
I.M.O.   International Maritime Organization
I.O.   International Organization
I.Y.B.I.A.   The Indian Yearbook of International Affairs
Int. Af.   International Affairs
Int. Conc.   International Conciliation
I.U.C.N.   International Union for the Conservation of Nature
J.A.G.Jour.   Judge Advocate General Journal
J.D.I.   Journal du Droit International
J.I.S.W.A.   Journal of Interamerican Studies and World Affairs
J. Int. Af.   Journal of International Affairs
J.I.L.   Journal of International Law
J.M.L.C.   Journal of Maritime Law and Commerce
J.W.T.L.   Journal of World Trade Law
J. Comp. Leg. I.L.   Journal of Comparative Legislation and International Law
Jap. An. I.L.   Japanese Annual of International Law
Law Pol. Int. Bus.   Law and Policy in International Business
M.T.S.J.   Marine Technology Society Journal
Mc. Gill L.J.   Mc Gill Law Journal
Mel. U.L.R.   Melbourne University Law Review
N.Z.I.R.   New Zealand International Review
N.Z.L.J.   New Zealand Law Journal
Nat. Res. J.   Natural Resources Journal
Ocean Dev. I.L.   Ocean Development and International Law
O.Z.F.O.R.   Osterreichische Zeitschrift fur Offentliches Recht
Phil. Trans. R. Soc. Lond.   Philosophical Transactions of the Royal Society, London
Pol. Rec.   Polar Record
Pol. Sci. Q.   Political Science Quarterly
Proc. A.S.I.L.   Proceedings of the American Society of International Law
R.B.D.I.   Revue Belge de Droit International
R.G.D.I.P.   Revue Générale de Droit International Public
R.I.A.A.   Reports of International Arbitral Awards
Rec. Cours Ac. D.I.   Recueil des Cours de l'Académie de Droit International

Rev. Hel. D.I.   Revue Hellenique de Droit International
Rev. Iran. Rel. Int.   Revue Iranienne de Relations Internationales
Riv. Studi Pol. Int.   Rivista di Studi Politici Internazionali
S.C.A.R.   Scientific Committee on Antarctic Research
S.C.L.Rev.   Southern California Law Review
S.I.   Statutory Instruments of the United Kingdom
San.D.L.R.   San Diego Law Review
Sci. Publ. Af.   Science and Public Affairs
S.I.P.R.I.   Stockholm International Peace Research Institute
Sov. Y.B.L.   Soviet Yearbook of International Law
Stan. J.I.L.   Stanford Journal of International Law
Sy. J.I.L.C.   Syracuse Journal of International Law and Commerce
U.B.C.L.R.   University of British Columbia Law Review
U.C.L.A.-Alas. L.R.   University of California Los Angeles, Alaska Law Review
U.C.L.A. L. Rev.   University of California Los Angeles Law Review
U.N.E.P.   United Nations Environment Programme
U.N.T.S.   United Nations Treaty Series
Univ. Mia. L. Rev.   University of Miami Law Review
U.N.I.T.A.R.   United Nations Institute for Training and Research
U.S. Nav. Int. Proc.   United States Naval Institute Proceedings
U.W.I.S.T.   University of Wales Institute of Science and Technology
Virg. J.I.L.   Virginia Journal of International Law
Virg. L.R.   Virginia Law Review
West. Ont. L.R.   Western Ontario Law Review
Wil. Quar.   The Wilson Quarterly
Wisc. L. Rev.   Wisconsin Law Review
Y.B.I.L.C.   Yearbook of the International Law Commission
Y.B.W.A.   Year Book of World Affairs
Y.L.J.   The Yale Law Journal
Z.A.O.R.V.   Zeitschrift für auslandisches öffentliches recht und volkerrecht

Part I

The international legal framework of Antarctic co-operation and the development of resources

1

The evolution of the system of Antarctic co-operation and the influence of the development of resources

1.1 Stages of development in the Antarctic

Man's presence in the Antarctic continent falls into a number of periods or stages which are well defined in terms both of the nature of the activities undertaken and of the corresponding legal and political requirements for the organization of human work in this territory.

The first of these stages was that of discovery and geographical exploration,[1] a period which has with considerable justification been termed the 'heroic' age of the development of the Antarctic;[2] then came the stage of scientific research[3] and, more recently, the stage of the utilization and exploration of the natural resources of the continent.[4] The first of these stages is now largely completed, at least as far as exploration of the traditional type is concerned. The second, however, is at present in process of development, taking a number of different forms. Indeed, it can be seen that the original emphasis on pure research has been gradually supplanted by a different emphasis, even more closely linked to resources-related applications.[5]

In the course of this development, the third of the stages mentioned has begun to emerge more clearly and can today be said to be the main topic of discussions on the Antarctic both between countries directly concerned in activities in that continent and within the scope of other forums of the international community.[6] What has occurred, therefore, is a progressive sequence of activities in the context of which a start has also been made on defining the legal and institutional regime regulating exploration for, and exploitation of, the resources of the continent and of the related marine areas.

Antarctic co-operation, on the one hand, and the arrangements that have been set up for administering resources policies, on the other, together constitute one of the aspects in which modern international law has seen major advances both in relation to its thematic content and in regard to the application of its concepts and principles to this new field.[7]

Given the evolution which has been referred to, and the sequence in which the various stages have occurred, it is not possible to explain the true nature or scope of a particular solution or approach without bearing in mind earlier events. In this sense, the processes of activity in the Antarctic are inter-related and cannot be segregated into watertight compartments. Whenever an attempt has been made to interpret the Antarctic in a compartmentalized way, the result has always been a static viewpoint which frequently leads to equivocal conclusions since it is incompatible with the eminently dynamic characteristics of those processes.

Legal and political effects of the various stages
The inter-relationship between these stages can be seen particularly clearly when it is seen in conjunction with their characteristic legal and political aspects at different points throughout history. Thus, for example, the emergence of territorial claims to the continent, on the one hand, and the position of countries that have reserved their rights or have refused to recognize such claims, on the other, is intimately bound up with the nature and results of geographical expeditions and other activities during the stage of discovery.[8]

National interests, whose content has been determined by these various positions, had a decisive influence on the development of Antarctic scientific research.[9] The latter, in its turn, contained the germ of the necessary international co-operation as the precondition of its own effectiveness which led to the setting up and consequent strengthening of the system of co-operation which has been the essential characteristic of the Antarctic process. For this reason, when the stage corresponding to the exploitation of resources began, its inspiration consistently came from the model of successful co-operation which had occurred earlier rather than from approaches associated exclusively with the national interest.

The complementary nature of sovereignty and Antarctic co-operation
The most important result of this interaction among and the reciprocal influence of the various interests involved has been that the inherent features of national sovereignty have never occurred in an absolute or pure form in the Antarctic but have always been combined with various procedures and forms of international co-operation.[10] In the last analysis, this phenomenon explains the unique characteristics of the Antarctic system. Even though, at certain periods, the passions of nationalism were

present in the Antarctic continent, this has never altered the essential features of the tendency we are describing.

This inter-relationship between sovereignty and international co-operation within the Antarctic framework also means that, far from being antagonistic or antithetical, they are, in fact, complementary processes with which it would be difficult to deal in an exclusive or isolated fashion. It can safely be said that, just as manifestations of sovereignty would be without effect unless there were simultaneously a high degree of inter-national co-operation, so the possible forms of co-operation would not achieve their real scope and significance if they did not rest in part on the presence of claims to sovereignty in the continent. From this point of view, it would seem that this is a new development in regard to the conflicting tendencies which often characterize the processes of co-operation, in the present-day international community.[11]

The territorial claims which have been asserted in this continent, as well as the other positions mentioned in regard to the reservation of rights or the non-recognition of sovereignty, when considered in conjunction with the rules introduced by the Antarctic Treaty of 1959, reveal an interesting development in recent decades within the system of Antarctic co-opera-tion. When one also adds to this the new dimension relating to the utilization of the Antarctic resources, additional needs for adaptation and understanding become apparent within the system. To the same extent, the organization of activities in Antarctica has required differing responses at various times, thus triggering the development of the particular international law governing it and also, where appropriate, of general international law. In the sections that follow an attempt will be made to identify the main aspects of this evolution.

1.2   Claims of sovereignty: the view of international law and the evolution of the Antarctic debate

From the time when the polar regions first came to the attention of international law in the early part of this century[12] they were the subject of substantial disagreement among authors. The principal questions at issue concerned the nature of the polar territories and, in particular, whether they constituted a type of *res nullius, res communis* or one of the other categories recognized in law.

In the course of these discussions a distinction gradually came to be drawn between the Arctic[13] and the Antarctic regions because, whereas the former consisted mainly of sea areas, the latter is typically a continen-tal territory. Although, from that time onwards, the legal regimes apply-ing to these regions have developed along separate lines, it is to be noticed that some degree of identity has been maintained in connection with certain problems and the answers suggested by international law; this is particularly evident in the case of natural resources and the related trend towards a measure of internationalization.

Antarctica as a form of international property

One interesting and perhaps symptomatic fact is that among the first authors to deal with the subject there was a noticeable tendency in favour of a type of international ownership of these regions and their resources. Balch, in noting that man would become established in the Antarctic in order to 'draw upon the mineral deposits', postulated that Greater and Lesser Antarctica should 'become common possessions of all of the family of nations'.[14] As Waldock correctly pointed out in his well-known article on sovereignty over the Falkland Islands, these and other positions were strongly influenced at that time by the example of the Svalbard case.[15] Balch referred to the latter as a 'joint possession of all mankind'.[16]

A. Pearce Higgins and other authors of the time took the view that the polar territories did not appear to be susceptible to acquisition by means of occupation.[17] Fauchille added the weight of his authority to the discussion, suggesting the internationalization of the polar resources in the following terms:

> As they are territories, the polar regions are susceptible of appropriation. But, as they are *frozen* territories, they are not truly habitable; they are merely exploitable. . . . Accordingly, the entire wealth of the poles belongs to all the states and it is for all of them to exploit it.[18]

Following the same line of thinking, Fauchille anticipated a number of initiatives which have now reappeared in the debate on the resources of the Antarctic: the formation of a company and the distribution of profits, the granting of a greater say in the administration and management of the task of exploitation to those that have participated in discovery and, interestingly, the possibility of dividing the system into regional units[19] which, as we shall see, is one of the bases of the present scheme for mineral resources.

The conditions for the exercise of sovereignty: the influence of decisions

A further group of authors, on the other hand, considered that the regions in question were susceptible to occupation and to the exercise of sovereignty in other ways. James Brown Scott, studying the situation of the Arctic in international law, reached the conclusion that it was a 'no man's land' unless it were to be occupied.[20] René Waultrin dedicated a large part of his pioneering studies on this subject to the discussion of the problem of polar sovereignty and the modalities for the acquisition of sovereignty under international law.[21] Smedal,[22] Waldock,[23] Gidel,[24] and others[25] also made important contributions in this field.

This second line of thinking ultimately prevailed in international law, as it was formulated during the first half of the twentieth century. A large number of studies were devoted during this period to the various ways of acquiring sovereignty under international law and to the application of sovereignty to the polar regions, with particular reference to the case of Antarctica.[26] Prominent among them was the question of historic titles, the effects of discovery and exploration, the requirements of occupation[27] and the variety of geographical criteria that had been developed in this context, such as continuity, contiguity and especially the theory of sectors as applied to the Arctic and the Antarctic.[28]

The most important contribution to international law in this respect was to be the decisions of the courts which were handed down in a period of only a few years between 1928 and 1933. The case of the *Island of Palmas*[29] clarified important issues relating to the requirements of occupation, as the *Clipperton Island* case[30] did in relation to the effects of symbolic annexation singling out the lasting nature of the effects of the original acts of acquisition even where authority has not been exercised in a positive way.[31]

Shortly afterwards, the case of the legal status of *Eastern Greenland*[32] was to complete this set of decisions, adding the authority of the opinion of the Permanent Court of International Justice. In this other case, Denmark's sovereignty was recognized in spite of the absence of a human settlement and the presence of Norwegian settlements at various periods.

Although two of the cases did not refer at all to polar territories and the third did so only in certain respects, the influence of the principles of international law which they embodied were to have an effect of the greatest importance on the treatment of the purely Antarctic question. On the basis of these decisions the intellectual and diplomatic debate would no longer be concerned so much with the admissibility or inadmissibility of claims to sovereignty but with the extent to which such claims were compatible or not with the requirements of international law. While the International Court of Justice has not had the opportunity to decide on issues of polar sovereignty, some of its decisions on different questions of state authority and occupation are of relevance in defining the state of international law in the matter. Examples of such contribution can be found in the case of *Minquiers and Ecrehos*[33] in regard to the emphasis that was put on the principle of effectiveness, or in the *North Sea Continental Shelf* cases[34] to the extent of their influence on the law of the continental shelf and the concept of natural prolongation.

The development of international law that took place in this field led influential authors of the time to reach a number of conclusions which remained definitive for a long period of time. Hyde stressed the concept of the requirement for the claimant to exercise the necessary control over its territory, although admitting that the requirements of international law might be mitigated in the polar regions.[35] Gidel, contradicting the thesis of Fauchille and other authors, postulated the principle that 'Any space in which human activities are carried out must be subject to a legal regime: if this were not so, anarchy would sooner or later prevail'; this legal regime was in his view none other than sovereignty.[36] Waldock, for his part, reached the conclusion:

> that the alleged impossibility of obtaining sovereignty by occupa-
> tion of polar lands on the ground of their uninhabitability is
> founded on a false legal premiss.[37]

1.3   Pre-eminence of Antarctic sovereignty and tendency towards conflict

National activities had begun to increase in the Antarctic region as the century moved along. Successive expeditions[38] were followed by various manifestations of economic activity, principally in connection with seal and whale hunting.[39]

As the legal, political and economic interest in the region took shape, it would not be long before territorial claims were vigorously asserted in various parts of the Antarctic continent.[40] The first British claim of 1908[41] was to be followed by similar acts on behalf of New Zealand and Australia, on the basis of which the national claims of the latter two countries were subsequently to be established.[42] More ambitious plans were also to be considered by the Imperial Conference of 1926;[43] there was also an early mutual recognition of Antarctic sovereignty among the member countries of the British Commonwealth of Nations.[44]

France[45] was to claim a sovereignty interest as a reaction to the imminent extensive claim of Australia, just as Norway was later so to do as a result of the claims envisaged by Germany.[46] Nor did these countries meet with any difficulty in having their positions recognized by the previously mentioned claimants, in spite of the fact that some serious questions were later to arise in regard to the delimitation of the French sector.[47]

Chile[48] and Argentina[49] for their part had had an interest in the

Antarctic region since the early days of their independence and this became particularly intense in the early twentieth century. The respective claims were to overlap to a considerable extent just as they overlapped with the British claim. In spite of the conflict of interest between the two South American countries they also managed to reach a mutual recognition of their respective claims in the Antarctic.[50]

Local and general conflicts

The strong emphasis on sovereignty in the Antarctic led inevitably to a tendency towards conflict, particularly in the context of the overlapping claims that have been mentioned. In the early 1950s this resulted in clashes between armed forces and other acts of force[51] which threatened not only the necessary harmony in the Antarctic but also the stability of peaceful relations in that continent.[52] The link between this problem and other territorial disputes, such as the one between Argentina and Great Britain in connection with sovereignty over the Falkland Islands or Islas Malvinas[53] or the conflict between Chile and Argentina in the case of the Beagle Channel and related maritime areas,[54] was to prove an additional complicating factor from then on, as it could well be again if there were to be a breakdown in the present system of co-operation in the Antarctic.

The controversy and potential conflict over the Antarctic peninsula was not to be the only one affecting the continent. The Second World War showed the potential usefulness of the region for military purposes[55] and at the same time prompted diplomatic measures to block any activities or claims by Germany and Japan. To take just one example, it may be mentioned that the Chilean decree of 1940 which specified the limits of the Antarctic claim was the direct result of an initiative by President Roosevelt.[56] Similarly, the inclusion of part of the Antarctic continent in the area of application of the Inter-American Treaty of Reciprocal Assistance had its origin in decisions related to the cold war and created a special legal relationship for Argentina, Chile and the United States, as the American countries actively involved in the Antarctic continent.[57]

The repercussions of the cold war also made themselves felt in the Antarctic, in the form of tensions and suspicions in regard to the possible intentions of the major powers. Several of the diplomatic initiatives and activities in the Antarctic undertaken by the United States in the 1940s are directly related to the confrontation of the cold war.[58] For its part, the Soviet Union, after a long period during which it was not involved in the Antarctic, placed its point of view on record in a memorandum of 1950: 'The Soviet Government cannot recognize as lawful any decision on the Antarctic regime taken without its participation'.[59]

Diversity of national positions

From that point onwards, the pattern of claims in the Antarctic became even more complicated since, in addition to the formal claims of sovereignty that have been mentioned, there was the special position of the United States[60] and the Soviet Union[61] both of which, without recognizing the claims of other nations, reserved their own rights as potential claimants. Even though it is doubtful, from the point of view of international law, that the effect of such a position could be maintained for a long period without the claim being made effective,[62] an important political fact thus became established which has had a significant influence on the characteristics of Antarctic co-operation and on the 1959 Treaty itself.

It is also important to bear in mind in this context that the United States and the Soviet Union actively considered the possibility of making an Antarctic claim.[63] In the case of the former, this took the form of various governmental studies and parliamentary initiatives.[64] The present unclaimed area lying between the sectors claimed respectively by Chile and New Zealand owes its existence to the purpose of facilitating an eventual claim by the United States.[65] An interesting diplomatic study made by Walter Sullivan lists the principal factors taken into account by the State Department in 1939 in its analysis of the possibility of an Antarctic claim. The list includes the following: (i) trans-Antarctic aviation; (ii) valuable mineral resources and fuels; (iii) strategic interest of the War and Navy Departments; (iv) measures taken by the Soviet Union and other governments to establish their own claims; and (v) the interest expressed by the governments of Germany and Japan in the intentions of the United States in regard to Antarctic claims.[66]

Notwithstanding the existence of a powerful political, strategic and economic interest, this initiative failed to materialize. At that time the United States conceived its Antarctic policy in a way that embraced the continent as a whole and certainly had no wish to become involved in the territorial conflicts of the Antarctic peninsula.[67] Similarly, the Soviet interest did not lead to the establishment of a claim of sovereignty.

Just as these two powers were at one time attracted by the idea of making such a claim, so Germany and Japan took an interest in the same possibility, although their aspirations were frustrated by the outcome of World War II.[68] It is also to be noted that Japan's renunciation of its Antarctic claim under the terms of the Peace Treaty with the United States has been interpreted by a Japanese author in a restrictive sense which would not affect claims based on activities subsequent to the date of that Treaty.[69]

Solutions based on co-operation

Even though the motive of the activity in the Antarctic during the ten years that followed the Second World War was set largely by national interest and the presence of actual or potential sovereignty claims, the needs of international co-operation never ceased to make their influence felt. This was particularly evident in the field of science which, as has already been said, implicitly contained the germ of co-operation.

In this sense the conflicts to which this situation gave rise had both a negative and a positive aspect. The former is clearly exemplified by the tensions and confrontations which occurred and which created an environment in which any judicial resolution of the disputes was made impossible; this was evident in the Antarctic cases brought by Great Britain before the International Court of Justice in 1955.[70]

However, the same situation also had a positive influence by creating the conviction that it was indispensable to organize and strengthen co-operation, not as a substitute for manifestations of sovereignty but as a means of correcting the imbalance which had arisen. On this basis, sovereignty and co-operation in the Antarctic were to develop progressively towards a new and harmonious relationship which has been the most striking feature of the Antarctic system.

Each of the conflicts that have been referred to at one time or another moved towards settlements based on the concept of co-operation. The conflict in the Antarctic peninsula, for example, underwent a major change of perspective with the signing of the Tripartite Naval Declaration of 1949 under the terms of which Argentina, Chile and the United Kingdom undertook not to send warships south of the latitude of 60° south, as a way of preventing armed incidents.[71]

The more general tensions stemming from world politics or from differences between claimant countries and those which held other positions also evolved towards a co-operative approach. The numerous post-war diplomatic initiatives, which were to serve as a background to the preparation of the 1959 Treaty offer ample evidence of this change of outlook. The advance of scientific co-operation, for its part, led to the realization of the wide-ranging programme of the International Geophysical Year.

Perhaps the most significant fact of all is that, simultaneously, the authors began to place a new emphasis on the ideas of Antarctic co-operation, a development that coincided with the high point of this line of thinking which saw the birth of the United Nations and other international organizations in the post-war period. This new orientation was also to have a major influence on the creation of the necessary climate for making co-operation under the Antarctic Treaty a reality.

1.4   The 1959 Treaty and its influence on the system of Antarctic co-operation

New approaches by the authors of international law
International law authors have never in fact ceased to dwell on the necessity for co-operation in the Antarctic continent, irrespective of whether or not they accepted the possibility of claims of sovereignty. The proposal that an Antarctic convention should be drafted arose, indeed, very early in specialized literature. J. S. Reeves, arguing that the status of Antarctica was, like that of the ocean, *res communis*, noted in 1934:

> The entire area is essentially international in fact, and its future international character might well be established by general agreement and the conservation of its resources guaranteed.[72]

At various times the opinion also prevailed that an Antarctic convention was indispensable as a means of preventing future disputes,[73] that the continent was ripe for internationalism should the experiment be tried,[74] or that an international solution should be found through agreement among the states directly concerned as the sole alternative to the problem of claims of sovereignty.[75] Similarly, there were frequent calls for, or initiatives in favour of, international understanding so that all states would renounce their political claims and regard the continent as 'neutral territory in perpetuity'.[76]

As the conflicts besetting the continent became ever more frequent, so the emphasis of authors on an international solution similarly became more marked, particular reference being made to the possible role of the United Nations. The idea of the 'common property of all nations' once again emerged in this context[77] as did the option of a type of trusteeship under United Nations auspices.[78] The Berlin Conference of 1885, which dealt with the problems of colonization in Africa, was also invoked as a precedent for an Antarctic conference and at the same time it was proposed that the International Court of Justice should give a ruling on the applicable law or that the General Assembly of the United Nations should request the Court to give an advisory opinion.[79]

This set of concerns induced a number of distinguished personalities in the academic world to put forward proposals of a more far-reaching nature concerning the organization of Antarctic co-operation. Although the substance of some of these proposals will be analysed in later chapters of this study, it is necessary for us to draw attention to their key ideas at this stage because of their relationship with the emergence of the 1959 Treaty.

Bertram envisaged as possibilities for the future the recognition of

Antarctic claims, the creation of a condominium, the establishment of a trust territory or various forms of functional co-operation.[80] It is interesting to note that he also suggested the possibility that governments that were experiencing economic hardship might sell certain Antarctic territories.[81] Daniel, for his part, identified a system which would guarantee private property and the freedom of fishing and prospecting and would respect international conventions on the protection of marine life. Freedom of exploration and scientific research would be ensured without prejudice to the existence of claims to sovereignty. Such a system would also be accompanied by demilitarization and by the establishment of a Permanent International Commission which would take its decisions by a two-thirds majority of its members. Jurisdiction could be exercised by any nation or, alternatively, the Antarctic might be divided into sectors which would be patrolled by a country mandated to do so by all the other states.[82] It will be appreciated that many of these ideas form part of the contemporary debate on the mineral resources regime.

Another author analysed the following four options as a means of solving the problem which had arisen in the Antarctic: (i) assimilation of Antarctica to the international public domain in the form of a supra-state institutionalization; (ii) delegated trusteeship; (iii) condominium subject to an agreement by the powers concerned; (iv) contractual internationalization in which rights and obligations would be defined by a treaty.[83]

Jenks contributed other ideas which are interesting in this regard; he was critical of proposals to create a United Nations trusteeship and of ideas which drew a parallel between the Antarctic case and that of Svalbard. As an alternative, he suggested a functional approach designed to establish certain joint international services particularly in fields such as the preservation of peace, the maintenance of law and order, aviation, communications and scientific research. The regime proposed also embraced the utilization of oceanic resources, the exploitation of mineral resources and problems which might arise in regard to the Antarctic continental shelf. In the case of mineral resources, there was some consideration of the idea that the title to the resources would be held by the United Nations or by some other special international body which would be able to grant permits for exploitation or that such permits might be granted by certain designated countries or by those countries exercising authority in the Antarctic continent.[84]

Jessup and Taubenfeld also favoured the establishment of a special regime which was to include the creation of an Antarctic Commission and the formation of a company for the exploitation of minerals. The regime would operate on the basis of responsibility delegated to certain states and the distribution of profits with other countries.[85]

The influence of the International Geophysical Year (IGY)

In parallel with this manifestation of academic initiatives, a start was made on serious efforts to develop scientific research and to advance the frontiers of knowledge about the Antarctic. This corresponded in part to a new expression of national interest but also had a genuine scientific objective.[86] One important result of this other line of action was the intensive co-operation that was achieved within the framework of the International Geophysical Year, a process which constituted a permanent landmark in the history of Antarctic co-operation and which was to have a great influence on the negotiation of the 1959 Treaty.[87]

The International Geophysical Year was not only a large-scale experiment but also, as various authors have pointed out, represented a political event of special international significance at a time when the difficulties of the cold war cast a shadow over relations between the principal powers. From this point of view, science had achieved a political transformation that was due to last. As Richard A. Lewis wrote: 'Perhaps the greatest experiment in this icy laboratory has been man himself and his ability to adapt his outlook and his drives to an environment which requires co-operation'.[88]

Diplomatic initiatives

In this intellectual and scientific climate which had gradually arisen in the context of the Antarctic theme, official moves in favour of co-operation in the continent did not take long to appear. A number of authors agree in identifying the various options available to the policy of the United States in relation to the Antarctic: (i) to make a claim with particular reference to the unclaimed sector; (ii) to undertake some form of collective action with other interested countries, for which purpose it would be necessary to reach an understanding with the countries of Latin America or with Australia and New Zealand or a combination of those countries; and (iii) to seek a wider form of international solution which might involve the United Nations or at least those countries directly interested in Antarctic co-operation.[89]

As has already been explained, the first of these options was actively considered on various occasions. The possibility of collective action with the Latin American republics was also raised by Roosevelt in 1939 through a diplomatic initiative which, as was mentioned further above, led directly to the promulgation of the Chilean Antarctic decree of 1940. The proposals made by the United States in 1948 were a particularly important step in the sequence of ideas that culminated in the 1959 regime.[90] They suggested the concept of the United Nations trusteeship or, alternatively, a condominium in which the claimants would participate[91] for which purpose the United States might possibly make its own claim.

In the same year, the government of Chile responded to that proposal with an important memorandum prepared by Professor Julio Escudero which contained the basic ideas that were subsequently to be reflected in the Antarctic Treaty.[92] Indeed, the 'Escudero memorandum' envisaged the principle of the temporary freezing of claims, the freedom of scientific research and demilitarization as the central points of an Antarctic regime. The Soviet reaction, summarized in the memorandum of 1950, has already been mentioned.

Other important initiatives appeared after the Korean war. Some of these envisaged the internationalization of the Antarctic under the auspices of the United Nations. In this context one should bear in mind the initiatives by India in 1956 and 1958 in the General Assembly of the United Nations which will be studied later. The idea of the Antarctic trusteeship, which was sponsored by New Zealand in spite of the fact that it was a claimant country, received particularly strong support.[93] The option of bringing the disputed Antarctic territories within the framework of the United Nations was also discussed in 1956 by the House of Commons in the United Kingdom.[94]

The decisive year for the formation of the Antarctic regime was 1958, due partly to the fact that the International Geophysical Year was coming to an end and partly because the failure to reach a quick solution to the existing conflicts threatened to make the situation unmanageable. In February of that year the British Prime Minister, Harold Macmillan, during a visit to Australia, announced the idea of establishing an international commission of countries directly interested in the Antarctic in conjunction with the demilitarization of the continent.[95] Although at one time this initiative was interpreted as a change of position intended to promote the internationalization of the Antarctic,[96] such does not seem to have been its purpose. A similar interpretation has been placed on the initiatives of Prime Minister Nash of New Zealand[97] who proposed an Antarctic regime which was to be administered in the same spirit as the International Geophysical Year and would have the approval of the United Nations, although not necessarily should be administered by it.[98]

In May 1958 the government of the United States sent out invitations to negotiations which were to culminate in the Antarctic Conference of 1959[99] and the signing of the Antarctic Treaty.[100] The complex process leading to that stage was influenced by a combination of political, scientific and other considerations, but, as John Heap pointed out in a recent study of Antarctic co-operation, it was, in the last analysis, the fear among all the Antarctic countries that chaos might result in the continent that provided the decisive motivation for agreement on the formulae for co-operation which have since then characterized the Antarctic system.[101]

Nature of the system of Antarctic co-operation and the opinion of authors
Even though the official sources concerning the negotiation of the 1959 Treaty are not generally available,[102] its provisions and the diplomatic history on which those provisions were based have been exhaustively analysed by eminent authors.[103] It is not therefore the purpose of the present study to revert to this subject except to the extent that those provisions have a bearing on the various problems that have to be faced by the regimes governing the natural resources of Antarctica. These will be dealt with in the following chapters.

It is particularly worth bearing in mind in this context the effect, already described, which this settlement had on the framework of Antarctic co-operation and on sovereignty issues. Could the system that was set up be described as being designed to ensure the primacy of the interest of the Antarctic powers, with particular reference to that of the countries claiming sovereignty, as frequently has been maintained at the present time?[104] Or could it be argued that those claims to sovereignty disappeared in the machinery for international co-operation, as the more nationalistic authors have persistently claimed?[105]

The true nature of the system of Antarctic co-operation created in 1959 cannot properly be fitted into the framework of either of these uncompromising assertions; the fact is that it responds to specific conditions arising from the background that has been described, as a result of which the system has characteristics common to both of these positions. On the one hand, there is no doubt at all that the system represents a form of internationalization, even though it is neither total nor comprehensive. On the other hand, it is explicitly stated that claims existing at the date of the Treaty, or positions which rely on a basis of a claim, or the non-recognition of any claim, are not affected by the Treaty and are legally protected by Article IV.

This eclectic approach of the Antarctic Treaty explains why it has proved so successful as a model of international co-operation and, at the same time, why the system is so enormously complex in terms of its practical development: a constant effort has been made to preserve the basic equilibrium and to consider the most appropriate way of adapting it to the circumstances which may constantly have been changing with the passage of time.

Authors have tended to give prominence to factors related to internationalization in the 1959 Treaty,[106] even though its contribution to the stability of the Antarctic situation which existed prior to the Treaty has always been acknowledged.[107] In the view of one author, the conclusion of the Treaty represented the first step towards the internationalization of the Antarctic region,[108] a view which implies the idea of progressive internationalization. Later in this study we shall have occasion to note that to some extent this process has occurred in practice.

Jessup and Taubenfeld, for their part, saw in the case of the Antarctic an important precedent for the internationalization of the Arctic and of outer space[109] and, at the same time, the example of the 1959 Treaty was invoked on several occasions during the preparatory work on the Sea-Bed Committee which preceded the Third United Nations Conference on the Law of the Sea.[110] It is curious to note that some commentators are endeavouring at the present time to reverse this influence, maintaining that the Antarctic should be internationalized as a consequence of the concepts contained in the Moon Treaty and in the 1982 Convention on the Law of the Sea,[111] concepts which, moreover, are different from those embodied in the system of Antarctic co-operation, as it will be seen further below.

Kelsen put forward in his Principles of International Law an interesting point of view on the effects of the 1959 Treaty:

> By the middle of this century, the only area of significance continuing to hold the status of no state's land was Antarctica. Since the coming into force of the Antarctic Treaty in 1961, however, Antarctica has become a major exception to the law concerning no state's land, although the territory still does not belong to any state.[112]

Even if the view that the Antarctic was *terra nullius* in the middle of this century may be questionable, the implication of this opinion seems to be that, under the terms of the 1959 Treaty, a form of joint jurisdiction over the region was created, an idea which, as will be seen later, is of some importance today in resolving certain difficulties of Antarctic co-operation.

Evolution of national standpoints

The coincidence of views on the positive effects of the Treaty in regard to co-operation in the Antarctic continent is borne out in practice by the development that has occurred in the principal national standpoints on this matter. In the first place, it must be emphasized that the position of those countries that do not recognize any claim of sovereignty has undergone a fundamental change. Prior to the 1959 Treaty this position implied a certain antagonism towards the claimant countries because the two approaches were incompatible. The 1959 Treaty provides a different legal basis for the conducting of activities in Antarctica since, in the light of Article IV, neither position can be interpreted to the prejudice of the other. A compatibility has thus been achieved which avoids the negative connotations of the original point of view of non-claimant countries.

This fact alone has done much to facilitate the accession to the Treaty of a large number of countries which do not now find themselves antagonizing the claimant nations.[113] Even more significant is the fact that this machinery has resulted in a reduction in the pressure exerted by certain countries which were contemplating the possibility of making an Antarctic claim in the mistaken belief that that was the only way in which they could acquire an active role in that continent. In spite of the fact that the Treaty prohibits the assertion of new claims while it is in force, this is an idea which a number of countries have studied with interest either because, as third party countries, they did not consider themselves bound by that instrument or because they took the view that the situation in the Antarctic could change in the future. Such countries include Brazil, Ecuador, Peru and Uruguay.[114] However, some of them have acceded to the Treaty and two have become a Consultative Party without having needed to make such a claim since the position of countries that do not recognize claims enjoys the same safeguards and opportunities as any other.[115]

Among the Treaty Parties not claiming sovereignty in Antarctica, the United States and the Soviet Union have been recognized on historic grounds as having a basis for a claim, a situation which is also safeguarded by the terms of Article IV of the Treaty. Here, too, it may be considered that the Treaty has made it more likely that these potential claims will not be asserted, partly by its specific prohibitions but also, to some extent, by virtue of the protection afforded to the political balance on which the system was founded. If the instrument did not exist it is certain that the picture would be very different in this respect.

Another category is that of countries claiming sovereignty, the position of which has also undergone major changes as a result of the entry into force of the 1959 Treaty. However, in spite of the fact that they all share a common position, it would be a mistake to assume that they all base it on the same criteria. In the first place, one must acknowledge that certain claimants take a sympathetic view of more comprehensive options for internationalization, including the possibility of abandoning their own claims. Norway and New Zealand may be mentioned in this context although it must be borne in mind that, as far as exploitation of the resources of the Antarctic is concerned, the policy adopted by them has tended to be more cautious.[116]

The other claimants would seem to identify themselves more closely with a 'territorialist' position but even here there are major differences between them. The policy of Australia, France and Great Britain would seem to favour a view of the Antarctic problem encompassing in many respects the continent as a whole, which has also become more marked in relation to resources. This can also be explained by the fact that Australia has the largest claim in the continent and that Great Britain at one time claimed vast areas. In the case of France the reason might be the opposite, namely that it has the smallest claim from the geographical point of view, although it must be pointed out that on several occasions France has favoured a more narrow or nationalistic approach, concentrating her efforts in the claimed area.

Although Argentina and Chile are generally depicted in specialized literature as being the most tenacious of the claimants, this view stems from the conflicts of the 1950s and no longer corresponds strictly to reality.[117] At least in the case of Chile, one can see an appreciable trend towards a view encompassing the continent as a whole in some matters, which gives due weight to the virtues of international co-operation.[118]

One particularly important fact is that co-operation has been able to develop intensely in areas which had previously been the scene of the most serious conflicts, such as the Antarctic peninsula. This complementarity between the positions of claimant countries or among them and those countries taking different positions has at various times led to proposals for an Antarctic condominium, whether formally declared or otherwise.[119] The concept of a general condominium has also been suggested in the context of resources policy.

These developments are a very positive trend and have only been possible within the framework of the 1959 Treaty which has facilitated a qualitative and quantitative change in the perception of Antarctic co-operation. What was previously a conflictive relationship marked by rivalries and confrontations has today become a co-operative system through which harmony is sought on the basis of common interests.

1.5 The development of Antarctic resources: the new requirements of co-operation

The 1959 regime was based on a complex set of compromises the essential purpose of which was to ensure the necessary co-operation in the continent without prejudice to the respective national standpoints. The subject of Antarctic resources was obviously not ignored, since, directly or indirectly, it has been a factor to take into consideration since the earliest human activities in the region.[120] However, the fact that consideration of the subject was not felt at that time to be a matter of urgency and, above all, the conviction that, if it had been dealt with, this would have made agreement more difficult to reach, meant that the question of resources was not directly addressed in the Treaty although, as we shall see, it was by no means totally overlooked.

During the early years of Antarctic co-operation under this new instrument efforts were therefore concentrated principally on improving opportunities for carrying out those activities that were directly related to the type of concerns that were perceived to be most urgent at the time when the Treaty was signed. Prominent among these concerns where the freedom of scientific research, demilitarization and utilization exclusively for peaceful purposes, the effective freezing of the problem of conflicts of sovereignty and the organization of the consultative system which made possible the effective operation of the entire scheme. Such concerns were the correct priority at that time.

For the very reason that the existence of resources remained the background to such co-operation, it was not long before the subject made its appearance in the context of negotiations between the Consultative Parties. As John Heap explains in his analysis of Antarctic co-operation, there were, in the early years, two schools of thought involved in this context.[121] One, which was passive in nature, was in favour of addressing and solving problems as and when they arose and became urgent. The other, which was more active in nature, 'saw Consultative Meetings as an opportunity to look for problems, none of which were urgent in themselves, and deal with them on an *ad hoc* basis'.[122] It was the latter school of thought, as the author himself points out, that ultimately prevailed.

This situation explains one of the most remarkable features of the Antarctic co-operation system, one which is not often seen in the framework of other systems of co-operation, namely its capacity for anticipating problems and responding to their demands before they become critical or urgent. The Agreed Measures for the Conservation of Antarctic Fauna and Flora,[123] the Convention for the Conservation of Antarctic Seals,[124] the Convention on the Conservation of Antarctic Marine Living Resources[125] and, more recently, the consideration that has been given to the regime for mineral resources, all form part of this scheme of anticipation. The negative historic experience that had occurred with regard to the hunting of seals and whales in the Antarctic,[126] together with growing international pressures about the conservation of resources and the preservation of the environment, had an important influence on the need to prevent serious effects on the Antarctic eco-system by means of the development of treaty-regulated systems of co-operation such as those dealing with resources.

Changes in the nature of Antarctic co-operation

Once the basic objectives that had been taken into account in the signing of the Treaty had been consolidated, a process which was completed fairly quickly, the question of Antarctic resources began to gain increasing prominence to the point where it has today become the over-riding issue within the system, although not to the neglect of the concerns stemming from the initial stage of the system's operation. The new emphasis placed on resources policy has been reflected in a necessary change of viewpoint by the States party to the Treaty, a change which in its turn implies new requirements for Antarctic co-operation. The original concerns to which the system was a response could be met through the relatively passive forms of co-operation, the main feature of which was a policy of absten-tion from interfering with the activities of others. This is particularly clear in the case of the political abstention required in relation to the problem of claims to sovereignty or on demilitarization; it also applies in the case of scientific research, since the corresponding obligation on the Parties to the Treaty is that they should refrain from interfering with the principle of freedom to undertake such research.

In the case of resources, where such forms of passive co-operation are not sufficient, what is needed is a regime of active co-operation to which the Parties must make an effective contribution if the desired goal of conservation and rational exploitation is to be achieved. Refraining from interference continues to play a significant role but it is by no means the only one. Positive co-operation is also necessary, partly for the adminis-tration of the respective regimes and partly in order to solve the new problems which occur and which, in many cases, are different in nature from the traditional problems.

Extending the legal framework of co-operation

These new requirements basically determine the present orientation of the system. This fact, as will be appreciated, has important implications for the legal framework of Antarctic co-operation.[127] On the one hand, the 1959 Treaty, which provided the basic means of organizing such co-operation, has had to be applied progressively to a growing number of subjects connected with resources or related matters. The law-creating competence of the consultative meetings has made it possible gradually to develop the initial framework. On the other hand, various special regimes have had to be devised for the purpose, some of which have required their own treaty regime. One of the major characteristics of the most recent regimes is their tendency towards increasing institutionalization. The set of instruments forming the present-day structure of Antarctic co-operation constitute what is known as the 'Antarctic system' to use the apt term originally conceived by Roberto Guyer.[128]

Given this changing situation, it has been necessary to apply new criteria to the problem of jurisdiction in the Antarctic continent, which is another of the areas in which the resources policy has had an impact on this system of co-operation. The limited provisions concerning this matter contained in the 1959 Treaty have now been amplified by more specific standards. It is interesting to note, as we shall have occasion to do in a later chapter,[129] that it is not claimed that these approaches are capable of solving the jurisdictional problems raised by the system: they merely deal, in a somewhat casuistical way, with the needs inherent in each particular regime. This is indicative of the permanent objective of maintaining the political and juridical equilibrium on which the system rests and of solving problems, as they occur, by applying pragmatic criteria. As an example of the latter we have seen the gradual development of a special form of joint jurisdiction.

The subject of the natural resources of the Antarctic has given the entire system a new geographical and legal dimension: the application of the Law of the Sea to the Antarctic continent.[130] Problems relating to the exploitation of living resources, in the first place, and subsequently the considerations which it has been necessary to bear in mind in preparing a regime to cover mineral resources, have ensured that the application of the Law of the Sea represents a particularly important area for the development of Antarctic co-operation and one which has only very recently been brought more systematically within the jurisdictional scope of the system.

The re-adaptation of initial balances: the internal accommodation
The change from relatively simple means of co-operation to others which are more advanced and complex has also necessitated the adaptation of the necessary balances of the system to these new dimensions. The question of how the different positions of the Consultative Parties can adjust to this new situation, without upsetting the balance of their relationship, has become a central point in contemporary Antarctic discussion, a process known as the 'internal accommodation'.[131]

In subjects which are relatively passive such as demilitarization, or relatively neutral such as scientific research, such an adjustment might be achieved through simple clauses such as those contained in the Antarctic Treaty. However, a task such as that of organizing the conservation and exploitation of natural resources requires arrangements that, of necessity, are of vastly greater complexity. Merely to resolve the incompatibilities between such widely differing political and economic philosophies as those represented by the Consultative Parties requires an imaginative response of a high order. In the same way, the harmonization of the interests of those concerned primarily with the conservation of resources and the preservation of the environment with those more interested in the exploitation of such resources is a matter of particular difficulty in the context of the respective regimes.

All of the regimes that have been prepared in the framework of the Antarctic system of co-operation have had to deal with the problems of internal accommodation in their respective fields. It is to be noted in this connection that this is an increasingly difficulty process not because there has been any reduction in the willingness of the Parties to co-operate but because of the nature of the problems that need to be solved. The situation has become particularly strained in the case of mineral resources where it has even been necessary to impose a moratorium on activities pending negotiation of an accommodation of interests.

Owing to the fact that any resources regime assumes the exercise of regulatory power to a greater or lesser extent, the question of the distribution of power within the system has often been crucial. The question of which powers may be invoked by countries claiming sovereignty and which may be invoked by those that do not recognize such claims is one that regularly occurs. But, at the same time, the question arises as to which powers properly belong to states, irrespective of their standpoint, and which powers should be granted as being proper to the institutions of the regime. These two types of question are obviously related since it often occurs that the required balance can only be achieved by recourse to multiple forms of distribution.

In this context, and without prejudice to what may be noted in the following chapters, two tendencies of particular relevance to Antarctic co-operation are to be observed. On the one hand, the exercise of sovereignty as traditionally conceived is tending to be attenuated and minimized in the framework of these developments. It is not that a claimant state has lost the rights attributable to its claim, or that its role has diminished, but that the state of itself forms part of a qualitatively different system. On the other hand, the nature of the Antarctic co-operation has changed in terms of institutional requirements; originally it sufficed with a simple machinery for co-ordination, but the most recent resources regimes have evidenced the need to develop to some extent the exercise of regulatory powers by the organs established, which entails some form of subordination of the member or participating states. These two tendencies have brought about considerable changes in the system of co-operation, leading to a more intense and co-operative scheme so as to achieve the sought-after internal accommodation in the context of resources policy.

Different approaches to the international links of the system: the external accommodation

The problems relating to the accommodation of interests under more highly structured forms of co-operation are not restricted to what have been described as 'internal' problems. From the outset, activity relating to the Antarctic continent has been markedly international in character[132] by virtue of the area being a space open to the activities of all individuals and nations that took an interest in it. The fact that the Antarctic Treaty was negotiated and signed by a limited number of countries which became known as the Consultative Parties was not due to any intention to exclude others but was the faithful reflection of the situation then prevailing in regard to activity in Antarctica. It is of some interest to note that of the many nations whose scientists took part in the International Geophysical Year – a total of sixty-seven – only the original twelve Consultative Parties displayed their interest by becoming directly involved in activities in the Antarctic continent.[133]

In any case, this other aspect of Antarctic co-operation has ensured that the development of such co-operation has always taken into account its links with, and effects on, the wider international community. The concept of the interest of mankind is embodied in the 1959 Treaty and was subsequently reflected in numerous instruments of the system. The way in which this concept is translated into specific measures and machinery constitutes the essential features of the process now referred to as 'external accommodation'. As will be examined in a later chapter, such concept is altogether different from the 'common heritage of mankind' approach followed in the Law of the Sea Convention.

On some subjects, the interest of the Parties to the Treaty is not really different from that of the international community in general. This is the case, for example, with the freedom of scientific research or the preservation of the environment. However, to the extent that the question of resources has become a priority issue within the system, external adjustment has necessarily involved consideration of solutions which are more difficult to achieve. The distribution of profits and access to the respective regimes governing resource exploitation are some of the more specific matters which remain to be solved.

This is where there are some different perceptions as to ways of achieving this accommodation. The Consultative Parties have gradually defined, through the process of co-operation which has taken place, what constitutes their 'special responsibility' for directing and administering the system, including its special regimes. This assumes some emphasis on participation in institutions and, above all, control by them of the decision-making process. Access is genuinely open to other countries to the extent that it does not affect these central criteria and, naturally, on condition that such countries accept to be governed by the basic premises of the 1959 Treaty, the applicable special conventions and the relevant decisions taken under them. Co-operation with international organizations is subject to similar requirements.

For other sectors, however, adjustment presupposes a more advanced form of internationalization. Among other proposals in this regard, some emphasis has been placed on the idea of bringing the Antarctic within a regime based on the concept of the common heritage of mankind with a view to extending the forms of participation with particular reference to decision-making. Although some of these possibilities have been raised in connection with the regime of marine living resources, it is the case of minerals that has given rise to the most intensive discussion. The operation at some stage of the International Sea-Bed Authority may possibly create further pressures in this context due partly to the precedent established by a different model of co-operation and partly because this organization and the Antarctic system may find themselves overlapping over the administration of mining activities in particular geographical regions.

Furthermore, it is necessary to bear in mind the different situations in which third countries and those countries which are Parties to the 1959 Treaty, but have not achieved the status of Consultative Parties, find themselves. Countries which are Parties to the Treaty are undoubtedly bound by the various obligations provided for by that instrument but the rights enjoyed by them so far have been somewhat limited. As we shall see later, there is at present a positive tendency to correct this imbalance.

Characteristics of the new Antarctic legal order
The development that has been described in this chapter indicates the major changes that have taken place in the nature and regulation of

activity in the Antarctic. The maximalist phase of sovereignty and of the conflictive relationship that arose from it was replaced by a system of co-operation that placed emphasis on the positive factors of activity in the continent. The 1959 Treaty has been the cornerstone of a framework of co-operation which has made possible the harmonization of diverse interests and their adaptation to changing circumstances. The emergence of the issue of natural resources gave the decisive impetus to this adaptation.

In looking at the process as a whole, we can observe three central and abiding characteristics. The first of these is the progressive development of international law in its application to Antarctic activity which has given rise, on the one hand, to the improvement of the original Treaty through successive recommendations approved by the consultative meetings and, on the other hand, to the creation of other special conventions to complement the original instrument. The second characteristic is the evident tendency towards growing institutionalization which has made possible intervention on a larger scale by specialized bodies for the administration of resources policy. The third major characteristic to be mentioned is the more effective linking of the Antarctic system with the international community both through the gradual accession of further countries and through the participation of various international organizations in Antarctic co-operation.

We have thus reached a stage in which the Antarctic order differs markedly both qualitatively and quantitatively from the forms of co-operation that prevailed up to the mid-1970s. In the first place, we have a system that is more open and detailed and that requires the active participation of the countries involved. In the second place, we have a much more comprehensive machinery which has been gradually extending the scope of its material competence. This development of the system and its changing nature has to be borne in mind in the study of the legal developments referring more specifically to the mineral resources regime.

Chapter 1 Notes

1. Eleanor Honnymill: *The Challenge of Antarctica*, 1984. Sir Vivian Fuchs: *Of Ice and Men*, 1982. Ian Cameron: *Exploring Antarctica*, 1984. See also American Geographical Society: *Antarctic Maps and Surveys 1900–1964*, Antarctic Map Folio Series, Folio 3, 1965.
2. Laurence M. Gould: 'Emergence of Antarctica: The Mythical Land', *Sci. Publ. Af.*, Vol. XXVI N° 10, December 1970, 5–10, at 7. Interesting historic accounts of the period can be found in the following works: Sir Ernest Shackleton: *South*, 1919; W. G. Burn Murdoch: *From Edinburgh to the Antarctic*, 1894 (reprinted in 1984); H. J. Bull: *The cruise of the 'Antarctic'*, 1896 (reprinted in 1984); Albert B.

Armitage: *Two years in the Antarctic*, 1905 (reprinted in 1984). See also: J. Gordon Hayes: *Antarctica, A Treatise on the Southern Continent*, 1928; and Armando Braun Menéndez: *Pequeña historia Antártica*, 1974.

3. V. E. Fuchs: 'Antarctica: its history and development', in Francisco Orrego Vicuña (ed): *Antarctic Resources Policy*, 1983, 13–19. A. L. Washburn: 'Focus on Polar Research', *Science*, Reprint Series, Vol. 209, 8 August 1980, 643–652. Charles R. Bentley: 'International Science Programs in Antarctica', in Lewis M. Alexander and Lynne Carter Hanson (eds): *Antarctic Politics and Marine Resources: critical choices for the 1980's*, 1985, 45–54. R. M. Laws: 'Scientific opportunities in the Antarctic', in British Institute of International and Comparative Law: *Whither Antarctica?*, 1985, 38–71 (draft version). See also American Geological Society: *History of Antarctic Exploration and Scientific Investigation*, Antarctic Map Folio Series, Folio 19, 1975.

4. See generally Francisco Orrego Vicuña, op. cit., note 3 supra.

5. Philip W. Quigg: *A Pole Apart. The emerging issue of Antarctica*, 1983, 69–74.

6. Fernando Zegers Santa Cruz: 'The Antarctic System and the utilization of resources', *Univ. Mia. L. Rev.*, Vol. 33 N° 2, December 1978, 425–473. See also Chapter 10 infra.

7. For a collection of Antarctic legal materials and diplomatic correspondence, W. M. Bush: *Antarctica and International Law*, 1982.

8. See generally, E. W. Hunter Christie: *The Antarctic Problem. An historical and political study*, London, 1951.

9. W. L. S. Fleming: 'Contemporary international interest in the Antarctic', *Int. Af.*, Vol. XXIII, 1947, 546–557.

10. Roberto E. Guyer: 'Antarctica's role in international relations', in Francisco Orrego Vicuña, op. cit., note 3 supra, 267–279, at 274–276.

11. For a comparison with other models of international co-operation, Gunnar Skagestad: 'The Frozen Frontier: Models for International Cooperation', *Coop. and Confl.* 3, 1975, 167–187.

12. For the point of view of authors of the period and early diplomatic practice, G. H. Hackworth: *Digest of International Law*, 1940, Vol. 1, 449–476. For a bibliography on Antarctic affairs prior to the Antarctic Treaty of 1959, with particular reference to national activities and claims, Robert D. Hayton: *National interests in Antarctica. An annotated bibliography*, United States Antarctic Projects Officer, 1959.

13. For a discussion of sovereignty in the Arctic in the early period, René Waultrin: 'La question de la souveraineté des terres arctiques', *R.G.D.I.P.* Tome XV, 1908, 78–125 (first part), 185–209 (second part), 401–423 (third part). Ibid: 'Le probleme de la souveraineté des poles', *R.G.D.I.P.* Tome XVI, 1909, 649–660. Ibid: 'La Mer Blanche est-elle une mer libre?, L'Affaire de *l'Onward Ho*', Chronique des faits internationaux, *R.G.D.I.P.* Tome XVIII, 1911, 94–99. W. Lakhtine: 'Rights over the Arctic', *A.J.I.L.*, Vol. 24, 1930, 703–717. Oscar Svarlien: 'The legal status of the Arctic', *Proc. A.S.I.L.* 1958, 136–144. David Hunter Miller: 'Political rights in the Arctic', *For. Af.*, Vol. IV, 1925–1926, 47–60.

14. Thomas Willing Balch: 'The Arctic and Antarctic regions and the law of nations', *A.J.I.L.*, Vol. 4, 1910, 265–275 at 274–275. See also Clyde Eagleton: 'International Law and Aerial discovery at the South Pole', *Air Law Review*, Vol. 1, N° 1, January 1930, 125–127. The argument for 'common property' is made at 127.

15. C. H. M. Waldock: 'Disputed sovereignty in the Falkland Islands Dependencies', *B.Y.B.I.L.*, 1948, 311–353. As early as 1930 a Spitsbergen type regime was suggested for Antarctica, particularly in the context of British, Norwegian and

Argentine interests; see Laura H. Martin: 'Sovereignty in Antarctica', *Journal of Geography*, Vol. 29, N° 3, 1930, 111–120 at 119.

16. Balch, loc. cit. note 14 supra, at 274. For the Spitsbergen settlement, see Treaty of February 9, 1920. *A.J.I.L.*, Supplement, Vol. 18, 1924, Official Documents, 199–208. See also Fred K. Nielsen: 'The solution of the Spitsbergen question', Editorial Comment, *A.J.I.L.*, Vol. 14, 1920, 232–235.

17. William Edward Hall: *A treatise on International Law*, Eighth edition, edited by A. Pearce Higgins, 1924 at 124 note 1 and 125–131.

18. Paul Fauchille: *Traité de Droit International Public*, Tome I, Deuxieme Partie, 1925, 658–659. Emphasis in the original. Translation by the author of this book.

19. Ibid. at 659. See also generally section V of Fauchille's work: 'Le domaine polaire ou glaciaire', 651–663.

20. James Brown Scott: 'Arctic exploration and International Law', *A.J.I.L.*, Vol. 3, 1909, 928–941 at 941.

21. See the articles by Waultrin cited in note 13 supra. See also René Dollot: 'Le droit international des espaces polaires', *Rec. Cours Ac. D.I.* 1949, II, Vol. 75, 115–200.

22. Gustav Smedal: *Acquisition of sovereignty over polar areas*, Oslo, 1931.

23. Waldock, loc. cit., note 15 supra.

24. Gilbert Gidel: *Aspects juridiques de la lutte pour l'Antarctique*, Academic de Marine, Paris, 1948.

25. See generally, Olaf M. Smith: *Le statut juridique des Terres Polaires*, 1934.

26. R. Y. Jennings: *The acquisition of territory in international law*, 1963. James Simsarian: 'The acquisition of legal title to terra nullius', *Pol. Sci Q.* Vol. 53, 1938, 111–128. Charles Rousseau: *Droit International Public*, 1977, Tome III: Les Competences, 217–230. William W. Bishop Jr.: *International Law, Cases and Materials*, 1962, 354–362. Charles G. Fenwick: *International Law*, Fourth edition, 1965, 416–419. J. F. Da Costa: *Souveraineté sur l'Antarctique*, 1958, Premiere Partie. See also Georg Schwarzenberger: 'Title to territory: response to a challenge', *A.J.I.L.*, Vol. 51, 1957, 308–324. Charles de Visscher: *Problemes de Confins en Droit International Public*, 1969, especially Chapter 6.

27. M. F. Lindley: *The acquisition and government of backward territory in international law*, 1926, especially 4–6. Roberto Ago: *Il requisito dell'effettivitá dell'occupazione in diritto internazionale*, 1934, especially 30–40. F. A. F. Von der Heydte: 'Discovery, symbolic annexation and virtual effectiveness in international law', *A.J.I.L.*, Vol. 29, 1935, 448–471, epecially 470–471.

28. E. H. Hall: 'The Polar regions and international law', Editorial notes, *International Law Quarterly*, Vol. 1, 1947, 54–58. J. F. da Costa: 'A Teoria dos setores polares', *Boletin da Sociedade Brasileira de Dereito Internacional*, Ano 7, Nos. 13–14, Janeiro–Dezembro 1951, 87–128. See also the work by the same author cit. note 26 supra. J. S. Reeves: 'Antarctic Sectors', Editorial Comment, *A.J.I.L.*, Vol. 33, 1939, 519–521, with particular reference to United States policy. On general strategic, geographical and economic interest and claims, see also Normal Hill: *Claims to territory in international law and relations*, 1945. For a discussion of the sector principle with particular reference to the Arctic, Oscar Svarlien: 'The sector principle in law and practice', *Pol. Rec.*, Vol. 10, 1960–1961, 248–263.

29. Island of Palmas Case (Netherlands–USA), Award of 4 April 1928, Max Huber Arbitrator, United Nations, *R.I.A.A.*, Vol. II, 829–871.

30. Affaire de l'ile de Clipperton (Mexique–France), Sentence du 28 Janvier 1931, Arbitre S.M. Victor Emmanuel III, United Nations, *R.I.A.A.*, Vol. II, 1105–1111.

31. Ibid. at 1110–1111.
32. Permanent Court of International Justice: Legal Status of Eastern Greenland, Judgment of April 5, 1933, Series A/B, *Judgments, orders and advisory opinions*, N° 53, 21–147.
33. International Court of Justice: The Minquiers and Ecrehos Case (France–United Kingdom), Judgment of November 17th., 1953, *Reports of Judgments, advisory opinions and orders*, 1953, 47–109. For a discussion of this case, Gerald Fitzmaurice: 'The Law and Procedure of the International Court of Justice, 1951–1954: points of substantive law', Part II, *B.Y.B.I.L.*, 1955–1956, 20–96, particularly at 44–76. For the influence of geographic circumstances in the application of the principles of international law, Gerald Fitzmaurice: 'The General Principles of International Law', *Rec. Cours Ac. D.I.*, Vol. 92, 1957–II, 1–227 at 144–145.
34. International Court of Justice: North Sea Continental Shelf Cases (Federal Republic of Germany–Denmark; Federal Republic of Germany–Netherlands), Judgment of 20 February, 1969, *Reports of Judgments, advisory opinions and orders*, 1969.
35. Charles Cheney Hyde: 'Acquisition of sovereignty over polar areas', *Iowa Law Review*, Vol. XIX, 1933–1934, 286–294 at 294. An enlargement of this article appears in the work of the same author: *International Law chiefly as interpreted and applied by the United States*, Vol. I, 1947, 347–355.
36. Gidel, op. cit., note 24 supra, at 5.
37. Waldock, loc. cit., note 15 supra, at 317.
38. Brian Roberts: 'Chronological list of Antarctic expeditions', *Pol. Rec*, Vol. 9, 1958, 97–134, 191–239.
39. For a comparison between this type of pioneering activity in the Antarctic and similar exploitations in other areas characterizing as 'resource frontier regions', see David Sugden: *Arctic and Antarctic. A modern geographical synthesis*, 1982, at 15, 429–433.
40. For a detailed discussion of national claims and other approaches see John Hanessian Jr: *National Activities and interests in Antarctica*, American Universities Field Staff, Reports Service, Part I: The Why of Antarctica; Part II: The Claimant Nations; Part III: The Nonclaimant Nations, Polar Area Series, Vol. II, N° 5, 6, 7, September 1962. Also Ibid.: 'National Interests in Antarctica', in Trevor Hatherton (ed.): *Antarctica*, 1965, 3–53. Robert E. Wilson: 'National interests and claims in the Antarctic', *Arctic*, Vol. 17, 1964, 15–32. See also C.I.A.: *Antarctic Treaty and territorial claims. A reference aid* (Map), April 1982, and by the same agency: *Antarctica: Research stations and territorial claims* (Map), 1984.
41. See generally Waldock, loc. cit., note 15 supra. Peter J. Beck: 'British Antarctic Policy in the early 20th century', *Pol. Rec*, Vol. 21, N° 134, 1983, 475–483. Harry L. Lillie: 'The Antarctic in world affairs', *Canadian Geographical Journal*, Vol. 36, 1948, 283–294. See also Peter J. Beck: 'Britain and Antarctica: the historical perspective', *The Journal of Polar Studies*, Vol. I, N° 1, 1984, 66–82. Ibid: 'Britain's Antarctic dimension', *Int. Af*, Vol. 59, N° 3, Summer 1983, 429–444.
42. A. H. Charteris: 'Australasian claims in Antarctica', J. Comp. Leg. I.L., Vol. XI, 1929, 226–232. A. C. Castles: 'The International Status of the Australian Antarctic Territory', in: D. P. O'Connell (ed.): *International Law in Australia*, 1965, 341–367. Diane G. Thatcher: *Australia and Antarctica*, Thesis, History Department, University of Queensland, 1961. Gillian Triggs: 'Australian sovereignty in Antarctica', *Mel.U.L.R.*, Vol. 13, 1981–1982, 123–158 (Part I), 302–333 (Part II). Stuart Harris (ed.): *Australia's Antarctic Policy Options*,

Australian National University, 1984. Cisca Spencer: 'The evolution of Antarctic interests', in Stuart Harris, op. cit., 113–129. John Brook: 'Australia's policies towards Antarctica', in Stuart Harris, op. cit., 255–264. Bruce Davis: 'Australia and Antarctica: Aspects of policy process', in Stuart Harris, op. cit., 339–354. W. A. Budd: 'Scientific research in Antarctica and Australia's effort', in Stuart Harris, op. cit., 217–247. Anthony Bergin: 'Recent developments in Australia's Antarctic policy', *Marine Policy*, Vol. 9, 1985, 180–191. For the New Zealand claim see Ivor L. M. Richardson: 'New Zealand's claims in the Antarctic', *N.Z.I.J.*, Vol. XXXIII, February 19, 1957, N° 3, 38–42. F. M. Auburn: *The Ross Dependency*, 1972. H. F. M. Logan: *Cold Commitment: The Development of New Zealand's Territorial Role in Antarctica*, Thesis in History, University of Canterbury, Christchurch, New Zealand, 1979. Nigel Roberts: 'New Zealand interests in Antarctica', *N.Z.I.R.*, Vol. VIII, N° 5, September–October 1983, 6–12.

43. For the statements of the Imperial Conferences on Antarctica, see *Imperial Conference 1926*, HMSO, Cmd. 2768, 1926; *Imperial Conference 1930*, HMSO, Cmd. 3717, 1930; *Imperial Conference 1937*, HMSO, Cmd. 5482, 1937. See also Peter J. Beck: 'Securing the dominant "Place in the Wan Antarctic Sun for the British Empire": the policy of extending British control over Antarctica', *Australian Journal of Politics and History*, Vol. 29, N° 3, 1983–1984, 448–461.

44. For the state of recognition of claims in Antarctica, see Bush, op. cit., note 7 supra, at 58–59 and related documents referred to therein.

45. Da Costa, op. cit., note 26 supra, Deuxieme Partie: 'La Politique australe de la France'.

46. See Hanessian, op. cit., note 40 supra. See also 'Norwegian sovereignty in the Antarctic', Proclamation of January 14, 1939, *A.J.I.L.*, Vol. 34, 1940, Supplement, 83–85.

47. For the diplomatic correspondence between France and the United Kingdom on the question of delimitation of Terre Adélie, Bush, op. cit., note 7 supra, Vol. II, 498–506.

48. Oscar Pinochet de la Barra: *Chilean sovereignty in Antarctica*, 1955. Enrique Cordovez Madariaga: *La Antartida Sudamericana*, Santiago, 1945. Antonio Hunneus Gana: *Antartida*, Santiago, 1948. Jaime Eyzaguirre: *La soberanía de Chile en las tierras australes*, Santiago, 1958. Liliana Nuñez: *El Territorio Chileno Antártico*, Memorandum prepared for the Ministry of Foreign Affairs, Mimeo, 1959. Robert D. Hayton: 'Chile, Argentina and Great Britain in the Antarctic', *Inter-American Juridicial Year-book*, 1955–1957, 119–125. Ministerio de Relaciones Exteriores: 'Participación de Chile en la Conferencia Antártica de Washington', *Memoria*, 1959, 684–704. Pablo Ihl C.: 'Relato sobre la antártica y la polinesia sur oriental según la obra "Narratio de Terra Australis Incognita", editada en Sevilla, en 1610', *Revista geográfica de Chile, Terra Australis*, Vol. V, N° 7, September 1952, 11–14. Ricardo Riesco: 'Geopolítica austral y antártica', *Boletín Antártico Chileno*, Vol. 4, N° 2, Julio–Diciembre 1984, 14–17. Julio Escudero Guzmán: 'El Decreto Antártico de 1940', Ministerio de Relaciones Exteriores, *Anales de la Diplomacia*, 1984, 279–281. Jorge Berguño: 'Chile y el descubrimiento de la antártica', Ministerio de Relaciones Exteriores, *Anales de la Diplomacia*, 1984, 274–279. Francisco Orrego Vicuña, María Teresa Infante, Pilar Armanet (eds): *Política Antártica de Chile*, 1985. Carlos de Toro Alvarez: 'Vinculación histórica del territorio continental y la antártica', in Francisco Orrego et al., op. cit., 51–65. Pedro Romero: 'Presencia de Chile en la Antártica', in Francisco Orrego et al., op. cit., 35–50. Ricardo Riesco: 'La geografía antártica como base de nuevas orientaciones políticas', in Francisco Orrego et al., op. cit., 103–114. Oscar Pinochet de la Barra: 'La contribución de Chile al

Tratado Antártico', in Francisco Orrego et al., op. cit., 89–100. Enrique Gajardo Villarroel: 'Antecedentes de la negociación diplomática previa al Tratado de 1959 y la posición de Chile', in Francisco Orrego et al., op. cit., 81–87. Juan Guillermo Valenzuela: 'La política antártica chilena y las bases de una estructura adminitrativa', in Francisco Orrego et al., op. cit., 297–305.

49. Juan Carlos Puig: *La Antártica Argentina ante el Derecho*, 1960. Juan Carlos Rodríguez: *La República Argentina y las adquisiciones territoriales en el continente antártico*, Buenos Aires, 1941. José Carlos Vittone: *La soberanía argentina en el continente antártico*, Buenos Aires, 1944. Comisión Nacional del Antártico: *Soberanía Argentina en la Antártida*, Buenos Aires, 1947. Carlos Berraz Montyn: *La soberanía argentina en tierras antárticas*, Santa Fé, 1948. Felipe Barreda Laos: *La Antártida Sudamericana ante el Derecho Internacional*, Buenos Aires, 1948. Raúl Martínez Moreno: *Soberanía Antártica Argentina*, Tucumán, 1951. Enrique Ferrer Vieyra (ed): *Antártida Argentina*, Buenos Aires, 1960. Primavera Acuña de Mones Ruiz: *Antártida Argentina, islas oceánicas, mar argentino*, Buenos Aires, 1948. Guillermo R. Moncayo: 'La situación jurídica de la Antártida', *Estrategia*, N° 43–44, November–December 1976, January–February 1977, 47–59. F. A. Milia et al.: *La Antártida, Un espacio geopolítico*, 1978. Jorge A. Fraga: *El Mar y la Antártida en la Geopolítica Argentina*, 1980. Peter J. Beck: 'Argentine postmarks in the South Orkneys', *Polar Post*, Vol. 14, N° 2, June 1982, 49. Mario Raúl Chingotto: *El Mar y los intereses argentinos*, 1982. Jorge A. Fraga: *La Argentina y el atlántico sur*, 1983.

50. See note 44 supra. Various early negotiations on delimitation of the Antarctic claims between Chile and Argentina were unsuccessful, for which see Oscar Pinochet de la Barra: 'Antecedentes históricos de la política internacional de Chile en la Antártica: negociaciones chileno–argentinas de 1906, 1907 y 1908', in Francisco Orrego et al., op. cit., note 48 supra, 67–80. For the discussion of Argentine–Chilean co-operation in the Antarctic, see Vicente A. Palermo: 'Latinoamérica puede más: geopolítica del atlántico sur', in F. A. Milia et al., op. cit., note 49 supra, 163–194, and Patricia A. Operti: 'Pretensiones chilenas en Antártida', *Revista de Derecho Internacional y Ciencias Diplomáticas*, Vol. XXIX, N° 50–51, 1981, 89–96.

51. Colin Bertram in *Arctic and Antarctic. A prospect of the Polar regions*, 1957, remarks at 105: 'It should not pass unremarked that the first and only shots so far fired in anger in Antarctica were in 1952, when Argentines attempted to affright a British party . . .'. Other incidents of the period are reported in Sir Vivian Fuchs, op. cit., note 1 supra, particularly at 75.

52. See generally Francisco Orrego Vicuña: 'Antarctic conflict and international cooperation', in U.S. Polar Research Board: *Antarctic Treaty System. An Assessment*, 1986, 55–64. See also James B. Oerding: *The Frozen friction point. A geopolitical analysis of sovereignty in the Antarctic peninsula*, M.A. Thesis, Department of Geography, University of Florida, 1977, Unpublished. Robert D. Hayton: 'The "American" Antarctic', *A.J.I.L.*, Vol. 50, 1956, 583–610. F. M. Auburn: *Antarctic Law and Politics*, 1982, 48–61. Trevor Hatherton: 'Antarctica prior to the Antarctic Treaty – an historical perspective', in U.S. Polar Research Board, op. cit., 15–32.

53. On the Falkland Islands dispute see generally: Julius Goebel: *The struggle for the Falkland Islands*, A study in legal and diplomatic history, 1927. Gerard Cohen Jonathan: 'Les Iles Falkland (Malouines)', *An. Fr.D.I.*, Vol. XVIII, 1972, 235–262. Raphael Perl: *The Falkland Islands Dispute in international law and politics: a documentary sourcebook*, 1983. E. Shackleton: *Falkland Islands economic study*, 1982, HMSO. Cmnd 8653, 1982. Peter J. Beck: 'Cooperative confrontation in the Falkland Islands Dispute. The Anglo–Argentine search for

a way forward, 1968–1981', *J.I.A.S.W.A.*, Vol. 24, 1982, 37–58. C. R. S. Symmons: 'Who owns the Falkland Island Dependencies in International Law? An analysis of certain recent British and Argentinian official statements', *I.C.L.Q.*, Vol. 33, 1984, 726–736. Enrique Ferrer Vieyra: *Las islas Malvinas y el derecho internacional*, 1984. On the relationship of this dispute to Antarctica, Russell W. MacKechnie Jr: 'Sovereignty in Antarctica: the Anglo-Argentine dispute', Comment, *Sy. J.I.L.C.*, Vol. 5, 1977, 119–148. F. M. Auburn: 'The Falkland Islands Dispute and Antarctica', *Marine Policy Reports*, Vol. 5, N° 3, December 1982, 1–4. D. W. H. Walton: 'The first South Georgia leases: Compañía Argentina de Pesca and the South Georgia Exploring Company Limited', *Pol. Rec.*, Vol. 21, N° 132, 1982, 231–240. Peter J. Beck: 'Britain's Falklands Future. The need to look back', *The Round Table*, 1984, N° 290, 139–152. Charles Swithinbank: 'The Antarctic Connection', in: The Geography of the Falkland Islands, *Geographical Journal*, 1983, Vol. 149, part I, 8–9. Enrique Ferrer Vieyra: *Problemática jurídica de la Antártida Argentina*, Lecture delivered on 28 April 1981, Department of Political Science, School of Law and Social Sciences, Universidad Nacional de Córdova, Mimeo. Ibid., op. cit., this note, Chapter 5, at 263–286. Lord Shackleton: 'The Falkland Islands and Antarctica', *Proceedings of the Royal Institution*, Vol. 56, 1984, 147–160. Christopher C. Joyner: 'Anglo-Argentine rivalry after the Falkland-Malvinas war: laws, geopolitics, and the Antarctic connection', *Lawyer of the Americas*, Vol. 15, 1984, 467–502. Robert Fox: *Antarctica and the South Atlantic. Discovery, development and dispute*, 1985. House of Lords: 'Debate on the Falklands and the Antarctic', *Official Report*, Parliamentary debates (Hansard), Vol. 462, N° 77, Monday 22 April 1985, Cols. 904–953. The idea of extending the Antarctic Treaty so as to include the Falkland Islands has been considered at various occasions, for which see 'U.K. materials on International Law 1983: Antarctic Treaty', *B.Y.B.I.L.*, Vol. 54, 1983, 488–495, at 488; and U.K. Liberal Party Foreign Affairs Panel: *The Falkland Islands. A secure and peaceful future*, 1984.

54. Jacqueline Dutheil de la Rochere: 'L'Affaire au Canal Beagle', *An. Fr.D.I.*, 1977, 408–435. Brigitte Bollecker-Stern: 'L'arbitrage dans l'affaire au Canal de Beagle entre l'Argentine et le Chili', *R.G.D.I.P.*, 1979, 7–52. See also Auburn op. cit., note 52 supra, at 57. See also the Treaty of Peace and Friendship between Chile and Argentina, signed on November 29, 1984, and related material, *I.L.M.*, Vol. XXIV, 1985, 1–31.

55. See, for example, 'German raiders in the Antarctic during the second world war', *Pol. Rec*, Vol. 6, N° 43, January 1952, 399–403. On strategic interests generally, James P. McDeritt Jr: *The geopolitical and geostrategic importance of the antarctic regions*, Dissertation, Institute of International Law and Relations, Catholic University of America, Washington, 1966. Laurence M. Gould: *Antarctica in World Affairs*, Foreign Policy Association, Headline Series, N° 128, March–April 1958. Chile: 'Declaración del Ministerio de Relaciones Exteriores sobre Ensayos nucleares en la antártica', 1 December 1959, *Memoria*, 1959, 704–705. Laurie Barber: 'Keeping New Zealand's back door closed', *N.Z.I.R.*, Vol. VII, N° 3, May–June 1982, 13–14. Deborah Shapley: 'Pax Antarctica', *Bulletin of the Atomic Scientists*, Vol. 40, N° 6, June–July 1984, 30–33. Ron Purver: 'Security and arms control at the poles', *International Journal*, Vol. 39, 1984, 888–910. Melvin A. Conant: 'Polar strategic concerns', *Oceans*, Vol. 28, 1985, 62–66.

56. Enrique Gajardo Villarroel: 'Apuntes para un libro sobre la Historia Diplomática del Tratado Antártico y la participación chilena en su elaboración', Instituto Antártico Chileno, *Revista de Difusión*, N° 10, 1977, 41–74.

57. See the Declaration concerning the Inter-American Treaty of Reciprocal Assistance made by Argentina, Chile and the United States on signing the Antarctic Treaty on 1 December 1959, Bush, op. cit., note 7 supra, at 44. See also the Declaration by Chile and the statements by Argentina and the United States with occasion of the signature of the Final Act of the Conference for the amendment of the Inter-American Treaty of Reciprocal Assistance, San José, Costa Rica, July 1975, *I.L.M.*, Vol. XIV, 1975, 1117–1132 at 1121. The defence obligations under the Inter-American arrangements has also been invoked by Peru as a justification of its Antarctic interest, for which see the Peruvian note of accession to the Antarctic Treaty of 10 April 1981 and the press communique of 11 April 1981, in Edgardo Mercado Jarrin et al.: *El Perú y la Antártida*, 1984, 259–261.

58. Walter Sullivan: 'Antarctica in a two-power world', *For. Af.*, Vol. 36, 1957–1958, 154–166.

59. Peter A. Toma: 'Soviet attitude towards the acquisition of territorial sovereignty in the Antarctic', *A.J.I.L.*, Vol. 50, 1956, 611–626. The Soviet Memorandum of June 7, 1950 is reproduced at 625. A slightly different translation is given in Marjorie M. Whiteman: *Digest of International Law*, Vol. 2, 1963, at 1255. See also Boleslaw A. Boczek: 'The Soviet Union and the Antarctic regime', *A.J.I.L.*, Vol. 78, 1984, 834–858.

60. See generally Hackworth, op. cit., note 12 supra and Whiteman, op. cit., note 59 supra. See also Lawrence M. Gould: *The Polar Regions in their relation to human affairs*, The American Geographical Society, 1958. John Hanessian Jr: 'Antarctica: current national interests and legal realities', *Proc. A.J.I.L.*, 1958, 145–164. O. J. Lissitzyn: 'The American position in outer space and Antarctica', Editorial Comment, *A.J.I.L.*, Vol. 53, 1959, 126–131. C. Hartley Grattan: *The United States and the Southwest Pacific*, 1961, particularly at 55–58, 240–247. CIA: *Polar Regions Atlas*, 1978. B. M. Plott: *The development of United States Antarctic Policy*, Ph.D. Thesis, Fletcher School of Law and Diplomacy, 1969. F. M. Auburn: 'United States Antarctic Policy', *M.T.S.J.*, Vol. 12, N° 1, February–March 1978, 31–36. Joseph Macknis: 'United States Policy in Antarctica', *Marine Policy Reports*, Vol. 2, N° 2, May 1979. Robert H. Rutford: 'United States Antarctic Program', in Lewis M. Alexander and Lynne Carter Hanson (eds): *Antarctic politics and Marine resources: critical choices for the 1980's*, 1985, 55–64.

61. See generally the works by Toma and Boczek cit., note 59 supra. See also S. Wolck: 'The Basis of Soviet claims in the Antarctic', *Bulletin of the Institute for the Study of the USSR*, Vol. 5, N° 4, April 1958, 43–48.

62. F. M. Auburn, op. cit., note 52 supra, at 105–106.

63. The background of a potential Soviet claim is discussed by the authors cited in note 61 supra. See in particular the Resolution of the All-Soviet Geographical Society of February 10, 1949, on rights of discovery and participation, reproduced in Appendix II of the Article by Toma, cit., note 59 supra.

64. John Hanessian Jr, loc. cit., note 60 supra, with particular reference to the resolution introduced in the United States House of Representatives claiming the area between 90° W and 150° W, *H.J. Res. 353*, 2nd. Session, 83rd Congress, January 1954. See also Joint Resolution on claim of sovereignty: *H.J. Res. 184*, 85th. Congress, 1st session, January 23, 1957.

65. F. M. Auburn, op. cit., note 52 supra, at 67.

66. Walter Sullivan, loc. cit., note 58 supra, at 156.

67. F. M. Auburn, op. cit., note 52 supra, at 65–67.

68. Walter Sullivan, loc. cit., note 58 supra, at 156. The possibility of a claim was also suggested in Belgium: Jean Van Asbroeck: 'L'Actualité des questions

antarctiques et la Belgique', *Bulletin de la Societé Royale de Geographie d'Anvers*, Tome LXI, 1946–1947, 42–58.

69. Kamae Taijudo: 'Japan and the problems of sovereignty over the polar regions', *Jap. A.N.I.L.*, N° 3, 1959, 12–17, at 15.

70. International Court of Justice: *Pleadings, Antarctica Cases* (United Kingdom v. Argentina; United Kingdom v. Chile), 1955.

71. Statement of the Foreign Office of January 18, 1949, in Whiteman, op. cit., note 59 supra, at 1238. See also David Winston Heron: 'Antarctic Claims', *For. Af*, Vol. 32, 1953–1954, 661–667.

72. J. S. Reeves: 'George V Land', Editorial Comment, *A.J.I.L.*, Vol. 28, 1934, 117–119, at 119.

73. T. E. M. McKitterick: 'The validity of territorial and other claims in polar regions', *J. Comp. Leg. I.L.*, Vol. XXI, 1939, 89–97.

74. G. C. L. Bertram: 'Antarctic Prospect', *Int. Af*, Vol. 33, 1957, 143–153, at 153.

75. A. P. Movchan: 'The legal status of Antarctica: an international problem', *Sov. Y.B.I.L.*, 1959, 342–359.

76. R. N. Rudmose Brown: 'Political claims in the Antarctic', *World Affairs*, October 1947, 393–401, at 401.

77. Beverly May Carl: 'International Law – claims to sovereignty – Antarctica', Comments, *S.C.L. Rev.*, Vol. 28, 1954–1955, 386–400, at 397.

78. L. F. E. Goldie: 'International relations in Antarctica', *Aust. Q.* Vol. XXX, 1958, 7–29. Robert D. Hayton: 'The Nations and Antarctica', *O.Z.F.O.R.*, Vol. X, 1959–1960, 368–412, with particular reference to a significant indirect role of the United Nations, at 410. See also Sullivan, loc. cit., note 58 supra, at 164. Hanessian, loc. cit., note 60 supra.

79. Philip C. Jessup: 'Sovereignty in Antarctica', *A.J.I.L.*, Vol. 41, 1947, 117–119.

80. G. C. L. Bertram: *Antarctica today and tomorrow*, University of Otago, Dunedin, 1957, 25–30.

81. Ibid.

82. J. Daniel: 'Conflict of sovereignties in the Antarctic', *Y.B.W.A.*, Vol. 3, 1949, 241–272.

83. René Jean Dupuy: 'Le Statut de l'Antarctique', *An. Fr.D.I.*, IV, 1958, 196–229.

84. C. Wilfred Jenks: 'An International regime for Antarctica?', *Int. Af*, Vol. 32, 1956, 414–426. Updated in *The Common Law of Mankind*, 1958, Chapter 8.

85. Philip C. Jessup and Howard J. Taubenfeld: 'Outer Space, Antarctica and the United Nations', *IO.*, Vol. XIII, 1959, 363–379. Philip C. Jessup and Howard J. Taubenfeld: *Controls for outer space and the Antarctic analogy*, 1959. See also for other proposal on U.N. Control, Edward Shackleton: 'Antarctica: the case for permanent international control, a possible solution', *World Affairs*, N° 243, May–June 1958, 23–25.

86. Hugh Odishaw: 'The International Geophysical Year and World Politics', *J. Int. Af.*, Vol. 13, 1959, 47–56. Gordon Brewster Baldwin: 'The Dependence of Science on Law and Government – The International Geophysical Year – A case study', *Wisc. L. Rev.*, 1964, 78–118. Robert H. Rutford: 'Summary of science in Antarctic prior to and excluding the IGY', in U.S. Polar Research Board, op. cit., note 52 supra, 87–101.

87. Walter Sullivan: *Quest for a Continent*, 1957. By the same author, 'The International Geophysical Year', *Int. Conc.*, N° 521, January 1959, 259–336. Also ibid.: *Assault on the Unknown. The International Geophysical Year*, 1961. See also U.S. House of Representatives, Committee on Foreign Affairs, Subcommittee on National Security Policy and Scientific Developments: *The Political Legacy of the International Geophysical Year*, prepared by Harold Bullis, November 1973.

88. Richard S. Lewis: 'Antarctic research and the relevance of science', *Sci. Publ. Af.*, Vol. XXVI, N° 10, December 1970, 2–4, at 4.

89. Robert D. Hayton: 'Legal problems and the political situation in the Polar Areas', Remarks by the chairman of panel, *Proc. A.S.I.L.*, 1958, 135–136, 171–174. See also Sullivan, loc. cit., note 58 supra, at 164. Hanessian, loc. cit., note 60 supra.

90. See generally F. M. Auburn, op. cit., note 52 supra, 84–94. See in particular the secret document PPS-31, prepared by the Policy Planning Staff, dated June 9, 1948, putting forward the U.S. proposals for Antarctica, in *Foreign Relations of the United States, 1948*, Vol. 1, Part 2, 1976, 977–987.

91. The possibility of a condominium as an alternative to individual claims has been raised a number of times, particularly in the context of New Zealand and United States co-operation. See in particular the following works by F. M. Auburn: 'The White Desert', *I.C.L.Q.*, Vol. 19, 1970, 229–256. 'The Ross Dependency – An undeclared condominium', *Auckland University Law Review*, Vol. I, N° 3, 1970, 89–106. 'A sometime world of men: legal rights in the Ross Dependency', *A.J.I.L.*, Vol. 65, 1971, 578–582. Also *The Ross Dependency*, 1972. On condominium in international law, D. P. O'Connell: 'The Condominium of the New Hebrides', *B.Y.B.I.L.*, 43, 1968–1969, 71–145, with particular reference to Antartica at 71.

92. For the diplomatic correspondence related to the Memorandum Escudero, Bush, op. cit., note 7 supra, Vol. II, 383–384.

93. The proposals for the internationalization of Antarctica will be examined in Chapter 10 infra. See also: 'Issues before the eleventh General Assembly: Antarctica', *Int. Conc.*, N° 510, November 1956, 135–143, particularly at 142–143.

94. For the Question at the House of Commons on April 25, 1956, and the reply by the Minister of State for Foreign Affairs, Whiteman op. cit., note 59 supra, at 1239.

95. Robert D. Hayton: 'Polar problems and international law', Notes and Comments, *A.J.I.L.*, Vol. 52, 1958, 746–765 at 755.

96. Ibid.

97. Barbara Mitchell: *Frozen Stakes. The Future of Antarctic Minerals*, International Institute for Environment and Development, 1983, at 93.

98. Hanessian, loc. cit., note 60 supra.

99. US Department of State: *The Conference on Antarctica*, 1960. See also *United States Policy and international cooperation in Antarctica*, Message from the President of the United States, 88th. Congress, 2nd. Session, House Document N° 358, 1964. For the interest of Poland in participating in the Conference, Jacek Machowski: *The Status of Antarctica in the light of international law*, National Centre for Scientific, technical and economic information, Warsaw, Poland, 1977.

100. Conference on Antarctica: *Final Act, A.J.I.L.*, Vol. 54, 1960, Official Documents, 476–483. The Antarctic Treaty, Washington 1 December 1959, *U.N.T.S.*, Vol. 402, 1961, N° 5778, 71–102. *United Kingdom Treaty Series*, N° 97, 1961, Cmnd. 1535. For United Kingdom legislation, The Antarctic Treaty order in Council, 1962, *S.I.*, 1962/401.

101. J. A. Heap: 'Cooperation in the Antarctic: a quarter of a century's experience', in Francisco Orrego Vicuña, op. cit., note 3 supra, 105–106.

102. Diplomatic material is, however, available in the collection of Papers of Admiral George Dufek at the George Arents Research Library, Syracuse University. See Quigg, op. cit., note 5 supra, at 145 and associated text to note 9. For a study based on this material see Peter J. Beck: 'Preparatory meeting for the Antarctic Treaty 1958–59', *Pol. Rec.*, Vol. 22, N° 141, 1985, 653–664.

103. Christopher Beeby: *The Antarctic Treaty*, New Zealand Institute of International Affairs, 1972. Paul C. Daniels: 'The Antarctic Treaty', *Sci. Publ. Af.*, Vol. XXVI, N° 10, December 1970, 11–15. Henry M. Dater: 'The Antarctic Treaty in Action, 1961–1971', *Ant. J.U.S.*, Vol. VI, N° 3, May–June 1971, 67–72. René-Jean Dupuy: 'Le Traité sur l'Antarctique', *An. Fr. D.I.*, 1960, 111–132. Costas P. Economides: 'Le statut internationál de l'Antarctique résultant du traité du 1 Decembre 1959:, *Rev. Hel. D.I.*, Vol. 15, 1962, 76–86. Roberto E. Guyer: 'The Antarctic System', *Rec. Cours. Ac. D.I.*, Vol. 139, 1973-II, 149–226. Edvard Hambro: 'A Noble experiment', *Norseman*, N° 1, 1975, 7–10. John Hanessian Jr: 'The Antarctic Treaty', *American Universities Field Staff*, Reports Service, Polar Area Series. Vol. I, N° 2, July 6, 1960. John Hanessian: 'The Antarctic Treaty 1959', *I.C.L.Q.*, Vol. 9, 1960, 436–480. Robert D. Hayton: 'The Antarctic settlement of 1959', *A.J.I.L.*, Vol. 54, 1960, 349–371. Adolfo Scilingo: *El Tratado Antártico*, 1963. K. R. Simmonds: 'The Antarctic Treaty, 1959', *J.D.I.*, 1960, N° 3, 668–701. Alfred van der Essen: 'Le probleme politico-juridique de l'Antarctique et le Traité de Washington du 1er decembre 1959', *Annales de Droit et de Sciences Politiques*, Tome XX, N° 3, 1960, 227–252. See also U.S. Senate, Committee on Foreign Relations, Hearing on *The Antarctic Treaty*, 86th Congress, 2nd session, June 14, 1960, USGPO, 1960. Henry S. Francis Jr: 'The Antarctic Treaty – a reality before its time', in Lewis M. Alexander and Lynne Carter Hanson, op. cit., note 60 supra, 87–98.
104. This argument is frequently associated with the initiatives related to declaring Antarctica the common heritage of mankind, which will be examined in Chapter 10 infra.
105. Bernardo N. Rodriguez: 'Soberanía argentina en la Antártida', in F. A. Milia et al, op. cit., note 49 supra, 195–216. Jorge A. Fraga: 'El futuro incierto político-económico de la Antártida', in Milia, op. cit., 225–235. For a campaign opposing the ratification of the Antarctic Treaty, Alberto M. Candioti: *El Tratado Antártico no debe ratificarse*, Buenos Aires, 1960. Ibid: *El Tratado Antártico y nuestras fuerzas armadas*, Buenos Aires, 1960.
106. J. H. W. Verzijl: *International Law in Historical Perspective*, Part IV, 274–276. Finn Sollie: 'The political experiment in Antarctica', *Sci. Publ. Af.*, Vol. XXVI, N° 10, December 1970, 16–21. Ye. K. Fedorov: 'Antarctica: Experimental proving ground for peaceful coexistence and International Collaboration', *Sci. Publ. Af.*, Vol. XXVI, N° 10, December 1970, 22–28. G. N. Barrie: 'The Antarctic Treaty: example of law and its sociological infrastructure', *Comp. I.L.J. South. Afr.*, Vol. VIII, 1975, 212–224. D. W. Greig: 'Territorial sovereignty and the status of Antarctica', *Australian Outlook*, 32, 1978, 2, 117–129. O. Khlestov, V. Golitsyn: 'The Antarctic: arena of peaceful cooperation', *Int. Af.* (USSR), August 1978, 61–66. G. I. Tunkin: 'An example of International Co-operation', *Int. Af.* (USSR), 1960, 2, 42–45.
107. Giovanni Kojanec: 'La situazione giuridica dell'Antartide', *La Communitá Internazionale*, Vol. 15, 1960, 21–48, at 48.
108. Taijudo, loc. cit., note 69 supra, at 17.
109. See the works by Jessup and Taubenfeld cited in note 85 supra. Also Howard J. Taubenfeld: 'A Treaty for Antarctica', *Int. Conc*, N° 531, January 1961, 245–322.
110. Francisco Orrego Vicuña: *Los Fondos Marinos y Oceánicos*, Santiago, 1976, at 259.
111. See Chapter 10 infra.
112. Hans Kelsen: *Principles of International Law*, 1966, at 337.
113. The following countries have acceded to the Antarctic Treaty, a list given in chronological order: Poland (8 June 1961), Czechoslovakia (14 June 1962), Denmark (20 May 1965), Netherlands (30 March 1967), Romania (15 September

1971), German Democratic Republic (19 November 1974), Brazil (16 May 1975), Bulgaria (11 September 1978), Federal Republic of Germany (5 February 1979), Uruguay (11 January 1980), Papua New Guinea (16 March 1981), Italy (18 March 1981), Peru (10 April 1981), Spain (31 March 1982), Peoples Republic of China (8 June 1983), India (19 August 1983), Hungary (27 January 1984), Sweden (24 April 1984), Finland (15 May 1984), and Cuba (16 August 1984). The following acceding countries became Consultative Parties on the dates shown: Poland (17 September 1977), Federal Republic of Germany (23 June 1981), Brazil and India (12 September 1983). See generally R. K., Headland: 'Antarctic Treaty; signatories and dates', *Pol. Rec.*, Vol. 22, N° 139, 1985, 438–439, as corrected in *Pol. Rec.*, Vol. 22, N° 140, 1985, 559. The People's Republic of China and Uruguay became Consultative Parties on 7th October, 1985.

114. See generally Hayton, loc. cit., note 95 supra, at 759. For the Brazilian interest in Antarctica see Clovis Ramalhete: 'A Antarctica e o Brasil', *Revista de Informacao Legislativa do Senado Federal*, Vol. 12, N° 48, 1975, 41–56; Joao Frank da Costa: 'Antártida: O problema político', *Revista Brasileira de Política Internacional*, Vol. 4, N° 15, 1961, 85–102; Joao Grandino Rodas: 'Brasil adere ao Tratado da Antártida', *Revista da Faculdade de Direito, Universidade de Sao Paulo*, N° 71, 1976, 151–161; José Enrique Greno Velasco: 'La adhesión de Brasil al Tratado Antártico', *Revista de Política Internacional*, N° 146, July–August 1976, 71–89. For the interest of Ecuador, see Jorge W. Villacres M: *Los Derechos del Ecuador en la Antártida*, Instituto de Diplomacia, 1979, Mimeo. For the interest of Peru, see Edgardo Mercado Jarrin et al.: *El Perú y la Antártida*, 1984, and particularly the following contributions therein published: Jorge del Aguila: 'Posibilidades de la primera expedición peruana a la Antártida', at 185–194; Edgardo Mercado Jarrin: 'La Antártida: intereses geopolíticos', at 107–146, including a graphic of the suggested Peruvian claim; José Herrera Rosas: 'Importancia geoestratégica de la antártida', at 87–106; Percy R. Cano: 'Aspectos técnicos, científicos y de recursos naturales sobre la Antártida', at 25–62; and Marcelino Alegría Amar: 'Aspectos geográficos y políticos de la Antártida', at 1–24, see also Comisión Nacional de Asuntos Antárticos, Decreto Supremo N° 009-83-RE, 11 July 1983, in *Revista Peruana de Derecho Internacional*, Vol. XXXV, July–September 1983, 63–65. For the interest of Uruguay, see Heber Arbuet, Roberto Puceiro and Belter Garré: *Antártida: continente de los más, para los menos*, 1979.

115. Material and discussion relating to the Italian accession can be seen in Giuseppe Vedovato: 'L'Antartide Oggi', *Riv. Studi. Pol. Int.*, Vol. XLVII, N° 2, 1980, 215–223; Felice Benuzzi: 'Il Trattato sull'Antartide', *Riv. Studi. Pol. Int.*, Vol. XLVII, N° 2, 1980, 224–236. Also 'Italian expedition worked off west coast of Antarctic Peninsula', *Antarctic*, Vol. 7, N° 9, March 1976, 304–305. On the accession of India, Deborah Shapley: 'India in Antarctica: international treaty still on ice', *Nature*, Vol. 301, N° 5899, 3 February 1983, at 362. See also Chapters 9 and 10 infra.

116. For an analysis of national values and priorities on a country by country basis, see generally William E. Westermeyer: *The Politics of Mineral Resource Development in Antarctica*, 1984, Chapter 6.

117. It is of interest to note that in the analysis by Westermeyer both Argentina and Chile would favour an Antarctic regime based on arrangements other than the territorial approach, most probably in the form of a consortium, at least in so far as mineral resources are concerned. Westermeyer, op. cit., note 116 supra, at 156–159, 162–163.

118. Francisco Orrego Vicuña: 'La proyección extracontinental de Chile', in: Francisco Orrego Vicuña, María Teresa Infante and Pilar Armanet (eds), op. cit., note 48 supra, 15–34.

119. See the works cited in note 91 supra.
120. Auburn, op. cit., note 52 supra, at 256.
121. Heap, loc. cit., note 101 supra, at 106–107.
122. Ibid.
123. Agreed Measures for the Conservation of the Antarctic Fauna and Flora, Recommendation III–VIII, adopted at the Third Consultative Meeting, Brussels, 2–13 June 1964, text in Antarctic Treaty: *Handbook of measures in furtherance of the principles and objectives of the Antarctic Treaty*, Third edition, April 1983, at 2101. Hereinafter cited as *Agreed Measures*.
124. Convention for the Conservation of Antarctic Seals, done in London on 1st June 1972, text in Antarctic Treaty, *Handbook* cit., note 123 supra, at 9301.
125. Convention on the Conservation of Antarctic Marine Living Resources, done in Canberra on 20th May 1980, text in Handbook cit., note 123 supra, at 9501.
126. Daniel Torres: 'Explotación y conservación de mamíferos marinos en la antártica', in Francisco Orrego Vicuña and Augusto Salinas A. (eds): *El desarrollo de la antártica*, 1977, 186–225.
127. See Chapter 2 infra.
128. Guyer, loc. cit., note 103 supra.
129. See Chapter 3 infra.
130. See Chapter 4 infra.
131. This aspect is discussed in Part II of this work.
132. Part III of this work discusses the international dimensions and relationships of the Antarctic system.
133. See the works cited in notes 86 and 87 supra.

2

The Antarctic legal system and the development of a norm-creating function in the field of natural resources

2.1   The Antarctic Treaty as a basic legal framework

The Antarctic Treaty deals primarily with those issues which at the time of its negotiation were a matter of concern for the countries active in the area. As was explained in the previous chapter, these concerns referred in particular to the freedom of scientific research, exchange of information, prevention of a military build-up and organization of elementary forms of co-operation among the countries involved. The aims of the Treaty, therefore, have been to ensure that the activities in Antarctica can be conducted without interference arising from political interests of the participating countries.

In this context, the issue of natural resources did not appear at the time to be of an important priority. The only specific reference to natural resources in the Antarctic Treaty is contained in Article IX, 1 (f), which provides that consultative Parties may formulate, consider and recommend measures in furtherance of the principles and objectives of the Treaty, including measures regarding 'preservation and conservation of living resources in Antarctica'. On this basis, there was gradually to develop an extensive norm-creating function concerning such resources and specific aspects of the preservation of the environment.

In the case of mineral resources, however, the 1959 Treaty is silent. The history of the negotiation of that instrument reveals incontrovertibly that this was not a chance omission but was the result of a deliberate intention not to include in the discussions a subject which would make it virtually impossible to achieve an agreement on the delicate question of claims to sovereignty and on the position of those who refused to recognize such claims.[1] Nevertheless, it was not long before the question of mineral resources arose, as it did in fact at the Sixth Consultative Meeting held in Tokyo in 1970 in connection with the interest which had been expressed to certain Governments by private companies in the possibility of prospecting in the Antarctic.[2]

From that moment onwards an important question of the interpretation of the Treaty was raised: namely, whether, and under what conditions, it was possible, under the provisions of the Treaty, to permit activities relating to mineral resources, or whether such activities were prohibited. The implications of the answer given to this question was undoubtedly of great importance not only for the resources policy which the Consultative Parties aspired to achieve but also, and especially, for defining the interpretative criteria applicable to the 1959 Treaty.

This question of interpretation also touches upon interesting aspects related to the applicable rules of interpretation under the Law of Treaties.[3] Because of the fact that the Antarctic Treaty has not set up an international organization, at least in a formal sense, the fundamental competence to interpret the 1959 Treaty belongs to the parties to it and not to any specific organ or tribunal; however, as will be mentioned further below, the development of the Treaty framework has resulted in certain legal effects which are not altogether different from the case of an international organization, thus explaining the role of the Consultative Meetings in a certain institutional sense.

Because of this preponderant interpretative role of the parties, the kind of subsequent agreement between those parties regarding the interpretation or application of the Treaty provisions, the subsequent practice in the application of the Treaty and other relevant rules of international law applicable in the relations between the parties, as provided for in paragraph 3 of Article 31 of the Vienna Convention on the Law of Treaties, have a decisive influence in supplementing a purely contextual approach to the interpretation of the Antarctic Treaty. It is thus necessary to analyse the object and purpose of the Treaty in the broader framework of the Antarctic system, including the recommendations and decisions of Consultative meetings and the conventions entered into by the Treaty parties. The practice of individual parties may also prove relevant in this regard.

This broader and evolutionary approach to the interpretation of the 1959 Antarctic Treaty provides a more flexible aid to the legal process of Antarctic co-operation than would otherwise be the case if narrower rules were applied. Not even the principle postulating a restrictive interpretation of provisions implying a limiting of state sovereignty has found much application in the Antarctic experience, as it neither has had in the decisions of courts generally. On the other hand, there is some evidence of the recourse to the principle of effective interpretation and to the teleological approach that tends to emphasize the need to give effect to the purposes of the Treaty, a tendency that will be further strengthened to the extent that the Antarctic system becomes identified with the concept and scope of a regional organization.

Criteria for interpretation of the Treaty in relation to minerals
The various positions that were adopted in relation to the question of minerals were fully explored at the meeting convened by the Fridtjof Nansen Foundation in 1973 to analyse the problems of exploration and exploitation of the mineral resources of Antarctica.[4] Three main points of view on the matter are summarized in the report of this meeting:[5]

(i) According to one point of view, the commercial exploration for mineral resources was not possible under the terms of the 1959 Treaty as it would be necessary for that purpose either to amend the Treaty or to adopt additional international measures.

(ii) According to another interpretation, the Treaty neither does directly prohibit the activities in question, nor does it permit them. For this reason, any unilateral or multilateral action that might be taken requires the prior consent of all the Consultative Parties, otherwise such action would be a violation of the Treaty and would be contrary to its aims and objectives.

It was pointed out, in particular, that such a situation would be incompatible with the provisions of the Preamble of the Treaty which specifies that Antarctica 'shall not become the scene or object of international discord' and that the intention of the instrument is to ensure that 'the continuance of international harmony in Antarctica will further the purposes and principles embodied in the Charter of the United Nations'. In the same way, according to this point of view, there would also be a violation of another important provision of the Treaty: that of Article X. This provision, which will be examined in Chapter 9, contains a fundamental undertaking by the Contracting Parties 'to exert appropriate efforts, consistent with the Charter of the United Nations, to the end that no one engages in any activity in Antarctica contrary to the principles or purposes of the present Treaty'.

During the discussion on this occasion, it was also pointed out that the standards relating to the protection of information customarily applied by mining companies are incompatible with the provisions of the Treaty on the freedom of scientific investigation (Article II), the exchange of information (Article III, 1 (a) and (c)) and inspections (Article VII). In other analyses, attention was also drawn to Article IV of the Treaty as the basis for a moratorium on activities that might contravene the scientific objectives and the stability of the Treaty regime.[6]

(iii) Others took the position that, as long as the Treaty does not prohibit exploration and exploitation of mineral resources, any Contracting Party or its nationals may undertake such activities, provided they are compatible with the provisions of the Treaty.[7] The proponents of this view were in favour of solving the question on a multilateral basis, using the consultative procedure of Article IX.

Among the Treaty provisions to be observed reference was made to those on peaceful purposes (Article I), freedom of scientific investigation (Article II), exchange of information (Article III), inspections (Article VII, paragraphs 1 to 4), notification of expeditions (Article VII, paragraph 5) and others which might arise from approved recommendations with reference to the protection of the environment. In this context, particular emphasis was placed on the argument that economic activities represent one of the peaceful purposes to which Article I of the Treaty refers, and on the idea that scientific investigation may include activities related to possible future exploitation of resources.[8] This last point, as we shall see, gave rise to serious difficulties in the negotiation of the regime on mineral resources.

The various points of view to which attention has been drawn thus reveal that the extreme position, according to which activities relating to minerals could under no circumstances be carried out, was never adopted since even the first of the points of view enumerated above assumes that such activities may be possible through amendment of the Treaty or the adoption of other international measures. There remained the separate problem of whether or not such action would be appropriate, but this involves considerations which are different in kind from the legal discussion with which we have been dealing.

The second interpretation was even more flexible since it held that an appropriate regime for organizing such activities could be drawn up by consent of the Consultative Parties. The only major limitation is that any initiative that is unilateral or is taken without previous consent, is considered to be a violation of the Treaty. This is the really contentious issue since the third point of view mentioned above, even though it favoured multilateral agreement within the framework of the consultative procedure of Article IX, did not exclude the option of individual action since it considered it as permissible under the Treaty regime. This difference of interpretation was particularly acute in the discussions on the subject of a moratorium on activities which will be considered below.

Restrictive interpretations and dynamic interpretation

Both the point of view held by some non-parties and commentators in the context of the present international debate about Antarctica – which will be examined in Chapter 9 – that maintains that action in relation to mineral resources is not possible under the present terms of the Treaty and the diametrically opposed point of view which postulates freedom of action on the grounds that it is not specifically prohibited are based on a somewhat literal interpretation of the 1959 Treaty. Such an approach is rather narrow and static since it is not truly in accordance with the trend of the system of Antarctic co-operation since its inception and, more dangerous still, it introduces in both cases serious causes of friction which would be very likely to affect the normal operation of the system.

The true nature and scope of the provisions of the Treaty and of the system of co-operation to which it gave rise can be more clearly perceived if we adopt a dynamic criterion of interpretation, that is to say, one which is capable of analysing the rules in force in the context of the intentions on which they were originally based and of the spirit which governs the progress of the system as a whole.

From this point of view, the most extreme positions that have been mentioned may reasonably be open to criticism. Indeed, even though it is a fact that the Treaty does not specifically prohibit mineral activities and does not even refer to them, to maintain that such activities cannot be conducted under the terms of the Treaty is to overlook the capacity for evolution and adaptation which has always characterized the system, particularly in the field of natural resources, as can be seen from what has been said in the previous chapter. Such an evolution and adaptation is also very much in line with the development of international law concerning the interpretation of treaties, which has resulted in a more flexible legal approach to the matter as has been examined above.

On the other hand, even though no one doubts that the intention of those wishing to conduct mining activities is of a peaceful nature, it cannot be concluded that, because they are compatible with Article I of the Treaty, such activities may be undertaken in total freedom. In this context, the drafting history of the Treaty becomes important since it makes clear that the subject of mineral resources was not included in the negotiation because it was felt that its inclusion would make it impossible to achieve an agreement on other priority matters such as sovereignty.[9] Given this background, it is difficult to justify the position of total liberty to exploit resources since there is every indication that, today, difficulties similar to those which were feared in 1959 would make their appearance, to say nothing of the fact that it is by no means easy to reconcile this approach with other requirements and provisions of the Treaty.[10]

A more reasonable view would, therefore, seem to be that such activities are possible, but in the context of a regime previously agreed by the Consultative Parties or through other procedures and negotiations which may involve other Treaty Parties and interested countries. The main task of such a regime, in addition to organizing these activities, is to harmonize the necessity of such operations with the requirements of the Treaty and thus to maintain inviolate the spirit of balance on which Antarctic co-operation is based.

The Antarctic Treaty as a 'framework convention' (traité-cadre)

From this point of view the Antarctic Treaty may be classified as a type of 'framework convention' (*traité-cadre*), category now frequently used in the case of the processes of regional economic integration.[11] This kind of treaty will normally set out the fundamental provisions and machinery, leaving the further detailed development of the law to the subsequent action of the parties.

The 1959 Treaty thus does no more than indicate the central purposes and objectives of the system, establishes the basic provisions and provides the minimum institutional machinery for achieving co-operation. The development of the system and its specific application to various subjects is a task for the Consultative Parties under the mandate given in Article IX and in other provisions of the Treaty, all of which provides a basis for the adaptation and the evolution which has been identified as one of the major characteristics of the Antarctic system. The basic framework is thus complemented by the norm-creating function of the Consultative Parties in a manner comparable to what Philip Allott has described in relation to the Law of the Sea Convention as the new legal reality of '*powers* delegated en masse and leading to a cascade of derived activity (legislative, decision making, enforcing)'.[12]

It is interesting to observe that, after initially encountering differences, the Consultative Parties themselves accepted the criterion of dynamic interpretation and the conception of the Antarctic Treaty as a basic legal framework that was capable of subsequent development.[13] None of these Parties questions the legal feasibility of approving a regime for mineral resources even though there have been differences as regards its specific modalities. In the same way, the norm creating function has gradually been exercised in regard to the exploration and exploitation of natural resources and other matters. This is an important case in which the subsequent conduct of the Parties serves as a valuable element in the interpretation of the legal regime that was set up in 1959.

2.2   Norm-creating activity in relation to natural resources
From the outset, one of the major concerns of the system of Antarctic co-operation has been to organize the activities relating to the utilization of natural resources and other activities which may have implications for the more general aims of environmental conservation.[14] The main fields in which this norm-creating function has been apparent are three in number: in relation to living resources, in relation to the impact of man on the Antarctic environment and, lastly, in relation to the exploration and exploitation of mineral resources.

The protection of fauna and flora
The first of these functions was undoubtedly facilitated by the mandate received by the Consultative Parties under the provision of Article IX, paragraph 1 (f), of the Treaty in which the 'preservation and conservation of living resources in Antarctica' are specifically envisaged.[15] The protection of the Antarctic fauna and flora emerged as an issue at the First Consultative Meeting held in Canberra in July 1961. Recommendation I-VIII acknowledged 'the urgent need for measures to conserve the living resources of the Treaty area and to protect them from uncontrolled destruction', and at the same time recommended the adoption, on a provisional basis, of standards of conduct in this regard which had previously been drawn up by the Scientific Committee on Antarctic Research (SCAR).[16] Recommendation II-II also insisted, one year later, on this need.[17]

One step of particular significance was the adoption of Recommendation III-VIII by the Third Consultative Meeting, held in Brussels in June 1964, which contains the Agreed Measures for the Conservation of Antarctic Fauna and Flora.[18] The area of application of the Antarctic Treaty was formally declared to be a 'Special Conservation Area' and the establishment of 'Specially Protected Areas' and of standards to be observed in order to achieve the protection of fauna and flora were also decided upon. These measures gave rise to intensive subsequent norm-creating activity undertaken by the Consultative Parties in order to apply them adequately, and the measures were also supplemented by additional recommendations.[19] Among the latter, it is worth mentioning as an example the recommendations on the establishment of 'Sites of Special Scientific Interest'.[20] The particular legal characteristics of this instrument will be commented on further below.

The conservation of seals

The conservation of the Antarctic seal has been another specific subject in which the norm-creating function of the system has been brought into play. In this case, however, because of difficulties of interpretation as to whether the 1959 Treaty could be applied to the living resources of the sea, the approach followed was different. In spite of some recommendations by consultative meetings on the need for voluntary regulations and for provisional measures to achieve that end,[21] sealing was finally regulated by a separate convention which was opened for signature on 1 June 1972.[22] This Convention established the important precedent of approving particular regimes on resources by means of a treaty which also forms part of the Antarctic legal order or system. The hunting of whales, which was also regulated by means of a treaty,[23] is a different case which, because of the global distribution of the resource, falls outside the specific Antarctic framework.

The conservation of the living resources of the sea

The above-mentioned steps facilitated in due course the comprehensive treatment of the problem of the utilization and conservation of the marine living resources of Antarctica. This other field of co-operation pre-supposed the adoption of a definitive ruling as to whether the system, as far as its participating States were concerned, was competent to regulate the utilization of resources in the related marine areas, a decision which was a gradual process as we shall have occasion to note in dealing with the law of the sea in Antarctica. In any case, since the subject was first raised at the Eighth Consultative Meeting in Oslo in 1975, appropriate action was undertaken in a systematic manner.

Recommendation VIII-10 adopted on that occasion cleared the way for recognition of 'the need to promote and achieve, within the framework of the Antarctic Treaty, the objectives of protection, scientific study and rational use of these marine living resources'.[24] Recommendation IX-2, for its part, formally introduced the important concept of 'special responsibility conferred upon the Consultative Parties in respect of the preservation and conservation of living resources in the Antarctic'. In compliance with this criterion, measures were recommended concerning scientific research, provisional guidelines for conservation and the convening of a Special Consultative Meeting to establish the appropriate regime.[25]

The delicate work of the Second Special Consultative Meeting led to the adoption of the Convention on the Conservation of Antarctic Marine Living Resources, adopted in Canberra on 20 May 1980.[26] This instrument, some of whose provisions will be considered in connection with precedents for problems of the regime on mineral resources, not only represented an important step forward in the improvement of co-operation in the field of resources[27] but also denoted a substantive change in the orientation of the system as a whole. From that moment onwards, the characteristics of the process of internal and external accommodation in the light of the needs of the resources policy can be clearly seen. Furthermore, it was through this instrument that the concept of Antarctica as an ecosystem was duly recognized while at the same time a considerable step forward was taken towards the institutionalization of the system.

The protection of the Antarctic environment

In parallel with these developments, the system of co-operation was establishing its competence to deal with the problems of the Antarctic environment in a broad sense, even though this subject is not specifically covered in the provisions of the 1959 Treaty. A number of recommendations on 'the impact of man in the Antarctic environment' have given expression to this other concern.[28] Recommendation VI-4 particularly highlighted the concept of the ecosystem and the need to protect the environment from human interference, insisting that the Consultative Parties 'should assume responsibility for the protection of the environment and the wise use of the Treaty Area'.[29]

Recommendation VIII-11 approved an instrument of particular importance in this respect, namely the Code of Conduct for Antarctic expeditions and the activities of Antarctic bases, which envisages, among other measures, the assessment of the environmental impact of major operations which it is proposed to conduct in the Treaty area.[30] Recommendation XII-4 on its part placed on record the necessity of revising the Code in the light of experience and of problems encountered in the treatment and disposal of wastes from the bases.[31]

The concern with environmental matters also brought into sharper focus the relationship between the Antarctic system and the interest that has been shown by certain international organizations. As we shall see in due course, FAO, UNEP and the United Nations have from time to time expressed views on the subject.[32] In this connection, the Antarctic Treaty Parties, operating within the Antarctic system, on the basis that Antarctica is a 'global climatic regulator of major importance', have shown interest in the possibility of co-operating with the competent organizations and, at the same time, have reaffirmed that special responsibility for environmental protection rests with the Consultative Parties, having also particularly emphasized that the measures adopted should be 'consistent with the interests of mankind'.[33] This competence of the Consultative Parties was recognized by the eighteenth Conference of FAO in 1975.[34]

Other recommendations approved on this subject have referred specifically to the question of the pollution of the Antarctic environment by oil, calling for studies on the matter and recommending the revision of obligations existing under other international conventions in the light of the hazardous nature of navigation in the Antarctic.[35]

2.3   The norm-creating function relating to Antarctic mineral resources

The third main field relating to natural resources in which the norm-creating function of the system has been used is that of the Antarctic mineral resources. As has already been said, the fact that the Antarctic Treaty was silent on this subject has not prevented its being dealt with by consultative meetings. This is an even clearer demonstration of the dynamic interpretation which the Consultative Parties have conferred on the Treaty and of the way in which its basic legal framework has progressively been extended through this normative process. Although the substantive content of the various recommendations approved will be analysed in conjunction with the various topics covered by the mineral resources regime, it is necessary at this point to identify the main guidelines established by this norm-creating activity within the Antarctic system.

This subject was dealt with for the first time at the Sixth Consultative Meeting in Tokyo in 1970, but on that occasion differences concerning interpretation of the Antarctic Treaty prevented the adoption of any recommendation.[36] This explains the importance of Recommendation VII-6, adopted at the following Consultative Meeting in 1972. Although this Recommendation apparently contains no more than statements of a general nature, the fact that it was a pronouncement on this particular subject was in itself of the greatest importance. Indeed, as Colson points out 'a major collective step was taken in Recommendation VII-6 when both claimants and non-claimants agreed upon the appropriateness of addressing the mineral issue within the Antarctic Treaty system'.[37]

It is interesting to note in the first place that the recommendation concerned constitutes a timid attempt to spell out the legal foundations of the competence which was beginning to be exercised on the matter.[38] Mention was made, in the first place, of the 'provisions and principles' of the Antarctic Treaty and, next, of the provision in the Preamble stating that it is in the interest of mankind that the Antarctic should be used exclusively for peaceful purposes and that it should not become a scene or object of international discord. Similarly, the recommendation invokes Article X of the Treaty, relating to the making of appropriate efforts to ensure that no one engages in activities contrary to the purposes and principles of the Treaty. Subsequent recommendations, in addition to reiterating these principles, added references to other provisions such as that in Article IV, or to concepts such as the responsibility of the Consultative Parties and the need for environmental protection.[39]

In this way, in the opinion of the above-mentioned author, this recommendation implicitly affirmed four central principles: (i) the undertaking to maintain the integrity of the Antarctic Treaty and to consider the problem of mineral resources within the framework of that Treaty; (ii) it institutionalizes consideration of the subject; (iii) it establishes a link between this subject and considerations relating to the Antarctic environment; and (iv) it initiates discussion of a moratorium or voluntary restraint in terms which will be indicated below.[40]

Later recommendations were to improve the terms of reference for the treatment of this important subject without prejudice to the criteria already specified. Recommendation VIII-14 indicates a concern to obtain appropriate scientific and technological information, with particular reference to environmental implications.[41] For this purpose, among other measures, the opinion of SCAR was sought, giving rise to an intensive process of interaction between the consultative machinery of the Treaty and the scientific community which has been of enormous benefit to the discussion of the Antarctic mineral regime.[42] At the same time, this recommendation convened a special preparatory meeting which took place in Paris in 1976.[43]

Basic principles of the system

From the time of this preparatory meeting onwards, discussion on the subject of mineral resources took a more specific focus. On that occasion, four basic principles were approved which clearly define the function of the Antarctic Treaty as perceived by the Parties, the role of the Consultative Parties, the environmental dimension and the link between the question of minerals and the interest of the international community. These principles are as follows:

   (i) the Consultative Parties will continue to play an active and responsible role in dealing with the question of the mineral resources of Antarctica;

  (ii) the Antarctic Treaty must be maintained in its entirety;

 (iii) protection of the unique Antarctic environment and its dependent ecosystems should be a basic consideration;

(iv) the Consultative Parties, in dealing with the question of mineral resources in Antarctica, should not prejudice the interests of all mankind in Antarctica.[44]

These principles were re-affirmed by Recommendation IX-1, which, in addition, listed other interesting criteria. In the first place, it expressed the conviction 'that the framework established by the Antarctic Treaty has proved effective in promoting international harmony in furtherance of the purposes and principles of the United Nations Charter, in ensuring the protection of the Antarctic environment and in promoting freedom of scientific research in Antarctica'.[45] This Recommendation also expressed the concern that 'unregulated activities related to exploration and exploitation of mineral resources could adversely affect the unique environment of the Antarctic and other ecosystems dependent on the Antarctic environment'.[46] Through the first of these considerations, recognition was given to the 'framework' character of the 1959 Treaty, while the second implicitly indicated the intention that there would be no exploration or exploitation activities without prior regulation.

Recommendation X-1 took this line of thinking even further, referring repeatedly to 'an agreed regime' which, among other things, should provide the means for determining the acceptability of activities related to mineral resources and for giving due protection to the environment.[47] Both this Recommendation and Recommendation IX-1 which preceded it refer to the reports of groups of experts which met on those occasions[48] which were annexed to the final reports of the respective consultative meetings, giving them what one author describes as a 'diplomatic status' within the system.[49]

The set of principles which were gradually elaborated through this process was systematically expounded in Recommendation XI-1 which laid down a specific basis on which elaboration of the detailed regime was to proceed, a task which was carried out through the various negotiating sessions of the Fourth Special Consultative Meeting. It is especially interesting to note that one more principle, in addition to the four principles adopted by the Paris meeting which were quoted above, was added in order to ensure the necessary political balance: 'the provisions of Article IV of the Antarctic Treaty should not be affected by the regime. It should ensure that the principles embodied in Article IV are safeguarded in application to the area covered by the Antarctic Treaty'.[50] In this manner, not only was the regime to be elaborated within the framework of the 1959 Treaty, but particular care was also to be exercised in order to ensure that the basic political compromises of the Treaty were not affected.

The supplementing of the basic framework: synthesis

The intensive norm-creating activity that has been described in relation to natural resources was important in three major ways in relation to the 1959 Treaty. In the first place, it effectively supplemented its basic framework, giving rise to a comprehensive system for organizing and regulating the relevant activities. Next this process of supplementing the framework of the Treaty clearly extended its field of competence to cover subjects which the Treaty itself did not expressly include, or which it referred to only indirectly. Its applicability to adjacent maritime areas and marine living resources, and the incorporation of the treatment of mineral resources are two outstanding examples among others which will be considered further below. Thirdly, the initial framework has been developed in such a way that, through this process, important interpretative criteria have been established. The most significant of these relates to the prohibition of unilateral activities, which will be examined next.

2.4   The moratorium on mineral activities

In the first part of this chapter it was pointed out that the main point of conflict between the various theses that have been described concerning the interpretation of the Antarctic Treaty, in relation to the subject of mineral resources, lies in determining whether or not unilateral activity by the parties is permissible under the terms of the Treaty. One point of view is that such mineral activities can only be undertaken subject to prior agreement by the Consultative Parties. According to another point of view, however, although such agreement is desirable, unilateral activity is possible even if such agreement is not reached, on condition that the basic provisions of the Treaty are respected.

When the subject of mineral resources was dealt with for the first time at the Sixth Consultative Meeting, discussion focussed on a more elementary point, namely whether such a subject could be dealt with within the framework of the system or whether it should be entirely excluded.[51] Although the problem was swiftly overcome since it was agreed in Recommendation VII-6 that it could properly be approached within the system, the division of opinion arose even more clearly in connection with the problem of a moratorium. The negotiations of the Seventh Consultative Meeting in 1972 devoted considerable time to the possibility, duration and conditions for such a moratorium, but without reaching agreement.[52]

However, as has been indicated, the mere fact that Recommendation VII-6 recognized the acceptability of dealing with the question of minerals within the system was itself significant. In the opinion of Colson, having agreed to deal with the subject jointly within the system 'The recommendation, therefore, effectively forecloses unilateral action related to minerals'. He added that this instrument implicitly 'enunciates a policy of unilateral restraint until an ultimate decision on the mineral issue is reached'.[53]

During the Eighth Consultative Meeting, discussion on the problem of the moratorium resumed with unabated intensity. A speech by the representative of the United States provides a good indication of the fundamental legal difficulties that existed:

> In the absence of a shared understanding, those countries who do not recognize claims to sovereignty would surely have to assert the right to commence mineral resource activities at their will, subject only to applicable provisions of the Antarctic Treaty. Those who have made claims to sovereignty would contest that view.[54]

Standards for a moratorium

In spite of the opposition expressed by certain countries to the declaration of a moratorium,[55] agreement was reached with regard to the wording on this matter contained in Recommendation VIII-14 which, in spite of being somewhat vague, nevertheless represented a positive point of departure. The preambular part of this Recommendation states:

> Convinced that further consultations on the questions concerning Antarctic mineral resources are desirable and, in the meantime, of the need for restraint while seeking timely agreed solutions by the Consultative Parties to problems raised by such questions; and noting the intention of their Governments to keep these matters under review in the light of possible action by others.[56]

According to one author's interpretation, this policy of voluntary restraint:

> went beyond the implied moratorium of Recommendation VII-6 and created express assurances among the Consultative Parties that unilateral actions will not be taken if timely progress is made towards a full agreement on the mineral issue.[57]

Confirmation of this interpretation will be found in the Final Report of the Eighth Consultative Meeting in which it is recorded that Governments 'urge States and persons to refrain from actions of commercial exploration and exploitation'.[58] This is a firmer undertaking, even if it does not form part of the text of the Recommendation.

Recommendation IX-1 marked a step forward of even greater importance since it addressed the moratorium in more direct terms. The wording is similar to that of the Final Report mentioned above although, significantly, the term 'commercial' has been excluded. Furthermore, the relevant paragraph was not included in the preambular part but appears among the operative clauses, stating the views of the parties in the following manner:

> 8. They urge their nationals and other States to refrain from all exploration and exploitation of Antarctic mineral resources while making progress towards the timely adoption of an agreed regime concerning Antarctic mineral resource activities. They will thus endeavour to ensure that, pending the timely adoption of agreed solutions pertaining to exploration and exploitation of mineral resources, no activity shall be conducted to explore or exploit such resources.
>
> They will keep these matters under continuing examination.[59]

This provision was subsequently repeated by Recommendation XI-1, paragraph 10 of which establishes the relevant point of reference.[60]

The norms for the moratorium that have been described have, as might have been expected, been subject to divergent interpretations. Thus it is not fortuitous that while one group of authors, following the precedent of the General Assembly Resolution on sea-bed mining moratorium, that of the 1972 United Nations Conference on the Human Environment or the agreements on the matter of the International Whaling Commission, refers to such norms as a 'moratorium',[61] another group prefers the expression 'policy of voluntary restraint'.[62] These two expressions have a different legal connotation which should not pass unnoticed.

Divergences of interpretation on the conditions of application

The first category of divergences relates to the procedures or conditions for applying the moratorium, with particular reference to its duration. Indeed, according to one point of view once a moratorium has been decided on in the terms indicated, it continues in force until the Consultative Parties decide otherwise.[63] According to the second point of view, however, the moratorium would require to be continually reaffirmed, failing which its effects would lapse.[64] While the first position seeks to establish a stable undertaking, the second clearly seeks to leave all options open, including that of unilateral action.

This divergence of opinion was expressed in a compromise formula under which the restriction on undertaking mineral activities is linked to the idea of 'timely agreed solutions' or 'timely adoption of an agreed regime', to use the expressions contained in the recommendations mentioned. In other words, from one point of view, the restriction would remain in effect while the negotiations proceed with a view to defining the regime on mineral resources. Who should determine such progress, and how they should do it, or what it should consist of, were questions that remain unanswered.

Both Recommendation X-1 and Recommendation XI-1 expressly refer to the need for progress in negotiations or to the fact of having achieved such progress.[65] This does not, of course, mean that each consultative meeting should place on record the progress achieved on mineral negotiations as a condition of the validity of the moratorium. The Twelfth Consultative Meeting, for example, adopted no recommendation to that effect and included a general paragraph in the Final Report referring to progress in these negotiations.[66]

However, the fundamental question is harder to solve. Does what has been said above mean that, in the light of provisions concerning the moratorium, if progress achieved in negotiations on minerals is not attested by a consultative meeting, Consultative Parties remain free to engage in unilateral action? Although this interpretation has been suggested,[67] it seems to have no justification because it would mean, in effect, that if one Party were to decide to dissociate itself from the consensus necessary to attest such progress this would be sufficient to undo all the work achieved by the system in the field of minerals since 1970. There is no doubt, moreover, that such an interpretation is not in accordance with the decision already adopted to resolve the question of minerals jointly within the system. From this other point of view, the moratorium would seem to have a more stable and lasting legal effect.

Divergences of interpretation on the legal nature of the moratorium
The discussion can only be resolved by analysing the legal nature of such a moratorium which is the other major field of disagreement which has arisen. Although, for those who are in favour of a 'moratorium', the relevant provisions are of a mandatory legal nature, for those who incline towards the policy of 'voluntary restraint' this is less clear.[68] Three main arguments have been invoked to support this latter point of view and they do not preclude the corresponding counter-arguments.

In the first place, it is argued that it was the intention of the Consultative Parties to approve a policy of voluntary restraint rather than a measure producing mandatory legal effects and it is also added that such was the interpretation adopted by the Parties. The history of the negotiations does not support this point of view, since opinions were divided on this point and the compromise finally reached cannot be interpreted as being favourable to one of these points of view to the detriment of the other. On the other hand, it may be pointed out that the interpretation which seems to have been most firmly established is the one which maintains that unilateral action in this field is unacceptable to the Parties.[69]

It is pointed out next that the Recommendation uses language which does not define clear legal obligations. This observation being appropriate, it must also be assessed within the context of the practice of the Antarctic system in which such a loose language commonly occurs; and, consequently, that fact does not provide a basis for concluding that the Recommendation is devoid of mandatory legal force.

Lastly, it is added that, in any case, this Recommendation could not have mandatory effects until such time as it was accepted by the Consultative Parties. This is a somewhat mechanistic approach which does not deal with the substance of the question, only its procedural aspects, and therefore, does not affect the nature of the problem. Furthermore, there have been many instances within the system in which recommendations have produced effects before the instrument going through the procedure for acceptance by Consultative Parties.

In the course of this discussion, an argument has also been made in that, although a moratorium could inhibit activities undertaken by Governments, it could not be invoked against natural or legal persons without the adoption of the corresponding domestic legislation.[70] It has also been pointed out that one advantage of the policy of voluntary restraint is that it does not require such national legislation.[71] These arguments, however valid they may be, do not in any way affect the nature of the problem in the light of international law, since it is well known that the provisions of domestic law cannot be invoked as an excuse for not complying with an international obligation.[72]

It has also been suggested that paragraph 8 of Recommendation IX-1 might not be applicable to Consultative Parties since it is directed towards 'their nationals and other States'.[73] This excessively literal interpretation cannot be sustained if the paragraph is considered as a whole, as its own proponents seem to admit.[74] In any case, it suffices to bear in mind the meaning of the negotiation to reach the conclusion that this cannot reasonably be its intention.

Another important problem concerns the applicability of such a moratorium to third States, a matter that will be considered in Chapter 9 in conjunction with the effects of the Treaty and of the Antarctic system with regard to third parties.

The principle of good faith

As often occurs in divergent interpretations of this type which are the result of provisions approved after a difficult process of political compromise, it is not easy to achieve a precise legal clarification of the problem. The discussion on the moratorium which took place in the context of the sea-bed regime provides a good illustration of this difficulty,[75] a precedent which of course had some influence in the Antarctic negotiations on this point.[76] Other decisions on moratorium that were mentioned further above, with particular reference to the case of the International Whaling Commission, equally prove the difficulty of a precise legal clarification of the matter.

The principle of international law which ultimately permits the reaching of a firm conclusion is that of good faith. Whether the recommendations on a moratorium are interpreted as legally binding or merely voluntary, it is clear from the principle of good faith that for the Treaty Parties mineral-related activities are not permissible and that unilateral action would be a violation of this principle. It is also clear that such a moratorium is meant to remain in force while appropriate solutions are sought to the problem of organizing the regime for the exploitation of mineral resources. The principle of good faith had an equally important role in the questions which arose about unilateral action in connection with the above mentioned sea-bed mining moratorium at the time of the Law of the Sea Conference negotiations.

In the opinion of Bilder, an author who has favoured the interpretation of the moratorium as a policy of voluntary restraint: 'even if the moratorium recommendation is not legally binding, the Parties can in practice be expected to observe it in good faith'.[77]

Another author appropriately reaches the conclusion that:

> If any party should decide to proceed unilaterally in order to explore and exploit the mineral resources, this would probably cause discord, which could disturb the basis for a further development of the law on a multilateral, consensual basis. This in turn, could endanger other achievements such as scientific co-operation, environmental protection and peace in the area.[78]

It is clear from what has been said above that for the Treaty Parties unilateral action is not only contrary to the principle of good faith but would also violate the principles of the Treaty itself, which the Consultative Parties have committed themselves to safeguard.

2.5   The norm-creating competence of consultative meetings and the practice of the system

In accordance with Article IX, paragraph 1, of the Antarctic Treaty, consultative meetings have competence in three main areas: exchange of information, consultation on matters of common interest and the adoption of measures. The first two purposes are of a general nature and, as such, are relatively simple to interpret. The only peculiarity to be pointed out in connection with them is that, in the exercise of the respective fields of competence, the consultative meetings have not confined themselves strictly to dealing with matters envisaged by the Treaty but have also included additional questions that were considered to be of interest.

The competence to adopt measures is undoubtedly the most important since it is through the adoption of such measures that the norm-creating capacity of the system is exercised. Although this competence is frequently understood as consisting solely of 'recommending' measures, the language of the Treaty could be read to indicate that it is in fact a more extensive competence. Indeed, the third purpose indicated in Article IX, paragraph 1, is that of 'formulating and considering, and recommending to their Governments, measures in furtherance of the principles and objectives of the Treaty'. The concept of formulating and considering would thus seem to be complementary to that of recommending and thus to confer a greater power of action which could be considered as a kind of legislative competence within the system. The fact that decisions adopted are termed 'recommendations' may be restrictive of the legislative functions which is many times actually exercised. It would probably be more appropriate to call them 'resolutions' as this term denotes instruments which may contain both measures which are recommendatory and others which are mandatory in nature. As will be discussed further below this is a phenomenon frequently occurring in the ambit of international organizations, being the United Nations Charter and the powers of the General Assembly to adopt recommendations a well-known case in point.

In order to appreciate the full extent and scope of the competence of the consultative meetings, a subject which, in addition to its academic interest, is important in that it explains how the basic framework of the 1959 Treaty has been developed to the point where it is now interpreted by the Parties as including difficult subjects in the field of natural resources, a study of the practice of the system is indispensable. In this connection, there are three outstanding aspects of this practice: the material scope of competence, the extension of the instruments and the available procedures, and the legal nature of the measures adopted. All these questions show that the system has made intensive use of the implied powers in its constitutive document and related treaties.[79]

Material scope of the competence

Article IX, paragraph 1, is structured broadly and deals with the measures falling within the competence of the consultative meetings. The central criterion of the provision is that it must deal with 'measures in furtherance of the principles and objectives of the Treaty'. Consequently, any measure that may reasonably be interpreted as being related to these principles and objectives comes within the competence of these consultative meetings.[80] Moreover, it must be borne in mind that the principles and objectives are extremely broad. The enumeration of subjects under subparagraphs (a) to (f) of paragraph 1 of this Article is not exclusive and it is thus permissible to deal with any other question that fulfils the criterion indicated, as can be concluded from the interpretation and practice followed by the Consultative Parties, which will be explained next.

Indeed, the practice of the parties to the system has been to include various other questions of particular importance in the context of the material competence. A recent comment on the Treaty refers to the following matters which are not mentioned in the Treaty but to which competence has been extended and which have been the subject of norms approved by the Consultative Meetings: assistance in cases of emergency, including questions of civil aviation; historic monuments; postal services; telecommunications; tourism; and the exploration and exploitation of mineral resources.[81] It may be appreciated that covering some of these subjects, such as the one relating to mineral resources, entails a significant extension of the principles and purposes of the Treaty.

In other cases the process may entail subjects indirectly indicated in the Treaty which acquire major importance through the exercise of such competence. One example of this are the norms concerning environmental protection of which an account has already been given. In either case, it is the recourse to implied powers which makes it possible to develop the relevant competence. One author aptly describes this flexible interpretation of the Treaty in the following terms:

> At times, the Consultative Parties have read the Antarctic Treaty itself with a certain amount of flexibility. They have used a broad reading of the Treaty's mandates in order to attain a common goal by agreement under Article IX. The parties have adopted a

number of recommendations that, although not dealing directly with matters mentioned in the Treaty, have not been challenged as being beyond their power under the Treaty.[82]

However, as will be examined in Chapters 9 and 10, there has recently been some degree of challenge by non-parties to the competence of the Antarctic Treaty Parties for dealing with the issue of mineral resources.

In any event, as Brownlie has mentioned in relation to the practice of organizations and its influence on issues of interpretation under the Law of Treaties, what really matters 'is the reasoning *behind* the practice, which can reveal its legal relevance, if any'.[83] Although this reasoning is not always available in the case of the practice of the Antarctic Treaty Parties, it would appear that on various occasions it has deliberately pointed towards the development of the framework of the Treaty, in order to strengthen the competence of the system in the matter eventually under consideration, as the various examples already given seem to confirm.

On the other hand, as the same author has commented about the *Reparation* case, 'in practice the reference to implied powers may be linked to a principle of institutional effectiveness',[84] what explains the Court's reference to those powers conferred upon the organization 'by necessary implication as being essential to the performance of its duties'.[85] While the Antarctic Treaty system is not an organization, and only recently one can recognize a trend towards a greater institutionalization within this system, the criteria of institutional effectiveness can anyhow be found in the practice of the Consultative Meetings, particularly in terms of interpreting the Treaty with greater flexibility as to ensure the availability of the necessary powers considered to be necessary to deal with a given matter. Thus *mutatis mutandis* the doctrine of implied powers can also serve to assess the extent and the limits of the development of the Antarctic legal framework by the Consultative Parties and the manner how this will result in the interpretation of the 1959 Treaty and related conventions.[86]

Variety of instruments
The second outstanding aspect of the practice of the Antarctic system is the extension of the available instruments and procedures as to ensure a greater variety. In addition to formal recommendations, consultative meetings have developed the practice of adopting 'decisions' of other types, introducing a new measure of flexibility in the legal arrangements of the system. These other decisions are recorded in the final report of each meeting.[87]

In spite of the fact that the Antarctic Treaty does not provide for this kind of instrument, Consultative Meetings have occasionally adopted 'decisions' on important matters relating to the development of the law, such as the criteria for admission as a Consultative Party or the moratorium on mineral activities. In this regard, the decision can have a very significant legal effect, including mandatory effects for the Parties. To the extent, however, that their content is kept within the limits of a permissible interpretation under the Law of Treaties or of a legitimate use of implied powers, they will not be objected to by the Parties or addressees.

The first type of decision takes the place of what would normally have been the subject matter of a recommendation. Thus, for example, the Final Report of the First Special Consultative Meeting contains the unanimous decision of the Consultative Parties concerning the procedure for admission of new Consultative Parties. In this case, use was made of the form of words: 'The Representatives of the Consultative Parties . . . unanimously decide'. In that same meeting Poland was admitted as a Consultative Party, for which purpose a decision was taken which stated: 'The Representatives of the Consultative Parties . . . record their acknowledgement that the Polish People's Republic has fulfilled the requirements. . .'. Although the type of decision is similar in both these cases, the latter seems to have a slightly different connotation as reflected in the language used. The Third Special Consultative Meeting used this precedent for admission of the Federal Republic of Germany as a Consultative Party.

Another type of decision which has been used has the purpose of considering and recording understandings on subjects which have not been directly dealt with in the recommendations adopted by a particular consultative meeting. One interesting case is related to the question of the moratorium; although the text of Recommendation VIII-14 contains a general reference to the idea in its preamble, the Final Report of the Eighth Consultative Meeting recorded a rather more decisive viewpoint whereby the Governments represented 'urge States and persons to refrain from actions of commercial exploration and exploitation'. With certain modifications, this understanding was subsequently incorporated in Recommendation IX-1.[88]

Depending on the scope which is conferred on this latter type of decision, it may assume a third function which is that of serving as an instrument for interpreting the adopted recommendation. One example is contained in the Final Report of the Ninth Consultative Meeting where the interpretation of the term 'conservation' is placed on record in relation to living resources,[89] an interpretation which was subsequently to be included in the Canberra Convention itself.[90] A somewhat similar approach was followed in relation to the problem of the Kerguelen Islands and Iles Crozet in the negotiations of the Convention mentioned above, in which the basic interpretation was established by means of a statement by the President of the Conference to which no objections were raised and which was recorded in its entirety in the Final Act of the Conference.[91]

The practice of the Parties to the Antarctic Treaty system has made use of various other alternatives as to the instruments that are employed to record their agreements. One such example is the case of decisions adopted by specialized technical meetings which are subsequently embodied in the form of a recommendation made to the governments by a Consultative meeting.[92] Final reports of the Consultative meetings occasionally refer to documents and other material prepared by groups of experts or other sources, thus endorsing them with the necessary diplomatic support.[93]

Because of the different use made of decisions and the different types of instrument which the practice examined reveals, it is not possible to reach a general conclusion about their binding or non-binding effect. In some cases, such as the admission of new Consultative Parties, the binding nature of the decision is beyond doubt; in other instances, such as the moratorium mentioned above, the point might be controversial; while still in other examples the non-binding character of the decision will be quite apparent. A case by case analysis of these decisions is thus the only approach possible as to the determination of their legal significance.

Similar legal problems can be found in the context of major international organizations. Thus, for example, while the United Nations Charter seems to offer a more clear-cut answer in contrasting the decisions of the Security Council with the recommendatory powers of the General Assembly and other organs, the practice of the organization is both richer and more complex and difficult to classify in rigid categories, providing for a variety of situations not foreseen in the Charter.[94] We shall refer again to this practice when discussing further below the legal nature of recommendations under the Antarctic Treaty.

Procedural innovation
In addition to making a greater variety of instruments available, this practice has given rise to interesting innovations in regard to the procedures followed. It is, of course, to be noted that, for the adoption of a final report, all that is required is a simple majority rather than unanimity,

a fact which means that, in principle, the decisions contained in the final report may be approved more easily than formal recommendations.[95] Even though this alternative has been used only once,[96] it offers interesting prospects with regard to the flexibility of the system. This greater procedural flexibility may explain the interest which the Parties have shown in diversifying the instruments available within the system, although, at the same time, the status of 'decisions' could have been undermined by the less stringent requirements applied to their approval.

More important still is the flexibility achieved with regard to the entry into force of the respective instruments. It is a requirement of the Treaty that the measures referred to in Article IX require the approval of all Consultative Parties for their entry into force. By means of the practice which has been mentioned, this procedure has begun to lose some of its rigour.

The unanimous decision relating to the procedure for admission of new Consultative Parties adopted by the First Special Consultative Meeting, and the 'acknowledgement' which was recorded in connection with the admission of Poland and the Federal Republic of Germany, were both types of decisions which did not require subsequent approval by the Consultative Parties and, consequently, entered into force immediately. As Bush points out, the same approach has been used for a 'recommendation', since the Second Special Consultative Meeting recommended that the various instruments relating to the negotiation of the regime on living resources should be referred to the Diplomatic Conference which met on the following day, without waiting for the recommendation to go through the confirmation procedure.[97]

In view of the inevitable slowness of any confirmation procedure of this nature, recommendations have provided fairly frequently for their application as provisional measures, pending compliance with the confirmation requirement.[98] The Agreed Measures, among others, have used this procedure. What is basically involved is a type of provisional entry into force, even if so is not formally expressed in the recommendation or instrument. Furthermore, the practice of the Parties, as commented upon by Colson,[99] evidences that Governments, as a general rule, consider that recommendations are effective from the time of their adoption and, in accordance with the principle of good faith, refrain from acting in a way incompatible with them. The fact that occasionally domestic legislation is required to put given measures into effect has not altered this practice. It should also be noted that, while sometimes the measures adopted relate to future activities of the Parties, thus making the question of the instrument being regarded as effective from the moment of adoption less relevant, in many other instances such measures refer to on-going activities which need to conform to the new norms enacted as quickly as possible.

Both the provisional application of recommendations and the fact that they may be regarded as producing specific mandatory legal effects have led to an interesting situation at the level of the domestic law of the Consultative Parties. In given matters, some of the Parties have proceeded to promulgate the relevant domestic legislation for the application of certain recommendations before the latter have entered into force internationally, or have done so only in the provisional sense mentioned above. An example of this can be found in the legislation promulgated by the United States imposing civil and penal sanctions on certain acts which violated the provisions of the Agreed Measures before the latter entered into force.[100]

In other cases, as occurs in Chilean practice, when the recommendations are confirmed, their publication is ordered in the Official Gazette (*Diario Oficial*),[101] which may result again in their full legal effects being produced domestically before the instrument becomes effective at the international level, what would only occur at a later date when all the approvals of the Consultative Parties have been secured.

This flexible practice with regard to the Antarctic legal order has at times been harshly criticized by some authors particularly with reference to decisions or procedures which make it possible to avoid subsequent confirmation at national level. Bush states in this regard that the practice 'seems to be a development of the competence of the consultative parties without any express justification in the Treaty'.[102] Auburn is even more categorical in concluding that 'the present practice is contrary to the Treaty'.[103]

Thus, once more, different interpretative criteria have arisen. If a narrow view is taken of the 1959 Treaty, the conclusion may well be reached that everything that is not strictly in accordance with the letter of the Treaty constitutes a violation of it. On the other hand, if the Treaty is analysed from a dynamic standpoint, it may be noted that the initial framework is capable of major development through the practice of its application, even if it is applied in a way that is not literally in accordance with its provisions. Here again, however, the limits imposed by a permissible interpretation under the Law of Treaties and by the necessary prudence in the recourse to implied powers, will need to be observed if the developments in question are to avoid all forms of arbitrariness.[104]

It should also be noted that this kind of legal development is rather frequent in such arrangements which seek to achieve international co-operation in specific geographical regions, as is evidenced by treaties of economic integration in Europe, Africa or Latin America.[105] While the Antarctic Treaty does not establish an international organization in a formal sense, the practice within the system which has developed under the original instrument does not differ greatly from that of such an organization, including the important question of the recourse to implied powers and the development of the framework treaty.[106]

So far, the analysis has referred to the case of the instruments, procedures and competences which are adopted and exercised within the framework of the consultative meetings. There are, however, other options open to the Antarctic system in its broader sense. In dealing with certain subjects of a particularly sensitive nature relating to resources regimes, recourse has also been had to the adoption of international conventions, as in the case of the Convention on Seals,[107] the Convention on the Conservation of Antarctic Marine Living Resources[108] and, most probably, the mineral regime. Although each Treaty is, of course, a separate and *ad hoc* legal instrument different from the Antarctic Treaty, the legal and institutional links established between them has come to constitute a network of arrangements within the system of Antarctic co-operation. This option, taken in conjunction with those already discussed, offers various interesting possibilities for the organization of the activities relating to natural resources and their respective regimes.

Although such conventions are adopted by a diplomatic conference and comply with the normal procedures of the law of treaties, it is interesting to note that the Consultative Parties are not absent from the negotiating process. It frequently occurs that the draft convention is discussed and prepared by the consultative meetings and is ultimately referred to the diplomatic conference by means of a recommendation.[109] Furthermore, as was mentioned above, it is customary for such conventions to contain provisions establishing substantive links between them and the 1959 Treaty and other relevant instruments.[110] For this reason, they themselves form part of the Antarctic legal order and represent a new and more formal expression of the norm-creating function of the system.

Legal nature of the recommendations

The legal nature of the recommendations is another question on which divergent opinions have been expressed by the commentators of the Antarctic Treaty system. The basic point at issue is whether or not such instruments should be assimilated to the type of resolution normally adopted by an international organization or whether they should be considered as a treaty. While the latter alternative has been raised, at least in the form of a question,[111] recommendations could hardly be identified with a separate treaty either in form or in substance, with the sole exception of the Agreed Measures for the very peculiar reasons that will be explained further below. The mandatory nature of the instruments is also linked to some extent with their legal nature.

Article IX, paragraph 4, of the Antarctic Treaty states that the measures adopted by the consultative meetings 'shall become effective' once they have been approved by the Consultative Parties. This expression, as Bush points out, is not normally included in treaty language, for the usual terminology in relation to treaties is 'entry into force'.[112] While this language could be interpreted as depriving the recommendation of legal force,[113] it may also denote the intention of achieving a measure of legal obligation since an instrument that is merely recommendatory does not need to 'become effective' or to go through a subsequent process of confirmation.

It is also to be pointed out that study of the language used by these instruments does not provide any basis for conclusions concerning their legal nature. While some recommendations use terms which appear to be devoid of any mandatory character, others, in contrast, clearly indicate their mandatory force, while some use both type of expression.[114] There is no uniformity or clear drafting practice on this matter. The fact that certain instruments have recommended 'voluntary' measures is equally inconclusive since the same subject has subsequently been covered by mandatory clauses contained in the international conventions concluded by the same parties, as occurred, for example, in the regime for the conservation of seals.[115]

Recommendation III-8 which contains the Agreed Measures, is the one which bears the greatest resemblance to a treaty. As we shall see, this is explained by the history of its negotiation: some Consultative Parties took the view that it should take the form of a treaty whereas others felt that it should be a recommendation, and the resulting instrument is something of a hybrid. As was said above, this recommendation and others had recourse to the technique of provisional application which tends to be more in keeping with treaty law, even though not restricted exclusively to it.

Another interesting indication of the practice to which Bush calls attention is that various countries publish the recommendations in their official gazettes or equivalent series. The United States does so in its Treaty Series, whereas Argentina and Chile use the official gazette (*Diario Oficial*). Other countries, on the other hand, do not follow this practice and none of them has registered the recommendations with the United Nations.[116]

An additional difficulty is that hitherto the Consultative Parties have been extremely reluctant to equate the Antarctic system with an international organization, a fact which makes it harder to establish comparisons. This reluctance is a survival of the disputes over sovereignty and has resulted in the absence of any organs, except to the extent that Consultative meetings perform some functions of an institutional nature. However, this has also been undergoing a process of change within the system, particularly in the context of the resources policy, with the result that a greater institutionalization is today apparent and that additional initiatives are coming to the fore to strengthen this trend.[117]

The fact that a recommendation may be equated with a resolution of an international organization does not necessarily affect its possible mandatory nature since such resolutions may also be binding, either because the constitutive instrument so determines or because of the subsequent practice of the parties. Although the legal effect of resolutions will vary from one organization to another, the study of decisions of international organizations in general and of resolutions of United Nations in particular, evidences an impressive practice pointing towards a greater development of mandatory effects of such instruments.[118] The procedure of subsequent confirmation of resolutions is also known in various international organizations, so there would be nothing strange in its application to the case of the Antarctic system. Furthermore, it is perhaps important to bear in mind in the case of the Antarctic system the necessity of avoiding more rigid and troublesome procedures such as those that might result if recommendations were regarded as falling strictly within the ambit of the law of treaties.

The final report of the Fourth Consultative Meeting contains a number of important interpretative considerations in this regard. In addition to certain elements which are specifically applicable to countries acceding to the Treaty, certain general criteria are defined with regard to the role of recommendations within the system: (i) The recommendations are, in accordance with the Treaty, 'measures in furtherance of the principles and objectives of the Treaty'; (ii) 'Approved Recommendations are an essential part of the overall structure of co-operation established by the Treaty'; and (iii) 'Approved Recommendations are to be viewed in the light of the obligations assumed by the Contracting Parties under the Treaty. . .'.[119]

These principles indicate clearly that, within the basic framework of the Treaty, the recommendations perform the role of developing and improving co-operation in compliance with its purposes, principles and objectives. In accordance with this interpretation, recommendations may have a mandatory legal effect as in fact has been confirmed by the practice of the parties on a number of occasions. Yet, this does not exclude the possibility that the same kind of instrument may be used on other occasions for mere recommendatory measures, which explains the existing confusion about the nature of recommendations and decisions and their comparison with either treaties or resolutions of international organizations. In any event, it is the specific content of a recommendation which will determine whether its legal effects are mandatory or merely recommendatory.

Schematic presentation of the Antarctic legal order
The Antarctic legal order that has been considered may be represented in a schematic way as follows:

                    Antarctic Treaty (basic framework)
    Recommendations   – mandatory   Special Conventions
                      – recommendatory
    Decisions   – taking the place of recommendations
                      – interpretative
                      – procedural
                      – others

2.6   The option of instruments for resources regimes
On the basis of what has been explained above, it will be appreciated that various options are available in regard to the legal instruments that it may be desirable to use for the preparation of a regime for natural resources. It must, of course, be pointed out that the process of preparation invariably begins with the approval of recommendations on the subject, a stage which is then followed either by a final recommendation containing the appropriate regime or by the corresponding diplomatic conferences which approve the text of a special convention on the subject.

The Agreed Measures offer an example of the first alternative since, as was mentioned, the process began at the first Consultative Meeting with the approval of recommendations on the protection of the Antarctic fauna and flora and culminated with the adoption of Recommendation III-8 which contains the corresponding regime, without prejudice to the subsequent action which has taken place. Although the form of a recommendation was chosen in this case, the desirability of a special convention was also discussed during the negotiations, an option which was not so much related to the legal effects of the regime but to the competence of the Consultative Parties to deal with certain marine areas, as will be explained below.

Because of this, the Agreed Measures use the language appropriate to a convention and, in some respects, are structured like a treaty. As Alfred van der Essen pointed out:

> Technically, these measures are merely arrangements adopted within the framework of the Treaty under the provisions of Article IX, paragraph 1; however, they are an anomaly in that they were presented as an international convention, with a preamble which mentions the governments, the articles and the types of final clauses.[120]

The regime on seals and the regime concerning the conservation of the Antarctic Marine Living Resources followed the second alternative mentioned, namely after the various initial recommendations, they opted for the form of a special convention. In the case of mineral resources a similar course of action is to be observed.

On the basis of the experience gained within the Antarctic system in this connection, it may be stated that the relevant option is determined by two basic considerations. The first relates to whether the adoption of the corresponding regime will involve a question of interpretation or the possible extension of the 1959 Treaty. The second is related to the participation of other countries in the regime.

The difference of points of view as to whether the Agreed Measures should adopt the form of a recommendation or of a convention was due principally to the fact that one view was that they should apply only to the fauna and flora of the continent without including the maritime areas, whereas the other maintained that the latter areas should also be subject to conservation.[121] The first case would have been adequately covered by a recommendation whereas the second required a convention which would provide a basis for resolving any obstacles or difficulties arising from Article VI of the Treaty in relation to freedom of the high seas. When the first view prevailed, the option of a recommendation was chosen although, as will be explained in Chapter 4, the maritime areas were not entirely excluded.

As a direct consequence of the fact that the Agreed Measures did not clearly include the protection of the marine fauna, it immediately became necessary to draw up the regime on seals and, for that purpose, it was necessary to opt for a convention including the maritime areas where the species lives, with particular reference to pack ice.[122] A similar criterion prevailed for the Convention on the Conservation of Antarctic Marine Living Resources and for the mineral regime, since both are strongly connected with the maritime areas surrounding the continent.

The option of a convention is also related to the participation of other countries in the regime in question since such an instrument allows a greater degree of access, including access by countries that are not Parties to the Antarctic Treaty. This consideration applied in the case of the Seal Convention,[123] even though, in the event, only Consultative Parties took part in the diplomatic conference. As we shall see in due course, participation by non-Consultative Parties has been an aspect of the utmost importance with regard to the regimes on living and mineral resources.

The fact that certain regimes opted for a special convention does not mean that they were distancing themselves from the Antarctic system since, on the one hand, such conventions are instruments which complement the Treaty and, on the other hand, particular care has always been taken to define clearly the links with the 1959 Treaty, reference frequently being made to the provisions of the Treaty and attention being given to seeking other linkage arrangements. In the case of the negotiation of the minerals regime, it was also suggested that the regime might be embodied in a Protocol annexed to the Antarctic Treaty as a way of further strengthening the links between the two instruments.[124]

Chapter 2 Notes

1. In the 1959 Antarctic Conference the Chilean delegation made a statement explaining its interest 'in the conservation and protection of natural resources, particularly those of the maritime areas', which was supported by South Africa; the British delegation expressed some concern about whether this initiative would also include the mineral resources, while Australia considered that the question of natural resources went beyond the purpose of the treaty under discussion; this debate led to the drafting of Article IX. 1 (f) of the Treaty; see the restricted official document of the Conference COM II/SR/6 (final) of 7 November 1959 as cited by Oscar Pinochet de la Barra: 'La contribución de Chile al Tratado Antártico', in Francisco Orrego Vicuña, María Teresa Infante and Pilar Armanet (eds): *Política Antártica de Chile*, 1985, 89–100, at 95. The Assistant Secretary of State of the United States has also stated in this regard that 'In 1959, during preparatory talks for the treaty conference, it became clear that resource questions were so contentious that the subject would not be addressed at the conference', see Statement by Mr Dixy Lee Ray, *Hearing on U.S. Antarctic Policy*, Subcommittee on Oceans and International Environment, Committee on Foreign Relations, United States Senate, 1975, at 5.
2. David A. Colson: 'The Antarctic Treaty System: the mineral issue', *Law Pol. Int. Bus*, Vol. 12, 1980, 841–902, at 884.

3. On the interpretation of treaties and the development of the rules of interpretation, see generally Ian Brownlie: *Principles of Public International Law*, 1979, 623–630. D. W. Greig: *International Law*, 1976, 476–488. Charles Rousseau: *Droit International Public*, Tome I, 1970, 241–305.

4. Report from the meeting of experts at the Fridtjof Nansen Foundation at Polhogda, May 30–June 10, 1973, text in Hearing cit., note 1 supra, 68–85.

5. Report of the Working Group on Legal and Political Questions, Report cit., note 4 supra, particularly at 79–80.

6. Richard B. Bilder: 'The present legal and political situation in Antarctica', in Jonathan I. Charney (ed.): *The new nationalism and the use of common spaces*, 1982, 167–205, at 186.

7. The US Department of State has stated in this respect that 'It is our view that exploration for and exploitation of mineral resources is permitted under the Antarctic Treaty', see State Department responses to additional questions submitted by Senator Pell, *Hearing on Exploitation of Antarctic Resources*, Sub-committee on Arms Control, Oceans and International Environment, Committee on Foreign Relations, US Senate, 95th Congress, 2nd. session, 1978, at 38.

8. Bilder, loc. cit., note 6 supra, at 186–187.

9. See note 1 supra and associated text.

10. Report cit. note 4 supra, at 79, with particular reference to the incompatibility of commercial and industrial secrets with Articles II, III i a) an c) and VII of the Antarctic Treaty.

11. See generally, Riccardo Monaco: *Lezioni di organizzazione internazionale*, Vol. II, Diritto dell'integrazione europea, 1968, 204–223.

12. Philip Allott: 'Power sharing in the law of the sea', *A.J.I.L.*, Vol. 77, 1983, 1–30, at 25. On the conduct of parties to a treaty generally, Jean-Pierre Cot: 'La Conduite subsequente des parties a un traité', *R.G.D.I.P.*, Tome LXX, 1966, 632–666.

13. An author writes in this regard: 'The Antarctic Treaty system is dynamic and capable of change and new interpretations. It has found new procedural forms and new substantive interpretations to meet the needs of the Consultative Parties. A whole range of understandings has flown from the Consultative Meetings themselves', Colson, loc. cit., note 2 supra, at 882. See also Finn Sollie: 'The Development of the Antarctic Treaty System. Trends and issues', in Rudiger Wolfrum (ed.): *Antarctic Challenge*, 1984, 17–37; and Yuri M. Rybakov: 'Juridicial nature of the 1959 Treaty System', in US Polar Research Board: *Antarctic Treaty System, An Assessment*, 1986, 33–45.

14. Antarctic Treaty: *Handbook of Measures in furtherance of the principles and objectives of the Antarctic Treaty*, Third edition, April 1983, hereinafter cited as *Handbook 1983*. Additional recommendations are included in Antarctic Treaty: *Report of the Twelfth Consultative Meeting*, Canberra, 13–27 September 1983, 1984.

15. See generally Brian B. Roberts: 'Conservation in the Antarctic', *Phil. Trans. R. Soc. Lond*, B, 279, 1977, 97–104. M. R. Clark and P. R. Dingwall: *Conservation of islands in the Southern Ocean: a review of the protected areas of insulantarctica*, document prepared for the IUCN Commission on National Parks and Protected Areas, February 1985. For the work of the Scientific Committee on Antarctic Research (SCAR) in the conservation of the Antarctic and other aspects of scientific research, see Tore Gjelsvik: 'Scientific research and cooperation in Antarctica', in Rudiger Wolfrum, op. cit., note 13 supra, 41–51; James H. Zumberge: 'The Antarctic Treaty as a scientific mechanism – SCAR and the Antarctic Treaty System', in US Polar Research Board, op. cit., note 13 supra,

153–168; Lucía Ramírez: 'El SCAR y el desarrollo de la cooperación en materia científica', in Francisco Orrego Vicuña et al., op. cit., note 1 supra, 131–146; Guido Pincheira: 'La investigación científica como fundamento de una política nacional antártica', in Francisco Orrego Vicuña et al., op. cit., note 1 supra, 121–130.

16. Recommendation I-VIII, *Handbook 1983*, at 2301.
17. Recommendation II-II, *Handbook 1983*, at 2302.
18. Recommendation III-VIII, *Handbook 1983*, at 2101.
19. For the measures related to the implementation of the Agreed Measures, *Handbook 1983*, 2201–2205.
20. Recommendation VII-3, VIII-3 and related measures, *Handbook 1983*, 3101–3120.
21. Recommendation III-XI, IV-21, IV-22 and V-7, *Handbook 1983*, 2401–2404.
22. Convention for the Conservation of Antarctic Seals, London 1 June 1972.
23. International Convention for the Regulation of Whaling, 1946. See also the *Schedule* to this Convention, as amended to June 1984, January 1985; and the *Rules of Procedure and Financial Regulations*, June 1984.
24. Recommendation VIII-10, *Handbook 1983*, at 2501.
25. Recommendation IX-2, *Handbook 1983*, 2502–2504.
26. Conference on the Conservation of Antarctic Marine Living Resources, Canberra, 7–20 May 1980, Final Act and text of the Convention in *ILM*, Vol. XIX, 1980, 837–859.
27. On the process of negotiations and discussion of the regime, Barbara Mitchell and Richard Sandbrook: *The Management of the Southern Ocean*, International Institute for Environment and Development, 1980. Daniel Vignes: 'La Convention sur la Conservation de la faune et de la flore marines de l'Antarctique', *A.F.D.I.*, 1980, 741–772. David M. Edwards and John A. Heap: 'Convention on the Conservation of Antarctic Marine Living Resources: a commentary', *Pol. Rec.*, Vol. 20, 1981, 353–362. James M. Barnes: 'The emerging convention on the Conservation of Antarctic Marine Living Resources: An attempt to meet the new realities of resource exploitation in the Southern Ocean', in Jonathan I. Charney (ed.): *The New Nationalism and the Use of Common Spaces*, 1982, 239–286. Ronald F. Frank: 'The Convention on the Conservation of Antarctic Marine Living Resources', *Ocean Dev. I.L.*, Vol. 13, 1983–1984, 291–345. See also Beatriz Ramacciotti de Cubas: 'Recursos naturales antárticos: problemas y posibilidades', in *Revista Peruana de Derecho Internacional*, Vol. XXXV, July–September 1983, 29–40.
28. Fernando Zegers Santa Cruz: 'The Antarctic System and the Utilization of Resources', *Univ. Mia. L. Rev*, Vol. 33, 1978, 425–473, at 443–451.
29. Recommendation VI-4, *Handbook 1983*, at 1101.
30. Recommendation VIII-11, *Handbook 1983*, at 1102–1104.
31. Recommendation XII-4, Report cit., note 14 supra, 37–38.
32. See Chapter 10 infra.
33. Recommendation VIII-13, *Handbook 1983*, 1104–1105. On the background of this Recommendation, with particular reference to the action taken by the United Nations Environment Program in 1975, F. M. Auburn: *Antarctic Law and Politics*, 1982, 124–125. See also Chapter 10 infra.
34. FAO: *Report of the Conference*, Eighteenth Session, Rome, 8–27 November 1975, Doc. C75/REP, 1975, at 39, par. 177. See also Chapter 10 infra and Zegers, loc. cit., note 28 supra, at 451.
35. Recommendations IX-6 and X-7, *Handbook 1983*, 1107–1108.
36. Colson, loc. cit., note 2 supra, at 884–885.
37. Ibid., at 886.

38. Recommendation VII-6, *Handbook 1983*, at 1501.
39. Recommendations IX-1, X-1, XI-1, *Handbook 1983*, 1503–1509.
40. Colson, loc. cit., note 2 supra, at 886.
41. Recommendation VIII-14, *Handbook 1983*, 1501–1502.
42. The most important documents of this scientific contribution are referred to in Chapter 6 infra in relation to the environmental policy. See also generally note 15 supra.
43. Antarctic Treaty, Special Preparatory Meeting for the IXth Consultative Meeting, Paris, 28 June–10 July 1976. This meeting dealt specifically with the question of exploration and exploitation of mineral resources.
44. These principles are transcribed in Recommendation IX-1, cit., paragraph 4.
45. Recommendation IX-1 cit., Preambular paragraph 3.
46. Ibid., preambular paragraph 6.
47. Recommendation X-1 cit., paragraphs 3 and 4.
48. See note 42 supra.
49. Colson, loc. cit., note 2 supra, at 891–892.
50. Recommendation XI-1 cit., paragraph 5 (e). The text of Article IV of the Antarctic Treaty is reproduced in full in the Appendix of this book.
51. Colson, loc. cit., note 2 supra, at 884–885.
52. Oscar Pinochet de la Barra: 'Evolución político-jurídica del problema antártico', *Estudios Internacionales*, Vol. XIV, No 55, July–September 1981, 380–393.
53. Colson, loc. cit., note 2 supra, at 886.
54. As quoted by John Lawrence Hargrove: 'Environmental problems of Antarctic Resources Management: legal and institutional aspects', American Society of International Law, 1976, unpublished, at 8. The statement is not reproduced in the report of the meeting, Antarctic Treaty: *Report of the Eighth Consultative Meeting*, Oslo, 9–20 June, 1975.
55. Auburn, op. cit., note 33 supra, at 259–263.
56. Recommendation VIII-14 cit. note 41 supra, preambular paragraph 6.
57. Colson, loc. cit., note 2 supra, at 890.
58. Antarctic Treaty: *Report of the Eighth Consultative Meeting*, Paragraph 15, Oslo, 9–20 June 1975. See W. M. Bush: *Antarctica and International Law*, 1982, at 296.
59. Recommendation IX-1 cit., note 39 supra, paragraph 8.
60. Recommendation XI-1 cit., note 39 supra, paragraph 10.
61. See for example Zegers, loc. cit., note 28 supra, at 469. For the resolution on sea-bed mining moratorium see U.N. General Assembly, Resolution 2574 (XXIV), 1833rd plenary meeting, 15 December 1969, the text of which is published in Lay, Churchill and Nordquist: *New Directions in the Law of the Sea*, Vol. II, at 737. The United Nations Conference on the Human Environment, Stockholm, 5–16 June, 1972, approved in the context of the environmental aspects of natural resources management Recommendation 33 on a ten year moratorium on commercial whaling, for which see *Report* of the Conference, New York, 1973, at 12. For the International Whaling Commission comparable agreement establishing a zero catch limit, see paragraph 10 (e) of the *schedule* cit. note 23 supra, at 13; see also the *Chairman's Report of the Thirty-fourth Annual Meeting*, Brighton, 19–24 July 1982, par. 6, at 21.
62. See, for example, Colson, loc. cit., note 2 supra, at 889.
63. Colson, loc. cit., note 2 supra, at 895, 899–900. For a proposal on an indefinite moratorium, see Antarctic and Southern Ocean Coalition: *An indefinite moratorium on all Antarctic minerals activities*, January 21, 1985. For similar approaches embodied in the proposals for Antarctica as a world park, see Chapter 10 infra.
64. Colson, loc. cit., note 2 supra, at 895, 899–900.

65. Recommendation X-1 cit., last preambular paragraph; Recommendation XI-1, paragraph 1.
66. Antarctic Treaty, *Report of the Twelfth Consultative Meeting*, loc. cit., note 14 supra, paragraph 48, at 18–19.
67. Colson, loc. cit., note 2 supra, at 900.
68. See for a discussion of the legal issues associated with the moratorium resolution, Bilder, loc. cit., note 6 supra, at 187–188.
69. See note 53 supra and associated text.
70. Bilder, loc. cit., note 6 supra, at 188.
71. Colson, loc. cit., note 2 supra, 889–890.
72. Brownlie, op. cit., note 3 supra, at 36–38.
73. Auburn, op. cit., note 33 supra, at 261.
74. Ibid.
75. Francisco Orrego Vicuña: *Los Fondos Marinos y Oceánicos*, 1976, 241–246. See also note 16 supra.
76. Recommendation XI-1, for example, reminds 'of the negotiations that are taking place in the Third United Nations Conference on the Law of the Sea', preambular paragraph 6.
77. Bilder, loc. cit., note 6 supra, at 188.
78. Rainer Lagoni: 'Antarctica's Mineral Resources in International Law', *Z.A.O.R.V.*, Vol. 39, 1979, 1–37, at 16.
79. On implied powers in international organizations see generally Manuel Rama-Montaldo: 'International legal personality and implied powers of international organizations', *B.Y.B.I.L.*, 1970, 111–155, with particular reference to 'non-expressed rights which can only be inferred from the purposes and functions of each organization', at 131; Rudolf L. Bindschedler: 'La delimitation des compétences des Nations Unies', *Rec. Cours Ac. D.I.*, 1963-I, 307–424; Finn Seyersted: 'United Nations Forces: some legal problems', *B.Y.B.I.L.*, 1961, 351–475.
80. See the work by Bush, cit., note 58 supra, at 91.
81. Ibid, at 91–92.
82. Colson, loc. cit., note 2 supra, at 883.
83. Brownlie, op. cit., note 3 supra, at 627.
84. Ibid., at 687.
85. International Court of Justice: Advisory opinion on Reparation for Injuries suffered in the service of the United Nations, *Reports*, 1949, at 182.
86. On the limits of legislation under implied powers, see Brownlie, op. cit., note 3 supra, at 687–688.
87. For a summary of this practice, see Bush, op. cit., note 58 supra, at 88–89. See also Auburn, op. cit., note 33 supra, at 161–165.
88. See notes 58 and 59 supra and associated texts.
89. Auburn, op. cit., note 33 supra, at 163.
90. Convention on the Conservation of Antarctic Marine Living Resources, Article II, *Handbook 1983*, 9501–9514. See also note 26 supra.
91. See Extract from the Final Act of the Conference on the Conservation of Antarctic Marine Living Resources, *Handbook 1983*, 9515; and also note 26 supra.
92. Bush, op. cit., note 58 supra, at 89.
93. Colson, loc. cit., note 2 supra, at 878, 891–892.
94. See generally Rosalyn Higgins: *The development of international law through the political organs of the United Nations*, 1963; Jorge Castañeda: 'Valeur juridique des resolutions des Nations Unies', *Rec. Cours Ac. D.I.*, 1970-I, 205–331; D. W.

Bowett: *The Law of International Institutions*, 1982. See also Bindschedler, loc. cit., note 79 supra.

95. Bush, op. cit., note 58 supra, at 88.
96. Colson, loc. cit., note 2 supra, at 877.
97. Bush, op. cit., note 58 supra, at 88.
98. Colson, loc. cit., note 2 supra, at 880–881.
99. Ibid., at 880.
100. Ibid., at 881. See United States: Antarctic Conservation Act of 1978, Public Law 95-541, 95th Congress, *I.L.M.*, Vol. 18, 1979, 131–136. The latest edition of the Handbook of Measures reports that the approval of the Agreed Measures by the Federal Republic of Germany and Japan is still pending; see *Handbook 1983*, Annex A, at 9101.
101. Bush, op. cit., note 58 supra, at 98.
102. Ibid., at 88.
103. Auburn, op. cit., note 33 supra, at 162.
104. See generally Brownlie, op. cit., note 3 supra, at 687–688, with particular reference to the statement that 'the process of interpretation cannot be subordinated to arbitrary devices' and to the dissenting opinion of Judge Hackworth in the *Reparation* case, cit. note 85 supra, at 198, restricting implied powers 'to those that are "necessary" to the exercise of powers expressly granted'. However, as Brownlie also points out, there is a wide power of appreciation in the matter, which needs to take into account the context of the issue and the interplay of various relevant principles, ibid., at 688. With regard to the practice of organizations in the interpretation of treaties, see ibid., at 627; and note 83 supra and associated text.
105. The development of framework treaties in the context of regional economic integration processes is analysed in Academie de Droit International de la Haye: *Legal Aspects of Economic Integration*, Colloque 1971, contributions by A. M. Akiwumi (Africa), Francisco Orrego Vicuña (Latin America), Joel Rideau (Europe) and A. Wasilkowski (socialist countries).
106. For a general survey of the law and practice of international organizations, see generally Frederic L. Kirgis, Jr: *International organizations in their legal setting*, 1977.
107. See note 22 supra.
108. See note 26 supra.
109. Auburn, op. cit., note 33 supra, at 209–210.
110. See, for example, Article 1 (1) of the Convention for the Conservation of Antarctic Seals and Articles III and IV of the Convention on the Conservation of Antarctic Marine Living Resources.
111. Bush, op. cit., note 58 supra, at 96, 98. An account of the legal status of recommendations is done by Bush at 96–98.
112. Ibid., at 96. Article XIII (5) of the Antarctic Treaty, Article 13 of the Seal Convention and Article XXVIII (1) of the Canberra Convention use the expression 'enter into force' for the respective treaties.
113. Bush, op. cit., note 58 supra, at 96.
114. Ibid., at 96–97.
115. See Recommendation IV-21 in conjunction with the Convention on the Conservation of Antarctic Seals, *Handbook 1983*, at 2402–2403.
116. Bush, op. cit., note 58 supra, at 98.
117. On the institutional developments of the Antarctic system, see generally Chapter 8 infra. For a recent initiative proposing measures of co-ordination within the system and the establishment of a *pro-tempore* secretariat, a centre for

information and documentation and other institutional developments, see Chile: *Operation of the Antarctic Treaty*. Doc.ANT/XII/PREP/7, 11 April 1983.

118. On decisions of international organizations generally, Stephen M. Schwebel (ed.): *The Effectiveness of International Decisions*, 1971. See also Lino Di Qual: *Les effets des Resolutions des Nations Unies*, 1967; Obed Y. Asamoah: *The legal significance of the Declarations of the General Assembly of the United Nations*, 1966, and Castañeda, loc. cit., note 94 supra.

119. Antarctic Treaty, Report of the Fourth Consultative Meeting, Santiago, 3–18 November 1966, paragraph 30, in Bush, op. cit., note 58 supra, at 195.

120. Alfred van der Essen: 'The application of the law of the sea to the Antarctic continent', in Francisco Orrego Vicuña (ed.): *Antarctic Resources Policy*, 1983, at 236. On the definition of treaty see generally Article 2.1 (a) and Article 3 of the Vienna Convention on the Law of Treaties, and see also Sir Ian Sinclair: *The Vienna Convention on the Law of Treaties*, 1984, at 6 and footnote 12.

121. Van der Essen, loc. cit., note 120 supra, at 236–237.

122. See the speech of welcome by Sir Anthony Kershaw on the occasion of the opening of the Conference on the Conservation of Antarctic Seals, 3 February 1972, in Foreign and Commonwealth Office: *Report of the Conference on the Conservation of Antarctic Seals*, London, 3–11 February 1972, at 5.

123. The purpose of including in the Convention nations which are not signatories of the Antarctic Treaty is also stated in the speech cited in note 122 supra, at 5–6.

124. Jorge Berguño: 'Criterios de aceptabilidad en un régimen para los minerales antárticos', in Francisco Orrego Vicuña et al., op. cit., note 1 supra, at 262.

3

Antarctic sovereignty and jurisdiction: new approaches for a resources policy

3.1   Antarctic sovereignty and co-operation: the need for reconsideration

The discussion on sovereignty in the Antarctic continent has traditionally been dominated by the question of territorial claims and the procedures for making such claims, and by the way in which the requirements of effective occupation are fulfilled.[1] This is adequate for the needs of a period in which territorial rivalries and the other positions that have been considered competed for control of the system of organization that was applied to the Antarctic continent.

However, the development that has taken place over the last twenty-five years has highlighted two cardinal elements. The first is that, in spite of the many existing difficulties, sovereignty has become an established fact in the Antarctic. But this is so only in a relative sense, since simultaneously there has also been the development of the second basic element, consisting in a powerful framework of international co-operation in Antarctica. The fundamental link between these two elements has been Article IV of the Antarctic Treaty, which by freezing formal claims to sovereignty and not prejudging on the issue has made possible the strengthening of the process of co-operation in the region. As was pointed out earlier, sovereignty has become inseparable from co-operation in the Antarctic since it would be difficult to maintain sovereignty unless it were closely linked with the factor of co-operation.[2] Conversely, it can also be said that co-operation on its own, if it does not rely on the support provided by national interests in the Antarctic, including those related to claims to sovereignty, would probably lack the necessary vitality.

In view of this new situation, discussion on sovereignty as traditionally conceived becomes largely irrelevant. The question that becomes relevant in this new context is how to reconcile the exercise of sovereignty with the growing requirements of Antarctic co-operation which embraces subjects of ever-growing complexity. At a time when such co-operation was restricted to a relatively simple subject matter, such as that with which the system was concerned during the first few years after the Treaty came into force, these other considerations did not specifically arise and the general safeguards set forth in Article IV of the Antarctic Treaty were adequate. When, however, the question arose of regulating and ordering the resources policy, the problem became progressively more acute and has become particularly intense in connection with the mineral resources regime.

The primacy of international law and the Antarctic order

The existing relationship between the sovereignty of the State and the international order has been a subject of constant concern to theoreticians of international law. In his Principles of International Law, Kelsen describes the State as a social order of a coercive type which cannot be other than a legal order.[3] The essential feature which differentiates this legal order of the State from that of the international community is the degree of centralization which each exemplifies. While the former is of a centralized nature, the second is decentralized but this is no reason why the legal order should be identified solely with the State. Even if it is considered from the point of view of the monopoly over the use of force, the international order, concludes Kelsen, is similar to the national order.[4]

Having established the legal nature of the international order, Kelsen turns to the problem of the relationship between the 'superiority and inferiority' of the respective orders. He concludes in this connection that these are figurative expressions and defines them in the following terms:

> In the social sphere it can mean only a specific normative relationship that is constituted by a normative order, a system of obligating and authorizing norms. . . . Hence the relationship of superiority and inferiority exists really not between the individuals themselves but between the individuals on the one hand, and the order regulating their conduct on the other. . . . Superiority and inferiority are only figurative expressions. They signify a normative bond, the relationship of the individual to the normative order.[5]

Once again it is observed that there are no differences between the two orders since when international law imposes a certain conduct on States, a relationship of subordination is established with regard to this law which is identical to the relationship between individuals and domestic law. Furthermore, it is pointed out that 'the power of the State' is equivalent to the power of the social order which consists solely in its effectiveness.[6]

On the basis of these concepts, Kelsen elaborates on the scope of the sovereignty of the State. In his General Theory, he says:

> The question of whether the State is sovereign or not thus coincides with the question whether or not international law is an order superior to national law. . . . If we accept the hypothesis of the primacy of international law, then the State 'is not' sovereign. Under this hypothesis, the State could be pronounced sovereign only in the relative sense that no other order but the international legal order is superior to the national legal order, so that the State is subjected directly to international law only.[7]

While Kelsen's theory may be open to criticism in the light of other jurisprudential assessments of the role of sovereignty in international law,[8] the fact is that a good number of authors coincide with the basic proposition that sovereignty is subordinated to international law and that, consequently, individuals can have a direct relationship with the international normative order. Brierly has criticized the notion of the state as a personality with a life and a will of its own, characterizing states as '*institutions*, that is to say, organizations which men establish among themselves for securing certain objects, of which the most fundamental is a system of order within which the activities of their common life can be carried on. . . . There are important differences between international law and the law under which individuals live in a state, but those differences do not lie in metaphysics or in any mystical qualities of the entity called state sovereignty'.[9]

Jessup also foresaw a system of law based on the concept of a 'community of interests' which would transcend the ideas of both independence and sovereignty.[10] On the basis of these conceptual developments a more precise separation between 'imperium' and 'dominium' has also been suggested, the former highlighting the relationship between sovereignty and persons, the latter assuming territorial rights which not always are of the essence of the sovereign state.[11] This was also the question which puzzled Robert Lansing when discussing the more extreme case of Spitzbergen while it was still considered '*terra nullius*':

> Upon what theory can a government be established over a territory owned by no nation? What basis is there for the exercise of sovereign rights? . . . The common conception of government carries with it the idea of a state and that idea seems to be

> inseparable from territory and from territorial sovereignty. . . .
> Now in Spitzbergen the proposition is to establish a government
> which can exercise its functions within a territory over which it
> has no sovereign powers, and which derives no authority from
> territorial dominion, for none exists. Can it be done? And if so,
> how can it be done?[12]

When this line of reasoning by the authors of international law is
applied to the case of the Antarctic legal order, certain important aspects
of the role played by the sovereignty of the State can be clarified. It is
meaningful to point out in the first place that national legal orders are
applied in the Antarctic continent in a far more decentralized manner
than occurs in other areas which are subject to the same national order.
This phenomenon is explained by reasons of a geographical and historical
nature but the fact is that the differences which might exist between these
national orders and the prevailing international order in the continent are
minimized to a significant degree.[13]

In this context, the concept of superiority and inferiority acquires an
even more figurative connotation than in the theoretical analysis of
Kelsen that has been given above. The normative link on which the
relationship between individuals and the normative order is based, or the
system from which the norms relating to obligations and authorizations
stem, is not only of a similar nature in the case of the national order and
in that of the international Antarctic order, but the latter is frequently the
only, or the more specific, normative source. The relationship of subordination of the individual is consequently more intense with regard to
the Antarctic international order than in regard to his national order,
without prejudice to the subordination of the State itself in this context.

A third observation concerns the effectiveness of the power of the
social order which, as mentioned above, provides the measure of the
power of the State itself. Given the difficulties inherent in activities in the
Antarctic, the effectiveness of the 'national' social order is extremely
limited and this is what has given rise to the existing high degree of
co-operation. It is clear from what has been said that it is the 'international' order which serves as a guarantee of the effectiveness of the
so-called power of the State.

The sovereignty of the State is not only subordinated in this way to
international law, thus confirming the conclusions of Kelsen's General
Theory and those of the other authors mentioned above, but it is this
international order that contains the condition of the effectiveness of
sovereignty and, in fact, of its validity. From this point of view,

sovereignty and the international Antarctic order cannot continue to be considered, within a traditional frame of reference, as antagonistic concepts but rather as complementary legal expressions of a social order which is constantly acquiring a greater degree of integration. A parallel phenomenon of integration occurs between the national legal orders of non-claimant States as applied to Antarctic matters and the international order governing the region. To the extent that this new frame of reference prevails, the Antarctic social order will be further improved.

The evolution of concepts of territorial sovereignty

The general analysis of sovereignty in international law may be carried out in the more specific realm of the problems raised by territorial sovereignty. One author aptly comments that 'modern developments have rendered sovereignty more relative also in its territorial aspects'.[14] The fundamental tendency to be observed in international law in this connection is the abandonment of theories based on a physical concept of territory or at least a reduction in their influence, and the espousal of theories based on specifically juridical concepts.[15]

Indeed, it is noticeable that the theory of 'territory-as-object', according to which the State exercises over its territory a *dominium* similar to that which, in private law, an owner exercises over his property, is now largely outdated even though it must be pointed out that it is still frequently reflected in the actual practice of States. Another approach is to consider territory principally as the constituent element of the State in which the power that is exercised is that of *imperium*.[16] But, as Suy points out in this connection: 'it is obvious that such power can be exercised only over persons'.[17] As was pointed out further above, it is on the basis of these differences that both concepts have come to be more clearly separated in current jurisprudential discussions about sovereignty.

The physical foundation which such theories assign to territory is, however, insufficient to explain the true nature of the legal relationships which exist in such space. Kelsen's approach, which is to consider territory as the sphere of validity of the legal order of the State, makes it possible to overcome certain of these limitations by introducing a strictly juridical notion. However, the problems are further complicated if it is borne in mind that in certain circumstances a State may exercise competence or jurisdiction over a particular territory without having sovereignty over it. Examples of occupation, leasing, military bases or specific forms of territorial administration are frequently cited in this context.[18] Jessup and Taubenfeld have included in their analysis of 'shared controls of political administration' such forms as condominium, joint belligerent occupation, the regime of Svalbard, neutralized and demilitarized areas, leases and military bases arrangements.[19] Other arrangements, such as that of the Aaland Islands, bear some resemblance to this type of shared controls of political administration, for while being under the control of a single power have been subject since 1856 to an international regime.[20] The case of Svalbard will be considered at a later point.

Suy in this matter reached the conclusion that:

> These few examples provide abundant proof that exclusive territorial competence over part of the territory may be transferred to another State while the territorial State still retains sovereignty. Furthermore, a State may exercise territorial competence in a territory in which sovereignty remains suspended. . . . Territorial competence may also be transferred either to a group of States or to an organ or to an international organization.[21]

The creation of specific international organizations to which member states transfer competences has further enhanced the phenomenon of interconnection between the territory of the State and international law to the point where the concept of the 'territory' of such an organization has been developed, as in the case of the European Economic Community (EEC).[22] The concept of 'territory' of an organization is mostly used in a functional sense, examples of this being provided by references to the 'customs territory' of the EEC,[23] vessels 'registered in Community territory',[24] or the more general concept of a 'zone communautaire des 200 milles'[25] and other similar approaches to the problems of fishing zones and Common Fisheries Policy in the ambit of the EEC.[26] The transfer of competences which takes place in this context is generally limited to the purposes and scope of a precise policy and does not involve a general renunciation of sovereignty. What we have here is, of course, a legal fiction since the State has not abandoned its sovereignty but has merely transferred specific competences, even though for a considerable period of time this process was interpreted as being inimical to national sovereignty.

Given the fact that the territorial competences of the State may vary both in extent and in intensity, the central question raised by Suy in his analysis is: What is the substantive content of the legal order of the State in a region and with what degree of intensity must it be exercised for such a region to be described as the 'territory' of the State? On this matter he makes the point that:

> When a given region remains under the sovereignty of a State, it

cannot become the 'territory' of another State unless the latter exercises its administration there, that is *all* the legislative, executive and judicial competences.[27]

In other words, as long as we are dealing with competences shared with or partly transferred to another State, or to an international organization, sovereignty remains an attribute of the territorial State. Only in the case of total transfer can this sovereignty be affected but even in such a case it would be necessary to consider whether such transfer is permanent or temporary, and on what conditions, since sovereignty could continue in existence as a *nudum jus*.[28]

The arguments that have been outlined above are of particular importance in the case of the Antarctic. It must, of course, be borne in mind that discussion of Antarctic sovereignty has always been relative in nature since, as was indicated in Chapter 1, in regions where, for geographical reasons, difficult conditions prevail authors and the decisions of international courts and tribunals have applied less rigorous conditions to the exercise of sovereignty than are generally required in normal situations.

As regards specifically territorial matters, there has also been an evolution which appears to coincide with the changes at the theoretical level which were discussed above. During the state of reaffirmation of territorial sovereignty in the 1940s and 1950s, the concept of 'territory-as-object' could be identified as the prevailing tendency in the practice of the States that claimed sovereignty in the Antarctic continent, at least to the extent that the idea of ensuring a *dominium* prevailed in the respective Antarctic policies of some claimant states.[29] However, since the entry into force of the Antarctic Treaty, it is noticeable that less emphasis has been placed on such notions and that others, in which *imperium* appears as the central element, have come to the fore, even though not necessarily in a strictly territorial sense but, as we shall see, directed more towards the exercise of jurisdiction over persons. In a way, this trend is parallel to the increasing sophistication of approaches which characterizes the jurisdiction over the sea and sea-bed.[30] The political and legal compromises on which the Treaty is based undoubtedly facilitated this change of approach.[31]

Once again, however, it was in relation to the resources policy that there occurred the most significant change which is still developing. Gradually the concept of Antarctic sovereignty has come closer to the interpretation of Kelsen and other authors whereby the Antarctic territory is regarded as a special sphere of validity of the legal order that has evolved under the Antarctic Treaty and related instruments. To some extent that is related to the territories which certain countries claim as their own, which in their view comes within the sphere of validity of the national legal order. However, the interesting fact is that this phenomenon is also related to Antarctic space considered as a whole and which, in this sense, represents the sphere of validity of the international Antarctic legal order. This explains, for example, the origin of the concept of joint jurisdiction within the Antarctic system.[32]

Since it is in relation to the administration and ordering of resources that the greatest degree of integration occurs between the national legal order and the international legal order that prevails in the continent, this is also where the process of transfer of competences has begun to occur. This, in its turn, coincides with the beginning of the process of creating Antarctic institutions for the management of such resources. The case of the Convention for the Conservation of Antarctic Marine Living Resources represents a first step in this direction since competences were distributed to some extent between the institutions that were created and participating States.

However, it is in the field of mineral resources that this new orientation acquires greater significance. As we shall see in due course, the essence of the internal accommodation of interests consists in determining how competences are to be distributed between the institutions of the regime and member States, while differentiating between the case of those which claim sovereignty and those which do not. Thus, what we are dealing with is not an exclusive choice between the national and international orders as might have been the case under the classical conception of sovereignty, but of a question of assigning and transferring competences and integrating these orders in a common regime. The latter's sphere of validity is the Antarctic space as a whole so that one may speak of an 'Antarctic territory' in a way which makes it comparable to the 'territory' of the European Economic Community, in the functional sense of the concept which has been explained above, although, of course, the competences and powers of the Antarctic minerals regime will not be as developed as that of a major organization of economic integration such as the EEC. The fact that in Antarctica sovereignty and territorial claims are disputed by the non-claimant countries has also added weight to the need of common regimes applicable to the area as a whole as a major factor of the internal and external accommodation of interests.

In a conception of this nature, territorial sovereignty does not disappear and is not abandoned as might have been expected in the light of classical theories, but it is interconnected in a different and complementary way with the international order prevailing in the Antarctic. The extent and intensity of the applicable national legal order becomes more relative but, at the same time, consolidates the necessity of its own effectiveness. Owing to this change of perspective, the problem in the Antarctic context arises not so much in terms of the 'exercise of sovereignty' as in terms of the exercise of 'jurisdiction', a fact which, in itself, is indicative of the evolution that has taken place.

3.2   The bases of jurisdiction in international law and the Antarctic case

Jurisdiction is a manifestation of sovereignty which has been defined as 'the capacity of a State under international law to prescribe or to enforce a rule of law'.[33] From this concept stems the traditional classification of jurisdiction into 'prescriptive jurisdiction' and 'enforcement jurisdiction',[34] to which yet a third category has been added, namely 'jurisdiction to adjudicate'.[35] However, since the main concern of jurisdiction is the allocation of competences between States,[36] it has also been suggested that it is legally possible to distinguish the competence to prescribe and enforce from the competence to apply the law, the latter saying nothing 'about the origin of the law (it may be the law of the forum or another law) – rather it is about the authority to apply law directly to specific persons, events or property'.[37] This distinction is helpful in the case of a complex jurisdictional situation, like that existing in Antarctica, for it will provide additional alternatives as to the manner how given competences may be allocated between States or between States and the institutions of a regime.

In the general theory, the relationship between the principal types of jurisdiction is well established. It has been summarized by Bowett as follows:

> There can be no enforcement jurisdiction unless there is prescriptive jurisdiction; yet there may be a prescriptive jurisdiction without the possibility of an enforcement jurisdiction. . . .[38]

To the extent that the jurisdiction to apply the law is accepted as a separate category, one could also add to Bowett's reasoning that such jurisdiction may exist independently from the competence to prescribe and enforce.

Even if this relationship also applies in principle to the case of the Antarctic, in view of the relative nature of the central concept of sovereignty in this context, one may also observe somewhat more complex situations in regard to the jurisdiction deriving from such sovereignty. Thus, the existence of prescriptive jurisdiction without the corresponding enforcement jurisdiction is perhaps more likely in the

Antarctic order than in other legal contexts, given the need to take into account a greater number of interests involved. But it should also be observed that, in the context of some of the Antarctic resources regimes, there is some indication that States have retained enforcement jurisdiction for certain purposes in circumstances that such States may no longer have the prescriptive jurisdiction, since they may have delegated the latter to the institutions of the regime. While this occurs only to a minimal extent in the case of the Convention for the Conservation of Antarctic Marine Living Resources, which in general follows the pattern of the international fisheries commissions, it is more evident in the approaches suggested for the regime on mineral resources as will be examined in the second part of this work. With every more reason the jurisdiction to apply the law can be retained by participating States irrespectively of the allocation of the competences to prescribe and enforce.

The authors of international law agree in identifying the main principles on which jurisdiction may be based though not all States use them all. These are: (i) the territorial principle; (ii) the principle of nationality; (iii) the principle of protection; and (iv) the principle of universality. The passive personality principle is generally added to these, albeit more cautiously.[39] Even if the substance of these principles of jurisdiction is in general well established, it is to be noted that they have a number of relative characteristics which may be particularly relevant to the case of the Antarctic.

Bowett emphasizes the factors of dynamism and adaptability which are at the present time characteristic of the territorial principle, which has been extended in various directions.[40] One of these has been its extension to movable objects such as ships, aircraft or space vehicles on the basis of their link with the territory of registry. It is interesting to note that, in Bowett's opinion, this type of 'flag State jurisdiction', which is common in the case of the Antarctic, is seen not as being incompatible with the principle of territorial jurisdiction but as being a special application of it.[41] While ships or artificial islands are not viewed as a kind of 'floating territory', functional relations with the territory of the State are anyhow still prevalent in the legal analysis, as can be evidenced by the concept of 'quasi-territorial' jurisdiction over ships or of 'flag State jurisdiction' over artificial islands.[42] Admittedly, the view of Bowett and other authors has a different starting point, namely the link with the territory of registry, but it is none the less important in that it avoids the perceptions of incompatibility with the territorial principle espoused by the majority of authors.[43]

The territorial principle has also been extended to various activities which are prejudicial to the community of States without recourse to other principles such as that of nationality or that of personality. Situations such as genocide, apartheid and various manifestations of terrorism have been dealt with through the application of the principle of territorial jurisdiction and of other principles associated with the territorial fiction, coupled with international principles, however. A similar approach has been adopted to protect interests in relation to resources which are located outside the territory *stricto sensu* but in respect of which international law recognizes the control of the State; outstanding examples of this are the continental shelf and the Exclusive Economic Zone.[44] In both cases what is involved is the exercise of a type of specialized jurisdiction which combines the territorial and the international aspects of the rights in question.

Mention must also be made of the exercise of jurisdiction based on the fact that a particular form of conduct produces effects within the territory of the State; this is yet another extension of the principle which is being commented upon.[45]

A number of interesting problems arise in connection with the application, scope or interpretation of the principles to which we have referred. Thus, for example, the concept of the 'genuine link' in the case of the principle of nationality involves determination of whether or not a specific type of behaviour should be the subject of jurisdiction by the State of nationality rather than the application of nationality as an automatic criterion of jurisdiction. In other words, the jurisdiction which is most appropriate to the case must be identified.[46] Leading cases on the questions of nationality have well defined the concept of genuine attachment and related issues, most notably the *Nottebohm* and *Flegenheimer* cases;[47] in other cases still, with particular reference to *Joyce* and *Kawakita*,[48] although differing on the approach followed, the flexible criteria for the exercise of jurisdiction has been an evident common feature, thus confirming the existence of multiple choices for the determination of jurisdiction and the avoidance of absolute rules in the field.

Furthermore, it must be borne in mind that the rigorous application of the principle of nationality and its extension to subsidiaries of foreign firms has given rise to serious conflicts in the case of the United States, particularly in regard to anti-trust legislation.[49] However, this situation has also prompted a vigorous discussion about the need of balancing the pertinent interests and introducing a degree of additional flexibility, which will be.commented on further below.

The main reason why the passive personality principle has been challenged is that it is not clear in what circumstances the damage suffered by the national of a State constitutes an adequate basis on which the State

may claim jurisdiction.[50] While the view of authors doubts whether the
Lotus case recognizes this principle,[51] the discussion in itself is a good
indication about the relativity of the nationality link as the basis of
jurisdiction.

*Inapplicability of the traditional principles: the necessity for a balance of
interests*
In view of the relativity of the traditional principles on which jurisdiction
is based, it does not seem entirely suitable to apply them to the case of the
Antarctic since it is difficult by doing so to reach a solution that avoids
conflictive situations. As one author correctly points out, 'traditional
guidelines for the exercise of jurisdiction developed from actual international practice in circumstances unlike the unique situation that prevails
in Antarctica'.[52] Similarly, another author explains that 'so-called traditional jurisdictional principles have been derived from experiences and
situations not relevant to Antarctica'.[53]

Any choice of one or other of the main traditional principles that have
been mentioned inevitably entails a pronouncement on the underlying
legal and political problem of the Antarctic, namely the question of claims
of sovereignty or the non-recognition of such claims. For this reason, even
though one or other principle may be applied to specific subjects, it is not
possible to choose one of them as the sole criterion to the exclusion of the
others.

Occasionally an attempt has been made to suggest different principles
for the polar regions but this does not overcome the obstacles just
mentioned. Thus, for example, it has been proposed that, for 'insulated
environments' such as the Arctic or the Antarctic, the law of the 'social
environment' should be applied, which in this case would be that to which
the respective expedition belongs.[54] In other words, the social and legal
environment in which the particular activity originates would be projected
on to the geographical environment in which the activity takes place;
however, this approach does not preclude a conflict of jurisdictions.
Specific studies on theories of jurisdiction in relation to extradition have
equally failed to come up with formulas that are appropriate to the case of
the Antarctic.[55] Similar difficulties affect the application of the 'flag-State'
jurisdiction to the Antarctic, particularly when it is conceived in the
context of a renunciation of sovereignty by claimant states in the area;[56]
even though the number of non-claimant parties to the 1959 Treaty is
increasing, and consequently the acceptance of a 'flag-State' approach
could become more general or widespread, in view of the provisions of
Article IV of the Treaty it could not be regarded as a substitute for

territorial sovereignty nor entail a prohibition of territorial jurisdiction, since this would upset the balanced formula of that article. Not even in the case of a formal amendment of the Treaty is it likely that this approach could be accepted as the overriding principle of jurisdiction. Perhaps it would be different if the principle is conceived in a manner not incompatible with territorial sovereignty, a solution which might also be helpful to solve the problems inherent to the present approach to the question in the United Nations and other discussions.

On the other hand, it is to be noted that in some analyses the concept of territory is greatly extended to include special situations; the Harvard Research in International Law, for example, includes in this concept the case of territories in dispute, condominium or joint occupation and areas administered by a State but under the nominal sovereignty of another State, in addition to the special cases such as that of the former Panama Canal Zone, protectorates and mandates.[57] Even though some of them may be assimilated to the Antarctic case, it remains true that the territorial principle alone leaves intact the fundamental problem that we have been discussing.

The existence of concurrent jurisdictions is a phenomenon that occurs frequently in international law. Referring to it in the context of the principles explained above, Bowett states:

> The answer cannot be that these rules serve to indicate the State which ought to exercise jurisdiction. For, generally speaking, situations of concurrent jurisdiction are normal enough, so the propriety of a given State exercising jurisdiction is rarely raised in an absolute sense. It is more commonly raised in a relative sense, in the form of a question whether jurisdiction ought to be exercised by State A rather than State B – without disputing that both States can invoke one or other of the principles of jurisdiction to support their claim.[58]

On the basis of this statement of fact, Bowett suggests the necessity of using the technique of the 'balancing of interests' as one way of determining the applicable jurisdiction. This approach has been used in part in connection with some of the conflicts caused by the anti-trust legislation of the United States, but the fact that final determination is made by the courts of one of the parties involved is in itself a difficulty that has rightly been criticized.[59] As Judge Wilkey has rightly observed in the case *Laker v. Sabena*, the usefulness of interest balancing 'breaks down when a court is faced with the task of selecting one forum's prescriptive jurisdiction over that of another'.[60]

In addition to the general criterion of 'restraint' which a court may always apply where there are problems of concurrent jurisdiction, in the case of *Mannington Mills v. Congoleum Corp.*, the Court of Appeals of the United States identified various factors relevant to its consideration of the 'balancing of interests'.[61] Among these, mention may be made of the following: degree of conflict with the foreign law or policy; nationality of the parties; relative importance of criminal behaviour under each of the jurisdictions; availability of judicial remedies abroad; possible impact on international relations if the court exercises jurisdiction; possibility of enforcing the judgement; and the existence of treaties regulating the matter. A number of elements were also identified in the decision on the *Timberlane* case[62] as well as in other precedents.[63] The matter has also been discussed in terms of its implications under customary international law.[64] These various criteria may assist in determining the most appropriate jurisdiction in those cases in which there is a legitimate concurrence of jurisdictions in the light of the principles of international law.[65]

It must also be remembered that, when this accommodation of interests is not satisfactorily achieved, it is customary for the country which considers that it is affected to have recourse to the application of 'blocking legislation' or other measures which seek to paralyse the exercise of foreign jurisdiction, particularly when it produces extraterritorial effects.[66] British legislation provides an illustration of this point.[67]

As Bowett explains, the approach which consists in seeking an agreement on the applicable principles of jurisdiction would seem unlikely to produce satisfactory results. The option of a judicial solution also has a number of limitations. For this reason, Bowett expresses a preference for seeking negotiated solutions in the following terms: 'the process of negotiation should be more flexible than the use of judicial process and eminently more suitable to the area of economic or commercial conflicts of interests'.[68] The specific role of diplomatic negotiations has also been encouraged in this field.[69] Even if some progress appears to have been made in the development of negotiation and consultation as a method of solving conflicts of jurisdiction, this approach has still not found general favour. Progress in this direction would certainly find support in international law, for as the International Court of Justice reminded in the *North Sea Continental Shelf Cases*[70] not only is there a duty to negotiate but also – referring to the Permanent Court Advisory Opinion on *Railway Traffic between Lithuania and Poland* – there is an obligation to pursue negotiations 'as far as possible with a view to concluding agreements'.[71]

The application of these considerations to the Antarctic case may provide interesting new insights since, as we have said, it is impossible to identify a single guiding principle for the exercise of jurisdiction in the Antarctic continent. In addition, given the existing nature of the Antarctic system, it is inevitable that there should be concurrent jurisdictions and this fact makes it necessary to seek different approaches. This aspect will be analysed in the sections that follow.

However, before doing this, it should be pointed out that there exist two schools of legal thought which have a number of important differences of approach. Within the legal thinking of 'common law', the theory of jurisdiction has undergone a markedly greater development than has occurred in the tradition of continental law. The different orientation is also apparent in the respective views of such schools on international law.[72]

The first school of thought, which recognizes jurisdiction as a manifestation of sovereignty, tends in practice to separate one concept from the other. On this basis, jurisdiction acquires greater autonomy as a subject and it may be analysed with a degree of flexibility. At the same time, this approach provides a basis for seeking more pragmatic solutions to problems that arise without such solutions being regarded as greatly affecting the concept of sovereignty which is more relative. In the continental tradition, on the other hand, the idea of jurisdiction is much more closely linked with that of sovereignty and at times becomes inseparable from it. As a consequence of this identification, the concept of jurisdiction has greater rigidity and solutions can only be conceived within a narrower framework of options which will be determined on the basis of how far they are seen as potentially affecting sovereignty. Sovereignty thus becomes a more absolute concept.

On occasions it even seems that we are dealing with different concepts, as a result of which the 'common law' school places greater emphasis on the existing link between the legal system and individuals whereas the continental school gives priority to the relationship between the legal system and the territory. As we shall see, these different traditions have also had an influence on the approach to jurisdiction in the Antarctic system.

Ultimately, the fundamental question on the problem of jurisdiction which is still unanswered in international law is, as Professor Higgins has asked in discussing the Lotus case implications, 'is it necessary to show a specific basis of jurisdiction, or may one assert jurisdiction without reference to a specific basis, so long as one is acting reasonably?'[73]

3.3   Jurisdiction in the Antarctic Treaty system

During the course of negotiations over the Antarctic Treaty the criteria for the exercise of jurisdiction were clearly stated. However, contrary to what might normally have been expected, national positions on the matter were not related to whether or not a country claimed sovereignty but to its espousal of one or other of the central principles of international law which we have been discussing, namely the principle of nationality or territoriality. It is possible that the different schools of thought that we have mentioned above explain this situation.

The system of jurisdiction based on the principle of nationality was proposed by Great Britain, a country claiming sovereignty, in the context of what was described as 'a proposal that would have provided for a more complete system of jurisdiction'.[74] Japan, which also made a proposal on the same lines, was a country which did not recognize claims of sovereignty and consequently its delegation made the following comment on Article VIII of the Treaty: 'the delegation of Japan continues in its belief that all personnel in Antarctica should be subject only to the jurisdiction of the country of which they are nationals'.[75]

The diplomatic documents that have been published on these negotiations show that the countries that do not recognize claims of sovereignty naturally favoured jurisdiction based on the principle of nationality. South Africa stated that 'the Government of South Africa is not able to foresee that it will be possible to renounce its jurisdiction over its nationals in any place in Antarctica'.[76] The Soviet Union, for its part, placed on record that: 'The Soviet Union has considered and continues to consider that Soviet citizens in the Antarctic are subject to the jurisdiction of the Soviet Union alone'.[77] Belgium also endorsed the statement by Japan.[78] As we shall see later this was also the position adopted by the United States.

In addition to Great Britain, another important country claiming sovereignty, namely Norway, endorsed the principle of nationality and made the following statement:

> We believe, nevertheless, that any person in the Antarctic should be subject solely to the penal jurisdiction of the country of which he is a national and that this principle should have been embodied in the Treaty. We are therefore disappointed that the principle which was outlined in the proposal of the United Kingdom and in that of Japan as well, has not found the necessary support of all Delegations.[79]

Other claimant countries, on the other hand, affirmed the territorial principle. The same diplomatic documentation contains an interesting statement by France in this connection:

> . . . the French Delegation wishes to make clear that it does not renounce any of the privileges of its sovereignty in Adélie Land,

especially those concerning the general power of jurisdiction which it exercises over the said territory.[80]

Chile and Argentina endorsed the statement by France.[81] These three countries, following the view of the continental school of law, have placed a greater emphasis on the concept of sovereignty – as the French statement clearly evidences – while jurisdiction is more closely associated with the territorial aspect of such sovereignty.

The limited jurisdictional formula of the Antarctic Treaty

The different positions that have been outlined were difficult to reconcile because acceptance of one or other basic principle would have entailed a prejudgement of the political and legal theses which the various groups of countries maintained in Antarctica. While certain countries that claimed sovereignty were not willing to relinquish the exercise of jurisdiction on the basis of the principle of territoriality, since they feared that some other formula might affect their rights, the countries that did not recognize such claims were equally disinclined to accept a principle different from that of nationality.

As a consequence of this, the system envisaged by Article VIII of the Treaty is basically a transactional formula which is intended not to prejudge the substantive problem. It has its origin in a proposal submitted by the United Kingdom when disagreement arose over its original proposal based on the principle of nationality. This was explained by the British delegation in the following terms:

> As this proposal was not generally accepted, we presented a compromise solution with reference to the immunity of observers and exchanged scientists which formed the basis of the proposal that was agreed to. We considered that this was a method of dealing with those cases which in practice will be those which were more likely to cause difficulties.[82]

Article VIII emphasizes at the outset that its purpose is not to prejudge, stating that its provisions are: 'without prejudice to the respective positions of the Contracting Parties relating to jurisdiction over all other persons in Antarctica'. Next, the Article applies only to three categories of persons, namely: (i) 'observers designated under paragraph 1 of Article VII', who are those responsible for carrying out inspections in Antarctica; (ii) 'scientific personnel exchanged under subparagraph 1 (b) of Article III of the Treaty', which forms part of the system of international scientific co-operation in the Antarctic continent; and (iii) 'members of the staffs accompanying any such persons'. One author has pointed out that the precise definition of these categories of persons might, in some circumstances, give rise to difficulties, particularly with regard to the scope of the third category mentioned.[83] However, it is to be noted that in practice this has not occurred and that the meaning of the provision is reasonably clear.

In accordance with the same Article, the system applies to such persons 'while they are in Antarctica for the purpose of exercising their functions'. Doubts have also been expressed on the scope of this point but it has reasonably been understood that the persons indicated are covered by the system throughout their stay in the Treaty area and not only when they are actually exercising their functions.[84]

These categories of persons 'shall be subject only to the jurisdiction of the Contracting Parties of which they are nationals in respect of all acts or omissions occurring while they are in Antarctica'. Owing to the different national positions that have been indicated, the approach followed by the Consultative Parties in applying this system has necessarily differed. Whereas for those countries that do not recognize claims of sovereignty it is sufficient to promulgate legislation which envisages the link of nationality for the exercise of jurisdiction over such persons, for those countries that have territorial claims the approach is more complex. On the one hand, they may do the same in respect of their nationals, but on the other they must establish the corresponding immunity of jurisdiction in relation to the nationals of other Parties in their respective Antarctic territories. This latter immunity has been compared to immunity of the diplomatic and consular type.[85]

It might even be appropriate to compare the situation of scientific personnel to a type of diplomatic immunity given the more general character of their functions, while the situation of observers, whose task is of a more functional nature, could be compared to the functional type of immunity provided for in the Vienna Convention on Consular Relations of 1963.[86] As we shall see later, special legislation has not in all cases been promulgated; in the absence of such legislation it is the actual text of Article VIII that applies in any case as the central criterion.

With regard to other persons or situations, the 1959 Treaty could not give an answer because of the disagreements that have been mentioned. This is where concurrent jurisdictions really arise since both those countries that apply the territorial principle and those that favour the principle of nationality will have a legitimate basis for their claim of civil or penal jurisdiction, as applicable. It is to be noted, however, that on this matter the Antarctic system of co-operation has observed a special spirit of 'restraint'. Thus, for example, both expeditions and bases in the

Antarctic have been governed by what has in general been described as 'flag jurisdiction'[87] and the legal discrepancies that are inherent in the Treaty have not hitherto given rise to any obstacle in this connection. It follows that the practice of the Treaty is just as important as its provisions.

Although the possibility of a conflict of jurisdiction cannot be ruled out, one must also bear in mind the highly important provision of paragraph 2 of Article VIII of the 1959 Treaty under which 'the Contracting Parties concerned in any case of dispute with regard to the exercise of jurisdiction in Antarctica shall immediately consult together with a view to reaching a mutually acceptable solution'. On the other hand, among the measures which may be considered by consultative meetings under the terms of Article IX, paragraph 1 (e) of the Treaty, 'questions relating to the exercise of jurisdiction in Antarctica' are specifically included.

In spite of the fact that the Treaty's system of jurisdiction has frequently been criticized as inadequate and incomplete[88] there are grounds for considering that its success has lain precisely in the fact that it has not attempted to resolve a jurisdictional situation which contemporary international law itself has been unable to organize adequately. Furthermore, the method of negotiation and consultation provided for in the Treaty is also the approach advocated by a number of authors as the most appropriate means of resolving conflicts of jurisdiction.[89] In connection with the subject of resources, an evolution of interest has also taken place, to which we shall return later.

Political and academic proposals on the Treaty system

The limited solution of the Antarctic Treaty in respect of jurisdiction has given rise to expressions of concern in various governmental and political circles as it has been feared that it might be a future source of difficulties. Britain made the following official statement during the treaty negotiations:

> We still believe that the general problem of jurisdiction, if not resolved as soon as possible, could well cause international disputes of the kind that this Treaty has as its objective to avoid. Consequently, we hope that pursuant to paragraph (1) of Article IX the designated representatives, in conformity with this article will consider and present recommendations to their Governments on this matter as soon as possible after they begin their meetings.[90]

In an analysis of the Treaty made some years later, Christopher Beeby identified the question of the exercise of jurisdiction as one of the three factors that might ultimately threaten the future of the Antarctic Treaty.[91]

Through these manifestations of concern, the first possibilities of a solution began to take shape. In an interesting and little known debate in the House of Lords on the ratification of the Treaty, a number of important ideas were expressed. Among the questions put by Lord Shackleton to the Government on this occasion there was one on 'whether they have any proposals for the settlement of questions relating to the exercise of jurisdiction and property rights in Antarctica'.[92] He pointed out that the major difficulty lay in the exercise of jurisdiction since there were no provisions governing this subject in the Treaty apart from the case envisaged in Article VIII.[93] Some of the questions seem to indicate a premonition of future events: 'And who, if somebody should find some valuable mineral rights, which I am sure will happen one day, is to establish not only national but individual ownership of these rights? Who will police the land? What courts will administer the law, if there be a law?'[94]

For his part, Lord Denning pointed out that the Treaty involves a limitation of sovereignty, adding that 'the only hope for the future of international law throughout the world is an agreed limitation of sovereignty'.[95] Having considered various examples of jurisdictional conflicts or vacuums, the distinguished judge concluded:

> No English court has jurisdiction over land abroad. No English court has jurisdiction over crimes abroad other than murder by British subjects. . . . Suppose that, in this great new continent, there is some question of property, of sinking a mine somewhere, or there is a cruel assault, or an observer goes from one place to another and is ill-treated and misused: what court can deal with such matters? Certainly no English court . . .; and I believe through all the laws of all the countries none of them have such jurisdiction. Who is to have jurisdiction in this territory in matters of property or person? . . . At present there is no law at all to cover individuals or property in the Antarctic.[96]

Some of the solutions proposed in this debate are of particular interest at the present time. Lord Shackleton proposed a formula for internationalization, referring to the initiatives both of Prime Minister Nash of New Zealand and of Nehru:

> My view is that there is only one long-term solution, which I hope the Government will support, namely, that the Antarctic should be fully internationalised and, indeed, that it should be the first United Nations territory. . . . A Board could be set up similar to the United Nations Agency for the peaceful uses of atomic energy.[97]

Lord Denning suggested, in the first place, the mandatory jurisdiction of the International Court of Justice for the settlement of disputes and as a long-term solution, agreeing with Lord Shackleton: 'if this territory could be made international territory, this could be an example to everyone in the way of the future law and order in the world itself'.[98]

The ideas put forward by Lord McNair in this important debate sought, on the other hand, more immediate solutions to the jurisdictional problem. This distinguished international lawyer stated:

> this country has had a good deal of experience in the past in dealing with foreign jurisdiction overseas . . . and I do not think that it is beyond legal abilities to find a solution of those private law difficulties which may arise . . . . Lord Shackleton, referred to the possibility of placing the Antarctic under the administration of the United Nations. That may well happen in time, but what I want to see happen at once is a meeting of this Committee (Consultative Meeting) to establish its procedure.[99]

The position of the Government, stated by the Marquess of Lansdowne, was that the Government had desired a broader system of jurisdiction and that it would raise the question again at the consultative meeting.[100] This initiative took place in 1962 with a proposal for the creation of a group of Experts, but it proved unsuccessful.[101]

Some aspects of the debate over jurisdiction were again raised on the occasion of parliamentary discussion of the Agreed Measures.[102] However, in this case there was agreement on the appropriate course of action which was to apply the principle of nationality; in the words of Lord Wilberforce, 'the Bill proceeds on the perfectly sound basis of founding jurisdiction on nationality'.[103] One point of interest that was made on this occasion was the need to harmonize the sanctions that might be applied under the Agreed Measures with those applied under British law to similar offences since, in the opinion of one Member of Parliament, the former would be more severe than the latter.[104] This posed the need for a certain degree of legislative harmonization in the framework of the Antarctic system.

Concerns expressed in other countries with regard to the Antarctic jurisdictional system are indicative of different orientations. In the debate on this subject that took place in the Senate of the United States, for example, the official replies do no more than note the existence of a potential controversy. In the example of a conflict of jurisdiction with Chile, it was stated:

> If we send a scientist or an inspector into the section claimed by

Chile, he can't be arrested by Chile. Our jurisdiction applies to
him no matter where he is in Antarctica but if there should be a
mining engineer who went down into the sector claimed by Chile
and he got into some trouble, Chile would claim that its laws
governed. We would claim that Chile's law did not govern
because we do not recognize Chile's claim, and there would be an
international controversy as to who had jurisdiction over the
individual.[105]

Although it was indicated that the United States favoured the mandatory jurisdiction of the International Court of Justice for certain situations, it was merely recorded that objections were raised, while no
alternative solutions were suggested.[106]

A third type of reaction was rather far-fetched in scope. An Argentine
author based a campaign of opposition to the ratification of the Antarctic
Treaty on the argument that the Treaty would prevent any possibility of
the exercise of national jurisdiction, both civil and penal, and that the
legal situation thus created:

excludes Argentine sovereignty and replaces it by an internationally shared sovereignty. . . . Sovereignty is not to be shared. It is
exclusive. It may or may not be possessed but it is inseparable
from its exercise.[107]

National legislations in regard to Antarctic jurisdiction

The fears expressed concerning the possibility of a jurisdictional vacuum
in Antarctica[108] have gradually been overcome by legislation on the
subject promulgated by various countries that are Parties to the 1959
Treaty. This body of legislation is neither comprehensive nor uniform but
it represents a first approximation to a solution of the problems that might
arise.

One type of legislation that has been promulgated extends the corpus
of national legislation to the respective Antarctic territory as a consequence of the fact that this territory is regarded as an integral part of the
national territory. In this case there is no special Antarctic legislation but
rather a straightforward process of assimilation into the national legal
order. The legislation promulgated by Argentina belongs to this category
as it declares that Antarctica is national territory.[109] Without prejudice to
this, Article VIII of the Treaty will continue to apply since the instrument
is in force.

In a second type of legislation, certain aspects of national legal arrangements are explicitly or implicitly extended to the Antarctic territory,

representing in both cases a special form of legislation. France has specially extended its penal legislation, penal procedures and regulations governing the civil status of persons to cover the Antarctic territory.[110] Chile has determined the administrative authorities and the competent courts to deal with civil and penal cases involving Antarctica and has thereby implicitly extended its administrative, civil and penal legislation.[111] This is, of course, without prejudice to Article VIII.

Yet another type of legislation is represented by the case of Norway; like the countries in the category just mentioned, Norway has extended its civil and penal legislation to its Antarctic territory but jurisdiction is specifically waived in the case of foreign nationals in those territories.[112] This exception may be a reference to the categories of persons mentioned in Article VIII of the Treaty, since the legislative text contains a special reference to what is required by 'international agreement',[113] but the language used seems to indicate a wider scope. In any case, Article VIII remains applicable.

One element that is common to the three categories mentioned is that none of them governs the conduct of its nationals when they are outside the claimed Antarctic territory, without prejudice once again, to the provisions of Article VIII, and to the position of these countries in questions of the Law of the Sea, which will be examined in the following chapter.

The legislation promulgated by Australia[114] and Great Britain[115] may be considered as forming a fourth category. In both cases, the civil and criminal law is extended in a general way to the appropriate territories, thus establishing the competence of the courts to deal with any cases that arise. The categories of persons covered by the terms of Article VIII of the Treaty, if they are of foreign nationality, are exempt from jurisdiction. However, it they are nationals of Australia or Great Britain, as appropriate, they remain subject to the relevant national jurisdiction whether the acts or omissions that are the subject of jurisdiction occurred in the territory itself or in any other place in Antarctica. It is to be noted that, as a consequence of the recognition of reciprocal claims between the countries of the British Commonwealth, the legislation of the United Kingdom excludes from this latter provision the Australian Antarctic Territory and the New Zealand Ross Dependency, thereby recognizing the competence of the jurisdictions of those countries in their own territories.[116]

The jurisdictional system envisaged in the legislation of New Zealand[117] is similar to that of Australia and Great Britain but has provided for a number of situations which are of interest. In the first place, the system applies to crimes committed by any person in the Ross Dependency as well as to crimes committed: 'in any part of Antarctica, other than the Ross Dependency, that is not within the jurisdiction of any country' by ordinary citizens or residents of New Zealand. However, in the case of crimes committed by foreign nationals in the Ross Dependency, or in certain circumstances, crimes committed by New Zealanders or residents of New Zealand in other parts of Antarctica, the prior consent of the Attorney General is required for the exercise of jurisdiction over them. Similarly, it is to be noted that in the case of persons covered by Article VIII of the Treaty, the Contracting Parties of which they are nationals may waive the immunity of such persons, thus conferring jurisdiction on the courts of New Zealand.

By means of bilateral agreements with the United States the Government of New Zealand has also dealt with some jurisdictional questions posed by the establishment of American Antarctic operational headquarters in New Zealand and by the transit through New Zealand of American personnel, ships and aircraft engaged in operations in Antarctica.[118] The normal requirements in relation to arrival and departure of ships or aircraft, as well as passports, visas and other immigration laws and regulations are waived by New Zealand in relation to such personnel, ships and aircraft; the goods imported or exported in relation to the operations envisaged are exempt from payment of taxes and customs duties, and salaries are not subject to taxation in New Zealand.[119] The jurisdictional clauses of these agreements are of special interest:

> (i) The New Zealand authorities, recognizing the problems arising from the concurrent jurisdiction in criminal matters over such personnel in New Zealand territory, will consider alleged offences affecting only United States personnel or property, or committed in the performance of official duty, as a matter for the United States authorities.
>
> (ii) Moreover, the New Zealand authorities will not ordinarily be concerned to institute proceedings in the New Zealand courts in respect of alleged minor offences which do not fall within the categories referred to in (i) above.[120]

While these provisions do not entirely exclude the jurisdiction of New Zealand, such jurisdiction is severely restricted, in a manner comparable to the agreements governing foreign military bases and similar installations.[121] It is also important to note that even though these agreements refer to the New Zealand territory *stricto sensu*, thus not including the New Zealand Ross Dependency, there is every reason to think that a similar or even broader approach would be followed in the case of concurrent jurisdiction arising from activities in the Ross Dependency, subject to the laws mentioned above and to the provisions of the Antarctic Treaty. This type of bilateral agreement can be considered as supplementary to the provisions of the Antarctic Treaty and related instruments, as is also the case with agreements concluded in other fields.

Among the countries that do not recognize claims of sovereignty, only South Africa has promulgated special legislation under which 'the laws from time to time in force in the Republic shall apply to any South African citizen while he is in Antarctica'.[122] Here we have a jurisdictional link based exclusively on the principle of nationality which applies to citizens of the country concerned in any place in Antarctica.

The position of the United States has been officially defined as follows: 'By virtue of recognizing that there is no sovereignty over Antarctica we retain jurisdiction over our citizens who go down there and we would deny the right of the other claimants to try that citizen'.[123] The legal situation at the level of domestic law, however, is highly complex since it is not clear under what provisions jurisdiction may be exercised and there are in addition a number of major procedural difficulties.[124] Various legislative proposals have tried to clarify the problem on the basis of the promulgation of special legislation but none of them has been approved.[125] In the opinion of one author, Article VIII, paragraph 1, of the 1959 Treaty is a 'self-executing' provision.[126] In spite of these difficulties the American courts have exercised jurisdiction in a number of cases dealing with events in the Arctic and Antarctic, which will be commented upon further below.

For other countries which do not claim sovereignty and which also have not promulgated special legislation, the only jurisdictional norm is that of Article VIII of the Treaty, subject to whatever interpretation they may make of the general scope of the Treaty in this field. It will be recalled, for example, that the Soviet Union only recognizes the application of the principle of nationality in relation to its own citizens in Antarctica.[127]

Two observations may be made on the basis of a study of national legislations. The first is that there is an evident difference between the tradition of continental law and that of 'common law'. Whereas in Argentine, Chilean or French legislation the idea of applying national legislation *in toto* to the Antarctic territory as an expression of sovereignty predominates, in the legislation of Australia, Great Britain or New Zealand there is a more functional approach which many times results in the enactment of legislation specifically designed to deal with the jurisdictional issues as required by the very special conditions of Antarctica.

The second observation arises from a study prepared by M. W. Holdgate and B. B. Roberts concerning legislation on conservation in the Antarctic.[128] These authors point out that one type of legislation applies to Antarctica merely as an extension of norms promulgated for the remainder of the national territory whereas another type, promulgated specifically for the Antarctic continent, is more restricted in scope. These authors conclude that it appears to be an almost universal policy for elaborate mainland legislation to be greatly simplified when it is applied to personnel working in Antarctica.[129] This comment may be applied *mutatis mutandis* to legislation on jurisdiction in the continent.

Jurisdictional vacuums in the Antarctic system

In spite of the fact that this legislative process has done something to overcome the jurisdictional vacuum in Antartica, this has mainly been designed to satisfy the chief concerns at national level but has not provided a solution either to the possibility of conflicts between these jurisdictions or concurrence of jurisdictions in the majority of foreseeable situations. Bush summarizes the existing situation as follows:

> If there is any consensus among consultative parties it is to the effect that a State may exercise jurisdiction over:
> (a) nationals of States exercising jurisdiction;
> (b) vessels and aircraft of the State exercising jurisdiction and
> (c) territorial jurisdiction of the State exercising jurisdiction over areas the sovereignty of which is not in dispute. This leaves undefined the extent to which any State may exercise jurisdiction over:
> (a) Nationals of:
> (i) other Consultative Parties; (ii) Contracting Parties who are not Consultative Parties; and (iii) States which are not Contracting Parties, who are not on a vessel or aircraft of a State exercising jurisdiction or who are not within an area of undisputed sovereignty;
> (b) vessels or aircraft of:
> (i) other Consultative Parties; (ii) Contracting Parties who are not Consultative Parties; and (iii) States who are not Contracting Parties, which are not subject to the territorial jurisdiction, in accordance with international law, while in an area claimed by the State exercising jurisdiction being an area of undisputed sovereignty.[130]

Although we shall have occasion in later chapters to revert to certain aspects of maritime jurisdiction and of jurisdiction over nationals of countries other than Consultative Parties, it cannot be denied that in substance the framework of Antarctic jurisdiction remains uncertain. Additional problems which must also be borne in mind are the problem of aerial jurisdiction and of private ownership in the region.

Aerial jurisdiction

As Brownlie observes, 'aircraft have not fitted very readily into the jurisdictional rules of either domestic or international law',[131] a comment which applies fully to the case of the Antarctic. Except in cases of reciprocal recognition of Antarctic claims, or of specific agreements covering air navigation over claimed Antarctic territories,[132] the problem of aerial jurisdiction is also undefined in that the territorial principle comes into conflict with that of the nationality of the aircraft. As early as 1930, one author pointed out in this connection: 'It would seem clearly preferable to make these territories common property rather than to subject them to the jurisdiction of any one nation'.[133] In a way, the concept of the Antarctic air space as a *res communis* has gained ground in practice, for the freedom of air navigation is well established and no permits of overflight are required, not even in the case of scheduled trans-Antarctic services. This freedom of overflight also applies to the high seas surrounding the continent and no exception has been made in law or fact regarding the territorial sea and other areas subject to national claims. Furthermore, aerial observation under the inspection clauses of the Treaty requires freedom of access to any point in the continent. It thus appears that the view expressed by an author in relation to the Arctic, arguing that the theory of sectors is inapplicable to aerial rights as such rights should be governed by the principle of the freedom of the high seas,[134] has had some recognition in the practice of Antarctica.

The increase in the use of the Antarctic air space will undoubtedly make it necessary to solve the jurisdictional problem, in which connection one author has studied the possible role of the International Civil Aviation Organization.[135] The idea of the 'airbus' as a common system of air transport in the Antarctic has also been proposed[136] and there have also been suggestions for joint control of Antarctic air traffic.[137] Because of the overlapping jurisdictions of the Argentine flight information region of Comodoro Rivadavia and the Chilean controlled region of Punta Arenas, both of which extend to the south pole, an early papal proposal in the mediation related to the Beagle Channel suggested 'that a system of terminal air control managed by both parties, should be established on Isla Nueva, in order to regulate air traffic to and from the Antarctic',[138] a suggestion which was not retained. The Mount Erebus air disaster[139] has also given place to important judicial proceedings in the United States which will be examined further below.

Private property in the Antarctic

The question of private property in the Antarctic is still more complex and has received very little consideration. Once various States have extended their legal system to the Antarctic continent, should it be understood that this includes provisions relating to private property? Or is the Antarctic a 'nationalized' territory? If so, on what legal authority did nationalization occur? These questions have a certain similarity with the case of maritime spaces, especially the continental shelf and the Exclusive Economic Zone where the question of private property has also arisen.[140]

In the debate in the House of Lords referred to earlier, Lord Shackleton raised the question of the situation with regard to property rights in Antarctica with special reference to what would happen in the case of individual ownership of mineral rights. He added: 'I am told that there is no possibility at the moment of owning your own property in the Antarctic' and he put forward the idea that the international organization to be established under United Nations auspices might also act as a 'Land Registry'.[141] Lord Denning, in his turn, commented: 'But what of the plane of private law, of individuals and properties? . . . who is to have jurisdiction in this territory in matters of property or of person? . . . At present there is no law at all to cover individuals or property in the Antarctic'.[142] An Argentinian author also referred to the appropriateness of applying in Antarctica the system of property embodied in the Argentine Civil Code, with particular reference to ownership of mines and buildings, concluding that 'it would seem appropriate that both civil and international law should begin to develop a regime referring to property ownership in Antarctica'.[143]

It is interesting in this regard to note that the State of Chile has opened up a register of Antarctic property in Punta Arenas, the first inscription of which established that the State is the 'owner of all land, islands, islets, reefs and other' within the limits of the claimed Antarctic area.[144] The constitution of private property over Antarctic land would require, in the light of this inscription, a concession or some form of transfer of title.

In addition to the questions that this approach to property might raise in terms of domestic law, there is also the question of how property rights of this kind might be reconciled with the Antarctic Treaty freezing of claims to sovereignty or the question of overlapping of claims.

Practical problems about property have already arisen in connection with the transfer of buildings in Antarctica[145] but the question is probably most relevant in the field of resources with reference both to their utilization and to the installations necessary for their exploitation. We shall return to this matter subsequently.

Judicial decisions on questions of jurisdiction

The case law relating to questions of jurisdiction in the Arctic or Antarctic is not abundant. However, three contemporary cases illustrate well the nature of the problems involved, not so much because of the answers given but rather because of the difficult questions raised.

The case of *US v. Escamilla* dealt with issues of criminal jurisdiction over the ice island T-3 in the Arctic,[146] where the leader of a research team was shot and killed by the defendant in this case. Most of the issues discussed in the trial and retrial of Escamilla referred to procedural questions and safeguards under the laws of the United States, on which ground the defendant was finally acquitted. However, two problems connected with this discussion had relevance for the exercise of jurisdiction by the United States. The first problem was the determination of the basis of jurisdiction: was the ice island a vessel?, or could it be assimilated to land?, or was it still a new category?[147] This determination could have triggered major discussions about the meaning of a vessel under American law or, worse, about claims to sovereignty over the floating island. While the principle of nationality might have provided a basis of jurisdiction, since the case involved only American citizens, it could also have conflicted with Canadian interests in the matter, in whose claimed sector the island was floating. The jurisdictional argument also dealt with the fact that the United States was the 'only State in a practical position to maintain order and apprehend offenders'.[148]

The second and related problem dealt with the potential concurrent jurisdiction by Canada, whose territorial relationship to the island has been the subject of discussion in that country.[149] While the United States does not claim sovereignty over the island and neither recognizes claims over it – a position similar to the one held in relation to Antarctic claims – it was evidently anxious to avoid any dispute with the Canadian Government on the matter.[150] The potential conflict was solved by a waiver of jurisdictional claims on the part of Canada, made in the following terms:

> The Canadian government continues to reserve its position on the question of jurisdiction over the alleged offence but would not object to having the drifting ice formation in question treated as a ship for the purposes of the particular legal proceedings concerned in order to facilitate the course of justice and if it is considered necessary for the purposes of the legal proceedings in

question the Canadian Government hereby waives jurisdiction.[151]

The international law implications of the case having been avoided, it then concentrated mainly on the discussion of the applicable American legislation and the procedural issues. Yet, as Auburn has concluded, this case has been inevitably regarded as unsatisfactory since the basic problem of the lack of a legal regime on jurisdiction for the Arctic or the Antarctic remains unsolved.[152] Furthermore, as that author remarks, 'a similar case on the Antarctic continent would shake the present status quo to its foundations'.[153]

In the case *Larry R. Martin v. Commissioner of Internal Revenue*, the Tax Court of the United States had to deal with a different but more straightforward question, namely, whether Antarctica qualified as a 'foreign country' in terms of the tax exemptions provided for in the Internal Revenue Code.[154] The Court relied on the American policy of not asserting claims of sovereignty in Antarctica and not recognizing claims of any other nation, while at the same time emphasizing that Article IV of the Antarctic Treaty had put in abeyance all questions of sovereignty and consequently the 'Department of State does not consider the Antarctica region to be under the sovereignty of any government'.[155] On this basis the Court concluded that Antarctica was not a 'foreign country' within the meaning of the tax regulations.

This case did not involve any question of conflict of jurisdiction for the petitioner was an American scientist who in any case would be covered by the flag-state approach followed in Antarctica in relation to stations and expeditions. However, should a similar case have come before the courts of a claimant country, most certainly the conclusions about the legal status of Antarctica and the meaning of Article IV of the 1959 Treaty would have been quite different from those of the American tribunal.

Difficult questions of interpretation have also been discussed in the case *Beattie v. United States*, in which British and New Zealand residents or citizens appointed as administrators of the estates of individuals killed in the Air New Zealand crash in Mount Erebus, Antarctica, on 28th November 1979, brought action before the US District Court for the District of Columbia alleging that negligence of US Navy personnel at McMurdo Station air traffic control facilities caused the accident.[156] Here again a basic issue was the determination whether Antarctica is or not a 'foreign country' in terms of the Federal Tort Claims Act. If it was held to be a foreign country the claims could not be cognizable under the Act for claims arising in a foreign country are exempted from its coverage; otherwise the United States courts would have jurisdiction on the matter.

The question was discussed of course in the light of that particular Act and of various other provisions of the American legislation referring to foreign countries,[157] bringing the court to the conclusion that 'Antarctica is not a foreign country; it is not a country at all; and it is not under the domination of any other foreign nation or country. . . . It is also true, on the other hand, that Antarctica is not part of the United States'.[158] The US Court of Appeals confirmed the conclusion of the lower court,[159] allowing the proceedings to move forward on the merits of the claim.

Beyond the issues appertaining to domestic law, these decisions have important implications in terms of international law. Again the American courts have had to discuss the international legal status of the Antarctic continent, following closely the position of the US Government on the matter, although occasionally reaching rather far-fetched conclusions, such as that 'to the extent that there is any assertion of governmental authority in Antarctica, it appears to be predominantly that of the United States'.[160] However, it is also interesting to note that the dissenting opinion of Judge Scalia during the appeals proceedings emphasizes the fact of the existence of sovereign claims and foreign jurisdiction in Antarctica so as to justify that Antarctica should be regarded as a foreign country for the purpose of the Federal Tort Claims Act. In this context, the meaning of Article IV of the Antarctic Treaty has also been discussed, for while for the majority of the court the signatory nations agreed 'not to exercise sovereignty in Antarctica',[161] for the dissenting judge that article 'merely provides that the treaty does not *prejudice* any nation's claim or basis for a claim to Antarctica'.[162]

More important still are the implications of the case in another respect. The District Court made the argument that since there is 'neither foreign sovereignty nor foreign law in Antarctica, the responsible parties could not be reached under the laws of any other nation', thus justifying the jurisdiction of the US Courts for determining the liability and damages.[163] Similarly, the Court of Appeals reasoned that 'among the two "forums" with the greatest interest in the outcome of this litigation – Antarctica and the United States – only one has any civil law to apply. And, in fact, Antarctica has no "forum" either; fundamentally, because Antarctica is not a "country", foreign or otherwise'.[164] But what about the potential jurisdiction of a claimant country like New Zealand, in whose claimed territory the air traffic control facilities are located and the accident took place and whose airliner was involved, killing many of its citizens? Under the New Zealand legislation examined above there is ground for the exercise of jurisdiction by this country, as there also is under the bilateral agreements with the United States,[165] particularly if the latter are regarded as applicable to Antarctica, as is the view of the dissenting appeals judge.[166]

While the existence of concurrent jurisdictions arising from different legal approaches to the status of Antarctica is perfectly natural, the reasoning of the court does in fact deny this possibility by arguing that the choice is between the American jurisdiction or nothing at all, thus entirely disregarding the role of other bases of jurisdiction in the matter. Perhaps more appropriately Judge Scalia remarked on this point: 'If "foreign country" is given its usual meaning, there will always be "civil tort law to apply" just as there will always be a district court with venue'.[167] It is possible to make the argument that the jurisdiction of the American courts can be established in this case by construing that Antarctica is not a foreign country in terms of the Federal Tort Claims Act, yet without disqualifying other views on the matter, for which purpose Article IV of the Treaty provides a very sound and effective legal foundation.

Solutions to problems of jurisdiction proposed by authors
Because neither the existing law or the decisions of courts provide clear answers to the problems of jurisdiction in Antarctica, various proposals have been made to resolve these difficulties. In the first place, an attempt was made to find a formula whereby the exercise of national jurisdiction might be organized appropriately in those cases in which the corresponding legislation either did not exist or was unclear. Thus, for example, Bilder proposed that Title 18 of the United States Code be amended to clarify the jurisdiction of that country in Antarctica.[168] In accordance with that suggestion, acts or omissions which take place in the Antarctic and which, had they occurred under 'the special maritime and territorial jurisdiction of the United States' would constitute a crime, would also be considered a crime in Antarctica and would be subject to the same penalties and procedures under that special jurisdiction.[169]

In this proposal, the situation of the Antarctic is equated with a pre-existing approach, namely that of the 'special maritime and territorial jurisdiction', which is a form of flag-state jurisdiction. The formula would be applied not only to nationals of the United States – whether civil or military – but also to foreigners who were in the Antarctic under the auspices of the United States Antarctic Research Program. However, persons privileged under Article VIII of the Antarctic Treaty would be excluded in that proposal and, in general, it was stated that the system 'shall not otherwise be applicable to any foreign national with respect to any act or omission as to which the state of which he is a national has asserted jurisdiction'.[170] This latter exception is an attempt to eliminate conflicts of jurisdiction in the case of concurrent exercise of jurisdiction, restricting to some extent the jurisdiction of the United States over foreigners who would otherwise have been included within the ambit of the proposed legislation. It is also to be noted that the formula would apply to the zone extending south of parallel 60 south, including the corresponding maritime spaces.

Another suggestion was an attempt to find an internationally uniform solution on the basis of a proposed amendment to Article VIII of the Treaty.[171] Under this formula, primacy is given to the jurisdiction of the State of nationality but if such State does not exercise jurisdiction it will then pass, on the basis of the 'passive personality principle', to the State whose national has suffered as a result of the act or omission. If none of these situations applied, jurisdiction might be exercised by any Consultative Party. Although the sequence of jurisdiction was an attempt to accommodate the various interests involved, in fact it minimized the possibilities of territorial jurisdiction.

A third model is even more elaborate as it proposes the promulgation of an Antarctic Criminal Code and the creation of a special court.[172] Under this scheme, disregarding the traditional principles relating to jurisdiction, 'the Treaty should simply declare that its tribunals shall have jurisdiction over certain enumerated crimes'.[173] By virtue of the mere fact that the crimes enumerated in the Antarctic Code were committed, the court would acquire jurisdiction, a situation which would be similar to the principle of universality applied at a regional Antarctic level.[174] Other writers also suggested the possibility of an International Criminal Court with Antarctic jurisdiction[175] or the intervention of international courts or reciprocal agreements to enable national courts to participate in the specific procedural acts.[176]

These various proposals have the merit of departing to some extent from the traditional bases of jurisdiction which rely either on territory or on nationality, introducing instead other bases such as the 'flag-state' approach, passive personality or universality. However, in most cases they would require a rather elaborate legal system to put those principles into effect, a situation which is unlikely to occur in the context of the present Antarctic legal arrangements. This is particularly difficult in the case of Codes or special tribunals. However, as it will be examined next, it is in connection with resource regimes that new criteria has begun to emerge to address the questions of jurisdiction within the Antarctic system. Some aspects of these new developments are related to the proposals conceived by writers.

3.4 Jurisdictional criteria in the light of the resources policy

The complex legal panorama that has been outlined acquires yet another dimension if it is considered from the point of view of the situation relating to resources. Both the formula in Article VIII of the Treaty and the orientation of the national laws that have been considered have their origin in a phase of Antarctic co-operation which was concerned basically with scientific research and certain other subjects which the 1959 Treaty included as priorities, such as demilitarization, inspections and others. For this reason such jurisdictional schemes are relatively simple and the fact that they have up to now given rise to no particular difficulties indicates that they have achieved their objective.

The present phase of Antarctic co-operation, closely bound up with the problem of natural resources, undoubtedly raises entirely different imperatives in the jurisdictional field.[177] For this reason, however imaginative the models for a solution which have been proposed may be, they do not generally meet this new situation but are still guided by the original outlook. To this extent their chances of success are very slender.

The starting point in the quest for appropriate responses lies in the special relationship between sovereignty and international co-operation that was indicated at the beginning of this chapter. The relativity of Antarctic sovereignty and its identification with international co-operation has determined not only the complementary nature of these two factors but also the emergence of powerful processes of integration between the national and international legal orders in relation to the continent. Within this framework, the transfer of competences between one order and another has taken place more readily and expeditiously than customarily occurs in other contexts.

One important consequence of this has been that the traditional principles on which jurisdiction is based in international law[178] are not applicable in the same way in the case of Antarctica. Thus, they cannot be conceived as antagonistic principles which may operate in a mutually exclusive way against each other. If concurrence of jurisdictions is a normal factor in international law and practice, it occurs in a still more acute manner in the case of this continent in view of the higher degree of integration that exists among national arrangements and between national arrangements and international Antarctic arrangements. Moreover, the political balance on which the 1959 Treaty is based and the system of co-operation would not, as we have indicated, permit one principle to predominate over another, even though in practice one particular principle may be used more frequently than another.

For these reasons, no formula of a general type will be able to solve the problem since such formulas inevitably tend to emphasize one principle at the expense of another as the consideration of the various models proposed has made clear. The only feasible approach is to proceed on the basis of resolving specific problems in the light of which the most effective means for safeguarding the balance of interests involved in the matter should be sought. From this point of view, as it was said earlier, the Antarctic Treaty was not misconceived since the endeavour to find a formula of a general type would have been an impossible exercise and would necessarily have resulted in serious conflicts. Thus, the frequently made criticism that the Treaty has not adequately dealt with the jurisdictional problem is unfounded since the only possibility of a solution lies in adopting the pragmatic and gradual approach which the system itself has developed.

The context for finding specific solutions has been that of natural resources arrangements and regimes. Within the framework of these arrangements there occurs the greatest degree of integration between the elements of sovereignty and international co-operation and this is conducive to solving more specifically jurisdictional problems. Furthermore, the fact that in the context of some of these arrangements institutions to administer them have been or are being set up has also introduced a new element in the quest for the corresponding jurisdictional solutions.

The jurisdictional regime of the Agreed Measures

The Agreed Measures constitute the first case of an arrangement for the administration of resources in Antarctica. As they were a first attempt in this direction, their approach to the jurisdictional problem was very cautious: the differences of opinion between the Consultative Parties with regard to the granting of permits produced serious difficulties in the negotiation as an expression of the existing problem of jurisdictions.[179] In order to avoid this difficulty, the Agreed Measures restrict themselves to prohibiting specific activities in Antarctica, other than on the basis of a permit issued by the 'appropriate authority' of the participating Governments.[180]

The system devised went no further than this so as not to prejudge the substantive positions on claims of sovereignty, or the non-recognition of such claims, concerning which the jurisdictional question was not resolved.[181] In this manner, one point of view was that permits could be issued by virtue of territorial jurisdiction in relation both to nationals and to foreigners, whereas the other point of view was that each Government remained responsible for regulating the conduct of its own nationals in

Antarctica. However, subsequent recommendations – one of which formally amended the Agreed Measures – specified that Governments would prohibit their nationals from entering the specially protected areas unless the appropriate permit had been obtained.[182] Even though it is once again not indicated who would grant the permits, the reference to a form of exercise of jurisdiction over nationals implied the adoption of a solution on the basis of the principle of nationality or eventually of flag state which has been interpreted as a measure adopted within the framework of the provision of Article IX, paragraph 1 (e), of the Treaty concerning jurisdiction.[183]

National laws enacted in compliance with the Agreed Measures have also been based on differing approaches. Some of these are based on a territorial concept. For example, Australian legislation applies 'to any persons and property, including foreign persons and property' in the territory claimed by Australia, and also to Australian citizens and property elsewhere in Antarctica.[184] The legislation of France applies to Terre Adélie without any qualification, thus presumably including foreigners but not extending to French citizens elsewhere in the continent.[185] New Zealand applies its legislation to citizens and residents in general, but in the Ross Dependency the exercise of jurisdiction over nationals of other Contracting Parties is excluded but not in relation to those of third States.[186] Under the legislation of Australia and New Zealand it is specifically indicated that it is not a crime to act in conformity with permits issued by other Contracting Parties.[187]

The British Antarctic Treaty Act 1967 applies to British citizens and subjects in general but is also extended to foreigners on a limited basis in the case of the 'master or a member of the crew of a British ship registered in the United Kingdom', in accordance with the general rules of flag-state jurisdiction over ships. This Act could potentially be extended to other categories of foreigners.[188]

The special legislation of other States shows an attachment to the principle of nationality. That of Belgium applies only to Belgian nationals but it recognizes an accusation made by a 'foreign competent authority' as a means of establishing that an infringement by a Belgian national has occurred.[189] The legislation of the United States also applies in principle to the nationals of that country but it may cover foreigners operating under permits issued by the United States and to other situations.[190] A draft bill that was considered by the United States Congress for the implementation of the Agreed Measures provided that the Act would apply to nationals of the United States and organizations incorporated in that country, but that in no event jurisdiction would be asserted 'over any foreign national if the state of nationality of the accused foreign national asserts jurisdiction prior to trial and so advises the Secretary of State'.[191] One can recognize here an effort to avoid problems of concurrent jurisdiction which partly follow the approach suggested by Professor Bilder examined further above, but this solution was not retained.

Even if, in the context of this early approach, a clear jurisdictional solution was not afforded, it will be appreciated that it was, in any case, a major step forward. Thus, a greater spirit of co-operation and restraint is apparent in the regime and in the way in which it operates and this has provided a basis for partial solutions such as the amendment adopted in 1975. The same spirit is apparent in certain national laws. But most important of all is the fact that, through its various mechanisms, the regime established a uniform international regulation which must necessarily be borne in mind for the exercise of the corresponding jurisdictions, a process which of itself avoids many conflicts which might otherwise arise in this field. The element of co-operation and restraint lessens the possible clash of national positions including their jurisdictional manifestations. It is on the basis of this uniform legal background that the practical application of the Agreed Measures has resulted in a positive achievement for the protection of fauna and flora in Antarctica, particularly through the control of potentially damaging activities. This also explains perhaps that no violations have been officially reported, although private organizations have called the attention to alleged violations, particularly in connection with the French airstrip at Pointe Géologie,[192] as some writers have been critical of activities that could amount to breaches of these arrangements in general.[193]

Jurisdiction in the conventional regimes

The regime for the conservation of the seal has a two-fold importance from the point of view of the exercise of jurisdiction. In the first place, it establishes for the first time a system of jurisdiction over the maritime spaces of Antarctica. Next, it opts for a specific formula whereby States have jurisdiction over 'their nationals or vessels under their respective flags', and this also applies to the issue of the corresponding permits.[194] This type of jurisdiction based on nationality and on the flag of registry is inherent in the regime of the high seas, thus being entirely compatible with the safeguard of high seas rights provided for in Article VI of the 1959 Treaty, without prejudicing other questions inherent in the maritime jurisdiction of the coastal State.

The Convention on the Conservation of the Antarctic Marine Living Resources signified a further advance in the establishment of the maritime jurisdiction under the Antarctic system even though the underlying differences of the various positions of States concerned prevented the adoption of specific formulas covering the jurisdiction of States parties. As one author points out, the same approach as under the Convention on Antarctic Seals presumably applies to the exercise of jurisdiction in the high seas, that is jurisdiction based on nationality and the flag of registry, even if this is not specifically indicated in the Canberra Convention and can only be inferred from certain indirect provisions and from national legislation and practice.[195] With regard to observations and inspections, the Canberra Convention follows the same approach as that of Article VIII, paragraph 1, of the 1959 Treaty, that is, the principle of nationality applies.[196]

With regard to the maritime jurisdiction determined by those territories the sovereignty over which is recognized by all the Contracting Parties, as is the case of French sovereignty over the Archipel de Kerguelen and Iles Crozet, the coastal state shall exercise his rights and duties in accordance with the general principles of international law and the law of the sea.[197] Nevertheless, as will be examined in Chapter 4, there is also a degree of international co-operation which is relevant in those areas as a consequence of the provisions and the regime of the Canberra Convention.

Maritime jurisdiction in connection with the other Antarctic territories must be seen in the context of what is known as the 'bifocal' approach, which will also be considered in the next chapter. Even though it may be assumed that a potential jurisdictional conflict may always arise under this approach, it must be borne in mind that the regime of the Canberra Convention envisages institutions for its administration and a procedure for the settlement of disputes, all of which may play a part in solving this particular conflict. As it advances, this greater degree of institutionalization inherent in some of the resources regimes facilitates the quest for jurisdictional solutions.[198]

In spite of the vacuums which still exist, it should not pass unnoticed that these regimes have resolved some of the most serious jurisdictional problems amongst the parties, in particular the problem of whether under the Antarctic Treaty system jurisdiction over the maritime spaces can be exercised. This highly complex question was answered in the affirmative by conclusion of the seal regime and that of the living resources, thereby clarifying one of the unknown factors that might have caused serious difficulties between the parties within the system. Once this fundamental step had been taken, the specific modalities for the exercise of jurisdiction by the States in this field have progressively been determined.

3.5   Models for the organization of a mineral resources regime

The fundamental conclusion that emerges from an analysis of Antarctic jurisdiction is that, owing to the multiplicity of interests involved and the diversity of political and legal positions, it is not possible to find solutions on the basis of general formulas. The carefully reasoned approach which has been followed up to now in the context of the resources regimes and other activities has made it possible to devise pragmatic choices which meet the requirements of each specific situation. In this context one may observe a positive tendency amongst the parties to put aside purely theoretical considerations arising from ideological standpoints and positions of principle.

In some recent international negotiations, such as the Third United Nations Conference on the Law of the Sea, many of the difficulties that arose on certain issues were due to the undue emphasis that was given to theoretical approaches and confrontational positions which made it impossible to seek solutions that might reasonably satisfy the various interests involved.[199] On other equally difficult points, however, the more pragmatic approach that was adopted made it possible to achieve the necessary agreements.

Just as Bowett observed in connection with jurisdiction in international law, in the case of the Antarctic the essential point is to ensure the 'balancing of interests' as the Antarctic Treaty itself did. The interests to be balanced have of course undergone changes since the Treaty was signed, particularly in the light of interest on resources, a reality which is precisely the essential point of the internal and external accommodation of interests that today characterizes the Antarctic system. To that end, the method that seems most appropriate is that of negotiation and consultation since this ensures that every solution evolves in the light of the specific circumstances of the subject or problem being dealt with. No universal formula could achieve this balanced result.

Accordingly, as was pointed out above, it is paradoxical that what has been assumed to be the greatest weakness of the Antarctic Treaty, namely the fact that it has not solved the problem of jurisdiction, has become a relevant factor of strength since it has made it possible for the system to evolve on the basis of negotiation and consultation, devising solutions appropriate to each area of interest as it arose. Rigid principles adopted *ab initio* might have produced the opposite effect by exacerbating conflicts and differences.

The case of mineral resources to some extent represents the culmination of this process because, in the framework of this new regime, it has been necessary to deal with the entire range of jurisdictional problems which characterize the Antarctic situation,[200] including aspects of territorial and maritime jurisdiction, claims of sovereignty and non-recognition of such claims and the policy specifically applicable to these resources. Given the magnitude of the problem, the subject of jurisdiction has arisen not as an isolated issue but rather in the context of the major options for organizing and administering these resources. Thus the principal debate has concentrated on the main models in terms of which this new important activity was to be organized, each one of which implies a jurisdictional solution. These models are briefly described below, for the purpose of identifying the respective jurisdictional approach, while the detailed suggestions based on them are fully discussed in Chapter 7.

The national, multilateral and universal options
The three basic options for organizing the mineral resources regime or for tackling, in a more general way, the solution of problems of jurisdiction in the continent have been defined as the 'unilateral approach', the 'limited multilateral approach' and the 'universal approach'[201] or, to use the formulation of another author, as the nationalistic, multinational or internationalization alternatives.[202]

The first of these options entails organizing the resources policy on the basis of territorial sovereignty, in regard not only to the present claimants but also to the other countries which maintain interests in Antarctica. Even though some opinions have been voiced in favour of this option,[203] the evolution of Antarctic co-operation makes it seem unlikely to prevail, although it might again come to the fore in the event of a collapse of the present system.

The limited multilateral approach, on the other hand, is a fundamental attempt to harmonize the various Antarctic interests on the basis of solutions which, while respecting individual positions, are capable of enhancing the necessary co-operation for the management of resources and the exercise of jurisdiction in this field. This model amounts to a degree of internationalization but without dissolving sovereignty or other manifestations of interest. A considerable number of formulae have recently been proposed in this category including various types of condominium, approaches similar to that of Svalbard, models of joint jurisdiction, forms of association and various schemes for partial internationalization.[204]

The option of general or universal internationalization aspires to a model of organization administered within the framework of an international organization which would have powers of decision and jurisdiction in the field of activity involved. The concept of the common heritage of mankind and the influence of the Third United Nations Conference on the Law of the Sea have been discernible in various proposals that have been put forward in that respect. The United Nations and other types of specialized body have also been considered as organizational models.

The second part of this study, dealing with the mineral resources regime, will analyse the problems associated with the unilateral option and with some of the procedures of the limited multilateral approach. The third part of the study will consider the options of general internationalization and other approaches proposed which have implications for the relationship between the Antarctic system and the international community.

Apart from the general approaches, it must also be remembered that certain proposals have attempted to devise special procedures for Antarctic jurisdiction based on the specific characteristics of the Antarctic continent. Although we shall revert to these later, it seems appropriate to draw attention at the present stage to two of these proposals which are to some extent an adequate indication of the trend of the Antarctic system: (i) *The principle of the Antarctic Community* This principle has been conceived as an intermediate option between the principle of territorial sovereignty and that of open use. It has been described as 'a significant third organizational principle for Antarctic law', which has the following characteristics:

> The principle suggests that a legal order in the Antarctic region should build upon the common interests of States active in Antarctic affairs – notably the interest in regional stability – while accommodating in so far as possible the divergent interests of such States.[205]

(ii) *The concept of Joint Antarctic Resources jurisdiction* This other approach also tends to highlight the unique nature of Antarctic co-operation, suggesting that 'the Consultative Parties declare joint exclusive resource jurisdiction over the continent and the continental shelf of Antarctica'.[206] This would be done in the context of a regime which would take into account the interests of the various countries active in Antarctica and those of the international community to the extent of the external accommodation that might take place in relation to the various matters with which the Antarctic system is concerned. In essence it would be a type of joint jurisdiction centralized within the framework of the minerals regime, or of other arrangements that may be based on a similar concept, and would be of a functional nature. However difficult the legal construction of joint jurisdiction might be, particularly should a dispute develop about its exercise among the various participating states, it is nonetheless a new and useful approach to overcome the existing legal differences in Antarctica in a more co-operative framework. As we shall see, some application of this concept has been suggested in relation to the law of the sea in Antarctica and, more importantly, in the negotiations about the minerals regime.

In this connection Brownlie has observed that, in principle, joint responsibility would flow from the 'joint occupation or administration of territory (whether of a third state, or an area the title to which is undetermined, such as Antarctica)',[207] a situation which needs to be kept in mind in the context of the responsibility for mineral activities or other undertakings in the area.

Chapter 3 Notes

1. See generally the discussion on sovereignty in Chapter 1 supra. See also Giovanni Battaglini: *La Condizione dell'Antartide nel Diritto Internazionale*, Padova, CEDAM, 1971. J. Peter A. Bernhardt: 'Sovereignty in Antarctica', *Cal. West. I.L.J.*, Vol. 5, 1975, 297–349.
2. See generally Chapter 1 supra.
3. Hans Kelsen: *Principles of International Law*, 1966, 182–184.
4. Ibid., at 184.
5. Ibid., at 185.
6. Ibid., at 186–189.
7. Hans Kelsen: *General Theory of Law and State*, 1949, at 384–385.
8. For a recent jurisprudential discussion of sovereignty in international law, see generally Bernard Gilson: *The conceptual system of sovereign equality*, 1984.
9. J. L. Brierly: *The Law of Nations*, 1963, Sixth edition, at 54–55. On the relationship between obligation and the sovereignty of States see also H. L. A. Hart: *The Concept of Law*, 1970, 215–221.
10. Philip C. Jessup: *A Modern Law of Nations*, 1949, at 36–37, 40–41.
11. Gilson, op. cit., note 8 supra, at 163–166.
12. Robert Lansing: 'A unique international problem', *A.J.I.L.*, Vol. 11, 1917, 763–771, at 764–765.
13. On the evolution of the Antarctic legal order see generally Chapter 2 supra.
14. Luzius Wildhaber: 'Sovereignty and International Law', in R. St. J. Macdonald and Douglas M. Johnston: *The Structure and Process of International Law: Essays in Legal Philosophy Doctrine and Theory*, 1983, at 443. On political aspects of sovereignty and current trends, see Alan James: 'Sovereignty: ground rule or gibberish?', *Review of International Studies*, 1984, 10, 1–18.
15. W. Schoenborn: 'La Nature juridique du Territoire', *Rec. Cours. Ac. D.I.*, Vol. 30, 1929-V, 81–189.
16. For a discussion of various theories on territorial sovereignty see Erik Suy: 'Reflexions sur la distinction entre la souverainete et la competence territoriale', *Internationale Festschrift für Alfred Verdross*, 1971, 493–508.
17. Ibid., at 493.
18. Ibid., at 496–499.

19. Philip C. Jessup and Howard J. Taubenfeld: *Controls for Outer Space and the Antarctic analogy*, 1959, 11–49. The cases of the condominium of Sudan, New Hebrides and Canton and Enderbury Islands are also discussed by these authors at 11–26.
20. Ibid., at 39–40.
21. Suy, loc. cit., note 16 supra, at 498–499.
22. Ibid., at 500–502.
23. European Communities: Regulation N° 1496/68 of the Council, 27 September 1968, H.M.S.O. 1969; Article 1 of this Regulation provides that 'The customs territory of the Community shall comprise the following territories . . .'.
24. See Article 2, par. 1, of the E.E.C. Council Regulation N° 101/76, of 19 January 1976, *Official Journal of the European Communities*, Vol. 19, No L 20, 28 January 1976, at 19–22.
25. Patrick Daillier: 'Les Communautés Européennes et le Droit de la Mer', *R.G.D.I.P.*, Vol. LXXXIII, 1979, 417–473, at 456.
26. See generally R. R. Churchill: *The common fisheries policy of the European Economic Community: a legal analysis*, Ph.D. Thesis, UWIST, 1984. See also Daniel Vignes: 'The problem of access to the European Economic Community's Fishing Zone as the cornerstone for the adoption of a common fisheries policy', in C. L. Rozakis and C. A. Stephanou (eds): *The New Law of the Sea*, 1983, 83–96. See also Chapter 4 infra.
27. Suy, loc. cit., note 16 supra, at 504. Emphasis in original text.
28. Ibid., at 506–507.
29. The policy of establishing military installations in the Antarctic responded to the idea of securing a territorial *dominium* in the area. See generally Chapter 1 supra.
30. See generally Philip C. Jessup: 'Jurisdiction', in Richard B. Lillich and John Norton Moore (eds): *Role of International law and an evolving ocean law*, U.S. Naval War College, International Law Studies, Vol. 61, 1980, 303–318.
31. Some authors tend to take this situation a step further, suggesting that territorial sovereignty has been altogether eliminated under the Treaty of 1959; Kish writes in this regard: 'The inadmissibility of territorial sovereignty constitutes the basis of the international regime of Antarctica', John Kish: *The Law of International Spaces*, 1973, at 79. But this does not appear to have a factual support nor to constitute a reasonable legal interpretation.
32. See section 3.5 of this Chapter.
33. American Law Institute: *Restatement of the Law* (Second), Foreign Relations Law of the United States, 1965, at 20.
34. Ibid., at 20–21.
35. American Law Institute: *Restatement of the Law*, Foreign Relation Law of the United States (Revised), Tentative Draft No 2, March 27, 1981, at 96.
36. Rosalyn Higgins: 'The legal bases of jurisdiction', in Cecil J. Olmstead (ed.): *Extra-territorial application of laws and responses thereto*, 1984, 3–14, at 3.
37. Ibid., at 4.
38. D. W. Bowett: 'Jurisdiction: changing patterns of authority over activities and resources', in R. St. J. Macdonald and Douglas Johnston, op. cit., note 14 supra, at 555.
39. American Law Institute, op. cit., note 33 supra, at 29–102. M. Cherif Bassiouni: 'Theories of jurisdiction and their application in extradition law and practice', *Cal. West. I.L.J.*, Vol. 4–5, 1973–1975, 1–61.
40. Bowett, loc. cit., note 38 supra, at 558–560.
41. Ibid., at 558.
42. N. Papadakis: *The international legal regime of artificial islands*, 1977, at 125, 152.

43. See for example Elizabeth K. Hook: 'Criminal jurisdiction in Antarctica', *Univ. Mia. L. Rev.*, Vol. 33, December 1978, 489–514, at 497. See also John Kish: *The Law of international spaces*, 1973, 116–127.
44. Bowett, loc. cit., note 38 supra, at 558–559.
45. Ibid., at 559–560.
46. Ibid., at 560–561. See also Ian Brownlie: *Principles of Public International Law*, 1979, 406–420, with particular reference to the principle of effective link in international law.
47. International Court of Justice: *Nottebohm Case*, Liechtenstein v. Guatemala, Second phase, Judgment of 6 April 1955, Reports of Judgments, Advisory opinions and orders, 1955, particularly at 22–23, 24–26. Italian–United States Conciliation Commission: *Flegenheimer claim*, September 20, 1958, *International Law Reports*, Vol. 25, 1958 I, 91–167.
48. In *Joyce v. Director of Public Prosecutions*, House of Lords, 1946, *The Law Reports*, 1946, 347–382, an alien holding British passport was held guilty of treason for service to the enemy during the war. In *Kawakita v. United States*, United States Supreme Court, 1952, 343 US 717, 96 L ed. 1249, an American citizen who at the same time was a citizen of Japan was held guilty of treason for maltreatment of American prisoners of war.
49. *United States v. Aluminum Co. of America et al.* (Alcoa), 148 F. 2d. 416, 1945. For comments on this case, the *Watchmakers* case and other precedents, see Brownlie, op. cit., note 46 supra, at 306–308. See also *British Airways Board v. Laker Airways Ltd. and others*, 1983 3 ALL ER 375; and *Laker Airways v. Sabena, KLM*, 731 F. 2d. 909 (1984). For comments on these cases and other material see Rosalyn Higgins, loc. cit., note 36 supra; A. V. Lowe: 'Blocking extraterritorial jurisdiction: the British protection of trading interests act, 1980', *A.J.I.L.*, Vol. 75, 1981, 257–282; R. W. Bentham: 'The oil industry and problems of extraterritoriality', in R. W. Bentham (ed.): *Recent developments in United Kingdom Petroleum Law*, University of Dundee, Centre for Petroleum and Mineral Law Studies, 1984, 50–71; Edmund Dell: 'Interdependence and the judges: civil aviation and antitrust', *Int. Af.*, Vol. 61, 1985, 355–373, see also generally A. V. Lowe: *Extraterritorial jurisdiction*, 1983, and Bowett, loc. cit., note 38 supra, at 561.
50. Bowett, loc. cit., note 38 supra, at 562.
51. Permanent Court of International Justice: *The case of the S.S. 'Lotus'*, Collection of Judgments, Series A, No 10, 1927. For comments see Brownlie, op. cit., note 46 supra, at 301–302, and Higgins, loc. cit., note 36 supra, at 12–14.
52. Eric W. Johnson: 'Quick, before it melts: Toward a resolution of the jurisdictional morass in Antarctica', *Corn. I.L.J.*, Vol. 10, 1976, at 192.
53. Richard B. Bilder: 'Control of Criminal Conduct in Antarctica', *Virg. L.R.*, Vol. LII, 1966, at 274.
54. O. Kahn Freund: 'Delictual liability and the conflict of laws', *Rec. Cours Ac. D.I.*, Vol. 124, 1968-II, 1–166, at 83–84.
55. See generally Bassiounni, loc. cit., note 39 supra.
56. Kish, op. cit., note 43 supra, at 117, 122.
57. Harvard Research in International Law: 'jurisdiction with respect to crime', *Supplement to the A.J.I.L.*, Vol. 29, 1935, 435–651, at 472.
58. Bowett, loc. cit., note 38 supra, at 565.
59. Ibid., at 568–571.
60. *Laker Airways v. Sabena*, decision cit., note 49 supra, at 948.
61. *Mannington Mills Inc. v. Congoleum Corporation*, 595 F. 2d. 1287 (1979) particularly at 1297–1298. See also Bowett, loc. cit., note 38 supra, at 569–570.

62. *Timberlane Lumber Co. v. Bank of America*, 549 F. 2d. 597 (1976), particularly at 614–615.
63. See generally the discussion of precedents in *Laker Airways v. Sabena*, decision cit., note 49 supra, at 945–955, and the comments by Lionel Kestenbaum: 'Antitrust's "extraterritorial" Jurisdiction: a progress report on the balancing of interest test', *Stan, J.I.L.*, Vol. 18, 1982, 311–346, and generally Lowe, op. cit., note 49 supra, particularly the material reproduced as No 15, 20 and 38.
64. Karl M. Meessen: 'Antitrust jurisdiction under customary international law', *A.J.I.L.*, Vol. 78, 1984, 783–810.
65. See also United States Department of Justice: *Guidelines for International Operations*, 1977, as commented and discussed in: Panel on International Restrictive Business Practices? *Proc. A.S.I.L.*, 1977, at 213–224.
66. Bowett, loc. cit., note 38 supra, at 571–572.
67. United Kingdom: Protection of Trading Interests Act, 1980, Public General Acts and Measures of 1980, Part I, Chapter 11, 243–249. See also the article by Lowe, loc. cit., note 49 supra.
68. Bowett, loc. cit., note 38 supra, at 573.
69. Harold G. Maier: 'Interest Balancing and Extraterritorial Jurisdiction', *American Journal of Comparative Law*, Vol. 31, 1983, 579–597.
70. International Court of Justice: *North Sea Continental Shelf Cases*, Judgment of 20 February 1969, Report of Judgements, Advisory opinions and orders, 1969, particularly at 47–48.
71. Permanent Court of International Justice: Advisory opinion on *Railway traffic between Lithuania and Poland*, Series A/B, No 42, 1931, at 116.
72. Compare for example the structure of the work by Ian Brownlie, *Principles of Public International Law*, third edition, 1979, with that by Charles Rousseau, *Droit International Public*, 5 Vol., 1971–1983.
73. Higgins, loc. cit., note 36 supra, at 14.
74. Statement by Great Britain in relation to Article VIII of the Treaty at the Plenary Committee of the Conference on Antarctica, 30 November 1959; see Chile, Ministerio de Relaciones Exteriores: *Memoria 1959*, 698–704, translation by Bush: *Antarctica and International Law*, 1982, 38–43.
75. Statement by Japan in relation to Article VIII, sources cit., note 74 supra.
76. Statement by South Africa in relation to Article VIII, sources cit., note 74 supra.
77. Statement by USSR in relation to Article VIII, sources cit., note 74 supra.
78. Statement by Belgium in relation to Article VIII, sources cit., note 74 supra.
79. Statement by Norway in relation to Article VIII, sources cit., note 74 supra.
80. Statement by France in relation to Article VIII, sources cit., note 74 supra. The author of this book has changed the translation given by Bush so that it will correspond more exactly with the Spanish original version.
81. Statements by Chile and Argentina in relation to Article VIII, sources cit., note 74 supra.
82. Statement by Great Britain cit., note 74 supra.
83. F. M. Auburn: *Antarctic Law and Politics*, 1982, at 198–199.
84. Bush, op. cit., note 74 supra, at 75–76. Auburn, op. cit., note 83 supra, at 198.
85. Bush, op. cit., note 74 supra, at 76.
86. Vienna Convention on Consular Relations, 1963, Article 43, 596 United Nations Treaty Series, 261.
87. See generally Kish, op. cit., note 43 supra, particularly at 116–127.
88. See, for example, Hook, loc. cit., note 43 supra, at 491–495.
89. Bowett, loc. cit., note 38 supra, at 572–574.
90. Statement by Great Britain cit., note 74 supra.
91. Christopher Beeby: *The Antarctic Treaty*, New Zealand Institute of International

Affairs, 1972, at 17–19; the other two factors mentioned by Beeby as potential threats to the continuity of the Antarctic Treaty were the entry into Antarctica on a large scale of a non party to the Treaty which refused to become a party or to abide by the Treaty rules, and the exploitation of economic resources.

92. House of Lords, *Official Report*, Parliamentary Debates (Hansard), Vol. 221, No 40, Thursday, 18 February 1960, cols. 158–191; statement by Lord Shackleton at col. 158.

93. Ibid., col. 166.

94. Ibid., at col. 166.

95. House of Lords, Official Report cit., note 92 supra; statement by Lord Denning, col. 178.

96. Ibid., at col. 180.

97. Statement by Lord Shackleton cit., note 92 supra, at cols. 167–168.

98. Statement by Lord Denning cit., note 95 supra, at col. 181.

99. House of Lords, Official Report, cit., note 92 supra; statement by Lord McNair at cols. 181–183.

100. House of Lords, Official Report cit., note 92 supra; statement by the Marquess of Lansdowne, at cols. 189–190.

101. Auburn, op. cit., note 83 supra, at 184. For an account of the work of Consultative Parties during this period, see generally Jeffrey D. Myhre: *The Antarctic Treaty System: Politics, Law, and Diplomacy*, 1986.

102. House of Commons: *Official Report*, Parliamentary Debates (Hansard), Vol. 737, No 109, Friday, 2 December 1966, cols. 892–899. House of Commons: *Official Report*, Parliamentary Debates, Standing Committee C, Wednesday, 22 March 1967, cols. 3–34. House of Commons: *Official Report*, Parliamentary Debates (Hansard), Vol. 744, No 179, Friday, 14 April 1967, cols. 1589–1594. House of Lords: *Official Report*, Parliamentary Debates (Hansard), Vol. 282, No 144, Monday, 1 May 1967, cols. 738–766. House of Lords: *Official Report*, Parliamentary Debates (Hansard), Vol. 285, No 184, Monday, 24 July 1967, cols. 622–626.

103. House of Lords, Official Report of 1 May 1967 cit., note 102 supra; statement by Lord Wilberforce, at col. 752.

104. House of Commons, Official Report of 22 March 1967 cit., note 102 supra; statement by Mr. Griffiths, at col. 12.

105. United States Senate, Committee on Foreign Relations: *Hearings on the Antarctic Treaty*, 1960, statement by Mr. Herman Phleger, at 61–62; reproduced in Bush, op. cit., note 74 supra, at 112–114.

106. Ibid., at 113.

107. Alberto M. Candioti: *El Tratado Antártico y el Derecho Público Argentino*, Buenos Aires, 1961, at 49.

108. See generally Gillian Triggs: 'The Antarctic Treaty system: some jurisdictional problems', in ibid. (ed.): *The Antarctic Treaty regime*, 1987, 88–109.

109. Argentina, Decree-law No 2191, 28 February 1957, cited in Bush, op. cit., note 74 supra, at 76.

110. France, Law No 71-569, 15 July 1971, reproduced in Bush, op. cit., note 74 supra, Vol. II, at 574–575.

111. Chile, Decree No 298, 17 July 1956, reproduced in Bush, op. cit., note 74 supra, Vol. II, at 407–410.

112. Norway's legislation is summarized in Bush, op. cit., note 74 supra, at 77.

113. Ibid.

114. Australian Antarctic Territory Act 1954 and Antarctic Treaty Act 1960, both reproduced in Bush, op. cit., note 74 supra, Vol. II, at 178–181, 192–193 respectively.

115. The following United Kingdom legislation is relevant to the exercise of jurisdiction in Antarctica: The British Antarctic Territory Order in Council, 1962 (South Atlantic Terrirories), SI 1962, No 400; The Antarctic Treaty Order in Council, 1962 (South Antarctic Territories) SI 1962, No 401; Instructions to our High Commissioner for the British Antarctic Territory, The Queen in Council, 26 February 1962.

116. United Kingdom Antarctic Treaty Order in Council, 1962, cit., note 115 supra, s. 4 (4).

117. New Zealand Antarctica Act, 1960.

118. New Zealand–United States: Agreement with memorandum of understandings concerning U.S. operations in Antarctica, signed at Wellington on December 24, 1958, *United States Treaties and other international agreements*, Vol. 9, 1958, 1502–1509; extended indefinitely by Agreement of October 18, 1960, *United States Treaties* cit., Vol. 11, 1960, Part 2, 2205–2207.

119. Ibid., pars. 2, 3.

120. Ibid, par. 4 (a).

121. On various types of agreements on the status of forces, see generally Marjorie M. Whiteman: *Digest of International Law*, Vol. 6, 379–427.

122. South Africa, South African citizens in Antarctica Act, 1962.

123. Statement by Mr Herman Phleger cit., note 105 supra, at 113.

124. See generally Bilder, loc. cit., note 53 supra, particularly at 244–259.

125. United States House of Representatives, H.R. 6148 and H.R. 7842. See *Extraterritorial Criminal Jurisdiction, 1977*, Hearing on H.R. 763, H.R. 6148 and H.R. 7842 before the subcommittee on Immigration, Citizenship and International Law, House Committee of the Judiciary, 95th Congress, 1st Session, 1977.

126. Bilder, loc. cit., note 53 supra, at 258.

127. See note 77 supra and associated text.

128. M. W. Holdgate and B. B. Roberts: *Wild life conservation laws relating to the Antarctic and subantarctic*, SCAR, July 1961, Mimeo.

129. Ibid., at 2.

130. Bush, op. cit., note 74 supra, at 78.

131. Brownlie, op. cit., note 46 supra, at 319.

132. For a comment on air agreements in Antarctica between the United Kingdom and France, and between Australia and New Zealand, see E. H. Wall: 'The polar regions and international law', *The International Law Quarterly*, Editorial Notes, Vol. 1, 1947, 54–58, at 58.

133. Clyde Eagleton: 'International Law and Aerial discovery at the South Pole', *Air Law Review*, Vol. I, No 1, January 1930, at 127.

134. John C. Cooper: 'Airspace rights over the Arctic', *Air Affairs*, Vol. 3, No 3, 1950, 516–540.

135. Stephen J. Lovergan: *The legal status of the Antarctic airspace*, Institute of Air and Space Law, McGill University, Theses, January 1972.

136. Philip M. Smith and John B. Dana: 'Airbus: an international air transportation system for Antarctica', *Ant. J.U.S.*, Vol. VIII, 1973, 16–19.

137. Javier Lopetegui: 'Infraestructura antártica y política de acceso al continente', in Francisco Orrego et al. (eds): *Política Antártica de Chile*, 1985, at 175.

138. Proposal of the mediator dated December 12, 1980, paragraph 4 B) b), *I.L.M.*, Vol. XXIV, 1985, 7–10, at 9.

139. See Speech by the Hon. Peter Mahon: 'The Antarctica air disaster – the role of the black box', *Law Institute Journal*, Vol. 56, No 12, December 1982, 1069–1071. See also Recommendation XI-3 on 'Air Disaster on Mount Erebus', *Handbook 1983*, at 1211.

140. The legislation implementing the 200 mile maritime zone in Chile gave rise to the question whether the fisheries resources had been nationalized – in the sense of having become state owned – or the provisions of the Civil Code on private property rights applied; see Alfonso Filippi: 'El régimen aplicable a los recursos pesqueros en la Zona Económica Exclusiva', in Francisco Orrego Vicuña and Jeannette Irigoin (eds): *La aplicación de la Zona Económica Exlusiva y el regimen de la pesca*, 1982, 115–137.

141. Statement cit., note 92 supra, particularly at col. 168.

142. Statement cit., note 95 supra, cols. 179–180.

143. Domingo Sabaté Lichtschein: *La cuestión de la soberanía estatal y del dominio privado en la antártida*, Santa Fé, 1960, at 29.

144. Register of Antarctic Property, Punta Arenas, inscription No 1, page 1, 9 March 1961. This inscription was practised before the Antarctic Treaty came into force. Law No 17.170, dated 8 August 1969, established a regime in bond for the supply of Antarctic stations and other operations; *Official Journal*, 20 August 1969. See also Decree No 1731, dated 31 July 1970, which enacts the regulations for the operation of the in bond regime; *Official Journal*, 7 September 1970. Law No 18.392, dated 10 January 1985, authorized a preferential customs and tax regime for the area extending between the Strait of Magellan and the South Pole, covering corporations in the business of industry, mining, exploitation of the resources of the sea, transport and tourism, with the exception of the oil industry; *Official Journal*, 14 January 1985. See also Resolution No 1057 of 25 April 1985, regulating some aspects of this preferential regime; *Official Journal*, 30 April 1985.

145. Henry M. Dater: 'Organizational developments in the United States Antarctic Program, 1954–1965', *Ant. J.U.S.*, Vol. I, No. 1, January-February 1966, 21–32, especially at 27. A transfer of an Antarctic station on Adelaide Island took place between the United Kingdom and Chile by exchange of notes effective 5 October 1984.

146. See generally: Ben Partridge: 'The White Shelf: a study of Arctic ice jurisdiction', *U.S. Nav. Inst. Proc.*, Vol. 87, No 9, September 1961, 51–57. Donat Pharand: 'State jurisdiction over Ice Island T-3: the Escamilla case', *Arctic*, Vol. 24, 1971, 83–89. Edward M. Silverstein: 'United States Jurisdiction: crimes committed on Ice Islands', Note, *Bos. U.L.R.*, Vol. 51, 1971, 77–89. David A. Cruickshank: 'Arctic Ice and International Law: The Escamilla case', *West. Ont. L.R.*, Vol. 10, 1971, 178–194. Daniel Wilkes: 'Laws for special environments: ice islands and questions raised by the T-3 case', *Pol. Rec.*, Vol. 16, No 100, 1972, 23–27. Lloyd W. Aubry Jr: 'Criminal jurisdiction over Arctic ice islands: United States v. Escamilla', *U.C.L.A. Alas. L.R.*, Vol. 4, 1974–1975, 419–440. F. M. Auburn: 'Problems in Polar Criminal Law', *Antarctic*, Vol. 7, No 1, March 1974, 27–29.

147. On the jurisdictional arguments of the case, see F. M. Auburn: 'International Law and sea-ice jurisdiction in the Arctic Ocean', *I.C.L.Q.*, Vol. 22, 1973, 552–557.

148. Ibid., at 557.

149. Cruickshank, loc. cit., note 146 supra, at 184–185; and Auburn, loc. cit., note 147 supra, at 553.

150. Auburn, loc. cit., note 147 supra, at 557.

151. Note from the Canadian embassy in Washington to the Department of State, dated 5 May 1971, as transcribed by Auburn, loc. cit., note 147 supra, at 555. For other aspects of the case see also Daniel Wilkes: 'Law for special environments: jurisdiction over polar activities', *Pol. Rec.*, Vol. 16, No 104, 1973, 701–705.

152. Auburn, loc. cit., note 147 supra, at 557.

153. Ibid., at 557.

154. United States Tax Court, *Reports*, Vol. 50, 1968, 59–62. See also *A.J.I.L.*, Vol. 63, 1969, 141–142.
155. Tax Court Reports cit., note 154 supra, at 61.
156. Martin John Beattie *et al.* v. United States of America, U.S. District Court, District of Columbia, June 25, 1984, 592 F. Supp. 780 (1984).
157. See particularly the Tariff Act of 1930, 19 U.S. Code, Sec. 1336 (h) (3), and Sec. 1338 (i); Interstate Transportation of Wagering Paraphernalia Act, 18 U.S. Code, Sec. 1953 (d); and State Conducted Lotteries Act, 18 U.S. Code, Sec. 1307 (c). In all these laws 'the term "foreign country" means any empire, country, dominion, colony, or protectorate, or any subdivision or subdivisions thereof (other than the United States and its possessions)'. In the Foreign Bank Participation in Domestic Market Act, 12 U.S. Code, Sec. 3101 (8) "foreign country" means any country other than the United States, and includes any colony, dependency, or possession of any such country'.
158. *Beattie v. United States* cit., note 156 supra, at 781, 782.
159. U.S. Court of Appeals for the District of Columbia, 31 December 1984, 756 F. 2d. 91 (1984).
160. Case cit., note 156 supra, at 783.
161. Case cit., note 159 supra, at 93.
162. Ibid., dissenting opinion of Judge Scalia, at 106; emphasis in original.
163. Case cit., note 156 supra, at 784, footnote 23 of this case.
164. Case cit., note 159 supra, at 105.
165. See notes 117 and 118 supra and associated text.
166. Case cit., note 159 supra, dissenting opinion of Judge Scalia, at 107.
167. Ibid., at 111.
168. Bilder, loc. cit., note 53 supra, at 282–285. See also note 125 above for bills based on this proposal.
169. Ibid., at 284–285.
170. Ibid., at 285.
171. Johnson, loc. cit., note 52 supra, at 194–198.
172. Hook, loc. cit., note 43 supra, at 503–514. For the various proposals on international criminal courts, see generally Benjamin Ferencz: *An international criminal court. A step towards world peace*, 1980.
173. Hook, loc. cit., note 43 supra, at 507.
174. For a proposal based on a type of universality principle under which the jurisdiction would be based not on an offence against the interest of a particular nation but on one against the interests of the international community, see Clare Coslett: 'United States criminal jurisdiction in Antarctica: how old is the ice?', *Brook. J.I.L.*, Vol. 9, 1983, 67–89, particularly at 88–89.
175. F. J. Klein and D. Wilkes: 'United Nations draft statute for an international criminal court: an American evaluation', in G. Mueller: *International criminal law*, 1965, at 526–587.
176. Wilkes, loc. cit., note 151 supra, at 702.
177. Finn Sollie: 'Jurisdictional problems in relation to Antarctic mineral resource in political perspective', in Francisco Orrego Vicuña (ed.): *Antarctic Resources Policy*, 1983, 317–335.
178. For a discussion of the traditional principles of international law on jurisdiction and the opinion of writers thereon, see George G. Wilson: 'Jurisdiction and polar areas', in: *International law situations with solutions and notes*, US Government Printing Office, 1939, 69–131.
179. Auburn, op. cit., note 83 supra, at 271–272.
180. Agreed Measures, Arts II, VI. For references to the legislation on implementation of the Agreed Measures, see Bush, loc. cit., note 74 supra, at 148–151.

181. Bush, op. cit., note 74 supra, at 160–161.
182. Recommendation VIII-5, *Handbook 1983*, at 2104. For references to the legislation on implementation of the Specially Protected Areas, see Bush, op. cit., note 74 supra, at 152–153.
183. Bush, op. cit., note 74 supra, at 317.
184. Australia, The Antarctic Treaty (Environment Protection) Act 1980, reproduced in Bush, op. cit., note 74 supra, Vol. II, 212–225.
185. France, Arrete No 17, 7 September 1966, reproduced in Bush, op. cit., note 74 supra, Vol. II, 555–558.
186. New Zealand Antarctica Amendment Act 1970, Sec. 2 (4). See also Antarctica (Fauna and Flora) Regulations 1971, in Bush, op. cit., note 74 supra, at 161–162.
187. Australia, Act cit., note 184 supra, s. 19 3 c); New Zealand, Regulation cit, note 186 supra, reg. 11 2 b).
188. Great Britain, Antarctic Treaty Act 1967, Sec. 1 (3).
189. Belgium, Loi relative a la protection de la fauna et de la flore dans l'Antarctique, 12 January 1978, reproduced in Bush, op. cit., note 74 supra, Vol. II, 268–271.
190. United States, Antarctic Conservation Act of 1978, I.L.M., Vol. XVIII, 1979, at 131–136.
191. H.R. 7749, June 13, 1977, Sec. 13, reproduced in U.S. House of Representatives, Committee on Merchant Marine and Fisheries, Subcommittee on Fisheries and Wildlife Conservation and the Environment: *Antarctic Fauna and Flora Conservation*, Hearing on H.R. 7749, 95th Congress, 1st session, 1977, 1978, 245–369, at 262.
192. Antarctic and Southern Ocean Coalition: *Background paper on the French airfield at Pointe Geologie, Antarctica*, March 1, 1985; ECO: 'The French blow it!', Vol. XXVI, No 2, Washington D.C., January 18–27, 1984; Jacky Bonnemains: 'Antarctique: les avions denicheurs', *La Sirena*, Regional seas programme of UNEP, No 26, December 1984, 21–26.
193. See, for example, Auburn, op. cit., note 83 supra, 270–277, particularly at 277.
194. Convention on the Conservation of Antarctic Seals, Art. 2.
195. Bush, op. cit., note 74 supra, at 428.
196. Convention on the Conservation of Antarctic Marine Living Resources, Art. XXIV 2(c). The questions concerning inspection will be examined in Chapter 5 infra.
197. See Statement of the Chairman of the Conference on the Conservation of Antarctic Marine Living Resources, reproduced in Bush, op. cit., note 74 supra, at 391–392.
198. The role of institutions in the exercise of jurisdiction in Antarctica will be examined in Chapter 8 infra.
199. This was particularly the case of the seabed regime; see generally Francisco Orrego Vicuña: 'Le regime de l'exploration et de l'exploitation de la zone internationale des fonds marins', in René-Jean Dupuy et Daniel Vignes (eds): *Traité du Nouveau Droit de la Mer*, 1985, 551–601.
200. See generally Rainer Lagoni: 'Antarctica's Mineral Resources in International Law', *Z.A.O.R.V.*, Vol. 39, 1979, 1–37.
201. Jonathan I. Charney: 'Development of Antarctica', Remarks, *Proc. A.S.I.L.*, 1979, at 268–271, including remarks of the other participants in panel.
202. Rudy J. Cerone: 'Survival of the Antarctic Treaty: Economic Self interest v. Enlightened International Cooperation', *Bost. Coll. I.C.L.R.*, Vol. 2, 1978–1979, at 115–129.
203. Roland Rich: 'A minerals regime for Antarctica', *I.C.L.Q.*, Vol. 31, 1982, 709–725, particularly at 718–719.
204. See generally William E. Westermeyer: *The Politics of Mineral Resource*

Development in Antarctica, Alternative regimes for the future, 1984, particularly Chapter 3. See also generally Chapter 7 infra.

205. Steven J. Burton: 'New stresses on the Antarctic Treaty: toward international legal institutions governing Antarctic resources', *Virg. L.R.*, Vol. 65, 1979, 421–512, at 474.

206. Frank C. Alexander, Jr: 'A recommended approach to the Antarctic Resource Problem', *Univ. Mia. L. Rev.*, Vol. 33, 1978, 371–423, at 417.

207. Ian Brownlie: *System of the Law of Nations, State Responsibility*, Part I, 1983, at 192.

4

The Law of the Sea in the Antarctic Treaty system: its evolution in the light of the resources regimes

4.1　The maritime extension of the Antarctic Treaty system

The national positions that have been explained have a determining influence on the approach of each country or group of countries to the problems related to the application of the law of the sea in Antarctica. The central question that has arisen in this regard is whether the subjection of maritime zones to national jurisdiction is a concept that can be made applicable to the situation of the Antarctic.[1] Given the close links between the concepts of the territorial sea, the exclusive economic zone and the continental shelf and the territory of a coastal State from which these concepts derive,[2] the territorial status of the continent is the starting point for developing a reply to this question.

The complexity of the problem is due not only to the different positions that have been adopted by the Treaty parties with regard to this territorial status but also to the fact that a process of rapid development in the international law of the sea itself was initiated simultaneously with the development of the Antarctic system.[3] It may reasonably be stated that, at the time when the Antarctic Treaty was signed, the continental shelf doctrine was already established in customary international law[4] in addition to the jurisdictional concepts governing traditional maritime areas such as the territorial sea and the high seas. Simultaneously there began to emerge the concept of a further maritime zone for the exploitation of resources under the jurisdiction of the coastal State which was later to become what is today known as the Exclusive Economic Zone.[5] The regime relating to the sea-bed beyond the limits of national jurisdiction was to take shape later like many other aspects of the law of the sea which have been reformulated or developed through the negotiations at the Third United Nations Conference on the Law of the Sea and in other specialized forums.[6]

Another factor adding to the complexity of the matter stems from the fact that the Consultative Parties to the Antarctic Treaty do not adopt a uniform attitude with regard to the law of the sea in general and this makes it harder to achieve agreement on its application to the Antarctic continent and its offshore maritime areas.

In any case, it was inevitable that the subject of the law of the sea would be considered within the framework of the Antarctic system. This was due in part to the importance of the Antarctic marine ecosystem which dominates all known forms of life south of latitude 60 degrees south.[7] But it was also partly due to the fact that the principal resources of Antarctica are to be found in the marine environment. The exploitation of living resources and the entire set of problems associated with their conservation are among the most topical issues as far as current resource questions are concerned.[8] A similar issue is that of mineral resources since the greatest potential for the exploitation of oil is on the Antarctic continental shelf.[9] For this reason, while interest in resources came to dominate Antarctic co-operation, the law of the sea also began to play a more active role. It is in the context of the various resources regimes that the required solutions on these issues have been achieved between the participating countries.

Positions of principle and new legal approaches

As a consequence of the different positions of the Treaty parties concerning the territorial status of Antarctica, the first approaches that were made to the law of the sea were also based on positions of principle. In the view of countries that claim sovereignty, each Antarctic territory generates its corresponding maritime zones by virtue of the principle of appurtenance.[10] Under the theory of inter-temporal law, as developed by Judge Huber in the *Island of Palmas* case,[11] these maritime zones should be those created by international law in the course of its evolution in time; it thus follows that not only those zones existing at the time of the preparation of the Treaty would be included in the principle of appurtenance, but those which came into existence at a later moment, such as the Exclusive Economic Zone, would be included in that principle as well. Some particular aspects of the doctrine of inter-temporal law as applied to Antarctica will be considered further below. The policy of the mutual recognition of territorial claims by countries making similar claims implies the recognition of their maritime jurisdictions, irrespective of whether or not this is specifically stated. The fact that some overlap will give rise to superimposed maritime jurisdictions but, in the view of claimants, this does not affect their validity in international law.

For the countries that do not recognize claims of sovereignty, the situation is entirely different. The non-existence of national territory in Antarctica means that for them the concept of maritime zones linked to national territorial jurisdiction is inapplicable to the Antarctic continent.[12] It follows that the continent is surrounded only by the high seas. Referring to the position of the United States as representative of this point of view, one author writes: 'The United States further argues that, owing to the absence of a recognized coastal sovereign (which is a legal prerequisite for an espoused territorial sea), the high seas extend up to Antarctica's coastline'.[13] However, as will be explained further below, the position of the United States does not seem to be as simple as is suggested by this author who, moreover, erroneously maintained that 'traditionally both claimants and non-claimants alike have regarded Antarctica's circumjacent waters legally to be the status of high seas'.[14]

These positions of principle gradually began to be revised in connection with the imperatives of the need for a resources policy. If the first standpoint had been strictly adopted, this might have impeded the development of co-operation in the management of these resources, to say nothing of the difficulties created by superimposed sovereignties and the fact that this approach also provides no adequate solution to the peculiar situation of the unclaimed sector of Antarctica.[15] Similarly, if the second standpoint had been rigorously adopted, this might have led to a situation in which the characteristic freedom of the high seas might have impeded efforts to devise rational management regimes, thus jeopardizing the stability of the Antarctic ecosystem.[16] Such a situation would, moreover, have made it impossible to control any activity in which third States might have engaged.[17]

This situation gave rise to an entirely different approach which Alfred van der Essen has termed 'the global jurisdiction of the Consultative Parties' over the maritime areas of Antarctica.[18] This form of joint jurisdiction seems to be in harmony with the balance of the Treaty and does not prejudice the question of territorial status while at the same time it also provides the basis for a satisfactory way of dealing with the unclaimed sector. Above all, this approach has made it possible to harmonize the various national positions of Consultative Parties on the basis of a common policy with regard to living and mineral resources which has been developed through the respective regimes. While this subject will be examined at a later point, it should be kept in mind at this stage that this point is vital for the correct interpretation of the evolution that has taken place in regard to the application of the law of the sea within the Antarctic system and to an appreciation of the purport of Articles IV and VI of the 1959 Treaty.

Article IV and the question of the new maritime zones

As Van der Essen points out in his contributions to the study of the law of the sea in Antarctica, the 1959 Treaty was concerned indirectly with the law of the sea in Article IV and more directly in Article VI.[19] In the case of the former, the decision on a freeze of claims of sovereignty and the provision that the Treaty did not prejudge such claims and other positions meant that, indirectly, the provision extended similarly to maritime claims that might have arisen from such territorial sovereignty. In this way, even though such maritime claims remain unaffected by the Treaty regime or by subsequent action, from this point of view, this Article cannot be regarded as prejudicing the other positions indicated. Van der Essen writes in this connection:

> A strict application in Antarctica of the principle by which a land jurisdiction is necessary in order to have jurisdiction over an area of the sea would reinforce only the position of the signatories which have claimed sovereignty.[20]

For this reason, he[21] and other authors[22] agree that the application of Article IV alone does not provide an adequate response to the problem of maritime jurisdiction, even though the various positions on the matter are duly safeguarded.

The interpretation of Article IV has given rise to other interesting questions one of which relates to the problem of whether specific maritime claims constitute in the language of the Article a 'new claim or enlargement of an existing claim', which is expressly prohibited by paragraph 2 of that Article. The other related issue concerns the application of the rules of inter-temporal law in this context.

A recent study of the matter by Lagoni has suggested that both the territorial sea and the continental shelf should be considered as maritime zones appended to Antarctic territory and that this is not in fact an extension of the claims existing at the date of entry into force of the Treaty.[23] The rationale for this is the fact that, even if the territorial sea were not formally claimed, it must be assumed to be appurtenant to the respective territorial claim.[24] The doctrine of the continental shelf is similarly regarded as an institution incorporated in general international law at that date which similarly requires no specific proclamation for its addition to Antarctic territory.[25]

Although this approach is confirmed by the principles of international law, the conclusions arrived at by that study in other respects appear questionable. In the first place, a question arises as to the breadth of the territorial sea, since by virtue of the inter-temporal law doctrine, any claim relating to the territorial sea must arguably have been valid at the time when it was asserted, which means that it could not exceed the maximum breadth recognized by international law at the date of entry into force of the 1959 Treaty. Given the then prevailing uncertainty as to what was the recognized breadth of the territorial sea, Lagoni concluded that 'any such claim exceeding 12 miles would be invalid'[26] which is undoubtedly a correct appreciation of the situation.

However, a further conclusion is added that if the territorial sea is extended from three to twelve miles, thereby reaching the maximum breadth accepted by the 1982 Convention on the Law of the Sea, this would be a prohibited enlargement under the provisions of Article IV, paragraph 2, of the Treaty. Similarly, it is argued that the proclamation of an Exclusive Economic Zone or exclusive fishing zone of the 200 miles would constitute an enlargement prohibited by the Treaty because these two concepts have only been recently recognized.[27]

However, the dimension given to the doctrine of inter-temporal law by arbiter Huber in the *Island of Palmas* case, suggests a different conclusion.[28] Following the same line of reasoning of that case, the national claims to a territorial sea related to the Antarctic territories must undoubtedly have fulfilled the conditions prevailing in international law at the time when they were proclaimed or established, but their specific breadth must be judged in the light of the evolution of the law of the sea, and Article IV, paragraph 2, cannot be interpreted as an exception which invalidates this rule. For this reason, extension of the territorial sea to 12 miles must not be regarded as being contrary to this Article if such an extension were to occur, particularly in circumstances in which, according to the author just quoted, only an extension beyond 12 miles would have been invalid at the date of entry into force of the Treaty.

The doctrine of inter-temporal law has been criticized on the ground that an eventual retro-active effect of the law would be highly disturbing for the security of title;[29] however, the situation that was considered in the *Island of Palmas* arbitration was entirely different from the one we are now discussing. From the point of view of claimant countries, once the title to territory has been established the right to the pertinent maritime areas follows by virtue of the principle of appurtenance, and this legal premise has not changed in the course of time; it is only the exercise of the right that has changed to the extent of the evolution of the Law of the Sea and the incorporation of new maritime zones to national jurisdiction, all of which can be considered the continued manifestation of the existence of the right. While non-claimant countries will of course have a different view with regard to the question of title, this is not due to a change in the law but to a legal standpoint held *ab initio* of the Antarctic question; in any case Article IV of the Treaty prevents the prejudice of the respective approaches.

In the case of the Exclusive Economic Zone, the situation is not very different from that of the territorial sea. Even though this concept was not generally recognized at the date of entry into force of the 1959 Treaty, its subsequent acceptance has meant that it has become a maritime zone appurtenant to any national territory and any coastal State has a right to proclaim or establish it. There is furthermore an increasing body of opinion that considers the Exclusive Economic Zone as having become a part of international custom, just as the practice of establishing fisheries zones and other similar areas points in the same direction of extending the resource jurisdiction of coastal states.[30] On the other hand, it must be remembered that at least one State claiming Antarctic territory had already proclaimed a maritime zone of 200 miles before the date of the 1959 Treaty and that consequently it would be difficult for Article IV, paragraph 2, to apply to it.[31]

One fact of greater importance still is that this paragraph applies solely to the claims of 'territorial sovereignty' which is certainly not the case of the Exclusive Economic Zone. The essential point of the negotiations that took place on this subject at the Third United Nations Conference on the Law of the Sea was precisely that the concept of the Exclusive Economic Zone was devoid of any possible territorial scope.[32]

In the light of these considerations, the Exclusive Economic Zone is also covered by the rule of inter-temporal law, as expressed above, being a right which derives from the status of coastal Statehood and which manifests itself in a way that is determined by the evolution of the law of the sea concerning the rights of coastal states. At a later point the practice that has developed in the framework of the Antarctic system will be considered, which tends to confirm the international legal validity of this zone, without prejudice to the existence of the special regimes.

The overall conclusion that emerges from what has been said is that, as a general rule, the maritime areas recognized by the law of the sea do not fall within the prohibition of Article IV, paragraph 2. Some of these areas fall outside this prohibition by reason of their pre-existence, as in the case of the territorial sea and the continental shelf; other, namely the Exclusive Economic Zone, is accepted partly because some elements pre-existed it; above all, the Exclusive Economic Zone is accepted because it cannot be regarded as a claim of territorial sovereignty. All these concepts are governed by the conditions imposed by the evolution of the law of the sea in general and by those of Antarctic co-operation in particular. Claims that might be incompatible with the current status of the law of the sea, one example of such claim being the eventual proclamation of a 200-mile territorial sea, would not only be contrary to the norms of inter-temporal law as applied to Antarctica under the suggestions made above, but would also incur in the prohibition of Article IV, paragraph 2.

Article VI and the scope of the regime for the high seas

The second basic provision of the Treaty relating to the law of the sea is that of Article VI, which is intended to safeguard the freedom of the high seas. The scope of this provision has also been subject to doubts. Even though doubt has been expressed concerning the exact meaning to be ascribed to the expression 'area' in this Article, i.e. whether or not it includes maritime areas,[33] the reference made in the last part of the provision to 'high seas within that area' clearly suggests that maritime areas are in general included within the meaning of 'area' in this provision,[34] subject to the determination of which maritime areas might be envisaged.

A more important difficulty is that of determining the scope of the expression 'high seas' in this Article. Does it mean that the entire maritime area south of latitude 60° south is to be considered as the high seas, as some have maintained?[35] Or does it mean that in the part of this area which constitutes the high seas the freedom which is proper to it exists but without precluding the existence of a territorial sea or other zones of the law of the sea linked to national jurisdiction? The language used by the Article does not lend substance to the first interpretation, above all, because such interpretation requires that countries claiming sovereignty renounce the maritime zones that they might have claimed, and this would necessitate a specific affirmation by them to that effect. Although there is no mention of the territorial sea either, this is probably due to the need not to prejudge the various positions.

Van der Essen points out an important fact in the legislative history of this Article. The original draft referred to the application of the basic principles of the Treaty to the area south of the above mentioned parallel 60 'with the exception of the high seas'.[36] The result of this would have been to exclude the high seas entirely from the provisions on demilitarization, prohibition of nuclear tests and other basic provisions of the Treaty. So as to ensure that this did not occur, the claimant and non-claimant countries suggested drafting changes designed to extend the norms concerning peaceful uses to the largest possible area. Van der Essen points out that 'the final version of Article VI was the product of amendments introduced to that end'.[37]

As a result, Article VI was intended to be entirely unrelated to problems of jurisdiction and of economic utilization, and its only objective was to apply to the maritime areas the general principles of the Treaty concerning peaceful uses. For this reason, Van der Essen concludes:

> The only effects of the current text, therefore, are to ban air and naval manoeuvres and weapons testing (stated in Article I), peaceful nuclear tests and the disposal of radioactive wastes (prohibited in Article V) in the Treaty zone, as well as to uphold the freedoms of fishing, navigation and over-flight in marine spaces.[38]

This interpretation is especially important because, in addition to safeguarding the recognized freedoms of the high seas such as navigation, overflight, fishing and scientific research, this Article brings other uses of the sea within the ambit of the Treaty regime, particularly in regard to demilitarization, the prohibition of nuclear tests and other measures connected with peaceful uses. At the same time, this background clearly explains that the Article was not intended to include questions of jurisdiction or economic problems. Problems of this other type have been dealt with through practice within the system and the development of its special regimes.

4.2   The Consultative Parties and the general regime of the Law of the Sea

Neither the range of the national legislation of the Consultative Parties concerning the Law of the Sea in general,[39] nor their participation in the various general or special treaties in this field,[40] points to uniform criteria which might facilitate the application of the law of the sea to the Antarctic continent.

With regard to the territorial sea, although there is general agreement concerning the legal nature of this space in the light of the rules of international law, there are enormous differences of opinion as to its breadth. Some of the Parties, including Australia, Belgium, Chile, the United States, Great Britain, Japan, New Zealand, Poland and the Federal Republic of Germany, claim and recognize a territorial sea of only three miles even though some of them might possibly extend it to twelve miles as a consequence of the 1982 Convention on the Law of the

Sea, either generally or in relation to specific areas; Norway has a territorial sea of four miles; South Africa of six miles; China, France, India and the Soviet Union claim 12 miles; Argentina, Brazil and Uruguay have a territorial sea of 200 miles, even though their claims have certain elements of ambiguity or qualification.[41] In some of these cases, contiguous zones or other equivalent zones are also asserted, varying in size and purpose.

As far as exclusive fishing zones or equivalent zones are concerned, historically speaking, important differences in the legislation of these Parties are to be noted since these zones in general range in breadth from twelve miles for one group to 200 miles for another, with various intermediate widths in between.[42] However, there is a tendency towards uniformity on this matter as a consequence of the negotiations of the Third United Nations Conference on the Law of the Sea and of practices which evolved during the last three decades. The adoption of zones of 200 miles has become a common practice of coastal States even though the content and scope of the various proclamations or statutes on the subject vary.[43] However, as it will be seen, the application of such zones in the case of the Antarctic has in general been subject to the regimes for natural resources and to other important qualifications.

Claims relating to the continental shelf have had in general a certain uniformity, partly due to the rapid incorporation of the doctrine of the continental shelf into international custom and partly to the influence exercised by the Continental Shelf Convention of 1958, which established the criteria for its outer limit. This has not, admittedly, prevented the existence of different criteria such as those which inspired the Chilean declaration of a 200-mile maritime zone which incidentally included the continental shelf or the epicontinental sea concept followed by Argentina.[44] The work of the Third United Nations Conference on the Law of the Sea and the 1982 Convention have given rise to new criteria on this matter, particularly in regard to the determination of the outer limit of the continental shelf.[45]

The other Geneva Conventions of 1958 similarly provide little further clarification for the case of the Antarctic. The Convention on the Territorial Sea and the Contiguous Zone has been ratified by only seven Consultative Parties; three other Parties are signatories of the Convention.[46] The Convention on the High Seas has been ratified by a larger number of parties, namely nine, and has been signed by a further four parties.[47]

The Convention on Fishing and the Conservation of the Living Resources of the High Seas has been less successful in attracting the support of the Antarctic Treaty Consultative Parties since it has been ratified only by six of them and signed by three others.[48] The Convention on the Continental Shelf has been ratified by nine Parties and signed by four others.[49] Lastly, it is to be noted that the Optional Protocol for the settlement of disputes has been ratified by seven Consultative Parties and signed by a further one.[50]

The provisions on fishing embodied in the above mentioned Geneva Convention did not attain a widespread application in the years following its signature and this fact, together with new issues that had arisen in connection with the use of the oceans, had an influence on the origins of the Third United Nations Conference on the Law of the Sea.[51] The important work carried out by this Conference made possible the progressive development of certain aspects of the law of the sea, the codification of other subjects and the preparation of a complete text which included the whole of the provisions governing the utilization of the oceans.[52] The 1982 Convention is the result of this effort.[53]

Even though the natural disagreements on the scope or interpretation of some of the provisions remain, this Convention has, in general, made an important contribution to the harmonization of the various national positions and, thereby, to the harmonization of their corresponding legislative expressions.[54] The general consensus that large parts of this instrument has attracted will thus provide the international community with a common legal basis. It is still too early to assess the extent to which the Convention will be implemented but the large number of signatories is indicative of this consensus.[55]

The 1982 Convention has been signed by an important number of the Antarctic Treaty Consultative Parties,[56] being the United States, the Federal Republic of Germany, Great Britain and South Africa the only four countries having this Consultative status that did not sign this instrument.

Although it is unlikely that the provisions of this Convention will be capable as such of resolving the complex issue of the implementation of the law of the sea in Antarctica, the greater level of uniformity which the Convention represents may well make this task easier as indeed it has already done in the context of the most recent resources regimes, since even most non-signatories accept large parts of the Convention, other than its deep sea-bed mining provisions. This promising aspect is capable of playing a particularly significant role on matters which are necessarily reflected in the Antarctic issues, such as the regime of the continental shelf or the control of marine pollution, to name but a few. It must also be remembered that the Convention is interconnected in regard to certain specialized subjects with other important treaties, a typical example being the control of pollution and the numerous instruments adopted under the auspices of the International Maritime Organization, as well as *ad hoc* conventions such as the London Dumping Convention.[57]

4.3   The regime of the Agreed Measures and the status of the territorial sea

The differences between the Consultative Parties in regard to Antarctic claims and related matters, and probably also the dissimilarity of the principles and approaches adopted by them in regard to the law of the sea in general, explain the caution which was displayed in connection with maritime questions at the outset. The provisions of the Antarctic Treaty do not provide a basis on which one can act with full confidence owing to the uncertainty of their scope. As Van der Essen points out in this connection with particular reference to Article IV of the Treaty, 'the least that can be said, in view of the different positions of signatory States on the matter and the fact that certain affirmations of sovereignty overlap, is that this Article does not provide a basis for the definition of the limits of jurisdiction at sea along the Antarctic coast'.[58]

In the development of their norm-creating function the Consultative Parties timidly provided, in Recommendation I-VI,[59] for the exchange of information on various topics of common interest which, *inter alia*, included the programme of work and scientific investigation that was envisaged for the Antarctic stations, ships and aircraft. This reference to ships was a first indication of an interest in activities that might be conducted in the maritime areas which were certainly covered by the freedom of scientific investigation provided for in the Treaty and which, as far as the high seas were concerned, were also covered by the general rules of the law of the sea which prevail in such area. From the geographical point of view, the recommendation confined itself to noting that the location of such ships 'in Antarctica' should be indicated without any reference to any individual maritime area.[60]

The extent to which the Law of the Sea had evolved was clearly apparent ten years later when Recommendation VI-13 requested 'information about those ships which are carrying out substantial oceanographic research programmes in the area south of 60° South Latitude'.[61] It must also be remembered in this connection that, in compliance with Article VII, paragraph 5 (a), of the Treaty, relevant information must be circulated concerning 'all expeditions to and within Antarctica, on the part of its ships or nationals'. On occasion, the request for information has been extended to zones located outside the Treaty area, thus prompting declarations by various Consultative Parties to protect their rights or positions with regard to these other zones.[62]

These expressions of interest in maritime areas have taken a particularly important form in relation to the subject of the conservation of fauna and flora,[63] a theme which for the first time provided a means of bringing the law of the sea into sharp focus. Recommendation I-VIII mentioned 'the urgent need for measures to conserve the living resources of the Treaty area',[64] which in itself indicated the intention to apply such measures to the Antarctic maritime areas. The discussion on this point had particular implications for the negotiations leading to the approval of Recommendation III-VIII, which contains the Agreed Measures.[65] As was explained earlier, the special modalities of the form of this instrument, in that it is a recommendation which uses the actual terms of a Treaty, arise precisely from the question of its area of application. One body of opinion held that, if the living resources of the maritime areas were included, it was necessary to opt for a Convention, since a strict interpretation of Article VI of the Treaty would have precluded such a development.[66]

Area of application and questions of jurisdiction

Article I of the Agreed Measures refers to the area of application which is the same as that of the Antarctic Treaty and in relation to which the rights on the high seas are safeguarded in terms similar to those of the Treaty itself. Nevertheless, this instrument was not specific as to its application to particular marine resources and this has given rise to difficulties of interpretation. The prevailing view has been that these Measures apply only to the continent and the ice shelves and that the high seas, an area which would have continued to be governed by the principles of the freedom of fishing and hunting, was altogether excluded.[67] In spite of this, doubt has remained as to some of the provisions of the Agreed Measures, in particular Article IX, to the extent that it prohibits the introduction 'into the Treaty area' of non-indigenous species, a provision which might include marine species, thereby bringing it within the regulatory competence of the Consultative Parties.[68]

These difficulties of interpretation also occur in the corresponding national legislation relating to the application of the Agreed Measures. As Bush observes, the legislation of New Zealand and that of the United Kingdom specifically excludes the high seas; that of Belgium in the main follows the Treaty language; while that of Australia and the United States applies to the entire area south of latitude 60° south, and consequently includes its maritime areas.[69]

Both the Agreed Measures and the implementing national legislation have also shed light on some aspects of the exercise of maritime jurisdiction. Article XI of the Agreed Measures provides that, should the expeditions use ships flying the flag of another nationality, each Government 'shall, as far as feasible, arrange with the owners of such ships that the crews of these ships observe these Agreed Measures'. This provision obviously implies a special type of jurisdiction over third parties. For its part, Australian legislation extends to ships 'in Australian control'; that of New Zealand to 'the owner or master or a member of the crew of a New Zealand ship', and that of the United Kingdom to 'the owner or master or a member of the crew of a British ship registered in the United Kingdom'.[70]

The territorial sea: national legislation and the practice within the system
From the point of view of the policy of differentiating the various maritime areas for jurisdictional purposes, the most important provision of the Agreed Measures is that of Article VII, paragraph 3, under which 'each Participating Government shall take all reasonable steps towards the alleviation of pollution of the waters adjacent to the coast and ice shelves'. Several authors agree that this clause suggests the existence of a territorial sea in Antarctica.[71] Van der Essen pointed out that on the basis of this Article 'it may be deduced that the Antarctic possesses a territorial sea',[72] adding in another study that, in any case, 'the formulation is purposefully vague and does not affect the position of those States not recognizing territorial seas'.[73] However, it is quite apparent that the practice of the Consultative Parties in connection with the territorial sea in Antarctica has entirely relied on a flag-state jurisdictional approach or, in any case, in the adoption of measures which are not enforced under a policy of restraint.

The national legislation of some States assumes the existence of a territorial sea appurtenant to the claimed territory. When Chile specified the limits of its claim in 1940, it specifically included 'all lands, islands, islets, reefs of rocks, glaciers (pack-ice), already known, or to be discovered, and their respective territorial waters'.[74] As for French legislation, initially there may have been doubts as to whether it applied to the Antarctic territory since the legislation was of a general type.[75] Decree 71-711 of 25 August 1971 restricted fishing rights of foreigners within a twelve-mile band but this was confined to the French Southern territories and consequently excluded the case of Terre Adélie.[76] However, by an order of 1 September of the same year, the decree was also promulgated with respect to the Antarctic territories.[77] Later, Order No. 5 of 13

January 1972 extended the territorial sea to twelve miles in the case of the French southern and Antarctic territories.[78] This is an example of the extension of the territorial sea which has not been considered by the State concerned to be incompatible with the provisions of the 1959 Treaty.

In addition to legislation concerning the territorial sea and applying specifically to Antarctica, one must take account of general legislative provisions on the subject which apply to the Antarctic continent by extension. Australian legislation affords an example of this. A distinguished Australian author writes:

> The territorial sea was not proclaimed separately for the Antarctic. It did not need to be since Australia claims a three mile territorial sea appurtenant to all its territory . . . If Australia should make a claim to a wider territorial sea, let us say one of twelve nautical miles as would be permitted under the Draft LOS Convention, then that claim would apply equally to the territorial sea adjacent to Australian Antarctic Territory.[79]

In spite of the existence of legislation reaffirming the application of the territorial sea, what was said earlier concerning the position of countries that do not recognize maritime areas under national jurisdiction in Antarctica and the restraint with which claimants have acted must also be remembered.[80] In the judicial case of *Martin v. Commissioner of Internal Revenue*, the Tax Court of the United States re-affirmed the position of the United States Government concerning the non-recognition of sovereignty in Antarctica and specifically on the non-recognition of the territorial sea in that continent. Similar implications can be seen in the case *Beattie v. United States*.[81]

Article VII, paragraph 3, of the Agreed Measures has also given rise to intensive legislative activity related to pollution control. Australia, France, New Zealand, Great Britain, the United States and Belgium have promulgated legislation which embraces Antarctic waters in order to exercise such control.[82] An important body of international treaty law, which will be examined in Chapter 6, is also relevant in this context.[83]

The provisions and scope of these Agreed Measures clearly reflect the underlying conflict between the positions of those States that favour the extension of the Antarctic system to adjacent maritime areas and those who have endeavoured to restrict it to the continental land mass. In spite of the difficulties of interpretation and the discrepancies that have been mentioned this instrument marked a clear step forward in giving prominence to this maritime extension. Since its purpose was the conservation of mainly marine species, there was no longer any possibility of restricting its application strictly to the Antarctic continent.

For this reason, in addition to those provisions in the Treaty and the Agreed Measures which bear upon maritime jurisdiction, some State practice in their implementation has also confirmed this tendency. Various Chilean initiatives intended to establish Specially Protected Areas (SPA) and Sites of Special Scientific Interest (SSSI) in maritime zones have obtained a measure of recognition within the system.[84] In another case, the establishment of a Specially Protected Area in an island was based on the fact that it 'provides a representative sample of the maritime Antarctic ecosystem'.[85] Auburn explains the ingenious devices that have been used on other occasions to include floating ice and various other features of this further projection of the Antarctic system in the surrounding maritime areas.[86]

4.4   The Seal Convention: clarification of the regime for the high seas
In spite of the efforts towards extension of the Treaty to maritime areas that have been mentioned, the Agreed Measures were never definitely extended to the protection of seals and other living resources of the marine environment. This was undoubtedly an anomalous situation since while the seals were on the continent they were covered by the regime of the Agreed Measures but when they were in the open sea – their main habitat – they would have been subject to the regime of the freedom of fishing in the high seas in accordance with the terms of Article VI of the Treaty. In order to overcome this difficulty, Recommendation III-XI, which was adopted simultaneously with the Agreed Measures, provided for a system of voluntary regulation which Governments were to apply 'when ships of their nationality engage in pelagic sealing or the taking of fauna on pack ice south of 60° South Latitude'.[87] Subsequent recommendations improved this voluntary regime.[88]

The fact that this Recommendation III-XI was adopted together with the Agreed Measures seems to evidence a restrictive interpretation in regard to the maritime scope of the measures themselves since it implied that pelagic sealing or activities on the pack ice were outside their protection regime.[89] This restrictive interpretation was made more explicit in the Final Report of the Sixth Consultative Meeting which indicated that the subject of pelagic sealing was to be regarded as falling 'outside the framework of the Antarctic Treaty, since the conservation of seals in the sea does not fall within the scope of the latter and is of interest to countries which are not Parties to the Antarctic Treaty'.[90] This reasoning explains why the seal regime was adopted by means of a special convention which made it possible, on the one hand, to overcome the limitations of Article VI of the Treaty and, on the other hand, to facilitate the access of third countries. This did not, of course, prevent the negotiation of the regime among the Consultative Parties nor the fact that only they participated in the London Conference in 1972 when the Convention was adopted.[91]

On the occasion of this Conference, Sir Anthony Kershaw, speaking on behalf of the British Government, offered the following criterion of interpretation:

> Conservation measures on land in the Antarctic can be dealt with satisfactorily under the Antarctic Treaty, but we need to be able to take in a wider circle of nations in order to extend these measures to cover possible future exploitation of Southern Ocean Resources. Otherwise, we may find ourselves in the position that we are restricting the freedom of action by Antarctic Treaty nations while there would be no way to prevent others coming in who would not be subject to any restrictions.[92]

This restrictive approach to the Antarctic Treaty was not generally favoured. At the Seventh Consultative Meeting, Chile 'expressed regret that the conservation of Antarctic seals should have been dealt with at a special conference, and trusted that this subject would again be brought within the scope of the Antarctic Treaty'.[93] This statement represented a re-affirmation of the view that the 1959 Treaty should have a more active role to play in the sphere of the law of the sea since it would thus include subjects which are clearly within the maritime domain, such as the conservation of seals. In any case, as was said in Chapter 2, it must be borne in mind that the special Treaty regimes have also come to form part of the Antarctic system and thus cannot be regarded as elements external to the Treaty but rather as factors which complement it.

Reformulation of Article VI of the Treaty

The adoption of the 1972 Convention[94] was a major advance in the process of linking the Antarctic system with the law of the sea. Its field of application extends 'to the seas south of 60° South-Latitude', including the pack ice and other floating ice formations even though some doubts have arisen as to its exact scope in relation to ice.[95] For certain purposes, the floating ice north of this latitude is also included.[96] Thus, a conservation regime is applied to Antarctic maritime areas and this in fact implies to some extent a reformulation of the scope of Article VI of the Treaty by making the freedom of the high seas subject to these conservation purposes. From then onwards the scope of the system was to be extended with ever-growing clarity to maritime areas. In the words of Van der Essen:

> But the fundamental difference with the Treaty obviously lies in the very purpose of the Convention which is a specific derogation from the freedom of fishing (or hunting) envisaged by the law of the sea.[97]

This reformulation of the scope of Article VI has proved an important means of covering the limitations which might otherwise affect the action of the Parties to the Antarctic Treaty in regard to the high seas as it is now clear that the system has a means of intervention in this maritime area. This particular arrangement will of course bind the Parties to the Seal Convention, but, as will be examined in Chapter 9, the eventual action of third parties in the Treaty area might be under some form of control on the part of the Antarctic Treaty system and the rules adopted within this system by the parties to it. The maritime trend of the Antarctic Treaty system was to become even more obvious with the Convention on the Conservation of Antarctic Marine Living Resources.

It was earlier explained that Article VI had its origin in the desire to extend the application of the principles relating to peaceful use, demilitarization and other basic principles embodied in the Treaty, but without dealing with issues relating to resources and other jurisdictional problems. It was through the Seal Convention that these latter issues began to be brought into the field of competence of the system particularly in regard to natural resources. This is a further example of the issue of natural resources initiating a qualitative change in the competence of the Antarctic system.

Once the maritime extension of the scope of the Antarctic Treaty system was accepted by the Consultative Parties, a further legal issue has been raised in relation to whether the rights on the high seas envisaged by Article VI were those in force at the time when the Antarctic Treaty was signed or whether they resulted from the evolution of the law of the sea.[98] The point is particularly important in connection with problems such as that of military uses or the regime of scientific investigation.[99] This issue raises questions no different in nature from those discussed earlier in connection with the doctrine of inter-temporal law and the appearance of new maritime areas subject to national jurisdiction. For this reason it needs to be stated once again that the law of the sea must be applied in a manner determined by its gradual evolution from time to time. This conclusion is also supported by the practice of the Antarctic system considered above.

The 1972 Convention followed the actual rules of the international regime of the high seas in regard to jurisdiction and was based on flag State jurisdiction, as is clear from Article 2 which refers to 'their nationals or vessels under their respective flags'.[100] In the same way, the legislation, regulations and other implementing measures which each member country promulgates in accordance with the Convention, including the corresponding hunting authorizations, are referred to as being 'for its nationals and for vessels under its flag'.[101] Even though Article 3 (1) (k) of this instrument envisages the possibility of a system of inspection, this has not been spelt out in detail.[102] The general provision of Article VII of the Antarctic Treaty, as far as ships are concerned, applies solely to 'all ships and aircraft at points of discharging or embarking cargoes or personnel in Antarctica', and it could thus not readily be used to control activities carried out in maritime areas. For this reason, the provision of Article 3 of the Seal Convention to which we have referred would seem to imply a different system that might be applied to such maritime areas, and this has indeed been established within the framework of the Convention on the Conservation of Antarctic Marine Living Resources.[103] The International Convention for the Regulation of Whaling also envisages an inspection system; initially this was done only by means of national inspectors but a subsequent Protocol amended the Convention to provide for appointment of international observers under bilateral agreements.[104] The issue of inspection will be discussed further in the context of the regime for mineral resources.

Safeguarding maritime jurisdictions

The Seal Convention introduced no distinctions based on the existence of different maritime areas in Antarctica for which reason it must be assumed to apply without exception to all such areas south of parallel 60° South latitude.[105] Nevertheless, the respective national positions have also been safeguarded in this respect. Thus, Article 1 of the Convention re-affirms the application of Article IV of the Treaty with respect to the Antarctic seas, thus entailing a general safeguarding of positions. More particularly, several Consultative Parties made specific declarations or reservations.

During the discussion of pelagic sealing at the Fifth Consultative Meeting, Argentina indicated that the approval of a recommendation on the subject 'must not be considered as a precedent affecting in any way whatsoever the application of the provisions of Article VI of the Antarctic Treaty'.[106] Does this declaration denote a desire to safeguard the freedoms of the high seas or, on the other hand, a desire to preserve the position adopted with regard to maritime areas linked to national jurisdiction?[107] The second possibility seems to be confirmed by a statement made by Argentina in depositing its instrument of ratification of the

Convention, declaring that the reference to Article IV of the Treaty 'means that nothing in the said Convention affects or impairs its sovereignty rights and maritime jurisdiction and its juridical position in this matter'.[108] Argentina has also made the point that research programmes of international organizations 'should be unanimously approved by the consulting (*sic*) parties when they refer to marine zones south of 60° S latitude',[109] a view which is not easy to reconcile with the safeguard of high seas rights under Article VI of the Treaty.

On signing the Convention, Chile also declared that the reference to Article IV of the Treaty 'signifies that nothing specified therein shall confirm, deny or impair the rights of the Consultative Parties as regards their maritime jurisdictions and their declared juridical position on this matter', an identical reservation having been made in the ratification decree.[110] A declaration made on the occasion of the deposit of the instrument of ratification referred to its 'territorial jurisdictions, whether on land or on sea';[111] however, this more extreme position does not form part of the corresponding decree of ratification.

The opposite point of view, however, was also expressed in a Soviet note reacting to the declaration made by Argentina on depositing its instrument of ratification. This note states that 'the Soviet Union has frequently announced that it does not recognize territorial claims which have been put forward by certain States in Antarctica' and that the reservation as to maritime jurisdiction 'is in conflict with paragraph 2 of Article IV of that Treaty according to which no extension of an existing claim to territorial sovereignty in Antarctica shall be made while the present Treaty is in force'.[112]

National practice concerning the application of this Convention shows that, in respect of nationals and ships under the jurisdiction of a Party, the corresponding legislation may impose conditions relating to conservation and measures stricter than those embodied in the Convention itself.[113]

4.5 The living resources regime and the issue of the Exclusive Economic Zone

The progression of application of measures to maritime areas of Antarctica which began with the Agreed Measures and continued with the Seal Convention was to reach a new phase with the Convention of Antarctic Marine Living Resources. Just as the first steps enabled the Antarctic Treaty system to embrace marine resources and other matters related to their conservation this further step represented an even more significant advance, partly because it provided for a more comprehensive regime and partly because its policies were more specific. In the context of the first regimes examined, the problem of the territorial sea and that of the regime of the high seas in the Treaty area were to some extent clarified since, even if definitive solutions were not achieved, the terms of the problems and the positions of the Parties were clarified. A similar process took place with this new Convention particularly in regard to the Exclusive Economic Zone and the fishery regime on the high seas.

It is interesting to note how closely this progression was linked to the potential exploitation of resources. The Agreed Measures restricted themselves to the protection of fauna and flora on the continent and in certain ice areas leaving some uncertainty with regard to the situation of individual species in the marine environment. In order to remedy this situation, the regime for the conservation of seals was negotiated and covered the entire range of marine areas. The Canberra Convention completed this cycle. On the one hand, since it applies in general to marine living resources,[114] it follows therefore that no species remain unprotected. Even though there are doubts as to whether the Convention also applies to seals and whales, both these species are specifically subject to other regulatory mechanisms.[115] On the other hand, the Convention applies to species in a geographical area larger than that of the Antarctic Treaty which also constitutes a geographical extension of the Antarctic system.[116]

Another characteristic of the seals and living resources regimes which should not pass unnoticed is that they have been developed in anticipation of large-scale commercial exploitation of the respective marine resources. This has been one of the factors which have made it possible to organize the Antarctic co-operation in a manner that satisfies the various interests and points of view since, once such commercial activities begin, it is always harder to find appropriate solutions, a point which is well illustrated by the experience of the Whaling Convention. Interest in Antarctic krill was already beginning to present a source of discord, due partly to the different principles applied on matters of maritime jurisdiction and partly to the different interests involved in the conservation or the exploitation of this resource.[117] The Convention made it possible to ensure that this discord did not turn into open conflict; new approaches to jurisdiction were developed and acceptable appropriate concepts were applied in connection with conservation, particularly as regards the recognition of an Antarctic 'ecosystem'.[118]

The positions of principle maintained by the countries that claim sovereignty and those that do not recognize such claims in relation to maritime jurisdiction have been mentioned earlier, as well as the problems that arise concerning the application of the rules of inter-temporal law, particularly in regard to the Exclusive Economic Zone. These positions have resulted in specific legislation or criteria which it is interesting to examine from the point of view of their implications for the Convention regime.

National legislations and the policy of restraint

The Chilean Antarctic decree of 1940 which specified the boundaries of Chile's territorial claim in Antarctica specifically included the territorial sea and the pack ice.[119] When, in 1947, that country issued its proclamation of a maritime zone of 200 miles, it was made applicable to the whole of the national territory.[120] Even though the Antarctic territory was not specifically mentioned on that occasion, it was included by extension.[121] It follows that when Chile signed the Antarctic Treaty it had already adopted this maritime zone. Various special Chilean laws have also referred to fishing and hunting activities in the Antarctic Seas.[122] This explains why Chile has consistently reserved its rights with regard to Antarctic maritime areas, as in the case of the declarations and reservations made in connection with the Seal Convention. Similarly, in ratifying the Whaling Convention of 1946, Chile reserved its jurisdictional rights in this maritime zone.[123]

In spite of this, the policy of Antarctic maritime jurisdiction has been applied with a considerable measure of restraint. It is, of course, a case of application of general legislation by means of its extension to the Antarctic continent, as also, it appears, is the case with Argentina.[124] Furthermore, a rigorous policy of enforcement has never been attempted by either country in Antarctica. All this has undoubtedly done much to promote the quest for harmonious solutions.

The approach followed by other Consultative Parties shows a similar concern for restraint. Although, as it was seen, France extended its twelve mile territorial sea to the southern and Antarctic territories, the French Exclusive Economic Zone has been applied only to the southern territories in the strict sense, thus not including Terre Adélie.[125] The example of Australian practice is even more interesting in this context since, by means of the proclamation of 20 September 1979, Australia extended its *Fisheries Act* of 1952 to 'All waters within 200 nautical miles outwards of the baselines by reference to which the territorial limits of an external Territory are defined'[126] and it was specifically stated that 'the waters up to 200 miles off the Australian Antarctic Territory are to be covered by the new proclamation'.[127] However, by another proclamation of 31 October 1979, these Antarctic waters were excepted from the system of 'proclaimed waters'.[128]

The result of this complex legislative relationship is that Australian fisheries legislation may be applied in Antarctica to Australian nationals but not to foreign persons or ships.[129] Australia has also refrained from applying to the Antarctic Territory its legislation on the movement of ships in the vicinity of naval establishments, because of its eventual incompatibility with the Antarctic Treaty.[130]

Other Consultative Parties have also refrained from extending their legislation concerning the Exclusive Economic Zone or fishing zones to the Antarctic territories, as in the case of Great Britain, Norway and New Zealand.[131] The last named country has specifically reserved its right to extend to the Ross Dependency its legislation over the Exclusive Economic Zone, although in other contexts it appears to have considered a different policy.[132] It is also interesting to note that New Zealand has made a policy of including the issue of the proper management and conservation of the living resources of the Sub-Antarctic and Antarctic Oceans in bilateral fisheries agreements; examples of this can be found in the Agreement with Korea and, subject to consistency with the Antarctic Treaty, in those with the USSR and Japan.[133] While these provisions are intended to apply beyond the New Zealand Exclusive Economic Zone, they evidence an interest in the activities undertaken in the vicinity of such Zone. The fact that consistency with the Antarctic Treaty is only mentioned in those agreements entered into with parties to that Treaty, suggests that non-parties like Korea would be subject to a different set of rules in Antarctica, but this is something that has changed with the entry into force of the Canberra Convention and its implications for the activities of third States in the terms that will be examined in Chapter 9.

The countries that do not recognize claims of sovereignty have also developed principles on this subject which are generally intended to deny the validity of national maritime jurisdictions. The position of the Soviet Union on this matter has already been considered in the context of the Seal Convention.[134] Similarly, a distinguished United States negotiator has stated:

> In the areas covered by the Antarctic Treaty, the United States, of course, with the possible exception of a couple of islands, clearly does not recognize sovereignty. Thus, we do not recognize the claims of sovereignty or maritime jurisdiction south of 60 degrees latitude.[135]

Nevertheless, it is to be noted that, just as in the case of the claimant countries, this position has always been stated with a considerable measure of restraint in an effort to achieve a satisfactory accommodation of interests within the framework of the Antarctic Treaty. The same negotiator, referring to the negotiations on the Living Resources Convention declared:

> With regard to those areas around the continent of Antarctica where there is a dispute as to whether territorial sovereignty or maritime jurisdiction exists, one of the major purposes of the Treaty is to work out a formula whereby claimants, (*sic*) non-claimants can agree on a system which will provide for adequate conservation, without, however, compromising their legal positions.[136]

In the same spirit, other authors have sought to make claims of maritime jurisdiction subject to the primacy of conservation needs. On this matter Barnes, for example, writes:

> The U.S. must not allow states with putative 200 mile economic zones off their asserted claims (*sic*) to do anything within those zones that is inconsistent with the conservation requirements of the convention. . . . In our view, the convention should make it clear that conservation measures will be applied over the entire area of the Antarctic marine eco-system, regardless of claims to economic zones.[137]

The view taken by other authors, however, seems to indicate a more inflexible position as they reject the very concept of maritime jurisdiction.[138] One of them writes: 'If there is no national sovereignty over the land area, still less can there be sovereignty over the adjacent marine areas, and therefore the concept of an exclusive economic zone has no application here'.[139] Another author states that if there is a proclamation of an economic zone or other types of maritime jurisdiction 'the propriety of their legal status would be questionable and highly suspect',[140] and similarly that 'the prerequisites in the UNCLOS III Draft Convention for the legal establishment of EEZs – presence of coastal State, recognized coastal baselines, effective occupation, and purposeful management of natural resources – are not found in Antarctica'.[141]

New approaches for the balance of interests

The various positions that we have indicated were to be confronted in the course of the negotiations on the Living Resources Convention.[142] There was not a great deal of difficulty at the level of general principles since they were based on a degree of scientific[143] and legal[144] consensus. For example, as Barnes points out, Recommendation IX-2 established as the central criteria of the new regime the concept of conservation of resources within the ecosystem, its application to areas north of latitude 60 degrees south to the extent necessary to ensure effective conservation and, above all, the safeguarding of the principles of Article IV of the Treaty 'in application to the marine areas south of 60° S latitude'.[145]

However, the difficulties of devising specific mechanisms were to be far greater than in the case of the other regimes referred to in this Chapter and at one time even produced a serious polarization of positions. In a well documented account of these negotiations, Barnes points out that at the session held in Buenos Aires in July 1978, Argentina proposed 'The establishment of a "reserved" zone around the continent (inside the 1000 fathom mark) in which all exploitation activities would be banned', which was interpreted as tantamount to an area of national jurisdiction.[146] Chile proposed a prohibition on 'the establishment of all land-based fishery facilities on the continent'.[147] Maintaining the opposing point of view, the Soviet Union proposed that it be clearly stated that the claimant countries were not entitled to establish maritime areas of national jurisdiction.[148] Another country sought to achieve a compromise formula on the basis of which economic benefits from fishing would be granted to the countries claiming sovereignty.[149]

The highly imaginative formula which made possible the accommodation of these different positions is contained in Article IV of this Convention. It provides in the first place that, in regard to the area of application of the Antarctic Treaty, all the Contracting Parties, whether or not they are Parties to the Antarctic Treaty, 'are bound by Articles IV and VI of the Antarctic Treaty in their relations with each other'. In this way, a general safeguarding of positions was established, including those relating to the question of maritime jurisdiction. It must be noted, however, that the safeguarding of rights relating to the high seas provided in Article VI of the Treaty must undoubtedly be understood as being subject to the objectives of the Canberra Convention which are to regulate fishing on the high seas or in other Antarctic maritime areas.[150]

It should also be pointed out that the close link that was established with these Articles of the Treaty, in addition to other provisions of the Convention which tend in the same direction, involves, on the one hand, the recognition of the maritime scope of the Treaty which had been placed in doubt as a result of the Agreed Measures and the Seal Convention; on the other hand, it means that the Canberra Convention must be regarded as an integral part of the Antarctic system. Even though these links with the Antarctic Treaty, to the extent that they are binding on all the Parties to the Living Resources Convention, have been criticized as 'unfortunate and unnecessary',[151] they form the cornerstone of the integrity of the Antarctic system and, as it will be seen later, in no way affect the progressive participation of other countries.[152] The combined effect of Articles IV and VI of the Antarctic Treaty, which as has been examined are closely related in the context of the maritime scope of the system, provides a solid safeguard for all the points of view relevant in the matter.

Article IV of the Convention reproduces in substance the terms of Article IV of the Antarctic Treaty whereby none of the provisions of the former or the activities engaged in under those provisions, may be interpreted as supporting or denying a territorial claim; at the same time, the prohibition on enlarging existing claims during the period while the Antarctic Treaty is in force is reaffirmed. From the point of view of maritime jurisdiction, the most significant aspects of this Article are in subparagraphs (b) and (c) of paragraph 2:

> 2: Nothing in this Convention and no acts or activities taking place while the present Convention is in force shall: (b) be interpreted as a renunciation or diminution by any Contracting Party of, or as prejudicing, any right or claim or basis of claim to exercise coastal state jurisdiction under international law within the area to which this Convention applies;
>
> (c) be interpreted as prejudicing the position of any Contracting Party as regards its recognition or non-recognition of any such right, claim or basis of claim.

These provisions have made it possible to deal with two central problems of the negotiation. In the first place, they represent the legal basis on which a solution was found to the problem of the maritime jurisdiction of France in relation to the Kerguelen Islands and Iles Crozet.[153] These maritime areas were included within the Convention area but France did not accept that its rights as a coastal State were to be thereby affected. Paragraph 2 (b) quoted above, allows France to retain its rights of maritime jurisdiction as a general principle. More specifically the declaration made by the president of the Conference on 19 May 1980 recognizes the right of France to maintain the conservation measures that it had promulgated for those areas – including the establishment of the Exclusive Economic Zone – to accept or reject the conservation measures approved under the Convention and to remain outside the inspection system. The declaration was incorporated in the Final Act of the Conference with a note to the effect that no objections had been raised.[154]

The understanding contained in this declaration 'also applies to waters adjacent to the islands within the area to which this Convention applies

over which the existence of State sovereignty is recognized by all Contracting Parties'. Australia, for example, has applied the fishing zone of
200 miles around the islands of Heard and McDonald.[155] Similarly, the
legislation that it has enacted in compliance with the Convention provides
for Australian jurisdiction over persons and ships located in the
Australian fishing zone, consequently including these islands.[156]

The location of these and other islands in relation to the Antarctic
Treaty area and the area of application of the Convention on the
Conservation of Antarctic Marine Living Resources is shown in the
attached map; this map will also help to explain the so-called jurisdictional
'bifocal approach' that will be examined next.

Legal scope of the bifocal approach
The second central problem which these provisions are designed to solve
is that of maritime jurisdiction in general on the basis of what some

Figure 1   Antarctic Treaty area and area of application of C.C.A.M.L.R.

--- Approximate position of
Antarctic Convergence

authors have termed the 'bifocal approach',[157] 'constructive ambiguity'[158] or 'chameleon-like wording'.[159] This formula has been explained in the following terms:

> It is these provisions that give rise to the 'bifocal' approach, an approach which allows claimants and non-claimants to interpret the same language differently. Claimants can interpret these provisions as referring to all land territory in the Antarctic Region. Thus under a claimant interpretation, the right to assert a coastal zone from the continent has been preserved, and such an assertion is not an enlargement of an existing claim but rather a recognition of a latent but inherent right to territorial sovereignty. In contradistinction, non-claimants can interpret these provisions as permitting coastal zones to be drawn for islands north of 60° S but proscribing any such assertions from islands south of 60° S or from the continent.[160]

This formula is endorsed by many commentators on the Convention[161] and has also been accepted in declarations made by official representatives.[162] Even though it is true that the history of the negotiation confirms the process whereby this difficult compromise formula was sought and found, from the strict point of view of international law the situation might be read differently. The distinction between areas north of or south of latitude 60 degrees south, on which this approach is mainly based, does not, of course, originate in the text of the Convention. On the contrary, specific objections were raised against drafting formulas that might have introduced this distinction since they would have prejudged the situation of maritime claims in relation to the continent.[163]

Moreover, the distinction between islands whose sovereignty is recognized by all Contracting Parties and others in respect of which there is no such recognition similarly does not arise from the Convention but from the declaration made by the President of the Conference to which reference has been made. Even though it forms part of the Final Act, it is a document whose legal status differs from that of the Convention. In this way, if Article IV of the Convention is interpreted in the light of its own terms, it explicitly recognizes the possibility of the exercise of jurisdiction by the coastal State, a fact which certain Parties affirm and others deny, while the Article itself does not prejudge these various positions. In this sense, even though the Article is neutral with regard to the positions of the Parties, it implies the possibility of coastal State maritime jurisdiction, just as Article IV of the Antarctic Treaty, which is also neutral with regard to these positions, implies the possibility of the existence of territorial sovereignty.

The provisions that have been discussed have two further implications which it is interesting to note. It must be observed that the reference to 'coastal State jurisdiction' is attended by the requirement that it should be 'under international law'. This means that it will be international law that determines the scope of maritime jurisdiction, an aspect which in principle resolves the question of inter-temporal law already mentioned since international law as it develops over time will establish the limits of this scope.

The second aspect refers to disputes over sovereignty. One author has pointed out in this connection that:

> the wording permits rival claimants of territory both north and south of 60° S latitude to assert that they may exercise jurisdiction themselves over territory they claim, yet deny that right to their rivals.[164]

The Convention's maritime jurisdictional scope could not in any case support the above mentioned view in relation to the Antarctic Treaty area, namely south of 60 degrees south latitude, since both Article IV of the Antarctic Treaty and Article IV of the Convention safeguard the positions of claimant and non-claimant countries, on the one hand, and of countries which have rival claims on the other.

The problem would be more likely to arise in connection with disputed islands outside the Antarctic Treaty area but included in the Living Resources Convention area. In this case, an interesting question arises with regard to the declaration of the President of the Conference quoted above which, as already said, also applies to islands 'over which the existence of State sovereignty is recognized by all Contracting Parties'. In the case of a dispute, there is no doubt that such an island would be susceptible to the existence of sovereignty, a fact recognized by all Parties, including those in dispute; what might be in doubt is which of the various claims to sovereignty is the one that should be exercised or recognized. Given the language used by paragraph 5 of this declaration it would seem that it refers only to the first situation mentioned and that, consequently, it is applicable even in those cases in which there are concurrent claims.

Clarification of the jurisdictional regime
In spite of all the difficulties of interpretation that may arise, the significant fact is that this Convention has managed, in the first place, to accommodate the divergent positions of the various countries engaged in Antarctic activity and, thereby, to resolve definitively the question of the

maritime extension of the Antarctic system. The technique of juridical ambiguity had already been successfully used in other difficult negotiations on maritime jurisdiction[165] and this was a further case in which its usefulness was demonstrated. This approach may be also of some importance in connection with another special regime where the question of maritime jurisdiction has been in dispute, namely that of Svalbard.[166]

The Canberra Convention also has implications for other problems relating to the exercise of jurisdiction in Antarctica. Owing to the underlying problems of national maritime claims, this instrument does not contain a specific clause to the effect that national jurisdiction on the high seas is restricted to the nationals of the State concerned and to ships flying its flag, as was the case with the Seal Convention.[167] However, one author deduces that jurisdiction based on nationality and flag-State jurisdiction are applicable in the light of the indirect scope of Articles X (1) and XXIV (2) (a) of the Convention.[168] In any case, a similar conclusion may be reached on the basis of the general principles governing jurisdiction on the high seas, a fact which should not, of course prejudge the possibility of exercise of jurisdiction by the coastal State in the maritime spaces which, in accordance with international law, are subject to its jurisdiction. Australian legislation follows these principles of jurisdiction to the extent that, outside its fishing zone, such jurisdiction is applied to 'Australian nationals and Australian vessels' and members of their crews.[169]

The Convention was undoubtedly explicit in connection with jurisdiction over any observers and inspectors that may subsequently be appointed and adopted the same criterion as the Antarctic Treaty.[170] Such persons 'shall remain subject to the jurisdiction of the Contracting Party of which they are nationals'. Australian legislation applying the Convention has also been mentioned as relevant in this regard since, on the one hand, it provides the system for the designation of inspectors and, on the other, it is 'subject to the obligations of Australia under international law, including obligations under any international agreement binding on Australia'.[171] This latter clause has been interpreted as sufficient to exclude from Australian jurisdiction observers and inspectors of foreign nationality.[172]

4.6   The minerals regime and the issue of the continental shelf in Antarctica

Just as each of the regimes that we have considered contributed in its own way to clarifying the terms and scope of the jurisdictional problems related to the various maritime areas, so the negotiations concerning the minerals regime have done much to elucidate the problems connected with the Antarctic continental shelf and its relationship with the international sea-bed regime. Although some of these problems will be considered in Chapter 5 in relation to the area of application of the minerals regime, it is interesting at this stage to point out some aspects of the evolution of the Law of the Sea on this subject as pertinent to the case of Antarctica.

The general position maintained by the claimant and non-claimant countries in regard to the question of national jurisdiction over maritime areas was repeated *mutatis mutandis* in discussions concerning the status of the continental shelf: for the former, the continental shelf is an area typically 'appurtenant' to the territorial sovereignty and does not need a specific proclamation or act of occupation, whereas for the latter it is a further aspect of territorial jurisdiction which they do not recognize. However, unlike the other maritime areas, there is in this case a somewhat different approach.

It is, of course, beyond doubt that, at the date when the Antarctic Treaty was signed, the concept of the continental shelf was already incorporated into international custom.[173] This fact, taken together with the specific details of the continental shelf regime spelt out in the 1958 Convention on the subject, has facilitated a universal understanding of the legal characteristics of the continental shelf. Thus, there are no conceptual differences like those affecting other areas or regimes such as the Exclusive Economic Zone. Nor are there in this case any divergent interpretations concerning the applicable inter-temporal law.[174] This being so, the safeguards of Article IV of the Treaty are, if anything, even further reinforced.

Furthermore, independently of the legal problems which arise, the continental shelf represents a specific geomorphological fact which cannot be overlooked.[175] From the point of view of mineral resources this would seem to be the Antarctic area with the greatest potential.[176] On this basis, the position of the Consultative Parties has shown perhaps a greater degree of agreement than on other subjects.

Some claimant countries have issued proclamations which directly or indirectly refer to the Antarctic continental shelf. The Chilean proclamation of 1947 on the national maritime zone of 200 miles specifically included the continental shelf.[177] As has been stated, this proclamation applies by extension to the Antarctic territory. The Australian proclamation of 1953 also applies to the 'continental shelf contiguous to any part of the coasts of territories under its authority'[178] which includes the Antarctic territory of Australia.[179] The Australian Seas and Submerged Lands Act 1973 follows a similar approach.[180] France, for its part, has also extended its legislation on the continental shelf to the southern and Antarctic territories[181] and this extension has also been mentioned in other provisions concerning the Exclusive Economic Zone.[182] Argentina has specifically legislated on the conduct of oil prospection on the Antarctic continental shelf.[183] The other claimant countries have no special legislation applicable to the Antarctic in this connection.

The countries that do not recognize claims of sovereignty have reiterated their position 'that no state now exercises over the continental shelf of Antarctica sovereign rights for the purpose of exploring it and exploiting its natural resources'.[184] But, at the same time, it has been pointed out that:

> Under these circumstances, the status of the Antarctic continental shelf is unclear. . . . It remains to be determined whether exploitation of the resources of the continental shelf would be subject to the same legal regime as that applicable to the resources of the Antarctic land mass, or whether such a regime is in general based upon the freedom of the high seas, subject, of course, to the environmental and other measures applicable in the Antarctic pursuant to the Treaty.[185]

This latter position involves a change with regard to the traditional view of non-claimants according to which the regime of the high seas was applicable up to the coast of the Antarctic continent.[186] This change of view involves an exception with regard to the continental shelf whereby the concept is recognized but not the regime that would be applicable to it. In the same way, in the Report of the meeting held in 1973 by the Fridtjof Nansen Foundation on the problems of mineral exploitation, the concept of the continental shelf is once again recognized in a geological and juridical sense while the disagreements are maintained as to its regime and its specific status.[187]

While from the point of view of non-claimants the argument could have been made to the effect that international law and the doctrine of the continental shelf are concerned only with the rights of a 'coastal State' to the exploitation of the resources of the shelf, and do not provide for situations where there is no coastal State as in Antarctica, this argument has not in fact been expressly invoked since it could have diminished the possibilities of considering the Antarctic continental shelf as 'appurtenant' not to individual states but to the continent as a whole under some form of joint jurisdiction or administration by a special regime. In any event, such argument could not have any effect in the light of Article IV of the 1959 Treaty and the manner how its scope has been extended to the maritime areas of Antarctica, including the continental shelf.

Distinctions of Recommendation XI-1

On the basis of this greater degree of understanding, it was an easy matter for the Consultative Parties to place on record in Recommendation XI-1 'the unity between the continent of Antarctica and its adjacent offshore areas' and also to recall 'the negotiations that are taking place in the Third United Nations Conference on the Law of the Sea'. More specifically, it was agreed that the regime would apply 'to all mineral resource activities taking place on the Antarctic continent and its adjacent offshore areas but without encroachment on the deep sea-bed'.[188]

In spite of the fact that the term 'continental shelf' was avoided, possibly because it would normally involve the exercise of coastal state jurisdiction under international law,[189] the use of the expression 'adjacent offshore areas' was tantamount to a recognition of the same concept but in the context of a special mineral resources regime. This more neutral term does not in any way prejudice the positions of the Parties on coastal State jurisdiction and these are, moreover, covered by Article IV of the Treaty which is pointedly invoked by this Recommendation.

The provisions mentioned also made it possible to distinguish between the situation of the continental shelf and that of the deep sea-bed. In the discussion concerning the area of application of the regime, which will be considered later, some of the ideas suggested envisaged no clear distinction between these two concepts; this might possibly have produced a conflict of jurisdiction and competence between the Antarctic system and the International Sea-Bed Authority[190] or other arrangements for the exploitation of sea-bed minerals. The question of the delimitation of the continental shelf and the question of the maritime projection of the unclaimed sector will also be analysed in the context of the regime's area of application.

Just as in the case of the Exclusive Economic Zone, the discussion on the Antarctic continental shelf has points of similarity with the problem which arose on the same subject in Svalbard.[191] Norway, as the sovereign country of this archipelago, maintained its right of exclusive jurisdiction over the continental shelf but the Soviet Union argued that this maritime projection was subject to the regime of the 1920 Treaty even though this Treaty was restricted to the islands and the territorial sea.[192] Other countries have reserved their positions on this subject.[193] This also raises an important problem concerning the application of inter-temporal law.

It is particularly interesting to recall in this connection that the negotiations on the mineral resources regime have provided a framework within which it is possible to resolve the situation of the Antarctic continental shelf as another of the important maritime areas in this region. Without prejudice to the safeguarding of national positions on the matter, the Antarctic Treaty parties have agreed in these negotiations to extend the system of Antarctic co-operation to minerals in general and to this new maritime area in particular; by means of the arrangements devised for the minerals regime the parties to such arrangements will be able to exercise competences in regard to the Antarctic continental shelf, in the terms that will be examined in Part II.

4.7 The legal regime relating to ice and other aspects of the Law of the Sea

The problems relating to the application of the law of the sea in Antarctica are not confined to the question of maritime areas. The legal regime relating to ice was one of the subjects that early attracted the attention of the authors of international law when they raised the question as to whether ice should be assimilated to the land or to the sea. Although there has at times been speculative consideration of a distinction based on the chemical composition of the water, whereby only water having a salt content would be assimilated to the regime of the sea, most of the authors have favoured differentiating the legal regime on the basis of the stability of the ice in question.[194]

On this basis, for example, Lakhtine assimilated floating ice to the regime of the polar seas while he extended the regime of the polar territory to the permanent ice formations.[195] Smedal, on the other hand, maintained that although the Arctic ice could not be subject to sovereignty, other formations, such as the Ross barrier, could be assimilated to the land regime, even in the case of those parts which were floating, on the grounds that they rendered navigation impossible.[196] Mouton, in his turn, distinguished between ice formations which rested on the continental shelf, which should be assimilated to the land, and those supported by the water which, in principle, belonged to the regime of the high seas.[197] In a curious case that was raised by the establishment of a gambling casino on the Alaskan ice, beyond the limits of the territorial sea, one author concluded that if the ice in question was permanent it should follow the land regime and, if that were not the case, it should be subject to the regime of the territorial sea even if such ice formations extended beyond three miles.[198] Colombos, on the other hand, did not consider that a different limit should be established for the territorial sea on account of the existence of ice formations.[199]

The Antarctic Treaty did not provide a definitive answer to these different points of view since the situation under the Treaty of the ice formations is not entirely clear. It is true that Article VI refers to the area south of 60° south latitude 'including all ice shelves' but doubt has been cast on the meaning of these areas. At one extreme, Japan has interpreted this provision as referring to 'all the zones more or less permanently covered by ice, including the airspace above and the waters below such zones' in relation to which the rights of the high seas are preserved.[200] At the other extreme, the Chilean decree of 1940 includes within the limits of its claim the pack-ice, which would thus remain subject to national jurisdiction.[201] The United States has taken the view that ice shelves are those which are fixed[202] or which are thick portions of ice attached to the land;[203] Great Britain has also taken the view that features such as the Ross barrier should follow the land regime.[204] The practice of the system has made it possible to clarify this matter to some degree but without a conclusive outcome being reached. The Agreed Measures, like the Treaty, apply to 'all ice shelves'[205] but the context of the negotiation on the Agreed Measures seems to indicate that they do not include the pack-ice.[206] In spite of this, the way in which they have been applied in practice has extended their coverage for certain purposes to the pack-ice and to other marine features.[207] The Seal Convention seems to exclude the ice shelves from its field of application but certainly includes the pack-ice and certain other floating ice formations including some to the north of the Treaty area.[208]

If one were to derive a general rule within the Antarctic system, it might be said that the stable ice formations, such as the large barriers, tend to be assimilated to the land regime. Bernhardt concludes in this respect that 'there is no logical or compelling legal reason, including navigational freedom, why the shelf and sheet ice of Antarctica should not be assimilated to a land regime governing that continent'.[209] On the other hand, the unstable formations such as pack-ice tend to be assimilated to the regime of maritime areas.

In addition to the scientific interest of Antarctic ice,[210] it has acquired growing importance in the context of environmental conservation. A large part of the difficulties associated with exploration and exploitation of Antarctic mineral resources is due to the risk of pollution in ice zones, which are particularly vulnerable. Article 234 of the Law of the Sea Convention recognizes the special situation of ice-covered areas by entitling coastal States to adopt and enforce non-discriminatory laws and regulations for the prevention, reduction and control of marine pollution from vessels in such areas within the limits of the Exclusive Economic Zone.[211]

Furthermore, the ice is also of growing interest as a resource in that it represents the largest concentration and reserve of fresh water to be found anywhere in the world.[212] The question of the exploitation of icebergs has been seriously considered.[213] The legal problems associated with such exploitation raise once again questions concerning application of principles relating to the freedom of the high seas and to coastal State jurisdiction as well as the territorial status and the competences that can be exercised within the Antarctic system.[214] Even though the ice is a mineral resource, it has not been included in the negotiations on the minerals regime, a point which will be discussed further in Chapter 5.[215]

The stable ice formations are also relevant to the determination of the baselines for the delimitation of the territorial sea and other maritime areas. As early as 1926 the report of the Committee on British Policy in the Antarctic, a Committee established in connection with the Imperial Conference of that year, considered a memorandum on establishing the boundary of the territorial sea in ice zones which proposed an exception to the normal baselines 'in the case of ice barriers which are to all intents and purposes a permanent extension of the land proper'.[216] The 1930 Codification Conference of The Hague also envisaged such an exception with respect to 'coasts ordinarily or permanently icebound'.[217] Similarly, Van der Essen explains that these lines 'cannot be located anywhere but on the outward face of the ice shelves, which are the seaward prolongation of the Antarctic continent'.[218]

The law of the sea could also have relevance in Antarctica in the context of island and archipelago regimes since, as one author pointed out, the South Shetland, South Orkney and South Sandwich Islands have archipelagic characteristics.[219] However, it must be noted that no claimant State would qualify as an 'archipelagic State' in the light of Article 46 of the Law of the Sea Convention. In any event, the geographical feature of archipelagos is present in the Antarctic, including some regions of the Antarctic 'continent' which are in reality archipelagos, frequently below sea level, which are joined together by large ice sheets.[220] The peculiar situation of the ice islands which has been considered in relation to the Arctic might also be applicable to the Antarctic case.[221]

All these situations might have an influence on the maritime delimitation between States with opposite or adjacent coasts. On various occasions problems of territorial delimitation in Antarctica have been discussed, particularly in the early part of the century, as in the negotiations involving Chile and Argentina[222] or Great Britain and France.[223] The same might well happen in connection with maritime boundaries, a subject that is beginning to attract the attention of writers.[224]

The problems of overlapping maritime jurisdictions between the sub-

Antarctic islands of Kerguelen and Heard and McDonald have been the subject of an Agreement on Maritime Delimitation between Australia and France.[225] This Agreement follows the median line between the respective territories, being its southernmost point at 53° 14′ 07″, thus not entering the Antarctic Treaty area; further delimitation of the continental shelf shall be effected by agreement, for, as one author has commented 'it was decided that because of uncertainty as to the configuration of the continental shelf south-west of the agreed line, it was not appropriate to delimit this area at this stage'.[226] Since this Agreement refers also to the Australian fishing zone and to the French exclusive economic zone it has implications in connection with the Convention on the Conservation of Antarctic Marine Living Resources, the geographical area of which relates to the sub-Antarctic islands mentioned.

The 1984 maritime settlement between Chile and Argentina makes applicable to their claimed Antarctic territories the general provisions on peace, non use of force and settlement of disputes (Articles 1 to 6), but expressly provides that 'the remaining provisions in no way affect, or may be interpreted in a sense that may affect, directly or indirectly, the sovereignty, rights or legal positions of the Parties or delimitations in the Antarctic or in their adjacent maritime areas, including the soil and subsoil thereof'.[227] This safeguard clause is clearly intended to separate the case of the Antarctic territories from that of the sub-Antarctic regions involved in the agreed settlement.

In Chapter 1, attention was also drawn to the relationship between the Antarctic situation and other territorial and maritime problems such as the one affecting Argentina and Great Britain in the South Atlantic.

4.8   The joint maritime jurisdiction within the Antarctic system

The jurisdictional difficulties that have been considered in regard to the application of the law of the sea in Antarctica, just like the problems of general jurisdiction to which attention was drawn in Chapter 3, have led to proposals of various models for a solution related to the way in which the respective resources regimes are organized. Thus, for example, one author has suggested as basic choices the national model, open exploitation of resources, condominium, trusteeship or the common heritage of mankind.[228] Another author has argued that in respect of the continental margin, the choices lie among the national, co-operative or international approach.[229] On these questions there are no fundamental differences from the issues and solutions discussed in Chapter 3; further-more, many of the principles and approaches that we have considered in the context of that chapter will also be applicable by extension to the maritime areas examined above. The various proposals and models for a solution will be examined further in Chapter 7.

What is especially interesting to note is that the entire evolution of the law of the sea which has been described has been closely linked with the development of the respective resources regimes and is in fact inseparable from them. In this framework there has been clarification of the concepts inherent in each maritime area and their corresponding jurisdictional approaches and also the manner of applying them to the particular situation prevailing in this region. On the basis of this clarification some interesting conclusions can be reached.

The first stems from the explanation provided by Roberto Guyer in relation to international law in Antarctica:

> . . . the normal rules of international law . . . are difficult to apply in Antarctica. There exists, therefore, an inevitable confrontation between legal norms – which were conceived to be applied in normal circumstances – and the possibility of their full application in the Antarctic case.[230]

If this line of argument is applied to the law of the sea, it will be appreciated that various of its concepts have been considered in the Antarctic deliberations but its modalities and scope of application have necessarily been different. The territorial sea, the exclusive economic zone and the continental shelf are not unknown doctrines in Antarctica but they are applied in a setting which differs from the traditional framework within which these concepts have been applied, namely the framework provided by the Antarctic resources regimes.

Given the fact that the resources regimes necessarily involve to some extent the exercise of shared and internationally regulated and administered competences, a second conclusion emerges. Jurisdiction over the Antarctic maritime areas has developed in a collective manner whereby it tends to be exercised jointly by the Consultative Parties or other countries participating in the regimes acting either through the machinery of the Consultative Meetings or through that of the specific resources regimes as the case may be. On this point Van der Essen has explained that the process of application of the law of the sea in Antarctica has resulted in the exercise of joint jurisdiction over maritime areas,[231] and has reached the conclusion that 'it is possible to view the Consultative powers as in fact exercising a global jurisdiction over the continent and its marine prolongations'.[232]

As was explained in Chapter 3, however difficult the exercise of joint jurisdiction might be it has the advantage of providing a new approach for the accommodation of interests within the Antarctic Treaty system, an approach which so far has been reasonably successful.[233] Of course, following Brownlie's observation, the models based on joint jurisdiction will also entail a joint responsibility of the parties.[234] On the other hand, the possibility that the Treaty Parties could exercise 'collective jurisdiction' over maritime areas of the Antarctic has prompted the remark by one government that 'then there would be a need for negotiations on a global scale under United Nations auspices';[235] this remark is linked with the issues of the external accommodation that will be examined in Part III.

The result of this process is, on the one hand, that one should not overlook the application of the concepts of the Law of the Sea in Antarctica, which are, moreover, safeguarded by Article IV of the Treaty; and, on the other hand, that the exercise of coastal State jurisdiction has been reconciled with the necessities of joint co-operation, particularly in the context of the regimes that have been mentioned. In this connection it has been stated that:

> In the context of these special regimes, the Consultative Parties accept limitation on the powers that might belong to them individually, in favour of the joint exercise of jurisdiction for the same purposes.[236]

The criterion of harmonization explains how both the claimant and non-claimant countries have reached agreement on the acceptance of these joint regimes and have integrated their respective positions on the question of maritime jurisdiction within such regimes. This approach does not, admittedly, solve all of the problems but it has made a significant contribution to avoiding what might otherwise have been a conflictive situation. The principal problem remaining is that of residual rights since, here again, the position of the Parties will diverge. The claimant countries will maintain that everything that has not been included in the common regime comes under the jurisdiction of the coastal State whereas those that do not recognize claims will argue in favour of the application of the freedom of the high seas. This situation is no different from that of the negotiations on residual rights of the Exclusive Economic Zone in the Law of the Sea Conference, without any clear solution having been found to the problems raised.[237] In any case the policy of restraint has meant that the problem has not hitherto arisen in Antarctica.

The formula of joint jurisdiction also has other important dimensions. It provides a basis for satisfactorily dealing with the peculiar case of the unclaimed sector in relation to which, even though there is no applicable national jurisdiction, there is a form of jurisdictional approach stemming from the resources regimes.[238] On the other hand, this joint jurisdiction is exercised not only in regard to the Consultative Parties or parties participating in the respective regimes, but also, as we shall see later, in regard to third States to the extent that the pertinent Treaty arrangements might have constituted objective regimes or might overwise have implications for such States in the terms that will be examined in Chapter 9.

The jurisdictional approach followed in the Antarctic arrangements in questions of the application of the law of the sea to the various maritime areas examined has some points of similarity with the Common Fisheries Policy of the European Economic Community. Under the Common Fisheries Policy certain resources and the rights over them are taken out of the ambit of exclusive national legislative competence and jurisdiction and incorporated in a policy of common access for purposes of exploitation subject to Community regulations which determine how, and under what conditions, such exploitation is to occur and lay down a common policy for the conservation of such resources.[239] While enforcement jurisdiction remains exclusively within the competence of the EEC member States, the division of the legislative powers between the community organs and the member States has been a matter of great controversy in the past, at any rate until the *Van Dam* case was decided.[240]

In so far as fisheries are concerned, another interesting point of similarity between the Antarctic and the EEC policies is that neither is restricted to areas under national jurisdiction such as the territorial sea, fishing zone or Exclusive Economic Zone, but apply equally to areas of the high seas; in the case of the former, this applies to a specific geographical region determined by the Antarctic convergence and the ecosystem approach embodied in the Canberra Convention, while in the case of the latter a more functional principle applies extending the community competences to the community vessels fishing in the high seas on the basis of the authority of the *Kramer* case.[241]

Because the Common Fisheries Policy is applicable to the above mentioned vessels fishing in the high seas, it can also apply to activities of those vessels in areas of the high seas included within the ambit of application of the Canberra Convention. In this case there could be a situation of concurrent jurisdiction between the EEC and the jurisdictional arrangements developed in Antarctica in this matter. The fact that the EEC is a party to the Convention minimizes, of course, the risk of a potential conflict. It is interesting to speculate, however, on which would be the attitude of the EEC if the issue ever arises of whether a given activity in Antarctica has taken place in the high seas or in a zone claimed to be under the national jurisdiction of a member State. If in the high seas, the Common Fisheries Policy can apply to such activity; otherwise it cannot apply, for that policy does not include the French Southern and Antarctic territories nor the British Antarctic Territory. A further complicating factor is that among the EEC member States one can find countries that are claimants of both territory and maritime areas in Antarctica, such as France; non-claimant countries, like the Federal Republic of Germany; and countries that are third-States in relation to the Antarctic Treaty arrangements. It should also be noted that the French and British Antarctic territories are listed in Annex IV of the EEC Treaty for some limited community purposes. The problems related to the EEC competences in connection with minerals will be discussed in Chapter 8.

In spite of the existing similarities, there are, however, important differences between the EEC and Antarctic approaches under discussion. The first difference is, of course, that while the Antarctic Treaty system represents only a very limited process of institutionalization, the EEC is a very highly developed experience in this regard, thus having specific community powers and the institutions necessary for their exercise. But, above all, the differences stem from the fact that, in the EEC, the zones under national jurisdiction are not themselves under discussion or subject to challenge, whereas in Antarctica there are disagreements on this very fundamental matter.

Chapter 4 Notes

1. On the application of the Law of the Sea to Antarctica see generally Francisco Orrego Vicuña and María Teresa Infante: 'Le Droit de la Mer dans l'Antarctique', *R.G.D.I.P.*, 1980, 340–350. Alfred van der Essen: 'L'Antarctique et le Droit de la Mer', *Rev. Iran. Rel. Int.*, N° 5–6, 1975–1976, 89–98. Ibid: 'The application of the Law of the Sea to the Antarctic continent', in Francisco Orrego Vicuña (ed.): *Antarctic Resources Policy*, 1983, 231–242. Ibid: 'Les regions arctiques et antarctiques', in René-Jean Dupuy and Daniel Vignes (eds): *Traité du Nouveau Droit de la Mer*, 1985, 463–496. Gregory P. Wilson: 'Antarctica, the southern ocean, and the Law of the Sea', *The J.A.G. Journal*, Vol. 30, 1978, 47–85. Scharnhorst Muller: 'The impact of U.N.C.L.O.S. III on the Antarctic regime', comment, in Rudiger Wolfrum (ed.): *Antarctic Challenge*, 1984, 169–176. Juan Miguel Bákula: 'La Antártida y el Derecho del Mar', *Revista de la Academia Diplomática del Perú*, N° 23, January–December 1984, 85–103. Other works on the law of the sea are cited in this chapter in connection with specific subjects.
2. For the principles of international law related to maritime areas, see generally Ian Brownlie: *Principles of Public International Law*, Third edition, 1979, 183–257.
3. For a recent analysis of the evolution of the law of the sea see generally Daniel Bardonnet and Michel Virally: *Le nouveau droit international de la mer*, Pedone, 1983. R. R. Churchill and A. V. Lowe: *The Law of the Sea*, 1983. René-Jean Dupuy and Daniel Vignes (eds), op. cit., note 1 supra.

4. In the *North Sea Continental Shelf* cases, the International Court of Justice holds the view that some provisions of the 1958 Convention on the Continental Shelf reflect customary law; International Court of Justice, *Reports*, 1969, p. 39.

5. F. V. García-Amador: 'The origins of the concept of an Exclusive Economic Zone: Latin American practice and legislation', in Francisco Orrego Vicuña (ed.): *The Exclusive Economic Zone. A Latin American perspective*, 1983, 7–25.

6. For an overview of the work and changes in the law introduced by the Third United Nations Conference on the Law of the Sea, see Bo Johnson Theutenberg: *The Evolution of the Law of the Sea*, 1984. Bernard H. Oxman: 'La Troisieme Conference des Nations Unies sur le Droit de la Mer', in René-Jean Dupuy and Daniel Vignes (eds), op. cit., note 1 supra, 143–216. See also note 3 supra.

7. M. W. Holdgate: 'The Antarctic ecosystem', *Phil. Trans. R. Soc. Lond.*, B. Vol. 252, 1967, 363–383. George A. Llano: 'Ecology of the Southern Ocean Region', *Univ. Mia. L. Rev*, Vol. 33, 1978, 357–369. Bruce C. Parker (ed.): *Environmental impact in Antarctica*, 1978. R. M. Laws (ed.): *Antarctic Ecology*, 1984. Ibid.: 'The Ecology of the Southern Ocean', *American Scientist*, January–February 1985, 26–40. W. N. Bonner: 'Conservation and the Antarctic', in R. M. Laws (ed.), op. cit., 821–850. George Deacon: *The Antarctic circumpolar ocean*, 1984. James N. Barnes, Thomas C. Jackson, Bruce Rich: 'An introduction to Southern Ocean Conservation issues', *The Oceanic Society*, 1980. James N. Barnes: 'Environmental protection and the future of the Antarctic: new approaches and perspectives are necessary', in Gillian Triggs (ed.): *The Antarctic Treaty Regime*, 1987, 150–158.

8. George A. Knox: 'The living resources of the Southern Ocean: a scientific overview', in Francisco Orrego Vicuña (ed.), op. cit., note 1 supra, 21–60. Dietrich Sahrhage: 'Present knowledge of living marine resources in the Antarctic, possibilities for their exploitation and scientific perspectives', in Rudiger Wolfrum (ed.), op. cit., note 1 supra, 67–88. Ibid.: 'Fisheries overview', in Lewis M. Alexander and Lynne Carter Hanson (eds): *Antarctic Politics and Marine Resources: critical choices for the 1980's*, 1985, 101–112. See further Section 4.5 of this chapter and the literature referred to therein.

9. Tore Gjelsvik: 'The mineral resources of Antarctica: progress in their identification', in Francisco Orrego Vicuña (ed.): op. cit., note 1 supra, 61–76, at 63. See further Chapter 5 infra.

10. Francisco Orrego Vicuña and María Teresa Infante, loc. cit., note 1 supra, at 340–341.

11. In the *Island of Palmas* case, Judge Huber stated the doctrine of inter-temporal law in the following terms:

> As regards the question which of different legal systems prevailing at successive periods is to be applied in a particular case (the so-called inter-temporal law), a distinction must be made between the creation of rights and the existence of rights. The same principle which subjects the act creative of a right to the law in force at the time the right arises, demands that the existence of the right, in other words its continued manifestation, shall follow the conditions required by the evolution of law;

Award of 4th April 1928, United Nations, *R.I.A.A.*, Vol. II, 829–871, at 845. On the doctrine of Inter-Temporal Law, see generally Brownlie, op. cit., note 2 supra, at 131–133, Philip C. Jessup: 'The Palmas Island Arbitration', *A.J.I.L.*, Vol. 22, 1928, 735–752; Wolfang Friedmann: *The Changing Structure of International Law*, 1964, 130–131.

12. Van der Essen, loc. cit. (1975–1976), note 1 supra, at 94.

13. Christopher C. Joyner: 'Antarctica and the Law of the Sea: rethinking the current legal dilemmas', *San. D.L.R.*, Vol. 18, 1980–1981, 415–442, at 436–437.
14. Ibid.: 'Antarctica and the Law of the Sea: an introductory overview', *Ocean Dev. I.L.*, Vol. 13, 1983–1984, 277–289, at 279.
15. On the question of maritime jurisdiction of the unclaimed sector, Francisco Orrego Vicuña: 'The application of the law of the sea and the Exclusive Economic Zone to the Antarctic continent', in Francisco Orrego Vicuña (ed.), op. cit., note 1 supra, 243–251, at 249.
16. On the need of rational management and conservation of the Antarctic ecosystem, George A. Knox: 'The Southern Ocean: an ecosystem under threat', *N.Z.I.R.*, Vol. VII, N° 3, May–June 1982, 15–18. See also John A. Gulland: 'The Antarctic Treaty System as a resource management mechanism – Living Resources' in U.S. Polar Research Board: *Workshop on the Antarctic Treaty System, An Assessment*, 1986, 221–234.
17. The legal relationship of the Antarctic Treaty system with third countries will be examined in Chapter 9 infra.
18. Van der Essen, loc. cit. (1983), note 1 supra, at 242. The expression 'global' jurisdiction is used by this author in the sense of 'joint' jurisdiction by the Consultative Parties. On the concept of joint jurisdiction in Antarctica see also Chapter 3 supra, section 3.5.
19. Alfred van der Essen, loc. cit. (1975–1976), note 1 supra, at 90–91.
20. Alfred van der Essen, loc. cit. (1983), note 1 supra, at 232.
21. Alfred van der Essen, loc. cit. (1975–1976), note 1 supra, at 91.
22. Francisco Orrego Vicuña and María Teresa Infante, loc. cit., note 1 supra, at 349.
23. Rainer Lagoni: 'Antarctica: German activities and problems of jurisdiction', *G.Y.I.L.*, Vol. 23, 1980, 392–400, at 399–400.
24. Ibid., at 398.
25. Ibid., at 399. See also note 4 supra.
26. Ibid., at 398.
27. Ibid., at 399–400.
28. The pertinent paragraphs of the award of 4 April 1928 on the *Island of Palmas* case are transcribed in note 11 supra. See also the text associated to that note.
29. Jessup,. loc. cit., note 11 supra, at 739–740. For other critical views and comments see also the opinions of Brownlie and Friedmann referred to in note 11 supra.
30. On the state of national legislation and other material, see generally F.A.O.: *Coastal State requirements for foreign fishing*, Vol. 1, Legislative study N° 21, Rev. 1, 1983. On the EEZ and customary international law, see generally René-Jean Dupuy: 'Politiques nationales et systeme juridique issu de la Troisieme Conference', Societé Française pour le Droit International: *Le Droit de la Mer apres la Troisieme Conference des Nations Unies*, 2–4 June 1983, at 7–15. See also Francisco Orrego Vicuña: *The Law of the Sea experience and the corpus of international law: effects and interrelationships*, in Robert B. Krueger and Stefan A. Riesenfeld: *The Developing Order of the Oceans*, 1985, 5–22. See also Continental Shelf (Libyan Arab Jamahiriya/Malta), Judgement ICJ Reports, 1985, p. 13, par. 33.
31. For a comment on the Chilean legislation in this regard, see Francisco Orrego Vicuña, loc. cit., note 15 supra, at 244–245.
32. See generally Reynaldo Galindo Pohl: 'The Exclusive Economic Zone in the light of negotiations of the Third United Nations Conference on the Law of the Sea', in Francisco Orrego Vicuña, op. cit., note 5 supra, 31–59.
33. Van der Essen, loc. cit. (1983), note 1 supra, at 233.
34. Ibid., at 233.
35. See note 13 supra and associated text.

36. Van der Essen, loc. cit. (1983), note 1 supra, at 233.
37. Ibid., at 233.
38. Ibid., at 233–234. The point of view that demilitarization of the Antarctic continent could not apply to the high seas if this interferes with the freedom of the high seas has also been held; similarly it has also been argued that denuclearization would apply only to the continent, ports, coastal waters and other related areas but not to the high seas; see B. Vukas: 'L'utilisation pacifique de la mer, denuclearisation et desarmament', in Dupuy and Vignes, op. cit., note 1 supra, 1047–1093, at 1079, 1088.
39. For tables of claims to the Territorial Sea, Exclusive Fishing Zones, continental shelf and other exclusive zones, see Lay, Churchill and Nordquist: *New Directions in the Law of the Sea*, Documents, Vol. II, 1973, 833–874; ibid., Vol. VI, 1977, 843–880; FAO, Doc. cit., note 30 supra, 25–30.
40. For tables of ratification of the major multilateral conventions on the law of the sea, see Lay, Churchill and Nordquist, op. cit., note 39 supra, Vol. II, 799–832.
41. F. V. García-Amador: *America Latina y el Derecho del Mar*, 1976, 48–54.
42. E. D. Brown: 'Maritime zones: a survey of claims', in Churchill Simmonds and Welch: *New Directions in the Law of the Sea*, Collected Papers, Vol. III, 157–192.
43. For a study on the current legislation on maritime zones, with particular reference to fishing requirements, see FAO, Doc. cit., note 30 supra. See also Hugo Caminos: 'El régimen de pesca y conservación de los recursos vivos en la Zona Económica Exclusiva: implicaciones jurídicas y económicas', in United Nations Economic Commission for Latin America and Institute of International Studies of the University of Chile: *Economía de los Océanos*, Vol. I, 1978, at 108–120.
44. García-Amador, loc. cit., note 5 supra, at 18–24.
45. See generally Lucius Caflisch: 'Les zones maritimes sous jurisdiction nationale, leurs limites et leur delimitation', in Daniel Bardonnet et Michel Virally, op. cit., note 3 supra, 81–104.
46. The following Consultative Parties have ratified the Convention on the Territorial Sea and the Contiguous Zone: Australia, Belgium, Japan, South Africa, USSR, United Kingdom and the United States. Argentina, New Zealand and Uruguay are signatories of this Convention. See note 40 supra.
47. The Convention on the High Seas has been ratified by the following Consultative Parties: Australia, Belgium, Federal Republic of Germany, Japan, Poland, South Africa, U.S.S.R., United Kingdom and the United States. Argentina, France, New Zealand and Uruguay are signatories of Convention. See note 40 supra.
48. The Convention on Fishing and Conservation of the living resources of the high seas has been ratified by the following Consultative Parties: Australia, Belgium, France, South Africa, United Kingdom and the United States. It has been signed by Argentina, New Zealand and Uruguay. See note 40 supra.
49. The Continental Shelf Convention has been ratified by the following Consultative Parties: Australia, France, New Zealand, Norway, Poland, South Africa, U.S.S.R., United Kingdom and the United States. Argentina, Chile, the Federal Republic of Germany and Uruguay are signatories of the Convention. See note 40 supra.
50. The optional protocol on the settlement of disputes has been ratified by the following Consultative Parties: Australia, Belgium, France, Federal Republic of Germany, New Zealand, the United Kingdom and Uruguay. It was signed by the United States. See note 40 supra.
51. Constantine A. Stavropoulos: 'The third conference on the Law of the Sea in a historical perspective', in C. L. Rozakis and C. A. Stephanou (eds): *The New Law of the Sea*, 1983, 11–20. See also notes 3 and 6 supra.

52. Jean Monnier: 'La troisième Confèrence des Nations Unies sur le droit de la mer', *Ann. Suisse D.I.*, 1983, 9–38.

53. United Nations Convention on the Law of the Sea, UN Doc. A/Conf. 62/122, 7 October 1982, opened for signature on 10 December 1982.

54. Dupuy, loc. cit., note 30 supra, at 28–37.

55. The Convention on the Law of the Sea was signed by 159 States and territories, for which see generally United Nations: *Multilateral Treaties deposited with the Secretary General, Status as at 31 December 1984*, 1985, 671–672. See also Dupuy and Vignes, op. cit., note 1 supra, 1397–1400; and M. J. Bowmann and D. J. Harris: *Multilateral Treaties: index and current status*, 1984, and Supplement 1984, at 476 and 46 respectively. For additional information on the status of the Convention, see Jean-Pierre Levy: *La Conférence des Nations Unies sur le Droit de la Mer*, 1983, particularly at 140–142; Kenneth R. Simmonds: *U.N. Convention on the Law of the Sea 1982*, 1983, at XXVI-XXX.

56. The 1982 Convention on the Law of the Sea has been signed by the following Consultative Parties to the Antarctic Treaty: Argentina, Australia, Belgium, Brazil, Chile, China, France, India, Japan, New Zealand, Norway, Poland, Uruguay and the USSR. See the sources cit. in note 55 supra.

57. See generally International Maritime Organization: *Status of multilateral Conventions and instruments in respect of which the International Maritime Organization or its Secretary-General performs depositary or other functions*, as at 31 December 1984, Doc. Misc. (85) 1. UN General Assembly Resolution 40/156A of 16 December 1985 requested the Secretary-General to report, *inter alia*, about the significance of the 1982 Law of the Sea Convention in the southern ocean; the ensuing report is contained in UN Doc. A/41/722, of 7 November 1986.

58. Van der Essen, loc. cit. (1975–1976), note 1 supra, at 91. Translation by the author of this book.

59. The text of Recommendation I-VI is reproduced in W. M. Bush: *Antarctica and International Law*, Vol. 1, at 122–123. For the role of recommendations in the Antarctic Treaty System, see Chapter 2 supra, Sections 2.2, 2.5.

60. Van der Essen, loc. cit. (1975–1976), note 1 supra, at 92.

61. Text of Recommendation VI-13 in Bush, op. cit., note 59 supra, at 242–243.

62. See the statement by Argentina, Australia, Belgium and the United Kingdom that 'references to areas situated outside the Treaty area do not affect any rights or claims which Consultative Parties may have in such areas', in *Report and Recommendations of the Sixth Consultative Meeting*, Tokyo, 19–31 October 1970, par. 12; text in Bush, op. cit., note 59 supra, at 227.

63. On conservation in the Antarctic see generally David Anderson: 'The Conservation of Wildlife under the Antarctic Treaty', *Pol. Rec.*, Vol. 14, N° 88, 1968, 25–32. Tore Gjelsvik: 'The work of SCAR for conservation of nature in the Antarctic', in Francisco Orrego Vicuña (ed.): *El Desarrollo de la Antártica*, 1977, 328–334. See also American Geographical Society: *Antarctic Mammals*, Antarctic Map Folio Series, Folio 18, 1974. See also the works cited in note 7 supra; and Chapter 2, note 15, supra.

64. Text of Recommendation I-VIII in Bush, op. cit., note 59 supra, at 124–125.

65. Agreed Measures for the Conservation of Antarctic Fauna and Flora, Recommendation III-VIII, in *Handbook of Measures 1983*, 2101–2121.

66. See Chapter 2 above, Section 2.6.

67. Bush, op. cit., note 59 supra, at 147.

68. Van der Essen, loc. cit. (1975–1976), note 1 supra, at 93.

69. Bush, op. cit., note 59 supra, at 147.

70. Ibid., at 161–162. On the jurisdictional aspects of these laws, see Chapter 3 supra, Section 3.4.

71. Orrego and Infante, loc. cit., note 1 supra, at 343–344. On the distinction between coastal waters and the high seas in Antarctica, see also Vukas, loc. cit., note 38 supra, at 1079.
72. Van der Essen, loc. cit. (1975–1976), note 1 supra, at 92.
73. Van der Essen, loc. cit. (1983), note 1 supra, at 236.
74. Chile, Decree N° 1747 of 6 November 1940 declaring the limits of the Chilean Antarctic territory; text in Bush, op. cit., note 59 supra, Vol. II, at 311.
75. France, Law N° 71-1060 of 24 December 1971 on the delimitation of French territorial waters, in UN Legislative Series: *National Legislation and treaties relating to the Law of the Sea*, ST/Leg./Ser. B/18, 1976, at 17.
76. France, Decree N° 711 of 25 August 1971; text in Bush, op. cit., note 59 supra, Vol. II, at 576–577.
77. Bush, op. cit., note 59 supra, Vol. II, at 577.
78. France, Order N° 5 of 13 January 1972; text in Bush, op. cit., note 59 supra, Vol. II, at 579.
79. Ralph R. Harry: 'The Antarctic Regime and the Law of the Sea Convention: an Australian view', *Virg. J.I.L.*, Vol. 21, 1981, 727–744, at 730.
80. See generally the studies cited in note 1 supra, and particularly Wilson, loc. cit., note 1 supra, at 66–68.
81. On these cases see generally Chapter 3 supra, Section 3.3, and citations in Chapter 3, notes 154, 156 and 159, supra.
82. For a summary of legislation on the implementation of Article VII (3) of the Agreed Measures and other provisions on marine pollution, see Bush, op. cit., note 59 supra, at 378–379.
83. See note 57 supra and Chapter 6 infra.
84. F. M. Auburn: *Antarctic Law and Politics*, 1982, at 132–133, 271.
85. Recommendation IV-13 on the establishment of Moe Island as a Specially Protected Area; text in Bush, op. cit., note 59 supra, at 184–185.
86. Auburn, op. cit., note 84 supra, at 131.
87. Recommendation III-XI, *Handbook 1983*, at 2401.
88. See Recommendation IV-21, IV-22 and V-7, *Handbook 1983*, at 2402–2404.
89. Bush, op. cit., note 59 supra, at 147.
90. Final report of the Sixth Antarctic Treaty Consultative Meeting, Tokyo, 19–31 October 1970, par. 10; text in Bush, op. cit., note 59 supra, at 227.
91. Van der Essen, loc. cit. (1983), note 1 supra, at 237.
92. Anthony Kershaw: Speech of welcome on the occasion of the opening of the Conference on the Conservation of Antarctic Seals, 3 February 1972, U.K. Foreign and Commonwealth Office: *Report of the Conference on the Conservation of Antarctic Seals*, London, 3–11 February 1972, at 5–6.
93. Report on the Seventh Antarctic Treaty Consultative Meeting, Wellington, 30 October–10 November 1972, par. 29; text in Bush, op. cit., note 59 supra, at 269.
94. See generally Evelyn Peyroux: 'Les reglementations internationales de protection des phoques', *R.G.D.I.P.*, 1976, 104–129. See also US Department of State: *Environmental impact statement on the Convention for the Conservation of Antarctic Seals*, August 8, 1974.
95. Bush, op. cit., note 59 supra, at 249.
96. See Article 5 (7) of the Seals Convention; also Bush, op. cit., note 59 supra, at 249.
97. Van der Essen, loc. cit. (1975–1976), note 1 supra, at 94.
98. On this question see generally Bush, op. cit., note 59 supra, at 66–70.
99. Ibid., at 67–68.
100. See Article 2 (1) of the Seal Convention and the comments thereon of Bush, op. cit., note 59 supra, at 250.
101. See Article 2 (2) of the Seal Convention.

102. In the opinion of the American delegation to the Conference of 1972 a US proposal for an international observer system was defeated, not by fear of interference with commercial interest 'but rather from States that feared the effect on their territorial or maritime positions'; Report of the US delegation to the Conference, Statement cit., note 94 supra, Appendix I, at 54. See also the US statement of February 11, 1972, *I.L.M.*, Vol. XI, 1972, at 417.
103. See Article XXIV of the Convention on the conservation of Antarctic marine living resources.
104. See Article IX of the International Convention for the regulation of Whaling of 2 December 1946 and the Schedule to the Convention as amended to June 1984, par. 21 (a), (b), (c). For comments on the matter, see Simon Lyster: *International Wildlife Law*, 1985, at 31–32; and generally James E. Scarff: 'The international management of whales, dolphins, and porpoises: an interdisciplinary assessment', *Ecology Law Quarterly*, Vol. 6, 1977, 326–427 (Part I), 574–638 (Part II). See also Cynthia E. Carlson: 'The international regulation of small cetaceans', *S.D.L.R.*, Vol. 21, 1984, 577–623, and Patricia Birnie: *International Regulation of Whaling*, 1985.
105. Bush, op. cit., note 59 supra, at 250.
106. Report of the Fifth Antarctic Treaty Consultative Meeting, Paris, 18–29 November 1968, par. 02; text in Bush, op. cit., note 59 supra, at 200.
107. While the official text of the Report refers to Article VI, a typing error should not be entirely excluded; in such case the reference could have been to Article IV of the Treaty. This kind of error is frequent in the literature on the subject; see, for example, Bush, op. cit., note 59 supra, at 201, note 9.
108. See the Argentine declaration of 7 March 1978 reproduced in Bush, op. cit., note 59 supra, at 259–260.
109. See the Argentine statement in FAO, Committee on Fisheries, 11th session, 19–26 April 1977, Item 4 (b): Review of the State of Exploitation of the World Fish Resources: Living Resources of the Southern Ocean, *Verbatim of Discussion* (21–22 April); a diplomatic note of January 1976 to the UNDP and of May 1976 to FAO is quoted in this statement, at 6–7.
110. Chilean statement of February 11, 1972, *I.L.M.*, Vol. XI, 1972, at 417; also reproduced in Bush, op. cit., note 59 supra, at 261. And Chilean Decree N° 191 of 21 February 1980, *Diario Oficial*, 24 April 1980. On these reservations see also Chile, 'Informe de la Dirección Jurídica del Ministerio de Relaciones Exteriores sobre la Convención para la Conservación de las Focas Antárticas', N° 157, 11 November 1978, *Memoria del Ministerio de Relaciones Exteriores*, 1978, 394–395.
111. Chilean declaration of 7 February 1980, reproduced in Bush, op. cit., note 59 supra, at 261.
112. Note of the Soviet Embassy in London to the Foreign and Commonwealth Office, dated 18 July 1978; reproduced in Bush, op. cit., note 59 supra, at 260.
113. See the comments on the scope of the US Marine Mammals Protection Act of 1972 in Bush, op. cit., note 59 supra, at 259.
114. On the question of Antarctic living resources, see generally the following technical and scientific works: American Geographical Society: *Circumpolar characteristics of Antarctic Waters*, Antarctic Map Folio Series, Folio 13, 1970. American Geographical Society: *Coastal and Deep Water Benthic Fishes of the Antarctic*, Antarctic Map Folio Series, Folio 15, 1971. Dayton L. Alverson: 'Tug-of-war for the Antarctic krill', *Ocean Dev. I.L.*, Vol. 8, 1980, 171–182. John L. Bengtson: 'Review of information regarding the Conservation of Living Resources of the Antarctic Marine Ecosystem', *Final Report to the U.S. Marine Mammal Commission*, July 1978, reproduced in US Senate: *Antarctic Living*

Marine Resources Negotiations, Hearing 1978, 87–234. Harm J. de Blij: 'A regional geography of Antarctica and the Southern Ocean', *Univ. Mia L. Rev*, Vol. 33, December 1978, 299–314. Roberto Cabezas Bello: 'El desarrollo de la explotación del krill antártico', in Francisco Orrego Vicuña (ed.): *El Dessarrollo de la Antártica*, 1977, 169–181. G. L. Kesteven: 'The Southern Ocean', *Ocean yearbook*, 1, 1978, 467–499. George Knox: 'Antarctic resources: implications for the Antarctic Treaty and New Zealand', *N.Z.I.R.*, July–August 1976, 18–22. James McElroy: 'Krill – still an enigma', *Marine Policy*, Vol. 6, N° 3, July 1982, reprinted in International Institute for Environment and Development: *Antarctica, a continent in transition*, 1983. Tetra Tech: *The Antarctic krill resource: prospects for commercial exploitation*, Final Report, February 1978, reproduced in U.S. Senate: *Antarctic Living Marine Resources Negotiations*, Hearing 1978, 237–379. R. B. Thomson: 'The development of living resources of Antarctic: krill', in Francisco Orrego Vicuña, op. cit. 182–185. World Wildlife Fund News: *The Question of krill*, N° 24, July–August 1983, reprinted in International Institute for Environment and Development: *Antarctica, a continent in transition*, 1983. Lee Kimball: 'La carrera por la pesca antártica está en marcha', in C. J. Moneta et al.: *Geopolítica y política del poder en el atlántico sur*, 1983, 195–223. Graham Chittleborough: 'Nature, extent and management of Antarctic living resources', in Stuart Harris (ed.): *Australia's Antarctic Policy Options*, 1984, 135–163. James K. McElroy: 'Antarctic fisheries. History and prospects', *Marine Policy*, Vol. 8, 1984, 239–258. Vladimir Kaczynski: 'Distant water fisheries and the 200 mile Economic Zone', Law of the Sea Institute, Occasional Paper N° 34, 1984. Vladimir M. Kaczynski: 'Economic aspects of Antarctic fisheries', in Lewis M. Alexander and Lynne Carter Hanson, op. cit., note 8 supra, 141–158. Roberto Cabezas Bello: 'Alternatives de política para la utilización de los recursos vivos marinos antárticos', in Francisco Orrego Vicuña et al.: *Política Antártica de Chile*, 1985, 237–248. See also note 8 supra.

115. Bush, op. cit., note 59 supra, at 401.
116. For a comment to the effect that the Convention applies not so much to a geographical area as to the resources of such area, see David M. Edwards and John A. Heap: 'Convention on the Conservation of Antarctic Marine Living Resources: a commentary', *Pol. Rec.*, Vol. 20, 1981, 353–362, at 354–355.
117. See generally on the interest in Antarctic krill William Y. Brown: 'The Conservation of Antarctic Marine Living Resources', *Environmental Conservation*, Vol. 10, N° 3, Autumn 1983, 187–196. O. G. Savin: 'Marine living resources of the Antarctic regions: experience with conventional regulation of conservation and use', *Sov. Y.B.I.L.*, 1981, 187–200. Finn Sollie: 'Trends and prospects for regimes for living and mineral resources in the Antarctic', in John King Gamble Jr: *Law of the Sea: Neglected issues*, 1979, 193–208. R. Tucker Scully: 'The Marine Living Resources of the Southern Ocean', *Univ. Mia. L. Rev.*, Vol. 33, 1978, 341–356. See also note 114 supra. On questions of jurisdiction, with particular reference to maritime areas, see Gillian Triggs: 'The Antarctic Treaty system: some jurisdictional problems', in ibid. (ed.): *The Antarctic Treaty Regime*, 1987, 88–109. Ibid.: 'The Antarctic Treaty Regime: a workable compromise or a "Purgatory of Ambiguity"?', *Case W.R.J.I.L.*, Vol. 17, 1985, 195–228.
118. Josyane Couratier: 'The regime for the conservation of Antarctica's living resources', in Francisco Orrego Vicuña, op. cit., note 1 supra, 139–148. Fernando Zegers: 'The Canberra Convention: objectives and political aspects of its negotiation', in Ibid., at 149–156.
119. See note 74 supra.

120. For a summary of the Chilean legislation on maritime zones, see Bush, op. cit., note 59 supra, Vol. II, at 448–450.
121. Orrego, loc. cit., note 15 supra, at 245.
122. See note 120 supra. See also the special legislation on economic incentives for activities undertaken south of the Strait of Magellan, including activities related to the utilization of ocean resources, cited in Chapter 3 supra, note 144. The first concessions granted by Chile in relation to sub-Antarctic and Antarctic areas were also related to the exploitation of ocean resources, for which see Pedro Romero Julio: *Síntesis de la historia antártica de Chile*, Instituto de Investigaciones del Patrimonio Territorial de Chile, Universidad de Santiago, 1985.
123. Bush, op. cit., note 59 supra, Vol. II, at 450. See also Chile: 'Informe de la Dirección Jurídica del Ministerio de Relaciones Exteriores sobre Ratificación de la Convención Internacional sobre la caza de la Ballena', N° 136, 18 October 1978, *Memoria del Ministerio de Relaciones Exteriores*, 1978, 388–391.
124. Bush, op. cit., note 59 supra, Vol. II, at 71.
125. France, Decree N° 78-144 of 3 February 1978, reproduced in Bush, op. cit., note 59 supra, Vol. II, at 586–588.
126. Australia, Proclamation by H.E. the Governor-General of the Commonwealth of Australia of 20 September 1979, reproduced in Bush, op. cit., note 59 supra, Vol. II, at 202–203.
127. Australia, Parliamentary statement concerning the establishment and extent of the Australian fishing zone, 25 September 1979, reproduced in Bush, op. cit., note 59 supra, Vol. II, at 203–205, at 204.
128. Australia, Proclamation declaring waters around the Australian Antarctic Territory to be excepted waters under the Fisheries Act 1952, 31 October 1979, reproduced in Bush, op. cit., note 59 supra, Vol. II, at 208–209.
129. Bush, op. cit., note 59 supra, Vol. II, at 209.
130. Ibid., Vol. I, at 53.
131. Bush comments in this regard that 'most claimant states have not extended their fisheries legislation to their claims on the Antarctic continent or to islands south of 60° S'; op. cit., note 59 supra, at 430. The British Fishery Limits Act 1976 applies to the United Kingdom, Channel Islands and the Isle of Man, Section 1 (1); text in Churchill, Nordquist and Lay: *New Directions in the Law of the Sea*, Vol. V, 1977, 123–140. The New Zealand Territorial Sea and Exclusive Economic Zone Act 1977 applies generally to New Zealand Territory, but its application to the Ross Dependency requires a declaration by Order in Council of the Governor-General, which can include 'such modifications and exceptions (if any) as he may specify in the order', Section 9 (3); text in United Nations Legislative Series: *National legislation and treaties relating to the Law of the Sea*, ST/LEG/Ser. B/ 19, 1980, 65–85. The Norwegian Law N° 91 of December 17, 1976, relating to the Economic Zone is subject to a determination by the King as to the waters to which it shall apply, Article 1; by Royal Decree of the same date the Economic Zone was established in the 'waters off the Norwegian mainland'; texts in Churchill, Nordquist and Lay, op. cit., 337–341.
132. See the New Zealand Territorial and Exclusive Economic Zone Act 1977 as cited in note 131 supra; see the pertinent comment in *New Zealand and Antarctica*, May 1983, at 46; and see also the comment by Bush, op. cit., note 59 supra, at 62.
133. See the Fisheries Agreement between New Zealand and the Republic of Korea of 16 March 1978, New Zealand Treaty Series 1978, N° 4, Article VI (1) (b); Agreement on Fisheries between New Zealand and the USSR of 4 April 1978, New Zealand Treaty Series 1978, N° 5, Article IX (1) (c); and between New

Zealand and Japan of 1 September 1978, New Zealand Treaty-Series 1978, N° 12, Article VII (2).

134. See also V. Ptitsyn: 'The legal regime in Antarctic waters and questions regarding the exploitation of marine resources', *Morskoy Flot*, 1965, N° 3, 17–18, translation from Russian.

135. Statement by R. Tucker Scully, in U.S. Senate: *Antarctic Living Marine Resources Negotiations*, Hearing of June 14, 1978, at 7.

136. Ibid., at 7. The text should read 'claimants and non claimants' in the line marked (*sic*). In the congressional hearing on Antarctic Fauna and Flora Conservation it was also stated that the Antarctic Treaty parties could extend a 200 mile zone around the continental mass of Antarctica for the purpose of protection of resources without touching on the question of sovereignty, what probably would require additional treaty action; see U.S. House of Representatives, Committee on Merchant Marine and Fisheries, Subcommittee on Fisheries and Wildlife Conservation and the Environment, Hearing on H.R. 7749, 95th Congress, 1st session, 1977, 245–369, at 291–292; this approach is similar to the proposals examined on joint jurisdiction.

137. Statement by James N. Barnes, in Hearing, op. cit., note 135 supra, at 37. The expression marked (*sic*) refers to asserted territorial claims.

138. See generally Joan E. Moore: 'The Polar regions and the law of the sea', *Case W.R.J.I.L.*, Vol. 8, 1976, 204–219. This author argues the case of a 'common heritage of all' for both the Arctic and the Antarctic, particularly at 215–219.

139. Barbara Mitchell and Richard Sandbrook: *The Management of the Southern Ocean*, 1980, at 19.

140. Joyner, loc. cit., note 14 supra, at 279.

141. Christopher C. Joyner: 'The Exclusive Economic Zone and Antarctica, *Virg. J.I.L.*, Vol. 21, 1981, 691–725, at 725.

142. Conference on the Conservation of Antarctic Marine Living Resources, Final Act and text of the Convention, Canberra, 7–20 May 1980, *I.L.M.*, Vol. XIX, 1980, 837–859.

143. On scientific aspects of the Convention, see D. L. Powell: 'Scientific and economic considerations relating to the conservation of marine living resources in Antarctica', in Orrego, op. cit., note 1 supra, 111–118. Takese Nagata: 'The Implementation of the Convention on the Conservation of Antarctic Marine Living Resources: needs and problems', in Orrego, op. cit., note 1 supra, 119–137. James Barnes: *Let's Save Antarctica!*, 1982. International Union for the Conservation of Nature: *Background statement and action plan for Antarctica and the Southern Ocean*, 1981. US Senate, Committee on Foreign Relations, Subcommittee on Arms Control, Oceans, and international environment: *Hearing on Exploitation of Antarctic Resources*, 95th Congress, 2nd Session, 1978. US Department of State: *Final Environmental Impact Statement on the Negotiation of a Regime for Conservation of Antarctic Marine Living Resources*, June 1978, in US Senate: *Antarctic Living Marine Resources Negotiations*, Hearing 1978, 45–76. George A. Knox: 'The key role of krill in the ecosystem of the Southern Ocean with special reference to the Convention on the Conservation of Antarctic Marine Living Resources', *Ocean Management*, Vol. 9, 1984, 113–156. William Y. Brown and Bruce S. Manheim: 'Conservation of Antarctic Marine Living Resources: the environmental perspective', in Lewis M. Alexander and Lynne Carter Hanson, op. cit., note 8 supra, 123–129. See also the works cited in notes 8 and 114 supra.

144. For background and analysis of the Convention see Daniel Vignes: 'La Convention sur la Conservation de la faune et de la flore marines de

l'Antarctique', *An. Fr. D.I.*, 1980, 741–772. James N. Barnes: 'The emerging
Antarctic living resources convention', *Proc. A.S.I.L.*, 1979, 272–292. Richard
B. Bilder et al.: 'Development of Antarctica', *Proc. A.S.I.L.*, 1979, 264–294.
Jeffrey E. Stone: 'Convention on the Conservation of Antarctic Marine Living
Resources', *Har. I.L.J.*, Vol. 22, 1981, 195–200. International Legal Notes:
'Convention on the Conservation of Antarctic Marine Living Resources, signed
at Canberra, 20th May, 1980', *Austr. L.J.*, Vol. 54, 1980, 432–434. International
Legal Notes: 'Preparatory meeting at Hobart, 10–24 September, 1981, to give
effect to the Convention of 1980 on the Conservation of Antarctic Marine Living
Resources', *Austr. L.J.*, Vol. 56, 1982, 49–50. N. D. Bankes: 'Environmental
protection in Antarctica: a comment on the Convention on the Conservation of
Antarctic Marine Living Resources', *Can. Y.B.I.L.*, Vol. 19, 1981, 303–319.
James N. Barnes: 'The Emerging Convention on the Conservation of Antarctic
Marine Living Resources: an attempt to meet the new realities of resource
exploitation in the Southern Ocean', in Jonathan I. Charney (ed.): *The new
nationalism and the use of common spaces*, 1982, 239–286. Ronald F. Frank: 'The
Convention on the Conservation of Antarctic Marine Living Resources', *Ocean
Dev. I.L.*, Vol. 13, 1983–1984, 291–345. Rainer Lagoni: 'Convention on the
Conservation of Marine Living Resources: A model for the use of a common
good?', in Rudiger Wolfrum, op. cit., note 1 supra, 93–108. Robert J. Hofman:
'The Convention on the Conservation of Antarctic Marine Living Resources', in
Lewis M. Alexander and Lynne Carter Hanson, op. cit., note 8 supra, 113–122.
See also the works cited in notes 116, 118 and 139 supra. On the process of
implementation of the Convention in the US see US House of Representatives,
Committee on Merchant Marine and Fisheries, Subcommittee on Fisheries and
wildlife conservation and the environment: Hearing on *Antarctic Marine Living
Resources* (H.R. 3416), June 30, 1983; see particularly the statements by Scully,
who holds the view of CCAMLR as a self-executing instrument, and Barnes, at
30 and 102 respectively. See also William H. MacKenzie and Rebecca S. Routes:
'Implementation of the Convention on the Conservation of Antarctic Marine
Living Resources: the legislative process', in Alexander and Hanson, op. cit.,
note 8 supra, 129–141. See also US Public Law 98-623 of 8 November 1984, Title
III: Antarctic Marine Living Resources Act 1984, as reported in *Ant. J. U.S.*, Vol.
XIX, N° 4, December 1984, 11–12, and US Code Annotated, Title 16, Chapter
44A.
145. Barnes, loc. cit. (1982), note 144 supra, at 248.
146. Ibid., at 252.
147. Ibid., at 252.
148. Ibid., at 253–254.
149. Ibid., at 254.
150. See also note 97 supra and associated text.
151. Mitchell and Sandbrook, op. cit., note 139 supra, at 131.
152. Keith Brennan: 'Recent international developments regarding Antarctica', in R.
A. Herr, R. Hall, B. W. Davis (eds): *Issues in Australia's Marine and Antarctic
Policies*, Public Policy Monograph, University of Tasmania, 1982, 91–99.
153. See Vignes, loc. cit., note 144 supra, at 757–758.
154. See note 142 supra.
155. See Parliamentary statement cit., note 127 supra, and comments by Bush, op.
cit., note 59 supra, Vol. II, at 205.
156. Australia, Antarctic Marine Living Resources Conservation Act 1981, Section 5
(2) (b), reproduced in Bush, op. cit., note 59 supra, Vol. II, at 251–264. See also
the comment by Bush at page 262, note 9.
157. Barnes, loc. cit. (1982), note 144 supra, at 265–266.

158. Van der Essen, loc. cit. (1983), note 1 supra, at 240.
159. Bush, op. cit., note 59 supra, at 429.
160. Frank, loc. cit., note 144 supra, at 307. See also Edwards and Heap, loc. cit., note 116 supra, at 360.
161. See generally note 144 supra, and Triggs, loc. cit., note 117 supra, in fine.
162. See the statement cit., note 135 supra; see also Edwards and Heap as cited in note 160 supra.
163. Van der Essen, loc. cit. (1983), note 1 supra, at 239–240.
164. Bush, op. cit., note 59 supra, at 406.
165. See, for example, Bernard H. Oxman: 'L'accord entre le Bresil et les Etats-Unis concernant la peche a la crevette', *An. Fr. D.I.*, Vol. XVIII, 1972, 785–803.
166. On the dispute about maritime jurisdiction in Svalbard, see generally Finn Sollie: 'Norway's Continental Shelf and the boundary question on the seabed', *Coop. and Conf.* 2/3, 1974, 101–113, particularly at 107–109; see also Theutenberg, op. cit., note 6 supra, at 52–54. The regime of Svalbard will be discussed in Part II of this book in connection with the minerals regime in Antarctica.
167. See note 100 supra and associated text.
168. Bush, op. cit., note 59 supra, at 428.
169. Australia, Act cit., note 156 supra, Section 5 (a); see the comment by Bush, op. cit., note 59 supra, at 428.
170. See Article XXIV of the Convention on the Conservation of Antarctic Marine Living Resources.
171. Australia, Act cit., note 156 supra, Section 5 (3) (a); see the comment by Bush, op. cit., note 59 supra, at 428.
172. Bush, op. cit., note 59 supra, at 428.
173. See note 4 supra and associated text.
174. See note 25 supra and associated text.
175. J. Michel Marcoux: 'Natural resource jurisdiction on the Antarctic continental margin', *Virg. J.I.L.*, Vol. 11, 1971, 374–404, particularly at 390–396.
176. See note 9 supra.
177. See note 120 supra.
178. Australia, Proclamation on the Continental Shelf of 10 September 1953, reproduced in Bush, op. cit., note 59 supra, Vol. II, at 172–173.
179. Harry, loc. cit., note 79 supra, at 730–732.
180. Bush, op. cit., note 59 supra, Vol. II, at 173–174.
181. France, Order N° 10 of 9 June 1971, promulgating decrees N° 71-360 and 71-361 of 6 May 1971 concerning the continental shelf; text in Bush, op. cit., note 59 supra, Vol. II, at 572–573.
182. France, Law N° 76-655 of 16 July 1976, Article 2; text in Bush, op. cit., note 59 supra, Vol. II, at 584–586. See also Decree N° 78-144 of 3 February 1978; text in Ibid., at 586–588.
183. Argentina, Law N° 21-024 of 4 September 1975; text in Bush, op. cit., note 59 supra, Vol. II, at 71. See also the comments by Bush at 71–73. Chile has legislated for economic incentives applicable, inter alia, to mineral activities south of the Strait of Magellan, with the exception of the oil industry; see Chapter 3 supra, note 144.
184. US Department of State: *Legal Status of areas south of 60° South Latitude*, in: US Senate: *US Antarctic Policy*, Hearing 1975, 18–20, at 19. See also the letter sent by the US Department of State to the Australian embassy in Washington DC, expressing its non-recognition of sovereignty over the Antarctic continental shelf, reproduced in *Digest of U.S. Practice in International Law*, 1975, at 110–111.
185. US Department of State, loc. cit. (Prima), note 184 supra, at 19–20.

186. See generally F. M. Auburn: 'Legal implications of petroleum resources of the Antarctic continental shelf', *Ocean Yearbook*, 1, 1978, 500–515, particularly at 506.

187. Report of the meeting of experts at the Fridtjof Nansen Foundation at Polhogda, May 30–June 10, 1973: Report of the working group on legal and political questions, in *U.S. Antarctic Policy*, cit., note 184 supra, 76–85, particularly at 77–78.

188. Recommendation XI-1, *Handbook 1983*, at 1507–1509.

189. For a study of the continental shelf in the Antarctic Treaty system, see María Teresa Infante: 'The Continental Shelf of Antarctica: legal implications for a regime on mineral resources', in Orrego, op. cit., note 1 supra, 253–264.

190. F. M. Auburn: 'Offshore oil and gas in Antarctica', *G.Y.I.L.,* Vol. 20, 1977, 139–173, particularly at 155–156. See also the work cit., note 186 supra, at 506; and work cit, note 15 supra, at 248–249. See also generally Kim Traavik: 'Antarctica and the International Seabed regime', *Internasjonal Politikk*, October–December 1974, N° 4, 783–800 (in Norwegian).

191. See note 166 supra.

192. For the present status of the Spitzbergen continental shelf question, see Robert W. Smith: 'National claims and the geography of the Arctic', in Robert B. Krueger and Stefan A. Riesenfeld (eds.): *The Developing Order of the Oceans*, 1985, 485–512, particularly at 503–505. Willy Ostreng: 'Delimitation arrangements in Arctic seas. Cases of precedence or securing of Strategic/Economic interests?', in Krueger and Riesenfeld, op. cit., 539–574. David A. Colson: 'Political and boundary issues affecting Arctic energy resources', in Krueger and Riesenfeld, op. cit., 513–523. See also note 166 supra.

193. Theutenberg, op. cit., note 6 supra, at 52–53.

194. On the question of the status of ice see generally, J. Peter A. Bernhardt: 'Sovereignty in Antarctica', *Cal. West. I.L.J.*, Vol. 5, 1975, 297–349, particularly section III. Gerald F. Graham: 'Ice in international law', *Thesaurus Acroasium*, Vol. VII, 1977, 489–495.

195. W. Lakhtine: 'Rights over the Arctic', *A.J.I.L.*, Vol. 24, 1930, 703–717. Sir Gerald Fitzmaurice also considered that ice covering the high seas should in principle rank as *res communis* but permanent or semi-permanent ice shelves or barrier should be regarded as part of the true land mass, while treating the question as still unsettled; see 'The general principles of international law considered from the standpoint of the rule of law', *Rec. Cours Ac. D.I.*, Vol. 92, 1957-II, 1–227, at 155.

196. Gustav Smedal: *Acquisition of sovereignty over polar areas*, 1931, 27–32.

197. M. W. Mouton: 'The international regime of the polar regions', *Rec. Cours Ac. D.I.*, 1962-III, 169–284, particularly at 209.

198. Louis Rolland: 'Alaska: Maison de jeu établie sur les glaces au delá de la limite des eaux territoriales', *R.G.D.I.P.*, Vol. XI, 1904, 340–345.

199. C. John Colombos: *The International Law of the Sea*, 1967, at 129.

200. Statement by Japan on Article VI of the Antarctic Treaty, Ministerio de Relaciones Exteriores de Chile: *Memoria*, 1959, 698–704, translation in Bush, op. cit., note 59 supra, at 40.

201. See note 74 supra.

202. Statement by Mr. Herman Phleger before the United States Senate on the scope of the Antarctic Treaty, 14 June 1960; extract published in Bush, op. cit., note 59 supra, at 112–114; reference to 'fixed ice shelves' at 114.

203. US Report on provisions of the Antarctic Treaty, 4 February 1960; extract published in Bush, op. cit., note 59 supra, 111–112, at 111.

204. Report of the Committee on British Policy in the Antarctic, *Imperial Conference, 1926*, Par. 31; text in Bush, op. cit., note 59 supra, 100–104, at 103.
205. See the comment by Bush, op. cit., note 59 supra, at 147.
206. See Recommendation III-XI and the comment by Bush, op. cit., note 59 supra, at 144–145.
207. See note 86 supra and associated text.
208. See the comments by Bush, op. cit., note 59 supra, at 249.
209. Bernhardt, loc. cit., note 194 supra, at 310.
210. See, for example, David A. Peel: 'Antarctic ice: the frozen time capsule', *New Scientist*, 1983, Vol. 98, N° 1358, 477–483.
211. On aspects of the negotiation of this article, see Colson, loc. cit., note 192 supra, at 21–24. D. M. McRae and D. J. Goundrey: 'Environmental jurisdiction in Arctic waters: the extent of Article 234', *U.B.C.L.R.*, Vol. 16, 1982, 197–228. Article 234 will be considered further in the context of environmental policies in Chapter 6 infra, section 6.1.
212. John M. Reynolds: 'On the history of the economic use of natural ice', *Iceberg research*, 1983, N° 3, 3–4.
213. A. A. Husseiny (ed.): *Iceberg utilization*, 1978. Peter Wadhams: 'The resource potential of Antarctic icebergs', *Iceberg research*, 1985, N° 10, 9–23.
214. On the legal issues related to iceberg utilization see the following works: Thomas R. Lundquist: 'The iceberg cometh? International law relating to Antarctic iceberg exploitation', *Nat. Res. J.*, Vol. 17, 1977, 1–41. Steven J. Burton: 'Legal-political aspects of Antarctic iceberg utilization', in Husseiny, op. cit., note 213 supra, 604–615. Jean-Pierre Chamoux: 'Some international implications of iceberg transfer', in Ibid., 597–603. William W. Bishop Jr: 'International law problems of acquisition and transportation of Antarctic icebergs', in Ibid., 586–596. Emil A. Zuccaro: 'Iceberg appropriation and the Antarctic's gordian knot', Comment, *Cal. West I.L.J.*, Vol. 9, 1979, 405–429. Curt Epperson: 'International legal issues regarding towing of icebergs and environmental effects of iceberg exploitation', in John King Gamble Jr (ed.): *Law of the Sea: Neglected issues*, 1979, 209–239.
215. On the scope of the minerals regime, see Chapter 5 infra.
216. See note 204 supra.
217. Societé des Nations: *Acte de la Conference pour la codification du droit international*, La Haye, 13 mars–12 avril 1930, Vol. I, Appendice II: Rapport de la sous-commission N° II: 'lignes de base', at 131.
218. Van der Essen, loc. cit. (1983), note 1 supra, at 234. See, however, for reference to cases where ice has not been taken into consideration as to the regime of the territorial sea, International Law Commission: 'Regime of the Territorial Sea', Doc. A/CN.4/53, 4 April 1952, Rapport par J. P. A. Francois, *Y.B.I.L.C.*, 1952, Vol. II, 25–43, at 32.
219. Joyner, loc. cit., note 14 supra, at 283.
220. US Department of State: *Final environmental impact statement on the negotiation of an international regime for Antarctic Mineral Resources*, 1982, at 5-1, 5-2. Because of limited scientific and geographical evidence, the Antarctic peninsula was considered during a long period to be an archipelago until exploration revealed its present continuous land and ice mass; see Colin Bertram and Alfred Stephenson: 'Archipelago to peninsula', *The Geographical Journal*, Vol. 151, 1985, 155–167.
221. The Arctic experience on the law of the sea is in general of interest for Antarctica in view of some of the existing similarities, though differences are also to be taken into consideration. For aspects of the law of the sea and other claims in the Arctic,

see generally: Ivan L. Head: 'Canadian claims to territorial sovereignty in the Arctic regions', *McGill L.J.*, Vol. 9, 1963, 200–226. Donat Pharand: *The Law of the Sea of the Arctic with special reference to Canada*, 1973. Douglas M. Johnston (ed.): *Arctic ocean issues in the 1980's*, Law of the Sea Institute, 1982. Kim Traavik and Willy Ostreng: 'The Arctic Ocean and the Law of the Sea', *Coop. and Confl*, 2/3, 1974, 53–67. Carl August Fleischer: 'The Northern waters and the new maritime zones', G.Y.I.L., Vol. 22, 1979, 100–118. J. A. Beesley: 'Rights and responsibilities of Arctic coastal States: The Canadian view', *J.M.L.C.*, Vol. 3, 1971–1972, 1–12. Donat Pharand: 'The Arctic Waters in relation to Canada', in R. St. J. Macdonald, Gerald L. Morris, Douglas M. Johnston: *Canadian perspectives on International Law and organization*, 1974, 434–448. Donat Pharand: 'L'Arctique et l'Antarctique: patrimoine commun de l'humanité?', *Annals Air and S.L.*, Vol. VII, 1982, 415–430. Donat Pharand: 'The legal status of the arctic regions', *Rec. Cours Ac. D.I.*, 1979-II, 53–115. Donat Pharand: 'The Continental Shelf redefinition, with special reference to the Arctic', *McGill L.J.*, Vol. 18, 1972, 536–559. Jacques-Ivan Morin: 'Le progrés technique, la pollution et l'evolution récent du droit de la mer au Canadá, particuliérement a l'egard de l'Arctique', *Can. Y.B.I.L.*, Vol. VIII, 1970, 158–248. Louis Henkin: 'Arctic Anti-Pollution: Does Canada make – or break – international law?', *A.J.I.L.*, Vol. 65, 1971, 131–136. Donat Pharand: 'The legal regime of the Arctic: some outstanding issues', *International Journal*, Vol. 39, 1984, 742–799. Willy Ostreng: 'Soviet–Norwegian relations in the Arctic', Ibid., 866–887. Kurt M. Shusterich: 'International jurisdictional issues in the Arctic ocean', in William E. Westermeyer and Kurt M. Shusterich: *United States Arctic interests. The 1980's and 1990's*, 1984, 240–267. Egil Bergsager: 'Oil and gas in the USSR', *Nor oil*, August 1984, reprint. Kurt M. Shusterich: 'International jurisdictional issues in the Arctic ocean', *Ocean Dev. I.L.*, Vol. 14, 1984, 235–272. See also Theutenberg, op. cit., note 6 supra; and ibid.: 'The evolution of the Law of the Sea with special regard to the polar areas', in René-Jean Dupuy (ed.): *The settlement of disputes on the new natural resources*, Academie de Droit International, Colloque 1982, 1983, 377–424. See also 'Chronique des Fait Internationaux', *R.G.D.I.P.*, 1970, 130–137; *R.G.D.I.P.*, 1970, 120–126; and *R.G.D.I.P.*, 1911, 94–99. See also notes 166 and 192 supra.

222. Oscar Pinochet de la Barra: 'Antecedentes históricos de la política internacional de Chile en la Antártica: negociaciones chileno-argentinas de 1906, 1907 y 1908', in Francisco Orrego Vicuña et al.: *Política Antártica de Chile*, 1985, 67–80. See Chapter 1 supra, note 50 and associated text.

223. For the diplomatic correspondence and comments on the delimitation between France and the United Kingdom in Adelie Land, see Bush, op. cit., note 59 supra, Vol. II, 498–504.

224. See generally J. R. V. Prescott: 'Boundaries in Antarctica', in Stuart Harris (ed.): *Australia's Antarctic Policy Options*, 1984, 83–111. Ibid.: 'Actual and potential political boundaries in the Antarctic region', *The Globe*, Journal of the Australian Map Circle, N° 21, 1984, 12–26.

225. Australia–France: Agreement on Maritime Delimitation, signed at Melbourne on 4 January 1982, *Australian Treaty Series*, 1983, N° 3. This Agreement delimitates the Australian fishing zone and French Economic Zone, and the areas of the continental shelf under the sovereignty of each country; see Article 2.

226. P. G. Bassett: 'Australia's maritime boundaries', *A.F.A.R.*, Vol. 55, March 1984, 186–191, at 190. See also Bush, op. cit., note 59 supra, Vol. II, at 211, 589.

227. Argentina–Chile: Treaty of Peace and Friendship of 29 November 1984, *I.L.M.*, Vol. XXIV, 1985, 11–28, Article 15. For a comment on the implications of this agreement for Antarctica, see Michael A. Morris: 'The 1984 Argentine–Chilean

Pact of Peace and Friendship', *Oceanus*, Vol. 28, 1985, 93–96. For an early discussion of the questions of Antarctic maritime delimitation between Chile and Argentina, see Joaquín E. Curtze Sancho: *Soberanía marítima nacional en la Antártica chilena*, thesis, Law School of the University of Chile, Valparaíso, 1959, particularly at 237–257.

228. Joyner, loc. cit., note 13 supra, 436–442.
229. Marcoux, loc. cit., note 175 supra, 398–404.
230. Roberto E. Guyer: 'The Antarctic system', *Rec. Cours Ac. D.I.*, 1973-I, at 153–154.
231. Van der Essen, loc. cit. (1975–1976), note 1 supra, at 96. See also note 18 supra and associated text.
232. Van der Essen, loc. cit. (1983), note 1 supra, at 242. As explained in note 18 supra, this author uses the expression 'global' jurisdiction to mean 'joint' jurisdiction.
233. See Chapter 3 supra, Section 3.5, in fine.
234. See Chapter 3 supra, note 207 and associated text.
235. United Nations: *Question of Antarctica*, Views of States, Vol. III, Reply from the Philippines, UN Doc. A/39/583 (Part II), 9 November 1984, at 45.
236. Orrego and Infante, loc. cit., note 1 supra, at 350.
237. See Article 59 of the 1982 Law of the Sea Convention. On the question of residual rights in the Exclusive Economic Zone see also R. R. Churchill and A. V. Lowe: *The Law of the Sea*, 1983, at 136; and Reynaldo Galindo Pohl: 'The Exclusive Economic Zone in the light of negotiations of the Third United Nations Conference on the Law of the Sea', in Francisco Orrego Vicuña (ed.): *The Exclusive Economic Zone, A Latin American Perspective*, 1984, 31–59, at 46.
238. Orrego, loc. cit., note 15 supra, at 249–250.
239. On the EEC Common Fisheries Policy, see Daniel Vignes: 'The EEC and the Law of the Sea', in Churchill, Simmonds and Welch, op. cit., note 42 supra, 335–347. Daniel Vignes: 'The problem of access to the European Economic Community's fishing zone as the cornerstone for the adoption of a Common Fisheries Policy', in Rozakis and Stephanou, op. cit., note 51 supra, 83–96. Albert W. Koers: 'The external authority of the EEC in regard to marine fisheries', *C.M.L.R.,* Vol. 14, 1977, 269–301. Ibid.: 'Participation of the European Economic Community in a new Law of the Sea Convention', *A.J.I.L.*, Vol. 73, 1979, 426–443. Ibid.: 'The fisheries policy', in Commission of the European Communities: *Thirty years of Community Law*, 1983, 467–475, Tullio Treves: 'The EEC and the Law of the Sea: How close to one voice?', *Ocean Dev. I.L.J.*, Vol. 12, 1982–1983, 173–189. European Economic Community: 'Watch on the fishing grounds', *Europe 1984,* N° 11, November 1984, 3–5. R. R. Churchill: *The Common Fisheries Policy of the European Economic Community: a legal analysis*, Ph.D. Thesis, UWIST, 1984, unpublished.
240. European Court of Justice: Criminal proceedings v. Firma J. *Van Dam* en Zoven and others, Judgment of 3 July 1979, *Reports*, 1979, 2, 2345–2371. In this decision the Court affirmed the exclusive authority of the Community in respect of fisheries after the transition period, at 2350.
241. European Court of Justice: Cornelis *Kramer* and others, Judgment of 14 July 1976, *Reports*, 1976, 2, 1279–1328. In this decision the Court held that '. . . the rule-making authority of the Community *ratione materiae* also extends – in so far as the Member States have similar authority under public international law – to fishing on the high seas', at 1309.

Part II

Alternative approaches to the conservation and development of Antarctic minerals: the process of internal accommodation

5

Basic elements of the regime for the exploration and exploitation of Antarctic mineral resources

5.1 The complexity of interests involved in the negotiation

When the Antarctic Treaty parties embarked on their consideration of mineral resources, the basic elements of the applicable regime
gradually began to take shape.[1] The principles approved by the preparatory meeting in Paris in 1976 were successfully taken up and developed by
Recommendations IX-1, X-1 and XI-1, which defined the essential
features of the content and scope of such a regime.[2] These instruments
were based on the deliberations of specialized working groups which were
convened either on the occasion of the various Consultative Meetings or
on an *ad hoc* basis.[3]

The detailed elaboration of the mineral resources regime has been the
result of the tasks undertaken by the Fourth Special Consultative Meeting
which began its work in 1982.[4] The negotiations that have taken place in
that context were of a highly complex nature since they involved a
confrontation of ideas that differed both on the nature of the Antarctic
Treaty system and on the specific problems relating to the management
and organization of mineral resources.[5]

The first type of conflicting interests involved in these negotiations was
the approach that has traditionally separated claimant countries from
those that do not recognize claims of sovereignty, a difference of point of
view which, in the case of mineral resources, is exacerbated by the fact
that the link between these resources and the question of sovereignty or
sovereign rights is stronger than in the context of other subjects. Whereas
the first group of countries takes the view that the appropriate regime
should give some prominence to the factor of sovereignty, for the second
group the regime should emphasize the features that are implied by an
international approach.[6]

Another important point at issue relates to differences of view concerning the development of the Antarctic. Certain countries tend to favour a type of regime that facilitates the exploitation of Antarctic natural resources, whereas others give high priority to the conservation of those resources within the framework of a policy of environmental protection.[7] To some extent, this difference of interests is bound up with the question of geographical proximity to the Antarctic, since the countries of the southern hemisphere that are closer to the Antarctic continent have a particularly keen awareness of the environmental factor.[8]

The specific characteristics of the mineral resources regime have also been influenced by the different economic philosophies of the Consultative Parties. The principles of the market economy and those of the centrally planned economy have been obliged to seek mutually agreed options within the framework of the regime.[9] Furthermore, although the differences between developing and industralized countries have not been overtly manifested to any significant degree, such differences underlie various important points in the negotiation.[10] In the same way, it is possible to note differences of approach on some subjects between the middle-ranking countries and the great powers, and this creates a further need for harmonization within the regime.[11]

Questions relating to institutional organization and the external accommodation also reflect differences of perception. In the first place, for example, one typical difference is the one that divides countries that seek a procedure for the adoption of decisions based on the traditional consensus within the Antarctic system and those other countries that favour the adoption of decisions on the question of resources policy by a majority.[12] The greater or lesser degree of openness of the regime or the extent of participation by third countries exemplifies the type of differences that may be observed in the context of the external accommodation.[13]

In addition to the inherent difficulties of the negotiation, it is also necessary to bear in mind that there are very few precedents for internationally organized regimes for the administration of mineral resources. The regime of Svalbard is one of these precedents but with the fundamental difference that, in the Svalbard case, the territorial sovereignty of Norway was recognized.[14] The regime established in Part XI of the 1982 Convention on the Law of the Sea, relating to the seabed, is another precedent but with another fundamental difference, namely that the area in question is one in which, by definition, the exercise of national sovereignty is prohibited.[15] Antarctica, in the light of the explanations given in earlier chapters, represents a unique case which cannot be assimilated to any of these precedents even though, on a considerable number of aspects, there are similarities which stem from the fact that the regimes under consideration are internationally defined.

The difficulties and complexities which the Antarctic system was to encounter in the elaboration of this regime had already been anticipated by various authors. As we have mentioned before, in his analysis of the Antarctic Treaty, Christopher Beeby pointed out in 1972 that the exploitation of resources would be the 'most probable source of trouble in the future'.[16] A Soviet author, in his turn, expressed the following opinion about the growing complexity of the issue of natural resources:

> The extensive drawing of Antarctic natural resources into the world's economic circulation will unquestionably upgrade the economic possibilities of mankind. It seems obvious that in the future Antarctica's economic and political status may change considerably. Interest in this part of the earth will continue to grow.[17]

Because of the various interests and positions involved in the matter and the international nature of the process of preparation of the regime on mineral resources, important issues of international law have also arisen during the discussions of this subject. These issues refer in part to the manner how given principles of international law can apply to the case of Antarctic mineral resources and related aspects, but also in part they refer to the fact that the regime under negotiation appears to be opening new ground in international law, particularly from the point of view of unprecedented problems and situations that require new legal approaches for their solution.

However, in spite of numerous problems with which the negotiation of the regime has had to contend, the spirit of co-operation which is characteristic of the Antarctic Treaty system has prevailed throughout. The processes of accommodation that will be examined in this chapter and in those that follow clearly demonstrate this spirit of co-operation.

Considerations relating to procedure

The procedure adopted in the negotiations on the mineral resources regime has a number of important characteristics which it is necessary to emphasize since they played a decisive part in the development of this spirit of co-operation. In the first place, it is to be noted that the procedure is an entirely flexible one which allows for whatever type of meeting is desirable at any particular time. In the initial stage, negotiations were conducted within the framework of the regular consultative meetings[18] and of *ad hoc* working groups,[19] but, when the complexity of the problems being dealt with made it necessary, work was continued within the framework of the Fourth Special Consultative Meeting.[20] The sessions of the latter were scheduled in accordance with the progress of work and on some occasions working groups were set up.[21]

The Scientific Committee on Antarctic Research (SCAR), a non-governmental organization devoted to Antarctic research within the framework of the International Council of Scientific Unions, has been periodically requested by the Consultative Meetings to make known its point of view on certain particularly delicate problems, such as that of environmental conservation, thus following its tradition of scientific and technical involvement in the preparation of all the resources regimes related to the Antarctic.[22] Some meetings organized by academic and official bodies have also helped to create a framework of discussion which has favoured the quest for solutions to fundamental problems.[23]

Another important characteristic of the procedure followed has been its informality and privacy. In spite of the fact that the Antarctic system has frequently been criticized for making available so little information concerning its work,[24] privacy in this respect has proved an important means of ensuring the frank interchange of views and facilitating the corresponding accommodation between divergent positions. Such accommodation would otherwise have been far more difficult to achieve and the progress of negotiations would have been impeded. The experience gained in earlier negotiations on other resources regimes in the Antarctic system, particularly in regard to living resources, confirms the desirability of this informality and privacy among the participating countries, particularly in the early stages of the process;[25] however, as will be examined in Chapter 10, this approach has also resulted in criticism to the Antarctic arrangements on the part of third countries, what has led to an important change of attitude as to the availability of information.

This framework of informality has not only made it easier to hold plenary meetings or negotiating groups, but also to arrange meetings and discussions concerning special interests. The separate meetings of claimant countries to co-ordinate their positions are a manifestation of such special interests and are a practice which is followed not only in the negotiations on minerals but also, in a general way, throughout the Antarctic system.[26]

The procedural feature which probably has the greatest importance is the use of personal reports prepared by the chairmen of meetings or of specific negotiations to record the degree of agreement and disagreement on the most outstanding issues.[27] These reports provide a means of bringing the positions of the parties somewhat closer together and contributing to the formation of a consensus as to the final solutions. On occasion, the exercise includes the presentation of compromise formulae and draft texts by the chairman which endeavour to interpret this consensus as faithfully as possible.[28] This procedure has become indispensable in highly complex negotiations, such as those on the mineral resources regime, since it constitutes the most effective means of stimulating the quest for the required agreement and accommodation.

These various procedural approaches to the negotiation on Antarctic mineral resources resemble to an important extent the procedural arrangements and practices of the Third United Nations Conference on the Law of the Sea, with particular reference to the role played by the groups representing special interests and the drafts prepared by the chairmen of negotiating groups and other bodies.[29] Even though the view has been expressed that consensus can only be used in a limited way in major multilateral negotiations and that important legal issues cannot be solved satisfactorily by means of this approach, Buzan has concluded after examining the experience of the Law of the Sea Conference that 'consensus procedure can be used to produce hard legal outcomes'.[30] The experience arising from Antarctic negotiations on the various regimes dealing with resources, including that on minerals, tends to confirm this conclusion in a context where the legal issues are particularly difficult to resolve.

Certain other important procedural aspects of this negotiation are truly inseparable from the taking of decisions on certain fundamental questions. This applies principally to the time-table for the elaboration of the regime and to the decision on the type of instrument to be used, subjects that will be examined next.

The political importance of timely approval of the regime

The various technical studies that have been made concerning the existence and possible location of minerals in the Antarctic, the technology necessary for their extraction and the conditions to be observed and the economic features of such activity, all reach the identical conclusion that it will take a considerable time for the extraction of such resources to become a reality, if it ever does so.[31] This being so, it would seem that the preparation of the corresponding regime should not be seen as a matter of urgency and might be undertaken in a more gradual manner. However, there has been a clear and increasing sense of urgency in dealing with this subject since the Consultative Parties began to consider it. Recommendation X1-1 concluded on this matter that: 'A regime on Antarctic mineral resources should be concluded as a matter of urgency'.[32]

This judgement is based not so much on technical and economic considerations but rather on reasons of a legal and political nature. As was stated earlier, one of the key features of the system of Antarctic co-operation has been its capacity for anticipating needs and problems and for seeking solutions before the question identified become urgent or critical. All the resources regimes approved within the framework of the Antarctic Treaty and related instruments have followed this model and the case of minerals is no exception. Other resources regimes governed by international law have also shown this capacity for anticipation, as was the case with the regime of the continental shelf between 1945 and 1958 or is presently the case with the regime for sea-bed minerals under the Law of the Sea Convention.

There were two powerful reasons why such foresight was necessary in the case of the Antarctic minerals regime. The first is that international awareness of the implications of the subject is now so great that a solution is required before any major discovery of resources is made since, if there is such a discovery before the framework of a regime is agreed, that might lead to a crisis that would irreparably damage the Antarctic Treaty system. The second reason is that, given the growing international interest in the subject, if understanding is not achieved promptly within the system, including on the questions inherent in the external accommodation, the situation might also lead to a crisis; that it would be advisable to avoid. Christopher Beeby has aptly identified these difficulties:

> The most important reason for doing the job quickly is that the issue of minerals in Antarctica, if it is left unresolved, may present a threat to the Antarctic Treaty and the Antarctic Treaty system. This is so because the issue has the potential to bring back to centre stage the disputes about sovereignty which the Antarctic Treaty successfully put to one side. Moreover, for so long as the Consultative Parties have not managed to complete the work needed to fill the gap in the Treaty about resources . . . they will continue to be poorly placed to resist criticism from countries which have not become party to the Treaty.[33]

The choice of instruments

The question of the choice of instruments by means of which the minerals regime is to be instituted is also linked to important decisions on matters of substance within the Antarctic system. As indicated in Chapter 2, there are three principal options in this connection. The first would be the use of a recommendation approved by the Consultative Parties along the lines of the Agreed Measures; the second option is that of an *ad hoc* international convention as in the case of the seal regime and the marine living resources regime;[34] the third possibility that has been suggested is that of a protocol attached to the Antarctic Treaty.[35]

The alternative of a recommendation is seriously limited in its capacity to introduce some of the major legal changes within the system which such a regime requires; for example, the need to address the problem of 'proprietary data' in respect of resources and other aspects of the operation of the regime poses a conflictive issue *vis à vis* the concept of freedom of research and exchange of information on which the 1959 Treaty is based, since 'proprietary data' is by definition characterized by the withholding of information.[36] Although recommendations have been used flexibly to develop the framework of the 1959 Treaty, they have certain limitations.[37] Moreover, this type of instrument is also limited with regard to the participation of third States which would in some respects be made more difficult. Although a recommendation establishes a close link between the regime and the Antarctic Treaty, the same effect could also be achieved by means of the other alternatives.

The suggestion of an additional protocol is also inspired by the aim of ensuring a close link between the regime and the 1959 Treaty since its effect would probably be that any accession by third countries would automatically make it necessary for them to accede to the Treaty. Although this might be a desirable objective, it is possible that it also limits the participation of such third countries. However, this alternative does not involve the difficulty of a restricted capacity to introduce significant legal changes.

Owing to these potential limitations or difficulties, the alternative of a convention has been regarded since the beginning of the negotiations, as having the most to recommend it since it is compatible both with the objective of introducing the required legal changes and with participation of third parties. The precedents of the seal and living resources regime were clearly significant in this respect. As early as the first negotiating session of the Fourth Special Consultative Meeting, it was decided that 'the regime should be concluded in a form that imposes obligations on the parties to it that are binding under international law,' thus spelling out with greater precision a point which Recommendation XI-1 had left unresolved.[38] Although this formula was not a definitive pronouncement on the type of instrument to be chosen it clearly pointed in favour of a convention. The second revision of the draft articles expressly opted for a convention to embody the minerals regime.

This last alternative, as we have explained earlier, fits into the Antarctic system as well as any other and does nothing to diminish the links with the 1959 Treaty and the system as a whole. These links, moreover, have been specifically safeguarded by the new regime. The choice of a convention confirms the system's practice of having recourse to such an instrument whenever important questions concerning interpretation of the Treaty or the extension of the Treaty subjects which may be of the interest of third countries are involved.

5.2   Nature and objectives of the regime

The nature of the regime
A preliminary decision which the Consultative Parties had to take at the outset of negotiations concerned the nature of the future mineral resources regime. The basic available options on that matter were to design a detailed regime which would constitute in practice a mining code and in which each and every one of the possible aspects of mining activity in the Antarctic would be defined, or of designing a regime which would contain all the necessary elements to determine clearly how it would function, entrusting the detailed regulation of activities to subsequent stages of its operation.

The negotiators of the sea-bed regime in the recent Law of the Sea Conference were confronted by a similar choice. Although many delegations would have preferred a basic regime, the United States demanded a detailed approach which would give a precise rule for all major problems and would thus avoid subsequent intervention by the organs of the system. The decision to opt for this latter alternative was a mistake since it unnecessarily complicated the negotiations and ultimately impeded the achievement of consensus. Moreover, this approach was based in mistrust on the part of certain negotiating parties of the possible intentions of the other parties involved in the negotiation.[39] The US policy in the Law of the Sea Conference was also moulded to some extent by the concern of being outvoted either in that Conference or in the arrangements for sea-bed mining, as well as by the need to ensure the congressional ratification of the results of the negotiation. While the former concern does not arise in the case of the Antarctic negotiations due to the consensus procedures and other institutional arrangements, the latter question of congressional approval has beyond doubt an influence on the positions adopted by the American negotiators.

This negative experience undoubtedly had an influence on the corresponding decision concerning the nature of the Antarctic regime; the approach of designing a regime which would contain the necessary elements only was, therefore, adopted in order to avoid the repetition of unnecessary confrontations and discrepancies. The different approach to this question taken by the continental and Anglo-Saxon legal traditions has also been noted in this regard; while the former has favoured a general statement of obligations, the latter has sought the development of specific rules governing mining activities in Antarctica.[40] This agreement on the nature of the regime reveals, moreover, the different attitude on which the negotiations within the Antarctic system have been based, characterized as they were by a greater degree of mutual confidence and understanding. At the first session of the Fourth Special Consultative Meeting understanding was reached that 'the regime should not be a comprehensive mining and environmental code constituting a complete resolution to all the issues which could arise'.[41] This approach adequately meets the reality of the Antarctic situation in which it is not possible to anticipate each and every one of the issues that would require establishment of a rule within the framework of the regime.

Nevertheless, the alternative of a basic regime does not imply an indecisive or indeterminate regime since, at the same time, there is an understanding that the provisions 'will provide all concerned with a clear picture of the way in which the decisions will be taken under the regime and the standards against which those decisions will be taken'.[42] Furthermore, the regime is founded on the additional principle of juridical stability, particularly with regard to 'security of title for the operator, the protection of investment and certainty of regulation'.[43] In other words this is a basic regime which seeks to be, at the same time, defined and stable.

From the moment when a choice was made in favour of this alternative in regard to the nature of the regime, the role to be played by its institutions automatically came to the fore and this, in turn, made it necessary to indicate certain preferences as to the means of achieving the process of internal accommodation. For this reason, consensus was simultaneously reached on the fact that the regime would have to be provided with new institutional machinery, an aspect that will be examined in Chapter 8. Furthermore, the option adopted certainly facilitated the development of the process of negotiation.

In this connection it is interesting to bear in mind the precedent of the Svalbard regime even though its legal context was different because of the recognition of the sovereignty of Norway. In this case, the 1920 Treaty also confined itself to establishing a kind of basic regime the details of which were to be regulated by Norwegian mining legislation.[44]

The objectives and principles of the regime: concordances and discrepancies

The definition of the objectives of the regime have been one of the most delicate topics of the negotiation since it is on this subject that the divergent positions of those that favoured the exploitation of resources and those that emphasized the preservation of the environment have had to be harmonized in the context of difficult compromises.[45] In the case of the sea-bed regime negotiated in the Law of the Sea Conference, the clash of interests between those that postulated the development of these resources and those that sought the ordered management of the international markets in primary commodities, including the participation in them of land-based producers, was so powerful that for a long time it left the corresponding definitions in a state of paralysis.[46]

However, the negotiations on the Antarctic minerals have started from the consensus that a central objective of the regime is the protection of the Antarctic environment;[47] all other considerations of national interest or policy have been from the outset subordinated to this consensus. This is explained, in the first place, by the existence of a genuine conviction that it is essential to preserve a unique ecological heritage while allowing at the same time for different points of view concerning the ways of achieving this objective and on its relationship to any activities that might be undertaken for the exploration and exploitation of minerals.[48] There is a close connection, therefore, between the objectives and principles of the regime and the basic principles governing the protection of the environment in this context, and the rules and procedures under which mineral activities might be authorized.

The priority given to the environmental objective of the regime may also be explained in terms of the problems inherent in the external accommodation. One of the fundamental principles, invoked most frequently by the Consultative Parties to explain their special competence and responsibility in managing the Antarctic system, and in particular the resources policy, has been the requirements of environmental protection.[49] For this reason it would have been inconceivable, in structuring the minerals regime, to have placed greater emphasis on the objective of the exploitation of resources, as this might have prejudiced the international credibility of the Antarctic system as a whole.

Recommendation X1-1 clearly embraced this environmental concern.

Prominent among the principles contained in paragraph 5 of the Recommendation is the principle that the 'protection of the unique Antarctic environment and of its dependent ecosystems should be a basic consideration'.[50] Several other provisions of this Recommendation also refer to environmental protection.[51] Similarly, the draft articles submitted by ambassador Beeby in 1983 included in the first place among the objectives of the regime '(a) assessing the possible impact upon the Antarctic environment of Antarctic mineral resource activities'.[52] This overriding objective has been supplemented by the principle embodied in the 1984 and following revisions of the draft articles providing that Antarctic mineral resource activities shall be conducted on the basis of the environmental principles of the regime.[53] Various other principles relate to this concern for the environment, which is also reflected in the proposed machinery of the regime; these aspects of the regime will be considered later.

The second main objective of the regime, which is subordinate to the foregoing, is that of determining whether mineral resource activities are or are not acceptable. It will be noted in this connection that the objective is not to exploit the resources but merely to ascertain whether activities are permissible in the light of the environmental priorities and other considerations. Recommendation X1-1 envisaged two criteria for this purpose. The first was that of '(a) assessing the possible impact of mineral resource activities on the Antarctic environment in order to provide for informed decision-making', whereby a procedure for decision-making is sought, based on adequate information. The second criterion is that of the decision itself for the purpose of '(b) determining whether mineral resource activities will be acceptable'.[54] These criteria are also reflected in similar terms in the draft articles to which we have referred.[55] Two other stated objectives of the regime reaffirms this policy of environmental safeguard. The first is that of 'ensuring that any Antarctic mineral resource activities are undertaken in strict conformity with the provisions of this regime, including the principles established by it'; and the second and related objective is that there should be no activities conducted outside the regime, what has been expressed in the following provision: 'No Antarctic mineral resource activities shall be conducted except in accordance with this regime and measures adopted pursuant to it. . . .'.[56]

The means of achieving the environmental objectives has clearly been one of the most difficult questions of the negotiation that has been embarked on, since this is a point on which the different interests involved have competed most strongly to influence the formulation of the principles on the basis of which the corresponding definitions were to be adopted or to control the process of adopting decisions through various institutional approaches.

As far as the principles in question are concerned, one school of thought holds that they should reflect strictly the concern for environmental protection whereas another maintains that they should satisfy the 'criteria of acceptability' which, although they obviously also recognize the environmental requirements, nevertheless imply a greater interest in the conduct of mineral activities.[57] The expressions 'environmental principles' and 'principles of acceptability' that have been used in the negotiation subtly convey this difference of emphasis. In any case, as Christopher Beeby has pointed out, there is a consensus that:

> the regime will need to provide effective procedures to meet the declared objective of ensuring that the Antarctic environment is protected against any adverse effects of mining. It will also have to contain environmental standards – high standards – against which specific proposals for prospecting, development or production can be measured.[58]

Among these 'environmental standards', complex subjects are envisaged such as the type of 'impact assessment' that is to be carried out and the specific effects which will have to be assessed; the identification of the possible risks and the means of preventing or remedying them; the need for monitoring required by this process; or the technological capacity that is to be required in order to authorize mineral activities in the Antarctic.[59] All this will also require provision of adequate information and a corresponding development of research in order to make the achievement of these objectives a reality.

Even though the process of decision-making in relation to acceptability will be considered in conjunction with the institutional aspects of the regime, it must be pointed out at this stage that, once a decision on the matter is required, a decision is thereby made automatically also on another important aspect concerning which choices face the negotiator. The concept of unrestricted and unqualified access to Antarctic mineral resources[60] is excluded by the fact that the related activity must, in all cases, be deemed to be acceptable. Furthermore, this approach also implies recognition of the role which the institutions of the regime must necessarily play in the control of this process.

In this way, one of the most complex questions that affected the negotiations on the sea-bed regime in the Law of the Sea Conference has been resolved in this other context, namely the idea of free and unqualified access and of the establishment of institutions with nominal powers against which was set the thesis of an all-powerful authority and of the conducting of activities solely under its exclusive control. Although these extreme positions ultimately gave rise to a compromise within the framework of the parallel system, the related negotiation was noticeably affected by this controversy.[61]

The fact that this negative confrontation did not occur in the Antarctic mineral regime indicates the different spirit of accommodation and co-operation existing within the system, as well as the fact that compromise is easier when there is a smaller number of States involved in the negotiation. As was mentioned before, neither is there in the Antarctic tradition a question of outvoting any relevant position on a matter of importance, such as the negotiations of the minerals regime. However, as we shall see, this does not mean that there were no major differences concerning the stages that were to be subject to acceptance, or the way in which acceptance was to be accorded or the degree of freedom and control that ought to apply to the corresponding operations.

Since the regime will govern the conducting of the mineral activities found to be acceptable, the various standards and principles defined in this regime, as well as the corresponding institutional and decision-making procedures, are an inseparable part of the above-mentioned objectives.[62] The principle that such activities 'shall be conducted in an orderly, safe, efficient and rational manner' is also an approach that needs to be taken into account by the various policies of the regime and the work of the institutions.[63]

The link with the 1959 Treaty and the Antarctic Treaty system
The objectives and principles of the regime must also be seen as being closely bound up with the question of the links with the 1959 Treaty and the Antarctic Treaty system in general. When the subject of mineral resources was first considered, it was clear that the corresponding regime was conceived by the Consultative Parties as an integral part of the Antarctic system and, consequently, intimately bound up with it. The principles approved by the Paris Meeting in 1976 and the recommendations which followed on this matter clearly indicate this other purpose of the regime.[64]

Recommendation X1-1 unequivocally proclaimed this closer link. In its preamble it expressly invokes earlier recommendations, both in the specific field of mineral resources and, more generally, in relation to the impact of man on the Antarctic environment and ecological protection in various fields.[65] It also invokes various substantive principles of the system. Among these, mention is made of 'the provisions of the Antarctic Treaty', with particular reference to the use for peaceful purposes and to the necessity of avoiding the transformation of Antarctica into an object of international discord; of the fact that the Treaty has contributed to international harmony in accordance with the purposes and principles of the Charter of the United Nations, above all in relation to demilitariza-tion, denuclearization and the freedom of scientific research and of the concept of the unity between the Antarctic continent and the associated maritime areas.[66]

The operative part of the Recommendation also contains important considerations on this matter. The principles set forth in paragraph 5 of the Recommendation include the active and responsible role of the Consultative Parties, the maintenance of the integrity of the Antarctic Treaty and the fact that the safeguards provided in Article IV of the Treaty remain unaffected.[67] As a consequence of this, paragraph 6 provides that the regime must be acceptable to the various positions of the Consultative Parties in regard to territorial claims and must not be prejudicial to any of them. Furthermore, the principle of the special responsibility of the Consultative Parties for environmental protection and the role that will devolve on SCAR for the conduct of the related studies are considered.[68] Also within the context of the link with the system, this Recommendation provides that third States acceding to the regime must observe the basic provisions of the 1959 Treaty – in particular Articles I, IV, V and VI – as well as the relevant recommendations approved by the Consultative Parties.[69]

On the basis of these precise terms of reference, the negotiations of the Fourth Special Consultative Meeting considered the link with the Ant-arctic system at three complementary levels: that of general principles, that of safeguards provided in Article IV of the Treaty and that of the general obligations to be observed by countries acceding to the regime, including third countries.

The general principles of the Antarctic system, just as in the case of the above-mentioned Recommendation, have consistently attracted a con-sensus among the Consultative Parties in the context of the negotiation of the regime on mineral resources. The Preamble of the 1984 Draft Articles begins by 'recalling the provisions of the Antarctic Treaty' and then lists the most important principles on which the Antarctic Treaty is founded, with particular reference to the promotion of international harmony, utilization solely for peaceful purposes, the freedom of scientific research, the protection of the environment and due respect for other uses of the

Antarctic.[70] Many of these principles are also reflected in the operative parts of the regime.

Another feature of these general principles is the role of the Consultative Parties in the preparation and administration of the regime, an idea which reaffirms the decision that the regime should be prepared within the framework of the Antarctic Treaty system and linked to it.[71] As we shall see later the institutional approach of the regime also embraces this principle in so far as it contemplates a significant role for the Antarctic Treaty Consultative Parties. This expression of the special responsibility of the Consultative Parties is also reflected in the Preamble mentioned above, which recalls their responsibility to ensure that any activities in Antarctica are 'consistent with all the principles and purposes of the Antarctic Treaty system';[72] as was already mentioned, one important consequence of this criterion is that mineral activities cannot be conducted in the Antarctic outside the regime defined under the Antarctic Treaty system since this would be an infringment of the principles and purposes of such system. The legal effects for third countries that flow from this approach will be discussed in Chapter 9.

Application of Article IV of the 1959 Treaty and the problems of interpretation

The safeguards of Article IV of the Antarctic Treaty represent one of the essential features of the mineral resources regime, as also was the case with the other treaty regimes governing resources. Both the basic recommendations that have been referred to and the draft articles[73] establish specific links between this regime and Article IV of the Treaty. This ensures that the positions of both claimants and non-claimants, and of those countries that have a 'basis of claim', are not juridicially compromised in any way by this new regime. At the same time, it is ensured that nothing in the regime should give rise to a new claim or extension of an existing claim as provided in Article IV, paragraph 2, of the 1959 Treaty. Only on this basis is it possible to achieve the agreement necessary to make the regime viable.

The terms in which the link with Article IV of the Antarctic Treaty has been conceived are almost identical with those that appear in Article IV of the Convention for the Conservation of Antarctic Marine Living Resources. This, of course, includes the concept of 'coastal state jurisdiction under international law' which had already been envisaged in the Canberra Convention. The so-called 'bi-focal approach', by means of which this latter concept has been interpreted, as repeated in connection with the mineral regime in the same terms as those that we have already discussed.[74]

However, there is also an interesting difference in the language used in the two cases. The Living Resources Convention provides that nothing shall be 'interpreted as a renunciation or diminution by any Contracting Party of, or as prejudicing, any right or claim or basis of claim to exercise coastal state jurisdiction under international law. . .'.[75] The draft articles on minerals contain the same concept, but applied to 'territorial sovereignty in Antarctica or to exercise coastal state jurisdiction under international law'.[76] In the former case, it was sufficient to refer to coastal state maritime jurisdiction since the Canberra Convention applies solely to activities in the marine environment or related thereto. On the other hand, given the fact that mineral activities may take place both on the continent and in the marine environment, it was necessary in the latter case to envisage both territorial sovereignty and maritime jurisdiction.

The link established with Article IV of the 1959 Treaty also raises an interesting problem of interpretation with regard to the latter. Paragraph 1 (a) of this Article refers to 'previously asserted rights of or claims to territorial sovereignty in Antarctica'. Although the expression 'previously asserted' could broadly be interpreted as embracing any act of claim performed at any time in the past, in a specific context it may also be interpreted as applying solely to claims prior to the date of the 1959 Treaty.

The Canberra Convention omitted this expression, possibly in order to avoid this second interpretation. Indeed, if a restrictive interpretation is applied in this other context, 'previously asserted' would imply a reference only to the period prior to 1959 and this might thereby prejudice maritime claims made subsequent to that date, as most such claims have been. In any case, the restrictive interpretation would have taken into account only the situation prior to 1959 and not the situation existing up to 1980.

Following a similar approach to that of the Canberra Convention, the draft articles also omit any reference to 'previously asserted' claims, and thus do not prejudice this question. It is to be noted that paragraph 6 of Recommendation XI-1 contained this expression, but only with reference to the case of territorial sovereignty since that paragraph does not refer to the question of maritime jurisdiction.

A restrictive approach in this connection would have the additional drawback that it might be interpreted as freezing the determination of the question of jurisdiction over maritime areas in Antarctica and leaving it to be decided only according to the legal rules applying in 1959 on conclusion of the Antarctic Treaty; this would also affect the discussion about the role of inter-temporal law in the development of the law of the sea that we have examined earlier.[77]

General obligations stemming from the Antarctic Treaty system
The third type of link that has been provided with the Antarctic Treaty system is that of general obligations which stem from the system and devolve on the Parties to the regime. Even though these obligations are a natural legal consequence as far as the Parties to the Antarctic Treaty are concerned, it is to be noted that the same obligations and other principles and objectives of the 1959 Treaty also apply to all the parties to the minerals and living resources regimes, as the case may be, irrespective of whether or not they are parties to the Antarctic Treaty, by way of the linkage that has been established between these various instruments. The Canberra Convention provided for an undertaking by Contracting Parties 'that they will not engage in any activities in the Antarctic Treaty area contrary to the principles and purposes of that Treaty' and also that they would be bound in their relations with one another by the obligations of Articles I and V of the 1959 Treaty and by the provisions of Articles IV and VI of that Treaty.[78] The basic principles of peaceful use, demilitarization, freezing of claims and not prejudice to the various positions, and the freedom of the high seas are thus expressly incorporated in the regime of that Convention.

Both Recommendation XI-1[79] and the draft articles[80] contain a formula which is equivalent to that of the Canberra Convention and is designed to ensure the same objectives. However, it is to be noted that the 1984 revision of this draft articles introduced a number of other references to provisions of the Antarctic Treaty that could thus be applicable to the parties to the minerals regime by way of this linkage. Some of these additional references can be regarded as establishing a link to articles that embody important principles of the Antarctic Treaty system, such as Article II, concerning the freedom of scientific research, and Article III, concerning international scientific co-operation. Other references have been made to Article VII of the 1959 Treaty, dealing with the question of inspection and related matters, and to Article VIII, which provides for the jurisdictional principles that we have examined in Chapter 3; both these questions are treated separately in the context of the minerals regime, and to an important extent differently, what makes the linkage of limited use and eventually might mean the introduction of an unnecessary complicating factor.

The instruments and drafts relating to the mineral resources regime also envisage that Parties to this regime that are not Parties to the Antarctic Treaty should recognize the special obligations and responsibilities of Consultative Parties with regard to the protection and preservation of the Antarctic environment,[81] once again following on this matter the example of the Canberra Convention.[82] The 1986 Draft Articles have been prepared on the assumption that parties to the mineral regime shall also be parties to the 1959 Antarctic Treaty.

Given the fact that the Antarctic Treaty system comprises a complex set of instruments and conventions concerned with conservation, the mineral resources regime, like the one on living resources, has had to endeavour to find ways of accommodating this interest, including in particular the Agreed Measures and other measures adopted by the Consultative Parties on environmental matters, the conservation measures promulgated within the framework of the Canberra Convention in regard to living resources and the Seal Convention.[83] It may be noted that, by means of this legal relationship, the various instruments and conventions of the system have become applicable to Parties to the mineral regime even if they are not Parties to the 1959 Treaty or to the special conventions. One consequence of this might also be that the instruments and conventions would apply to the entire area embraced by the minerals regime and not only to the geographical area which they originally envisaged and that this could represent in some cases a special extension of the system by indirect or functional means.[84]

The co-ordination of the Antarctic system and the respect for other uses of Antarctica
This complex network of legal relationships that has grown up within the system has created an additional need for co-ordination between the different mechanisms and institutions responsible for its administration so as to avoid situations of incompatibility or interference in the respective regimes. Although the consultative meetings of the Antarctic Treaty cannot technically be regarded as an institution, particularly because of the lack of a permanent organ, there is a marked evolution towards a greater institutionalization, as we shall examine in Chapter 8; this evolving machinery, together with the Commission established under the Canberra Convention and the Commission being discussed in the context of the minerals regime all have a part to play in such co-ordination.

Furthermore, it is necessary to ensure that the economic activity that is beginning to grow up in the Antarctic and which is likely to become more intense as a result of mineral activities, takes place in a manner that is compatible with the other uses of Antarctica. In addition to the traditional uses, such as use for scientific research, stations and navigation, there are now other activities such as tourism and the developing fishing industry all of which necessitate some degree of harmonization within the system. The principle that economic activities must respect and be compatible with the other uses of Antarctica is thus beginning to be adopted within the system. The 1984 revision of the Draft Articles has recognized as a matter of principle that any activities in Antarctica, including mineral activities, must be consistent with all the principles and purposes of the Antarctic Treaty system, including among them those of the special resources regimes. More importantly it has been specifically mandated that mineral activities shall be conducted so as to protect and respect other uses of Antarctica which are consistent with the 1959 Treaty, particularly stations and associated installations, programmes of scientific investigation, conservation and rational use of living resources, tourism, historic monuments and navigation.[85]

Although, as we have mentioned earlier, there has occasionally been criticism of the links between the resources regimes and the Antarctic system,[86] it would seem to be essential from every point of view that the basic principles of the Treaty and other key aspects of the system are duly applied within the framework of the special regimes. If that does not take place there might begin a gradual erosion of the fundamental principles of the Treaty that would do nothing to promote the preservation of a stable regime and co-operation in the continent. Moreover, if these links were broken, the necessary accommodation between divergent legal positions would become impossible and this would particularly affect the problem of claims of sovereignty. The viability of the resources regimes is inseparable from the adequate safeguard of the principles of the Antarctic Treaty and their continuing application in the practice of the system.

5.3 The area of application of the regime

The area of application of the mineral resources regime has proven to be one of the most difficult questions to resolve in the negotiations of the Fourth Special Consultative Meeting.[87] It may be argued that that is a traditional difficulty within the Antarctic Treaty system since discussion at the 1959 Conference on Article VI of the Treaty ran into considerable difficulties on the question of the precise definition of the Antarctic, and the extent to which it covers ice shelves and the high seas.[88] A similar problem occurred in the case of the Agreed Measures particularly in relation to their potential maritime application and also in connection with ice shelves; these doubts were only partly resolved by the Seal Convention.[89] The Convention on the Conservation of Antarctic

Marine Living Resources also was not an exception in this respect since, although there was agreement concerning its application up to the northern limit of the Antarctic convergence, the question of the inclusion of the maritime areas of the Kerguelen islands and Iles Crozet proved to be a particularly contentious point.[90]

In the case of mineral resources, in addition to these traditional difficulties, there were a number of intractable questions arising from legal differences between the Consultative Parties and from the requirements of the external accommodation. With regard to the former, the policy of claims of sovereignty and of the non-recognition of such claims undoubtedly has an effect on the nature of jurisdiction over the continental shelf and on the way in which it may be defined for purposes of the application of the regime.[91] Another problem that arises in this context concerns the unclaimed sector. As far as the external accommodation is concerned, there is the additional difficulty of defining the area of application of the Antarctic minerals regime in a manner so as not to become superimposed on the area that might come under the deep sea-bed regime agreed within the framework of the Law of the Sea Convention or other arrangements. These various issues will be discussed next.

Application to the continent and the unclaimed sector
The first point to be borne in mind concerns the application of the regime to the Antarctic continent proper. There would not seem to be any doubts on this matter among the Consultative Parties as studies concerning the location of minerals indicates the existence of major deposits in the Antarctic continental territory.[92] Paragraph 7, IV of Recommendation XI-1 and Article IV of the 1984 Draft Articles referred clearly to the application of this regime to the Antarctic continent. However, there are three related problems that are more difficult to solve: they concern the unclaimed sector, the ice shelves and the Antarctic islands.

Although some authors have expressed doubts as to whether the Consultative Parties could exercise jurisdiction over the unclaimed sector[93] or other areas of the continent that might be in a similar situation,[94] the practice of the Antarctic system unequivocally indicates that these sectors have been included in all the legislative enactments of the system, even when they are not specifically mentioned.[95] This criterion has also invariably been followed by the resources regimes.[96] On this basis it may be confidently affirmed that these sectors are not excluded from the mineral regime.[97] The reference made by the above mentioned Recommendation and Draft Articles to the Antarctic continent certainly includes the unclaimed areas.[98] The concept of the joint jurisdiction of the Consultative Parties constitutes for some authors the legal basis for this inclusion of the unclaimed zones.[99]

The situation of the ice shelves or barriers forms part of the discussion on the legal status of the ice which we have already considered.[100] In this connection as well, the practice of the system is important since the stable ice barriers are assimilated to continental territory under the concept of '*terra firma–glacies firma*'.[101] Even though Recommendation XI-1 did not specifically refer to such barriers they may also be considered as being included in the term 'continent'; in any event the 1984 Draft Articles clarified any remaining doubts on the point by expressly including 'all ice shelves' in the area of application of the minerals regime.

Application to islands and archipelagic configurations

The case of the islands is also of special importance, owing above all to the projections of the continental shelf which will be discussed later. On the one hand, from a technical point of view, the islands could not be regarded as being included in the term 'continent' and it might therefore be thought that the mineral regime would not be applicable to them. But, on the other hand, the consistent practice of the system has always been to include all land south of latitude 60 degrees south, whether mainland or islands.[102] Recommendation XI-1 did not explicitly answer this question since it provided that 'the precise limits of the area of application would be determined in the elaboration of the regime'.[103] From a strict legal point of view, the fact that islands are included within the Antarctic Treaty area and in the subsequent practice under this Treaty may not have sufficed for having them included in the minerals regime, since in spite of the various linkages that we have examined these are separate treaty arrangements. However, Article IV of the 1984 Draft Articles has expressly included, in addition to the continent, 'all other land areas south of 60° south latitude', thus including all islands within the Antarctic Treaty area and, at the same time, excluding those to the north of that latitude.

In this connection it must be also be borne in mind that certain areas of the Antarctic have from a geographical point of view an archipelagic configuration. In some cases these are archipelagos covered by glacial shelves, and they are thus physically part of the continent.[104] In the cases of rocks incapable of sustaining 'human habitation or economic life of their own' there might be grounds for considering the application of the principle contained in Article 121 of the Law of the Sea Convention whereby they would have no exclusive economic zone or continental shelf.[105] However, it is doubtful whether this principle applies in the case of Antarctica since it is a region which, in general, is incapable of sustaining human habitation or economic life of its own except under very special circumstances.[106] For this reason, the question of maritime spaces ought not to be affected by principles that have arisen for application in other latitudes and under other conditions.

Application to the continental shelf

The second important area to be taken into consideration with regard to the application of the regime concerns the Antarctic continental shelf. In Chapter 4 consideration was given to the points of view of claimant and non-claimant countries on this concept within the framework of the Antarctic Treaty system and the way in which they have achieved harmonization.[107] Once the principle was accepted that this system is applicable in general to the Antarctic continental shelf, the way was cleared for the mineral resources regime to include this area within its ambit of application.

Objections have never been raised within the framework of the Antarctic system to the geological concept of the continental shelf and in some documents the term 'continental margin' has also been explicitly used.[108] Difficulties have arisen concerning the question of its legal regime since, while claimants have acted on the premise that this area is 'appurtenant' to the jurisdiction of the coastal State, the non-claimants do not accept this approach and prefer to seek a basis which implies no connotation of sovereignty.[109] The concept of the joint jurisdiction of the Consultative Parties has also been applied to this matter since, on the one hand, it makes it possible to harmonize these difficulties and, on the other, it adequately solves the problem of jurisdiction over maritime areas in relation to the unclaimed sector.[110] The latter sector and its continental shelf undoubtedly form part of the area of application of the regime in the light of the considerations set out above.

The existing legal differences have strongly influenced the negotiations on the mineral resources regime. Although the use of the term 'continental shelf' would probably have been more simple, and would have been in accordance with universal practice, it was probably objected to on the grounds that it might be seen as implying a link with the jurisdiction of the coastal State.[111] Recommendation XI-1, while recognizing that this area was included within the ambit of application of the regime, sought a more neutral formulation and referred to 'adjacent offshore areas'.[112] The 1984 and 1986 Draft Articles kept within brackets both the expression 'continental shelf' and 'offshore areas', thus indicating the difference of views existing on this issue at the time. Whichever the terminology used in this context it does not, of course, affect the basic legal standpoints, which are moreover safeguarded by Article IV of the Antarctic Treaty.[113] It must also be noted that the expression 'offshore areas' has a broad connotation and could be interpreted to include the Exclusive Economic Zone or the minerals of the water column; because it appears that this is not the intention of the negotiators, perhaps 'submarine areas' or other equivalent terminology might be more precise.

These same differences have also raised problems in regard to the method of establishing the outer limit of the Antarctic continental shelf. Concerning the substance of this matter the Consultative Parties appear to agree on the formula contained in Article 76 of the Law of the Sea Convention which establishes the criteria for fixing this outer limit, and one active Consultative Party has formally proposed this approach.[114] However, the express invocation of that article which might possibly be the most appropriate solution, could once again raise difficulties from the point of view of the link with the concept of coastal State jurisdiction.[115] The fact that the Federal Republic of Germany, the United Kingdom and the United States have not signed that Convention could also prove to be an obstacle for the reference to Article 76, although this provision in particular is not one of those objected to by any of these three countries. In order to overcome this difficulty, it might be possible to adopt an alternative wording which, while being consistent with the formula contained in that article, would avoid expressions that might have a particular legal connotation. It would also be possible to introduce variations in the criterion of this article but this would be likely to constitute a further complicating factor in the negotiations; it might also be argued that if this is done it could amount to a policy of 'pick and choose' certain convenient aspects of the Convention, thus undermining the package deal and the unitary approach to that instrument.[116]

Yet another alternative is to establish this other limit on the basis of geographical co-ordinates which avoid the use of any wording that might compromise one or the other position. An additional possibility is to refer to the continental shelf or 'adjacent offshore areas' in a generic way, without becoming involved in precise wording or fixing its outer limit, a solution which would be understood as a reference to the general principles of international law or to a future agreement on delimitation. Article IV, paragraph 2, of the 1984 Draft Articles has in a way endorsed this last approach by providing that 'to the extent necessary the Parties to this regime shall establish, by agreement, the precise northern limits of the area. . .'. It is interesting to note that the requirement of an agreement between the parties means in fact that the decision on this matter will no longer depend on the national jurisdiction of claimant countries, thus confirming the trend to deal with the question of Antarctic maritime areas in a collective or joint manner. However, it is also possible that this latter approach might prove to be a future source of controversy concerning the precise limit, whether in the framework of the regime or in relation to questions of the external accommodation, particularly in view of the eventual participation of a number of countries that have not attained the consultative status under the 1959 Treaty.

Whichever formula is selected, it must be borne in mind that under Article 76, paragraph 8, of the Law of the Sea Convention, when the outer limit of the continental shelf is beyond 200 nautical miles from the applicable baselines, the relevant information must be submitted to the Commission provided in Annex II of the Convention. Article 84 of the same Convention also provides that the charts or lists of geographical co-ordinates shall be deposited with the Secretary-General of the United Nations and, in the case of the outer limit of the continental shelf, also with the Secretary-General of the Authority. Even if these obligations applied only to States Parties to the Convention, it is possible that they would cause difficulties with regard to their application in the Antarctic case. The claimant countries will have to provide this information so as not to prejudice their Antarctic title, whereas the non-claimants might refrain from doing so, a situation which might give rise to reciprocal objection or to objections by third countries. The situation of the non-signatories of the Convention is another complicating factor in this matter. These difficulties might perhaps be minimized if the Consultative Parties, either jointly or through the institutions of the regime, were to provide the required information with respect to the Antarctic continental shelf in its totality without distinctions concerning its legal status and safeguarding the respective national positions. This would represent a new manifestation of joint jurisdiction.[117]

The geomorphological configuration of the Antarctic continental shelf and the presence of islands are the cause of a number of additional difficulties concerning the precise identification of the regime's area of application. This is due in particular to the fact that some parts of the continental shelf extend north of latitude 60 degrees south; similarly, there is also the reverse phenomenon whereby some sub-Antarctic islands project their continental shelf south of the same parallel, in other words into the area of application of the 1959 Treaty.[118] The first situation mentioned should in principle be included in the regime's area of application since it involves a natural extension of the continent or of the

Antarctic islands. The second situation, on the other hand, should remain outside the regime and its area of application since it involves a natural extension of islands or territories that are not included within the area of the Antarctic Treaty and do not share its particular legal conditions. Taking into account the pertinent differences, the situation is analogous to that of the Kerguelen islands and Isles Crozet in the context of the living resources regime which we have examined earlier.

This complex configuration may also give rise to controversies concerning delimitation between countries or between them and the Antarctic minerals regime, just as we have examined in relation to the Exclusive Economic Zone.[119]

The situation of the sea-bed

Having established that the regime will be applied to the continent and to its adjacent off-shore areas, a third question still remains to be answered. Should this regime also be applied to the area of the sea-bed beyond the continental shelf but located south of latitude 60 degrees south? Various arguments might be advanced in favour of this option which has been discussed by some authors.[120] In the first place, the Consultative Parties have a special responsibility in the area of application of the Antarctic Treaty which cannot simply be renounced, and this might provide a justification for making the areas of the Treaty and the regime identical. Moreover, the requirements of environmental protection extend to the Treaty area as a whole and cannot easily be restricted to smaller areas.[121]. The fact that Antarctica constitutes a special case, different from those which the Law of the Sea Convention took into account, might also be invoked as an argument.

On the other hand, however, such a solution would have created the risk of conflict with the sea-bed regime and the Authority to be established under the Law of the Sea Convention and this would certainly not have made it easier to solve the problems of the external accommodation.[122] Although the deep sea-bed regime of the Law of the Sea Convention is different from that of the high seas, a number of countries regard it as being based on the principle of the freedom of the high seas;[123] as this is safeguarded by Article VI of the Antarctic Treaty, it could not be affected by the mineral regime. Furthermore, the Canberra Convention had already established the precedent that the area of the special regime need not coincide with that of the Antarctic Treaty. An early academic suggestion had envisaged that the Antarctic Treaty area should coincide with the 200-mile breadth of the economic zone for the purpose of delimitation with the international sea-bed regime.[124]

For all these reasons the Consultative Parties were not slow in agreeing that the regime should apply, as stated by Recommendation XI-1, 'without encroachment on the deep sea-bed'.[125] The term 'encroachment' would not seem to be the most appropriate in this context as it has a certain negative connotation.[126] The precise delimitation between the area of the Antarctic minerals regime and that of the deep sea-bed under the Law of the Sea Convention will have to be determined in accordance with some of the criteria that have been considered for establishing the outer limit of the continental shelf.

Although the Consultative Parties have accepted the need to restrict the area of application of the mineral regime, this does not entail a renunciation of certain types of special responsibility, particularly as regards the environment. Recommendation XI-1 provides in this connection that such special responsibility shall be ensured in the Treaty area 'taking into account responsibilities which may be exercised in the area by other international organizations'.[127] In this way, the Consultative Parties will continue to discharge their responsibilities throughout the Treaty area and, to the extent that international organizations empowered to intervene exist, as, for example, in the case of the Authority established under the Law of the Sea Convention, this fact will also need to be taken into consideration. The 1984 Draft Articles have mandated the Commission to be established under the minerals regime to 'seek to develop a co-operative working relationship with any international organization which may have competence in respect of mineral resources in areas adjacent to those covered by this regime'.[128]

The discussion on the area of application of the Antarctic minerals regime has also made it possible to clarify the point that any such international organization having competence in respect of mineral resources in areas adjacent to those under the Antarctic regime, will be confined strictly to the deep sea-bed area. As will be examined in Chapter 10, there have been suggestions for a type of inverse 'creeping jurisdiction' whereby the sea-bed regime and the Authority under the Law of the Sea Convention might be extended to the Antarctic continental shelf or the continent itself, with particular reference to the unclaimed sector. This possibility has now been entirely excluded. It should also be noted that in view of the fact that the Federal Republic of Germany, the United Kingdom and the United States have not signed the Law of the Sea Convention, particularly because of objecting to the sea-bed regime under Part XI of the Convention, there might also be a case for different points of view as to which, if any, is the competent international organization in the deep sea-bed adjacent to the area of the Antarctic minerals regime.

There is also another point of view which needs to be taken into consideration. Although, in the framework of the Law of the Sea Convention, the regime of the continental shelf is independent of, and separate from, that of the exclusive economic zone,[129] the latter also comprises the resources of the sea-bed and its subsoil. In the case of those countries that claim an exclusive economic zone in the Antarctic this matter is important since even if the continental shelf might in some cases not extend to the distance of 200 miles, the sea-bed and the subsoil would in any case remain subject to national jurisdiction as part of the exclusive economic zone. This is particularly relevant in view of the reasoning of the International Court of Justice in the *Libya–Malta* case as to the application of the distance criterion to the continental shelf as well as to the exclusive economic zone and the close link between the two concepts.[130] In this case, the sea-bed regime would begin not at the limit of the continental shelf but at that of the exclusive economic zone. This is not so when the continental shelf exceeds the distance of 200 miles, in which case it is the outer limit of the shelf that determines the dividing line between the shelf and the deep sea-bed regime.

The definition of mineral resources

The fact that the area of application of the regime was specified also helped to clarify the problem of defining the 'mineral resources' that would be included in the regime. At an early stage of the negotiations it was thought that only certain types of resources (with particular reference to oil) should be included.[131] However, once it had been decided that the regime would cover the continent and the continental shelf in the terms that have been outlined, the mineral resources could be more broadly defined. The 1984 Draft Articles defined mineral resources to mean 'all non-living natural non-renewable resources, including but not limited to, fossil fuels, metallic and non-metallic minerals'.[132] Consequently, the regime will cover any type of non-living and non-renewable natural resources.[133] The only type of resource that apparently falls outside this broad definition are the icebergs since, although they are technically a mineral resource, they are also of a renewable nature. In view of the potential importance of icebergs as a resource they will probably require in the future an addition to the regime to enable their eventual development to be controlled.[134]

Another idea that was initially envisaged was that of establishing different standards and procedures for the various types of minerals to be included in the regime, the main aim being to separate the case of petroleum from that of solid minerals. However, this approach was later abandoned since it did not have sufficient technical justification and.

moreover, the special needs of each type of potential exploitation will always be dealt with in the framework of the process of issuing the required authorization.[135]

5.4   The system of exploration and exploitation

The nature, rules and procedures of the specific system in which mineral resources activities are to be organized were naturally central to the negotiations of the regime.[136] This aspect involves complex questions affecting both the internal and the external accommodation, particularly in so far as it once again raises the question of the fundamental standpoints of the claimant and non-claimant countries. Irrespective of the manner in which powers are distributed within this regime, including the question of powers of States, an aspect that will be examined in Chapters 7 and 8, the basis of the system is that there shall be a recognized 'authority' em-powered to grant the required authorizations and, in general, to be responsible for administering the system;[137] while claimants have sought to identify this authority with the powers of the State claiming territory in Antarctica, other countries have favoured a privileged role for the State sponsoring applications for mineral activities and yet others have aspired to a prominent role on the basis of the size of their general Antarctic operations; on the other hand, the institutions being established by the regime – a Commission, Advisory Committee and Regulatory Commit-tees, which will be examined in Chapter 8 – will certainly have also a major role to play in the process of authorization and administration, sharing some powers with participating States.

The different economic philosophies and traditions of the Consultative Parties were very much in evidence in discussions on the design of the system for organizing such activities. One point of view maintained that the main objective was for the system to be an open one which would ensure prompt access to resources and would involve the minimum of regulation and intervention by the 'authority' in order to achieve the objectives of the regime, particularly in regard to environmental protec-tion. Another point of view held that the system should provide all safeguards to guarantee that the activities would be conducted in an orderly and safe manner, with particular attention to the requirements of the environment.[138]

The same somewhat divergent approaches that we considered in relation to the objectives of the regime similarly determine these different points of view concerning the nature of the system. Notwithstanding these legitimate differences, it must be borne in mind that they do not have the antagonistic ideological connotations that were characteristic of the negotiations on the deep sea-bed regime in the Law of the Sea Conference.[139] Concepts such as the unitary or parallel system of exploitation were absent in the case of the Antarctic.[140] This difference can be accounted for partly by the spirit of co-operation and accommodation that is inherent in the Antarctic Treaty system but it is also due specifically to the fact that it was felt desirable to avoid a repetition of the experience of the negotiations on this subject at the Law of the Sea Conference.[141]

Thus, those that favour an open access system accept the existence of an 'authority' endowed with the necessary powers. Those that favour a system provided with ample safeguards also agree that the powers invested in the 'authority' cannot represent a bureaucratic and arbitrary hindrance to activities. All sides also accept the basic principle that the system should make no discrimination of any kind on the basis of nationality.[142] It was on the basis of this same understanding that the institutions of the regime were conceived in a more functional and practical and less bureaucratic manner than is commonly exemplified in some manifestations of contemporary international practice as we shall have occasion to examine in Chapter 8.

Once the basic criterion that the Antarctic mineral activities are subject to the controls and powers provided for under the regime has been accepted, the question arises as to the nature of these controls and the extent of the corresponding powers. The consideration of the stages of mineral activity and the conditions attaching to them will help to explain the main alternatives and approaches that arise in this connection.

Stages of mineral activity and necessary distinctions
Recommendation XI-1 provided that the regime should apply 'to all mineral resource activities' thus assuming that all stages of mineral activities would be included.[143] This criterion was subsequently confirmed when the draft articles defined 'Antarctic mineral resource activities' in a broad manner, including specifically the stages of prospecting, exploration and development of mineral resources, and excluding, as clarified by the 1984 revision, scientific research activities, the latter being governed by the provisions of the 1959 Treaty as regards both the freedom of scientific investigation and the obligation to publish findings.[144]

A recent technical study identified four stages into which mineral resource activities are generally divided: (i) regional geological exploration which is basically a scientific activity intended to identify possible areas of interest; (ii) basic commercial exploration, the purpose of which is to identify structures that might contain hydrocarbons in commercial quantities, a stage which, in general, coincides partly with prospecting activities and partly with exploration activities; (iii) exploratory drilling by means of which the hydrocarbon content is verified; and (iv) exploitation or development which will take place if the previous stage is successful.[145]

The principal difficulty that arises in this connection is that, as pointed out in the study, 'there is no sharp distinction between the four stages'.[146] Current activities in the Antarctic mainly correspond to the first stage and use the methods of scientific, geological and geophysical investigation.[147] To this extent, these activities are naturally permitted under the Treaty. However, some of these activities border on the second stage.[148] As long as they are authentically scientific activities they will continue to be compatible with the Treaty, but to the extent that they may be classified as prospecting or exploration activities, that would create a different situation. The possibility that this has already occurred has given rise to considerable controversy, above all because the moratorium provisions might thereby be compromised.[149]

The problem of how to distinguish scientific investigation activities from those of prospecting is a difficult one in view of the fact that, in general, similar methods are used in both types of activity. However, the respective regimes are entirely different since, while the former involves an obligation to publish the results, the second is covered by the standards relating to 'proprietary data' which are confidential. The mineral regime naturally envisages guaranteeing this latter.[150] There is, moreover, the difficulty that certain prospecting activities might be carried out under the guise of scientific investigation without all the data being made available which are required for meaningful interpretation of the results.

One possible way of achieving this distinction would be to establish a data centre for mineral-related scientific investigation to which it would be mandatory to provide full information on the results of scientific investigation, which would certainly be compatible with the Treaty regime. This centre might form part of the regime and might comprise the machinery for verifying whether the information made available is reasonably comprehensive and for dealing with objections on the matter. The idea of a scientific research institute or fund within the Antarctic system is an old one[151] and such a data centre might be associated with it. If the entity undertaking research opted to provide comprehensive information, the activity in question would be classified under the scientific investigation regime. If, on the other hand, it opted to withhold the information or a significant proportion of usable data, it would be regarded as coming under the prospecting regime and would have to abide by the rules and conditions established under the regime. In this way, scientific research activities would not be hindered, the availability of their findings would be ensured and prospecting activities that might be carried out on the fringe of the regime would be prevented.

The prospecting regime: conceptual difficulties

Having distinguished between scientific investigation and prospecting on the basis of a particular criterion, it is necessary to determine which specific activities are to be included under the latter category and are, therefore, to be subject to the rights and obligations of the regime. The use of the ordinary methods of geological and geophysical investigation, including the use of remote sensors and the gathering of test samples, raises no difficulty at all as it is the same type of technique as is used in scientific investigation.[152] If some of these methods were to have an environmental impact it would be minimal and could be controlled in the same way as the possible effects of scientific research under the Treaty.[153]

The case of other techniques such as dredging, excavation and, above all, drilling is different. Although they may be methods that are useful at the prospecting stage, they already begin typically to resemble the exploration phase. Furthermore, these methods have a potentially greater impact on the environment, ranging from localized situations to others on a large scale.[154] Owing to those difficulties, it must be assumed that while the environmental point of view might have sought their exclusion or restriction, the developmental criterion would have to some extent favoured their inclusion.[155] It must also be pointed out that it is always possible to distinguish between different types of excavation and drilling, in accordance with their objectives, location, depth and other criteria, and that on this basis some may be accepted and others prohibited.

The problem of drilling raises the additional question of whether such activity is permitted under the scientific investigation regime of the Treaty or whether it should be regarded as a commercial aspect which is prohibited. Recommendation XI-1 refers indirectly to this matter since the definition of commercial exploration in paragraph VI includes the activity of 'non-scientific exploratory drilling'.[156] Thus it would seem to postulate the existence of 'scientific exploratory drilling' which would not be defined as commercial exploration and which, accordingly, might be a scientific investigation activity. It is well known that the ship *Glomar Challenger* was engaged in drilling on the Antarctic continental shelf, and this seems to indicate that the United States favours this latter interpretation.[157] However, as we have mentioned earlier, this point of view does not seem to be generally shared.

Owing to the existence of different points of view, the 1983 Draft Articles did not define 'prospecting'; this was done, however, in the 1984 revision in a careful manner which, on the one hand, includes but is not limited to, geological, geochemical and geophysical means and field observation, the use of remote sensing techniques and collecting of surface and seafloor samples; but, on the other hand, it does not include dredging or other surface or subsurface excavations, except for the purpose of obtaining samples, or drilling other than shallow drilling not exceeding a depth yet to be defined.[158] According to Article XXIV (*ter*) of this revision, when an area has been identified for exploration and development, the Commission may apply the rules governing prospecting to drilling activities at a greater depth, thus expanding the scope of prospecting in specific cases and subject to such conditions as this organ may establish. This definition involves an effort to differentiate the activities which are characteristic of prospecting and generally aimed at the identification of areas of mineral resource potential, from the activities that are part of the phase of exploration.

The second major problem relating to prospecting is whether the activities should be subject to prior authorization in the context of the regime or whether they could be engaged in freely. Various alternatives or models have been suggested for the specific organization of prospecting activities taking into account the basic options mentioned above. In the case that prior authorization is required, the study by Bergsager indicates four principal models[159] under which: (i) prospecting is carried out by the Authority through a subsidiary organ, an arrangement which, although it permits full control of the activity, is costly and is generally inefficient as regards results and procedures; (ii) the Authority undertakes regional prospecting and entrusts the more detailed prospecting to interested companies, an approach that is applied in the continental shelf oil development of Norway[160] and which also requires substantial investment; (iii) regional prospecting is carried out on an individual basis while the Authority merely plays a supervisory role, an approach which has also been used in the continental shelf of Norway; and (iv) prospecting is carried out consistently on an individual basis. The same author proposes the third alternative for Antarctica, while seeing some merit in the fourth, in view of the high risk factor and the substantial investment that is required.[161]

The free prospecting model, which only requires notification and an undertaking to comply with certain environmental or other requirements, has been provided for, as far as the sea-bed is concerned, in Part XI of the Law of the Sea Convention.[162]

The decision on this matter in the case of the Antarctic has once again divided the proponents of development and the environmentalists, subject to the relativity of their respective positions. While the former have favoured prospecting without prior authorization, the latter have been more inclined to make such authorization a requirement.[163] This aspect is also bound up with the types of activities which are ultimately to be included within the definition of prospecting; the greater the environmental risk involved, as occurs with some kinds of drilling, the stronger will be the case for a mandatory prior authorization.

Recommendation XI-1 included prospecting within the regime since, on the one hand, it refers to 'all mineral resources activities' and, on the other, it defines commercial exploration as 'activities related to minerals involving, in general, retention of proprietary data and/or non-scientific exploratory drilling'.[164] Although the question of drilling has been discussed in the terms that have been explained above, prospecting certainly comprises the case of 'proprietary data'. It is interesting to note that in this Recommendation the prospecting stage is clearly assimilated to commercial exploration and not to scientific investigation activity. However, it is not specified whether or not that stage of activity would require prior authorization.

The draft articles chose the option of not requiring authorization for prospecting activities and envisaged a straightforward system whereby the sponsoring State shall notify the Secretariat established under the regime.[165] On the other hand, as we have mentioned earlier, because of the existing disagreement about which activities should be included under the concept of prospecting, the 1983 draft articles did not define prospecting and the 1984 revision attempted a compromise formula.[166] The approach chosen has been sharply criticized since, if no more than a simple notification were required, activities might be undertaken which were potentially hazardous for the environment and were not subject to strict prior control by the regime.[167] This situation would be particularly delicate in the case of drilling, which although limited to certain types and depth can anyhow be somewhat expanded by the Commission.[168]

In view of the serious differences of opinion on this matter, the 1984 Draft Articles introduced a procedure for the review of prospecting whereby any Party to the regime can request the sponsoring State to provide further particulars of prospecting activity; if a Party considers that any such activity may be inconsistent with the regime or conflict with other uses of Antarctica or, in the case of drilling, dredging, excavating or establishing installations, present a hazard to the Antarctic environment, it may request this review. The procedure would require the support of the request by other Parties, in a number yet to be determined; the Commission could then recommend measures to ensure consistency with the regime or reduce or eliminate other conflicts or environmental hazard.[169] While this review mechanism is not quite strong enough to satisfy the concerns of the environmental point of view, it is in any case a step forward in the right direction. It should also be noted that this mechanism is without prejudice of the procedures for the settlement of disputes under the regime, which will be discussed in Chapter 8.

Under the draft articles, notification requires the simultaneous provision of various types of information to identify the area in which prospecting is to take place, its duration and the resources to be prospected for. Additional requirements have been introduced with the general aim of environmental protection, including an assessment of the environmental impact of such activities and the provisions of appropriate information on the methods to be used, the installations necessary, and other aspects.[170] The Commission to be established under the regime will have the power to designate those areas where for historic, ecological, environmental or scientific reasons prospecting or other mineral activities should be prohibited; this could of course include the Specially Protected Areas and the Sites of Special Scientific Interest designated under the Antarctic Treaty arrangements.[171]

It must also be borne in mind that, in any case, mineral resource activities must be conducted in a way that is compatible with the other uses of Antarctica and this implies various restrictions as to the area and other matters.[172] The Commission, under the procedures for reviewing prospecting will have the duty of verifying such compatibility and it will be generally empowered *inter alia* to impose additional requirements for environmental protection or other needs.

In accordance with the common standards governing this activity, prospecting does not confer 'any rights or title to resources',[173] which can be acquired only by means of a licence or contract. As we have explained earlier, prospecting is covered by the concept of 'proprietary data'; however, this does not prevent the circulation of reports of a general nature to all parties without compromising the necessary confidentiality; full information may be made available if the prospecting is terminated and, after a lapse of time, is not continued in the form of exploration activities.[174]

Exploration and the identification of areas
The exploration stage involves major changes as compared with the preceding stage of prospecting because its objective is to identify and

evaluate specific mineral deposits. For that purpose, it requires the use of techniques which differ considerably from those proper to scientific investigation and prospecting, in particular, various types of drilling – including some in depth – and excavation. Only pilot projects or commercial production are customarily excluded from this stage as they form part of the phase of exploitation or development of the resource. Given the different nature of exploration, it is desirable to avoid any confusion between its techniques and those of prospecting, as has occurred in connection with drilling. The 1984 Draft Articles defined exploration along these lines and specifically included among its activities 'exploratory drilling, dredging and other surface or subsurface excavations required to determine the nature and size of mineral resource deposits and the feasibility of their development. . .'.[175] Unlike prospecting, there is no limitation of depth for such drilling nor other exclusions as to the type of activity undertaken.

The stage of exploration requires, in the first place, the identification of specific areas which will normally be smaller in size than those previously prospected.[176] To that end it is desirable to identify the areas where all mineral activity will be excluded for ecological and other reasons. Such an exclusion has been declared in the case of Svalbard and Greenland.[177] As we have examined, in the case of Antarctica the Commission to be set up under this regime will be generally empowered to designate areas where mineral activities shall be prohibited;[178] the areas protected under various Antarctic resource regimes are likely candidates for this exclusion.[179] On this basis, unnecessary investment in the prospecting and exploration of areas which will not ultimately be open may be avoided.[180]

The decision to open up areas of Antarctica has been described as 'a small technical step but a giant political step'[181] owing to the expectations that it would produce with regard to the potential development of resources. Perhaps for this reason, the arguments that were initially put forward as regards the extension of the areas that might be made available appear to be diametrically opposed. Some ecological groups have argued for the exclusion of areas comprising complete ecosystems,[182] an approach which is sometimes linked with the concept of an 'Antarctic park' or other initiatives that will be considered later.[183] This would result in only small areas, if any, remaining available for mineral activities. The Consultative Parties, acknowledging the need for excluded areas, tend in general to restrict these to the cases provided for in the special regimes or other very specific situations, an approach which would make available vastly extended areas for the conduct of mineral activities.[184]

The opening up of areas also raises the problem of which State or entity should instigate this process, a question which, to some extent, is related to the distribution of powers within the regime. As we shall examine below, the basic options are that the pertinent identification be undertaken by the institutional machinery of the regime, the State claiming sovereignty over the area, the sponsoring State or the entity interested in undertaking the exploration, all of what relates in turn to the need of arranging for an acceptable internal accommodation.[185]

Models for the organization of exploration

The exploration stage, and also the exploitation phase which follows it, are subject to the essential requirement of prior authorization in the context of the Antarctic minerals regime. Although in many cases under domestic legal systems the exploration phase and the production phase are clearly separate, the latter requiring different rules and undertakings, in the Antarctic regime this distinction has become somewhat blurred and has tended to rely more on the idea of integrated operations covering both phases, as is also the case with the sea-bed regime under Part XI of the Law of the Sea Convention.[186] As we shall examine later, this approach has met severe criticism.

The requirement of prior authorization is due not only to the nature of the activities undertaken and their greater environmental risk but also to the type of rights and duties that are comprised in regard to resources, legal commitments and other matters. These rights and duties must be specified in the corresponding contract or authorization including the definition of the relevant financial arrangements, the withholding of the necessary confidential information and other aspects.

Exactly in what legal form this authorization will be granted is something not yet entirely clear in the Antarctic minerals regime. If it is in the form of a licence the arrangement can be described, following Cameron's analysis of the British petroleum licence, as 'the legal link between the State's possession of rights to offshore petroleum resources and the exploration and exploitation of those resources by the oil companies';[187] the transfer of rights that takes place involves the 'exclusive licence and liberty . . . to search for and bore for, and get, petroleum'[188] under defined obligations set out in the model clauses,[189] but does not involve the transfer of a title to the resources *in situ*.[190] If the pertinent legal arrangement is that of a concession, as was stated in the *Aramco* case, 'it involves, first, a State act, and, second, rights of ownership vested in the concessionaire';[191] in the more traditional form of concessions the transfer of the right of ownership could refer to the resources *in situ* and was usually accompanied by rather broad stabilization clauses. It is quite unlikely that the Antarctic regime will follow the option of a concession and, as we shall examine further below, it is rather probable that a kind of licensing or other modern contractual approach will be favoured.

Assuming that the Antarctic minerals regime will follow a licence system or some form of modern contractual arrangement, there are three principal models used in international practice to this effect. One model is that of 'open negotiations' in which the State or the competent authority chooses the area opened for applications, evaluates the qualification of applicants, negotiates contracts with the interested parties and grants the pertinent authorization, including the specific legal rights involved.[192] This option has been used, according to Bergsager, in Norway and Chile and to some extent in Great Britain and the Soviet Union, but, in the view of the same author, the terms of each negotiation vary considerably and consequently raise the problem of the lack of uniformity in the application of the regime; also from the financial point of view this alternative usually entailse high initial investments.[193]

A second model is that of 'auction bidding' in which areas are selected, evaluated and then auctioned among the interested parties. This approach has the advantage of stimulating competition but also involves the difficulty of requiring a high initial investment and consequent risks. This system has been used in the United States and to a limited extent in Great Britain.[194]

The third model is that of the 'automatic' licensing or qualification for a contract on the basis of complying with certain technical conditions defined in the regime. The role of the licensing authority is, in general, limited to that of verifying compliance with these conditions, studying and negotiating the programme of work and, if necessary, determining certain characteristics of the rights such as the area or duration. This is the approach used in the Svalbard regime and in the case of the deep sea-bed regime under the Law of the Sea Convention.[195]

The choice in the Antarctic case has certainly not been an easy one because of the peculiar legal characteristics of the Antarctic continent and its maritime areas. This decision is closely linked to the options of the internal accommodation including the various institutional approaches that we shall consider later. The open negotiation model might be an attractive option if the relevant authority of the regime for the granting of licences or contracts were the State maintaining a territorial claim since, as Bergsager points out, 'such a system works well in areas where there is a clear national jurisdiction'.[196] However, as we shall examine in Chapters 7 and 8, it is clear that the competences to this effect will be differently conceived to meet the requirements of the internal accommodation. For this reason, the model would be difficult to apply in Antarctica and might impede the process of accommodation. It would, moreover, have implications for the uniformity of the regime since this option might be applied in radically different ways from one negotiation to another, giving rise to unnecessary competition between the various territorial claimants. This is not to say that there should be no negotiation at all since it may serve a useful purpose in specific cases or at particular stages of the process. The 'auction bidding' model has also been recommended for the Antarctic case, with a number of possible variants or adjustments.[197]

The model that has been chosen in the Antarctic minerals negotiations is principally the automatic one but so qualified that the applicant concerned would have a large measure of initiative while the institutions of the regime would retain the power of verification and decision. It seems clear that a compromise between the exploitational and environmental approaches has once again been reached in this scheme, since, while the proponents of development gain a considerable degree of initiative, the environmentalist pressures have ensured that the institutions to be established will control environmental aspects of the activity proposed or undertaken. It must, however, be noted that the concept of 'automatic' in this case is relative since, in the last analysis, the organs have the important power of accepting the application or of rejecting it if it fails to comply with the applicable general or specific standards.

The system envisaged in the Antarctic mineral regime has four principal stages which will be considered in turn: the preliminary stage of applying for exploration and for opening up the area; the stage at which the formal application is submitted and the operators selected; the stage of evaluating the application selected on the basis of general and specific criteria; and the stage of elaboration and approval of the management scheme.

The exploration application: preliminary stage

The preliminary stage begins when the interested party notifies the Secretariat to be set up under the regime of its interest in exploring a particular area and requesting the pertinent authorization to this effect. This notification must include all relevant details concerning the area, the resources to be explored, the methods to be used and the environmental assessment of the possible effects, together with measures to minimize any environmental impact.[198] It must be pointed out that, as a consequence of the type of model chosen, the general identification of the exploration area is made by the interested party, and not by the institutions of the regime or States parties as generally occurs with other models.

However, under the 1984 Draft Articles, the Regulatory Committee has been entrusted with the important task of identifying the specific blocks for the exploration activities within the general area proposed by the applicant.[199]

It must also be noted that there is a subtle but important change in the approach followed by the various draft articles on the question of the precise scope of the authorization for exploration. While the 1983 draft articles envisaged that the decision of the Commission would refer to the opening of the area requested, the 1984 version has clarified that such decison is to make a determination authorizing the submission of applications, that does not necessarily entail that the exploration or exploitation will be permitted;[200] the decision to authorize activities will depend on the subsequent stages. This change of approach means in fact that the automatic nature of the model chosen has been diminished to allow a greater role of the institutions in the process of authorization.

The fundamental decision to be made by the Commission at this stage is to determine whether, in relation to the area in question, authorization should be given for submission of exploration applications or whether, on the contrary, such authorization would not be appropriate because the activity envisaged involves an unacceptable risk for the environment. Given the importance of this determination it has been envisaged that it shall be made by consensus, not majority voting, and that the opinion of the Advisory Committee will also be required.[201] As we shall examine in Chapter 8, a Special Meeting of States Parties has also been envisaged as a part of this procedure for the identification of areas.

If the Commission makes an affirmative determination, it will have to specify the necessary technical details relating to the area approved.[202] It is particularly important that the area can be treated as a single unit from the point of view of the exploration and exploitation of the resource,[203] since it often occurs that deposits extend across different exploitational or jurisdictional areas.[204] The resource to be explored and the procedure to be followed for requests covering different resources will also be specified at this stage. These problems are common to all mineral administration regimes.[205]

Various functions of the Commission, which will be considered in Chapter 8, are related to this and following stages. An affirmative determination by the Commission will also trigger the convening of the Regulatory Committee, which shall undertake the necessary preparatory work, particularly in connection with the identification of specific blocks and the establishment of fees.[206]

The selection of applicants: criteria

If the determination made by the Commission at the preliminary stage is positive, the formal application for exploration may then be submitted by interested parties in relation to specific blocks that have been identified. Such applications must contain all relevant technical details to facilitate the decision of the Commission on whether to accept or not the activities proposed.[207]

The principal function of the Commission in this phase is that of selecting the applicant. In the first place, it must be established that the applicant is of sufficient technical and financial standing to be able to assume rights and duties within the regime. The first evaluation on this matter will have to be made by the sponsoring State but it will naturally be verified by the Commission. If the applicant is a State Party, this condition will have to be kept in consideration, as is also the case in the deep sea-bed regime under Part XI of the Law of the Sea Convention;[208] this does not denote the granting of any privilege or exception, but merely that a treatment is required that will be in keeping with the public nature of the State applicant.

Given the fact the model is generally of the automatic type and that the initiative lies with the applicant, it is possible that several applications will be submitted in respect of the same approved blocks. In this case, the Commission will have to make its own selection, without prejudging the possibility that it might prove appropriate to impose a general restriction on the number of applications should the size of the block or the nature of the deposit make this advisable.[209] One of the first selection criteria will always be the technical and financial standing of the applicant, as well as his compliance with the requirements concerning sponsorship and other similar matters. Next, consideration will have to be given to the customary standards concerning priority in relation to the order in which applications have been submitted,[210] the determination as to whether the background information is sufficiently comprehensive and other similar considerations. On this matter the auction bidding system that we mentioned earlier might prove an important option as a means of deciding between several similarly qualified applicants. Alternatively, the selection of applicants might take into account the degree of international participation involved in the proposed contract, through joint ventures or other appropriate arrangements. This latter approach has been followed by the 1986 Draft Articles in terms of assigning priority to applications involving broader participation.

Some other considerations will probably have an influence in the selection process. If one sponsoring State or applicants of its nationality get to the point of dominating most of the blocks available for exploration and exploitation, the need to examine the problem in terms of anti-monopoly policies will arise; this and other special policies of the regime will be examined in Chapter 6. On the other hand, it is also probable that the countries that have made a greater contribution to the development of research and technology in the Antarctic will seek to ensure that this is taken into account in the selection process.

Evaluation of the application and policy decisions
The third stage of the process is the most complex in that it involves the power of the institutions to be set up under the regime to evaluate the application and to approve or reject it. The relevant Regulatory Committee and the Advisory Committee will be the main participants in this phase, without prejudice to the role devolving on the Commission. The task of the Advisory Committee during this stage will be that of advising whether or not the application, if approved, would involve an unacceptable risk for the Antarctic environment, for which purpose the application will have to be evaluated in the light of the environmental principles of the regime and of any decisions or guidelines adopted by the Commission.

In the context of the more automatic approach followed by the 1983 Draft Articles, the Advisory Committee had a rather weak role, which was limited in general to the preparation of scientific, technical and environmental guidelines for the activities proposed. This role was later strengthened so as to assess the application, reach a determination on the risks involved and prepare guidelines for the conduct of activities.[211]. This evolution appears to evidence the need for more articulate scientific advice in the process of evaluation of applications, an aspect which has also been reflected to some extent and for other purposes in the regimes for the Continental Shelf and the Deep Sea-bed in the Law of the Sea Convention; in the case of the Antarctic minerals regime, however, the scientific and technical information is mostly provided for by the applicant and the sponsoring State, and only in a limited manner by the Advisory Committee, a situation that, as we shall examine in Chapter 8, has led to criticism of the institutional arrangements.

If it is advised that the risk is unacceptable, the Regulatory Committee will have the option of either to reject the application or to refer it to the Commission which may authorize the Regulatory Committee to proceed with its consideration in order to find a way of overcoming the environmental shortcomings that have been established.[212] In this latter case additional conditions will be required and it is probable that a type of negotiation with the applicant would take place, thus escaping the general automatic nature of the procedure.

If the determination of the Advisory Committee is that the application does not involve an unacceptable risk, or the problems are otherwise solved, the Regulatory Committee shall proceed with the preparation of the management scheme, taking fully into account the guidelines mentioned, thus opening the next stage of the process.[213]

It has also been tentatively suggested that during this stage the Regulatory Committee should define the specific terms and conditions to be applied to the application and activities under consideration, but this is more properly a task which belongs to the management scheme. The difference between defining the terms and conditions beforehand and defining them in each management scheme is not so much of a technical nature but stems from the inherent problems of the internal accommodation. While the first approach favours the intervention of the institutions of the regime, with particular reference to the Regulatory Committee and the Commission, the second facilitates the intervention of the State maintaining a territorial claim in the area to which the application refers in the preparation of such management scheme; as will be examined next, the claimant State may be entrusted by the Regulatory Committee with the task of preparing the draft management scheme, which would then be discussed and approved with the participation of the institutions.[214]

Approval of the management scheme
The preparation and approval of the management scheme is a task of the greatest importance since, in effect, it entails defining the specific terms and conditions that will form part of the authorization. From the institutional point of view, this phase has raised difficult problems of accommodation and it has accordingly been provided in the negotiating texts that the draft scheme will be prepared by a Member State of the Regulatory Committee, or occasionally by more than one such State, designated by the Committee. This Member State may be the State maintaining a territorial claim in the area in question, an approach which has been disputed by other States aspiring to have either a more powerful role for themselves or a greater role for the institutions to be established under the regime.[215] It has also been suggested that the draft scheme might be prepared by a Subcommittee of the said body.

The approval of the draft management scheme will be granted or withheld by the Regulatory Committee itself but its decision must subsequently be referred to the Commission for final consideration. The granting of the exploration authorization, which represents the culmination of the process, is authorized only after the Commission has approved the management scheme. Similarly, it has been provided that if the scheme is not approved by the Commission it will be referred back to the Regulatory Commission for reconsideration and possible revision.[216] Even though it is possible that the Commission may ultimately reject the scheme and, consequently, will not grant the corresponding authorization, this is most unlikely to occur in this phase, since the application has passed through the crucial determinations of earlier stages. In any event, as we shall examine when dealing with the institutional aspects of the regime, there has also been a struggle in the negotiations between those supporting the approach that the final power and decision should stay with the Commission and those who favour that such should be a function of the Regulatory Committee. The 1986 revision of the draft articles to some extent reflects the latter point of view, since the Regulatory Committee will issue the exploration permit, subject eventually to a review of the management scheme by the Commission if this is requested on the ground of a violation of the rules of the Convention or abuse of power.

From the point of view of the relationship existing between the principles and standards of the regime, the approval of the management scheme entails a detailed and precise application of these principles and standards to the activities authorized. The first and more general level is represented by the basic objectives and principles of the regime; the second by the standards approved by the Commission as part of its functions in compliance with these objectives and principles; the third normative level is that of the guidelines to be established by the Advisory Committee in a manner that is compatible with the above; and lastly, the management scheme will lay down the specific details deriving from this hierarchy of principles and standards.

For this reason, its specific content will include a wide range of matters to be encompassed. The regime will merely enumerate these matters which subsequently will be fully developed in each scheme. This approach is strictly in accordance with the decision that the Antarctic minerals regime should not constitute a detailed mining code and will thus differ also on this point from the deep sea-bed regime under the Law of the Sea Convention which provides for the full detail of the conduct of exploration and exploitation activities.[217]

The enumeration of subjects reveals the scope of the management scheme as foreseen by the draft articles; the list of subjects included in the 1984 draft articles follows, with indication in parentheses of the corresponding 1983 version when relevant to evident changes of approach: the law applicable to the applicant and persons employed by him; arrangements for the grant of authorization (licensing arrangements); inspection and enforcement; levies payable by the successful applicant (reimbursement by the successful applicant of the costs of implementation of the management scheme); taxes, royalties or payments in kind; technical and safety specifications; monitoring; depletion policy; time limits and diligence requirements; duration of permits; data collection and reporting; contingency plans to deal with accidents; liability, bonding and insurance; assignment or relinquishment of permits; decommissioning; procedures for modification; suspension, modification or cancellation of the management scheme.[218]

Even though we shall come back later to some of these points, it should be noted at this stage that they involve delicate questions of jurisdiction, of applicable policy and of accommodation between divergent positions. Only in the context of a regime of this nature is it possible to achieve the necessary understanding between the Treaty parties on these delicate subjects to enable exploration and exploitation to take place in the future.

The authorization for exploitation or development

As we have mentioned earlier, the Antarctic minerals regime, unlike some domestic models, opted for the approach of closely linking the phase of exploration with that of exploitation or development in a kind of integrated operation.[219] This substantive integration applies even though, as a further environmental precaution, provision has been made for separate authorization for the exploitation stage.[220] This should not prevent an applicant who desires to confine his activity to the exploration phase from doing so.[221]

The entity concerned is required to apply for a development permit during the period in which the management scheme and the exploration permit are in force, an application which must be accompanied by the relevant comprehensive and up-to-date information.[222]

The Advisory Committee shall review this application and determine whether it reveals any significant modifications to the development activities envisaged at the time the management scheme was adopted; this body will also determine whether there are environmental considerations that were not initially foreseen. If modifications to the management scheme are required, the Advisory Committee will adopt new guidelines on the basis of which the Regulatory Committee will consider these modifications and will refer the modified scheme to the Commission. If no modifications are required, the management scheme referred to the Commission shall be the original one.[223]

In either case, the Commission 'shall, without further review, authorize the issue of a development permit'.[224] This indicates the extent to which exploration and exploitation are integrated within the management scheme and explains why, in the view of the proponents of this approach, it is unnecessary for the Commission to review in detail everything that has been done in earlier stages since the examination of the matter made by the Advisory Committee and by the Regulatory Committee in the terms indicated will be adequate enough. This approach, however, has been criticized on the grounds that it does not ensure adequate environmental protection and it cannot fully take into account the many changes that may have intervened since the adoption of the original management scheme; suggestions have accordingly been made that there should be a procedure for more detailed discussion of the exploitation application.[225]

5.5   The contractor and the required conditions

The discussion of the requirements for qualifying as a contractor under the Antarctic minerals regime needs, in the first place, clarification of a question of terminology. Under the British legislation, for example, the licence will normally be awarded to a number of companies forming a 'consortium' which takes the form of a joint venture; this legal entity will hold the rights and assume the obligations under the licence; one of these companies will be appointed as the single 'operator' for the consortium, that entails a number of other legal relations.[226] The 1984 Draft Articles have identified the 'Operator' of this regime as any participant in Antarctic mineral resource activities meeting the requirements laid down by these articles, which will be examined below; in this regime the expression 'operator' is used in a way as a synonym of 'consortium', that is, the entity holding the rights and assuming the obligations under the licence or contract, but in another way is also used to mean the entity which will actually undertake the operations, all of it without prejudice to joint venture arrangements.[227] So as to avoid confusions we shall use the expression 'contractor' to identify the entity which will be awarded the licence or contract, which in any event, as we shall examine, is likely to take the form of a contract under the regime, and which can constitute a joint venture; 'operator' will thus be the entity actually undertaking the mineral activities.

The agreement on the general criteria relating to the nature and procedures of the system for exploration and exploitation has also made it easier in the Antarctic negotiation to determine who should be the contractors under the regime. This determination was one of the complex questions that had to be solved by the deep sea-bed regime under the Law of the Sea Convention in view of the widely differing points of view concerning the applicable exploitation system, with particular reference to the question of its 'unitary' or 'parallel' nature, or the alternative 'joint ventures' approach.[228]

Although this ideological discussion was absent in the case of the Antarctic, it is interesting to note that moves were made, in any case, to ensure a collective scheme of operation, which, by its nature, also implied a centralized system of exploitation. An initial proposal to that end, of academic origin, was that responsibility for the operation should be borne by an international company formed by the Consultative Parties within a system of exploitation by consortium; this concept is comparable to that of the enterprise in the deep sea-bed regime mentioned, a model which was specifically taken into account in that connection, even though, in the Antarctic case, it would not be independent of governments and was conceived as a means of helping to channel private enterprise.[229]

At the time of the Law of the Sea Conference negotiations, an academic proposal was also made to the effect of following the model of Intelsat, Comsat and Inmarsat for overcoming the deadlock,[230] a proposal which points in the same direction as that examined above. It must also be noted that the idea of an Antarctic enterprise was raised during the first discussions concerning the regime to be set up in the Antarctic continent.[231]

Another initiative was of an official nature: it has been described in the following terms:

> A different and, as yet, minority view looks to having Antarctic mining undertaken on the basis of some form of collective arrangement . . . what can best be described as compulsory joint venture arrangements under which any entity applying for a licence to explore and exploit minerals in Antarctica would be obliged to accept, as partners, other entities, whether governmental or private, wishing to have this status.[232]

However, this approach did not find support as it was incompatible with the chosen system of exploitation, although this does not, of course, affect the important role to be played by joint ventures of a voluntary type.[233]

The collective option having been excluded, the scheme of contractors is of a diversified nature. Consequently, State Parties to the regime will be able to undertake activities either directly or through the intermediary of their State companies or agencies of various types. Similarly, such activities may be undertaken by individuals or by legal entities, provided they meet certain conditions. The way will also be open for various types of joint venture or consortium with the voluntary participation of any of the above-mentioned categories or combinations thereof.[234]

Except in the case of a State Party undertaking activities directly, a prerequisite for contractors will be the sponsorship of a State Party to the regime. This condition is also imposed for State companies or agencies participating in such activities. The exception which is made in the case of a State Party becoming involved directly is justified on the grounds that it is a State and will act as its own sponsor.

For the above purposes, the contractor must have a substantial and genuine link with the sponsoring State. In the case of an individual, the link must be that he has the nationality of a State Party. In the case of a legal entity, the link takes the form of two cumulative requirements: it must 'have its central management and control and substantial resources located in the territory of a Party and be established under the laws of such Party'.[235]

In the case of the nationality of individuals, the major legal problems that may arise are relatively few. The main one probably occurs in the case of dual nationality. If the two States to which he is linked by nationality are both Parties to the regime, he will probably be able to opt for the sponsorship of one of them. Should only one of those States be a Party to the regime, only that State may act as a sponsor.

As far as the legal entities are concerned, it is interesting to note that the regime has taken note of the problems of nationality that have arisen in international law.[236] In this connection, the first requirement under this regime is that there should be a formal link by virtue of the fact that the entity is established under the laws of the sponsoring State.[237] However, a substantive link is also required, namely that it must have its central management and control in the territory of that State.[238] In addition, it is required that the entity should also have 'substantial resources' in that territory.[239] The purpose of all these requirements is, of course, to ensure that a link is 'substantial and genuine' and to avoid relations that are merely formal and do not represent an actual administrative and economic control.[240]

The consortia and joint venture arrangements[241]

The regime relating to joint ventures, consortia and other legal entities gives rise to more complex situations. Here again there is a need to clarify certain questions of concept and terminology. Under the British system, the arrangements related to the organization of a consortium made up of a partnership of oil companies is usually known as a 'joint venture';[242] the precise legal form of this joint venture is defined in the Joint Operating Agreement, which will deal basically with the rights and obligations of the participating entities, including such questions as percentage interests, joint or several liability, financial arrangements, appointment of the operator and the like.[243]

In the case of the Antarctic minerals regime, the concept of joint venture is somewhat broader. As far as participation in this type of entity is concerned, there may be combinations involving any of the categories of contractors mentioned;[244] the type of joint venture concerned is open in that they may be equity joint ventures, contractual joint ventures or any other type since no limitations on this matter are envisaged. The concept of joint venture thus appears to encompass in this regime both that of the consortium and the Joint Operating Agreement mentioned above.

Whatever combination is chosen, the consortium must certainly have the same genuine and substantive link with the sponsoring State. Special situations may arise in this connection such as the need to determine in which State Party the entity has its central management, control and substantial resources, given that it may be composed of participants of various national origins or, in the case of a joint venture formed by States, it will have to be determined which of those States will act formally as the sponsor.[245]

At one stage in the negotiations there was consideration of the idea of establishing a special regime for State joint ventures which were termed 'co-operative ventures'.[246] The purpose of this was to accommodate the positions of those Parties that favoured a collective system of contracts based on compulsory joint venture arrangements which was mentioned above; although this system was not adopted, a variant of this other type was conceived which would be compatible with the nature of the regime and for which special standards would apply. However, the broad interpretation of the term 'joint ventures' permits various forms of State partnership and of partnership between States and other entities which do not in fact require special standards. It is also possible that if the States Parties, or some of them, voluntarily agree, they may form a collective or co-operative consortium to conduct mineral activities, an approach which is similar to the idea of the Antarctic enterprise that was initially proposed and to which we have referred earlier.

The main problem raised by these consortia arrangements is that related to the participation of entities that have no genuine and substantive link with any State Party to the regime. This question involves complex policy decisions which have implications for the options of the regime's external accommodation. On the one hand, it might be thought that participation in consortia might be restricted to entities that have links with States Parties since, if that were not the case, the benefits of the regime might indirectly be extended to those that do not belong to it. If this were to occur, each of the partners in the consortia would have to meet the requirements of having a formal and substantive link with a State Party.

On the other hand, however, it must also be borne in mind that broader participation in such consortia might, in fact, facilitate such an external accommodation by progressively enabling entities that had not had the required experience of research, technology and operation to participate in activities in the Antarctic.[247] This is probably the most effective and practical means of opening up the Antarctic system.

It may be necessary to make a distinction in this connection. If the entity outside the system that desires to participate in it is a State or a State enterprise or agency, it would be justifiable to require such a State to accede to the regime since, if this were not done, it would, in fact, be a case of extending the benefits of the regime to third parties without requiring them to assume the corresponding obligations.[248] In the case of an individual or private legal entity, the participation criterion might be more flexible, as, indeed, it might be in the case of participation by certain suitably qualified developing countries. In any case, it would seem reasonable to envisage in this case a minority participation in the consortium, perhaps by keeping to a predetermined percentage, since the consortium holding a contract would be obliged, as far as the greater part of its composition was concerned, to meet the requirements that have been mentioned concerning the link with a State Party.

To the extent that this type of broader participation is open in a consortium, it would also be interesting to envisage the possibility of participation in such consortium of international organizations that might qualify on the basis of the nature of their activities or fields of action.

The consortia arrangements have other important implications in regard to the general operation of the regime. These arrangements provide a suitable means of promoting the active participation of the developing countries acceding to the regime in the actual exploration and exploitation of mineral resources. The participation in a joint venture fulfils an integrative function within the regime in that it permits access to relevant experience and technology which would be of enormous benefit to the countries that have hitherto had no access to these advantages.[249]

It must be remembered in this connection that the negotiations on the deep sea-bed regime in the Law of the Sea Conference considered the option of a joint ventures system in place of the parallel system of exploitation which was ultimately adopted.[250] If the first of the options mentioned had been approved, that might have given a more positive and integrative direction to co-operation since the second, as its name indicates, tends to keep the activities undertaken separate in accordance with the type of contractor involved. Although this matter is not up for discussion in the Antarctic case and the context of the negotiation is altogether different, the integrative function of joint venture arrangements might contribute positively to the operation of the regime.

Role of the sponsoring State

The requirement of a substantive link with the sponsoring State is of particular importance in the context of this regime in view of the active role to be played by the sponsor. The sponsoring State has the function in the first place of assessing the technical and financial standing of the entities interested in conducting activities and on the basis of its assessment it will grant or withhold its sponsorship. It is also the sponsoring State that submits to the Secretariat the notifications concerning prospecting, exploration and development, as well as the relevant applications, acting either on its own behalf or as the representative of an entity sponsored by it. In general, the relations with the institutions of the regime are entirely conducted by such a sponsoring State. A similarly important role is performed by the sponsoring State in the context of the deep sea-bed regime under Part XI of the Law of the Sea Convention.

On the other hand, the sponsor plays an important role in regard to monitoring compliance with the obligations of the regime by the entities under its patronage, and this requires the existence of a strong link.[251] Most important of all is the fact that as a consequence of the nature of the system, the sponsor will have responsibility for activities that may cause damage even though such responsibility may ultimately be borne by the contractor. As we shall see, one possibility is the establishment of a regime of objective or strict responsibility. All these considerations make it imperative that the requirements concerning the link in question are very strictly applied in order to ensure the effective exercise of these functions and responsibilities.

As it has so often happened before, the participation of corporations and other private legal entities in activities of an international character has contributed in an important manner to the development of international law, and what we have examined in connection with consortia arrangements in the Antarctic minerals regime does not seem to constitute an exception in this regard.[252]

5.6   The legal regime of contracts

The legal regime of contracts is of special interest in the Antarctic case because it offers a means of resolving difficult questions relating to title to resources and the nature of rights and duties. An initial consideration is that the instrument establishing the mineral regime cannot pronounce explicitly as to any title to resources that may exist since this would produce an irreconcilable difference of opinion between claimant and non-claimant countries. While, for the former, this title would be an expression of sovereignty and national jurisdiction, for the latter, the title could be based only on the norms of international law and their application to the Antarctic case.[253]

However, once it has been agreed that mineral resource activities can be undertaken only within the regime, the question of title loses its importance to a great extent. The Consultative Parties have accepted that the exercise of their respective rights over resources, on whatever grounds of title they are based, shall be conducted solely in the context of this regime.[254] It could also be argued that, this being so, the various titles that might be invoked within the framework of the regime have been merged into one since the Parties have, in a sense, renounced their right to invoke any title that might belong to them individually.[255]

The really important matter is to determine the existence of the right to explore and develop the mineral resources of Antarctica. While there could be doubts and differences of view in relation to the existence of this right under the Antarctic Treaty, a problem that we have examined in Chapter 2, the point will be clearly settled by the entry into force of the regime on mineral resources, under which the existence of the right and the manner in which it can be exercised shall be no longer discussed as a point of controversy. Similarly, the moratorium arrangements that we have discussed do not affect at all the existence of the right to mine, but only its exercise until a regime governing the matter comes into force. All of the foregoing will be, of course, lawful arrangements under international law, thus making very unlikely the success of eventual legal challenges. This is not to say, however, that there are not political difficulties involved, as evidenced by the current international debate on Antarctica, or that there are no differences of view about the rules which should govern mining in Antarctica. Given that rights shall be exercised only within the regime, this represents an adequate legal basis for the granting of licences and approval of contracts under the terms and procedures of the regime. Similarly, it is unnecessary for the right in question to be conceived as a form of ownership right in the traditional sense, an approach which, once again, raises the difficulties inherent in the concept of territorial sovereignty. The right can be described as an entitlement to explore and develop these resources, which is not necessarily associated with territorial sovereignty, but, at the same time, it does not exclude it, and this facilitates the corresponding accommodation within the regime.

This situation is not entirely new in international law since in connection with the continental shelf, for example, the right of a coastal State over resources is not comparable to the right of ownership but merely represents the right recognized by international law to explore and exploit such resources.[256] As it has been explained in connection with the regime of the continental shelf of the United Kingdom, 'while this is perhaps less than full legal ownership in the sense that petroleum *in situ* on land might be, it is a jurisdiction sufficient to found the grant of licences to search for, bore and get petroleum'.[257]

The above-mentioned observation also applies to some extent to the Antarctic case since even if the right recognized by the regime is not typically a right of ownership it is, nevertheless, sufficient for the granting of the relevant authorizations and for entering into contracts for the exploration and exploitation of Antarctic mineral resources. It is to be noted, of course, that the sovereign rights of the coastal state over the continental shelf are not disputed by third States, as the concepts of contiguity and natural prolongation of the land territory have been generally accepted in international law, a fact that makes an important difference with the situation of Antarctica where recognition of claims is rather limited. In spite of these differences, however, the Antarctic mineral regime will have the necessary legal strength as to prevent that the resources of the area could be regarded as *res nullius*.

The nature of the licence

The nature of the licence that may be granted for the conduct of mineral activities is also an important matter requiring clarification. A recent comparative study of legislation relating to licences in the petroleum sector points out that a licence, whatever it is called, 'has broadly the same effect and content'.[258] In particular:

> Over a defined period and area, it gives the licensee exclusive exploration and production rights, and operates to transfer to him title in any petroleum he extracts. As a counterpart the licensee pays to the granting state certain fees together with a royalty on production, and accepts a wide range of obligations,

and powers of State supervision, as to the way in which he carries out operations under the licence.[259]

Bearing in mind the differences between licensing arrangements under national sovereignty and jurisdiction and the Antarctic case, it can be noted that the relationship between the licensee or authorized contractor and the regime established is similar to what has been described. This conceptual similarity was reflected in the 1983 Draft Articles, which referred to the management scheme as prescribing terms and conditions for 'licensing arrangements'; although this was later changed to read 'arrangements for the grant of authorization to conduct activities', it does not change the nature of the arrangements.[260]

Under national legislation, different responses have been given to the question of the precise nature of the licence or arrangement that produces these rights and obligations.[261] In some cases the nature of the licence has been that of an administrative permit whereas in other schemes it has been considered as a contract of an administrative type. More frequently, however, the nature of the licence is identified with a contract between parties, a tendency which, although not universal, is beginning to predominate in national practice and in the interpretation of the courts.[262] In the Antarctic case, the contractual nature of the authorization or licence is very marked as could be seen from the discussion of the proposed rules for governing the exploration and exploitation of resources. For this reason, it would be more appropriate in the Antarctic regime to refer to a 'contract' rather than to a 'licence'.[263] The drafting change in the Draft Articles mentioned above already suggests this approach.

It is clear from a comparative study of the petroleum production legislation that, in addition to the specific terms of the contract, there is always included a set of legislative and regulatory provisions which determine various aspects of the rights and obligations of the parties. This combination of elements does not follow a single model. In Australia, all the essential elements are defined in the legislation; in Canada, the terms of the contract are contained in part in regulatory legislation and in part in the licence itself; in Great Britain, all the terms are contained in the licence but this incorporates 'model clauses', laid down in the Petroleum Production Regulations, and Statutory Regulations which are an integral part of it and are of a regulatory nature.[264]

It cannot be inferred, from the contractual nature of the authorization, that negotiated criteria or a bargain will be predominant since the presence of the regulatory elements that have been referred to ensures that the public interests, as represented by the States Parties and the institutions of the regime, is always safeguarded in the agreed arrangements.[265] The Antarctic model has a strong regulatory component established in the principles and objectives of the regime, the standards promulgated in compliance with these and the specific guidelines that are approved for the granting of the corresponding authorization. Moreover, specific terms and conditions need to be defined for this authorization. Whether the latter are established in a general way and are incorporated automatically in the management scheme or whether they are defined individually for each management scheme, in accordance with the options proposed, the regulatory element is a permanent feature.

It is also interesting to note that if the terms and conditions are established in a general way and are automatically incorporated in each contract, this creates a situation comparable to that of the British 'model clauses', as also is done in the deep sea-bed regime under the Law of the Sea Convention.[266] Other alternatives resemble the case of Canada and possibly that of Australia.[267] In any case, it would seem that, in the Antarctic, the elements open to negotiation are relatively few in number since the management scheme always has to be approved by the corresponding Regulatory Committee and by the Commission and is subject to the principles, standards and criteria of the regime; however, these elements open to negotiation may refer to very important matters, such as jurisdiction, financial arrangements and other questions; this particular aspect of the regime will be discussed in Chapters 7 and 8.

The nature of the Antarctic contract may be identified with the terms in which one author has described the British licences: 'The licences which the Crown may grant are more than mere administrative regulations. They are contracts, albeit contracts with a strong regulatory component'.[268]

Exclusivity of the rights granted
The principal right granted by the Antarctic contract, and by any other similar contract relating to minerals, is the exclusive right to explore and exploit the mineral resources authorized by the contract in the block which is defined and for the scheduled period.[269] In this way the objective of 'security of tenure' and 'certainty of regulation', which one author has defined as essential criteria of the regime, is ensured.[270] One important point made in the 1984 Draft Articles is that such rights shall be subject to compliance with the regime and the measures adopted pursuant to it, including the approved management scheme;[271] a consequence of this is, as we shall see, that the rights under the contract can lapse in case of serious violation of the rules governing mineral activities in Antarctica.

The exclusivity of the right has of course important implications as regards the title to the minerals. Under the terms of traditional concessions, the title would normally refer to the surface and the mineral or petroleum *in situ,* usually for a long period of time and accompanied by strong stabilization clauses; this has of course radically changed under modern forms of contract and licensing arrangements, which will approach the question of title on different basis, usually opting for solutions other than that of transferring title to the minerals or petroleum *in situ.*[272] In the United Kingdom, for example, title will pass upon reduction of the resources into possession, which in the case of oil is understood to happen at the well-head.[273] In the case of the deep sea-bed regime under Part XI of the Law of the Sea Convention, title similarly passes upon recovery.[274]

It is very important that the Antarctic mineral regime makes clear how the question of title will be approached. Because of the contractual form of the licence or authorization that we have discussed, it can be safely assumed that there will be no connection in this regard with the traditional concessions, and therefore title shall not refer to the minerals or petroleum *in situ.* This last approach would also be inconvenient from the point of view that it would highlight the different interest and legal policy of claimants and non-claimants of Antarctic territory; since the grantor of the right will be the 'regime', which has no sovereignty, it is less controversial if the title passes upon recovery. The question of when has the mineral or oil been recovered can follow the solution provided by national legislation, like the above-mentioned British well-head point of recovery for oil.

Under the approach suggested, similarly to what happens under the British licence arrangements, the kind of property rights acquired by means of the contract resemble the English *profit à prendre.* As Cameron has explained 'this is simply a right to take the produce of another's land (for example, to fell and take away timber, or to catch fish), and is a right of property in the sense that it can be invoked against any third parties that interfere with its exercise'.[275]

The clarification of the matter in the Antarctic mineral regime is important not only for the sake of legal precision but also in regard to two other issues: the first is the implication that the question of title has for securing the bank financing and guarantees required by Antarctic mineral activities; the second issue is that of domestic legislation of claimant countries which specifically prohibits the State of transferring title over minerals or oil *in situ,* a legislation which if applied to the claimed Antarctic territory could conflict with a regime based on different principles.[276]

The exclusive nature of the right imposes a number of additional requirements which the regime will have to govern through its regulatory norms. One of these is that the contractor is not entitled to transfer his exploration and exploitation rights to a third party, or to make any other arrangements relating to participation without specific authorization since not only would this involve a change in the contract, but the institutions of the regime would need to ascertain that such a third party was a qualified entity. This situation might also produce difficulties in regard to the procedures for the selection of applicants. The terms of the contract must also specify the conditions for total or partial relinquishment.[277]

Another aspect of the matter to be borne in mind is that the participation of different contractors in a given area must be compatible with the exclusivity of the rights granted and must ensure, in particular, that there are no prejudicial interferences.[278] Although the identification of the relevant blocks must take into consideration the need to ensure the unity of the deposit, it is possible that problems may arise in this connection, as for example, when a given deposit extends across several blocks or areas. In addition to the economic difficulties arising from the concept of the 'common pool',[279] it produces complex legal situations. If this occurs, the principles and agreements that have been arrived at within the framework of extensive international practice in this field may serve as a model for resolving the difficulties in the Antarctic, including the case of deposits which extend across national boundaries.[280] An adequate solution could also be to empower the institutions of the regime to require the various contractors to develop the field as a unit, following the concept of 'unitisation' under British legislation.[281]

The question of private ownership in Antarctica, which we have examined in Chapter 3, might also be relevant in connection with the exercise of exclusive rights.[282] This matter does not arise so much in regard to resources, since these are governed entirely by the provisions of the regime in respect of title, rights, registration and other topics, but rather in relation to auxiliary installations and other back-up facilities for operations. It may, at some future time, be necessary to define the property regime applicable to structures of this type and the respective land, thus once again raising the problem of sovereignty and jurisdiction. As was also mentioned in Chapter 3, a number of authors have raised the question of the extension of national property regimes to Antarctica, which would raise new and complex questions including that related to private or State ownership of mineral resources and their corresponding legal bases. The International Union for Conservation of Nature and

Natural Resources has suggested in this regard that the regime should grant rights only in relation to minerals and not give title to surrounding land or sea areas.[283] The only way that can be envisaged of avoiding this type of difficulty, which stems from the civil, mining and administrative legislation of member countries, is to organize the entire system relating to minerals within the framework of the regime and its regulatory norms.

Stability of the Antarctic contract

In international and comparative law there is an important relationship between the nature of the licence and the question of stability of the rights and obligations that it contains. In so far as it might be similar to a permit or an administrative contract, that would seem to increase the likelihood that the granting Government will regard itself as being entitled to modify the agreed terms. If it is identified with a contract, that would tend to give prominence to the concept that the licence can only be modified by joint agreement between the parties.[284] Provisions to this effect are incorporated in some of the specific stabilization clauses incorporated in petroleum development contracts and the same approach has also been recognized in a number of important arbitral awards.[285]

From the point of view of its stability, the Antarctic contract will be fully in accordance with this latter tendency because the concept of security of tenure means that the contract cannot in general be modified or amended without the consent of both the contractor and the institutions of the regime.[286] The guarantee afforded in this case by an international regime is comparable to the type of constitutional guarantees of ownership provided by several countries[287] and is further strengthened by means of an international convention. In the case of the deep sea-bed regime under the Law of the Sea Convention, a similar system to ensure the stability of the contract has been provided for.[288]

It is also important to bear in mind that in the context of a multilateral convention establishing a regime of this kind, the reasons which generally prompt unilateral action in a domestic context are less likely to happen. These reasons usually relate to political disputes, need for revenue, public emergency, nationalization and the like.

Notwithstanding this contextual and built-in stability of the Antarctic contract, as we have mentioned earlier, the rights will always be subject to compliance with the obligations provided in the regime and in the specific terms laid down by the contract. In case of non-compliance, therefore, sanctions will be applied, subject probably to a review procedure under the procedures for the settlement of disputes. These sanctions may entail fines or other financial penalties, but may also involve the suspension or termination of the contract, depending on the seriousness of the failure to fulfil the contract.[289]

In the case of the deep sea-bed regime under the Law of the Sea Convention a number of situations have been envisaged which illustrate the type of problems that must be borne in mind in the Antarctic regime. The first is a situation in which activities are carried out in such a way as to result 'in serious, persistent and wilful violations' of the contract and of the applicable standards.[290] Although it is difficult to imagine a situation in which a contractor or operator could behave in such a way and exemplify all the cumulative features of such a violation, the regime must retain this power of sanction in case problems of this nature occur. Another situation calling for sanctions would be the failure of the contractor to comply with the final and mandatory decision of the machinery for the settlement of disputes.[291]

Other situations need to be envisaged in which the institutions of the regime might decide to suspend or terminate a contract. One such situation would occur if the contractor ceased to qualify as such by ceasing to have a link with the sponsoring State, for example by moving the headquarters of his central management and control or by no longer holding substantial resources in a country participating in the regime.[292] More important still would be a case in which the activity undertaken has an impact on the environment of such a nature as to constitute an unacceptable risk that could not originally have been foreseen. The deep sea-bed regime of the Law of the Sea Convention to some extent contemplates this environmental situation since the Council is empowered to adopt emergency orders to prevent damage to the environment which might include suspension of operations without prior recourse to the machinery for the settlement of disputes.[293] Given the ecological concerns of the Antarctic regime, the subsequent environmental risk would have to be regarded as justifying suspension, modification or termination of contracts, in a duly qualified way and probably subject to the final determination of the machinery for the settlement of disputes. This criterion was, of course, recognized in the course of negotiations.[294]

Expropriation and other action affecting rights
Nationalization or expropriation and their complex legal consequences have figured prominently in the literature of international law in relation to investments in the development of natural resources,[295] giving rise to major discussions in the law of State responsibility with particular reference to the protection of property rights under international law.[296] Is a situation of this kind likely to arise in the context of an internationally agreed regime on Antarctic mineral resources?

The answer to this question is clearly negative. This is due in part to the fact that the Antarctic regime in question is not a State and thus lacks the sovereign attributes under which nationalization might take place. It is also partly due to the fact that the States participating in the regime have agreed, by virtue of their sovereignty, that mineral activities will be governed solely by the provisions of the regime; there are thus no other express or implied powers that might be invoked in this connection. Moreover, as we shall see, the regime is, by definition, subject to international law.

These considerations have an important bearing on the discussion of the subject of permanent sovereignty over natural resources[297] and its relationship with the stability of contracts.[298]States participating in the Antarctic mineral regime will do so in the exercise of their sovereign right to conclude a treaty; among them are some claimant countries, like Argentina or Chile, that have to some extent espoused the concept of permanent sovereignty over natural resources. It can be argued in this regard that the participation of the latter is on the basis or in application of the concept of permanent sovereignty over natural resources; it follows that for these countries the contracts entered into under the regime must be seen and understood as being compatible with the concept of permanent sovereignty. On the basis of this criterion, the view put forward in the *Aminoil* case to the effect that the prohibition of the right to nationalize, if it is to be regarded as applicable, must be specifically included in the stabilization clauses of the contract,[299] is irrelevant in the context of the Antarctic regime for nationalization will anyhow be ruled out under the above-mentioned argument. In any event, as we have mentioned earlier, the reasons which usually prompt nationalization or expropriation in a domestic context are not likely to occur in an international arrangement like the Antarctic mineral regime.

Even if the nationalization possibility is excluded, it is still necessary to ask oneself if situations could occur within this regime comparable to those occurring in Great Britain under the 1975 Petroleum and Submarine Pipeline Act.[300] The model clauses approved by this Act were applied retroactively to licences granted before such clauses were approved and which consequently modified the terms of the prior licences. This has been explained by an author as follows: 'the United Kingdom Government took the view that its sovereign right to legislate in respect of the natural resources on its shelf was in no way impeded by contracts that it had previously entered into with foreign licensees'.[301] Even though the fact that there are no stabilization clauses in the British system made it easier to offer this justification for amendment, the same argument was also put forward in other cases in which there were clauses of this type, thus indicating that a State, by virtue of its sovereignty, cannot enter into contracts which lay down obligations in perpetuity or, alternatively, that the concept of executive necessity makes it permissible to alter contracts.[302]

Although this line of reasoning has gained some measure of recognition in a decision of a national court,[303] the criterion maintained by international law is stricter in regard to the protection of acquired rights.[304] While it may be admitted that opinions vary widely in studies concerning State rights in this respect and their relationship with the requirements of international law,[305] in the case of an internationally agreed regime such as the Antarctic mineral regime, which is subject specifically to international law, the type of protection afforded by international law will clearly prevail. It is also clear that an acquired right is not only based on a title of ownership but also on contractual rights[306] such as specifically occurs in the framework of the Antarctic mineral regime.

For the above reasons, a situation such as the British one under the Submarine Pipelines Act could not occur in the Antarctic mineral regime where the concept of security of tenure and stability prevails over that of any form of legislative sovereignty. The only modifications that may be envisaged in the contract are those stemming from situations expressly contemplated in the treaty and the terms and conditions, enacted pursuant to the treaty, and, consequently, in the contract itself. Moreover, the regime itself is covered by that supreme stability clause *'pacta sunt servanda'*.[307] There is certainly a place for differing opinions on certain aspects, such as the precise content of what is to be understood by acquired right, the specifically applicable standards and principles of international law, or if a case arises, the appropriate compensation – always a difficult question – even though, in any event, this will be covered by a procedure for settlement of disputes of a typically international nature.

Indirect taking and the question of regulatory powers

There are many other situations in international law in which acquired rights may be affected by the action of a State, not only in the form of deprivation of ownership but also in an indirect way. The legal issues arising from indirect taking and the ample international practice in the matter have been extensively analysed by Christie, García-Amador, Higgins and Weston.[308] A particularly important source of difficulties in this field is the exercise of regulatory powers by the State; as we have seen, problems have occurred under the British legislation, similar situations having occurred in Canada and other cases;[309] important arbitral and judicial decisions have also been pronounced on the matter, with particular reference to the *Revere Copper v. Opic*[310] and the *Murphyores*[311] cases.

As we shall examine in Chapters 7 and 8, the institutions of the Antarctic mineral regime will have some important regulatory powers, including those related to financial arrangements and the payment of fees, royalties and the like. The question therefore arises as to whether these powers could be used in such a way as to constitute a form of indirect taking of the rights under the contract.

Again this question must be answered in the negative. In the first place, the regulatory powers of the institutions of the regime may only be exercised in the context of the provisions of the regime, which will establish precise limits and specific guarantees such as security of tenure, to which we have already referred. Second, it must be borne in mind that the financial obligations are defined beforehand among the terms and conditions which must be contained in the management scheme which can subsequently be modified only with the consent of the parties.

There is no doubt that the regulatory powers will give greater weight to environmental considerations. As has been mentioned above, the institutions of the regime must be empowered to adopt emergency orders and other measures in order to be able to deal with situations not originally foreseen, even if this entails varying a contract. This power would not, however, be exercised in an unpredictable manner since it must be regarded as being among the specific powers of the institutions and, as such, forms part of the contract and of its terms and conditions. Thus, there will not be an unforeseen change in the rules as occurred in the *Murphyores* case. Furthermore, the qualified exercise of this power and the fact that it should be subject to the machinery for the settlement of disputes means that any form of arbitrary action would be avoided.

Some of the major obstacles to achieve a consensus on the deep sea-bed regime under the Law of the Sea Convention are related to the concern of potential mining States about the stability of contracts in the light of the powers of the Authority; because some of these countries do not regard such stability as fully guaranteed under the convention, they have sought to restrict the powers of the Authority and in the meanwhile have abstained from signature of or accession to the convention.

The only situation in which an alteration of the stability of the regime of Antarctic contracts would be conceivable would occur in the highly unlikely event of an agreement by all the parties to the regime to modify the regime and introduce a different system. But even in this case the question of non-retroactivity and the protection of acquired rights in international law would arise and this would remain subject to an international machinery for the settlement of disputes. The concept of the revision conference provided for in the Law of the Sea Convention for the deep sea-bed regime is comparable to this hypothetical case,[312] but it has not been contemplated in the case of the Antarctic mineral regime; there is of course a revision mechanism under the 1959 Antarctic Treaty, which we shall examine later, but this is unrelated to the mineral regime.

The law applicable to the contract

The law governing the contract is another important question to be clarified in a regime of this nature.[313] The fundamental problem in this regard is that as of the moment there is no clause on the law applicable to the contract, and it is quite unlikely that a general clause of this kind might be agreed on in the near future for this would certainly raise the issue of the conflictive views of the parties on jurisdiction; as we shall see, however, there is an indirect clause on the mattter. Even where there is this type of general clause, the argument is usually made as to whether it excludes international law. In the absence of such a clause the governing law should be deduced from the contract and the relevant circumstances. In any event the question will still remain as to whether international law applies or only the law of the national entities engaged in the contract shall govern the matter, or still there might be a mixture of international and domestic law.

Oil contracts offer a wide variety of answers in this regard, ranging from 'nationalistic' solutions to 'internationalist' approaches.[314] The Institut de Droit International has also attempted to arrive at the definition of rules generally acceptable in the proper law of contracts: Article 1 of the Resolution adopted in the Athens session suggests that 'contracts between a State and a foreign private person shall be subjected to the rules of law chosen by the parties or, failing such a choice, to the rules of law with which the contract has the closest link', while Article 2 gives a clear indication of the many choices available:

> The parties may in particular choose as the proper law of the contract either one or several domestic legal systems or the principles common to such systems, or the general principles of law, or the principles applied in international economic relations, or international law, or a combination of these sources of law.[315]

Because of the international character of the Antarctic mineral regime, the contract, as a general proposition, will be governed by rules of international law. These include the clauses of the contract itself, the terms and conditions of the management scheme, the standards and rules and regulations adopted by the institutions of the regime and the pro-visions of the Convention that establishes the regime. Other treaty rules may be applicable through the regime's links with the Antarctic Treaty system and the same could be said of the applicable rules, principles and standards of general international law that are compatible with this particular regime. From this point of view, the contract in question is an 'internationalized' one and is subject to international law. To this extent international law will control not only procedural matters related to the contract but substantive questions as well, particularly due to the fact that the rules of the Antarctic mineral regime are themselves part of interna-tional law.

In spite of this, the Antarctic contract, on the other hand, may be brought into relationship with national law. The matters to be contained in the management scheme include 'the law applicable to the operator and persons employed by the operator in connection with the proposed exploration and development activities'.[316] This applicable law may be the domestic law of a country party to the regime, whether that of a country that has a claim over the area of the contract, that of the sponsoring State or some other system of law determined in the manage-ment scheme. Even the law of a third country could be chosen in this regard. The role of national law governing the contract could prove to be very significant in view of the fact that international law will not always provide substantive rules beyond the clauses of the mineral convention. This choice does not necessarily have implications with regard to the jurisdictional problem but it is thought preferable to keep it open and to not prejudge the substance of the matter. According to this approach the problem will be resolved on a case-by-case basis since, for example, while a Soviet contractor will probably insist on being governed by the appro-priate law of the Soviet Union, a French contractor engaged in activities in Terre Adélie will probably be governed by the legislation of his country both on the basis of nationality and of territorial sovereignty. Given the difficulty in agreeing on a general clause, each contract will decide the matter by means of the terms defined in the management scheme.

The above-mentioned approach could also mean that the national law of a claimant country could apply to a contract entered into by an entity of different nationality, but this would again raise the question of jurisdiction. In such event probably a negotiation with the sponsoring State would be required. It is also possible that the law of the claimant might apply only to given aspects of the contract, such as conditions of employment. In a situation of overlapping claims, such as those over the Antarctic peninsula, the choice of the law of the claimant is still more complex and might suggest the need for an agreement among the various claimants. Where reciprocal recognition of claims has intervened the choice of law will be facilitated.

The application of the national law which is determined will, in any case, be complementary or auxiliary to the standards of international law governing the contract and will relate mainly to those aspects that are not regulated directly by international law or by the specific rules of the regime and the contract.

It must also be borne in mind that a national law will not necessarily be chosen for this purpose since other standards of international law may be selected if they are appropriate.

The national law, however, will always have a role to play in this regime whether through the determination of the management scheme, the requirements of nationality, incorporation and sponsorship or in other ways, a situation that will raise a number of problems of compatibility with the regime. Consideration must thus be given to the necessity of ensuring that no State Party imposes conditions on the contractor which are incompatible with the regime, an idea which was taken into account in the deep sea-bed regime under the Law of the Sea Convention.[317]

Another interesting situation is that in which national law may impose more stringent requirement than the Antarctic mineral regime in regard to environmental matters or other aspects of operations. This situation is likely to arise frequently within the Antarctic Treaty system. In the deep sea-bed regime such a situation was not regarded as being incompatible with the rules laid down under Part XI of the Law of the Sea Convention[318] and it is only reasonable that a similar criterion should be followed in the Antarctic case.

As we shall examine in Chapter 8, the clauses on applicable law have also relevance for the purposes of the arrangements for the settlement of disputes.

5.7   Compliance with, and the enforcement of, the regime

As we have examined, the central principle governing all aspects of compliance with the regime and its enforcement is that no mineral activities shall be conducted except in accordance with the provisions of the regime and the measures adopted pursuant to it.[319] This principle will of course apply both to the Parties to the regime and to third countries, in the terms we shall examine in Chapter 9.

Given the somewhat decentralized nature of the regime, the participating States have an active role to play in this connection. In the first place, there is an obligation, which is applied in a general way to all participating

States, to adopt appropriate measures within their competence in order to ensure compliance with the regime and with the measures adopted within its framework.[320] It was also mentioned above that certain types of measures adopted by States more stringent than those of the regime should not be considered as incompatible with it, particularly in connection with the environment.[321]

The corresponding obligations of States Parties will be to notify the Secretariat of the regime of all the measures taken to ensure compliance with the regime. The Commission of the regime will in turn be empowered to draw the attention of all Parties to the regime to any activity which affects the implementation of the objectives or principles or the compliance by any Party with its obligations under the regime, thus opening up a procedure for institutional participation in the compliance and enforcement mechanisms of the regime.[322]

Next there are more specific obligations which devolve on the sponsoring State since it must make the initial assessment of the interested applicants and ensure that they meet the conditions of the regime.[323] In the same way, it will be the sponsoring State that has to take action if the institutions of the regime determine and bring to its attention any failure to comply on the part of the contractor, without prejudice to the powers and duties of these institutions as regards sanctions. In this sense, there is an obligation to co-operate with the institutions in the question of compliance and control of the measures of the regime.

One interesting question in this regard is whether the contractor as a private entity will have rights and duties directly binding on it as a result of the regime, or these rights and duties will only apply to them indirectly through the role of intermediation of the sponsoring State. While the Draft Articles show some inclination towards an indirect role of contractors, in practice the direct standing of contractors will be of importance, not only in technical issues but also on very relevant points of substance, such as financial payments, the settlement of disputes and the like. For this very reason, in case of sub-contracts or other forms of delegated operations, any additional entity must equally be subject to the requirements of compliance and enforcement.

The question of which are to be regarded as appropriate measures within the competence of the State is something closely bound up with the issue of jurisdiction in this regime, with particular reference to questions of nationality and territorial claims. The solution to this problem will have to be found within the distribution of competences in the regime and, above all, in terms of the procedures for the settlement of disputes, to which we shall return later.

Various procedures have been established throughout the regime for the purposes of reporting on the activities undertaken and the different stages of work at which a contract may be proceeding.[324] Similarly, monitoring requirements have been considered with a greater institutional participation in order to keep a close watch on the progress and problems which the mining activities might encounter.[325] But of course the inspection system will be in a better place to verify about the compliance with the regime.

Problems of the inspection system in relation to mineral activities
The rules concerning inspection established by Article VII, paragraphs 1 to 4, of the Antarctic Treaty and the related practice that has developed thereunder correspond basically to the stage of Antarctic co-operation linked to the development of scientific investigation and the promotion of peaceful uses.[326] In spite that these inspection mechanisms have been generally successful, the period relating to the development of resources raised different needs. A similar phenomenon occurs with the provisions on the exchange of information provided in Article VII, paragraph 5, of the Treaty, which in certain resource-related activities have had to defer to the protection of proprietary data.[327]

As illustrated in Chapter 4, the Seal Convention timidly hinted at the need for an inspection system that might be applied to the essentially marine environment of sealing but such a system did not come into being.[328] Some of the inspections carried out under the terms of the 1959 Treaty were also concerned with the conservation of living resources but their scope was very limited.[329] The Canberra Convention provides a more comprehensive system for the living marine resources regime[330] but it displays a number of weaknesses stemming from the fact that the system is not a strongly centralized one and the inspectors and observers are designated by the Member countries of the Commission, reports are referred to the Commission through those countries and a type of flag State prosecution is envisaged.[331] The nature of the system is related to the jurisdictional problems that we considered earlier and to the fact that at least in part, the Convention of Living Resources applies to fishing in the high seas. As we examined in the previous chapter, in the case of the International Convention for the Regulation of Whaling the original inspection was based only on national appointments, but a subsequent amendment authorized observers under bilateral agreements, thus opening the way for a greater institutional role in the enforcement procedures.[332]

Because of the underlying problems of jurisdiction, it has been proposed that the inspection arrangements for the Antarctic mineral regime follow those of Article VII of the 1959 Treaty with the necessary adjustments.[333] This might result in a somewhat limited approach given the particular needs of the mineral regime. It will obviously be necessary for inspections to take place not only in the continent but also throughout the area of the regime, covering all facilities and equipment used for mineral-related activities, and in particular off-shore oil rigs.

The main limitation to be foreseen in this connection concerns the inspection of ships and aircraft. Article VII, paragraph 3, of the 1959 Treaty specifies that such inspections may only be made at points 'in Antarctica' where cargoes or personnel are discharged or embarked, a clear reference to points in the Antarctic continent.[334] Nevertheless, in the case of the mineral regime, embarkation and discharging may take place not only in the continent but also at facilities and installations which may exist in the sea and on the continental shelf. Since the facilities will be subject to inspection, the same must necessarily apply to ships and aircraft at these other points. This is innovatory with respect to the principle of the Treaty.

Another aspect to be considered concerns the need to carry out the inspection in a way that is compatible with the development of operations and, above all, with the protection of proprietary data and other justifiable requirements of confidentiality.[335] Both for this purpose and to ensure the necessary impartiality of inspections, it might perhaps be more appropriate to set up an inspection system that depended more directly on the institutions of the regime than on the member countries.[336] This would also provide a means of overcoming some of the weaknesses of the existing system. In any event it might be appropriate for the Commission to have the power to designate observers, particularly in conjunction with its monitoring functions.

The aggregate of the provisions on reporting, monitoring, inspection and bringing situations of non compliance to the attention of the institutions, States parties and contractors, should provide a satisfactory means for detecting any failure to implement the regime and the management scheme or any difficulties that might have to be remedied. However, in view of some of the shortcomings we have mentioned the powers of the institutions of the regime in this connection have been criticized as being inadequate.[337]

Should a situation of non-compliance be established, the appropriate corrective measures will have to be put into effect. These might include penalties and other sanctions or might even involve the action of the institutions and States Parties to ensure that the regime is complied with adequately. These enforcement aspects are closely related to the question of settlement of disputes, which we will examine in Chapter 8.

Liability for Antarctic mineral activities
Under the traditional law of State responsibility, the question of liability for certain kinds of activity has always been very much linked to the concept of damage, fault or in any event breach of an international obligation.[338]. Even though the *Trail Smelter* arbitration helped in an important manner to clarify some of the issues associated with transboundary pollution damage, it did so mostly within the framework of the traditional law on the matter.[339] Discussions as recent as that of the deep sea-bed regime in the Law of the Sea Conference, opted in this matter for a traditional and restricted type of responsibility, confined to cases of 'wrongful acts' and limited to the actual amount of the damage caused.[340]

However, in view of the hazardous nature of important activities undertaken by men in an evolving technological world, the law has also begun to evolve in order to introduce more stringent requirements that have generally become identified with the concept of strict liability. The law governing activity in outer space[341] and in some respects the law dealing with the pollution of the marine environment[342] have evidenced this trend for change. Recent proposals have suggested no-fault climate insurance that would compensate all victims of adverse climate changes, regardless of cause[343] or that those who affect the condition of commonly used realms should be answerable for their actions to the international community.[344]

Given the extremely delicate nature of Antarctic mineral activities and the top priority of environmental concerns in the deliberations of the negotiations underway, the traditional approach mentioned above was clearly inappropriate for this particular regime. A strict liability approach might be more in accordance with the needs of this regime, particularly from the point of view of environmental conservation where damage, if it does occur, will be impossible to quantify in economic terms. This particular aspect is yet to be elaborated upon by the draft articles.[345]

The option of linking compensation to damage arising from a breach of the regime, or when damage is related to fault, has not been generally favoured in the negotiations, which show some inclination to a regime based on absolute or strict liability.[346] However, the idea of establishing a limit to the liability which may result has also been sounded out with a view to minimizing the cost of insurance. Other suggestions have proposed a regime of strict liability for environmental damage only, whereas other types of damage would be linked to the concept of fault or other restrictions.

The question of which entity shall be held liable in case needed is likely to be very relevant in the context of the Antarctic mineral regime. There could be no doubt that, in the first place, the contractor will be liable for any damage caused by its activities; whether this will be a form of joint or several responsibility it is to be determined by the joint venture agreement.[347] But next, given the very prominent role of the sponsoring State in the management of the regime, it should also be responsible to some extent, even if only in a residual manner. Furthermore, the argument made earlier that because Antarctica is a case of joint administration there might be ground for joint responsibility,[348] should also be borne in mind in this context.

The draft articles have indicated that the management scheme shall in each case contain requirements relating to the 'liability, bonding and insurance' of the contractor,[349] but this is only one of the elements to be taken into consideration in the broader spectrum of liability for Antarctic mineral activities. On the other hand, the necessary remedial action will probably need the involvement of the institutions of the regime, the sponsoring State and other States especially concerned, an aspect which in turn is linked to the procedures for the settlement of disputes.

5.8 Evaluation of the system of exploration and exploitation: the quest for equilibrium

As may have been apparent, the regime proposed for organizing mineral-related activities in Antarctica seeks to find a balance between two main tendencies: one that gives priority to the development of resources within a framework of environmental safety and one that gives primacy to environmental preservation above all other considerations. This is the basis, moreover, on which efforts are made to achieve internal accommodation between divergent legal standpoints. The enormous legal complexity of this exercise is a factor that cannot pass unnoticed.

The whole of the discussion that we have been considering concerning the powers of the regime is based on the quest for this equilibrium within the new treaty. The terms and conditions for the accomplishment of the various phases of mineral activity, for example, seek to establish a system which is sufficiently rigorous to guarantee the safety of operations but, at the same time, is sufficiently effective to prevent any artificial bureaucratic obstruction. In this manner, the requirements of public control over operations are harmonized with those of private enterprise and the economic production of potential resources.

Within this scheme, the environmental question is certainly the most delicate. As there is full agreement on the need to ensure environmental protection, the differences stem rather from the extension of and intensity of the powers of the institutions of the regime required to achieve it. Once again, the approach proposed seeks to balance the demands made in both directions on the basis of providing appropriate powers and objective procedures without ending up with a situation that would make all mineral-related activity impossible. Similar considerations underlie the regime of contracts and many other essential aspects of the system that has been devised.

The regime proposed has been criticized on various grounds, depending on the underlying assumptions on which the analysis has been based. The most contentious aspects have been the system provided for conducting prospecting, the relatively automatic transfer from the phase of exploration to that of exploitation and the powers of the institutions for verifying and enforcing compliance with the regime.[350] The institutional approaches that will be considered later have also given rise to various difficulties. As the analysis in this chapter has shown, provisions on all these aspects are, of course, capable of improvement, a fact which has also been largely confirmed in practice in the course of negotiation.

There is also another type of criticism which has the objective, not so much of improving certain mechanisms within the system provided as of replacing the entire system by a wholly different conception. Certain ecological groups have made proposals along these lines. Thus, for example, the Antarctic and Southern Ocean Coalition has proposed that the current negotiations be abandoned and that the matter be referred for consideration to the United Nations.[351] The concept of Antarctica as an international park also belongs to such alternative approaches.[352] Another recent suggestion has been 'a non-commercial approach to Antarctic minerals' whereby prospecting and exploration activities would be carried out directly by Governments and the information obtained exchanged in accordance with the provisions of the Antarctic Treaty.[353]

The evolution of mineral agreements and the Antarctic case
The conceptions underlying these various points of view are related to some extent to the basic models for mineral agreements that have been developed in international practice.[354] The basic option of organizing mineral activity on the basis of a Mining Code or of *ad hoc* agreements which allow in a more flexible way for the special conditions of each project,[355] is reflected in the Antarctic case in discussion as to whether all the terms and conditions should form part of the pre-established regime or whether they should be specially defined in each management scheme. Practice demonstrates the desirability of a measure of flexibility, subject,

of course, to the basic principles and conditions provided in the legislation.[356]

In the same way, the approaches inherent in the concept of traditional concession[357] may be recognized in certain positions that have been adopted in relation to the Antarctic regime. The characteristic feature of those concessions were that they excluded the Government concerned from the ownership, control and operations of the mineral development that had been undertaken as a result of which benefits were restricted almost entirely to the concessionaire. The unrestricted nature of the rights granted, the vast areas covered by the concession and its long duration were other important characteristics.[358] Although no proposal has gone to this extreme in the Antarctic case, those initiatives that tend to exclude any form of control or of profit-sharing or to seek unrestricted rights, excessively large areas or indefinite time-scale, have similarities with the philosophy on which these traditional concessions are based.

International practice, as we have seen, has gradually been rectifying this original extreme form of concession which was also used in early continental shelf licences.[359] The changes introduced first into the system of taxation and, in general, the resulting closer link with the national economy have determined a development that has led to a greater degree of participation by the host Government in the ownership of the mining firm or to greater control of operations.[360] The concept of permanent sovereignty over natural resources has formed part of this process although certain ideological excesses have given rise to sharp conflict in this field.[361]

Licensing arrangements and other modern contracts have been the legal expression of these tendencies. Greater participation through forms of equity sharing and various kinds of financial arrangements, as well as greater control over the administration of the oil or mining companies have become common characteristics of many modern contracts.[362] In all these cases, the rights and obligations of the licensee are defined by *ad hoc* agreements whose terms generally contain a strong element of State regulation. When control by the State over mining activity is very intensive, recourse has also been had to work or service contracts and to agreements on participation in production or co-production.[363]

These new tendencies may also be discerned in the system designed for Antarctica, even though they respect the limits imposed both by the international nature of the system and by the fact that the proposed institutions, whatever their powers, are not in any sense a State and have none of the attributes of a State. The trend in regard to financial arrangements, which will be considered in the next chapter, is representative of the new approaches as is the greater control which the regime has to exercise over operations, particularly in the context of the environmental policy. There is also a link between these tendencies and the nature of the Antarctic contract.

Owing to the international nature of the system, there has been no discussion of forms of co-ownership of the companies involved or ways of linking them more closely with the local economy[364] which, in the Antarctic case, is non-existent. For the same reason, no consideration has been given to forms of work or service contracts or co-production arrangements. It must, however, be remembered that these approaches have not been entirely absent from the positions adopted by some countries. The initiative which is designed to set up a 'compulsory joint venture' system among participating States, the various forms of sharing in operations or the requirement of firm links between the contractor and the sponsoring State are concepts which have much in common with the philosophy which inspires the new trends that have been mentioned. Particularly important in this regard are the joint-ventures arrangements.

In the same way, the desire of the countries which maintain territorial claims to benefit from mineral activities taking place in the Antarctic territory is also an illustration of the necessity for greater State participation and forms part of the problems relating to the internal accommodation.

In the case of the Law of the Sea Conference deep sea-bed regime, the international nature of the system did not prevent the launching of initiatives designed to ensure total control by the Authority over the resources and operations, including forms of work or service contracts, co-production arrangements and other aspects.[365] This was one of the factors which eventually prevented achievement of a consensus on the deep sea-bed regime. The greater similarity of views that prevails within the framework of the Antarctic system, the smaller number of States involved at present and the more marked spirit of co-operation which inspires it, have made it possible to avoid a repetition of such confrontations in this other context.

Chapter 5 Notes

1. See generally David A. Colson: 'The Antarctic Treaty System: the mineral issue', *Law Pol. Int. Bus.*, Vol. 12, 1980, 841–902. Also chapter 2 supra, section 2.3.
2. For the text of the relevant recommendations on mineral exploitation, see Antarctic Treaty: *Handbook 1983*, section 1.5. For comments on the issues that

were to be discussed at the 1976 Paris Special Meeting, see P. Jones: 'Whose oil resources? The question of Antarctic sovereignty', Note, *Geography*, N° 272, Vol. 61, Part 3, July 1976, 167–168.

3. See particularly, Antarctic Treaty: 'Report of the Group of Experts on Mineral Exploration and Exploitation', *Report of the Ninth Consultative Meeting*, Annex 5, Foreign and Commonwealth Office, 1977; also reprinted in U.S. Senate: *Hearing on Exploitation of Antarctic Resources*, 1978, 118–148. See also Antarctic Treaty: 'Report of the working group on the question of Antarctic Mineral Resources. Legal and Political aspects', *Final Report of the Tenth Consultative Meeting*, Annex 5, reproduced in Jonathan I. Charney (ed.): *The New Nationalism and the use of common spaces*, 1982, 304–312. See also Chapter 6, infra, section 6.1, for the reports dealing specifically with environmental and other questions of the minerals regime.

4. For a background note on these negotiations, see C. D. Beeby: 'Towards an Antarctic mineral resources regime', *N.Z.I.R.*, Vol. VII, N° 3, May–June 1982, 4–6. Ibid.: 'The Antarctic Treaty System as a resource management mechanism – Non-living resources', in U.S. Polar Research Board: *Antarctic Treaty System, An Assessment*, 1986, 269–284. US Department of State: 'International regime for Antarctic mineral resources, proposed negotiation', *Federal Register*, November 8, 1982, Vol. 47, N° 216, 50598–50599. A. D. Watts: 'Antarctic mineral resources: negotiations for a mineral resources regime', in Gillian Triggs (ed.): *The Antarctic Treaty Regime*, 1987, 164–175.

5. María Teresa Infante: 'Los recursos minerales antárticos y su régimen', in Francisco Orrego Vicuña, María Teresa Infante and Pilar Armanet: *Política Antartica de Chile*, 1985, 225–236. Jorge Berguño: 'Criterios de aceptabilidad en un regimen para los minerales antárticos', in Orrego et al., op. cit., 249–274. Alfredo Bruno Bologna: 'La Antártida: aspectos políticos y jurídicos de la explotación de los recursos naturales', in Asociación Argentina de Derecho Internacional: *El Derecho Internacional en los congresos ordinarios*, 1981, 275–314. For earlier views on the various approaches to resources' regimes, see also G. Battaglini: *I diritti degli Stati nelle zone polari*, 1974; P. Antonsen: 'Natural resources in Antarctica', *Internasjonal Politikk*, 1974, N° 4, 801–816 (in Norwegian). Other works are cited in this and following chapters in relation to individual subjects.

6. See Beeby, loc. cit. (1982), note 4 supra, particularly at 5–6. See also C. D. Beeby: 'An overview of the problems which should be addressed in the preparation of a regime governing the mineral resources of Antarctica', in Francisco Orrego Vicuña (ed.): *Antarctic Resources Policy*, 1983, 191–198.

7. R. B. Thomson: 'Antarctic mineral resources: possibilities and problems', *N.Z.I.R.*, Vol. VII, N° 3, May–June 1982, 7–8.

8. For a discussion of environmental protection in Antarctica and its effect on 'related ecosystems' of neighbouring countries, Fernando Zegers: 'The Antarctic system and the utilization of resources', *Univ.Mia.L. Rev*, Vol. 33, 1978, at 443–451. See also Chapter 6 infra, section 6.1.

9. For a discussion of the various interests involved in the process of accommodation, see Francisco Orrego Vicuña: 'The definition of a regime on Antarctic mineral resources: basic options', in Francisco Orrego Vicuña, op. cit., note 6 supra, 199–215. On general interests relating to political and strategic aspects, see also Harry H. Almond Jr.: 'Demilitarization and arms control: Antarctica', *Case West. Res, J.I.L.*, Vol. 17, 1985, 229–284.

10. This aspect will be discussed in Chapter 6 infra in relation to the principle of 'full and fair opportunity' in the participation in Antarctic mineral activities.

11. See for example Rudiger Wolfrum: 'The Use of Antarctic Non-Living Resources:

the search for a Trustee?', in Rudiger Wolfrum (ed.): *Antarctic Challenge*, 1984, 143–163, at 151.

12. On the institutional aspects of the regime, see Chapter 8 infra.

13. On the issues relating to the external accommodation, see generally Part III of this work.

14. Treaty relating to Spitzbergen, Paris, February 9, 1920; text in *A.J.I.L.*, Supplement, Vol. 18, 1924, Official Documents, 199–208. For a comment, see Fred K. Nielsen: 'The solution of the Spitzbergen question', *A.J.I.L.*, Vol. 14, 1920, 232–235. For a detailed discussion of the regime, see Willy Ostreng: *Politics in High Latitudes. The Svalbard Archipelago*, 1977; Carl August Fleischer: 'Le regime d'exploitation du Spitsberg', *An.Fr.D.I.*, 1978, 275–300.

15. For a discussion of the sea-bed regime, see Francisco Orrego Vicuña 'Le regime de l'exploration et de l'exploitation des fonds marins', in: René-Jean Dupuy et Daniel Vignes (eds.): *Traité du Nouveau Droit de la Mer*, 1985, 551–601. E. D. Brown: *Sea-bed energy and mineral resources and the Law of the Sea*, 1984.

16. Christopher Beeby: *The Antarctic Treaty*, New Zealand Institute of International Affairs, 1972, at 17–19.

17. S. B. Slevich: *Basic problems of Antarctica Exploitation*, Joint Publications Research Service, Arlington, Virginia, 6 June 1974, translation from Russian, at 29.

18. See particularly recommendations VII-6, VIII-14, IX-1, X-1, and XI-1, source cit., note 2 supra; the 1976 Paris Special Preparatory Meeting on mineral resources was also held in connection with the Ninth Consultative Meeting.

19. See note 3 supra. A special meeting on mineral resources was also held in Washington D.C., December 8–12, 1980.

20. Recommendation XI-1, paragraph 3.

21. The fourth Special Consultative Meeting has held the following meetings: Wellington, 14–25 June 1982; Wellington, 17–28 January 1983; Bonn, 11–22 July 1983; Washington D.C., 18–27 January 1984; Tokyo, 22–31 May 1984; Rio de Janeiro, 26 February–12 March 1985; Paris, 23 September–4 October 1985; Hobart, 14–25 April 1986; Tokyo, 27 October–12 November 1986; Montevideo, 11–20 May 1987.

22. On the constitution, procedure and structure of SCAR, see generally W. M. Bush: *Antarctica and International Law*, Vol. I, 1982, 5–27; see particularly the list of recommendations and other references by means of which the Consultative Parties have requested the opinion of SCAR on various subjects, compiled at 24–27.

23. The Institute of International Studies of the University of Chile convened a Conference on Antarctic Resource Policy held at the Antarctic Station Teniente Marsh, October 6–9, 1982, which was the first conference ever to be held in Antarctica; the proceedings have been published in Francisco Orrego Vicuña, op. cit., note 6 supra. The US Polar Research Board convened the second meeting of this series on the Antarctic Treaty System, held at the Transantarctic Mountains, January 7–13, 1985; the proceedings have been published in US Polar Research Board: *Antarctic Treaty System, An Assessment*, 1986. For a comment on this second meeting, see M. W. Holdgate: 'International workshop on the Antarctic Treaty System, 7–13 January 1985', *Pol. Rec.*, Vol. 22, 1985, 538–539. For the proceedings and comments of other recent academic meetings on Antarctica, see: Rudiger Wolfrum (ed.): *Antarctic Challenge*, 1984; also commented in Harald Heimsoeth: 'Antarctic mineral resources', *Environmental Policy and Law*, Vol. 11, N° 3, November 1983, 59–61; Lewis M. Alexander and Lynne Carter Hanson (eds.): *Antarctic politics and marine resources: critical choices for the 1980's*, 1985; Gillian Triggs (ed.): *The Antarctic Treaty Regime*, 1987; Rudiger Wolfrum (ed.): *Antarctic Challenge II*, 1986.

24. On the problem of Antarctic 'secrecy', see F. M. Auburn: *Antarctic Law and Politics*, 1982, at 156–159.
25. It is difficult to imagine that delicate compromises on the issue of jurisdiction, for example, could be achieved by means of a public discussion of the matter. For the case of the 'bifocal approach', as a relevant example of this situation, see Chapter 4 supra, Section 4.5.
26. See the statements by Barnes and Heap in Rudiger Wolfrum, op. cit., note 11 supra, at 62. While the former statement implies a criticism of the meetings of claimants, the latter reply clarifies the role of such meetings.
27. The Chairman of the Special Preparatory Meeting held in Paris in 1976 submitted three *Working Documents* to the Ninth Consultative Meeting (London, 1977), which are restricted. The Chairman of the Working Group on legal and political aspects of mineral exploitation which met during the Tenth Consultative Meeting (Washington D.C., 1979) issued a *personal report* on the discussions, known as the 'Wulf Report', which is also restricted. The Chairman of this Group was Mr Norman A. Wulf. A similar restricted report was issued by the Chairman of the meeting on mineral resources (Washington D.C., 1980), known as the 'Busby Report'. During the work of the Fourth Special Consultative Meeting various reports have been issued by Mr Christopher D. Beeby, who has presided over different meetings, which will be referred to further below.
28. The Chairman of the informal session of the Fourth Special Consultative Meeting (Wellington, 17–28 January 1983) and of various other meetings of the negotiating process, Ambassador Christopher D. Beeby, has prepared in a personal capacity the Draft Articles and Draft Convention on the Antarctic minerals regime, which have served as a basis for the negotiations on the matter. The first Draft Articles (MR/17), though being a document of a restricted nature, were published in the periodical *E.C.O.*, Vol. XXIII, N° 1, Bonn, July 11–22, 1983, at 5–12; and in *Environmental Policy and Law*, Vol. 11, 1983, 47–52, the latter including the personal report by the Chairman (hereinafter cited as *1983 Draft Articles*). The revised Draft Articles (MR/17, Rev. I) were issued by Mr Beeby on 29 March 1984, and though also restricted were published in Greenpeace International: *The future of the Antarctic. Background for a second UN debate*, 22 October 1984, Appendix 8 (hereinafter cited as *1984 Draft Articles)* A second revision of the Draft Articles (MR/17, Rev. II) was issued on 19 September 1986. MR/17, Rev. III was issued on 2 April 1987. On the 'brokerage role' which New Zealand has sought to perform in the negotiations on Antarctic mineral resources, see Roderic Alley: 'New Zealand and Antarctica', *International Journal*, Vol. 39, 1984, 911–931, at 931.
29. On the procedure of the Law of the Sea negotiations, see Helge Vindenes: 'Procedimientos y técnicas de negociación en la Tercera Conferencia de las Naciones Unidas sobre el Derecho del Mar y su repercusión en la búsqueda de un acuerdo substancial sobre el tema', in Instituto de Estudios Internacionales de la Universidad de Chile, CEPAL: *Economía de los Océanos*, Vol. 1, 1978, 29–44. See also Jean Monnier: 'La Troisieme Conference des Nations Unies sur le droit de la mer', *Ann.Suisse D.I.*, Vol. XXXIX, 1983, 9–38.
30. Barry Buzan: 'Negotiating by consensus: developments in technique at the United Nations Conference on the Law of the Sea', *A.J.I.L.*, Vol. 75, 1981, 324–348, at 346. Critical views on consensus negotiation or specific aspects of it are cited in this article, particularly at 345–347.
31. See generally N. A. Wright and P. L. Williams: *Mineral Resources of Antarctica*, U.S. Geological Survey, Circular 705, 1974, in: US Senate: *U.S. Antarctic Policy*, Hearing 1975, 35–67. John F. Splettstoesser: 'Mining in Antarctica: Survey of mineral resources and possible exploitation methods', in *Third International Conference on Port and Ocean Engineering under Arctic Conditions,*

11-15 August 1975, Vol. II, 1137-1155, University of Alaska. Special Preparatory Meeting (Paris, 1976): *Antarctic Mineral Resources*. Document RPS-10, submitted by the U.S. Delegation, published in U.S. Senate, Committee on Foreign Relations: Hearing on *Exploitation of Antarctic Resources*, 95th Congress, 2nd Session, 1978, 109–117. Phillip Law: 'Possibilities for Exploitation of Antarctic Resources', in Francisco Orrego Vicuña (ed.): *El desarrollo de la Antártica*, 1977, 24–37. Oscar González Ferran: 'El continente antártico. Sus recursos no renovables', in Francisco Orrego Vicuña, op. cit., this note, 1977, 228–251. Mort D. Turner: 'Antarctic mineral resources', *Frontiers*, Vol. 43, N° 1, Autumn 1978, 27–29. Nestor H. Fourcade: 'Algunas consideraciones sobre los recursos no renovables del antártico', in F. A. Milia et al.: *La Atlantártida. Un espacio geopolítico*, 1978, 217–224. Marcello Manzoni: *Rapporto Informativo sulle risorse minerarie ed energetiche dell'Antartide*, Instituto de Geología Marina, Rapporto Tecnico N° 16, Bologna, 1981. British Antarctic Survey: *Metallic Mineral Resources of Antarctica*, Memorandum, in House of Lords select committee on the European Communities: *Strategic minerals, with minutes of evidence*, Session 1981–1982, 20th report (217), London HMSO, 267–274. Tore Gjelsvik: 'The mineral resources of Antarctica: progress in their indentification', in Francisco Orrego Vicuña, op. cit., note 6 supra, 61–76. John C. Behrendt (ed.): *Petroleum and Mineral Resources of Antarctica*, U.S. Geological Survey, Circular 909, 1983. Patrick Quilty: 'Mineral resources of the Australian Antarctic Territory', in Stuart Harris (ed.): *Australia's Antarctic Policy Options*, 1984, 165–203. Franz Tessensohn 'Present knowledge of non-living resource in the Antarctic, possibilities for their exploitation and scientific perspectives', in Rudiger Wolfrum, op. cit., note 11 supra, 189–210. D. J. Drewry: 'The Antarctic physical environment', in Triggs, op. cit., note 4 supra, 6–27. Dennis E. Hayes: 'An overview of the geological history of Antarctica with regard to mineral resource potential' in Lewis M. Alexander and Lynne Carter Hanson, op. cit., note 23 supra, 173–184. John C. Behrendt: 'Are there petroleum resources in Antarctica?, in Alexander and Hanson, op. cit., note 23 supra, 191–202. See also note 133 infra.

32. Recommendation XI-1, par. 2.
33. Beeby, loc. cit., note 6 supra, at 192.
34. On these options see generally Chapter 2 supra, Section 2.6
35. See Chapter 2 supra, note 124 and associated text.
36. The problems raised by proprietary data in the light of the 1959 Treaty provisions were mentioned as a case of incompatibility between the mineral regime and Articles II, III (i) (a) and (c) and VII of that Treaty at the meeting of experts at the Fridtjof Nansen Foundation, May 30–June 10, 1973; see the 'Report of the Working Group on Legal and Political Questions', in US Senate: US *Antarctic Policy*, Hearing, 1975, par. 23, at 79.
37. See generally Chapter 2 supra, Section 2.6
38. Beeby, loc. cit., note 6 supra, at 193.
39. Francisco Orrego Vicuña: 'The definition of a regime on Antarctic mineral resources: basic options', in op. cit., note 6 supra, at 202. See also note 15 supra.
40. I. E. Nicholson: *Address* to a conference on Antarctic Mineral resources organized by the Australian Mining and Petroleum Association, Sydney, 20 March 1985, mimeo, at 3-4.
41. Beeby, loc. cit., note 6 supra, at 193.
42. Ibid., at 194.
43. Ibid., at 194.
44. Norway: Act of 17 July 1925 relating to Spitzbergen; text in Willy Ostreng, op.

cit., note 14 supra, 105–108. Norway: The Mining Code (The Mining Regulations) for Spitzbergen, Royal Decree of 7 August 1925, as amended by Royal Decree of 11 June 1975; in Willy Ostreng, op. cit., note 14 supra, 108–116.
45. Orrego, loc. cit., note 9 supra, at 204, 206.
46. See generally Orrego, loc. cit., note 15 supra.
47. Beeby, loc. cit., note 6 supra, at 192.
48. See generally Jonathan I. Charney: 'Future strategies for an Antarctic Mineral Resource Regime – Can the environment be protected?', in Jonathan I. Charney: *The new nationalism and the use of common spaces,* 1982, 206–238. G. W. Schroff: *Antarctica: politics & resources,* Seaford House Papers, 1982, 99–125, Royal College of Defence Studies.
49. Recommendation XI-1, Par. 7, V.
50. Ibid., Par. 5 (c).
51. Ibid., Preambular paragraph 2; Par. 7, I; Par. 7, V; Par. 7, VII; Par. 8; Par. 9.
52. *1983 Draft Articles,* Article II (a); letter (d) of this Article also refers to the establishment of rules for the protection of the Antarctic environment. See also *1984 Draft Articles,* Article II 1 (a).
53. *1984 Draft Articles,* Article II, 2 (c), and Article III. The environmental principles and policies of the regime will be further discussed in Chapter 6, section 6.1, infra.
54. Recommendation XI-1, par. 7, I (a) (b).
55. *1983 Draft Articles,* Article II (a) (b). *1984 Draft Articles,* Article II, 1 (b). *1986 Draft Articles,* Article 2, 1.
56. See *1983 Draft Articles,* Article II, (c), (e); and *1984 Draft Articles,* Article II, 1, (c) (d). The principle that no activities should be conducted outside the regime is established in the *1984 Draft Articles,* Article III bis; the 1983 version of this Draft contained a comparable provision in Article VI, 2, which was a case of specific application of Article X of the 1959 Treaty to the extent that it involved the collective responsibility of the Parties to the regime to exert appropriate efforts, consistent with the Charter of the United Nations, to the end that no-one engages in Antarctic mineral activities contrary to the objectives and principles of the regime.
57. For a discussion of these points of view, see generally Berguño, loc. cit. Chapter 2 supra, note 124.
58. Beeby, loc. cit., note 6 supra, at 194.
59. See generally Article III of the *1983 Draft Articles,* which deals with environmental principles, and the footnote thereto to the extent that such listing is only indicative and subject to further development. See also Article III of the *1984 Draft Articles,* where these principles have in fact been developed to an important extent, and Article 4 of the *1986 Draft Articles.*
60. The concept of an 'open use regime' has not been officially sponsored but has been considered in various academic and other propositions. See William E. Westermeyer: *The politics of mineral resource development in Antarctica,* 1984, 63–67. For an early expression of concern in this regard, Earthscan: *The future of Antarctica,* Press briefing document N° 5, 1977, reproduced in *U.S. Senate: Hearing on Exploitation of Antarctic Resources,* 1978, 189–224. See also Chapter 7 infra where this approach is further discussed.
61. See Alexandra M. Post: *Deepsea Mining and the Law of the Sea,* 1983, at 164–171.
62. *1984 Draft Articles,* Article II, 1 (c).
63. Ibid., Article II, 2 (b). See also Article 2 of the *1986 Draft Articles.*
64. See generally Chapter 2 supra.
65. Recommendation XI-1, Preambular paragraphs 8, 9.

66. Recommendation XI-1, Preambular paragraphs 1, 2, 3, 4, 5.
67. Recommendation XI-1, Paragraph 5 (a) (b) (e).
68. Recommendation XI-1, Paragraph 7, V, and par. 9.
69. Recommendation XI-1, Paragraph 7, II (a).
70. See generally the Preamble of the *1984 Draft Articles;* the 1983 version did not contain this preambular part. See also Beeby, loc. cit., note 6 supra, 191–193. See further the Preamble of the *1986 Draft Articles.*
71. Recommendation XI-1, Preambular paragraph 4 and paragraph 5 (a). See also *1984 Draft Articles,* Article II, 2 (d), and *1986 Draft Articles,* Article 2.
72. *1984 Draft Articles,* Preamble, par. (f).
73. Recommendation XI-1, Preambular paragraph 4 and paragraph 5 (e). *1983 Draft Articles,* Article VII. *1984 Draft Articles,* Article VII. *1986 Draft Articles,* Article 11.
74. See Chapter 4 supra, Section 4.5. For a discussion of the links of the various Antarctic conventions to Article IV of the 1959 Treaty, see generally also Gillian Triggs: 'The Antarctic Treaty Regime: a workable compromise or a "Purgatory of Ambiguity"?', *Case W.R.J.I.L.,* Vol. 17, 1985, 195–228.
75. Convention on the Conservation of Antarctic Marine Living Resources, Article IV, 2 (b).
76. *1983 Draft Articles,* Article VII, (b). The same provision has been kept by the 1984 revision of the Articles, and in Article 11 of the *1986 Draft Articles.*
77. On the question of inter-temporal law and its application to Antarctic maritime claims, see Chapter 4 supra, Section 4.1. A further legal complication raised by this question of interpretation is whether the new maritime jurisdictions, such as the Exclusive Economic Zone or the outer limit of the continental shelf including the margin, exist *ipso facto* dependent on prior territorial claims or they need to be asserted separately; if the 'appurtenance' operates *ipso facto* the difficulty of the interpretation might be circumvented, otherwise conflictive views about the resolution of the matter will certainly come to the fore. It should be noted also that while the rights over the continental shelf are independent from any express proclamation (Article 2, par. 3 of the Convention on the Continental Shelf and Article 77, par. 3 of the Law of the Sea Convention), no comparable provision has been made for the EEZ.
78. Convention on the Conservation of Antarctic Marine Living Resources, Article III.
79. Recommendation XI-1, Paragraphs 5 (b), 7 II (a).
80. *1983 Draft Articles,* Article VIII, 1. An amended provision to this effect appears in the same Article in the 1984 revision. A more extensive linkage is provided for in Article 12 of the *1986 Draft Articles.*
81. *1983* and *1984 Draft Articles,* Article VIII, 2. Recommendation XI-1, par. 7, V.
82. Convention on the Conservation of Antarctic Marine Living Resources, Article V, 1.
83. *1983* and *1984 Draft Articles,* Article VIII, 3 and *1986 Draft Articles,* Article 12. See also the Convention on the Conservation of Antarctic Marine Living Resources, Articles V, 2 and VI.
84. Article VIII, 3 of the *1983 Draft Articles* referred in this connection to activities 'in the Antarctic Treaty area', which in many cases is broader than that of the resources regimes, particularly in relation to the Agreed Measures; the comparable provision of the *1984 Draft Articles* changed this reference to 'the area to which this regime applies', but this latter area is also broader than that of the Agreed Measures. For a discussion of the areas of application of the respective regimes, see Chapter 4 supra, and section 5.3 of this Chapter.

85. *1984 Draft Articles,* Article IX (bis), and Preamble, par. (f). See further *1986 Draft Articles,* Article 16.
86. For a criticism in this regard of the Living Resources regime, see Barbara Mitchell and Richard Sandbrook: *The Management of the Southern Ocean,* 1980, 130-131.
87. Orrego, loc. cit., note 9 supra, at 202–203.
88. W. M. Bush: *Antarctica and International Law,* 1982, Vol. I, 64–70.
89. See Chapter 4 supra, sections 4.3 and 4.4.
90. See Chapter 4 supra, section 4.5.
91. See generally María Teresa Infante: 'The Continental Shelf of the Antarctica: legal implications for a regime on mineral resources', in Francisco Orrego Vicuña, op. cit., note 6 supra, 253–264.
92. See generally the scientific and technical studies on the mineral resources of Antarctica cited in note 31 supra.
93. Christopher Pinto: Remarks and questions at the discussion of the Symposium on Antarctic Challenge, in Rudiger Wolfrum, op. cit., note 11 supra, at 59–60.
94. The southern limit of the Norwegian claim has not been defined, a situation that has given rise to the view that there is an unclaimed triangle in this area extending to the South Pole. For the unclaimed areas of Antarctica see the map published in Steven J. Burton: 'New stresses on the Antarctic Treaty: toward international legal institutions governing antarctic resources', *Virg. L.R.,* Vol. 65, 1979, at 512.
95. For the norm-creating functions of the Antarctic Treaty system and its development see Chapter 2 supra. None of the many expressions of this practice has ever excluded the unclaimed sector from its ambit of application.
96. See generally the question of the area of application of the various resource regimes discussed in Chapter 4 supra.
97. John Heap: Remarks at the discussion of the Symposium on Antarctic Challenge, in Rudiger Wolfrum, op. cit., note 11 supra, at 60–61.
98. Paragraph 7, IV of Recommendation XI-1 and Article IV, par. 1 of the *1984 Draft Articles* refer generally to the Antarctic 'continent', an expression that can only be taken to mean the continent as a whole; any exclusion of a part of the continent would have to be done on express terms. See also Article 5 of the *1986 Draft Articles.*
99. See Chapter 3 supra, section 3.5, and Chapter 4 supra, section 4.8.
100. See Chapter 4 supra, section 4.7.
101. Ibid. See also in relation to the application of this principle in the Arctic, Bo Johnson Theutenberg: *The Evolution of the Law of the Sea,* 1984, at 35–36.
102. The norm-creating function referred to in note 95 supra has not differentiated between land and insular territory for the purpose of its application.
103. Recommendation XI-1, par. 7, IV.
104. See Chapter 4 supra, section 4.7.
105. 1982 Convention on the Law of the Sea, Article 121, par. 3.
106. On the evolution of Antarctic settlements, see David Sugden: *Arctic and Antarctica,* 1982, 389–421.
107. See Chapter 4 supra, section 4.6.
108. Report of the Group of Experts on Mineral Exploration and Exploitation, in Antarctic Treaty: *Report of the Ninth Consultative Meeting,* UK Foreign and Commonwealth Office, 1977, Annex 5, at 62, footnote.
109. See generally the study cit. in note 91 supra.
110. See note 99 supra.
111. Francisco Orrego Vicuña: 'The application of the law of the sea and the Exclusive Economic Zone to the Antarctic continent', in Francisco Orrego Vicuña, op. cit., note 6 supra, at 247. See also the discussion on the link between the concept of the continental shelf and coastal state jurisdiction in Chapter 4 supra, section 4.6.

112. Recommendation XI-1, Par. 7, IV.
113. On the legal issues related to resource exploitation in the Antarctic continental shelf, see also J. Michel Marcoux: 'Natural resource jurisdiction on the Antarctic continental margin', *Virg. J.I.L.*, Vol. 11, 1971, 374–404. F. M. Auburn: 'Offshore oil and gas in Antarctica, *G.Y.B.I.L.*, Vol. 20, 1977, 139–173. F. M. Auburn: 'Legal implications of petroleum resources of the Antarctic Continental Shelf', *Ocean Yearbook*, 1, 1978, 500–515. Renzo G. Follegati: *The Exploitation of the Antarctic oil and its environmental and legal implications*, Master of Marine Affairs Major Paper, University of Rhode Island, 1982. Oscar Pinochet de la Barra: 'Algunas reflexiones sobre el problema de la Antártica en el año 2000', in Francisco Orrego Vicuña (ed.): *La Antártica y sus recursos*, Santiago, 1983, 355–367.
114. The New Zealand government has stated that 'the outer limits of the minerals regime in respect of the continental shelf of the Ross Dependency will not extend beyond the limits prescribed in article 76 of the 1982 United Nations Convention on the Law of the Sea'; United Nations: *Question of Antarctica*, Views of States, U.N. Doc. A/39/583 (part II), Vol. III, 9 November 1984, at 20. For an explanation of Article 76 of the Law of the Sea Convention and the criteria which influenced the consensus reached, see Lucius Caflisch: 'Les zones maritimes sous juridiction nationale, leurs limites et leur delimitations', in Daniel Bardonnet et Michel Virally (eds.): *Le Nouveau Droit International de la Mer*, 1983, particularly at 85–92. See also J. F. Pulvenis: 'Le plateau continental, definition et regime', in R. J. Dupuy and D. Vignes: *Traité du Nouveau Droit de la Mer*, 1985, 275–336.
115. See note 111 supra.
116. On the problems related to the effects of the 1982 Convention on the Law of the Sea in customary international law, see generally Francisco Orrego Vicuña: 'The Law of the Sea experience and the corpus of international law: effects and interrelationships', in Robert B. Krueger and Stefan A. Riesenfeld: *The Developing Order of the Oceans*, 1985, 5–22.
117. Francisco Orrego Vicuña and María Teresa Infante: 'Le Droit de la Mer dans l'Antarctique', *R.G.D.I.P.*, 1980, at 348.
118. Ralph L. Harry: 'The Antarctic regime and the Law of the Sea Convention: an Australian view', *Virg. J.I.L.*, Vol. 21, 1981, at 732.
119. See Chapter 4 supra, section 4.7. The delimitation agreement on the EEZ and the continental shelf between Australia and France of 4 January 1982 does not extend south of 53° 14' 07" because of the uncertainty as to the configuration of the continental shelf south of that point; see Chapter 4 supra, notes 225 and 226 and associated texts.
120. For a favourable point of view see Frida M. Pfirter de Armas: *La situación jurídica de la Antártica y el nuevo Derecho del Mar*, Facultad de Derecho y Ciencias Sociales, Rosario, Argentina, 1982. See also the discussion of this point in Scharnhorst Muller: 'The impact of UNCLOS III on the Antarctic Regime', in Rudiger Wolfrum, op. cit., note 11 supra, 169–176, at 175.
121. See generally Orrego, loc. cit., note 111 supra, at 248–249.
122. María Teresa Infante, loc. cit., note 91 supra, at 259.
123. See generally L. F. E. Goldie: 'A general international law doctrine for seabed regimes', *The International Lawyer*, Vol. 7, 1973, 796–824. Shigeru Oda: *International Law of the resources of the sea*, 1979, particularly at 122–123. Barry Buzan: *Seabed politics*, 1976, particularly at 162–177.
124. Kim Traavik: 'Antarctica and the International Seabed regime', *Internasjonal Politikk*, October–December 1974, N° 4, 783–800 (in Norwegian).

125. Recommendation XI-1, par. 7, IV. See also *1984 Draft Articles,* Article IV, par. 1, and Article 5, para. 1 of the *1986 Draft Articles.*

126. The word 'encroachment' has been translated in the Spanish version of Recommendation XI-1 as 'usurpar', which in fact means to 'usurp', or take without right.

127. Recommendation XI-1, par. 7, V.

128. *1984 Draft Articles,* Article XXXVI, par. 3. *1986 Draft Articles,* Article 52, par. 3.

129. See articles 56, par. 3, and 76 of the United Nations Convention on the Law of the Sea. See also the works cited in note 114 supra.

130. International Court of Justice: *Continental Shelf (Libyan Arab Jamahiriya/Malta),* Judgment of 3 June 1985, pars. 26–35,

131. Orrego, loc. cit., note 9 supra, at 203.

132. *1984 Draft Articles,* Article I, 1, k and *1986 Draft Articles,* Article 1, b). See also Recommendation XI-1, par. 7, IV. Article 133 of the United Nations Convention on the Law of the Sea has defined resources as 'all solid, liquid or gaseous mineral resources *in situ* in the Area at or beneath the sea-bed, including polymetallic nodules'.

133. See the technical studies cited in note 31 supra. See also, with particular reference to petroleum: American Geographical Society: *Geological maps of Antarctica,* Antarctic Map Folio Series, Folio 12, 1969, 1970. American Geographical Society: *Marine sediments of the Southern Oceans,* Antarctic Map Folio Series, Folio 17, 1973. D. J. Drewry: *Antarctica: Glaciological and Geophysical Folio,* Scott Polar Research Institute, 1983. Neal Potter: *Natural resource potentials of the Antarctic,* The American Geographical Society, 1969. U.S. House of Representatives, Committee on Science and Technology, Subcommittee on Energy research, development and demonstration: *Polar Energy Resources Potential,* Report prepared by the Congressional Research Service, 94th Congress, 2nd session, 1976. John F. Splettstoesser: 'Offshore development for oil and gas in Antarctica', *Fourth International Conference on Port and Ocean Engineering under Arctic conditions,* Memorial University of New Foundland, Sep. 26–30, 1977, Vol. II, 811–820. P. J. Cameron: 'The petroleum potential of Antarctica and its continental margin', Australian Petroleum Exploration Association Journal, Vol. 21, N° 1, 1981, 99–111. Oscar Gonzalez Ferran: 'Geologic data and its impact on the discussion on a regime for mineral resources', in Francisco Orrego Vicuña, op. cit., note 6 supra, 159–166.

134. See generally the studies cited in Chapter 4 supra, notes 212, 213 and 214.

135. Orrego, loc. cit., note 9 supra, at 203. On the authorization of mineral activities see generally section 5.4 of this Chapter.

136. See generally Beeby, loc. cit., notes 4 and 6 supra; Orrego, loc. cit., note 9 supra. See also 'Antarctica and the question of the exploitation of its resources', *Australian Foreign Affairs Record,* December 1977, 604–611; David C. McEwan: *The future political and economic development of the Antarctic,* Dissertation, Diploma in Polar Studies, Scott Polar Research Institute, 1978; Anthony Bergin: *Frozen assets–resource problems and Antarctica,* Dyason House Papers, Melbourne, Vol. 6, N° 1, September 1979, 7–12; Finn Sollie: 'Trends and prospects for regimes for living and mineral resources in the Antarctic', in John King Gamble Jr.: *Law of the Sea: Neglected issues,* 1979, 193–208; William Westermeyer 'Resource allocation in Antarctica. A review', *Marine Policy,* Vol. 6, 1982, 303–325; Christopher Beeby: 'A negotiator's view, in *The Antarctic: preferred futures, constraints and choices,* New Zealand Institute of International Affairs, 1983, 58–62; Antarctic and Southern Ocean Coalition: *Report on the Antarctic Mineral Meeting,* (Washington D.C. 18–27 January

1984), February 6, 1984; Antarctica briefing: *Status of Antarctic Minerals negotiations,* N° 1, April 3, 1984.

137. Various technical studies have identified the hypothetical organisation as 'the authority', without prejudging its nature on juridical basis. See for example M. W. Holdgate and Jon Tinker: *Oil and other minerals in the Antarctic,* 1979, p. 23, par. 84.

138. Orrego, loc. cit., note 9 supra, at 205.

139. See the studies cit. in note 15 supra.

140. One author has proposed the option of a parallel system for the Antarctic regime: Rainer Lagoni: 'Antarctica's mineral resources in international law', *Z.A.O.R.V.,* Vol. 39, 1979, at 35.

141. Charney, loc. cit., note 48 supra, at 219.

142. *1984 Draft Articles,* Article IX. See also the same article in the 1983 version. Article 15 of the *1986 Draft Articles* has enlarged this concept in order to exclude any form of discrimination affecting the Parties or operators.

143. Recommendation XI-1, Par. 7, IV.

144. *1984 Draft Articles,* Article I, 1, d; *1983 Draft Articles,* Article I, 1 c. See also Article 1 (d) of the *1986 Draft Articles.*

145. Egil Bergsager: 'Basic conditions for the exploration and exploitation of mineral resources in Antarctica: options and precedents', in Francisco Orrego Vicuña, op. cit., note 6 supra, at 169–170.

146. Ibid., at 170.

147. See generally Takesi Nagata: 'The advancement of scientific research as the basis of Antarctic development', in Francisco Orrego Vicuña (ed.): *El desarrollo de la Antártica,* 1977, 70–131. See also Gjelsvik, loc. cit., note 31 supra, at 64.

148. Bergsager, loc. cit., note 145 supra, at 170–171.

149. F. Auburn: 'Antarctic minerals and the third world', *F.R.A.M.: The Journal of Polar Studies,* Winter 1984, 201–223, at 205. See also the statement by Mr R. Tucker Scully in reply to a congressional question about whether there have been site specific types of geological exploratory works in Antarctica, in which he says 'To my knowledge, almost none'; see also the statement to the same effect by Dr Todd; both in U.S. House of Representatives: Committee on Merchant Marine and Fisheries, Subcommittee on fisheries and wildlife conservation and the environment: *Hearing on Antarctic Marine Living Resources* (H.R. 3416), 30 June 1983, at 59–60. Could 'almost none' be taken to mean that some activity of this kind has taken place?

150. *1984 Draft Articles,* Article IX (ter); *1983 Draft Articles,* Article XXIV, 6. See also Articles 17 and 35 of the *1986 Draft Articles.*

151. On the policy of scientific research and the institutions that have been proposed to this effect, see Chapter 6 infra, Section 6.4.

152. Bergsager, loc. cit., note 145 supra, at 175.

153. Ibid., at 175.

154. Ibid., at 177–178.

155. Alistair Graham: 'Environment hazards in the Antarctic', in *The Antarctic: preferred futures, constraints and choices,* New Zealand Institute of International Affairs, 1983, 25–30, at 29.

156. Recommendation XI-1, par. 7, VI.

157. Barbara Mitchell: *Frozen Stakes. The future of Antarctic minerals,* 1983, at 7. But see also the statements cit., note 149 supra.

158. *1984 Draft Articles,* Article I, 1 (j). The *1986 Draft Articles* have suggested to this effect a depth not exceeding 25 metres or such other depth as the Commission may establish; see Article 1 (j).

159. Bergsager, loc. cit., note 145 supra, at 176–177.
160. Ibid., at 177.
161. Ibid., at 177.
162. Convention on the Law of the Sea, Annex III, Article 2.
163. This aspect of the discussion appears to a limited extent in some of the criticism that has been made to the *1983 Draft Articles*. See in particular *E.C.O.: Antarctic Minerals Regime*, Vol. XXIII, N° 1, Bonn, July 11–22, 1983, at 1; Antarctic and Southern Ocean Coalition. Report cit., note 136 supra, at 5; Alistair Graham, loc. cit., note 155 supra, at 29. See also Lee Kimball: 'Environmental issues in the Antarctic minerals negotiations', in Lewis M. Alexander and Lynne Carter Hanson, op. cit., note 23 supra, 204–214; and Lee Kimball: 'The future of the Antarctic Treaty System. Environmental community suggestions', in Alexander and Hanson, op. cit., 237–247.
164. Recommendation XI-1, par. 7, IV and 7, VI.
165. *1984 Draft Articles,* Article XXIII; *1983 Draft Articles,* Article XXIII. Under the 1983 version notification was to be done to the Commission. See further Article 35 of the *1986 Draft Articles,* where notification is to be made to the Commission with an anticipation of nine months.
166. See note 158 supra and associated text.
167. See note 163 supra.
168. See note 154 and associated text. On the implications of exploratory drilling on the environment and the required powers of control, see also Bergsager, loc. cit., note 145 supra, at 177–178. On the environmental impact of seismic testing, see Antarctic and Southern Ocean Coalition: *Impacts of seismic testing,* October 1, 1985, Assoc Paper N° 3, ANT SCM/7.
169. *1984 Draft Articles,* Article XXIV (bis). For a comment on the revised Draft Articles of 1984, see E.C.O., Vol. XXVII, N° 3, Tokyo, May 22-31, 1984. Article 36 of the *1986 Draft Articles* has devised a more complete and flexible proceeding for consideration of prospecting by the Commission which can be activated by any member of this body.
170. *1984 Draft Articles,* Article XXIII; *1983 Draft Articles,* Article XXIII. See further *1986 Draft Articles,* Article 35.
171. *1984 Draft Articles,* Article XIII, 1 c; *1983 Draft Articles,* Article XIII, 1 c and Article XXIV, 1, with particular reference to Specially Protected Areas and Sites of Special Scientific Interest. See also *1986 Draft Articles,* Article 14.
172. See note 85 supra and associated text. See also *1984 Draft Articles,* Article XXIV, 5 b.
173. *1984 Draft Articles,* Article XXIV, 1; *1983 Draft Articles,* Article XXIV, par. 3. See also *1986 Draft Articles,* Article 35, e.
174. *1984 Draft Articles,* Article XXIII, par. 5, 6; *1983 Draft Articles,* Article XXIV, par. 5, 6. Article 35 of the *1986 Draft Articles,* pars. 9, 12, 13 has also provided detailed and more complete rules as to proprietary data.
175. On the definition of exploration, see *1984 Draft Articles,* Article I, 1, g; see also generally Bergsager, loc. cit., note 145 supra, at 169–170, 177–178. See also *1986 Draft Articles,* Article 1 (g).
176. Bergsager, loc. cit., note 145 supra, at 174–175.
177. Ibid., at 174. For mineral activities and regimes in the Arctic, see generally J. Peter A. Bernhardt: 'Spitzbergen: Jurisdictional friction over unexploited oil reserves', *Cal. West I.L.J.,* Vol. 4, 1973, 61–120; John C. Ausland: 'Spitsbergen: who's in control?', *U.S. Nav. Inst. Proc.* Vol. 104/11/909, November 1978, 63–70; P. Miles and N. J. R. Wright: 'An outline of mineral extraction in the Arctic', *Pol. Rec.,* Vol. 19, 1978, 11–38; Desmond Nicholas Morton: *Present political attitudes*

towards non-renewable resource development in selected northern areas. Thesis,
Diploma in Polar Studies, Scott Polar Research Institute, 1980; Clive Archer and
David Scrivener: 'Frozen frontiers and resource wrangles: conflict and
cooperation in northern waters', *Int. Af,* Vol. 51, N° 1, Winter 1982/83, 59–76;
Egil Bergsager: *Arctic Experiences,* Introductory talk at ONS Advance Projects
Conference, 15–17 November 1983, Stavanger, NDP- Contribution N° 15,
Oljedirektoratet, March 1984; John A. Dugger: 'Arctic oil and gas: policy
perspectives', in William E. Westermeyer and Kurt M. Shusterich: *United States
Arctic interests. The 1980's and 1990's,* 1984, 19–38; William E. Westermeyer:
'Energy from the polar regions', *International Journal,* Vol. 39, 1984, 721–741.

178. See note 171 supra and associated text.
179. See generally Antarctic and Southern Ocean Coalition: *Protected areas in the
Antarctic,* Workshop, Washington D.C., January 23, 1984. Also Antarctica
briefing: *Protected areas in the Antarctic,* N° 4, April 23, 1984.
180. Bergsager, loc. cit., note 145 supra, at 174.
181. Ibid., at 175.
182. See studies cited in note 179 supra.
183. See Chapter 10 infra.
184. See notes 171 and 172 supra and associated texts.
185. This aspect is also related to the various models for the conducting of prospecting,
on which see note 159 supra and associated text.
186. On British legislation and the specific separate requirements of the production
phase, see generally T. Daintith and G. Willoughby: *United Kingdom oil and gas
law,* 1984, Chapter 7, particularly pars. 1–703 to 1–713. For the integrated
operations under Part XI of the Law of the Sea Convention, see Annex III,
Article 3, par. 4 (c) of this Treaty. See also Chapter 4 of the 1983 and 1984 Draft
Articles of the Antarctic minerals negotiations.
187. Peter D. Cameron: *Property rights and sovereign rights. The case of North Sea oil,*
1983, at 50. See also Daintith and Willoughby, op. cit., note 186 supra,
Chapter 2, pars. 1–201 to 1–205.
188. Cameron, op. cit., note 187 supra, at 50, citing the Petroleum Regulations, 1976,
Schedule 5, clause 2; for the current text of these regulations see Petroleum
(Production) Regulations, 1982, Schedule 5, Clause 2, reproduced in Daintith
and Willoughby, op. cit., note 186 supra, par. 5–176.
189. Cameron, op. cit., note 187 supra, at 50. For the Model Clauses see Petroleum
(Production) Regulations 1982, cit., note 188 supra, Schedule 4.
190. Cameron, op. cit., note 187 supra, at 50.
191. Saudi Arabia v. Arabian American Oil Company (ARAMCO case), decision of
23 August 1958, *International Law Reports,* Vol. 27, 117–233, at 158.
192. Bergsager, loc. cit., note 145 supra, at 178.
193. Ibid., at 178. Under the British legislation the areas and blocks available for
licensing are generally determined by the Secretary of State for Energy, who will
allocate licences on discretionary bases but with indication of the criteria to be
taken into account; negotiation will proceed only to a limited extent under the
Model Clauses. See generally Daintith and Willoughby, op. cit., note 186 supra,
pars. 1–206 to 1–216.
194. For a reference to the case of the United States, see Bergsager, loc., cit., note 145
supra, at 179. In Great Britain cash premium bidding has been used to determine
allocation of blocks in three occasions (1971, 1982, 1984), in each case limited to
15 blocks; see Daintith and Willoughby, op. cit., note 186 supra, par. 1–217.
195. For a reference to the Spitzbergen case in this context, see Bergsager, loc. cit.,
note 145 supra, at 179. For the deep sea-bed regime, see generally Convention on
the Law of the Sea, Annex III; see also studies cit., note 15 supra.

196. Bergsager, loc. cit., note 145 supra, at 178.
197. Ibid., at 179.
198. *1984 Draft Articles,* Article XXV; *1983 Draft Articles,* Article XXV. In the 1983 version notification was to be made to the Commission. See also Article 37 of the *1986 Draft Articles.*
199. *1984 Draft Articles,* Article XXVI (bis), 2, a. *1986 Draft Articles,* Article 41.
200. See the statement by Beeby to this effect summarized in loc. cit., note 169 supra, at 4, under the subheading 'Exploration'. See also the changes made in the *1984 Draft Articles* to Article XXVI, par. 1, as compared with the 1983 version.
201. See generally Article XXVI of the *1983* and *1984 Draft Articles.* See also Articles 38, 39 of the *1986 Draft Articles.*
202. *1984 Draft Articles,* Article XXVI, par. 3.
203. Ibid., Article XXVI, par. 4. See generally also Articles 39, 40 of the *1986 Draft Articles.*
204. On common deposits see generally William T. Onorato: 'Apportionment of an international common petroleum deposit', *I.C.L.Q.,* Vol. 17, 1968, 85–102; Alan E. Friedman: 'The economics of the common pool: property rights in exhaustible resources', *U.C.L.A.L. Rev.,* Vol. 18, 1971, 855–887; Gunther Handl: 'The principle of "equitable use" as applied to internationally shared natural resources: its role in resolving potential international disputes over transfrontier pollution', *R.B.D.I.,* Vol. XIV, 1978–1979, 40–64; Rainer Lagoni: 'Oil and gas deposits across national frontiers', *A.J.I.L.,* Vol. 73, 1979, 215–243.
205. See, for example, Convention on the Law of the Sea, Annex III, Article 17, 2, (d).
206. *1984 Draft Articles,* Article XXVI (bis). *1986 Draft Articles,* Article 41.
207. *1984 Draft Articles,* Article XXVII; *1983 Draft Articles,* Article XXVII. Among other matters the application shall provide details about the resources to be explored, a description of the methods to be used, and an assessment of the environmental impact.
208. The different treatment accorded to State Parties is evident in the *1984 Draft Articles,* Article XXVII, par. 2 (g), which imposes additional requirements on applicants other than a Party. See further *1986 Draft Articles,* Article 42, 1 (g). See also Convention on the Law of the Sea, Annex III, Article 4, par. 5.
209. Bergsager, loc. cit., note 145 supra, at 180. The Commission is also empowered to establish rules on maximum block sizes: *1984 Draft Articles,* Article XIII, 1 m; *1986 Draft Articles,* Article 22, 1 m.
210. *1983 Draft Articles,* Article XXVII, par. 2. While this is the only criteria for selecting among competing applicants mentioned in this article, a footnote to it clarifies that other methods may be taken into account. The *1984 Draft Articles,* however omitted this footnote and in Article XXVIII par. 2, referred only to the selection criteria of the order of presentation of applications. More complete criteria have been developed by the *1986 Draft Articles,* Article 43, including the agreement among applicants and a priority for applications involving broader participation.
211. *1984 Draft Articles,* Article XXVIII; *1983 Draft Articles,* Article XXVIII. Among other matters, the guidelines of the Advisory Committee shall include the detailed measures for the protection of the environment, the technical and safety standards, monitoring procedures and contingency plans. See also *1986 Draft Articles,* Article 43.
212. *1984 Draft Articles,* Article XXVIII, par. 8. See also *1986 Draft Articles,* Article 43, par. 9.
213. *1984 Draft Articles,* Article XXVIII, par. 9. See also *1986 Draft Articles,* Article 43, par. 9.
214. Ibid., Article XXVI (bis), par. 3. This aspect of the internal accommodation is discussed in Chapters 7 and 8 infra.

215. The institutional aspects of the Regulatory Committees and related mattters will be discussed in Chapter 8 below, together with the question of the role of claimant States and other approaches to the issues of internal accommodation in this regime.
216. *1984 Draft Articles,* Article XXI; *1983 Draft Articles,* Article XXXI.
217. See note 39 supra and associated text.
218. *1984 Draft Articles,* Article XXX; *1983 Draft Articles,* Article XXX. See also *1986 Draft Articles,* Article 45.
219. See note 186 supra and associated text.
220. *1984 Draft Articles,* Article XXXIV, par. 1; *1983 Draft Articles,* Article XXXIV, par. 1. The 1984 revision has defined 'Development' to mean 'those activities which take place following exploration which are aimed at or associated with exploitation of specific mineral resource deposits, including but not limited to, pilot projects and support processing storage and transport activities'; see Article I, 1 (h). See also *1986 Draft Articles,* Article 1 (h).
221. A situation of this kind is envisaged in the Law of the Sea Convention, Annex III, Article 3, par. 4 (c) and Article 10.
222. *1984 Draft Articles,* Article XXXIV; *1983 Draft Articles,* Article XXXIV; *1986 Draft Articles,* Article 50.
223. See generally the *1984* and *1983 Draft Articles,* Article XXXV. It is to be noted that in the 1984 version in case of modifications being required in the management scheme these, in accordance with par. 4 of this Article, in no case shall relate to the financial obligations specified in the management scheme; in the 1983 version this exclusion referred also to questions of inspection and enforcement. This safeguard has been built in toensure the accommodation with the claimant state that might have intervened in the preparation of the Draft management sheme and in order not to upset the initial balance. This safeguard can also be compared to a stabilization clause in that it will freeze the question of payments made by the applicant. See also Article 51, par. 4, of the *1986 Draft Articles.*
224. *1984 Draft Articles,* Article XXXV, par. 6; *1983 Draft Articles,* Article XXXV, par. 7. Under the terms of the *1986 Draft Articles,* Article 51, par. 5 provides for the development permit to be issued by the Regulatory Committee.
225. Graham, loc. cit., note 155 supra, at 27.
226. See generally Daintith and Willoughby, op. cit., note 186 supra, 1–517, 1–801; and Cameron, op. cit., note 187 supra, at 57–58.
227. *1984 Draft Articles,* Article I, 1 i, and Article V; *1986 Draft Articles,* Article 1, i and Article 6.
228. See generally Orrego, loc. cit., note 15 supra.
229. Leigh Ratiner: Statement at Earthscan Press briefing seminar on the Future of Antarctica, 25th July, 1977, New Zealand High Commission, London, at 13.
230. G. J. F. van Hegelsom: 'The argument for an interim arrangement', *Marine Policy,* Vol. 5, 1981, 260–264.
231. See Chapter 1, Sections 1.2 and 1.4, supra.
232. Beeby, loc. cit., note 6 supra, at 198.
233. Orrego, loc. cit., note 9 supra, at 209.
234. *1984 Draft Articles,* Article V, par. 1; *1983 Draft Articles,* Article V, par. 1, 2; *1986 Draft Articles,* Article 6.
235. *1984 Draft Articles,* Article V, par. 2; *1983 Draft Articles,* Article V, par. 3; *1986 Draft Articles,* Article 6, par. 2.
236. On the principles of international law relating to nationality, see generally Ian Brownlie: *Principles of Public International Law,* 1979, Chapters XVIII and XIX.
237. *1984 Draft Articles,* Article V, par. 2; *1983 Draft Articles,* Article V, par. 3.

238. On the concept of effective link of nationality in international law, see generally the *Nottebohm* case, International Court of Justice, *Reports,* 1955, and the comments made on this and other cases on nationality in Chapter III supra, notes 46 to 49 and associated texts; see also Brownlie, op. cit., note 236 supra, at 406–420.

239. On the nationality of corporations, with particular reference to the questions of ownership and control, see Brownlie, op. cit., note 236 supra, at 421–422.

240. A requirement of incorporation in the United Kingdom was in force until 1976 for companies applying for U.K. licences; see Daintith and Willoughby, op. cit., note 186 supra, 1–207. See also Rosalyn Higgins: 'The taking of property by the State: recent developments in international law', *Rec. Cours Ac. D.I.,* Vol. 176, 1982-III, at 313. The last mentioned author has described this requirement as licensees having their 'mind and management' in the UK; see ibid.: 'Ten years of State involvement in the offshore petroleum industry – the UK experience', *Cambridge II Seminar Proceedings, IBA Energy Law,* 1979, Reprint, at 4.

241. On joint ventures in international law see generally Wolfang G. Friedmann and George Kalmanoff (eds): *Joint International Business Ventures,* 1961; Ahmed Sadek El Kosheri: 'Le regime juridique cree par les accords de participation dans le domaine petrolier', *Rec. Cours Ac. D.I.,* 1975-IV, 219–393; Samuel K.B. Asante: 'Restructuring transnational mineral agreements', *A.J.I.L.,* Vol. 73, 1979, 335–371; Gunther Jaenicke, Erich Schanze and Wolfang Hauser: *A joint venture agreement for seabed mining,* 1981.

242. Cameron, op. cit., note 187 supra, at 57; Daintith and Willoughby, op. cit., note 186 supra, 1–517.

243. Cameron, op. cit., note 187 supra,. at 57; Daintith and Willoughby, op. cit., note 186 supra, 1–615 to 1–649, with particular reference to Joint Operating Agreements.

244. *1984 Draft Articles,* Article V, 1 e; *1983 Draft Articles,* Article V, 2. This last article refers to 'any joint venture or consortium involving any of the foregoing'; the 1984 version has omitted the reference to consortia. See also *1986 Draft Articles,* Article 6.

245. See generally *1984 Draft Articles,* Article V, pars. 3, 4. See also *1986 Draft Articles,* Article 6, pars. 3, 4.

246. *1983 Draft Articles,* Article V, 1 (b) and 4.

247. Orrego, loc. cit., note 9 supra, at 209.

248. A situation of this kind is envisaged in Article 36 of the Vienna Convention on the Law of Treaties. This article requires, however, that the parties to the Treaty intend the provision to accord rights to a third State and, under paragraph 2 of the article, the state exercising the right shall comply with the conditions for its exercise provided for in the treaty or established in conformity with the treaty. The participation of third states in Antarctic activities will be examined generally in Chapter 9 infra.

249. Orrego, loc. cit., note 9 supra, at 209. The participation of developing countries in the minerals regime is further discussed in Chapter 6 infra, Section 6.3.

250. See note 15 supra.

251. See Section 5.7 on the problems of compliance and enforcement.

252. On the effects of transnational corporate activities in the development of international law see generally Jonathan I. Charney: 'Transnational corporations and developing public international law', *Duke Law Journal,* Vol. 1983, 748–788; D. Kokkini-Iatridou and P. J. I. M. de Waart: 'Foreign investments in developing countries – legal personality of multinations in international law', *Netherlands Yearbook of International Law,* Vol. XIV, 1983, 87–131.

253. On the different approaches to the question of claims and jurisdiction, see generally Chapters 1 and 3 supra.
254. On the principle that no activities can be undertaken outside the regime, see *1984 Draft Articles,* Article III (bis); and *1986 Draft Articles,* Article 3.
255. On the proposals relating to Joint Antarctic Resource Jurisdiction and other similar approaches see Chapter 3, supra, Section 3.5, and Chapter 7 infra, Section 7.3.
256. Rosalyn Higgins: 'The taking of property by the State: recent developments in international law', *Rec. Cours Ac. D.I.,* Vol. 176, 1982-III, at 306.
257. Ibid., at 306. See also Cameron, op. cit., note 187 supra, at 46–47.
258. Terence Daintith (ed.): *The legal character of petroleum licences: a comparative study,* University of Dundee, Centre for Petroleum and Mineral Law Studies, 1981, at 9.
259. Ibid., at 9.
260. *1983 Draft Articles,* Article XXX (b); *1984 Draft Articles,* Article XXX, 1 (b); *1986 Draft Articles,* Article 45 (b).
261. See generally the study directed by Daintith, op. cit., note 258 supra, and the discussion of the following national licensing systems contained therein: Michael Crommelin: 'The legal character of petroleum production licences in Australia', 60–100; Rowland J. Harrison: 'The legal character of petroleum production licences in Canada', 101–162; Uggi Engel: 'The legal character of the Danish sole concession', 163–175; Asger Thylstrup: 'The legal character of petroleum licences in Greenland and the Faroe Islands', 176–184; John A. Rein: 'The legal character of petroleum production licences in Norway', 185–199; Terence Daintith: 'The petroleum production licence in the United Kingdom', 200–225. See also R. W. Bentham (ed.): *Recent developments in United Kingdom petroleum law,* University of Dundee, Centre for Petroleum and Mineral Law Studies, 1984; Comisión Chilena del Cobre: *Contribución al estudio de la concesión minera en el derecho comparado,* 1981, mimeo.
262. Higgins, loc. cit., note 256 supra, 298–301.
263. For a similar reason, the deep sea-bed regime has used the concept of a contract; see Convention on the Law of the Sea, Annex III, Article 3, par. 5.
264. Daintith, op. cit., note 258 supra, Chapter 1: 'Petroleum licences: a comparative introduction', 9–10. For the text of the Petroleum (Production) Regulations 1982 and Statutory Regulations, see generally Daintith and Willoughby, op. cit., note 186 supra, part 5.
265. For a discussion of the bargaining and regulatory element in the comparative perspective of licensing arrangements, see generally Daintith, op. cit., note 258 supra, 8–12.
266. The terms and conditions of the sea-bed contract are generally established in Annex III of the Convention on the Law of the Sea and the rules and regulations which the authority will enact on these bases.
267. See the pertinent studies cit. in note 261 supra.
268. Higgins, loc. cit., note 256 supra, at 306–307.
269. See generally *1984 Draft Articles,* Article XXXII; *1983 Draft Articles,* Article XXXII; *1986 Draft Articles,* Article 48.
270. Beeby, loc. cit., note 6 supra, at 194.
271. *1984 Draft Articles,* Article XXXII, par. 2; *1986 Draft Articles,* Article 48, par. 2.
272. For a discussion about forms of traditional concessions and modern contracts, see generally section 5.8 of this Chapter. For a description of the traditional concession see also C. J. Lipton: 'Forms of agreement', in United Nations: *Negotiation and drafting of mining development agreements,* 1976, 92–102, at 92–93.

273. Cameron has explained the British licence rights in the following terms: 'In the light of the uncertainty surrounding the Crown's rights in international law, it is hardly surprising that there has been some doubt as to the exact nature of the exclusive right which each licensee is granted. It is certainly not a title to the resources *in situ*. Title does not follow from the licence itself but rather from the reduction of the resources into possession'; op. cit., note 187 supra, at 50.

274. For the seabed regime concept of passing of title upon recovery, see Convention on the Law of the Sea, Annex III, Article 1.

275. Cameron, op. cit., note 187 supra, at 51. See also Higgins, loc. cit., note 256 supra at 307. For a discussion of the concept of profit a prendre and usufruct in relation to sea-bed mining, see L. F. E. Goldie: 'Title and use (and usufruct) – An Ancient distinction too oft forgot', *A.J.I.L.*, Vol. 79, 1985, 689–714.

276. Under Article 19 of the Chilean Constitution of 1980, oil and other mineral resources are defined as not being subject to concession on the part of the State; they can, however, be exploited by means of administrative contracts or operational contracts. This approach in fact means that the State will not be able lawfully to transfer title to such resources *in situ,* but it can do so at the well-head or other points established in the contract. If this clause is made applicable to the Chilean Antarctic Territory it would have to be made compatible with an Antarctic mineral regime that does not itself transfer title to resources *in situ*.

277. The management scheme has to prescribe terms and conditions relating to decommissioning and relinquishment; see *1983 Draft Articles,* Article XXX (m), (n); and *1984 Draft Articles,* Article XXX, 1 (n), (o); *1986 Draft Articles,* Article 45 (n) (o).

278. Under Article XXXII, par. 3, of the *1984 Draft Articles,* the exercise of rights has to be done with due regard to the rights of other operators; *1986 Draft Articles,* Article 48, par. 3.

279. See studies cit., note 204 supra.

280. See in particular the studies by Onorato and Lagoni, cit., note 204 supra.

281. On the British unitization system, see Daintith and Willoughby, op. cit., note 186 supra, 1–717/1–719.

282. See Chapter 3 supra, Section 3.3.

283. International Union for Conservation of Nature and Natural Resources: *Conservation and development of Antarctic ecosystems,* paper submitted to the United Nations Political Affairs Division, 1984, at 35.

284. Rosalyn Higgins: 'The International Law perspective' in Daintith, op. cit., note 258 supra, 37–40.

285. Higgins, loc. cit., note 256 supra, at 298–305. See in particular the following cases: Saudi Arabia v. Arabian American Oil Company (ARAMCO), August 23, 1958, *International Law Reports,* Vol. 27, 117–233; Texaco v. The Government of the Libyan Arab Republic, 27 November 1975, 19 January 1977, *International Law Reports,* Vol. 53, 389–511; Liamco v. Government of the Libyan Arab Republic, 12 April 1977, *International Law Reports,* Vol. 62, 141–219; B.P. v. Government of the Libyan Arab Republic, 10 October 1973, 1 August 1974, *International Law Reports,* Vol. 53, 297–388; Government of Kuwait v. American Independent Oil Co. (Aminoil), 24 March 1982, *International Law Reports,* Vol. 66, 519–627. See also Robert B. von Mehren and P. Nicholas Kourides: 'International arbitration between states and foreign private parties: the Libyan nationalization cases', *A.J.I.L.,* Vol. 75, 1981, 476–552.

286. For the concept of security of tenure, see *1983 Draft Articles,* Article XXXII.

287. Daintith, loc. cit., note 258 supra, 17–24.

288. Convention on the Law of the Sea, Annex III, Article 19, par. 2.

289. The management scheme has to provide terms and conditions relating to the

suspension, modification or cancellation of the management Scheme. *1984 Draft Articles,* Article XXX, 1 (q); *1983 Draft Articles,* Article XXX (l). If this kind of maximum penalty is allowed, lesser penalties, such as monetary penalties and the like, would also be applicable in spite of not being mentioned specifically in that article. See also *1986 Draft Articles,* Article 45 (g).

290. Convention on the Law of the Sea, Annex III, Article 18, 1 (a).

291. Ibid., Annex III, Article 18, 1 (b).

292. Under Clause 39 (2) (g) of the British Petroleum (Production) Regulations 1982, the licence may be revoked because of ceasing to have the company's central management and control in the United Kingdom; for the tax implications of this clause, see Daintith and Willoughby, op. cit., note 186 supra, at 5–205. See also Higgins, loc. cit., note 256 supra, at 313, referring to Article 33 (2) (g) of the Model Clauses, Petroleum (Production) Regulations 1966.

293. Convention on the Law of the Sea, Article 162, 2 (w).

294. See note 289 supra.

295. Higgins, loc. cit., note 284 supra, at 44–51. On expropriation in international law see also generally: S. Friedman: *Expropriation in International Law,* 1953;
B. Wortley: *Expropriations in Public International Law,* 1959;
F. V. García-Amador: *The Changing Law of International Claims,* Vol. II, 1984, Chapter X.

296. For a discussion of the principles of international law governing State responsibility, see Ian Brownlie: *System of the Law of Nations. State Responsibility,* Part 1, 1983; García-Amador, op. cit., note 295 supra;
F. V. García-Amador: 'The proposed new International Economic Order: a new approach to the law governing nationalization and compensation', *Lawyer of the Americas,* Vol. 12, 1980, 1–58; F. V. García-Amador: 'Current attempts to revise international law – a comparative analysis', *A.J.I.L.,* Vol. 77, 1983, 286–295.

297. See generally Ria Kemper: 'The concept of permanent sovereignty and its impact on mineral contracts', in United Nations: *Legal and institutional arrangements in mineral development,* 1982, 29–36.

298. Higgins, loc. cit., note 284 supra, 44–51.

299. For comments on this approach of the award, Higgins, loc. cit., note 256 supra, at 301–305.

300. For a discussion of this Act, Ibid., at 307–309.

301. Ibid., at 309.

302. Ibid., at 309–311.

303. For a discussion of *The Amphitrite* case, see Ibid., at 310–311.

304. Ibid., at 311; see also Higgins, loc. cit., note 284 supra, at 40–44. On the concept of acquired rights in international law, see generally Georges Kaeckenbeeck: 'La protection internationale des droits acquis', *Rec. Cours Ac. D.I.,* Vol. 59, 1937 – I, 317–419; Ko Swan Sik: 'The concept of acquired rights in international law: a survey', *Netherlands International Law Review,* Vol. 24, 1977, 120–142; Rudolf Dolzer: 'New foundations of the law of expropriation of alien property', *A.J.I.L.,* Vol. 75, 1981, 553–589. See also notes 295–296 supra.

305. See generally note 296 supra.

306. Higgins, loc. cit., note 284 supra, at 43.

307. This is perhaps another important reason why the regime should be embodied in a Convention as opposed to a Recommendation. On this discussion see this Chapter, Section 5.1 supra.

308. See generally Higgins, loc. cit., note 256 supra, 322–354. See also G. C. Christie: 'What constitutes a taking of property under international law?', *B.Y.B.I.L.,*

Vol. 38, 1962, 307–338; Burns H. Weston: 'Constructive Takings' under international law: a modest foray into the problem of 'creeping expropriation', *Virg. J.I.L.,* Vol. 16, 1975, 103–175; Burns H. Weston: 'The Charter of economic rights and duties of States and the deprivation of foreign-owned wealth', *A.J.I.L.,* Vol. 75, 1981, 437–475. See also García-Amador, op. cit., note 295 supra, Vol. 1, Chapters II–V.

309. Higgins, loc. cit., note 256 supra, at 352–354. On the Canadian policy see also Glenn S. Kirby: *Economic rent and leasing policy choices for petroleum development in northern Canada,* Dissertation, Diploma in Polar Studies, Scott Polar Research Institute, 1975–1976; J. Ross Tolmie: 'Canadian mineral landholding system, royalties, rentals and taxation', in United Nations: *Negotiation and drafting of mining development agreements,* 1976, 55–80.

310. For a discussion of this case, see Higgins, loc. cit., note 256 supra, at 331–337.

311. *Murphyores Incorporated Pty. Ltd. and Another v. The Commonwealth of Australia and others, The Australian Law Journal Reports,* Vol. 50, 1976, 570–580.

312. Convention on the Law of the Sea, Article 155.

313. On the choice of law see generally Roland Brown: 'Choice of law provisions in concession and related contracts', in Roland Brown and Mike Faber: *Some policy and legal issues affecting mining legislation and agreements in African Commonwealth countries,* Commonwealth Secretariat, 1977, 82–107.

314. See generally El-Kosheri, loc. cit., note 241 supra, particularly Chapter II. See also Higgins, loc. cit., note 284 supra, at 37–40; and Higgins, loc. cit., note 256 supra, at 311–314.

315. Resolution on the proper law of the contract in agreements between a State and a Foreign Private Person, adopted by the Institut de Droit International, Athens session, 11 September 1979, *Annuaire,* Vol. 58-II, 1979, 193–195; see also the Resolution on Multinational Enterprises of 7 September 1977, *Annuaire,* Vol. 57-II, 1977, 339–343; Resolution on contracts concluded by international organizations with private persons, 6 September 1977, *Annuaire,* Vol. 57-II, 1977, 333–337; and the 'Projet definitif de resolution sur le droit applicable aux entreprises internationales communes', *Annuaire,* Vol. 60-I, 1983, 103–106.

316. *1984 Draft Articles,* Article XXX, 1, (a); *1983 Draft Articles,* Article XXX (a). As explained earlier, 'operator' as used in the Antarctic mineral regime means the contractor. See also *1986 Draft Articles,* Article 45, par. a.

317. Convention on the Law of the Sea, Annex III, Article 21, par. 2.

318. Ibid., Annex III, Article 21, par. 2. It should be noted in this regard that the Law of the Sea Convention has often encouraged the coastal state in environmental matters relating to conservation of resources or prevention of pollution to legislate more strictly than provided for in the Convention.

319. *1984 Draft Articles,* Article III (bis); *1986 Draft Articles,* Article 3.

320. *1984 Draft Articles,* Article VI; see also the same provision in the *1983 Draft Articles,* and *1986 Draft Articles,* Article 8.

321. See note 318 supra and associated text.

322. *1984 Draft Articles,* Article VI, pars. 2, 3; *1983 Draft Articles,* Article VI, par. 3; *1986 Draft Articles,* Article 8, par. 3.

323. Although the Draft Articles do not contain a specific provision on the matter it is of the essence of the role of the Contracting Parties in ensuring compliance to do so when approving the sponsorship of a contractor.

324. Reporting procedures can be found, inter alia, in the following provisions of the *1984 Draft Articles:* Article VI, par. 2; Article XXIII, par. 4, c; Article XXX, par. 1, k.

325. Provisons on monitoring are contained, inter alia, in the following Articles of the *1984 Draft Articles:* XIII, par. 1, q; XXX, par. 1,g; XXXIII. See also in particular *1986 Draft Articles,* Article 49.

326. On inspection in Antarctica see generally the following works: James Simsarian: 'Inspection experience under the Antarctic Treaty and the International Atomic Energy Agency', *A.J.I.L.,* Vol. 60, 1966, 502–510; Truls Hanevold: 'Inspections in Antarctica', *Coop. and Confl,* 2, 1971, 103–114; Michel Voelckel: 'L'Inspection en Antarctique', in Georges Fischer et Daniel Vignes (eds.): *L'Inspection Internationale,* Bruxelles, 1976, 223–246. See also UK House of Lords, Statement by Baroness Phillips on the Antarctic Treaty, Parliamentary Debates (Hansard), *Official Report,* Vol. 282, N° 144, 1 May 1967, cols. 761–765. On some aspects of the practice in this regard see: US Department of State: 'Statement concerning the United States decision to conduct an Antarctic inspection', Department of State Press Release N° 469, Sept. 13, 1963, *A.J.I.L.,* Vol. 58, 1964, 166–167; United States: 'Report of United States observers on inspection of Antarctic Stations', 1963–64 austral summer season, *I.L.M.,* Vol. III, 1964, 650–661; C.I.A.: 'U.S. Antarctic Inspection, 1983', Map, 1984. For a list of US inspections see also the U.S. reply to the views requested by the UN Secretary General on the *Question of Antarctica,* Doc. UN A/39/583 (Part II), 9 November 1984, at 111–113.

327. See note 150 supra and associated text.

328. See Chapter 4 supra, Section 4.4.

329. See United States Report of observers cit., note 326 supra, at 652.

330. Convention on the Conservation of Antarctic Marine Living Resources, Article XXIV.

331. James N. Barnes: 'The emerging convention on the conservation of Antarctic marine living resources: an attempt to meet the new realities of resource exploitation in the Southern Ocean', in Jonathan I. Charney: *The New Nationalism and the Use of Common Spaces,* 1982, at 267.

332. See Chapter 4 supra, note 104 and associated text.

333. *1984 Draft Articles,* Article VIII (bis). The *1983 Draft Articles* did not contain any provision on inspection. It was reported, however, at the time that most Consultative Parties favoured the extension of the Antarctic Treaty inspection system to the minerals activities. See *E.C.O.,* Vol. XXVII, N° 1, Tokyo, May 22–31, 1984, at 3. See also *1986 Draft Articles,* Article 13.

334. See Article VII, par. 3 of the 1959 Antarctic Treaty.

335. It has been reported in this regard that the compatibility of inspections with commercial secrets is one source of difficulty in agreeing on the inspection system; see *E.C.O.* cit., note 333 supra, at 3.

336. A centralized system of inspection has been discussed in relation to the Canberra Convention; see Barnes, loc. cit., note 331 supra, at 267. For the case of the International Convention on the Regulation of Whaling, see note 332 supra.

337. Graham, loc. cit., note 155 supra, at 29.

338. On the principles of State responsibility, see generally note 296 supra, and also see Eduardo Jimenez de Arechaga: 'State responsibility for the nationalization of foreign owned property', *New York University Journal of International Law and Politics,* Vol. 11, 1978, 179–195.

339. *Trail Smelter Case* (United States v. Canada), Awards of 16 April 1938 and 11 March 1941; *United Nations Reports of International Arbitral Awards,* Vol. III, 1949, 1905–1982. This case, however, has also been cited as evidence of the existence of a principle of strict liability for ultrahazardous activities in international law; see *Encyclopedia of Public International Law,* Vol. 2, 1981,

276–280, and L. F. E. Goldie: 'Liability for Damage and the progressive development of international law', *I.C.L.Q.*, Vol. 14, 1965, 1189–1264.

340. Convention on the Law of the Sea, Annex III, Article 22.

341. See generally S. Brown, N. W. Cornell, L. Fabian and E. B. Wiess: *Regimes for the Ocean, Outer Space, and Weather*, 1977. See in particular Article VII of the Treaty on Principles governing the activities of States in the exploration and use of outer space, including the moon and other celestial bodies, 1967.

342. See generally Melissa B. Cates: 'Offshore oil platforms which pollute the marine environment: a proposal for an international treaty imposing strict liability', *S.D.L.R.*, Vol. 21, 1984, 691–708. See also Goldie, loc. cit., note 339 supra. The Norwegian Petroleum Act on Liability for Pollution Damage (1985), is based on the concept of strict liability under which a licensee is liable for pollution damage regardless of fault and without limitation.

343. Brown et al., op. cit., note 341 supra, at 232.

344. Ibid., at 242.

345. Article VI (bis) of the *1984 Draft Articles* is reserved for the question of 'Responsibility and Liability', but the contents of which have not yet been defined. This is also the case of the *1986 Draft Articles*, Article 10.

346. *E.C.O.:* 'Liability: who pays?, Vol. XXXIII, N° 2, Paris, 23 September–4 October 1985, at 1–2.

347. Daintith and Willoughby, op. cit., note 186 supra, at 1–751.

348. Brownlie, op. cit., Chapter 3 supra, note 207 and associated text.

349. *1984 Draft Articles*, Article XXX, 1, m; *1983 Draft Articles*, Article XXX, (k); *1986 Draft Articles*, Article 45, m.

350. See generally Graham, loc. cit., note 155 supra. See also Alastair Machin: 'Preferred futures: an environmental view', in the work by the New Zealand Institute of International Affairs op. cit., note 155 supra, 69–74. But see also the reply by Christopher Beeby: 'A negotiator's view', in ibid., 58–62.

351. See *E.C.O.* Editorial, Vol. XXIII, N° 1, Bonn, July 11–22, 1983, at 1.

352. See generally James N. Barnes: *Let's Save Antarctica!*, 1982. See also Chapter 10 infra.

353. Antarctica briefing: *A non-commercial approach to Antarctic minerals*, N° 2, April 9, 1984.

354. See generally Ian Brownlie: 'Legal status of natural resources in international law', *Rec. Cours Ac. D.I.*, Vol. 162, 1979-I, 245–317. Mohamed Bennouna: 'Le Droit International relatif aux matieres premieres', *Rec. Cours Ac. D.I.*, 1982, IV, 103–191. See also David N. Smith and Louis T. Wells Jr: *Negotiating Third World mineral agreements*, 1975.

355. David N. Smith and Louis T. Wells Jr: 'Mineral agreements in developing countries: structures and substance', *A.J.I.L.*, Vol. 69, 1975, 560–590, at 563–565.

356. Ibid., at 565.

357. Samuel K.B. Asante: 'Restructuring transnational mineral agreements', *A.J.I.L.*, Vol. 73, 1979, 335–371, at 337–341.

358. Lipton, loc. cit., note 272 supra, at 92–93.

359. Erich Schanze and others: 'Mining Agreements in Developing Countries', *J.W.T.L.*, Vol. 12, 1978, 135–173. See also Roland Brown and Mike Faber: *Some policy and legal issues affecting mining legislation and agreements in African Commonwealth countries*, Commonwealth Secretariat, 1977.

360. Smith and Wells, loc. cit., note 355 supra, at 566–572. See also Samuel Asante and Albrecht Stockmayer: 'Evolution of development contracts: the issue of effective control', in United Nations, op. cit., note 297 supra, 53–67.

361. See generally F. V. García-Amador: 'Current attempts to revise international law – a comparative analysis', loc. cit., note 296 supra, at 286–295.
362. Smith and Wells, loc. cit., note 355 supra, 572–582.
363. Ibid., 582–588; see also Asante, loc. cit., note 357 supra, 341–369.
364. Schanze, loc. cit., note 359 supra, at 143–149.
365. See generally Orrego, loc. cit., note 15 supra.

6

Special policies pursued by the mineral resources regime

6.1   Environmental conservation policy

On the basis of the provisions of the Antarctic Treaty which have a rather indirect bearing on environmental questions,[1] the Consultative Parties have undertaken an intensive norm-creating function in this field.[2] It has taken the form, in the first place, of the adoption of various recommendations relating to the topic of the Impact of Man on the Antarctic Environment,[3] and recently has focussed more specifically on the problem of oil pollution.[4] As we had the opportunity to examine in Chapter 2, the measures enacted by the Consultative Parties can have either a recommendatory or a binding nature depending on the specific contents of the instrument in question. In the environmental field the trend has been generally to introduce measures of a binding nature, particularly by means of the resources regimes; the fact, however, that many times there are no adequate institutional procedures for enforcement has determined that State practice has become the single most important controlling factor of this policy, sometimes leading to abuses or distortions, a case in point being the recent discussion about the French airstrip at Pointe Géologie.[5]

The competence of the Consultative Parties in the environmental sphere is largely founded upon the concept of the 'special responsibility' of the Treaty Parties in this field.[6] Concurrently, the steps that have been taken in respect of the separate but linked resources regimes have been closely associated with the concerns existing in relation to environmental protection.[7] The Agreed Measures were the first expression of these regimes; these were followed by the Convention on Seals and that on Marine Living Resources, all being instruments whose principal aim, as we have examined, has been to safeguard conservation in their respective spheres. Thus the protection of the Antarctic ecosystem has become a central concept of the system's environmental policy.[8] A similar concern has prompted the negotiations on the mineral resources regime which, as part of this process, has been described as follows:

> The current discussions of a regime for Antarctic mineral resource management is the last in this sequence and would complete the picture, and the Antarctic Treaty forms a kind of linking framework within which all these sectoral management systems can be interrelated.[9]

Complementary provisions in national legislation

In addition to the instruments of the Antarctic Treaty system itself, various rules and regulations originating in national legislation or in international treaties are susceptible of application in the case of Antarctica in the environmental context. Australian legislation, for example, establishes the necessary powers for regulating or prohibiting pollution of the Antarctica environment.[10] France[11] and Belgium,[12] in order to implement the Agreed Measures make provisions in their respective legislations for powers to adopt measures preventing pollution of 'waters adjacent to the coast' and 'ice shelves'. In the terms of New Zealand's legislation, Antarctic pollution is classified as an offence when it is 'wilfully or negligently' caused.[13] British legislation making an offence the discharge of petroleum in territorial waters has been applied to the Falkland Islands Dependencies at the time when these included the claimed British Antarctic Territory.[14] United States legislation shows equal concern with control of Antarctic pollution.[15] In the case of countries asserting claims, general legislation in the environmental field might also be applicable by extension to the corresponding Antarctic territory; in some cases, such as that of the United Kingdom, this extension would have to be done by specific legislative authority, while in other cases, such as that of Chile or France this might occur automatically.

There has previously been occasion to refer to certain requirements in respect of harmonizing legislation within the Antarctic Treaty system.[16] When the British Parliament debated the approval of the Agreed Measures, one of the issues raised was whether specific acts committed in Antarctica might incur a severer penalty than if they had been committed in the United Kingdom, it having been underlined that the penalties for the same offence should everywhere be equal.[17] The opposite case has also been mentioned, that is the possibility that national legislation may contain stricter measures than those established in the Antarctic Treaty system. In the environmental sphere this latter situation should not be regarded as incompatible with the rules of such system, a matter of importance in the case of the mineral resources regime.[18]

The role of treaties, customs and principles concerning marine pollution
The application of treaties on marine pollution is another question that has been borne in mind in the deliberations of the consultative meetings. Recommendation X-7 was based on the recognition 'that the presence of ice in Antarctic waters gives rise to particular hazards for the operation of ships.[19] In connection with mineral resources an author has warned 'that perhaps the greatest risk of all to the Antarctic Oceanic ecosystem from oil exploration lay in the wreck amid icefields of a very large crude carrier'.[20] On the basis of these considerations, it was recommended to Consultative Parties that they should review their obligations in the light of treaties on marine oil pollution with a view to 'consider whether their compliance with these obligations adequately minimizes the risk of oil contamination of the Antarctic marine environment.[21]

It is of interest to note that this recommendation recognizes the potential applicability of international conventions on prevention of marine pollution in the case of Antarctica, in so far as the Consultative Parties are parties to such Conventions. Consultative Parties would of course have to enact individually each Convention to be applied to its claimed Antarctic territory, as we shall see that in fact it has been done in some cases. To the extent that such Conventions involve some linkage with the concept of a coastal state or similar territorial elements, this may prove to be an obstacle for their application to Antarctica by non-claimant countries, since it could contradict their basic legal approach to the issue of claims in that continent. On the other hand, while claimants do not face such a difficulty, there might be a situation in which such Conventions could collide with the freezing of claims under Article IV of the 1959 Treaty.

In any event, this kind of potential legal conflict has not arisen so far in the context of the environmental policy within the Antarctic Treaty system. On the contrary, on the basis of the review mentioned above, the Consultative Parties concluded at their eleventh meeting that such conventions, in the light of the nature of current shipping operations in Antarctica, 'provide for the time being an adequate and sufficient basis for minimizing risks of pollution.[22] This conclusion, of course, leaves open the possibility that if the nature of these operations were to change, as would happen if supertankers were to operate in the region, special regulations of a stricter character might be required.

A proposal in this last connection was put forward by Argentina on the occasion of the eleventh consultative meeting, suggesting that the 1954 International Convention for the Prevention of Pollution of the Sea by Oil, as amended in 1962 and 1969, should be supplemented 'in order to adapt its application to the special characteristics of the Antarctic ecosystem.'[23] One writer has also pointed out that Antarctica does not figure among the 'special areas' to which reference is made in the 1973 International Convention for the Prevention of Pollution from Ships and in respect of which more stringent measures are required, implying that if supertanker traffic were to operate this necessity might arise.[24]

Besides the conventions to which reference has just been made, many other instruments adopted within the framework of the International Maritime Organization are of interest for the case of Antarctica.[25] Special mention should be made of the 1969 International Convention on Civil Liability for Oil Pollution Damage[26] and its subsequent amendments,[27] with particular reference to the amendments introduced in 1984,[28] as well as of the International Convention on the Establishment of an International Fund for Compensation for Oil Pollution Damage signed in 1971,[29] and its subsequent amendments,[30] including those of 1984.[31] To the extent applicable, these conventions could provide a supplementary mechanism to the provisions on responsibility and liability that we have discussed in relation to the regime on mineral resources.[32]

As we have mentioned above, several of the Consultative Parties have applied international conventions specifically to their claimed Antarctic territories. Thus, for example, the above-mentioned 1954 Convention and some of its subsequent amendments have been applied by Australia to its external territories which include the Antarctic territory, and by France to its Southern and Antarctic territories.[33] These two countries[34] have also applied to their Antarctic territories the 1969 Convention on Civil Liability and the International Convention relating to Intervention on the High Seas in cases of Oil Pollution Casualties, also dated 1969.[35] The 1972 Convention on Dumping of Wastes and Other Matter[36] has been applied to the territories in question by Australia,[37] while France has other types of legislation for the same purpose.[38] The United Kingdom, for its part, has applied some conventions to the Falkland Islands Dependencies, but not specifically to the Antarctic territories claimed.[39] In the case of yet other Consultative Parties, these conventions may prove applicable by extension to their Antarctic territories, without need of express mention.

Some rules agreed upon by means of regional conventions could be relevant to Antarctica for the 1959 Treaty parties participating in such conventions. A case in point might be the system of inspection established in the 1982 Paris Memorandum of Understanding, which could allow the parties to this Memorandum to inspect in European ports their ships bound for Antarctica.[40] The Agreement for the protection of the marine environment and coastal zones of the southeast Pacific and related instruments, done under the auspices of the Permanent Commission of the South Pacific,[41] can be applied beyond the areas under the national jurisdiction of the Contracting Parties, and specifically to the high seas, up to a distance in which the pollution of the latter might affect the zones under national jurisdiction; these provisions could eventually be of interest for the maritime areas claimed by Chile in Antarctica or for the Antarctic high seas in the case envisaged.

The Convention on the Law of the Sea contains another set of important rules on marine pollution, which are likewise of interest as regards Antarctica. These provisions are of broader scope since they assemble the basic principles and criteria applicable in this field, and at the same time are related to the special conventions on marine pollution.[42] Some writers have upheld the view that the pertinent rules established in the 1982 Convention reflect the existing international custom, or else that they determine the general application of the rules laid down in the special conventions referred to;[43] in either case obligations of a general character would be implied which might affect the conduct of the Consultative Parties in the framework of the Antarctic system.

The only rule in this Convention which relates specifically to icefields is that contained in Article 234. Under this provision coastal States have the right to adopt and enforce laws and regulations for the prevention, reduction and control of marine pollution from vessels in ice-covered areas within the limits of the exclusive economic zone, where particularly severe climatic conditions and the presence of ice create obstructions or exceptional hazards to navigation, and pollution of the marine environment could cause major harm to or irreversible disturbance of the ecological balance.[44] This rule had its origin in negotiations between Canada, the United States and the Soviet Union, in their capacity as three important Arctic States,[45] and relates to the measures which the first of these countries had introduced to control pollution deriving from shipping operations in such areas.[46] The fact that this is a general rule of the Convention, not restricted to a particular geographical area like the Arctic, makes it potentially applicable to Antarctica. However, because this article is limited to the exclusive economic zone, it could be argued that the application of the norm assumes a recognized exclusive economic zone, which does not of course happen in Antarctica. The different views on the matter would have in any case to be interpreted in the light of the safeguard of positions established in Article IV of the Antarctic Treaty.[47]

It must also be noted that in the sphere of environmental law the existence of some rules of international custom has been suggested particularly as regards the obligation to avoid causing damage to the environment of other States in areas beyond the limits of national jurisdiction.[48] To the extent that they there exist, such norms would also be applicable to Antarctica.[49]

Environmental concerns relating to the regime on mineral resources
The concern for the environment began to deepen concurrently with the conduct of the negotiations on the mineral resources regime, since this represents the greatest challenge that the system has yet encountered in the field in question.[50] When New Zealand first brought up the subject of mineral resources in 1975, it did so in the context of a regime endowed with substantial powers in the environmental sphere while at the same time seeking the participation of the United Nations in order to ensure the support of the international community and ways and means of sharing benefits with the latter, though at the same time keeping the Antarctic system at all times intact.[51] Together with a broad international concern for the adverse environmental effects that could affect the global climate and other factors, there has also been an expression of concern on the part of the countries of the Southern Hemisphere, which given their position as neighbours to the Antarctic continent, have generally been sensitive to its ecological management problems.[52] The environmental issue can today be described as a shared pre-occupation of the Antarctic Treaty parties.[53]

The main difficulty in connection with environmental policy has been appropriately described as follows: 'In practical terms, the crucial question is how can we evaluate the likely impact of resource development on the Antarctic environment and so judge whether such developments are tolerable, and how they should be managed and monitored.'[54] The extreme sensitiveness of the Antarctic ecosystem, the variety of ecological situations which it contains, and the special risks involved in the development of mineral and petroleum resources in icefields and areas of difficult climate, make the precise identification of environmental conservation criteria a key element in the formulation of the regime.[55]

This complexity of environmental conditions in Antarctica has led to the preparation of a body of studies on scientific policy which are of the greatest importance in the formulation of the environmental criteria of the regime. The reports of SCAR[56] and of its groups of experts,[57] particularly those known by the acronyms of EAMREA[58] and AIMEE,[59] are of special value in this respect, and the same is true of independent working groups,[60] studies by academic institutions[61] and government assessments.[62]

On this basis a start has been made on defining the concepts of 'environmental impact assessment' and of 'environmental risk assessment' with precise reference to Antarctica,[63] while at the same time recognition has been accorded to some practical requirements of the process. One study has identified five central concepts in this connection: (i) the necessity of taking into account the inherent variability of Antarctic ecosystems; (ii) the recognition that resource development will evolve in relation to technological and economic criteria and that consequently continuing monitoring will be required; (iii) the impracticability of measuring all environmental variables; (iv) the need for a conceptual model to serve as a framework for the conduct of selective research; and (v) the scant possibility of predicting the exact result of a given development, so that the objective of the system should be the logical examination of broad relationships.[64]

Approaches of this kind are of importance for the realistic determination of what requisites the regime must incorporate in this respect. Given the fact that little is known of the Antarctic environment and that there is an obvious need for information, the regime will require to have at its disposal an appropriate flow of data on which to base decision-making. But it is one thing for the regime to count on enough relevant information for this purpose, and quite another to conceive of a type of information that will cover all imaginable angles and problems; this latter alternative does not seem realistic, and might bring matters to a needless standstill.[65]

A similar phenomenon occurs with respect to risk assessment criteria. To think of an absolute scheme, designed to guarantee that there will be no risk whatsoever, would be tantamount to banning any kind of resource development, since there will always be some degree of risk, difficult to predict beforehand. In contrast, the aim of a more realistic approach will be, in the first place, to distinguish between the unacceptable and the reasonably tolerable risk, and then to look for ways of minimizing or eliminating the latter.[66]

All the foregoing may also have a significant bearing on discussion of the environmental powers of the regime, particularly from the standpoint of deciding whether or not to authorize a particular activity and, if it is authorized, on what terms and conditions. In Chapter 5 there was occasion to review, in this context, the criteria relating to the requisites which the applicant must meet, the process of assessing the application and, above all, the essential decision as to whether the proposed activity does or does not represent an unacceptable risk to the environment – a decision which is the cornerstone of the whole regime.[67] Such is its importance, that it has been conceived in terms of an 'ecological veto', since it has been proposed that it should require a consensus in the Commission.[68] The need for the regime to possess sufficient powers and adequate enforcement capacity is another associated issue, especially where there is a possibility that unforeseen conditions and risks might supervene.

Ecological objectives and principles of the regime

It is in relation to this ecological concern that the environmental objectives and principles of the regime must be conceived on strict but at the same time realistic lines. As we have examined earlier, among the main objectives and principles of the regime there is that of assessing the possible impact on the Antarctic environment of mineral resource activities, on the basis of which a determination will be made about whether such activities are acceptable.[69] To this end, the mineral activities shall be conducted on the basis of the specific environmental principles which have been developed in Article III of the 1984 Draft Articles[70] and correspondingly in Article 4 of the 1986 version.

The essential point of the environmental principles is that no mineral activity shall take place until an impact assessment has been completed and a judgement has been made that the activity in question will not cause significant degradation of the Antarctic environment and associated ecosystems, have any but minimal local effects, affect global or regional climate or weather patterns or have other disturbing effects. Provision of the appropriate data and basic studies for assessing environmental risks also form part of these principles. Related to all this, too, is the need for contingency plans in the event of accidents, monitoring requirements and other questions. At the same time, the principles established have required additional standards in respect of provision of appropriate technology and other requirements for their proper implementation.[71]

No major objections have been made to these environmental objectives and principles, although of course much discussion has taken place among the parties to the negotiation and among interested organizations about the specific wording, extent or requirements associated with each principle.[72]

The greatest difficulty occurs, however, at two other levels. The first is that of the specific rules that will be incorporated in the exploration and exploitation system examined in the preceding chapter, and the effect they will have on environmental questions.[73] Special concern has been generated by the possibility of prospecting taking place without prior authorization and the fact that it might involve environmentally sensitive or dangerous activities. A further criticism that has been made in this context is that the operator will be able to pass from the exploration phase to that of exploitation by means of a simple procedure which does not entail an in-depth review of the original management scheme.[74] Other criticisms of the system are based on similar considerations.[75]

The second level at which difficulties arise is that of the institutional procedures for putting the aforesaid objectives and principles into effect. Notwithstanding what will be discussed in the following chapters, the basic question is how to ensure that the legitimate environmental criterion which may emanate from specialized bodies is respected by interests more closely bound up with the resource development objective.[76] This institutional relationship has already caused concern in the case of the Convention on Living Resources.[77] Moreover, the possibility that the controlling authority may be fragmented into various Regulatory Committees has been considered inappropriate for efficient environmental management.[78] Procedures before the Regulatory Committee, the machinery for decision-making and the enforcement powers of the Commission have also been objects of criticism in this connection.[79]

There are various measures of an institutional character which might be considered with a view to increasing the efficacy of environmental protection policy. A first group of such measures relates to the strengthening of the links between the relevant institutions of the regime.[80] Thus, for example, consideration might be given to the idea that the Advisory Committee should pronounce upon the environmental acceptability of the applications submitted and should recommend to the Regulatory Committee the action to be taken. While it is true that this approach enhances the pre-eminence of environmental considerations, it is no less the case that such a decision has a strong political and economic component which falls more within the province of the Regulatory Committee or the Commission. One solution proposed is that the Advisory Committee should not adopt a decision in this connection, but should submit its several points of view to the Regulatory Committee, on organized lines, so as to avoid a dispersion of opinions.[81]

In this context some form of linkage is also conceivable between the machinery for the adoption of decisions by the Regulatory Committee or by the Commission and the recommendatory processes of the Advisory Committee, by requiring, for example, that only by consensus can this recommendation be set aside, or by making alternative provisions whereby the opinion of the Advisory Committee may be given greater weight.[82] The aim, of course, should be to ensure the reliability and efficacy of the procedure, in order that the environmental viewpoint may be given due consideration. It will also be of interest to bear in mind the criticisms that have been levelled at the provisions concerning the transition from the exploration phase to that of exploitation, and an additional environmental assessment could be required for the latter, especially as the development phase will always involve changes in relation to what was originally foreseen when exploration was begun.[83]

A second order of measures to which thought could be given with a view to strengthening the representative character of the environmental opinion of the Advisory Committee is that this latter should to some extent bring into association with its work ecological or other organizations holding a relevant and responsible opinion on the subject.[84] To that end it has been suggested by some commentators that the Committee should give due publicity to its deliberations – taking care, of course, to ensure that the confidential nature of commercial information is respected – and perhaps invite comments and criticism.[85] This has been a long-standing aspiration of non-governmental organizations,[86] which often issue pronouncements on the Antarctic environment.[87]

A third type of measure bears on the creation of specialized institutions for environmental protection. At this level, the action considered might range from simple measures, such as the creation of a sub-committee or an advisory committee specializing in environmental questions, to others of a more complex nature, such as the establishment of an environmental tribunal to settle disputes arising with the contractor or between the institutions of the regime, *inter alia*.[88] A coalition of non-governmental organizations has also proposed the creation of an Antarctic Environmental Protection Agency, which, among other functions, could undertake independent studies and research and could be represented on the Regulatory Committees.[89] The creation of an organization parallel to the regime does not seem to meet the political interest of the Consultative Parties, which would make the feasibility of this idea rather difficult, but several of the purposes of such an organization could be served by strengthening the environmental mechanisms of the regime itself.[90]

The essence of the discussion on environmental policy and its various alternatives is, once again, the means of striking a proper balance between the demands of ecology and those of resource development. Just as the first should not arbitrarily obstruct the second, neither should the latter overlook the values of effective preservation to which environmental policy aspires. The whole system and its institutional expression pivot delicately upon this quest for the necessary equilibrium.[91]

6.2   Financial aspects of the regime

The specialized literature on the subject has hitherto devoted but little attention to questions relating to the financial aspects of the regime and the specific arrangements which will be applicable to contractors.[92] The negotiations conducted to date have apparently given only general consideration to this matter. The reason is partly that it is as yet too early to foresee the economic conditions in which a potential exploitation may be carried out, and partly also that this topic is linked to important criteria regarding the nature of the regime and to questions of internal and external accommodation.

It is the unanimous opinion of authors writing in this field that the economic cost of mineral production in Antarctica is much higher than that of a comparable activity in other continents. An estimate based on 1976 prices places the capital cost at double that of a comparable mine in South Africa,[93] an estimate which has been considered extremely conservative.[94] Taking other factors into account this same estimate gives an overall cost of producing the minerals which is close to three times the cost of purchasing the same minerals in the international market.[95] The cost differential is the natural result of the difficult environmental and technological conditions in Antarctica, the higher costs of production and transport determined by distance, the absence of any form of infrastructure, the costs of discovery, the more exigent demands in terms of management, and, in a very important degree, the greater risk represented by operations in so hostile an environment.[96]

To arrive at a precise estimate of the economic costs and conditions of exploitation, attention has been drawn to the need to obtain information on such varied problems as the richness, extent and other physical characteristics of the resource, to evaluate the cost of obtaining this information, to calculate in detail the production costs, to estimate changes in world supply and demand and to assess the real prices situation, and to take into account a variety of suppositions with respect to technological development.[97] In the words of one author:

> The economic future of Antarctic mineral resource exploitation depends on a great many unknowns: future world oil prices; the costs of alternative types of energy; the nature and extent of Antarctic mineral resources; the rate and direction of technological development; the terms of the regime devised for Antarctic mineral activity; and other political, legal and environmental constraints.[98]

On the basis of these considerations it has been estimated that costs might considerably exceed benefits and the conclusion has been reached 'that under a market system there will be no development of Antarctic resources in the near future'.[99] However, neither can the possibility be dismissed that mineral deposits or oilfields of giant proportions, wealth and even accessibility might be discovered, and that this might dramatically alter the conclusion aforesaid.[100] Besides, decisions concerning exploitation are not always founded on market criteria, since considerations of security of supplies or mere political expediency may intervene.[101] There will always be the possibility, too, of subsidies for high-risk or advanced-technology operations, such as these, and that may also make a difference to market conditions. Taking the experience in connection with the deep sea-bed into account, one writer remarks:

> . . . the economic reasons for assuming zero or very limited resource development in Antarctica dominate the situation. Nevertheless, the impact of the question of deep sea mining on the Law of the Sea Conference clearly suggests that a political grab for control of real or metaphysical resources in Antarctica might occur.[102]

Modalities for financial contributions

These considerations will of course influence whatever financial approaches are ultimately adopted by the Antarctic regime. The proposals formulated hitherto envisage three main types of financial contributions which the contractor will have to make. The first is that relating to reimbursement of the costs of implementation of the management scheme, an item which more generally could be identified with the payment of an administration fee.[103] The submission of an application for authorization to explore also normally involves a payment of this type. Normally this fee will have to be paid to the institutions of the regime which are those providing such administrative aspects. A second financial contribution consists in the payment of royalties and the third in tax payments or payments in kind.[104]

These last two financial obligations are harder to define exactly because of their incidence on a number of other issues of substance. The most delicate of these is undoubtedly the question of who is to collect the contributions, a subject on which claims to territorial sovereignty will once again come into conflict with non-recognition of the sovereignties concerned.[105] This is one of the problems that will have to be settled in the process of internal accommodation.[106] In addition, the idea of a distribution of benefits to the rest of the international community has also been borne in mind as a matter for external accommodation.[107]

The distinction between administration fees, royalties and taxes is consonant with the evolution shown in this respect by agreements on minerals in international practice.[108] The payment of royalties which was characteristic of traditional mining concessions has given rise to various forms in which royalties are combined with taxes or, in other cases, royalties have been replaced by taxation, since in this way the State obtains a bigger share in the economic benefits of the project.[109] The profit-sharing approach has begun to acquire special importance. Payment in kind is also conceivable, as well as other expedients. Equity sharing, that is, participation in the capital shares of the project, is another approach adopted in contemporary practice which is also aimed at wider distribution of benefits.[110] It must also be borne in mind that this practice has placed special emphasis on the linkage between mining projects and the local economy,[111] a criteria which in the case of Antarctica could be of special interest for the countries neighbouring the continent, since they will serve as the base points for Antarctic activities.

Various national models may be of interest for particular aspects of the tax arrangements applicable to Antarctic mineral activities. The United States outer continental shelf leasing system, based on a combination of bidding and royalty payment, and the British and Norwegian 'excess' profits taxation in relation to the exploitation of North Sea oil, have been mentioned as eventual models in this regard.[112] Question of tax deductions and tax credits in the home country for payment of taxes in the context of the Antarctic regime, may also be extremely important considerations for the financial strategies of the firms involved in Antarctic mineral activities.[113]

International precedents in this field are of course more limited. In the regime of Svalbard, taxes are only applied by Norway for the purposes of local administration and the financement of administrative services to the islands.[114] More relevant has been the recent Law of the Sea experience in terms of the financial arrangements applicable to deep sea-bed mining under Part XI of the 1982 Convention, partly because it is an instance of establishing an international tax system applicable to a mineral activity and partly because it provides an example of successful and pragmatic negotiation which contrasts with what happened in other aspects of that regime.[115] This system provides for a levy for administrative costs, which has to be paid only once, and also for payment of a fixed annual fee. Consideration is also given to an option between a production charge and a combination of this charge with profit-sharing, provision being made in the regime for the corresponding percentages and their variations through time.[116] The formula of a single production charge was introduced in order to accommodate the socialist countries, whose economic system is not governed by the profits concept.[117]

In the case of the Antarctic regime, until more precise information is available on the economic and other costs conditions in which mineral activity could be carried out, and which will also vary in terms of the type of development concerned, it might prove too early to establish at this date specific procedures for financial arrangements applicable to the contractor. One author has appropriately defined the general criteria which must be taken into account as follows:

> . . . revenues will undoubtedly be required for administrative expenses and to provide an economic benefit to a few or many States, selected by criteria yet to be established. One would expect that payments for the right to exploit minerals in Antarctica would be set at a level which would permit profitable development.[118]

Policy options and different models of regulation

Notwithstanding what has just been said, some of the major policy options existing in this field can be readily identified. A first question that arises, in common with that already discussed in relation to the terms and conditions on which mineral activities must be carried out, is whether the terms of financial arrangements should be defined in advance and on general lines within the regime, or whether they might be established in each management scheme on a mainly *ad hoc* basis. In favour of the first option, arguments may be invoked relating to the need for standard norms known for certain beforehand, which are non-discriminatory, and which forestall negotiations that might involve excessive concessions or incentives. This is the somewhat automatic approach that prevails in the deep sea-bed model.[119]

There are also important considerations in favour of the second option. From the economic standpoint it will be necessary to take into account the different conditions that may characterize projects bearing on different minerals. For example, the case of copper mining in the trans-Antarctic mountains will not present the same problems and considerations as petroleum production on the continental shelf. These differences must be reflected in the terms of the management scheme.[120] From the point of view of internal accommodation, as explained in Chapter 5, importance attaches to the role that the territorial State will have to play in the preparation of a management scheme, which includes provision for royalties and taxation. This could not happen if general or financial terms and conditions were defined beforehand.

There is nothing here to prevent due account being taken of the criteria for uniformity, non-discrimination and other issues which the regime establishes, and in the light of which the negotiations on each case will be conducted. In this connection it must be recalled that in general the management scheme will have to follow the guidelines laid down by the organs of the regime and will also have to be approved by these institutions. It is on this basis that the regime will be able to establish criteria whereby exaggerated benefits in favour of one party or the other can be prevented. Thus, for example, it will be possible to define the amount of total government take, or total regime take where appropriate, by means of which criteria for a precise limit can be set to the financial contributions of the contractor; or, again, to provide a mechanism for tapping windfall profits if they should happen to occur, which mechanisms generally take the form of a sliding scale of profit-sharing.[121]

The Antarctic regime seems to incline towards the second option described,[122] although prior definition of terms and conditions has not been entirely excluded as an alternative. Given the characteristics of this regime, the flexibility inherent in the second option seems to be more desirable providing limits which can be objectively established by the convention and the rules and regulations to be enacted under it. In any event, as we shall examine in Chapter 7, the main issue behind this policy question is that of the necessary internal accommodation between claimants and non-claimants as to the allocation of revenues under the regime.

A second policy question which arises is that of the financial policy objectives of this regime. One author has commented in this regard that in general such a regime can have three purposes: deriving revenue from the resource, affecting the behaviour of the firms involved in Antarctic mineral activities – particularly in terms of location, capital investment and other decisions – and making a political statement about the status of claims in their relationship to financial questions.[123] There can be no doubt that at least the first and third purpose mentioned are very much present in the current negotiations. However, no objective has been expressly defined by this regime as to financial aspects, for which reason they must be interpreted as according with the general objectives of the regime and the proper balance which it is sought to strike between resource development and ecological protection. In this context, it must be understood that financial policy will avoid placing artificial obstacles in the way of development or generating such additional costs as may make mineral activities economically inefficient. At the same time, it must also be understood that appropriate contributions will be required in accordance with international practice, with a view to a reasonable degree of profit-sharing. At this level fresh importance is acquired by the concept of 'total regime take', which will make it possible to establish levels of financial contribution in keeping with the balanced objectives in question.

This approach differs significantly from that adopted in the case of the deep sea-bed, where the objectives were expressly defined, and clearly reveals the conflict existing between those who aimed at giving priority to resource development and those who wanted to maximize the income of the Authority.[124] At the same time, owing to the fears of discrimination which also haunted those negotiations, emphasis was placed on the uniform and non-discriminatory character of the financial arrangements and on the equality of treatment of the various contractors. The Antarctic regime has also enshrined the general principle of non-discrimination,[125] but no stress is laid on uniformity as an absolute criterion; in principle this allows the parties more room for manoeuvre, always provided that whatever common and uniform parameters the regime may define are duly respected. The different spirit inspiring Antarctic co-operation largely accounts for this more flexible approach.

Nor has there been a repetition in the case of Antarctica of the discussion that characterized the negotiations on the deep sea-bed with regard to the activities that should be specifically included in the financial mechanisms. On that occasion, one position supported the criterion that financial contributions should cover not only the phase of actual mining but also those of transport, processing and marketing, since the biggest profits could be obtained in these last named stages. In contrast, another opinion was that only extraction activities were covered by the regime and its financial machinery.[126] It was the latter criterion that ultimately prevailed, just as has happened in the case of the Antarctic regime, in consequence of its being the most consonant with the practice of mineral agreements.

This discussion is related up to a point with the tendency of some producer countries to require that mining projects comprise not only extraction activities in their territories but also some processing activities, with the aim of benefiting by the greater value added.[127] This point of view might also appeal to countries claiming sovereignty which are nearest to the Antarctic continent.

Another important problem of policy that should be borne in mind is that of stipulating the exact time at which the different types of financial contributions must be made, a situation in relation to which various approaches have also been adopted in international practice. Administration fees, payments that must accompany the application for exploration permits and other similar contributions are of course made at the start of operations, but they should not be a special problem because their total amount is generally small. The position as to royalties and taxes may be different. Normally payments of royalties are a periodical contribution which is unrelated to whether the project is or is not producing profits. In the initial phases this type of so-called 'front-end' payment may come to represent an onerous financial burden for the contractor. An alternative is to concentrate taxes and other forms of contribution on the more advanced operational phases, relating them to the project's effective profits. A system of this latter kind is that of profit-sharing, which affects the contractor only in so far as he obtains profits. In the case of the deep sea-bed regime, a combination of these systems was used, with some measure of emphasis on the latter alternative.[128] This might also be justifiable in the Antarctic regime, especially as an activity of high economic risk is involved.

Precedents for financial participation and purchase options
The policy for State participation in licences raises some interesting financial and legal questions, particularly in the light of the British Petroleum and Submarine Pipelines Act of 1975,[129] and the establishment of the British National Oil Corporation (BNOC). Although the latter was privatized in 1985, State oil companies have still a very major role in many of the countries parties to the 1959 Antarctic Treaty, thus making of the problems of State financial participation in joint-ventures and other schemes a rather common situation.[130] BNOC was empowered to produce and market petroleum and, furthermore, the initial legislation provided that the State would hold, through this Corporation, a majority share in existing and future licences. The way in which this share would be purchased was left to individual negotiations with each company. To avoid paying enormous compensation for what might constitute a kind of nationalization the government adopted the position that it was a matter for negotiation and voluntary arrangements, and that the legislation did not constitute an act of expropriation *per se*.[131]

The formula finally adopted was that although the rights and obligations pertaining to the licence would not be affected BNOC would have the option to purchase at market prices 51% of the petroleum produced. Thus the participation objective was attained without the necessity for a formal act of expropriation which would have entailed the payment of compensation. This procedure has been explained in the following terms:

> In an unusual formula, BNOC has become a co-licensee in every licence comprising a commercial oil field; but it has been usual for the oil company to retain the obligations and benefits of the licence. Thus BNOC's 51 per cent entitlement has been not as a

percentage interest owner of the licence, but rather through a guaranteed option to purchase 51 per cent of petroleum as it became produced.

This avoided paying compensation to the companies for the loss of vast property rights: BNOC became entitled to purchase 51 per cent of *their* oil – oil to which they continued to have title as it was produced and reduced into possession . . . In this innovative manner the State acquired secure access to vast quantities of petroleum without depriving the licensee of the essential attributes of property rights.[132]

As far as Antarctica is concerned, as has already been explained, the alternative of expropriation or nationalization really does not exist, since the need for stability of contracts prevents it, in accordance with the guarantees established, and, what is more important, the regime organs do not have the attributes of statehood, though the participating States have agreed to be governed exclusively by the provisions of the regime as regards mineral activities. But the approach represented by an option to purchase, as BNOC initially had in the United Kingdom would be extremely attractive in the Antarctic context.

In this connection there would be nothing to prevent the regime from offering the participating States a priority option to purchase in respect of any minerals or petroleum that might be produced. This could be done in accordance with some preferential criterion, which might possibly include preference for the territorial State itself. The purchase would be made, of course, at market prices and 'buy-back' mechanisms might be provided for as in the British experience.[133] This approach would encourage adherence to the regime, inasmuch as it facilitates security of supplies, while at the same time the alternatives of internal accommodation might be made easier.

The concept of a Resource Adjacent Nation has been used in relation to fisheries and the Exclusive Economic Zone as indicative of the existence of a special interest and even of a preference;[134] it has also been used in relation to adjacent deposits of sea-bed minerals.[135] The recognition of this concept by the Antarctic regime would provide one more instance in which the special interest of adjacent or participating States would acquire a relevant expression.

Other aspects of the financial arrangements

The Antarctic regime touches upon several other subjects which have a direct or indirect bearing of financial arrangements. Depletion policy constitutes one of the aspects which the management scheme will have to define.[136] In international practice this policy consists in granting a tax concession in respect of the exploitation of non-renewable resources, allowing the deduction of 'a certain amount from gross income in computing taxable income',[137] which is generally considered as a 'repayment on capital'.[138] Normally the deduction of a percentage of gross income is authorized by the taxing agencies, although other systems are also applied.

Deductions of this kind are authorized in all important mining countries, albeit it must be borne in mind that the concept has been a subject of controversy. Since it implies a certain valuation of the resources *in situ,* which are susceptible to exhaustion, this gives rise to discussions as to who is really the owner of the resource concerned, a domain in which the question of permanent sovereignty over natural resources once again comes to the fore. In this context, it has been argued that since the State holds entitlement to the resources *in situ,* it is this State that should benefit by the depletion allowance.[139] Moreover, this topic is connected with the debate as to whether the resource has any instrinsic value – the line that the State will favour – or whether it acquires value only in so far as capital and technology makes its extraction possible, which is the approach favoured by investor companies.[140]

To the extent that the above-mentioned discussion might relate also to the resources of the Continental Shelf, its terms can somewhat vary. This is so because the State does not have full sovereignty over such resources, but only sovereign rights for the purpose of their exploration and exploitation; it follows that the question of permanent sovereignty and rights over the resources *in situ* is more relative in the case of the Continental Shelf. However, in practice the State tends many times to regard the latter situation in terms similar to those applicable to the resources in its land territory.

As was explained in Chapter 5, in the case of Antarctica the question of the title to resources is not of a major importance, since what is really of interest is the organization of the right to exploit within the framework of the Antarctic regime.[141] Nor, strictly speaking, does the discussion as to permanent sovereignty arise, since the regime has been accepted by the supporters of this concept only as a manifestation of the exercise of that sovereignty. In the absence of any doctrinal discussion of this kind, the common international practice has been followed, and depletion policy recognized.

The method of establishing the specific amount of the deduction will be related to the calculation of the project's internal rate of return, since the tax concession, together with other mechanisms such as depreciation and amortization strongly influences the determination of the cash flow. In this connection, too, the overlapping of concessions deriving from the various concepts[142] will have to be avoided. All these calculations, in their turn, are related to the type of financing of the project in question.[143]

Another aspect of the problem which has a more indirect relationship with financial policy is that of the time limits and diligence requirements of the project, which again will have to be defined by the management scheme.[144] On this level the rules of international practice will probably be followed,[145] with due regard to the special difficulties of Antarctic operations.

The budget of the regime's institutions also has some bearing on financial policy.[146] In so far as this regime obtains income of its own, mainly through the payment of administration fees and other financial contributions of this type, the budget can be partly financed therewith. Direct contributions from the States members of the Commission will also be needed. In this regime provision is made for an equal contribution on the part of the members of the Commission, in contrast to the Canberra Convention, which established equality only for the first five years after its entry into force, to be followed subsequently by a system which would also take into account 'the amount harvested'.[147] Budget decisions will be adopted by consensus.[148]

The aspects relating to the transfer of technology which made the negotiation of the sea-bed regime so difficult have not been directly tackled by the Antarctic regime. That does not mean that the matter is entirely disregarded since through the different options open to contractors under the regime the transfer in question can be ensured, especially where participation in joint ventures is concerned. Moreover, the facilitation of participation by developing countries in Antarctic activities, which includes a technological dimension, is an important element both within the Antarctic system and in relation to the external accommodation. Because of the different nature of Antarctic co-operation compared to the deep sea-bed regime, this subject is deprived of negative ideological connotations.

It may also be possible, likewise, to consider in the context of the Antarctic regime the establishment of special rules for preparatory investments, including their administrative, operational and financial aspects, if this is warranted in the light of the rules concerning the entry into force of the complete regime.[149]

6.3 Anti-trust policies and the question of other restrictive practices

The need for an anti-monopoly policy in the context of this regime has not gone unnoticed. Among the functions proposed for the Commission is that of adopting by consensus appropriate measures 'in order to avoid monopoly situations'.[150] Although anti-monopoly policies are generally resisted by powers abundantly endowed with capital and technological resources, since they are concerned that their operational possibilities will be restricted, such policies have been a point of key importance in the position of other countries, especially France. For the deep sea-bed regime detailed provisions in this field were ultimately established.[151]

In the case of Antarctica the definition of precise rules will be a function of the Commission, for which reason the Convention, in principle, will not devote any detailed attention to the matter. This is in keeping with the nature of the regime, inasmuch as the Convention will not lay down a fully elaborated mining code. In any event, detailed rules will have to be formulated from the outset, since they will have an effect on criteria for selecting contractors and on other operational machinery of the regime. These rules will of course have to draw distinctions in terms of the different mineral resources which are to be the object of operations.

Another of the Commission's functions is related to the regime's key principle of non-discrimination, which will have to be reflected in specific rules to ensure 'full and fair opportunity' for participation in mineral activities.[152] Although the principle of non-discrimination was at one time mainly thought of as applying to the nationality of the contractor,[153] it is also linked to the necessity of avoiding unfair trade practices which result in the obstruction of the said 'full and fair opportunity'.

The problems connected with subsidies and other methods that distort free competition might be the object of attention on the part of the institutions of the regime, in accordance with the scope given to the rules that will have to be laid down by the Commission.[154] This aspect of the question has in reality two dimensions. On the one hand, distortion of competition may occur within the regime, and will normally have to be corrected by its institutions. On the other hand, specific practices followed under the regime might be reflected in distortion of competition in international markets for raw materials and this in turn could affect countries which are exporters of the minerals concerned, some of which will actually be parties to the Antarctic regime itself.

This last issue was raised by Australia and Canada in the context of the deep sea-bed regime, on which occasion it was proposed that the rights and obligations deriving from relevant multilateral trade agreements should be applied to the production, processing, transport and marketing of minerals extracted within the area covered by the regime. On this basis a linkage was sought with the GATT mechanisms and its procedures for the settlement of disputes in so far as the avoidance of subsidies and other distortions was concerned.[155] This idea could also be of interest *mutatis mutandis,* for Antarctica; a large number of the Consultative Parties are participants in the GATT.[156] For those who were not members of GATT, *ad hoc* mechanisms of similar scope might be considered.

Another very delicate question discussed in the context of the deep sea-bed regime was that of limitation of production and other mechanisms designed to prevent adverse economic effects on land-based producers of the same minerals mined in the area.[157] At the same time, rules were laid down to ensure that the possible incentives granted to contractors would not take the form of subsidies that would give them an artificial competitive advantage over land-based producers.[158] A writer who at the time represented the Government of the United States brought up this discussion in relation to Antarctica in the first debates on the mineral resources regime, observing that the marketing of minerals 'should not be subject to artificial production restrictions or price controls',[159] while at the same time postulating 'a free market philosophy' for this regime.[160]

The question has not been raised as a principal issue in the course of the negotiations, partly because of the deeper agreement that has existed among the Consultative Parties as to the nature of the regime and its specific mechanisms, and partly because in general the kind of production that has been taken most into account is that of petroleum, supplies of which are of special interest for all the Parties.

The principle of full and fair opportunity for participation in mineral activities has yet another dimension of which mention should be made: that relating to the participation of the developing countries. This aspect is of course of interest for facilitating internal accommodation, inasmuch as Argentina, Brazil, Chile, India and Uruguay are developing State Consultative Parties. It is also of importance with respect to external accommodation, since that may facilitate the participation of other developing countries.

Through this application of the principle, this group of countries may be encouraged, by means of special incentives or facilities, to participate in programmes of scientific research, in the appropriate technological training or preparation, and above all, in different forms of joint ventures with other parties to the regime.[161] It must also be borne in mind that in the framework of many international economic arrangements and institutions special measures in favour of developing countries are not regarded as discriminatory against the other parties.[162] The *1986 Draft Articles* have embodied this principle by means of encouraging co-operation and international participation in Antarctic mineral activities, particularly by developing countries (Article 7). The Commission is also entrusted with the function of promoting measures to this effect, including financial measures (Article 22, 1, (j), (p)). This body is also mandated to provide incentives and opportunities in this regard (Article 39, 1, (d)). Still more importantly, in case of competing applications priority is to be granted to those involving broader participation, in particular of developing countries (Article 43, 3, (b)).

It is of special interest to stress that in the framework of Antarctica this dimension of the principle has been adduced as a positive expression of the prevailing spirit of co-operation, divested of connotations of negative confrontation and of the rhetoric which has so often characterized the proceedings of other international forums or negotiations. It is in this same spirit that appropriate and reasonable solutions for the problems that cause concern can be found.

6.4   New dimensions relating to the policy of scientific research

The policy of scientific research is another of the regime's concerns. Without prejudice to the scientific activity carried on under the aegis of the principle of freedom established in the Treaty, the regime must also promote certain special lines of research to ensure that it will be able to adopt the pertinent decisions concerning mineral exploitation in the light of all the necessary information, especially in the environmental field. In the first connection, the freedom in question is of course re-affirmed, while at the same time special protective measures are established for areas where mining will be excluded, whether for environmental or for scientific reasons.[163]

As regards the promotion of special lines of research, which constitutes an important general objective, the institutions of the regime will have to undertake certain important functions. One of the tasks envisaged for the Commission is that of facilitating and promoting research projects with a view to assessing possible environmental impacts of mineral activities,[164] while another is that of determining the areas where such activities will be prohibited on scientific and other grounds.[165] As stated before, participation in scientific research is also a point of interest for developing countries.

This more active institutional role in scientific research implies that specialized mechanisms are needed to serve this end. As early as 1958 Chile proposed the creation of an Antarctic institute of scientific research linked to the Treaty, with the potential participation of SCAR, but the idea was never approved.[166] In the context of the negotiation of the mineral regime this important initiative has been brought forward again as a stimulus to Antarctic research under the regime and to the co-operation of other international organizations, still with the participation of SCAR; some of the financial contributions deriving from mineral activities could be used to support such research programmes and projects.[167]

As we shall examine in Chapter 10, the policy of scientific research has also been a matter of concern for a number of non-governmental organizations. The Antarctic and Southern Ocean Coalition has proposed the creation of an Antarctic Fund,[168] which would be partly concerned with scientific research and the environment, and various non-governmental organizations have made the argument for the need to have independent scientific research as a basis for their involvement in Antarctic activities or institutions. As we shall also see, this argument has been made too by international organizations, particularly FAO and UNEP.

While it might be thought that mineral activities could potentially interfere with scientific research in the Antarctic, it must be borne in mind that such activities are governed by the key principle of due respect for the other uses of Antarctica. In relation to these uses the regime guarantees, first and foremost, freedom of scientific research.[169]

In conclusion it may be realized that the various special policies pursued by the Antarctic mineral regime provide an important set of rules and standards which are supplementary to the mechanisms examined in Chapter 5 as to the organization of mineral activities in Antarctica. These special policies will govern decisions and the criteria of the regime in the crucial fields of environmental issues and financial arrangements, without prejudice to associated questions like anti-monopoly clauses and scientific research.

Because of the importance of the matters covered by these policies it can also be expected that they will concentrate heavily the attention of the parties involved in this regime, either at the state of negotiation or later during the work of the institutions which will be established under these arrangements. This has already happened to a large extent with the environmental issues and it is certainly bound to happen in the future with the financial aspects of the regime, including the most contentious issue of the distribution of benefits and profits.

In any event, it is through the application of the special policies that the institution of the regime will be able to manage the mineral activities in Antarctica with a sense of equilibrium, combining the necessary safeguards to the environment with the basic development goals, and the required revenue – raising aspirations with the sound financial standing of the contractors and firms – among other examples.

Chapter 6 Notes

1. See in particular Article IX, 1, (f) of The Antarctic Treaty which refers to the 'Preservation and conservation of living resources in Antarctica'.
2. See Chapter 2 supra, Section 2.2.
3. Recommendations VI-4, VII-1, VIII-11, VIII-13, IX-5, XII-3 and XII-4. See generally Antarctic Treaty: *Handbook of Measures,* 1983, Section 1.1.
4. Recommendations IX-6 and X-7.
5. See Chapter 3 supra, note 192 and associated text.
6. W. M. Bush: *Antarctica and International Law,* Vol. 1, 1982, at 84–86.
7. On conservation in Antarctica see the following works: M. W. Holdgate: 'The Antarctic ecosystem', *Phil. Trans. R. Soc. Lon,* B, Vol. 252, 1967, 363–383; M. W. Holdgate: 'Terrestrial ecosystems in the Antarctica', *Phil. Trans. R. Soc. Lon,* B, Vol. 279, 1977, 5–25; David Anderson: 'The conservation of wildlife under the Antarctic Treaty', *Pol. Rec.,* Vol. 14, N° 88, 1968, 25–32; B. C. Parker (ed.): *Conservation problems in Antarctica,* 1972; Sierra Club: *Environmental Policy considerations in the Antarctic region,* meeting held at the American Society of International Law, 15 June 1976, summary; Tore Gjelsvik: 'The work of SCAR for conservation of nature in the Antarctic', in Francisco Orrego Vicuña (ed.): *El Desarrollo de la Antártica,* 1977, 328–334; Brian B. Roberts: 'Conservation in the Antarctic', *Phil. Trans. R. Soc. Lon,* B, Vol. 279, 1977, 97–104; R. M. Laws (ed.): *Antarctic Ecology,* 2 vols, 1984; T. Antezana, K. Ray and C. Morales: 'Ecosistema antártico: naturaleza, impacto y conservación', in Francisco Orrego Vicuña and María Teresa Infante: *Política Antártica de Chile,* 1985, 181–189; Beatriz Ramacciotti de Cubas: 'Algunas consideraciones sobre la explotación de los recursos naturales de la antártica y la protección del medio ambiente', in Edgardo Mercado Jarrin et al.: *El Perú y la Antártica,* 1984, 63–86. See also Hugh A. Brown: 'Antarctic Disaster', *Fate Magazine,* May 1956, 28–34; M. J. Dunbar: *Ecological development in Polar Regions. A study in evolution,* 1968; National Wildlife Federation: *Ranger Rick,* Special issue on Antarctica, February 1984.
8. Fernando Zegers: 'The Antarctic system and the utilization of resources', *Univ. Mia. L. Rev.,* Vol. 33, 1978, 426–473, at 449, 451.
9. M. W. Holdgate: 'Environmental factors in the development of Antarctica', in Francisco Orrego Vicuña (ed.): *Antarctic Resources Policy,* 1983, 77–101, at 97.
10. Australia, Antarctic Treaty (Environment Protection) Act 1980, Section 29 (2) (c); text in Bush, op. cit., note 6 supra, Vol. II, at 212–225.
11. France, Arret N° 17 reglementant la protection de la faune et de la flore dans le district de Terre Adélie, 7 September 1966, Art. 10; text in Bush, op. cit., note 6 supra, Vol. II, at 555–558.
12. Belgium, Loi relative a la protection de la faune et de la flore dans l'Antarctique, 12 January 1978, Art. 7; text in Bush, op. cit., note 6 supra, Vol. II, at 268–271.
13. For a summary of the New Zealand legislation, see Bush, op. cit., note 6 supra, at 378.
14. For a summary of the British legislation, see Bush, op. cit., note 6 supra, at 379. See in particular the *Oil in Navigable Waters Act,* 1955, as amended; text in United Nations Legislative Series, *National legislation and treaties relating to the territorial sea . . . .,* ST/LEG/Ser.B/15, 1970, 520–540.

15. For a summary of US legislation, see Bush, op. cit., note 6 supra, at 379.
16. See Chapter 3 supra, Section 3.3.
17. United Kingdom, House of Commons, *Official Report,* Parliamentary Debates, Standing Committee C. Wednesday 22 March 1967, statements by Mr Griffiths and Lever, at 12–13.
18. See Chapter 5 supra, Section 5.6.
19. Recommendation X-7, *Handbook* 1983, at 1107–1108. On the legal issues related to iceberg utilization, see Chapter 4 supra, note 214 and associated text.
20. Holdgate, loc. cit., note 9 supra, at 85.
21. Recommendation X-7 cit., note 19 supra.
22. Antarctic Treaty, Final Report of the Eleventh Consultative Meeting, par. 15; text in Bush, op. cit., note 6 supra, at 438.
23. Argentina, Draft Recommendation on the oil contamination of the Antarctic marine environment, Doc. Ant/XI/23, 26 June 1981; reproduced as Annex 7 of the Report cit., note 22 supra; text in Bush, op. cit., note 6 supra, at 448–449.
24. Boleslaw Adam Boczek: 'The protection of the Antarctic ecosystem: a study in international environmental law', *Ocean Dev. I.L.,* Vol. 13, 1983–1984, 347-425, at 391.
25. See generally International Maritime Organization: *Status of Multilateral conventions and instruments in respect of which the IMO or its Secretary General performs depositary or other functions,* 31 December 1984. In appendix II of this book the status of the most important of these and related conventions is given for the Antarctic Treaty parties. See also generally the following works: Patricia Birnie: 'Developments in the law for prevention of marine pollution from petroleum during 1983–1984', in R. W. Bentham (ed.): *Recent developments in United Kingdom Petroleum Law,* University of Dundee, Centre for Petroleum and Mineral Law Studies, 1984, 72–127; Christopher C. Joyner: 'Oceanic pollution and the Southern Ocean: rethinking the international legal implications for Antarctica', *Natural Resources Journal,* Vol. 24, N° 1, January 1984, 1–40; Christopher C. Joyner: 'The Southern Ocean and Marine Pollution: problems and prospects', *Case W.R.J.I.L.,* Vol. 17, 1985, 165–194; William Y. Brown and Bruce S. Manheim: 'Conservation of Antarctic Marine Living Resources: the environmental perspective', in Lewis M. Alexander and Lynne Carter Hanson (eds.): *Antarctic Politics and Marine Resources: critical choices for the 1980's,* 1985, 123–129.
26. International Convention on Civil Liability for Oil Pollution Damage, Brussels, 29 November 1969; for the status of signature, ratification and other as at 31 December 1984, see IMO doc., op. cit., note 25 supra, 145–160.
27. Protocol to the International Convention on Civil Liability for Oil Pollution Damage, 1969, done at London, 19 November 1976; for the status of signature, ratification and other as at 31 December 1984, see IMO doc., op. cit., note 25 supra, 161–168.
28. IMO: *Protocol of 1984 to amend the International Convention on Civil Liability for Oil Pollution Damage,* 1969, Doc. LEG/CONF. 6/66, 25 May 1984. For a comment on this amendment, see Clifton E. Curtis: 'Recent developments under special environmental conventions', in Robert B. Krueger and Stefan A. Riesenfeld: *The Developing Order of the Oceans*, 1985, 117–132.
29. International Convention on the Establishment of an International Fund for Compensation for Oil Pollution Damage, done at Brussels, 18 December 1971; for the status of signature, ratification and other, as at 31 December 1984, see IMO doc., op. cit., note 25 supra, 187–194.
30. Protocol to the International Convention on the Establishment of an

International Fund for Compensation for Oil Pollution Damage, 1971, done at London, 19 November 1976; for the status of signature, ratification and other as at 31 December 1984, see IMO doc., op. cit., note 25 supra, 195–200.

31. IMO: *Protocol of 1984 to amend the International Convention on the Establishment of an International Fund for Compensation for Oil Pollution Damage,* 1971, Doc. LEC/CONF. 6/67, 25 May 1984; for a comment see Curtis, loc. cit., note 28 supra, 119–123.

32. See Chapter 5 supra, Section 5.7.

33. Bush, op. cit., note 6 supra, at 379–380.

34. Ibid., at 380–381.

35. International Convention relating to Intervention on the High Seas in Cases of Oil Pollution Casualties; done at Brussels, 29 November 1969; for the status of signature, ratification and other as at 31 December 1984, see IMO doc. op. cit., note 25 supra, 127–138.

36. Convention on the Prevention of Marine Pollution by Dumping of Wastes and Other Matter, 29 December 1972; for the status of signature, ratification and other as at 31 December 1984, see IMO doc., op. cit., note 25 supra, 275–281.

37. Bush, op. cit., note 6 supra, at 381.

38. Ibid., at 382.

39. This is the case of the Civil Liability Convention of 1969, cit., note 26 supra, and the Convention on the Dumping of Wastes and Other Matter, cit., note 36 supra; see Bush, op. cit., note 6 supra, at 381, 382.

40. Memorandum of understanding on Port State control in implementing agreements on maritime safety and protection of the marine environment, Paris, 26 January 1982; the following Antarctic Treaty Consultative Parties are parties to this agreement: Belgium, France, Federal Republic of Germany, Norway and the United Kingdom. Text in David C. Jackson (ed.): *World Shipping Laws,* International Conventions, VIII – Marine Pollution, VIII/23/CONV, May 1984.

41. Permanent Commission of the South Pacific: Agreement for the protection of the marine environment and coastal zones of the Southeast Pacific, Lima, 12 November 1981; related agreements were signed on 12 November 1981 and 22 July 1983; United Nations, 1984 (in Spanish).

42. Mario Valenzuela: 'IMO: Public International Law and Regulation', in D. M. Johnston and N. Q. Letalik (eds): *The Law of the Sea and Ocean Industry: new opportunities and restraints,* 1984, 141–151.

43. Louis B. Sohn: 'Implications of the Law of the Sea Convention regarding the protection and preservation of the marine environment', in Krueger and Riesenfeld, op. cit., note 28 supra, 103–116. See also E. D. Brown: 'Pollution from seabed mining: legal safeguards', *Environmental Policy and Law,* Vol. 10, 1983, 122–134. For a schematic analysis of the responsibilities deriving from the Law of the Sea Convention in relation to the environment, see Dalhousie Ocean Studies Programme: *Conservation and Management of the marine environment: responsibilities and required initiatives in accordance with the 1982 U.N. Convention of the Law of the Sea,* 1984. The Convention on Conservation of Antarctic Marine Living Resources is referred to in relation to Art. 234 of the Law of the Sea Convention, at 6.

44. See generally D. M. McRae and D. J. Goundrey: 'Environmental jurisdiction in Arctic waters: the extent of Article 234', *U.B.C.L.R.,* Vol. 16, 1982, 197–228; John Warren Kindt and Todd Jay Parriott: 'Ice-covered areas: the competing interests of conservation and resource exploitation', *S.D.L.R.,* Vol. 21, 1984, 941–983.

45. David A. Colson: 'Political and boundary issues affecting Arctic energy

resources', in Krueger and Riesenfeld, op. cit., note 28 supra, 513–523, at 522–523.

46. Jacques-Yvan Morin: 'Le progres technique, la pollution et l'evolution recent du droit de la mer au Canada, particulierement a l'egard de l'Arctique', *Can. Y.B.I.L.,* Vol. VIII, 1970, 158–248; Louis Henkin: 'Arctic Anti-Pollution: Does Canada make – or break– International Law?', *A.J.I.L.,* Vol. 65, 1971, 131–136.

47. See generally Chapter 4 supra.

48. For a comment on the Principles of the Stockholm Declaration of the United Nations Conference on the Human Environment of 1972 and associated developments, and their relationship to general international law, see Boczek, loc. cit., note 24 supra, at 388–390.

49. Other international conventions are also relevant in relation to the protection of fauna and flora in Antarctica. The following have been cited: (i) International Convention for the regulation of Whaling, 2 December 1946; (ii) Convention on International Trade in Endangered Species of Wild Fauna and Flora, 3 March 1973; (iii) Convention for the Protection of the World Cultural and Natural Heritage, 23 November 1972; (iv) International Convention for the Protection of Birds, 18 October 1950; (v) Convention on Nature Protection and Wild Life Preservation in the Western Hemisphere, 12 October 1940; (vi) Convention on the Conservation of Migrating Species of Wild Animals, 23 June 1979; for reference to these and other agreements on the matter, see Bush, op. cit., note 6 supra, at 162–168. Particular programmes of international organizations might also be relevant in this context; see, for example, United Nations Environment Programme: 'Prospects for global ocean pollution monitoring', Regional Seas Reports and Studies N° 47, UNEP 1984. On the general aspects of the Law of the Sea Convention in relation to the marine environment, see also P. M. Depuy and M. Remond-Gouilloud: 'La preservation du milieu marin', in Rene–Jean Dupuy et Daniel Vignes (eds): *Traite du Nouveau Droit de la Mer,* 1985, 979–1045.

50. See generally M. W. Holdgate and Jon Tinker: *Oil and other minerals in the Antarctic. The environmental implications of possible mineral exploration or exploitation in Antarctica,* 1979; J. H. Zumberge (ed.): *Possible environmental effects of Mineral Exploration and Exploitation in Antarctica,* SCAR, 1979; James H. Zumberge: 'Potential mineral resource availability and possible environment problems in Antarctica', in Jonathan I. Charney (ed.): *The new nationalism and the use of common spaces,* 1982, 115–154; Renzo G. Follegati: *the exploitation of the Antarctic oil and its environmental and legal implications,* Major paper, Master of Marine Affairs, University of Rhode Island, 1982; Víctor A. Gallardo: 'El impacto ambiental del posible desarrollo de los recursos mineros antárticos', in Francisco Orrego Vicuña et al.: *Política Antártica de Chile,* 1985, 191–222. See also Holdgate, loc. cit., note 9 supra; M. W. Holdgate: 'The use and abuse of polar environmental resources', *Pol. Rec.,* N° 136, January 1984, 25–49; M. W. Holdgate: 'Regulated development and conservation of Antarctic resources', in Gillian Triggs (ed.): *Antarctic Treaty Regime,* 1987, 128–142; John A. Heap and Martin W. Holdgate: 'The Antarctic Treaty System as an environmental mechanism – an approach to environmental issues', in U.S. Polar Research Board: *Antarctic Treaty System, An Assessment,* 1986, 195–210.

51. John Hill: *New Zealand and Antarctica,* 1983, at 58.

52. See generally Zegers, loc. cit., note 8 supra.

53. See generally R. B. Thomson: 'United States and New Zealand co-operation in environmental protection', *Ant. J.U.S.,* Vol. VI, N° 3, May–June 1971, 59–62; John Lawrence Hargrove: 'Environmental problems of Antarctic Resource Management: legal and institutional aspects', unpublished paper, American

Society of International Law, 1976; F. M. Auburn: 'The Antarctic Environment', *Y.B.W.A.,* 1981, 248–265.

54. Holdgate, loc. cit., note 9 supra, at 80.
55. Ibid., at 81–85.
56. SCAR: 'Antarctic Resources – Effects of Mineral Exploration', initial response by SCAR, dated May 1976, to Antarctic Treaty Recommendation VIII-14, *Pol. Rec.,* Vol. 18, N° 117, 1977, 631–636.
57. See 'Report of the group of experts on mineral exploration and exploitation', Antarctic Treaty: *Report of the Ninth Consultative Meeting,* London, 19 September–7 October 1977, Foreign and Commonwealth Office, 1977, Annex 5, 56–72; also published in U.S. Senate: *Hearing on Exploitation of Antarctic Resources,* 1978, 118–145. Also see 'Report of the Working Group on the question of Mineral Resource Exploration and Exploitation: legal and political aspects', Antarctic Treaty: *Report of the Tenth Consultative Meeting,* Washington D.C., 17 September–5 October 1979, Annex 5, at 101; and 'Report of the Group of Ecological, Technological and other related experts on mineral exploration and exploitation in Antarctica', in Ibid., Annex 6, at 102–120.
58. SCAR Group of Specialists on the Environmental Impact Assessment of Mineral Exploration and Exploitation in Antarctica (EAMREA): *A preliminary assessment of the environmental impact of Mineral Exploration and Exploitation in Antarctica,* August 1977. See also the edited version by J. H. Zumberge, SCAR, 1979, op. cit., note 50 supra.
59. SCAR Group of Specialists on Antarctic Environmental implications of possible mineral exploration and exploitation (AIMEE): *Report N° 1,* University of Nebraska, Lincoln, 26–29 May 1981; *Report N° 2,* The University of Texas at Dallas, September 30–October 2, 1982.
60. For an account of the work of various groups on the subject, see Victor A. Gallardo, loc. cit., note 50 supra.
61. Institute of Polar Studies, Ohio State University: *A framework for assessing environmental impacts of possible Antarctic mineral development,* Part I, II, January 1977, US Department of Commerce, National Technical Information Service; Katherine A. Green Hammond: *Environmental aspects of potential petroleum exploration and exploitation in Antarctica: forecasting and evaluating risks,* Final Report to the US Marine Mammal Commission, February 1982.
62. US Department of State: *Final Environmental impact statement on the negotiation of a regime for conservation of Antarctic Marine Living Resources,* June 1978; (also reproduced in *US Senate: Antarctic Living Marine Resources Negotiations,* Hearing 1978, 45–76); US Department of State: *Final Environmental impact statement on the negotiation of an international regime for Antarctic mineral resources,* 1982; see also US Antarctic Conservation Act of 1978, Public Law 95–541, 95th Congress, *ILM,* Vol. 18, 1979, 131–136; US National Science Foundation: *US Antarctic Program final environmental impact statement,* June 1980, reprinted October 1984.
63. Holdgate, loc. cit., note 9 supra, at 86.
64. Ibid., at 88.
65. For a discussion of this point, ibid., at 86–87.
66. For the concepts of 'risk estimation' and 'risk evaluation', see ibid., at 86.
67. See generally Chapter 5 supra.
68. On decision-making in the institutions of the regime, see Chapter 8 infra.
69. *1984 Draft Articles,* Article II, 1, a, b; *1983 Draft Articles,* Article II, a, b; see also *1986 Draft Articles,* Article 2 (objectives) and Article 4 (Principles).
70. The 1983 version of the Draft Articles contained some principles on the

environmental aspects of the regime in Articles II and III, but these were conceived mostly as provisional approaches given by way of example.

71. For a discussion of the technology for the exploitation of Antarctic mineral resources, see John A. Dugger: 'Exploiting Antarctic Mineral Resources–Technology, Economics and the Environment', *Univ. Mia. L. Rev,* Vol. 33, 1978, 315–339; John F. Splettstoesser: 'Underground technology for offshore hydrocarbon development in Antarctica', *Fifth International Conference on Port and Ocean Engineering under Arctic conditions,* Norwegian Institute of Technology, 1979, Vol. 3, 233–245; E. F. Roots: 'Resource development in polar regions: comments on technology', in Francisco Orrego Vicuña (ed.): *Antarctic Resources Policy,* 1983, 297–315.

72. A publication of ecological non-governmental organizations has described the environmental objectives and principles of the regime as espousing 'strong sentiments in favour of protection of the environment', while at the same time the hope has been expressed that such principles will be expanded and more precisely defined; see *E.C.O.,* Vol. XXIII, N° 1 Bonn, July 11–22, 1983, at 3. For a summary of the views of US environmental organizations and the discussion of related issues, see Lee Kimball: 'Environmental issues in the Antarctic minerals negotiations', in Alexander and Hanson, op. cit., note 25 supra, 204–214.

73. See generally Chapter 5 supra.

74. Alistair Graham: 'Environment hazards in the Antarctic', in *The Antarctic: preferred futures, constraints and choices,* New Zealand Institute of International Affairs, 1983, 25–30, particularly at 27–30.

75. See the environmental considerations contained in *E.C.O.* cit., note 72 supra, at 1, 15–16; see also Alastair Machin: 'Preferred futures: an environmental view', in op. cit., note 74 supra, at 69–74; see also the report of the proceedings of the Seminar of the New Zealand Institute of International Affairs on *The Antarctic: preferred futures, constraints and choices,* op. cit., note 74 supra, held at the Victoria University of Wellington, 17–18 June 1983, in *N.Z.I.R.,* Vol. VIII, N° 5, Sept.–Oct. 1983, 2–5; and Lee Kimball: 'The future of the Antarctic Treaty System, Environmental community suggestions', in Alexander and Hanson, op. cit., note 25 supra, 237–247.

76. See Chapter 8 infra in relation to decision-making and functions of the institutions; on the question of regulated development and conservation see the Article on this matter by Holdgate, loc. cit., note 50 supra.

77. James N. Barnes: 'The emerging Convention on the Conservation of Antarctic Marine Living Resources: an attempt to meet the new realities of resource exploitation in the Southern Ocean', in Jonathan I. Charney (ed.): *The new nationalism and the use of common spaces,* 1982, 239–286, at 266–267.

78. Graham, loc. cit., note 74 supra, at 28–29.

79. Ibid., 28–30; see also Kimball, loc. cit., note 72 supra.

80. See note 76 supra.

81. The 1983 Draft Articles provided in this regard for the presentation of minority reports by the Advisory Committee, Article XVI, par. 6; this was changed, however, by the 1984 version so that the reports of the Advisory Committee reflect the views expressed by all its members, Article XVIII, par. 3; see also *1986 Draft Articles,* Article 26, par. 2.

82. For this and other proposals, see *E.C.O.,* Vol. XXVII, N° 1, Tokyo, May 22–31, 1984, at 2–3.

83. Graham, loc. cit., note 74 supra, at 27.

84. The participation of non-governmental organizations is discussed in Chapter 10 infra.

85. On this point see Chapter 8 infra.

86. See for example the Non-paper on the role of NGOs presented by interested groups on the occasion of the session of the Fourth Special Consultative Meeting in Tokyo, published as ANT 84/IV SCM/5 (NGO 4), Tokyo, May 28, 1984; see also Antarctic and Southern Ocean Coalition: *The role of NGOs,* ASOC Paper Nº 2, ANT SCM/7, October 1, 1985, published on the occasion of the Paris session.
87. See *NGO Non-paper on environmental principles,* ANT 84/IV SCM/5 (NGO 1), Tokyo, May 24, 1984; also *NGO non-paper on protected areas,* ANT 84/IV SCM/5, (NGO 2), Tokyo, May 24, 1984. Resolutions on Antarctica have also been adopted by the National Wildlife Federation, Sierra Club, National Audubon Society and other organizations; on these and other developments, see James N. Barnes: *Let's save Antarctica!,* 1982, particularly its appendixes.
88. *E.C.O.* cit. note 82 supra, at 2.
89. See *Non-paper on an Antarctic Environmental Protection Agency,* ANT. 84/IV SCM/5 (NGO 3), Tokyo, May 28, 1984; also *How might an AEPA work in a minerals regime?* ANT. 84/IV SCM/5 (NGO 5. Rev. 1), Tokyo, May 28, 1984; see also Antarctica briefing: *An Antarctic Environmental Protection Agency,* Nº 3, April 16, 1984.
90. Various proposals deal also with the concept of international measures for the conservation of Antarctica. See for example Auckland District Law Society: 'How strong is New Zealand's claim to the Ross Dependency?, *N.Z.L.J.,* 1980, Nº 4, 76–77, considering the alternative of a world campaign for Antarctic conservation; Edith Brown Weiss et al.: 'Protection of the global heritage', Panel discussion, *Proc. A.S.I.L.,* April 1981, 32–55; see further Chapter 10 infra for proposals on an Antarctic park.
91. The role and activities of various international organizations in the environmental field and related aspects will be discussed in Chapter 10 infra, with particular reference to UNEP, FAO and the United Nations.
92. On economic aspects of the development of Antarctic minerals, see the following works: Neal Potter: 'Economic potentials of the Antarctic', *Ant. J.U.S.,* Vol. IV, Nº 3, May–June 1969, 61–72; Neal Potter: 'The Antarctic: any economic future?', *Sci. Publ. Af.,* Vol. XXVI, Nº 10, December 1970, 94–99; John A. Dugger, loc. cit., note 71 supra; Giulio Pontecorvo: 'The economics of the resources of Antarctica', in Jonathan I. Charney (ed.): *The new nationalism and the use of common spaces,* 1982, 155–166; John Norton Garrett: 'The economics of Antarctic oil', in Alexander and Hanson, op. cit., note 25 supra, 185–190; Institute of Polar Studies, op. cit., note 61 supra; James K. Sebenius: 'Financial aspects of Antarctic mineral regimes', in Barbara Mitchell: *The Management of Antarctic Mineral Resources,* International Institute for Environment and Development, January 1982, appendix. See also generally Maarten J. De Wit: *Minerals and Mining in Antarctica,* 1985. For a discussion of the Arctic, see John Norton Garrett: 'Conventional hydrocarbons in the United States Arctic: an industry appraisal', in William E. Westermeyer and Kurt M. Shusterich: *United States Arctic interests. The 1980's and 1990's,* 1984, 39–58.
93. Pontecorvo, loc. cit., note 92 supra, at 157–158, citing the report by the Institute of Polar Studies, op. cit., note 61 supra.
94. Pontecorvo, loc. cit., note 92 supra, at 158.
95. Institute of Polar Studies, op. cit., note 61 supra, as commented on by Pontecorvo, loc. cit., note 92 supra, at 158.
96. Pontecorvo, loc. cit., note 92 supra, at 156–157; see also Dugger, loc. cit., note 71 supra, at 335–336.
97. Pontecorvo, loc. cit., note 92 supra, at 159.
98. Dugger, loc. cit., note 71 supra, at 339.

99. Pontecorvo, loc. cit., note 92 supra, at 158.
100. On the economic dimensions of giant and supergiant reserves that would justify their development in Antarctica, see Garrett, loc. cit., note 92 supra, at 188–189.
101. Stephen Zorn: 'The security of mineral supplies: impacts on developing countries', in United Nations: *Legal and institutional arrangements in mineral development*, 1982, 123–131.
102. Pontecorvo, loc. cit., note 92 supra, at 163.
103. *1983 Draft Articles,* Article XXX (d); the concept of reimbursement of costs of implementation of the management scheme was changed to 'levies' in the *1984 Draft Articles,* Article XXX, 1, d; see also *1986 Draft Articles,* Article 45, d.
104. *1984 Draft Articles,* Article XXX, 1, e; *1983 Draft Articles,* Article XXX (e); *1986 Draft Articles,* Article 45, e.
105. For a proposal on paying royalties into a central fund with a preferential distribution to claimants and the gradual elimination of the preferential treatment, see Frank Pallone: 'Resource exploitation: the threat to the legal regime of Antarctica', *Conn. L. Rev.,* Vol. 10, Nº 2, Winter 1978, 401–417, at 414 (also published in *Manitoba Law Journal,* Vol. 7, 1976, 597–610). For the policy of discouraging exercises of 'sovereignty' which might impede the flow of capital, see Nicholas de B. Katzenbach: 'Sharable and strategic resources: outer space, polar areas, and the oceans', *Proc. A.S.I.L.,* 1959, 206–212, at 211.
106. See Chapter 7 infra.
107. See Chapter 10 infra.
108. See generally Raymond F. Mikesell: 'Financial considerations in negotiating mining development agreements', in United Nations: *Negotiation and drafting of mining development agreements,* 1976, 7–20; Mike Faber: *Some policy and legal issues affecting mining legislation and agreements in African Commonwealth countries,* 1977, 30–81; Michael Faber: 'Some old and new devices in mineral royalties and taxation', in United Nations: *Legal and institutional arrangements in mineral development,* 1982, 104–122.
109. David N. Smith and Louis T. Wells Jr: 'Mineral agreements in developing countries: structures and substance', *A.J.I.L.,* Vol. 69, 1975, 560–590, at 566–571.
110. Ibid., at 572–577. On the effects of different tax instruments, including profit sharing, see Sebenius, loc. cit., note 92 supra, at 17–27.
111. David N. Smith: 'Conduct of operations and development goals', in United Nations: *Negotiation and drafting of mining development agreements,* 1976, 139–154.
112. Sebenius, loc. cit., note 92 supra, at 29–32; for the United Kingdom tax legislation, see generally Daintith and Willoughby: *United Kingdom Oil and Gas Law,* 1984, 1–1101 to 1–1194; see also J. A. Marshall: 'UK Petroleum Taxation: Where we stand in 1984– a look back and a look ahead', in Bentham, op. cit., note 25 supra, 1–21.
113. Sebenius, loc. cit., note 92 supra, at 28–29.
114. Ibid., at 30.
115. See generally Francisco Orrego Vicuña: 'La minería de nódulos: hacia la definición de un nuevo orden económico internacional para los recursos mineros', in CEPAL, Instituto de Estudios Internacionales de la Universidad de Chile: *Economía de los Océanos,* Vol. II, 1978, 293–325, particularly at 319–323; Giulio Pontecorvo: 'Reflections on the economics of the common heritage of mankind: the organization of the deep-sea mining industry and the expected benefits from resource exploitation', *Ocean Dev. I.L.,* Vol. 2, 1974, 203–216; Vincent J. Nigrelli: 'Ocean mineral revenue sharing', *Ocean Dev. I.L.,* Vol. 5, 1978, 153–180; Lance N. Antrim and James K. Sebenius: 'Incentives for ocean

mining under the Convention', in Bernard H. Oxman et al (eds): *Law of the Sea. US policy dilemma,* 79–99.

116. See 1982 Convention on the Law of the Sea, Annex III, Article 13.
117. Orrego, loc. cit., note 115 supra, at 321.
118. Dugger, loc. cit., note 71 supra, at 337–338.
119. Some incentives may be granted in the sea-bed regime by the Authority but subject to strict conditions of uniformity and non-discrimination; see Convention on the Law of the Sea, Annex III, Article 13, par. 1, (f), N° 14.
120. The approach of establishing separate Regulatory Committees of different geographical areas of Antarctica and other variations is founded on the need to take into consideration the existing differences as to resources, conditions, and other; see Chapter 8 infra.
121. For the deep sea-bed approach, see Orrego, loc. cit., note 115 supra, at 319 and see Convention on the Law of the Sea, Annex III, Article 13, par. (c).
122. *1984 Draft Articles,* Article XXX, 1, (e); *1983 Draft Articles,* Article XXX (e); *1986 Draft Articles,* Article 45 (e).
123. Sebenius, loc. cit., note 92 supra, at 2–5.
124. Convention on the Law of the Sea, Annex III, Article 13, par. 1.
125. *1984 Draft Articles,* Article IX; *1983 Draft Articles,* Article IX. These provisions, however, refer to non-discrimination only in relation to nationality. But see *1986 Draft Articles,* Article 15, which has enlarged the concept of non-discrimination in a substantive manner.
126. Orrego, loc. cit., note 115 supra, at 321.
127. See note 111 supra.
128. Convention on the Law of the Sea, Annex III, Article 13.
129. United Kingdom: *Petroleum and Submarine Pipelines Act 1975,* Public General Acts and Measures of 1975, Part III, Chapter 74, 2435–2593; see also Daintith and Willoughby, op. cit., note 112 supra, 3–062 to 3–115.
130. On State participation in the oil industry, see generally Daintith and Willoughby, op. cit., note 112 supra, Part 1, Chapter 3; see also Peter D. Cameron: *Property rights and Sovereign rights, The case of North Sea Oil,* 1983, 138–171.
131. Rosalyn Higgins: 'The taking of property by the State: recent developments in international law', *Rec. Cours Ac. D.I.,* Vol. 176, 1982-III, 263–391, at 351–352; see also Cameron, op. cit., note 130 supra, 80–85.
132. Higgins, loc. cit., note 131 supra, at 352.
133. Ibid., at 352.
134. On the concept of Resource Adjacent Nation, see James Joseph: 'The management of highly migratory species', *Marine Policy,* Vol. 1, 1977, 275–288.
135. Convention on the Law of the Sea, Article 142.
136. *1984 Draft Articles,* Article XXX, 1 (h); *1983 Draft Articles,* Article XXX, h; *1986 Draft Articles,* Article 45 (h).
137. Pierre Ch. A. Legoux: 'Depletion allowance', in United Nations, op. cit., note 111 supra, 34–42, at 34.
138. Ibid., at 34.
139. On this discussion, see ibid., at 39–40.
140. Ibid., at 39–40.
141. See Chapter 5, Section 5.6.
142. Legoux, loc. cit., note 137 supra, at 40–41.
143. See generally David Suratgar: 'International project finance and security for lenders', in United Nations: *Legal and institutional arrangements in mineral development,* 1982, 144–157; Philip Wood: *Commercial Bank project finance agreements,* Commonwealth Law Students' Conference, British Institute of International and Comparative Law, March 1984; Alexander J. Krem: *Financing*

ocean mineral developments: feasible under what terms?, in Krueger and Riesenfeld, op. cit., note 28 supra, 319–331.

144. *1984 Draft Articles,* Article XXX 1, i; *1983 Draft Articles,* Article XXX (i); *1986 Draft Articles,* Article 45, i.

145. Jorge Walter Friedrichs: 'Granting of rights, work obligations, waiver, stages of the agreement and time limits', in United Nations, op. cit., note 111 supra, 173–183.

146. *1984 Draft Articles,* Article XXII; *1983 Draft Articles,* Article XXII; *1986 Draft Articles,* Article 34.

147. Convention on the Conservation of Antarctic Marine Living Resources, Article XIX.

148. The institutional aspects of the budget will be discussed in Chapter 8 infra.

149. On preparatory investment in the sea-bed regime, see Resolution II of the Third United Nations Conference on the Law of the Sea.

150. *1984 Draft Articles,* Article XIII, 1 (k); *1983 Draft Articles,* Article XIII, 1 (h); *1986 Draft Articles,* Article 22, par. 1 (k).

151. Convention on the Law of the Sea, Annex III, Article 6, par. 3 (c), 4.

152. *1984 Draft Articles,* Article XIII, 1, l; *1983 Draft Articles,* Article XIII, 1, i; *1986 Draft Articles,* Article 22, par. 1, l.

153. See note 125 supra.

154. The problems of subsidies have been considered to a limited extent by the financial policy of the deep sea-bed regime; see particularly Convention on the Law of the Sea, Annex III, Article 13, par. 1 (f).

155. See the proposal by Australia and Canada contained in the following document of the Law of the Sea Conference: A/CONF. 62/L. 98, 13 April 1982; for a comment see Francisco Orrego Vicuña: 'Le regime de l'exploration et de l'exploitation de la zone internationale des fonds marins', in Dupuy and Vignes, op. cit., note 49 supra, 578–579.

156. The following Consultative Parties are parties to the GATT: Argentina, Australia, Belgium, Brazil, Chile, France, Federal Republic of Germany, India, Japan, New Zealand, Norway, Poland, South Africa, United Kingdom, United States and Uruguay; see John H. Jackson: *Legal problems of international economic relations,* 1977, at 410.

157. Orrego, loc. cit., note 115 supra; Antrim and Sebenius, loc. cit., note 115 supra.

158. See note 154 supra.

159. Leigh Ratiner: Statement at the Earthscan press briefing seminar on *The future of Antarctica,* 25th July 1977, New Zealand High Commission, London, at 16.

160. Ibid., at 16.

161. See Chapter 5 supra, Section 5.5.

162. See Nguyen Quoc Dinh, Patrick Daillier, Alain Pellet: *Droit International Public,* 1980, at 766–767, with particular reference to non-reciprocity; see also Antonio Remiro Brotons: *Derecho Internacional Público,* 1983, at 81–84, 330–332, with particular reference to the compensation of unequal economic conditions.

163. *1984 Draft Articles,* Article VIII, ter; *1983 Draft Articles,* Article III; *1986 Draft Articles,* Article 14.

164. *1984* and *1983 Draft Articles,* Article XIII, par. 1 (b); *1986 Draft Articles,* Article 22, 1 (b).

165. *1984* and *1983 Draft Articles,* Article XIII, par. 1 (c); *1986 Draft Articles,* Article 22, 1 (c).

166. See the Chilean report of the proceedings during 1958 of the preparatory working group for the Conference on Antarctica; text in Bush, op. cit., note 6 supra, at 27–28.

167. A proposal of this kind was introduced by Chile at the Fourth Special Consultative Meeting; see *E.C.O.*, Vol. XXVII, N° 1, Tokyo, May 22–31, 1984, at 3. This approach is reflected in the *1986 Draft Articles*, Article 22, 1, j, in which the Commission has the function to decide upon the disposition of funds, *inter alia*, by promoting scientific research related to Antarctic environment and resources.

168. Antarctic and Southern Ocean Coalition: *The Antarctic Fund*, 26 February 1985.

169. On the principle of protection of other uses of Antarctica, including scientific research, see *1984 Draft Articles*, Article IX, bis. On general aspects of scientific research in Antarctica, see Takesi Nagata: The advancement of scientific research as the basis of Antarctic development', in Francisco Orrego Vicuña et al. (eds): *El desarrollo de la Antártica*, 1977, 70–131; Lucía Ramírez: 'El SCAR y el desarrollo de la cooperación en materia scientífica', in Francisco Orrego Vicuña et al. (eds): *Política Antártica de Chile*, 1985, 131–146.

7

The distribution of powers within the regime: models and alternatives for accommodation

7.1 Basic interests and participation in the exercise of powers

Once there is no consensus as to who has jurisdiction over the mineral resources of Antarctica,[1] the problem arises that it is not enough to identify the powers to be exercised in the context of the regime, it is also necessary to determine by whom they are to be exercised, and how. It is on this point that all the interests of basic importance involved in the issue must be satisfied, and these therefore are the key questions which the internal accommodation has to settle.

Writers are in agreement upon the main interest groups that must be taken into account in order to effect this accommodation, together with the inescapable realities linked to each interest and the corresponding legal positions, with particular reference to the problem of jurisdiction. A study by Keith Brennan calls attention to four basic interest groups in this regard.[2] The first of these relates to those claiming sovereignty. In this connection Brennan observes: 'That sovereignty is real. It remains real notwithstanding the fact that other states do not acknowledge that it is validly exercised; and it would be quite unrealistic to entertain the belief that sovereignty will be abandoned either in form or in substance'.[3] The second fundamental interest group is that of the other Treaty Parties which neither exercise sovereignty nor recognize the validity of its exercise by others, in which connection the author remarks that 'it is equally unrealistic to believe that they can be persuaded to recognize the sovereignty of others or to submit to the exercise of sovereignty by others'.[4]

Within the last group there is yet another interest group, i.e. States which have a 'basis of claims', in relation to which 'again it would be unrealistic to believe that these States will abandon their bases of claim or agree to their extinction in form or in substance'.[5] The fourth basic interest group relates to a situation proper to the external accommodation, and covers the case of those States which consider that the resources of Antarctica are a part of the common heritage of mankind.[6]

In Brennan's view, the viability of the mineral resources regime depends upon whether a consensus can be reached by these several interests; he concludes:

> So let us understand at the outset that there are four groups of States, with differing positions, none of which will abandon its position. There is, moreover, a dimension to the position of each of them which we have to take into account. Each group has a political and diplomatic armoury sufficient to prevent an outcome which extinguishes or ignores its position. There is, in short, a four-way veto.[7]

The necessity of striking a complex balance of this kind between the different interests has also been the conclusion reached by several other writers. Barbara Mitchell has identified among the requisites for a minerals regime its acceptability to claimants, to non-claimants, to the signatories of the Antarctic Treaty as a group and to the broader international community.[8] Referring to the specific problem of sovereignty she indicates the terms of a possible understanding:

> However, acceptability to claimants need not entail recognition of their full sovereignty in the claimed sectors. If a claimant were to insist on its right to absolute sovereignty but be unable to assert control over mineral exploration and exploitation in its claim, the basis of any form of claim at all would be whittled away. On the other hand, if a claimant were to agree in advance to an abatement of certain aspects of its assertion of absolute sovereignty, mineral activities in its claimed territory need not be prejudicial to all its asserted rights.[9]

In an interesting contribution concerning the Antarctic system, Brian Roberts issued a similar warning that 'none of the Treaty signatories can possibly hope to obtain recognition of their exclusive rights to resources, wherever these may be found in the Antarctic. The other signatories simply will not give this recognition; nor, indeed, would the rest of the world'.[10] In quest of the balance of interests, this author also observed:

> It is not impossible to envisage a situation in which the Antarctic Treaty Consultative Parties continue to reserve all their claims to jurisdiction, but at the same time agree not to raise the question

of resource ownership. They could set up a joint licensing authority and establish a special regime with the necessary stipulations for protecting the environment, financial arrangements for licences, etc.[11]

In addition to the interests directly linked to the matters of sovereignty and jurisdiction, several writers have also identified some functional interests which must be taken into account in the accommodation formula respecting mineral resources. Charney underlines in this connection environmental needs, scientific research, military interests and the requirements of resource economics.[12] To all this is added, moreover, the need for the regime likewise to be acceptable to those interested in the exploration and exploitation of resources.[13]

The powers that must be taken into consideration for the purposes of effecting a distribution among the several interests mentioned and thus achieving the basic accommodation are easier to establish in the light of what was set forth in Chapter 5 on the content of a regime and in Chapter 6 on certain special policies. Brennan has identified five main powers of which an investor will require to have a clear knowledge: '(1) an undisputed authority for determining who shall have access to the area; (2) an undisputed licensing authority; (3) an undisputed regulatory authority; (4) a policing authority with undisputed powers; and (5) an undisputed revenue collecting authority'.[14] Some important additional powers are subsumed in the listing mentioned above, such as that relating to ecological protection[15] or that relating to the participation in various forms of economic arrangements.[16] How these powers are to be distributed among the interests identified is really the central question that the internal accommodation must settle.

The several theoretical models that have been put forward, together with other solutions, will be examined below, and will be followed by a discussion of the approaches and alternatives pursued by the Antarctic minerals regime.

7.2   Jurisdictional models and proposals for assignment and distribution of powers

The several general models for organization of mineral activities which seek to resolve the problems relating to the exercise of jurisdiction in the framework of the Antarctic system have already been examined.[17] These models have also been taken into consideration in the various proposals made with a view to ensuring the process of internal accommodation. Their different approach to the jurisdictional issue determines a similarly diverse effect on the questions proper to this accommodation.

Preservation of the status quo and absence of a solution

One option that has been proposed is that relating to the preservation of the status quo.[18] This approach had already been propounded as an option prior to the formulation of the 1959 Treaty, in which claims to sovereignty would have been maintained as they stood at that time;[19] Jessup and Taubenfeld, however, noted in this respect that it would have inevitably led to mounting international friction in the region.[20] In contemporary terms this option has been described as a strategy whose results 'would be to forego any legal arrangements for the purposes of resource and resource-related environmental management'.[21]

Although some writers recognize that maintenance of the status quo could be of benefit to the environment, scientific research and other values embodied in the present Antarctic system,[22] in practice it has serious drawbacks. Charney commented in this connection that 'the underlying jurisdictional issues, however, would remain unresolved, and no detailed rules of behaviour would be developed except pursuant to fairly low key understandings'.[23] This situation would bring a dangerous pressure to bear on the Antarctic system, and might be reflected in a renewal of the race for territorial claims, in imperilling the Treaty itself and even in the introduction of factors producing a military imbalance hitherto non-existent.[24] At the same time, pressure for a wider international participation would become unrestrainable.[25]

The establishment of a permanent moratorium, which would be the expression of this status quo, has been considered by many writers to be an unrealistic alternative. Roberts described it as 'wholly unrealistic in a world urgently seeking new sources of raw materials'.[26] From another point of view, in contrast, it would have the advantage of allowing change by stages within the system.[27] It has likewise been suggested that currently the Antarctic nations could clear the way to an international or regional consensus 'on the customary law for the area'.[28]

Weighed from the standpoint of the internal accommodation, this alternative really offers no solution. Partly because it does not resolve the jurisdictional questions, and partly because in practice it prevents approval of a regime which would enable mineral resources management. In this sense there would be no clearly defined powers to distribute among the various interests groups and no mechanisms or institutions for the purpose. The result of a 'non-solution' would obviously be negative for the Antarctic system.[29]

The territorial model and the claimants' benefit

In a model based on territorial sovereignty, the jurisdictional issue would automatically be settled entirely in favour of the State exercising that sovereignty. The five basic powers that were considered earlier would all pertain to that State, with no distribution among other bodies.[30] In the past this model has been much to the fore among the options for Antarctic organization, and it should be recalled that at one time, in addition to the traditional claimant, the United States and the Soviet Union have considered the possibility of making such a claim.[31] The category of States which have a 'basis of claim' derives precisely from this situation.

The alternative of a regime based on territorial sovereignty really admits of two different versions. From one point of view it is simply a parcelling-out of territory, which would lead to a 'segmented Antarctica'[32] or to this continent's being 'carved up into slices'.[33] Generally speaking, this approach is too simplistic and would undoubtedly create an atmosphere of confrontation both within the Antarctic system and *vis-à-vis* the rest of the international community.[34] Conflicts over sovereignty, overlapping of claims and other thorny questions would be further exacerbated.[35] This would call for a revival of the suggestion that recourse should be had to a decision of the International Court of Justice or other mechanisms in order to settle such conflicts,[36] an idea which has not been entirely absent from the contemporary literature.[37] Be that as it may, an approach that carries these negative implications would of course be prejudicial to the existing Antarctic system, which might be seriously affected.[38]

A different approach, on the other hand, is that which conceives of sovereignty in the context of a special regime. Jessup and Taubenfeld originally proposed the option of a 'limited national solution',[39] which 'would accept the national divisions but would attempt to ameliorate this solution by imposing various limitations on the sovereigns and placing servitudes on the area'.[40] The idea of neutralization and de-militarization was particularly favoured.[41] To some extent, the Antarctic Treaty takes up this proposition.

In the context of mineral resource activities, several proposals have some relation to this approach. One writer discusses the idea of a mutual recognition of sovereignties which might lead to reciprocal rights of access to the mineral resources of the area for nationals of the States concerned.[42] Another has proposed an outline regime under which claims to sovereignty are recognized, but their exercise is made subject to conditions with respect to mineral resources, including accepting the pre-eminence of decisions adopted by the Consultative Parties and the possibility of having recourses against measures taken by the territorial

State.[43] Fundamentally, the latter would enjoy the power of 'enforce-ment' and that of collecting economic benefits, but the regulatory powers would pertain to the Consultative Parties.[44]

Although several writers have rejected the territorial option out of hand,[45] the point must be made that in the opinion of others it has appreciable advantages. Charney explains in this connection that 'if by some means or another the territorial regime were to be established in Antarctica, the advantages of such a regime would be considerable',[46] mainly because the position as to the exercise of power would be made clear and because it would mean following the normal practice in respect of mining operations the world over.[47] In another writer's view, this model has the additional advantage of overcoming the difficulties involved in a regime of common property, especially as regards fore-stalling the activities of a 'free rider' and the economic problems associated with the exploitation of a 'common pool' of resources.[48]

Nevertheless, the difficulties raised by this model have also been acknowledged. In the opinion of several writers, de-militarization might be affected, scientific research might be hampered and, above all, protec-tion of the environment might be somewhat inefficient: all of which might ultimately make the Antarctic Treaty inoperable.[49] This will depend, of course, upon the specific approach adopted, for in another writer's version of the matter none of these situations would occur, and, on the contrary, all the relevant interests could be accommodated in the context of a regime based on territorial sovereignty.[50] Such a regime might even be, according to its modalities, 'the most effective vehicle for implement-ing the appropriate environmental controls'.[51]

From the standpoint of the requirements of internal accommodation, the main difficulty attaching to this model is that, although it adequately satisfies one of the interests that must be taken into account, it does not take equal care of the other interests actively involved in this field, especially as regards non-claimant countries and the international community.[52] Neither does this approach settle the problem of which territorial claims are valid in international law in an Antarctic context. That is why this alternative by itself is not a viable means of ensuring the necessary accommodation. Of course, the implication is not that there should be no room for the interests of the claimant countries, but that they will be recognized in a different way.[53] Furthermore, it must be borne in mind that the territorial model is not necessarily given absolute prefer-ence by claimant countries, since it may restrict their prospects, as will be mentioned further below.[54] There are also elements in this model which may be of interest to non-claimant countries.[55] Thus, the role played by the territorial issue will be important, though neither exclusive nor absolute.

Proposals for an Antarctic condominium
The establishment of an Antarctic condominium has been one of the recurrent ideas within the present system. It was given active considera-tion prior to the negotiation of the 1959 Treaty, mainly as a result of the diplomatic initiatives undertaken by the United States with a view to the creation of a general or partial condominium, but nothing concrete ever came of it.[56] In the contemporary phase of the discussion on the Antarctic this option has been put forward afresh by various writers,[57] and would also seem to have interested some governments.[58] Models such as general condominium, a *de facto* condominium[59] or a functional condominium applied to mineral resorces[60] or to specific ocean areas[61] have been some of the variants suggested.

The essence of this model is the joint exercise of State sovereignty over a given territory.[62] As in the case of territorial sovereignty, the several competences mentioned are assigned to a single body, which in this instance is the condominium. The jurisdictional problem is thus auto-matically resolved, since 'title to the mineral resources and the power to regulate their exploration and exploitation would rest with the con-dominium'.[63] To this extent the model has the same advantages that might attach to territorial sovereignty as regards the necessary certainty respect-ing jurisdiction, regulation and other powers. At the same time, it would mean that the conflicts among the several existing claims could be settled, and would allow Antarctica to be considered as a single State, or a single coastal state, for the purposes of territorial and maritime jurisdiction.[64]

However, the drawbacks of this model too have been duly analysed in the recent literature. To begin with, it has frequently been stressed that all recent cases of condominium have created difficult administrative situations,[65] one instance of which has been described as 'an administra-tive nightmare'.[66] Moreover, albeit it has been thought that a fusion of Antarctic claims would not be incompatible with Article IV of the Treaty,[67] the creation of a general condominium over resources signifies a more complex step, which according to some would necessarily entail an amendment of the Treaty.[68] Attention has also been drawn to the unfavourable reaction that such an initiative might trigger off in those countries that would have to formally renounce their claim.[69] Further-more, doubt has been cast on the efficiency of this model as regards the fulfilment of environmental preservation, de-militarization and other objectives, particularly on account of the political conflicts that would probably arise in the management of the condominium, and the fact that the rate of development would possibly be determined by the countries that were technologically least advanced.[70]

From the point of view of international law, Oppenheim has described the condominium as a piece of territory consisting of land or water 'under the *joint tenancy* of two or more States, these several States exercising sovereignty conjointly over it, and over the individuals living thereon';[71] until a settlement is reached on the question of individual sovereignty, the participating States agree upon a joint administration under their conjoint sovereignty.[72] However, Brownlie has cautioned in this regard that because the particular regime will depend on the facts of each case it is 'unsafe to rely on any general theory of the community of property';[73] in particular the analogies of joint tenancy and tenancy in common do not give satisfactory results.[74] This caution is particularly necessary in the case of Antarctica, where joint administration will not be founded on conjoint sovereignty for all the participating States, since some of them do not recognize the concept of sovereignty in relation to this area.

The main stumbling-block lies in the accommodation of the different Antarctic interests. While the interests of claimants and non-claimants would be to some extent met, since for the first the model would be an expression of sovereignty and for the second it would imply recognition of their right of access to the entire continent, the interests of the international community would not be similarly accommodated.[75] Problems would spring up in respect of participation and distribution of benefits that would be difficult to resolve in a model of this type. In this connection it has been said that of several solutions 'a condominium would probably be the least acceptable to the wider international community because it so blatantly and explicitly excludes outsiders'.[76] The mere fact that this approach involves a new claim to sovereignty would produce a highly unfavourable international reaction.[77] For these reasons, a condominium does not seem to be a viable alternative for ensuring the accommodation sought, and in practice the idea can be dismissed.

The open-use model and the non-claimants' benefit

The model based on the concept of open use is directly opposed to those founded on territorial sovereignty, since in this former case Antarctica is regarded as a type of *res nullius* or *res communis,* or a special area in which there is no place for the exercise of sovereignty.[78] Consequently, access to resources is open and, as we examined in Chapter 3, jurisdiction normally follows the principle of nationality or a special type of 'flag state jurisdiction'. In practice this approach implies extending the high seas regime to the Antarctic and its open spaces, an eventuality which in the opinion of one writer might also stem from a regime based on international custom.[79]

In this model the basic powers are exercised by the non-claimant States or by others that may be the beneficiaries of the open access in question,[80] so that the interests of the claimant countries are obviously disregarded. Nor could this alternative satisfy the interests of the international community, since open use benefits only the most technologically advanced countries. Moreover, the fact that a regime of this type signifies little or no institutionalization or regulation means that such values as those relating to the environment may be seriously threatened.[81] According to one writer, 'states are well aware of the potentially disastrous consequences of the free-for-all that could occur in an open use regime'.[82] Inasmuch as it fails to satisfy all the relevant interests, this other model likewise has no possibility of being accepted as a solution.

The Svalbard models: contributions and limitations

The several arrangements made in the case of Svalbard have also served as a source of inspiration for the proposal of solutions in relation to Antarctica.[83] A 1912 Protocol, which never came into force, established that the archipelago in question would have the status of *terra nullius* and would be under the administration of a Commission; access to resources would be tantamount to open use, subject to whatever regulations might be adopted.[84] While some authors have looked at this model with interest in relation to the Antarctic situation,[85] its identification with the open-use alternative makes it equally difficult to accept as a basis of accommodation.

The 1920 Treaty, on the other hand, which is still in force, was based on an entirely different principle, since besides recognizing Norwegian sovereignty it established some elements of internationalization to meet the interest of the forty States that are parties to the Svalbard Treaty, particularly with regard to freedom of access to resources, equality of treatment and financial administration.[86] This regime has been rightly described as one of 'tempered sovereignty'.[87] In this instance some distribution of powers was effected, for although they would normally be exercised by the territorial sovereign, the Treaty laid down precise limits for their exercise, which guarantee the interests of the other participant countries. Norwegian legislation on the exercise of jurisdiction also recognizes these limitations, in the following terms:

Norwegian civil and penal law and the Norwegian legislation relating to the administration of justice apply to Spitzbergen, where nothing to the contrary has been provided.

Other statutory provisions do not apply to Spitzbergen, unless specifically provided.[88]

The special rules of the Mining Code that are applicable also recognize some of the conditions deriving from this legal regime.[89]

The practical application of the regime in question has not been altogether easy and has given rise to several controversies of which the most important is that relating to the new maritime zones, of which an account was previously given.[90] On the basis of this situation, several writers have remarked that the possible application of the regime to Antarctica would be still more complex and fraught with difficulties.[91] Nevertheless, it is a first sketchy attempt at accommodating different interests, which as such has its merits. One author has aptly commented in this connection:

It is, however, impossible to apply the Svalbard solution in its entirety to Antarctica . . . . What can be lifted from the Svalbard model and applied to an Antarctic minerals regime, is the idea of an accommodation which recognises the sovereignty or sovereign rights of a state or states while spelling out the limitations on these rights and according specific rights to other parties.[92]

In different shapes and forms this is the type of accommodation that is being looked for in the framework of the negotiations regarding the mineral resources regime. At least from the standpoint of the basic interests of claimants and non-claimants, this model represents an approximation which excludes neither, and is thus differentiated from other models examined in which one or other interest is excluded by definition. It is in this sense that the approach seems more viable. That does not mean, of course, that it will not be attended by other difficulties, such as its complexity, the reactions that it might encounter on the part of the international community or its implications for the management of environmental policy, which in the opinion of some writers might be affected.[93]

7.3   Jurisdictional models of a functional type

Given the limitations inherent in the traditional approaches, another set of options concentrates on jurisdictional solutions that are not so inflexible. Thus the application of functional criteria can be seen as an effort to seek different ways of accommodating the relevant interests. In all these proposals, as formulated, the distribution of powers is more complex and never results in the assignment of all the competences to a single interest group.

Among the several academic propositions that were put forward in the period immediately preceding the negotiation of the 1959 Treaty, the functional alternative took a prominent place.[94] Jenks suggested a functional model 'which would reserve the views of all parties concerning questions of principle and particular historical claims without in any way impairing the effectiveness of the scheme . . . . The parties to the scheme could, so to speak, merge their claims and interests in Antarctica'.[95] Other authors suggested ways of contractual internationalization,[96] of internationalization in line with precedents set by certain waterways,[97] or other models.[98] This approach directly influenced the Antarctic Treaty itself, which is inspired by a similar criterion.

Proposals relating to shared or joint jurisdiction
The same tendency has recently found expression in other functional proposals which aim at working out a new jurisdictional formula for organizing the exercise of competences in Antarctica, with special reference to the question of mineral resources. The concept of 'Joint Antarctic Resource Jurisdiction' which was explained further above,[99] would be taken to mean that the parties 'declare joint exclusive resource jurisdiction over the continent and the continental shelf of Antarctica'.[100] In the context of this approach, the claimant countries would acquire rights over the mineral resources of the entire continent and the maritime areas, and at the same time could exercise specific management controls. This would also be a means of obviating the overlapping of sovereignties and resolving the situation of the unclaimed sector. The non-claimant countries, on their side, would obtain non-discriminatory access to resources and the exercise of rights under the regime. All this would be accompanied by a system of distribution of benefits for developing countries, with the object of thus satisfying this other interest.[101]

The proposition based on the 'principle of Antarctic community', which has also been previously explained,[102] pursues similar objectives. It proposes distributing decision-making powers between plenary bodies, and more limited bodies for the implementation of the decisions in question, and instituting procedures for the settlement of disputes, while at the same time different majorities for the adoption of decisions are suggested. Enforcement powers would be exercised through a system of reciprocal delegation between claimant and non-claimant countries which would prevent prejudgement of basic legal approaches. The distribution of benefits would also be one of the elements to be taken into consideration.[103]

The concept of a form of joint jurisdiction in the Antarctic sphere has also been worked on by other writers. Van der Essen has proposed joint jurisdiction of the Consultative Parties, with particular reference to jurisdiction over maritime areas.[104] Similarly, a co-operative approach has been suggested for the exercise of sovereignty in relation to the continental margin.[105] Several German writers have recently given their support to propositions of this kind. One author has remarked that 'the only approach feasible is to accept that the Consultative Parties exercise a joint administering authority over the Antarctic Continent which is equivalent to sovereignty and thus imparts the resource jurisdiction over off-shore areas'.[106] Another writes that the different positions in respect of the law of the sea,

> should not preclude a common stance in asserting Antarctic shelf and economic zone resource jurisdiction. There should be no fear of indirect recognition of claims to territorial sovereignty, if we justify Antarctic Treaty powers' authority not by individual or multiple sovereignty but by the concept of an evolving regime *sui generis* based on effective international administration.[107]

The identification of joint administration with sovereignty is perhaps a far-fetched proposition which would be more appropriate in the case of a condominium or even in a regime like that of Svalbard, since in either case sovereignty is formally recognized. In the case of Antarctica it is safer to delink the concept of joint administration from that of sovereignty as to facilitate the internal accommodation.

Another suggestion put forward on the basis of functional considerations refers to the 'jurisdictional ambiguity' model,[108] in which the aim would not be to resolve the jurisdictional problem but to find formulae acceptable to the different positions, as occurred in the case of the Canberra Convention and other precedents. In the latter case this approach was facilitated by the fact that jurisdiction under that Convention is more closely related to high seas rights than to territorial or sea-bed jurisdiction; in the case of the mineral regime, however, the territorial and sea-bed jurisdiction will have a greater weight, thus making 'jurisdictional ambiguity' somewhat more difficult to apply.

From a geographical standpoint, functional variants have been proposed which would distinguish between different areas. One model would be based on the establishment of 'zones' where the national authorities are granted certain restricted rights of sovereignty, combined with special international obligations.[109] It has been similarly proposed in relation to the Arctic that zones should be created outside national jurisdiction, under limited national jurisdiction and under exclusive national jurisdiction, although not prejudicially to other forms of inter-national co-operation.[110] In the negotiations on the living resources regime, too, a distinction based on geographical areas was suggested.[111]

The feature common to all these proposals is the search for formulae whereby the distribution of powers can satisfy the different interests and thus guarantee the internal accommodation. In the last analysis, it is a question of a multinational or of a limited internationalization approach, which is clearly differentiated from the national or total internationaliza-tion approaches, and has been appropriately described as 'pooling of all historic and legal rights and interests acquired by the Antarctic States in favour of a regime'.[112] Although other writers have expressed their apprehensions that this might affect national jurisdiction,[113] or conversely might be prejudicial to international settlements,[114] it is undoubtedly a pragmatic and as such a more realistic approach.

While some of these proposals are deliberately vague, like that based on 'ambiguity', or rather difficult to implement, as is the case of a distinction between various geographical areas, the basic approach of forms of joint jurisdiction and joint administration is very much in agreement with the fundamental trends that can be observed within the Antarctic Treaty system and its various resource regimes. No single jurisdictional formula is likely to emerge in relation to any matter of importance within this system, but joint exercise of jurisdiction provides a framework which has proven to be both viable and flexible.

The Antarctic consortium model

A variant of the functional approach is what is known as the consortium model. In the opinion of one writer this other model resembles the idea of 'Joint Antarctic Resource Jurisdiction' inasmuch as it involves joint and exclusive resource control by the Consultative Parties, but, on the other hand, it differs in that those countries 'would *jointly develop* the resources of Antarctica'.[115] In another formula, the consortium has been defined as a proposition by virtue of which 'states active in the Antarctic would merge claims to jurisdiction over resource activities and regulate them jointly while otherwise leaving questions of sovereignty aside'.[116]

In this connection it should be recalled that among the first proposals for organizing the mineral resources regime, the idea of an 'international stock company for the Exploitation of the Minerals of Antarctica' was put forward by Jessup and Taubenfeld.[117] Another proposal advocated the creation of an Antarctic corporation which would have the support of the Consultative Parties and the participation of private enterprise.[118] It has also been suggested that a consortium should be established to distribute capital subscription and shares on a broad international basis, and at the same time to serve as a mechanism for the transfer of technology and for environmental protection.[119] Several of the questions relating to the management of common spaces,[120] such as that of 'the common pool' could certainly be raised in the framework of a consortium.[121]

While this other model does something to help overcome the difference between claimant and non-claimant countries, since in general the exercise of powers is transferred to the consortium, it does not resolve the basic jurisdictional problem, nor does it satisfy the interest of any countries that might remain outside the consortium in question.[122] In this sense it is a partial rather than a general arrangement.

Models based on institutional arrangements
Many of the models of a functional type have found expression in institutional proposals, in relation to which it is sought to effect the distribution of the basic powers. Some of the suggestions that have been studied also contain institutional elements. Initiatives prior to 1959 were marked by strong emphasis on the institutional approach. In this connection Jenks pointed out that the functional approach could be reflected in the creation of 'common international services'.[123] One of the alternatives which this writer envisaged for the specific case of Antarctic minerals was that, setting aside the question of title over the resources, licences could be granted by certain designated States, which as a general rule might be those exercising authority in the continent.[124] Conditions for the granting of licences 'would be reasonably uniform and would be based on international rules'.[125]

Jessup and Taubenfeld also proposed, among several other alternatives, 'surrender of national claims to sovereignty to a supranational body'.[126] This body might have a limited character or be representative of the international community in a broad sense of the term. The several models that these authors have taken into account, in relation to the matters that would be the object of this form of organization, include the International Civil Aviation Organization, the administrative commissions of certain European rivers, the Caribbean Commission created in 1946, the South Pacific Commission, the International Maritime Organization, the International Whaling Commission, Eurochemic, UNESCO,

WHO and others.[127] As noted above, a consortium has also been proposed with respect to minerals.[128]

Some of the initiatives directed towards organizing Antarctic co-operation comprised proposals for the creation of commissions or similar managing bodies. One writer suggested in this connection the establishment of a Permanent International Commission and a system of jurisdiction based on the principle of nationality, or else the division of Antarctica into sectors for delegated policing on behalf of all the other States.[129] The proposals for an Antarctic regime made by Prime Minister Macmillan during his visit to Australia in 1958,[130] as well as the parliamentary debate upon them which followed,[131] also contained ideas relating to its institutionalization or the participation of international organizations, with particular reference to the United Nations. Other parliamentary speeches of the time also alluded to United Nations participation.[132]

The consultative mechanism of the Antarctic Treaty represents the institutional approach which stemmed from this group of proposals, albeit, of course, with a very limited character which stops short of intervening in the question of distribution of powers. Nevertheless, in comparison with co-operation mechanisms existing in the Arctic, it reveals a greater degree of institutionalization which has recently shown signs of strengthening.[133]

The current discussion of the mineral resource regime has also given rise to various institutional propositions in the quest for this internal accommodation. Some of them still tend to favour the assignment of powers to one of the basic interests, making no attempt at distribution proper. The model based on recognition of national sovereignty has included, in one version, that a decision of the Consultative Parties should be automatically binding on the sovereign State, including in respect of such matters as the payment of royalties, but this State would incorporate such decisions into its national legislation and would have the function of enforcing them.[134] Another proposition was based on the opposite viewpoint, visualizing an international authority which could conduct mining operations on its own account, and alternatively putting forward the idea of a 'parallel system providing the authority itself with the capacity to explore and exploit the mineral resources, besides its functions of a mere administrative and regulatory body'.[135]

Most of the institutional models, however, take into account the need for more complex arrangements to satisfy the several interests involved in the issue. In 1976 New Zealand officially proposed the creation of a Regulatory Committee, formed by the Consultative Parties, to monitor mineral operations.[136] This body would decide upon the establishment of zones in which such activities would be prohibited. Dealing with applications for exploration or exploitation would be one of the functions of the Committee, whose decisions would have to be unanimous, and it could also collect certain financial contributions. The Committee would undertake the necessary environmental evaluation of the various applications. Several writers have assumed that this model would be based on a private understanding between the contractor concerned and the claimant country in whose territory the activities would be carried out, whereby the benefits to be received by the latter would be negotiated, in return for which the risk of its veto in the Committee would be avoided.[137] This proposal by New Zealand was supplemented by other academic suggestions.[138] Commentators of this proposal agreed, however, that it would not succeed in satisfactorily harmonizing the several interests mentioned;[139] in spite of this negative view it should be noted that the approach of the New Zealand proposal was not altogether different from what is being discussed in the current negotiations, giving then a greater priority to environmental protection; given the combination and balance of interests involved it could well have provided a basis for finding a solution to the question of mineral exploitation.

Charney has analysed the several forms that could be taken by limited multilateral action, with particular reference to the establishment of a 'comprehensive international organization', or alternatively, an 'umbrella organization'.[140] This latter could confine itself to adopting uniform rules and handing over their implementation either to the sponsoring States or to a 'zonal enforcement' mechanism.[141] This zonal approach, which basically might coincide with the zones claimed in Antarctica, is a novel suggestion inasmuch as it tries to satisfy the interests of both claimant and non-claimant countries. The former could interpret their authority for enforcement and management as deriving from their claim, while the latter would understand it to represent a mere administrative expedient of the regime. While this approach is not without difficulties, it does approximate to the type of pragmatic accommodation which is necessary, and, as will be seen, is reflected in the minerals regime.[142]

Another recent proposition has aimed at the distribution of regulatory, executive and financial powers through an institutional system which could satisfy claimants and non-claimants alike.[143] The first of these powers would be invested in a Commission of which all the Consultative Parties were members and which would have to act by consensus. An alternative proposed is the establishment of a 'chamber system' for each of the categories of interests, under which decisions would have to be adopted by each Chamber's vote in favour, although the voting could be by simple or qualified majority. The executive powers, including the granting of licences, would pertain to the Commission, to smaller groups under the Commission's authority – such as an Executive Committee – or to governments appointed as agents. Financial powers would be exercised by the Commission, but income could be channelled to claimant governments, without detriment to the position of non-claimant countries.

As we shall examine in Chapter 8, the institutional arrangements within the Antarctic Treaty system and particularly those discussed in relation to the mineral regime, have in many ways reflected the institutional suggestions made by writers or governmental proposals. The active intellectual discussion that has taken place in relation to the organization of activities in Antarctica has influenced heavily the diplomatic outcome of the pertinent negotiations at various points in time.

However varied and diversified these suggestions might be, they all have one important point in common: the distribution of powers necessary to achieve the internal accommodation cannot be done in a vacuum but needs of an institutional framework within which that distribution might be undertaken and materialized. As we shall also see, the institutional component of the mineral negotiations has become the crucial factor in achieving this process of balance, compromise and accommodation.

7.4   Criteria of the Antarctic regime: the quest for equilibrium

In addition to all the models described, it must be borne in mind that various solutions relating to the total internationalization of the Antarctic regime have also been proposed. This approach, which will be discussed in Chapter 10, implies resolving the jurisdictional question by disregarding the interests of claimants altogether and satisfying only the viewpoint of the broader international community, albeit that recognition might be accorded to some expressions of those other interests. This option, of course, represents the opposite extreme to territorial sovereignty and the related models.

The prevailing tendency, however, is to seek middle-way alternatives which avoid extremes and contribute balanced solutions in which all the interests in question, including those of the international community, are represented. In this connection Edvard Hambro contrasted the option of a condominium *sui generis,* provided with common institutions, with the alternatives of taking no action whatever or of total internationalization, reaching the following conclusion:

These two extremes will probably not be easily acceptable to the contracting parties of the Antarctic Treaty. It is also improbable that the Antarctic states will prefer to return to the pre-treaty uncertainties. The remaining alternative is to develop collaboration under the treaty and to accept the advantages and burdens of closer collaboration in the hope that a wise pragmatism will prevent the states from shying back from fear of the spectre of a condominium *sui generis*.[144]

Similar conclusions have been reached by Brian Roberts,[145] Charney[146] and other writers[147] as regards underlining the expediency of these forms of limited collective action. In practice, these middle-way alternatives represent a form of partial and gradual internationalization, which, however, guarantees the accommodation of the several interests involved and is in general acceptable to the claimant countries. One author has aptly commented:

> The fact that the Antarctic model has the character of being a *de facto* internationalization model does not preclude, however, that the model leaves room, at the same time, for an at least implicit preservation of an – albeit limited – concept of *national* sovereignty.[148]

On this point yet another author has concluded:

> There is little doubt that, if the Antarctic regime continues to evolve as it has in the last twenty years, there will develop in the Antarctic something very akin to a condominium . . . . In such a situation, claims to sovereignty may well become a little academic. However, it is hard to see them being formally surrendered.[149]

It is this line that is followed in the current discussion on the mineral resource regime, and attention must now be devoted to the way in which this negotiation has approached the problem of distribution of powers.

Initial positions and evolution toward compromise
On the basis of the models described, it is not hard to identify the initial positions of the Parties in the negotiations on the mineral resources regime.[150] For the claimant countries the logical corollary of their exercise of sovereignty is to demand that all basic powers be placed in their hands. Among these powers special priority attaches to those connected with financial arrangements since the main interest of every claimant will necessarily be to obtain the economic benefits of exploitation, on the basis

of taxation or other mechanisms. At a second level of priority might be placed the regulatory powers, such as participation in the selection of applications or reception of licensing applications. Among these the granting of licences of course takes a leading place. The question of implementation or enforcement possibly commands a more relative priority, since it is not so sensitive an aspect as those mentioned above.

For non-claimant countries the point of departure is to envisage the exercise of all these powers under the regime, without recognizing implications of sovereignty. Beeby has offered the following explanation of these positions:

> The initial non-claimant answer to that question has been that, for the most part, regulation would have to be undertaken by the parties to the regime acting collectively through its institutions. No special role is envisaged for claimant states. The initial claimant response has been that, for the most part, regulation would have to be undertaken by States acting individually, even if in a manner envisaged by and consistent with the regime or possibly, in certain instances, pursuant to authority delegated by the institutions of the regime. In respect of areas of Antarctica subject to claims to sovereignty, the individual States having a major regulatory role would be those claiming sovereignty.[151]

But, as Brennan points out in relation to the five basic powers, 'it is not realistic to believe that consensus could be found for a regime which recognized one State's competence in all five of these areas . . . . On the other hand, it is not realistic to believe that consensus could be found for a regime which gave to a claimant State in claimed territory no power in relation to any of these five competences . . . . We would therefore have to look for some arrangement which claimant States felt did not extinguish sovereignty and which non-claimants felt did not amount to a recognition of sovereignty'.[152]

For this reason, the essence of the negotiations has consisted in seeking a distribution of powers under the regime which ensures the attainment of the above objective. A particularly notable fact is that States with each of the basic positions have been willing to take a step towards facilitating the accommodation sought. This is why in reality these initial positions were not over-emphatically urged and an early move was made towards consideration of the possible alternatives.

In reality, these choices are as many as imagination allows. The diverse functional models that have been mentioned reveal a variety of possible solutions. What matters is to bear in mind that whatever distribution of competences is effected will include the rules corresponding to the claimant State, to non-claimant countries and to the institutions of the regime. As there will be occasion to comment further below, this type of arrangement cannot be achieved unless institutions play a preponderant part, which explains why they figure as the third decisive factor in the accommodation.

The basic options for carrying out the distribution of powers under the regime can be summed up as follows: (i) that the powers proper to the regime be collectively exercised through the institutions; (ii) that they be exercised by the governments acting individually on the basis of a collective decision; and (iii) that they be exercised by the government alone, on the basis of the provisions of the regime but without the intervention of a collective decision. Given the fact that the first choice minimizes the role of the claimant countries and that the last in some measure maximizes it, the inclination to compromise began to steer towards a formula including elements of the first two options.[153] Within this framework, regulatory powers and other competences would have a strong institutional component,[154] but at the same time would leave room for some powers to be exercised by individual States in the context of the regime and of decisions adopted under its aegis.

Once this premise is accepted, the role of the individual States itself acquires a marked institutional significance, since in practice they act by authorization or delegation from the regime, albeit in the last analysis this is based on the question of claims to sovereignty. Presumably the interest of the claimant States will have been to secure specific recognition of their claims in this context, but obviously this would have meant a recognition, although indirect, which the other parties or interests would have refused to accept. In actual fact, given the strong institutional significance referred to, the point is not of any very great importance, since the claimants could dispense with this identification and accept that the same function be recognized in the framework of the powers of the institutions and of the designations or delegations which they may effect among the member countries. As regards the distribution of powers, the result is the same, but a structure is chosen which facilitates the necessary accommodation. In this way, while the Commission of the regime retains the collective institutional power, the Regulatory Committee provides the framework in which the claimant States act in a specific management function, all this within the institutional system and the equilibria that will be discussed in the next Chapter.

A point of importance in this accommodation would be the question of residual rights. In this connection it might be thought that the powers incorporated in the regime are only those to which that regime makes specific reference, while the other powers remain under national jurisdiction. Nevertheless, the tendency of the Antarctic resource regime is to be, in the main, all-embracing, i.e. including everything relating to the regulation of the resource concerned.[155]

Formulae for distribution of specific powers

It is the spirit of compromise described above that has predominated in the discussions of the distribution of specific powers under the regime. The respective approximation formulae can be appraised in relation to each of the five powers identified as essential.

As regards access to resources, the point of departure was a system sufficiently open to satisfy the interests of the Consultative Parties concerned to develop resources, but at the same time safeguarded fully to satisfy the interests linked to the region's ecological protection. The broad framework within which contractors may participate in Antarctic development and the functions invested in the sponsoring State are undoubtedly satisfactory to the non-claimant countries and to the contractors themselves. The procedure chosen to identify prospecting and exploration areas, as well as to determine whether they can be open for this purpose, likewise meets these interests.

In general, the claimant countries do not seem to have raised any objections to this approach, except in respect of some specific mechanisms such as the one which has been explained in connection with prospecting and the need for it to be authorized. The interest of this group will be met through its participation in the institutions and in decision-making. More specifically, this interest will play a part through the functions of the Regulatory Committee, which will begin its work as soon as the Commission accepts the application presented for a given area. This Committee will be empowered to identify precise blocs, to establish some initial payments and to discharge other functions, which, subject to the provisions of the regime, may well represent a special role for the claimant countries concerned.

This institutional accommodation does, however, have one limitation for the claimant countries, which Brennan explains in the following terms: 'A claimant State could not possibly tolerate a situation in which it or its nationals could be precluded over its objection from access to resources in territory which it claimed'.[156] It is for this reason, among others, that resolution of the question of decision-making procedure in the several institutions is essential to the accommodation under discussion. The writer cited comments that if this power were not recognized compensation would have to be given in the form of a clear benefit as regards general access to resources, on preferential terms in relation to those obtained by the other parties to the regime.[157]

This last question also raises an interesting consideration relating to the scope of the economic presence of the claimant State. Generally speaking, the initial premise is that the interest of the claimant is circumscribed to its own sector, mechanisms being sought to reflect this situation. On the other hand, it is also presupposed that non-claimants must have access to the resources of the whole region. This undoubtedly places the former at a disadvantage.[158] In the context of resources, the claimant must make sure of an equally broad interest, albeit it may be a specific one in relation to the sector it claims. Brian Roberts wrote in connection with his own country's interest:

> I have often thought that it might be best for the United Kingdom to look upon itself as a non-claimant state in all but name. In the long run, claimant states might well benefit most by helping to create a regime enabling them to have non-discriminatory access under license to the minerals of the *whole* area. Might this not be preferable to claiming exclusive ownership of minerals in a sector where exploitation can never be practical without international agreement?[159]

In Brennan's opinion, it is the licence-granting power that perhaps allows of most flexibility, and could be vested either in the Commission or in the governments.[160] In this latter case, it might be assigned to the claimants in their sector, or else to the sponsoring States. The regime has once again provided that in this field it should be the institutions that play the central part, so as to forestall interpretations that might favour one interest or another.[161] Nevertheless, it should be recalled that here too the Regulatory Committee has an active role to play, especially as regards the management scheme, an instrument which contains the specific terms and conditions of authorization.[162] As proposed, the draft management scheme is prepared by one or more States designated by the said Committee, possibly the State or States laying claim to the sector concerned. A function is thus recognized which these latter will interpret as pertaining to their sovereign status and the non-claimants will consider to be simply an administrative expedient. In any event, this procedure will be subject to the decisions of the institutions of the regime.

The regulatory competence is a more sensitive matter because of its impact on the sovereignty factor. Hence Brennan has deemed that it must necessarily be a shared power.[163] The negotiations of the mineral regime have approached this problem on two levels. The first relates to participation in the adoption of decisions on approving regulations or on enforcing them in relation to the authorizations specified in each contract. As regards the ecological dimension, which is the determining factor, agreement has been reached on the concept of the ecological veto, by virtue of which a decision by consensus is a prerequisite for opening areas to exploration. In other respects, as will be seen, opinions are divided as to whether a consensus or a majority will be required for the corresponding decisions. Some claimant countries haved been inclined to favour consensus as a manner of controlling any authorizations that may relate to their sector, but this is not a position exclusive to the countries in question.[164] For this group the ideal would probably have been to obtain that express consent on the part of the claimant be required for activities affecting its sector, but other institutional formulae, such as consensus, the positive vote of the claimant or some other majority, may set this uneasiness at rest.

The second level of distribution of the regulatory powers relates to the type of rule that must be approved by each institution. In addition to the basic rules contained in the regime, for every contract the corresponding guidelines must be drawn up, on the basis of which the management scheme will be formulated. These guidelines and other criteria are only of a general order, since the specific terms and conditions pertain to the management scheme; this means that it is the State designated to prepare the draft scheme that will be empowered to discuss those terms and conditions in the first instance, so that in principle, the claimant's interest is satisfied. It must be recalled that a further suggestion was that the terms and conditions should be approved beforehand by the Regulatory Committee, but there has been opposition to this since it would modify the aforesaid distribution of powers to the detriment of the claimants in question.[165]

Enforcement powers are easier to deal with, as they do not have so much bearing on questions of sovereignty and allow for a higher degree of delegation. According to Brennan's analysis, they might be assigned to the Commission, to the claimant State or to the sponsoring State, although the writer suggests the practical desirability of their being this last-named.[166] Various combinations of these bodies are also conceivable. The regime has granted functions in this respect to the institutions and to the participant States, with special emphasis on the role and responsibility incumbent upon the sponsoring State. This does not exclude the tasks that might fall to the claimant, especially if the Commission calls its attention to a specific situation. In any case, it should be recalled that these powers have been criticized as being unduly weak.[167] Furthermore, it must also be borne in mind that the applicable law has to be determined in the management scheme, and that this may have effects at the enforcement level. The comments made on the subject of inspection also relate to this other type of power.

The powers related to economic benefits: the crux of the matter
Of the five basic powers which have been discussed, the most decisive as regards achieving the necessary accommodation is probably that relating to the identity of the future beneficiary of financial payments and contributions.[168] For the contractor this is in general a matter of indifference, as long as the 'total regime take' is clearly determined. Nor are there any major difficulties as to who formally collects the payment or under what entitlement, since all this admits of many solutions. The determining factor is who, in the last instance, will benefit by this financial flow.

This power is closely linked with sovereignty and territorial jurisdiction. The territorial State will logically expect to have access to part of the minerals produced – perhaps in terms similar to those of the right held originally by BNOC[169] – or to obtain royalties, tax revenue or a share in the economic benefits. If production in Antarctica were to develop on an important scale the problem will be proportionally exacerbated. Consequently, Brennan points out that 'revenue collection would be an area in which claimants would have minimal scope for flexibility'.[170] This writer also stresses, however, that normally States do not impose payment of royalties or other charges on operations conducted outside their jurisdiction, for which reason there will possibly be no pressure on the part of the non-claimant countries to impose or share in such contributions.[171] However, even if non-claimants were to adopt such a liberal attitude with respect to financial benefits, they certainly would not take it so far as to recognize the claimants' exclusive right to tax mineral activities in the respectively claimed areas; the option of an express recognition of this right must, therefore, be realistically excluded.

On this basis, consideration might be given to the possibility of a pragmatic accommodation, whereby part of the benefit would be channelled to the claimant concerned, but without this involving recognition of its sovereign right. Brennan suggests that it may be described in a neutral fashion, as payment for services.[172] Among various options pointing in the same direction, it could also be thought of as a special share in the revenues of the regime for the claimant countries, which would be distributed according to some criteria to be defined; this recognition of the claimants' right to a special share could be understood as some form of compensation for the derogation of sovereign rights involved in the regime. Although this approach comes closer to the type of accommodation sought by the negotiations, neither it seems very likely to be accepted in view of the recognition, albeit indirect, of claimants' rights involved in this scheme.

According to Brennan the arrangement might be summarized in the following two conclusions:

> (1) It would be easier for claimant States to share power in regard to licensing, regulation-making, environmental questions and enforcement in claimed territory than to forego economic benefits . . . . (2) It would be easier for non-claimants to accept disguised economic benefits for claimants than to accept that regulations, including environmental regulations, or licensing, including the enforcement of the conditions of licenses, should be, or should appear to be, acts of sovereignty.[173]

Because of this situation, the idea that claimants might forego economic benefits of one kind or other must be equally ruled out.

The question of benefits is a crucial point not only in this internal accommodation but, as will be seen later,[174] in the external accommodation too, which means that distribution will have to take account of more complex interests. Similarly, part of the benefits will have to be used for administrative expenditure, promotion of research, and other requirements. Hambro's suggestion, to the effect that financial payments should be made to a common fund, might find its justification in this context.[175] This common fund could be distributed in accordance with priorities and by percentages among these several interests and needs.

The regime has provided for the types of contributions that will have to be made and the way in which they will be determined. Taxes and royalties will be defined in the management scheme, which opens up the prospect that the claimant State might obtain benefits by these means. However, there is no reference whatever in the regime to the idea of a distribution of those benefits. Beeby has explained that to facilitate the accommodation some of its elements will be 'hammered out *after* the regime has been adopted, through a continuing process of negotiation, on a case by case basis'.[176] Probably the distribution of economic benefits will be one of these questions that will be deferred. While this will facilitate the negotiations under way, the time will come when the issue will have to be faced, and possibly on conflictual terms, if no satisfactory solution is reached. Auburn has given a clear explanation of the problem:

The Beeby draft does not contain any direct provisions for methods of payment of royalties and taxes. However it would be suprising if non-claimants and superpowers consented to special payments to the claimants. The eventual outcome would seem likely to be an international grouping of States forming the Commission with relatively limited concessions to claimants. If this proves to be the case, then in effect sovereignty over territory such as that claimed by Australia in the Antarctic would be reduced to a mere vestige of rights.[177]

The choice of a postponement of the solution to this issue is inevitably linked to the various institutional arrangements related to the Regulatory Committee and the process of preparation and approval of the management scheme. If claimants are granted a veto in this context, or some other voting arrangement that will safeguard their role, the negotiation of financial arrangements in the management scheme will be ensured since the contractor will face the need to avoid a blocking vote in that process. The various institutional arrangements that have been proposed in this connection will be examined in Chapter 8.

Jurisdiction over minerals: pragmatism, combination and integration of principles

The approach adopted under this regime in relation to the distribution of powers does not settle once and for all, the problem of jurisdiction as regards mineral activities, nor does it attempt to seek a single guiding formula. As was explained before, the complexity of the Antarctic problem means that it is impossible to agree upon one jurisdictional principle only as a solution, and a pragmatic approach is preferable which tries to find the best choice for each situation.[178] In this sense, the minerals regime follows the Antarctic tradition and seeks to define formulae which meet the main interests concerned in the matter.

It may be noted that to some extent the principle of nationality is recognized, particularly as regards rules relating to sponsorship, responsibility of the sponsoring State and monitoring of the implementation of the rules of the regime, *inter alia*. Concurrently, a role is recognized for exercise of territorial jurisdiction, although it is not mentioned by name.

Participation in the Regulatory Committee, the designation of the State that is to prepare the draft management scheme and, above all, the determination of the applicable law which must be effected by this latter instrument – possibly including the territorial law – are expressions of the territorial principle in an institutional context which makes it possible to by-pass the question of formal recognition. The problem of financial benefits just discussed also stems from the principle of territorial jurisdiction. The delicate question of criminal jurisdiction will also be settled through determination of the applicable law mentioned above, whether the law chosen is that of the State of nationality, of the territorial State or of any other concept.

On the other hand, the strong institutional approach of the regime, and other mechanisms of a similar kind, facilitate the exercise of forms of joint jurisdiction over specific activities or procedures. To this extent, the regime transcends the rivalry of traditional principles by merging them in a common institutional ambit. As a result of the sum of all these factors, the regime is legally viable without the necessity of making a single pronouncement on the jurisdiction applicable, various criteria and procedures being satisfactorily combinable.

As has been made apparent, the feasibility of the accommodation and of the jurisdictional solution is heavily dependent upon the institutional system and the decision-making mechanisms. Without this other element it would be impossible to accommodate claimants and non-claimants, or to put the external accommodation into effect. This institutional system will be discussed in Chapter 8.

The approach followed by the Antarctic mineral regime is not really different from what has generally been the normal attitude of international law in comparable situations where national jurisdiction cannot be the single controlling factor for the attainment of a solution which will allow for the accommodation of competing or divergent interests of States.

The exercise of jurisdiction by the coastal State in the territorial sea is one instance where typically national jurisdiction will take into consideration the need to accommodate to some extent the interests of the international community, or at least of third States, thus allowing for some exceptions in favour of the jurisdiction of the latter. The whole concept of innocent passage and the stronger jurisdictional exceptions in the case of passage of warships though the territorial waters, stem from this attempt at a compromise between those different interests of the coastal State and third States.[179]

Transit through straits used for international navigation is likewise an example of jurisdictional compromise between the riparian State and the third States making use of such right under international law, a compromise that has emerged with greater clarity as a result of the negotiations of the Third United Nations Conference on the Law of the Sea.[180]

Even in conflictual situations affecting the right of innocent passage and the legality of certain activities under international law, such as those that took place in the *Pueblo* and *Mayaguez* affairs,[181] it can be seen that there has been an effort to reach a compromise settlement of the dispute by means of diplomatic negotiations, and only failing this has confrontation become the prevailing attitude.

By its very nature international law tends to keep away from extreme views or approaches and seeks to take into account the various interests that contribute to the formation and development of its rules. While historically this orientation could have been different, the contemporary system of international law no doubt exercises a moderating influence in the organization and rule of law in the international community. The Antarctic Treaty system and the orientation prevailing in the current negotiations on a mineral regime are no exception to this attempt at compromise and moderation.

Chapter 7 Notes

1. On the question of jurisdiction in Antarctica see generally Chapter 3 supra.
2. Keith Brennan: 'Criteria for access to the resources of Antarctica: alternatives, procedure and experience applicable', in Francisco Orrego Vicuña (ed.) *Antarctic Resources Policy,* 1983, 217–227. A corrected version of this study appears under the title of 'International Constraints' in *The Antarctic: Preferred futures, constraints and choices,* New Zealand Institute of International Affairs, 1983, 12–24. All citations herewith are to the original version.
3. Ibid., at 218.
4. Ibid., at 218.
5. Ibid., at 218.
6. On the proposals related to the common heritage of mankind, see generally Chapter 10 infra.
7. Brennan, loc. cit., note 2 supra, at 218.
8. Barbara Mitchell: *Frozen Stakes. The future of Antarctic minerals,* 1983, 57–71; see also a draft version of this study in Barbara Mitchell: 'The Management of Antarctic mineral resources', International Institute for Environment and Development, January 1982.
9. Mitchell, *Frozen Stakes,* op. cit., note 8 supra, at 58.
10. Brian Roberts: 'International cooperation for Antarctic development: the test for the Antarctic Treaty', in Francisco Orrego Vicuña: *El Desarrollo de la Antártica,* 1977, 336–356, at 342. This article was also reproduced in *Pol. Rec.,* Vol. 19, 1978, 107–120. All citations herewith are to the original version.
11. Ibid., at 343.
12. Jonathan I. Charney: 'Future strategies for an Antarctic Mineral Resource Regime – Can the environment be protected?', in Ibid. (ed.): *The New Nationalism and the use of common spaces,* 1982, 206–238, at 207–213.
13. Barbara Mitchell, *Frozen Stakes,* op. cit., note 8 supra, at 68–71.
14. Brennan, loc. cit., note 2 supra, at 219–220.
15. Ibid., at 220.
16. Charney, loc. cit., note 12 supra, at 212.
17. See Chapter 3 supra, Section 3.5.

18. William E. Westermeyer: *The politics of mineral resource development in Antarctica. Alternative Regimes for the future,* 1984, at 57–59. For a summarized version of this work see Ibid.: 'Alternative regimes for future mineral resource development in Antarctica', *Ocean Management,* Vol. 8, 1982–1983, 197–232.

19. The United States diplomatic initiative of 1958, which led to the convening of the Antarctic Conference and negotiations, expressly mentioned the concept of a status quo for the region. For comments see Philip C. Jessup and Howard J. Taubenfeld: *Controls of Outer Space and the Antarctic analogy,* 1959, 172–175.

20. Jessup and Taubenfeld, op. cit., note 19 supra, at 176.

21. John Lawrence Hargrove: 'Environmental problems of Antarctic resource management: legal and institutional aspects', *American Society of International Law,* 1976, Unpublished, at 11.

22. Charney, loc. cit., note 12 supra, particularly at 207; also see Westermeyer, op. cit., note 18 supra, at 58.

23. Charney, loc. cit., note 12 supra, at 221.

24. Ibid., at 222–223.

25. For a general criticism of the status quo in Antarctica, see also Frank C. Alexander, Jr.: 'A recommended approach to the Antarctic Resource Problem', *Univ. Mia. L. Rev.,* Vol. 33, 198, at 398–404.

26. Roberts, loc. cit., note 10 supra, at 343.

27. Westermeyer, op. cit., note 18 supra, at 58.

28. Charney, loc. cit., note 12 supra, at 221.

29. Francisco Orrego Vicuña: *El futuro de la Antártica,* Instituto de Estudios Internacionales de la Universidad de Chile, Serie de Publicaciones Especiales, N° 48, 1980, at 7, with particular reference to the problems of sovereignty; see also by the same author: 'La proyección extracontinental de Chile', in Francisco Orrego et. al. (eds): *Política Antártica de Chile,* 1985, 15–34.

30. Brennan, loc. cit., note 2 supra, at 220.

31. See Chapter 1 supra, notes 59 and 60 and associated texts; see also U.S. government: 'Antarctica', secret paper prepared by the Department of State, June 9, 1948, *Foreign Relations of the United States,* 1948, Vol. 1, Part 2, 1976, 977–987.

32. Christopher C. Joyner: 'Antarctica and the Law of the Sea: rethinking the current legal dilemmas', *San D.L.R.,* Vol. 18, 1980–1981, 415–442, at 435.

33. M. J. Peterson: 'Antarctica: the last great land rush on earth', *I.O.,* Summer 1980, 377–403, at 391.

34. See note 29 supra.

35. For a general criticism, see Westermeyer, op. cit., note 18 supra, at 59–63; see also Gerard A. Bertrand: 'Antarctica. Conflict or compromise?, *Frontiers,* Vol. 43, N° 1 Autumn 1978, 9–12.

36. For the early initiatives in this regard, see J. Daniel: 'Conflict of sovereignties in the Antarctic', *Y.B.W.A.,* Vol. 3, 1949, 241–272.

37. J. Michel Marcoux: 'Natural Resource Jurisdiction on the Antarctic Continental Margin', *Virg. J.I.L.,* Vol. 11, 1971, 374–404, at 399.

38. Rudiger Worfrum: 'The use of Antarctic Non-Living resources: The search for a trustee?', in ibid. (ed.): *Antarctic Challenge,* 1984, 143–163, at 143–144.

39. Jessup and Taubenfeld, op. cit., note 19 supra, at 177.

40. Ibid., at 177.

41. Ibid., at 177.

42. Rainer Lagoni: 'Antarctica's Mineral Resources in International Law', *Z.A.O.R.V.,* Vol. 39, 1979, 1–37, at 29–30.

43. Roland Rich: 'A Minerals regime for Antarctica', *I.C.L.Q.,* Vol. 31, 1982, 709–725, at 720–721.

44. Ibid., at 721.

45. See for example Peterson, loc. cit., note 33 supra, at 391–395.
46. Charney, loc. cit., note 12 supra, at 223–224.
47. Rich, loc. cit., note 43 supra, at 719–720.
48. Westermeyer, op. cit., note 18 supra, at 60–61.
49. Charney, loc. cit., note 12 supra, at 224; Westermeyer, op. cit., note 18 supra, at 61–62.
50. Rich. loc. cit., note 43 supra, at 720.
51. Charney, loc. cit., note 12 supra, at 224.
52. See note 29 supra.
53. Jorge Berguño: 'Criterios de aceptabilidad en un régimen para los minerales antárticos', in Francisco Orrego Vicuña, op. cit. (1985), note 29 supra, at 266–267.
54. See also Westermeyer, op. cit., note 18 supra, Chapter 6 on country analysis.
55. Rich, loc. cit., note 43 supra, at 719–720.
56. For a discussion of this approach, see, for example, Robert D. Hayton: Remarks of the chairman of panel on 'Legal problems and the political situation in the Polar Areas', *Proc. A.S.I.L.*, 1958, 135–136, 171–174; René-Jean Dupuy: 'Le Statut de l'Antarctique', *A.F.D.I.*, Vol. IV, 1958, 196–229; G. C. L. Bertram: *Antarctica today and tomorrow,* University of Otago, Dunedin, 1957, particularly at 25–30; US government, op. cit., note 31 supra. Jenks' views on the subject will be commented upon further below.
57. See, for example, Jessup and Taubenfeld, op. cit., note 19 supra, at 179; Barbara Mitchell: 'Antarctic riches – for whom?', Forum, *Mazingira,* August 1977, 71–77, reprinted in US Senate: *Hearing on Exploitation of Antarctic resources,* 1978, 70–76; Peterson, loc. cit., note 33 supra, at 395–397; Joyner, loc. cit., note 32 supra, at 437–438; Westermeyer, op. cit., note 18 supra, at 71–75. An author has identified the following five options for a mineral resources regime: World park, condominium, global regime, tempered sovereign rights and jurisdictional ambiguity, see Kurt M. Shusterich: 'The Antarctic Treaty System: history, substance, and speculation', *International Journal,* Vol. 39, 1984, 800–827, at 821–825.
58. Julia Rose: 'Antarctic condominium: building a new legal order for commercial interests', *M.T.S.J.,* Vol. 10, N° 1, January 1976, 19–27, at 26.
59. See generally Wolfrum, loc. cit., note 38 supra, at 144–145.
60. Edvard Hambro: 'Some notes on the future of the Antarctic Treaty Collaboration', *A.J.I.L.,* Vol. 68, 1974, 217–226; Rose, loc. cit., note 58 supra, at 26–27.
61. Marcoux, loc. cit., note 37 supra, at 400–401; Gregory P. Wilson: 'Antarctica, the Southern Ocean, and the Law of the Sea'. *J.A.G. Jour,* Vol. 30, 1978, 47–85, at 75.
62. On the condominium and other forms of divisibility of territorial sovereignty, see L. Oppenheim: *International law. A Treatise,* Vol. I, Peace, Eighth Edition, edited by H. Lauterpacht, 1962, 452–460; for a reference to Antarctic occupation, see ibid. at 556–557 in footnotes.
63. Lagoni, loc. cit., note 42 supra, at 30.
64. Westermeyer, op. cit., note 18 supra, at 73.
65. Jessup and Taubenfeld, op. cit., note 19 supra, at 11, particularly expressing criticism of the Condominium of the New Hebrides. For a favourable opinion of this experience see, however, D. P. O'Connell: 'The Condominium of the New Hebrides', *B.Y.B.I. L.,* Vol. 43, 1968–1969, 71–145. The experience leading to the independence of Vanuatu in 1980 also reveals the difficult relations existing between the administrating powers and the local communities; see generally Ron Crocombe and Ahmred Ali: *Foreign Forces in Pacific Politics,* 1983, particularly Chapter 1.

66. Rich, loc. cit., note 43 supra, at 717.
67. For a discussion of Article IV of the Antarctic Treaty in the context of a merger of sovereignties and related aspects, see W. M. Bush: *Antarctica and International Law,* 1982, Vol. 1, at 60–61.
68. Lagoni, loc. cit., note 42 supra, at 30.
69. Ibid., at 30–31.
70. Ibid., at 31.
71. Oppenheim, op. cit., note 62 supra, at 453; emphasis in the original.
72. Ibid., at 454.
73. Ian Brownlie: *Principles of Public International Law,* 1979, at 119.
74. Ibid., at 119.
75. Westermeyer, op. cit., note 18 supra, at 74.
76. Mitchell, op. cit., note 8 supra, at 89.
77. Ibid., at 89.
78. See generally Westermeyer, op. cit., note 18 supra, at 63–67; see also Jessup and Taubenfeld, op. cit., note 19 supra, at 178–179.
79. Charney, loc. cit., note 12 supra, at 224–225.
80. For a comparison with the Antarctic Treaty provisions on scientific research, see Mitchell, loc. cit., note 57 supra, at 77.
81. For the concept that open access can be environment degrading, see International Union for Conservation of Nature and Natural Resources: *Conservation and development of Antarctic ecosystems,* paper submitted to the United Nations Political Affairs Division for consideration at the General Assembly debate on Antarctica, 1984, at 34.
82. Westermeyer, op. cit., note 18 supra, at 64; see also Barbara Mitchell: 'Cracks in the ice', *Wil. Quar,* Autumn 1981, 69–84, at 84.
83. See generally Gunnar Skagestad and Kim Traavick: 'New problems old solutions', *Coop. and Confl.,* 2/3, 1974, 39–51; see also Lincoln P. Bloomfield: 'The Arctic: last unmanaged frontiers', *For. Af,* Fall 1981, 87–105.
84. For the text and analysis of the 1912 Protocol see generally Louis H. Gray: *Spitsbergen and Bear Island,* Government Printing Office, 1919; see also for comments on the approach of this Protocol, Robert Lansing: 'A unique international problem', *A.J.I.L.,* Vol. 11, 1917, 763–771; Fred K. Nielsen: 'The solution of the Spitsbergen question', *A.J.I.L.,* Vol. 14, 1920, 232–235. See also generally Mitchell, op. cit., note 8 supra, at 87–88, where the 1912 Protocol is compared to a condominium.
85. Jessup and Taubenfeld, op. cit., note 19 supra, at 181.
86. Treaty concerning the archipelago of Spitsbergen, signed at Paris, February 9, 1920, *League of Nations Treaty Series,* Vol. 2, 1920, N° 1, 8–19 (N° 41); also published in *A.J.I.L.,* Supplement, Vol. 18, 1924, 199–208. For the status of ratifications, see Clive Parry and Charity Hopkins (compilators): *An index of British Treaties, 1101–1968,* HMSO, 1970, Vol. 2, 605–606; it is of interest to note that all the present Antarctic Treaty Consultative Parties, with the exception of Brazil and Uruguay, are parties to the 1920 Spitsbergen Treaty. For the texts of treaties and regulations, see also Willy Ostreng: *Politics in High Latitudes. The Svalbard Archipelago,* 1977, in appendixes; see also Carl August Fleischer: 'Le regime d'exploitation du Spitsberg (Svalbard)', *A.F.D.I.,* 1978, 275–300.
87. Mitchell, op. cit., note 8 supra, at 105; see also Westermeyer, op. cit., note 18 supra, at 67.
88. Norway: Act of 17 July 1925 relating to Spitzbergen, Article 2, text in Ostreng, op. cit., note 86 supra, at 105–108.
89. Norway: The Mining Code (the Mining Regulations) for Spitzbergen, laid down by Royal Decree of 7 August, 1925, as amended by Royal Decree of 11 June 1975; text in Ostreng, op. cit., note 86 supra, at 108–116.

90. See Chapter 4 supra, Section 4.5, note 166 and associated text; see also Willy Ostreng: 'Soviet – Norwegian relations in the Arctic', *International Journal,* Vol. 39, 1984, 866–887, where a package deal settlement is proposed in terms of agreeing upon a line favourable to the USSR in the Barents Sea area in exchange for accepting the Norwegian view about the Svalbard maritime areas, at 884–887.

91. For a criticism of the analogy of Spitsberg and Antarctica, see Hambro, loc. cit., note 60 supra, at 224.

92. Mitchell, op. cit., note 8 supra, at 109; emphasis in the original.

93. Westermeyer, op. cit., note 18 supra, at 70–71.

94. See generally Jessup and Taubenfeld, op. cit., note 19 supra, 171–190, 251–282; see also Jessup and Taubenfeld: 'Outer Space, Antarctica, and the United Nations', *I.O.,* Vol. XIII, 1959, 363–379; Philip C. Jessup: 'Sovereignty in Antarctica', *A.J.I.L.,* Vol. 41, 1947, 117–119; Howard J. Taubenfeld: 'A Treaty for Antarctica', *Int. Conc.,* N° 531, January 1961, 245–322; Walter Sullivan: 'Antarctica in a two-power world', *For. Af.,* Vol. 36, 1957–1958, 154–166.

95. C. Wilfred Jenks: *The Common Law of Mankind,* 1958, Chapter 8: 'An international regime for Antarctica?', 366–381 at 369; see also the article by the same author: 'An International Regime for Antarctica?', *Int. Af.,* Vol. 32, 1956, 414–426. For comments on this approach see also Bertram, op. cit., note 56 supra at 25–30.

96. Dupuy, loc. cit., note 56 supra, at 216–218.

97. Hayton, loc. cit., note 56 supra, at 173.

98. For a general description of various early models proposed for the organization or internationalization of Antarctica, see L. F. E. Goldie: 'International relations in Antarctica', *Aust. Quar,* Vol. XXX, N° 1, March 1958, 7–29.

99. See Chapter 3 supra, Section 3.5.

100. Alexander, loc. cit., note 25 supra, at 417; see also Westermeyer, op. cit., note 18 supra, at 75–78.

101. For a general description of this proposal see also Kurt Michael Shusterich: *Resource Management and the oceans. The policital economy of Deep Sea-bed Mining,* Particularly Chapter 6: 'Precedents for other global commons', at 161–193 and Appendix 14, at 290–293.

102. See note 99 supra.

103. See generally Steven J. Burton: 'New stresses on the Antarctic Treaty: toward international legal institutions governing Antarctic resources', *Virg. L.R.,* Vol. 65, 1979, 421–512.

104. Alfred van der Essen: 'The application of the law of the sea to the Antarctic continent', in Francisco Orrego Vicuña, op. cit., note 2 supra, 231–242, at 242.

105. Marcoux, loc. cit., note 37 supra, at 400–401.

106. Wolfrum, loc. cit., note 38 supra, at 150–151.

107. Scharnhorst Muller: 'The impact of UNCLOS III on the Antarctic Regime', in Rudiger Wolfrum, op. cit., note 38 supra, at 175.

108. Mitchell, op. cit., note 8 supra, at 114–125.

109. Skagestad and Traavik, loc. cit., note 83 supra, 39–51, at 49.

110. Finn Sollie: 'The new development in the Polar Regions', *Coop. and Confl.,* N° 2/3, 1974, 23–37, at 36.

111. See Chapter 4 supra, Section 4.5, note 146 and associated text.

112. Rudy J. Cerone: 'Survival of the Antarctic Treaty: economic self-interest v. Enlightened International Cooperation', *Bost. Coll. I.C.L.R.,* Vol. 2, 1978, 115–129, at 128.

113. Finn Sollie: 'Arctic and Antarctic. Current problems in the Polar Regions', *Coop. and Confl.,* N° 2, 1969, 124–144.

114. Bernard H. Oxman: 'The Antarctic Regime: an introduction', *Univ. Mia.L.Rev,* Vol. 33, 1978, 285–297.

115. Westermeyer, op. cit., note 18 supra, at 78; emphasis in the original.
116. Peterson, loc. cit., note 33 supra, at 397.
117. Jessup and Taubenfeld, op. cit., note 19 supra, at 188.
118. Leigh Ratiner: Statement at press briefing Seminar on the Future of Antarctica, *Earthscan,* 25 July 1977.
119. Westermeyer, op. cit., note 18 supra, at 78–79.
120. For the concept of a 'joint economic zone' around the Antarctic land mass and the ownership of the resources by Consultative Parties, see Mitchell, loc. cit., note 57 supra, at 76.
121. See generally Garrett Hardin and John Baden (eds): *Managing the commons,* 1977.
122. Westermeyer, op. cit., note 18 supra, at 79.
123. Jenks, op. cit., note 95 supra, at 371.
124. Ibid., at 377.
125. Ibid., at 378.
126. Jessup and Taubenfeld, op. cit., note 19 supra, at 180.
127. Ibid., at 183–190.
128. See note 117 supra and associated text.
129. Daniel, loc. cit., note 36 supra, at 271.
130. Robert D. Hayton: 'Polar problems and international law', Notes and Comments, *A.J.I.L.,* Vol. 52, 1958, 746–765, at 755.
131. United Kingdom, House of Commons: Questions on the Prime Minister's statement on international control of Antarctica, *Hansard,* 18 February 1958; see also *Hansard,* 19 February 1958; House of Lords: Statement by Lord Shackleton on neutralization of Antarctica, and reply by Earl Attlee, *Hansard,* House of Lords, Vol. 216, N° 70, 4 May 1959, ast 42–43, 54.
132. United Kingdom, House of Commons: Question on United Nations and Antarctica, *Hansard,* 13 June 1956.
133. On institutional aspects of the Antarctic Treaty system, see Chapter 8 infra. With regard to developments in the Arctic, see generally Bo Johnson Theutenberg: *The evolution of the Law of the Sea. A study of resources and strategy with special regard to the Polar areas,* 1984.
134. Rich, loc. cit., note 43 supra, at 720–721.
135. Lagoni, loc. cit., note 42 supra, at 35.
136. For discussion of this proposal, see Barbara Mitchell: 'Resources in Antarctica. Potential for conflict', *Marine Policy,* Vol. 1, 1977, 91–101, particularly at 101.
137. Westermeyer, op. cit., note 18 supra, at 80.
138. Mitchell, op. cit., note 8 supra, at 120–125.
139. Westermeyer, op. cit., note 18 supra, at 80–81.
140. Charney, loc. cit., note 12 supra, at 225–229.
141. Ibid., at 226, 228–229.
142. See in particular Chapter 8 infra.
143. Burton, loc. cit., note 103 supra, at 485–497.
144. Hambro, loc. cit., note 60 supra, at 226.
145. Roberts, loc. cit., note 10 supra, at 343.
146. Charney, loc. cit., note 12 supra, at 229.
147. Jonathan I. Charney: 'Development of Antarctica', Remarks, *Proc. ASIL,* 1979, 268–271; see also Stuart Harris: 'A review of Australia's Antarctic Policy options', in Stuart Harris (ed.): *Australia's Antarctic Policy Options,* 1984, 1–28; US Department of State: 'Statements by US representatives at the Eighth Consultative Meeting on the question of Antarctic mineral resources', *A.J.I.L.,* Vol. 70, 1976, 113–115 (also published in *Digest of US Practice in International Law,* 1975, 104–107).

148. Gunnar Skagestad: 'The frozen frontier: models for international cooperation', *Coop. and Confl,* 3, 1975, 167–187, at 180.
149. R. H. Wyndham: 'The Antarctic', in Coral Bell (ed.): *Agenda for the eighties,* Australian National University Press 1980, 179–196, at 196.
150. See generally Francisco Orrego Vicuña: 'The definition of a regime on Antarctic mineral resources: basic options', in: Ibid., op. cit., note 2 supra, 199–215.
151. C. D. Beeby: 'An overview of the problems which should be addressed in the preparation of a regime governing the mineral resources of Antarctica', in Francisco Orrego Vicuña, op. cit., note 2 supra, 191–198, at 195.
152. Brennan, loc. cit., note 2 supra, at 220. Similar arrangements are often needed in international law in order to attain an acceptable settlement of contentious issues, a case in point being the *Manhattan's* voyage through Canadian Arctic Water Zones and the ensuing discussion about the rights of the parties; on the legal issues see generally Louis Henkin: 'Arctic anti-pollution: does Canada make – or break – International Law?', *A.J.I.L.,* Vol. 65, 1971, 131–136.
153. See generally Beeby, loc. cit., note 151 supra.
154. Ibid., at 195.
155. See generally Chapter 2 supra.
156. Brennan, loc. cit., note 2 supra, at 222.
157. Ibid., at 222.
158. Orrego, loc. cit., note 150 supra, at 209.
159. Roberts, loc. cit., note 10 supra, at 343; emphasis in the original.
160. Brennan, loc. cit., note 2 supra, at 222–223.
161. See generally Chapter 5 supra and Chapter 8 infra.
162. See Chapter 8 infra.
163. Brennan, loc. cit., note 2 supra, at 223.
164. The question of consensus also played a very important role in the negotiations of Part XI of the Law of the Sea Convention and the pertinent institutional arrangements; on consensus in the Conference on the Law of the Sea, see generally Giuseppe Barile: 'The way of negotiating at the Third United Nations Conference on the Law of the Sea', in C. L. Rozakis and C. A. Stephanou (eds): *The New Law of the Sea,* 1983, 21–31.
165. See Chapter 5 supra.
166. Brennan, loc. cit., note 2 supra, at 223.
167. See Chapter 5 supra.
168. On the financial aspects of the regime, see Chapter 6 supra, Section 6.2.
169. See Chapter 6 supra, Section 6.2, note 129 and associated text.
170. Brennan, loc. cit., note 2 supra, at 224.
171. Ibid., at 224.
172. Ibid., at 224. The *1983 Draft Articles* had introduced in Article XXX the concept of reimbursement by the contractor of the costs of implementation of the management scheme, a concept which could imply the recognition of a management role of claimant countries in the context of the management scheme and the pertinent financial payment for this service; this concept was not retained in the *1984 Draft Articles* or later revisions.
173. Brennan, loc. cit., note 2 supra, at 227.
174. See Chapter 10 infra.
175. Hambro, loc. cit., note 60 supra, at 224.
176. Beeby, loc. cit., note 151 supra, at 196; emphasis in the original.
177. Francis Auburn: 'Antarctic Minerals and the Third World', *FRAM: the Journal of Polar Studies,* winter 1984, 201–223, at 208.
178. See generally Chapter 3 supra.
179. Brownlie refers to innocent passage as 'a sensible form of accommodation

between the necessities of sea communication and the interests of the coastal state', op. cit., note 73 supra, at 204; for the legal regime of the territorial sea, see Ibid., at 203–209.

180. For a discussion of the regime of Straits in international law, see Brownlie, op. cit., note 73 supra, at 279–283.

181. See generally Adeoye Akinsanya: 'The "Pueblo" Affair and international law', *Indian Journal of International Law,* Vol. 15, 1975, 485–500; Stephan B. Finch Jr: 'Pueblo and Mayaguez: a legal analysis', *Case West. R.J.I.L.,* Vol. 9, 1977, 79–116; Robert E. Ward: 'The *Mayaguez;* the right of innocent passage and the legality of reprisal', *S.D.L.R.,* Vol. 13, 1975–1976, 765–778; Eleanor C. McDowell: 'Contemporary practice of the United States relating to international law: SS Mayaguez incident', *A.J.I.L.,* Vol. 69, 1975, 875–879.

8

The institutional system of the mineral regime

8.1 Institutional development in the framework of the Antarctic Treaty system

The institutional approach followed by the Antarctic Treaty has been of a rather elemental nature. In spite of the fact that the academic and diplomatic debate that preceded this instrument had a strong institutional emphasis,[1] the negotiators of the Treaty opted for the machinery of Consultative Meetings, i.e. for the Consultative Parties to meet periodically on a rotational basis, without the support of permanent organs.[2] This decision was certainly closely related to the question of the disputed claims of sovereignty since certain countries feared that any form of institutionalization might, as a concomitant, signify a process of internationalization that would affect their claims or rights.[3]

Within this approach, the central role in the management of the Antarctic Treaty system devolves on the Consultative Parties, whether founder members or whether admitted subsequently.[4] Even though the latter, in accordance with the Treaty, participate only during such time as they demontrate an interest in Antarctica by conducting substantial scientific research there,[5] the exercise of rights is identical for all the Consultative Parties. Furthermore, there is little likelihood in practice that a State that has acceded as a Consultative Party would subsequently be deprived of that status. This predominant role of the Consultative Parties in the management of the system is one of the basic characteristics of its institutional arrangements and has given rise to the concept of their 'special responsibility' in this and in other fields;[6] as we shall see, the consultative status has also been one of the features provoking most objection from third States.

The machinery for decision-making in the framework of the Consultative Meetings generally conforms to the same philosophy whereby a central role is played by each of the Consultative Parties. The Treaty does not, strictly speaking, deal with decision-making but only with the way in which the measures approved by these meetings are to enter into force by providing that they 'shall become effective when approved by all the Contracting Parties' which have the status of Consultative Parties.[7] The requirement of unanimity for the entry into force of the approved measures has been made more flexible through the practice within the system.[8] In spite of the fact that Consultative Parties have in practice a veto both at the stage of approval of recommendations at Consultative Meetings and subsequently at the stage of confirmation,[9] this does not necessarily mean that unanimity is required for the approval of such measures at Consultative Meetings.

The rules of procedures provide, indeed, that recommendations be approved 'by all the representatives present', which means that the absence of one Consultative Party does not prevent the approval of a decision.[10] This is inherently different from unanimity which would require an affirmative vote of all the Consultative Parties, without exception. On the basis of this rule it might further be inferred that an abstention cannot impede the approval of a decision since it involves a situation comparable to that of not being present. Thus, it might also be inferred that what is required is not unanimity but the absence of any formal objection, or of a negative vote, as occurs in several other Antarctic instruments.[11]

On this point the voting arrangements in international organizations provide interesting precedents,[12] particularly in relation to the questions raised by abstention in the voting procedures;[13] the practice of the United Nations Security Council in so far as abstention and absence is concerned is highly relevant in this regard.[14]

One author points out in connection with the Antarctic arrangements that the procedure for the adoption of decisions has always been interpreted in the practice of the system as a 'mechanism of consensus – and it is precisely this interpretation which has made all the achievements of the Antarctic System possible'.[15] It is well known that the concept of consensus, as embodied in various aspects of contemporary practice, differs from the idea of unanimity or of a simple power of veto.[16] This approach is of course designed to give greater flexibility and institutional effectiveness to the Antarctic system.

The institutional arrangements of the 1959 Treaty have been criticized as inadequate, particularly on account of the fact that the Treaty has no secretariat or permanent archive of its own.[17] However, in looking beyond the formal aspects, it is necessary to ask whether this institutional lack has affected the substantive operation of the system. Haas has described the concept of a regime as 'norms, rules, and procedures agreed to in order to regulate an issue area',[18] or, to use the words of another author, 'regimes are social institutions governing the actions of those interested in specifiable activities'.[19] With regard to these regimes, it has also been said that 'like other structures, regimes may be more or less formally articulated, and they may or may not be accompanied by explicit organizational arrangements'.[20] Commenting on the institutional experience of the International North Pacific Fisheries Convention, one author concluded that 'this suggests that decentralized systems of compliance mechanisms may be workable in specific, real world situations . . . there is nothing in the record of the INPFC to lead to the conclusion that a centralized public authority with substantial enforcement capabilities is necessary to achieve high levels of compliance with prescriptions of this sort'.[21]

These views, which are largely looking into the internal operation of the respective systems analysed, will not necessarily influence the perception of third States in regard to those arrangements, which based on an external perspective can be highly critical of the arrangements in question. On the other hand, there is of course a difference between having an institution with limited enforcement powers, like the Commission of INPFC, and not having any institution at all; in the first case, enforcement powers are left to States parties nationally, which is a common feature of many international organizations, while in the second situation there might be a vacuum as to the very existence of enforcement powers of any kind. However, as we shall see, this is a situation that the Antarctic Treaty system has been gradually correcting in the course of its evolution.

Analysing the operation of the Antarctic Treaty system from the point of view of its effectiveness, it may be pointed out that it has not been generally impaired by the lack of institutions. On the contrary, this very feature has helped the flexibility of the Antarctic Treaty system since, as Scully concludes, 'the lack of institutional provisions in the Treaty, therefore, appears to stem more from an intentional desire to provide flexibility in future institutional development rather than an inability to agree upon institutional mechanisms'.[22] In similar vein, Van der Essen describes the Consultative Meetings as 'the dynamic element of the Treaty' and concludes:

> above all, it has created and maintained what has been termed 'the spirit of the Antarctic Treaty'. The latter is characterized by the systematic refusal of any confrontation, the quest for compromise whereby the views and interests of all parties are taken

into account, the constant endeavour to understand the sometimes divergent positions of delegations.[23]

Approach adopted by the first resources regimes
The characteristics that have been described have proved adequate for
the type of co-operation originally envisaged by the Antarctic Treaty.
However, with the gradual development of this co-operation towards the
regulation of resources and the devising of special regimes for that
purpose, the institutional needs consequently took a different form.
Through the close links between the Consultative Meetings and SCAR,
this scientific body became 'a primary source in identification of issues
requiring collective treatment by the Consultative Parties'[24] many of
which were concerned with living and non-living resources and with the
needs of environmental conservation and preservation. It was these
problems that gave rise to the institutional evolution of the system.

The Agreed Measures, which were the first of the approved regimes,
maintained the fully decentralized system that has been described, giving
the central role in the administration of this regime to each of the
participating Governments and, to a limited extent, to the Consultative
Meetings of the Treaty.[25] Given that what was involved was a recommendation and not a separate instrument of the Treaty, the Consultative
Meetings gradually assumed a more prominent institutional role in the
management of the regime.[26] This was a first symptom of the need for
greater institutional participation in the management of these regimes,
however simple they might have been.

The Seal Convention represented a further step in this evolution. On
the one hand, the decentralized system was maintained together with the
leading role of the Contracting Parties, whether acting individually or, for
certain purposes, collectively.[27] But, on the other hand, it was provided
that, after commercial exploitation of the seal had begun, a meeting of
Contracting Parties could be convened for the purpose of 'establishing a
commission to perform such functions under this Convention as the
Contracting Parties may deem necessary'.[28] In a meeting of this type,
consideration might also be given to other institutional aspects such as a
'scientific advisory committee' which would assume some of the functions
which the Convention entrusted to SCAR or the establishment of a
system of inspection and control.[29]

In this manner, consideration was given to the possibility of establishing
a governing body and another scientific body for the regulation of the
regime, but subject to the condition that a start had been made on the
commercial exploitation of the resource, which has not occurred so far.

The importance of this criterion was that it accepted the concept of a formal institutional machinery but, at the same time, did not actually bring it into existence until it was necessary, thus avoiding expenses and superfluous functions in the meanwhile. This formula probably represented a middle way between the option of institutionalizing and that of continuing on an entirely decentralized basis.

The institutional evolution represented by this rather modest step given by the Seal Convention is more significant than what might appear to be at first sight. Indeed, since in fact the Convention is calling for the establishment of a fisheries commission, this means in due course a major change in the role of the Antarctic Treaty Consultative Parties, who will be required to develop a conservation and development policy for the resource in question.

Once the need for the establishment of a fisheries commission is recognized, other consequences will immediately follow. The first consequence is perhaps the need to have a permanent organ that might deal with the problems of quotas, protective measures and other aspects of the policy in connection with that particular resource. Ever since the Behring Fur Seals Arbitration[30] established in its award regulations for the protection and preservation of fur-seal, acting in fact as a fisheries commission, this need has been the inescapable consequence of any fisheries management. This will lead in turn to the various institutional issues and requirements that have come to characterize contemporary fisheries commissions.[31]

Furthermore, an evolution of this kind necessarily determines the linkage between the Antarctic Treaty system and the whole range of problems appertaining to the field of international institutional law,[32] since that system will become every passing day more institutionalized. The experience of the Convention on the Conservation of Antarctic Marine Living Resources, the negotiation of the mineral regime and the Antarctic Treaty itself points clearly in this evolutionary and institutionalized direction.

Institutional provisions of the living resources regime
The regime for the conservation of living resources represented a more fully developed regulation of the resource in question which, in its turn, required a permanent institutional system. Within the framework of this Convention a set of permanently established bodies was set up for the first time comprising the Commission, the Scientific Committee and the Secretariat, which form the structure of an international organization for co-operation and administration in this field.[33] This situation represents a

substantive change in the criterion that previously prevailed in the Antarctic Treaty system.

The composition of the Commission reflects some of the prevailing criteria in the framework of this Antarctic Treaty system. On the one hand, there is provision for the permanent participation of the States that took part in the Canberra Conference, which were in fact the Consultative Parties of the Treaty and others which were specially invited, a category which once again represents the concept of special responsibility and the leading role of the Consultative Parties.[34] On the other hand, there is provision for the temporary participation of acceding States[35] and the very special case of participation by organizations for regional economic integration,[36] all of which is subject to certain demands and requirements. This differentiated participation also corresponds to the different types of Consultative Parties envisaged in the Antarctic Treaty and probably reflects requirements that are likely to be repeated in other regimes where this trend is reflected. It must, however, be pointed out that certain countries that were particularly interested in participating were excluded from the Canberra Conference.[37]

The procedure for decision-making is also representative of the substantive legal and political difficulties within the system. While certain countries proposed the adoption of decisions by a two-thirds majority, thus seeking to avoid a repetition of the formula of the Consultative Meetings, other countries insisted on this latter formula or on similar alternatives.[38] The first option was supported by those countries that were interested in developing the resource but, at the same time, wished to set up an expeditious institutional system that would not paralyse the procedures.[39] The second option was supported by certain claimant countries and by other powers that saw in it a more effective way of safeguarding their interests.[40]

Ultimately, the formula that was approved required a consensus for decisions of substance including a decision as to whether or not a question is one of substance. Decisions on other matters are to be adopted by a majority.[41] In this context, consensus has been interpreted by one author in a manner that is similar to the procedure of the Law of the Sea Conference, and which is thus distinct from a simple veto.[42] However, at the first session of the Commission, difficulties of interpretation arose in this connection and the requirement of consensus was extended on that occasion to procedural matters.[43] Furthermore, a system for raising objections was envisaged by the Convention with regard to the approved conservation measures, and this has been interpreted by another author as a double veto system.[44]

It should be pointed out in this connection that majority voting is quite common in fisheries organizations which have rule-making powers, but this arrangement is usually accompanied by objection procedures.[45] Such objection procedures do not paralyse the decision-making procedures of the meetings but they can become an obstacle for the operation of the conservation regime. The aggregate of decision-making by consensus and objection procedures is in fact a double safeguard built in the Canberra Convention which can make the operation of the conservation measures difficult.

Although the Convention does not specify the procedure for the adoption of decisions by the Scientific Committee, an identical procedure based on consensus has been incorporated by that Committee in its Rules of Procedure.[46] However, if no consensus is reached, the Committee informs the Commission of all the points of view that have been voiced concerning the matter under consideration.[47]

The Committee's ability in practice to function appropriately as a scientific and technical advisory body of the Commission has been regarded with scepticism by certain authors. Specifically, the fear has been expressed that 'ultimately, the Scientific Committee could be ignored by the politicians, without the Commission even being required to explain the reasons why it chooses not to follow Scientific Committee recommendations'.[48] The adoption of conservation measures, however, has not met so far with this kind of obstacle in the work of the institutions.[49] As was pointed out earlier, some measures of an institutional nature might be considered within the mineral regime in order to ensure that the opinion of the Advisory Committee on environmental matters cannot be lightly set aside.[50]

Although the living resources regime has a number of major weaknesses of an institutional nature[51] it nevertheless represents a highly significant change in the development of the Antarctic Treaty system. The leading role of the Parties is maintained in various matters such as participation, decision-making, enforcement, jurisdiction, inspection and others, but at the same time this role is incorporated within the institutional framework whose functions, although weak, serve as a means of channelling co-operation and producing the necessary uniformity in the applicable criteria. This arrangement may eventually evolve towards higher forms of control and institutionalization but it must be borne in mind that it represents only a first step.

One author has aptly described the direction in which the Antarctic Treaty system has evolved in this respect:

The favourable attitude towards the Treaty shown by the signatory States ought to make it possible to carry out innovations and changes in the treaty structure without impeding the dynamics of Antarctic Treaty co-operation.[52]

8.2   The new institutional requirements of the mineral regime

The necessity for institutions became even more evident in the context of the mineral resources regime.[53] This was partly due to the fact that the administration of a regime of this type is more complex than that of fishery regimes or of regimes for the conservation of living resources and implies greater institutional demands, particularly in view of the fact that institutions will have important powers and competences in dealing with the decision to authorize mineral activities, approve contracts and supervise the practical operation of the regime.

In part, however, these new needs arise from the fact that the institutional system proved itself to be the key element in the internal accommodation within this regime without which it would have been impossible to reconcile the interests of claimant and non-claimant countries. This fact explains why many of the jurisdictional models that were considered in Chapter 7 contain a strong institutional component. The entire problem of the distribution of competences thus became closely bound up with the institutional framework which Beeby describes in the following terms:

> . . . it would be wise not to view this question of the location of the necessary regulatory powers in isolation. It would be better to consider it along with the two other issues to which it is closely linked . . . These two issues concern the membership of the institutions of the regime and the means by which those institutions will take decisions.[54]

For these reasons, the conception of an entirely decentralized scheme, such as the Antarctic Treaty, had no place in this other context. The solution adopted in the Seal Convention whereby a simple institutional scheme was envisaged for activation at some future time was also inappropriate in this case. The institutional model of the Canberra Convention, which is the one that might have come closest to meeting this other situation, also has major limitations and required significant changes. All these precedents have certainly exercised some influence but none of them taken on their own offer a solution in the case of the minerals regime.

The discussions on the nature of the institutional system have been strongly influenced by the different points of view concerning the objectives of the regime and the protection of some of the basic interests involved. One point of view has maintained that the institutions should be endowed with relatively minor powers and have a restricted role in the administration of the system, the aim being to maintain the criteria of decentralization. This outlook has been reflected in the design of an institutional structure which is highly decentralized and embodies organs which, like the Regulatory Committees, refer to given zones or regions of Antarctica and not to the area as a whole. At the same time, the system for decision-making would, in such proposals, be designed in such a way as to facilitate operations, the aim being partly to establish a procedure for decision-making by majority and partly a procedure which is also decentralized. This approach also tends to assign more extensive competence to the zonal organs mentioned than to those of a centralized nature, without prejudice to the major role to be played by States Parties, with particular reference to the sponsoring State of mineral activities.[55]

This approach has, in general, been favoured by those States that give priority to developing resources. One author has proposed, to that end, that the mineral regime should, from the institutional point of view, follow the model of the Antarctic Treaty, particularly by adopting a gradual evolutionary approach to the solving of problems as they arise, a pragmatic and flexible approach for the creation of institutions and an approach based on intensive scientific studies as the basis for the adoption of decisions.[56] With regard to the institutions, the following has been suggested specifically:

(a) establishment of the minimum machinery necessary,
(b) development of new institutions only as and when necessary, and
(c) decentralization of institutions whose components, though linked, may address distinct subject areas, may involve differing participants and may establish relationships with differing sets of non-Antarctic institutions.[57]

It must, however, be pointed out there are also other interests that are attracted by the idea of decentralization and by the restriction of the powers of the institutions. This applies to certain claimant countries which, of course, see the role of each individual State as being of prior importance in the management of the regime.

There is another point of view, however, that considers that for the adequate management of the system, the role of the institutions should be strengthened. As a consequence, in such proposals, priority is given to the operation of organs of a centralized type and a procedure is envisaged for the adoption of decisions which signifies greater control over operations, principally through the machinery of consensus. This approach is mainly adopted by those countries or authors that give priority to the objective of ecological protection[58] even though other interests may also make themselves felt, particularly in the case of those countries which have always favoured the role of consensus as a means of ensuring their part in the decision-making process. This approach also includes a number of claimant countries, at least as far as the adoption of decisions by consensus is concerned.

The sets of formulae, points of view and interests needs to be harmonized within the framework of a mutually acceptable institutional scheme. Once again, this is an exercise of particular complexity which explains why the negotiations placed increasing emphasis on the consideration of institutional arrangements. This writer has stated elsewhere that: 'In the light of existing experience in the field of Antarctic co-operation, it seems desirable and appropriate that the institutions of the regime should have an effective role to play in its management, since otherwise the system would resemble one in which unilateral action predominates rather than one characterized by international co-operation among its member countries. Without prejudice to the role that may be played by auxiliary or functional mechanisms, possibly including those of a zonal character, the essential work of administration would have to be centralized and under the control of the Consultative Parties. The rule of consensus would also have a significant part to play. All this may in the event be accompanied by an effective system for the settlement of disputes, whereby an unjustifiable paralysis of proceedings or mining operations can be avoided'.[59] We shall be considering later how this difficult institutional construction has been approached in the negotiations.

The basic approach: centralized organs and those of a regional nature
Recommendation XI-1 did not contain provisions that were related directly to the institutional scheme, since it concentrated principally on the elaboration of the principles of the regime. However, the negotiations that followed in the Fourth Special Consultative Meeting saw the early emergence of an institutional scheme consisting of three main organs: the Commission, the Scientific, Technical and Environmental Advisory Committee and the Regulatory Committees.[60] A Special Meeting of States Parties was also envisaged as a part of the institutional machinery. In addition, a Secretariat and other institutional arrangements of a general nature were envisaged. The idea of establishing a Special Meeting of States Parties to adopt certain crucial decisions related to the identifica-

tion of areas and other conditions has also been considered in the negotiations.

The Commission and the Advisory Committee are both organs of a centralized nature within this institutional scheme and serve as common mechanisms for all parties to the regime. The former is an organ of a political type responsible for the adoption of specific decisions and for carrying out other governing functions within the regime, whereas the latter is an organ of a scientific and technical nature, responsible principally for advisory tasks as will be explained below. This part of the institutional structure is not different from what is envisaged by the Canberra Convention and, potentially, by the Seal Convention.

The idea of establishing organs of a regional or zonal nature is, however, a departure from the institutional precedents of the Antarctic system. Such an approach had already been anticipated in the early years of the twentieth century when the first steps were taken with a view to organizing an Antarctic regime. Fauchille had proposed to this end the creation of regional units forming part of his proposed system of Antarctic organization.[61] Various contemporary authors also enlarged upon this idea, suggesting a number of alternatives and variants.[62] All these proposals have in common that such organs would be related to specific areas of Antarctica and not to the continent as a whole.

In the context of the negotiations on the mineral regime, this approach has proved particularly attractive owing to the way in which it facilitates the problems of the internal accommodation. In the first place, it allows for organs of a more limited type which accommodate the varying geographical and ecological features of the Antarctic continent, which is highly conducive to a more efficient resources policy. Furthermore, it allows greater scope for the distribution of powers within the institutional system itself whereby the functions of the respective Regulatory Committee and of the Commission are combined. Above all, this type of organ makes it possible to balance the participation of the various national interests, including those of claimant States, within the system itself. This is a means of ensuring a measure of decentralization which accommodates the interests of States, but this does not occur entirely outside the framework of the institutional system but on an integrated basis within the scope of the respective Regulatory Committee.

Once the idea of including this type of organ within the institutional system was accepted, the question arose as to how many of those organs were to be established and on what criteria they would be based. Various ideas have been considered in this latter connection. A proposal made by the United States in June 1982 conceived of the division of Antarctica into four sectors, each of which would be administered by a regional panel.[63] The proposed division is illustrated in the diagram below.[64]

The draft articles of 1983 conceived a different system, whereby a Regulatory Committee would be established for every application for an exploration permit that was submitted.[65] This meant that there would be as many Regulatory Committees as there were projects in hand, a formula that was criticized on the grounds that it entailed a fragmentation of authority and a departure from the principles of the 'ecosystem

Figure 2   1982 U.S. proposal to divide Antarctica in four sectors for minerals regime.

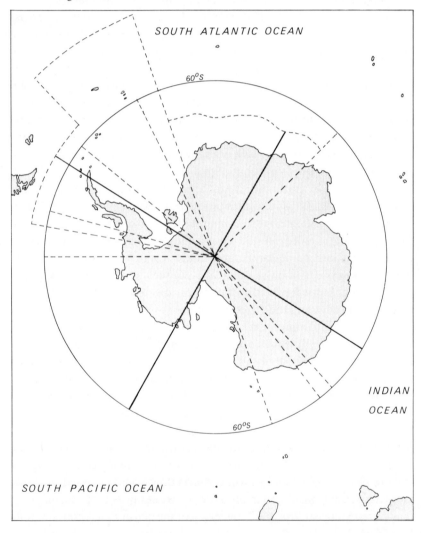

management'.[66] In the words of one author: 'if this principle were applied in New Zealand, we would have a dozen different regulatory authorities off the Taranaki coast alone'.[67] In the revision of these draft articles, this approach was altered and the establishment of a Regulatory Committee for each area opened for the submission of exploration and exploitation applications was proposed.[68] This approach permits the administration of broader areas within which there may be different blocks for specific projects all of which would remain under the same regional authority. It will be possible to specify the limits of each area only as they are gradually identified by the Commission.

The most complex part of the institutional structure designed refers to the composition of the organs, the decision-making and competence, subjects that are intimately bound up with the distribution of competences and the internal accommodation within the system. These aspects will be considered next.

8.3   The composition of the Commission and other organs

The composition of the Commission has, in general outline, followed the model of the Antarctic Treaty in that it distinguishes between a category of 'permanent' members and another of 'temporary' members. Under the terms of the 1983 Draft, the former category comprises the Consultative Parties of the Antarctic Treaty, thus once again expressing the idea of the special responsibility of these Parties.[69] The temporary category would comprise those countries acceding to the regime 'during such times as it, or an operator which it has sponsored, is engaged in Antarctic mineral resource activities'.[70]

Each of these sets of criteria entails a number of problems which it will be necessary to solve. In the case of the Canberra Convention, in addition to the Consultative Parties, it was necessary to recognize the permanent interest of other countries that did not have Consultative status and this gave rise to the recognition of the permanent membership of those countries that participated in the Conference at which the Convention was approved.[71] In the 1984 Draft Articles an approach similar to that of the Canberra Convention was adopted on this point, a decision that was also necessary in view of the fact that, with effect from 1985, the negotiating sessions were opened to the participation of observers.[72] In this sense, the formula of the Canberra Convention is broader and would consequently give rise to less resistance by other interested countries. In the event that all the parties might be entitled to participate in the Special Meeting of States Parties that has been proposed for certain purposes and to which reference has been made further above, the Commission, according to these suggestions, might have a more limited participation following in general the approach of the 1983 Draft Articles, that is, would be composed by Consultative Parties and parties sponsoring applications for mineral activities; this approach is the one reflected in the *1986 Draft Articles* (Article 19).

On the other hand, it is necessary to provide for the case of parties acceding to the regime which subsequently acquire the status of Consultative Party. In this case, it would be necessary to ensure their participation in the Commission, even if it is a country not carrying out or sponsoring mineral-related activities. The fact that, in accordance with the provisions of the 1959 Treaty, the Consultative Parties other than the original Consultative Parties have a temporary status probably justifies their participating in the Commission on a temporary basis also for as long as they retain that status. This is the criterion which has been followed since the 1984 revision of the draft articles.[73] It is also necessary to envisage what would occur in the hypothetical situation in which a Consultative Party other than an original one which had been admitted as a permanent member of the Commission loses its status as a Consultative Party. Even though such a case is highly theoretical,[74] it is necessary to bear it in mind and to envisage, as an alternative, that such a Party would have to terminate its membership of the Commission so as not to discriminate among the temporary Consultative Parties; or, as another option, deriving from the above-mentioned formula of the Canberra Convention, to provide that its permanent membership would continue on the basis of its participation in the meeting at which the regime was approved. This would mean in practice distinguishing between the various types of temporary Consultative Parties.

The temporary membership of States carrying out or sponsoring mineral-related activities also raises a number of difficulties. One of these is that such States will probably be interested in the Commission not only when mineral activities begin but, more importantly, when the Commission is faced with a decision either on applications to open up areas or on specific exploration authorizations, since these are, in fact, the initial phases of the intervention of the institutions. In such a case, temporary participation ought, it is suggested, to be envisaged as beginning with the start of the appropriate procedure until such time as the procedure has run its course, a criterion which again has been incorporated in the 1984 revision.[75]

The temporary membership also raises one difficulty of balance in the composition of the Commission. Given that the number of temporary members may increase indefinitely, to the extent that States carry out or sponsor mineral related activities, the Commission is likely to become dominated by this interest group. The fact that this situation may reduce or upset the balance of the ecological or other relevant interests has already attracted criticism.[76] A possible solution might be to restrict the representation of this interest in exploitation to a certain number of members determined on a basis of balance with other interest represented within the Commission.

The scheme that is being described also provides for the participation of observers in the Commission. The formula for determining this restricted participation category includes any country that is a party to the regime, any country that is a party to the Antarctic Treaty and such international organizations as may be specified by the Commission. The participation, albeit restricted, of observers that are parties to the regime is a positive approach that may help to facilitate the various aspects of the internal and external accommodation. The same may be said of the relevant international organizations that may be identified and invited to participate by the Commission. On the other hand, the suggestion that countries that are Parties to the Antarctic Treaty but are not parties to the regime should participate in the latter did not seem to have the same justification since, if such countries are interested in these activities, they ought to begin to achieve status in it by acceding to the regime.[77]

The problems that have been discussed also give an idea of the different situations that will need to be provided for by the terms governing accession to the regime.[78] These should provide for the accession of countries that may, in the future, achieve the status of Consultative Parties, of countries that are Parties to the Antarctic Treaty and of other countries that may be interested in mineral activities. With regard to the latter, the question of the links between the regime and the Treaty and the Antarctic system will have to be reflected in the relevant linking clauses and will have to accommodate the types of relations that were discussed earlier.

In the case of the mineral regime, unlike that of the Canberra Convention, the Draft Articles have made no provision for accession or for participation in the institutions by organizations of regional economic integration, a mechanism which in the case of that Convention was specifically designed to cover participation by the EEC. The reason explaining this difference between the two regimes is that while the EEC has competence to act in its own capacity as an organization deriving from the Treaty of Rome and subsequent developments with regard to fishing and living resources arrangements – a matter which we have already discussed – such competences are not entirely clear in regard to minerals and the role that national jurisdictions continue to perform in this other field.

The situation at present is that the EEC does not have competence in relation to the production or extraction of minerals, except for the very special case of the European Coal and Steel Community; it follows that such activities remain under national jurisdiction, including of course the case of the continental shelf. However, the EEC does have certain competence with regard to the commercial policy and related aspects of mineral trade, including the problems associated with the condition of world markets. The Community also has competence with regard to various environmental matters. On this basis it is that several authors have concluded that the EEC has competence with regard to the sea-bed regime under Part XI of the Law of the Sea Convention and for participation in the Sea-bed Authority,[79] an aspect which in any event requires a precise definition of such competences as mandated by Article 305 and Annex IX of the Law of the Sea Convention.

On signing the latter Convention on 7th December 1984, the EEC made the required declaration concerning its competence, which, with regard to Part XI, refers to the 'competence in matters of commercial policy, including the control of unfair economic practices', a competence which is also declared to be subject to continuous development.[80] The competence for the protection and preservation of the marine environment is also expressly stated. Various resolutions of the European Parliament on sea-bed mining,[81] as well as written questions on the matter,[82] had in fact offered a clear indication of a trend towards the establishment of EEC competences in this field, particularly with references to the coordination of national legislation at Community level and the need to avoid distortions of competition.

These developments are highly relevant for the question of an eventual EEC interest in the Antarctic mineral regime. Several questions have already been made in the European Parliament, including one on the competence of the EEC to participate in the mineral negotiations.[83] Although apparently the issue has not been discussed at community level,[84] it is not difficult to foresee that at some stage the EEC will express an interest in these negotiations and eventually will affirm certain aspects of its competence in the field of commercial policy. The competence in environmental matters might also be invoked to justify some form of involvement in the Antarctic mineral negotiations.

The composition of the Advisory Committee

The composition of the Advisory Committee has proved relatively easier to define since it has a direct relationship with the composition of the Commission. Just as in the case of the Canberra Convention, it has been proposed that all the members of the Commission should also be members of the Committee. The 1983 draft made a distinction in this regard between the Consultative Parties of the Antarctic Treaty and the members of the Commission that do not have Consultative status, but such a distinction is in fact unnecessary since all the Consultative Parties are also members of the Commission, the corresponding changes having been introduced.[85] The members of the Commission are interested in participating in the work of the Advisory Committee in order to ensure that their point of view is also reflected in the advice emanating from the Committee.

It has also been provided that parties to the regime that are also parties to the Antarctic Treaty and have carried out scientific investigation relevant to mineral-related activities shall also be members of the Advisory Committee.[86] This approach differs from that of the Canberra Convention, being the purpose of this broader participation to recognize a more prominent role for Parties to the Antarctic Treaty that do not have the status of Consultative Parties but are involved in the subject matter of the new treaty. Another interesting innovation has been the establishment of the status of observer in the Committee, a category that is open to any country that is a party to the regime, to any Party to the Antarctic Treaty and also to such international organizations as may be specified by the Commission, including non-governmental organizations.[87] Yet another option considered in the negotiations has been to open the membership in the Advisory Committee to all the States parties to the mineral regime, an approach which has been incorporated in the 1986 revision of the draft Convention (Article 24, par. 2).

The Committee may also request the advice of other scientists and experts and may establish subcommittees with the approval of the Commission.[88] In the 1984 revision of the Draft Articles, an important piece of machinery was added to ensure the openness of discussion within the Committee according to which the subjects being considered by the Committee must be publicly announced and the opinion of international organizations of a scientific, technical or environmental nature must be sought.[89] While the Advisory Committee is not bound to take into account these opinions, the procedure envisaged will facilitate a greater interaction of points of view and will also facilitate the external accommodation of this regime.

Proposals relating to the composition of the Regulatory Committees
The composition of the Regulatory Committees has been one of the most difficult matters to resolve within the regime since this is a subject on which a balance satisfactory to the various interests involved must be achieved. The formulae proposed have followed the various options that were considered in regard to the criteria for establishing these organs.

In the original proposal of the United States, based on division of Antarctica into four geographical areas, the starting point was that each Committee might be composed of half the members of the Commission plus one, with the additional provision that no member might participate simultaneously in more than two Committees.[90] The purpose of this approach was undoubtedly that of ensuring that each organ represented the relevant claimant, the sponsoring State and other relevant interests, within a restricted participation structure.

The 1983 Draft Articles, based on the concept of one Committee for each application submitted, provided for a different system which would, however, pursue the same objectives of a balance of interests. In this system, two central interest groups were recognized: that of the sponsoring State and of other States that do not have the status of claimants, on the one hand, and that of the claimant States, on the other.

The first group would be represented, in the first place by the sponsoring State that had submitted an exploration application and, next, by the two States which, prior to the entry into force of the Antarctic Treaty, 'had asserted a basis of claim in Antarctica', which is, in effect, an indirect reference to the United States and the Soviet Union. This group would also have to designate up to two other Parties as members of the Committee, provided that the total number representing the group did not exceed four members.[91] In practice, the formula means that if the sponsor is a country other than the United States or the Soviet Union, an additional member may be designated to make up the total of four. If the sponsor is one of these two powers, two other members may be designated to make up a total of four members.

The second interest group would be represented by the Party or Parties 'which maintain rights of or claims to sovereignty in the block to which an application . . . refers'. This Party may designate up to three other members, similarly provided that the group does not exceed four members of the Committee.[92] This other formula means that, if there is only one claimant, it may designate three additional members; if there are, for example, three claimants, as occurs in the Antarctic peninsula, they will all be members of the Committee and will be able to designate only one additional member to make up the total of four.

Although this formula tends, in general, to represent the interests in exploitation in the first group and the interest in sovereignty in the second – a situation which has been graphically described as a kind of 'four-a-side football' with one team of 'miners' and another of 'owners'[93] – in actual fact there is likely to be some intertwining of interests, although probably only to a limited extent. Thus, for example, a sponsor which figures in the first group may happen to be a claimant country, or the interests of the two powers that have been mentioned may not always be identified with that of exploitation; on the other hand, in the second group, it may happen that among the additional members that are to be designated there is included a country that is not a claimant.

The formula described entails a number of important problems. In the first place, it is to be noted that the members of the Regulatory Committee are not explicity required to be members of the Commission. Even if membership of the Committee will normally imply membership of the Commission, it would have been preferable to make an explicit requirement in order to ensure a measure of continuity in the work of the institutions. Perhaps this omission was due to a simple drafting problem, for it was later corrected. A more difficult problem is that of the recognition of privileged participation by the countries that have 'a basis of claim', which would be members of all Regulatory Committees. In fact this approach meant the recognition of a special role for the US and the USSR, a criterion which is not part of the Antarctic tradition and has already attracted criticism from several German authors,[94] which may, perhaps, indicate that other powers are not satisfied with this distinction.[95] On the other hand, this type of composition ensures that while an interest may be expressed in relation to Antarctica as a whole, that of the claimants tends to be restricted to the area which is the subject of the claim, a fact which has certain drawbacks, as it was explained earlier;[96] while some claimants might prefer the advantage of conducting mineral activities close to their Antarctic stations or other facilities, some others that have a greater technological capacity will prefer to have a broader geographical scope for their activities in the area.

It should also be noted that if 'basis of claim' is recognized as a special interest group by this regime, in fact this could amount to a recognition of a kind of territorial interest throughout Antarctica, a situation that might not be entirely compatible with Article IV of the 1959 Antarctic Treaty. With even more reason other territorial claims would aspire to a recognition of a similar kind.

The 1984 revision of the draft articles changed the manner of establishing the Regulatory Committees, and provided that a Committee was to be set up for each general area and not for each application. This new situation necessitated an adjustment in the composition of the Committee although not in its general structure or in the basis chosen for ensuring a balance of interest. The representation of the interests of the claimants was maintained in almost identical form with the sole exception that, if the State requesting the opening of an area or the sponsoring State, is a claimant, this fact will be taken into account to ensure that the total membership of the group does not exceed four.[97] The potential problem inherent in the earlier formula that a given category might be more strongly represented on the Committee than another is thus avoided.

The representation of the other interest group has undergone a number of major changes owing to the new approach inherent in this revised formula. The first change is that when the Committee is established there will be no sponsoring State, but merely a State requesting that a particular area be opened for the submission of exploration applications. In other words, the Committee will be established in the initial phase of the regime's procedure. For this reason it will be this requesting State that will be a member of the Committee and may subsequently be replaced by the sponsoring State, should the two not be identical.[98]

A second major change is that the designation of additional members of this group will be made neither by the sponsoring nor by the requesting State but by the Chairman of the Commission in consultation with the Chairman of the Advisory Committee.[99] This greater degree of institutionalization of the system ensures that not only are the interests associated with exploitation represented on the Committee but also that the representation of other interests may be considered too. As was pointed out earlier, the formula embodied in the 1983 Draft Articles did not entirely exclude this possibility, but it has now been reinforced.

On the other hand, the number of members designated to represent this category will no longer be restricted to four, but the equal representation of claimants and non-claimants on the Committee will be ensured.[100] A similar principle will be followed if the balance might be upset as a result of the replacement of the requesting State by the sponsor.[101] The purpose of these provisions is to ensure equality of representation, with adjustments being made if the requesting State or the sponsor is at the same time a claimant State. The representation of the two great powers continues to be ensured in this group.[102] It must also be noted that all additional nominations for either of the two interest categories must be made among members of the Commission, a requirement which overcomes the difficulty in this connection that was inherent in the first formula.[103]

Other suggestions have also been made occasionally for the representation of non-claimants in the Regulatory Committeees. According to one suggestion, developing countries should be recognized an adequate representation in this category, since all such countries that have acceded to the Antarctic Treaty and the mineral negotiations, with the exception of Argentina and Chile, are non-claimants. In yet another view, the group of non-claimants participating in a Regulatory Committee should be composed only of countries having a concrete interest in mineral activities. The most controversial suggestion has been that the US and the USSR should be represented in this organ in addition to the four members of the non-claimant interest group, and not included in such group, what would make a total of six members sharing the non-claimant approach; this, of course, would seriously upset the balance between the interest groups that has been explained above.[104]

Some of the latter suggestions are reflected in Article 29 of the 1986 revision, which provides for membership of the Regulatory Committee according to the following categories: (a) members of the Commission which assert rights or claims in the identified area; (b) the two members which at the time of entry into force of the Antarctic Treaty maintained the largest presence in Antarctica; and (c) additional members of the Commission designated by its Chairman so as to include four claimants and four non-claimants, the latter being additional to the US and the USSR since these two countries are included under (b) above.

Under this approach there would be a larger representation of non-claimants, a situation which could upset the delicate balance being sought. Some criteria are made available for the designation of members of the Committee: inclusion of members of the Commission which have contributed substantial scientific, technical or environmental information relevant to the identification of areas; equitable and adequate representation of developing countries; and rotation in the membership.

8.4 The mechanism for decision-making in the institutions

The rules relating to decision-making are another of the difficult problems with which the negotiation of the regime has had to contend. As happened in the negotiation of the Canberra Convention, the two basic theses have been one that postulates a formula based on consensus and one which favours a qualified majority. The positions of the countries have tended to follow those that were adopted in the negotiation on the living resources regime.[105] Each of these theses is based on arguments concerning both form and substance, even if the substantive arguments are not always made explicit.

Consensus is always supported by the formal argument that it is necessary to preserve the tradition of the Antarctic Treaty system, but the purpose of the formula is clearly to ensure that each country retains control over decisions. There are a number of interests which concur on this approach. The Soviet Union supports consensus as a norm of a general policy in international negotiations. Certain claimant countries favour this position as a means of safeguarding their rights. A number of countries, also including a number of claimants, see consensus as the best means of safeguarding the ecological values associated with the process; it should be noted, however, that while this argument is valid in so far as it concerns the original decision to authorize mineral activities, it can well produce the opposite effect during the conduct of operations since consensus would be required to issue emergency orders or other protective measures. In any case, as has been explained, a distinction has begun to be drawn between the concept of consensus and that of unanimity.[106]

The qualified majority is justified in formal terms in that it makes possible a more effective policy for the administration and conservation of the resource but its purpose is also to ensure that no country or group of countries is able to paralyse the decision-making process in order to develop this resource. The interests associated with exploitation, possibly including certain claimant countries, favour this formula which follows the general trend in other international organizations.

Decisions within the framework of the Commission
The 1983 draft envisaged a voting procedure for the Commission which was an attempt to satisfy, to some extent, each of the basic points of view. The transactional formula established that, as a general rule, decisions on matters of substance were to be adopted by a two-thirds majority of members present and voting. This same principle was to be applied in deciding whether a question is to be regarded as a matter of substance. Other matters could be decided by a simple majority.[107] However, this general rule was subject to an important exception: certain key matters indicated in the text of the draft should be decided by consensus. Thus, compatibility is sought between the various positions that have been mentioned, and different majorities, or a consensus, are required, depending on the nature of the matter to be decided.

Decisions which, in accordance with this draft, must be adopted by consensus were those concerned with five subjects. The most important of these is the decision as to whether a specific area is to be opened for the submission of exploration and exploitation applications or whether such a step would represent an unacceptable risk for the environment.[108] As has been explained earlier, this mechanism has been described as 'an ecological veto'. There is no doubt that this is the most crucial determination of the entire procedure. Other subjects refer to determination of the size of blocks,[109] the adoption of measures to avoid monopoly situations,[110] the adoption of principles relating to participation under the concept of 'full and fair opportunity',[111] and budgetary matters.[112] Not all these subjects are of equal importance and for this reason the requirement of a consensus will probably have to be reviewed later.

The revision of the draft made in 1984 and 1986 did not alter this formula even though it was clearly understood at the outset that it would be considered during the final stages of the negotiation.[113] In complex negotiations such as this, the formula for decision-making is customarily the last crucial point to be resolved. The insistence of the USSR on the consensus requirement as a matter of policy and the fact that there are a number of precedents within the Antarctic system itself means that it is not easy to accept an approach whereby decisions are to be taken by a qualified majority or, if such a voting method is accepted, it will probably be in the context of a compromise based on some type of *quid pro quo* concession.

If such a compromise does take place, it is likely that the system for decision-making will continue to be based on the idea of requiring a consensus for subjects of decisive importance, various forms of qualified majority for other objects depending on their importance, and a simple majority for other matters. A similar approach was followed in the formula adopted toward the end of the negotiations on the sea-bed regime under the Law of the Sea Convention in relation to decisions of the Council.[114] Various proposals of academic origin have also suggested systems involving chamber voting[115] and other alternatives.[116]

The final decision on the voting arrrangements in the Commission will also be related to whether or not there shall be established a Special Meeting of States Parties for the adoption of certain key decisions. In this context it has been suggested, for example, that the latter meeting should decide by simple majority including the concurrent vote of the Consultative Parties, an approach which in fact would grant a veto to such Consultative Parties. If this were the case the Commission would probably decide by majority, except for given matters within its competence that would still require consensus. The Special Meeting of State Parties has indeed been established in the 1986 Draft Articles, which shall be opened to all parties to the Convention (Article 28) and which shall examine whether the identification of an area by the Commission is compatible with the Convention, reporting to the Commission all the views expressed in such a meeting (Article 38).

Decisions of the Advisory Committee

The same formula as that designed for the Commission has been applied to the adoption of decisions in the Advisory Committee.[117] Even though the possibility is mentioned that certain provisions should contemplate different procedures, such as consensus, none of the articles of the draft departs from the general rule in the case of the Advisory Committee. This does not, of course, mean that exceptions to the rule may not eventually be contemplated in the definitive formula.

This approach differs from that of the Canberra Convention since, in the case of the Scientific Committee, the Convention did not provide rules for the adoption of decisions; these were defined subsequently in the rules of procedure of this Committee. As was pointed out earlier, the procedure ultimately chosen was that of consensus, with the additional provision that, if no consensus was reached, all the points of view that had been taken into consideration would be submitted.[118] On this point, the regulations are to some extent in conflict with the provisions of the Convention which indicates that procedures should be envisaged for the submission of minority reports whereas the regulations only allow either for a consensus or for the submission of all points of view, without specifying whether these are majority or minority views. An equivalent provision to that of the Canberra Convention was included in the 1983 draft, an approach which was subsequently changed to bring it into line with the solution adopted for the Scientific Committee under that regime.[119] The 1986 revision has simplified decision-making in this body, providing that reports shall reflect all the views expressed by members and that decisions on other matters shall be taken by a simple majority (Articles 26 and 27).

The question of the voting procedure in this body is closely bound up with the type of institutional relations that are to be established with the Commission, since the opinion of the Advisory Committee will normally have an influence on the decisions of the Commission. In the case of the Canberra Convention, various mechanisms were contemplated to achieve this end, in particular the fact that the Scientific Committee was described as a 'consultative body' and, above all, that the Commission must 'take full account' of the recommendations of this body. In addition, provision was made for publicity measures and for the requirement that the Commission should give effect to the objectives and principles of the Convention, thus establishing a more objective scientific framework for its implementation.[120] However, as has been pointed out, these mechanisms have attracted criticism on the grounds of their potential weakness.[121]

In the case of the mineral regime, equivalent machinery has been established for organizing this institutional relationship. Both the Commission and the respective Regulatory Committee must take full account of the opinion and guidelines drawn up by the Advisory Committee in the preparation of the decisions or instruments entrusted to these other bodies.[122] A function of the Advisory Committee is also to advise these other bodies, and its role is therefore equivalent to that of a 'consultative body' as under the Canberra Convention.[123] The intervention of the Commission within the framework of the objectives and principles of the Convention is also a provision identical to that of the Canberra Convention,[124] with similar arrangements being made for a set of publicity measures for the intervention of the Advisory Committee.[125]

In spite of this, the fear has also been expressed that such mechanisms might, in the case of this regime, prove inadequate to ensure that due weight is given to the opinion of this body. An interesting mechanism has been proposed in order to deal with this difficulty, whereby a consensus or a substantial majority within the Commission would be required before it would be possible to set aside the opinion expressed by the Advisory Committee.[126] This formula would ensure a close link between the respective procedures for decision-making.

As has been explained, all the points of view expressed in the Advisory Committee will be submitted to the Commission, thus constituting a further mechanism for ensuring that all relevant approaches are weighed. It may then be necessary to organize these opinions in a coherent manner with the aim of ensuring that they represent useful options for the decision of the Commission, thus avoiding a dispersion of points of view.

Decision-making in the Regulatory Committee: the key to the internal accommodation

Decision-making in the Regulatory Committee constitutes another of the key aspects of the internal accommodation. The general rule that has been provided for the Regulatory Committee is the simple majority[127] whereby the needs of prompt administration are met and the positions of those that support this approach are satisfied. However, an additional requirement is established in regard to two specific matters whereby this majority must include the State or States making a claim in the area in question and the State sponsoring the corresponding application. These two mattters are the designation of the member or members which will prepare the draft management scheme[128] and the approval of this instrument in the Regulatory Committee.[129]

The latter machinery is a highly ingenious means of providing the guarantees necessary for the internal accommodation. In effect, it grants a special type of right of veto to two categories of interest that are most directly involved in the decision made by the Committee, and thus fully safeguards their respective points of view. But, as this is a reciprocal veto, it obliges both interests to reach an understanding. This understanding must not only be of a preliminary type, which ensures the designation of the member that is to prepare the draft management scheme, but also of a definitive nature, so as to ensure the approval of the instrument. This is the stage at which the ultimate decisions will be taken on such delicate matters as: the applicable law and, consequently, the jurisdiction that is to prevail; the amount of taxes, fees and other financial charges which will determine the potential profit that will be earned by the claimant or by other interests that may be defined; and the specific authorization to proceed with exploration and exploitation. On all these questions, and on the other terms and conditions, this understanding will have to be reached between the claimant and the applicant so as to ensure a mutually satisfactory result. This is the principal reason why these terms and conditions cannot be defined beforehand by the Regulatory Committee, as one approach has suggested, but must remain subject to a measure of negotiation within the general lines of the regime. Only in this way is it possible to achieve the internal accommodation.

It can be seen that the fundamental compromise that should occur is the granting of the corresponding authorization on the basis of the agreement concerning financial benefits, jurisdiction and other terms and conditions. In this way, the interest of the claimant is satisfied, but not on the basis of an individual exercise of its jurisdiction but in terms of the operation of an institutional mechanism of the regime. The interest of the applicant is also satisfied; here again, not on the basis of unrestricted access to resources but in terms of the operation of the same institutional machinery. Other relevant interests are also satisfied through the decision of the Regulatory Committee and of the other organs of the regime in which these interests will be represented.

However, as anticipated by an author,[130] it was quite unlikely that non-claimants would accept an arrangement whereby claimants were granted a straightforward right of veto, even if the sponsoring State would have the same right. This suggested arrangement not only involved a recognition of certain legal effects of claims but also meant the acceptance of a very prominent role for one interest group in the operation of the regime. Non-claimants, including some leading developing countries, objected to this approach in the negotiations. On the other hand, if a right of veto was granted to any given interest group, it would automatically trigger a similar demand by the USSR in view of its traditional policy on the matter.

The arrangement that has been explored as an alternative is based on a high-qualified majority that would include a majority of both claimants and non-claimants. This approach in fact amounts to a system of chamber voting: a majority of three out of four claimants and a majority of three out of four non-claimants composing the Regulatory Committee would be needed to adopt a decision, which would represent an overall majority of six over eight members, that is, a two-thirds overall majority. Although the right of veto is eliminated, each chamber would virtually enjoy a blocking power through the operation of such majorities. The fundamental interests in the negotiation are thus safeguarded in a manner that should prove satisfactory to all. The 1986 revision has opted for a simple majority, which in the two crucial matters referred to shall also include the members of the Committee asserting rights or claims to the area identified and the Party lodging an application for exploration (Article 32 and Article 44, par. 3, and 46, par. 1). Under the latter approach the reciprocal veto is kept.

The approach to decision-making in the Regulatory Committee has attracted a number of criticisms stemming principally from environmental organizations. One of these criticisms is directed chiefly at the nature of the system on the grounds that 'this fragmentation of regulatory authority among restricted groups of countries in restricted geographical areas is a major departure from the principles of ecosystem management'.[131] In order to overcome this situation, the creation of a single Regulatory Committee for the Antarctic as a whole has been proposed.[132] Another type of criticism, which is certainly related to the foregoing, impugns the fact that the decision by the Regulatory Committee may be adopted by only eight countries, or in certain cases by a slightly larger number of members, of which five votes could constitute a simple majority. In this connection it has been pointed out that, in the last analysis, mining operations in the Antarctic would be controlled by only five countries and that, consequently, certain highly important decisions would be taken without participation of all the Consultative Parties in the decision-making process.[133]

The starting point of all these criticisms is chiefly a concern for certain ecological values and principles which are in themselves respectable and necessary, particularly in that they are relevant to the concept of an Antarctic ecosystem. Nevertheless, it cannot strictly be maintained that the idea of a regional Regulatory Committee necessarily constitutes a threat to those principles. On the contrary, it is arguable that a regional authority will be better placed to put those environmental principles into practice in the light of the specific problems of smaller geographical areas than would be an organization of continental scope. On the other hand, it must be remembered that the Regulatory Committee will always have to comply with the principles and standards of the regime, including the guidelines stemming from the Advisory Committee, and that consequently the basic elements of a common policy will always be present. This includes, of course, compliance with the rules on liability for environmental damage and related issues that we have examined earlier.

It must also be borne in mind in this connection that, in addition to safeguarding environmental interests, the regime must maintain a balance between other problems, one of the most important of which is the question of claimants and of those committed to the development of resources. The approach adopted by the Regulatory Committees and their decisions are intended to deal with this set of factors, thus facilitating the internal accommodation. If the nature of the institutional system were to change, the whole picture would be far more complex and the likelihood of its being accepted would correspondingly recede. As will be examined next, this accommodation is also related to the competences of the organs and their reciprocal relationships.

8.5   The basic competences of the organs of the regime
The competences of the Commission

As was examined in Chapter 7, the competences of the regime have been distributed in a complex manner among the various interests involved. Some competences have been entrusted directly to States, whereas others have been recognized as institutional competences. Among the latter there are some which are typically the functions of an international body and others which represent certain functions which might have been exercised by States but have been institutionalized in order to simplify questions relating to the internal accommodation. The assignment of functions to particular organs has also been related to an important extent to these problems of the internal accommodation.

The Commission, as the central organ of the regime, has important regulatory, executive and administrative competences. Although the content of these functions has been considered in earlier chapters,[134] the main ones must be mentioned again in order to enable the competence of this organ to be fully appreciated.

The regulatory competence, like the other functions, must be exercised for the purpose of complying with the objectives and principles of the regime, which provides a specific framework for the Commission in discharging its tasks.[135] Within this framework the Commission must formulate, adopt and review measures for the protection of the Antarctic environment and for the promotion of techniques of exploration and exploitation which are both safe and effective, thus giving specific content to the environmental principles of the regime.[136] The Commission must also identify the areas in which mineral-related activities will not be authorized in accordance with the various criteria of the regime relating to this matter.[137]

Another expression of the regulatory competence of the Commission is the adoption of standards to complement certain provisions or principles of the regime so as to make possible its application in practice. In this context, the Commission has to adopt standards relating to the type of information to be included in notifications and applications concerning the exploration process; for the reimbursement of administrative costs incurred by the institutions in relation to the processing of the relevant applications; measures to avoid monopoly situations; and standards to give effect to the principle of 'full and fair opportunity' to participate in the regime, including questions relating to the participation of developing countries.[138] Similarly, the Commission must consider measures for the participation of the international community in the benefits of the regime, which is an essential function in the context of the external accommodation.[139]

On certain subjects, the regulatory functions of the Commission will be of decisive importance to the internal accommodation and will resolve some of the situations which are unlikely to be dealt with in detail in the negotiation of the regime, as part of the policy of not engaging in discussion of a detailed mining code. The adoption by the Commission of the standards relating to prospecting activities and the role of this organ in a possible machinery for registering objections in this field will be of decisive importance in satisfactorily resolving this difficult problem.[140] In the same way, the acute problem of how the economic benefits of the regime are to be distributed, and on the basis of what criteria, will probably require the intervention of the Commission in the future.[141] To some extent it is already provided that the Commission should regulate the payment of fees and other financial contributions to be made by contractors, which will affect the concept of 'total regime take' and the determination of the taxes and fees specified in the management scheme.[142]

The executive competence of the Commission includes the crucial decisions that must be taken in the operation of the regime. In the main,

these concern the determination of whether the proposed activity constitutes an unacceptable environmental risk,[143] granting authorization for
exploration and exploitation activities[144] and keeping mineral-related
activities under review.[145] Other associated competences are those of
facilitating and promoting research projects in order to determine the
likely environmental impact of mineral-related activities[146] and that of
specifying the size of the blocks for such activities.[147] The aggregate of
these executive competences ensure that the Commission exercises precise control over the beginning and development of the process.

The administrative competences also refer to important matters which
impinge on the substantive policies of the regime. The consideration of
monitoring reports and the adoption of the budget of the institutions are
among the subjects to be included in this type of competence.[148]

Without prejudice to the functions expressly indicated in the corresponding draft articles, it is envisaged that the Commission will have such
other functions as are 'necessary to fulfil the objectives and principles of
the regime'.[149] This clause will make it possible to develop within the
regime the concept of implied powers, a development which has frequently occurred within the Antarctic system.

In the event that a Special Meeting of States Parties is established in
conjunction with the institutional machinery of the regime it will probably
be entrusted with some of the competences that the Draft Articles have
assigned to the Commission, particularly in relation to the identification
of areas, block sizes and the definition of some modalities of contracts or
operations. The major function of this Special Meeting in accordance
with the 1986 Draft Articles is that of considering whether a determination of the Commission to identify an area would be compatible with the
Convention (Article 38, para. 3).

The competences assigned to the Commission have attracted a certain
amount of criticism. One type of criticism is based on the view that these
competences are inadequate to ensure control over the conduct of
mineral activities and to provide adequate protection for the environment.[150] In some respects this is a valid criticism, for example in regard to
prospecting and the more or less automatic manner in which it is possible
to pass from the exploration phase to that of exploitation. In Chapter 5,
various suggestions involving strengthening the role of the Commission in
order to deal with these difficulties were considered. It has also been
suggested that the competence of the Commission should be reinforced to
enable it to make a regular analysis of the effectiveness of the measures
adopted,[151] but this is a matter which the Commission will be in a position
to consider within its normal function of reviewing the progress of mineral
activities.

A second type of criticism is also aimed at the inadequacy of the Commission's competence but is concerned with the functions entrusted on this matter to the sponsoring State, which amounts, in effect, to a criticism of the way in which these competences have been distributed. This applies particularly to the competences relating to securing compliance with the decisions of the regime since, while the Commission has a general power of monitoring activities and observance of the regime, the basic responsibility has been entrusted to the State Parties and to the sponsoring State.[152] The rules relating to inspection that we have examined in Chapter 5 also follow in general the approach of the Antarctic Treaty, which of course is not sufficient in the case of mineral-related activities; probably a greater institutional role would be appropriate in this matter, but the fact that proprietary data and other confidential information might be affected is also likely to raise difficulties between the point of view of the contractors and that of the institutions concerned. To the extent that measures to meet this kind of criticism would involve strengthening the competence of the Commission, that would entail a corresponding curtailment of the competence of States which could eventually impair the balance of the internal accommodation. However, as we have indicated, it is essential that the institutions have sufficient powers for the adequate management of the regime.

There is also a third type of criticism which is similarly directed at the inadequacy of the Commission's powers, but from the point of view of the distribution of competences between the Commission and the Regulatory Committee. This aspect will be examined further below.

The competence of the Advisory Committee
The normal competence of the Advisory Committee is to advise both the Commission and the Regulatory Committee so as to assist them in the discharge of their functions.[153] Thus its general activity has been described as providing 'a forum for consultation and co-operation concerning the collection, exchange and evaluation of ecological, technical and other information' relating to mineral activities.[154] To perform this function it must identify the necessary types of information, recommend possible research projects, recommend those areas where the conduct of mineral activities is to be prohibited, identify the types of information to be contained in exploration notifications and applications and perform other similar technical functions.[155]

Some of its advisory functions are so important that they may correctly be regarded as an initial phase of the legislative and regulatory process that culminates with the Commission. This applies to the recommendation which it is called upon to make as to whether a particular area may be opened for exploration applications or whether such a step would entail an unacceptable risk for the environment.[156] Of equal importance are the recommendations that are to be made to give substance to the environmental principles in Article III, including various technical aspects concerning equipment and operations.[157]

Furthermore, it must be pointed out that the Committee has a regulatory and executive competence of its own. As far as the former is concerned, it has the highly important function of preparing 'scientific, technical and environmental guidelines' which will be the main criterion on the basis of which the Regulatory Committee will, in its turn, prepare the management scheme.[158] The executive function is exemplified by the Committee's responsibility for monitoring the operator's compliance with the corresponding management scheme on which it has the duty to report regularly to the Commission.[159] In addition to the above, it has other functions assigned to it under the regime or entrusted to it by the Commission, enabling this organ to develop its competence to the extent necessary to perform an efficient advisory function.[160] Among other functions it has been entrusted with the task of providing advice about the availability to Parties of information, training programmes and opportunities for co-operation.

Given the close link between the work of this organ and that of the Commission, the aspects of its competence that have come under criticism refer to the relations between these two organs. As we saw earlier, there is a trend of opinion that would like to ensure that the recommendations of the Advisory Committee cannot easily be rejected by the Commission. In general, the links between these two bodies follow the model of the Canberra Convention although, in the mineral regime, the Advisory Committee has more important functions than does the Scientific Committee under the other Convention. Similar considerations may perhaps be borne in mind in connection with the relations between the Advisory Committee and the Regulatory Committees from the point of view of strengthening their institutional links.

The competence of the Regulatory Committee

The functions of the Regulatory Committee are, in general, linked with the exercise of competences of the executive type, to the extent that this body is bound to give practical application to the standards and principles of the regime and to the regulations promulgated by the Commission or, where appropriate, to the guidelines issued by the Advisory Committee. The Regulatory Committee has important competences of this type to exercise in identifying specific blocks for the purpose of exploration applications; to evaluate them and to verify that they qualify under the provisions in force and to determine the fees that are to be paid on submission of an application; or to designate one or more of its members to prepare the draft management scheme.[161]

The actual adoption of the management scheme may be described as a function of the executive type.[162] However, in this connection the competence of the Regulatory Committee is simultaneously identified with a regulatory function owing to the large number and importance of the subjects to be dealt with in that scheme – such significant items as taxes and fees, applicable law and jurisdiction, and other subjects.[163] This is not, of course, a regulatory competence of general application since it refers specifically only to each separate scheme, but in any case the Regulatory Committee fulfils a function of a normative type. If the terms and conditions are defined by this body beforehand, as has been proposed, the competence will become one of a general type. The competence of this organ to examine the management scheme and, if appropriate, to amend it also belongs to this special category of regulatory function.[164] Under the 1986 revision, the Regulatory Committee has acquired the important function of issuing exploration permits (Article 31, e).

Like the Advisory Committee, the Regulatory Committee has monitoring functions in connection with exploration and exploitation activities and, in general, these functions belong to the category of administrative competences.[165] It must be noted that, in the case of the Regulatory Committee, apart from the functions assigned to it under the regime, there is no general provision enabling it to develop its competence, as occurs in the case of the Commission. This apparently means that the residual competence within the regime, to the extent that it refers to institutions, belongs to the Commission as the body which has to decide whether it is necessary to exercise additional competence within the objectives and purposes of the Convention and, if that is the case, to decide also by which organ such competence is to be exercised. This differs from the problem of allocation of residual rights in the relationship between States and the institutions, a more complex situation which we have already considered.[166]

The competence of the Regulatory Committee has been criticized in respect of its institutional relations with the Commission. It has been pointed out in general terms that the Commission has few competences since the most important of them will have been entrusted to the Regulatory Committees.[167] Although the latter undeniably have important competences in relation to the management scheme, these are not functions that are exercised outside the framework of the provisions of the Convention. On the contrary, the Regulatory Committee is bound by the Convention always to act within the limits established by the Commission and the Advisory Committee. This criticism does not, therefore, appear to be justified, particularly because authorization for exploration and exploitation is, in the last analysis, granted by the Regulatory Committee but subject to a procedure of review by the Commission.

More specifically, the criticism has been made that the Commission has no power to modify the terms and conditions of the management scheme although it may refer it back to the Regulatory Committee for reconsideration. Similarly, the fact that the Commission apparently has no right to examine the decisions of the Regulatory Committee has also been criticized.[168] The first of these criticisms touches upon a major issue of the internal accommodation: since the fundamental negotiation between the claimant State and the applicant will take place in the context of the preparation of the management scheme, and the voting arrangements that we have examined are geared to ensure this end, if all of it is reviewed by the Commission it might completely upset the balance sought at the Regulatory Committee level. Because of this the possibility of a review by the Commission has been opposed by most claimants, as they have opposed too the suggestion that the management scheme should be formally adopted by the Commission. A review mechanism has been established, however, in the 1986 Draft Articles on limited grounds (Article 47).

In accordance with this mechanism, a review by the Commission in case of *abus de pouvoir* by the Regulatory Committee, or on the grounds that the requirements of the Convention have not been met in the negotiation and approval of the management scheme, is provided for; however, this review would only lead to a request by the Commission that the Regulatory Committee reconsider the scheme, and not to a modification of its terms and conditions by the Commission itself. It has also been suggested that if there is no veto in the voting arrangements of the Regulatory Committee there should be no review at all before the Commission, except in a situation of *abus de pouvoir*. Some pending problems are whether the initiation of a review procedure entails the suspension of a permit for exploration and the situation that could arise if the Regulatory Committee does not decide on a management scheme, either positively or negatively.

If the difficult process of negotiation leading to approval of the terms and conditions of the management scheme takes place within the Regulatory Committee, it is entirely logical that any subsequent reconsideration should take place in the same organ since otherwise the accommodation that has been sought might be entirely altered. This in no way affects the higher competence of the Commission which in the Draft Articles has the power to accept or reject these terms in the course of the review procedure. The second criticism would seem to have no justification since the Commission has the general competence to examine the question of compliance with the regime and the conduct of mineral activities, and this may include the case of the management scheme and the related decisions. If, in exercising this competence, it encounters difficulties, it may always bring them to the attention of the Regulatory Committee so that it may consider them, just as it may bring them to the attention of the Member States. The purpose of the monitoring functions and of the reports that are made to the Commission is precisely to facilitate such examination. What the Commission cannot do is to assume the competences which the regime confers on the other organs or on States.

For the above reasons, it does not appear that the competence of the Regulatory Committee impairs the institutional balance which the regime was designed to ensure, bearing in mind its specific nature and the necessities of the internal accommodation. If the purpose were to establish a centralized structure, these criticisms would be fully justified but such is not the case. In any event, the very nature and purposes of the institutional structure has been to some extent challenged by means of this criticism, a situation that requires the present approach to achieve a satisfactory balance of interests so as to demonstrate its institutional effectiveness and its contribution to an adequate internal accommodation.

8.6 Other institutional aspects of the regime

The convening of organs

The draft convention has also provided for various other interesting institutional features. One of these refers to the time and requirements for the convening of organs, a concern which can be traced back to the stage at which the original Antarctic Treaty Parties were not interested in suggestions that institutions should be established, preferring to delay this until they were shown to be strictly necessary. The Seal Convention, for example, provided that the Commission that was specified in that Convention would be convened only when a start was made on commercial exploitation of the resource.[169] The Canberra Convention, provided, on the other hand, that its Commission may be convened more expeditiously on account of its important function of putting this regime into operation,[170] which has already been done successfully.

In the case of mineral resources a different system has been provided for convening the Commission. One approach was that this must be requested by a certain number of parties to the regime, although the precise number was not determined. A second approach was that the Commission be convened automatically when a notification of exploration is submitted by a sponsoring State. Once this first meeting has taken place, the frequency of subsequent meetings would be decided.[171] However, because there are other situations that justify automatic convening, the 1984 Draft Articles introduced a more flexible approach to provide for these. This flexible approach would be particularly appropriate if there is some objection to the prospecting activities or, more importantly, it is decided that prospecting will require authorization. Moreover, the Commission must meet promptly once the regime has entered into force in order to organize its work and to adopt decisions within its competence for the operation of the regime. In the light of this, everything points to the desirability of ensuring flexibility in the requirements for the convening of meetings,[172] an approach which has not been generally accepted.

The procedure for convening the other organs is more simple. The Advisory Committee may be convened by decision of the Commission, or at the request of a number of parties to the regime.[173] It is also desirable in this context that the Advisory Commmittee should make an early start on its work in view of its important role in the operation of the regime and for this purpose it has been provided that it should be convened promptly, in conjunction with the start of work of the Commission.[174] The corresponding Regulatory Committee in its turn, must be set up within a certain period after the Commission has opened an area for the submission of applications.[175]

In this connection it is apparent that the growing institutionalization of the Antarctic system, which requires the active intervention of appropriate organs, has made it increasingly necessary that the approach of deferring the convening of an organ should be replaced by a more flexible approach whereby early operation of those organs is ensured.

The regime has also provided a number of norms of a procedural type relating to the election of the Chairman and Vice-Chairmen of the organs, the elaboration of rules of procedure, the establishment of subsidiary organs and official languages.[176] Given the important institutional function which devolves on the Chairmen of the Commission and of the Advisory Committee – whose duties include that of appointing some members of the Regulatory Committees – the appointment of these Chairmen is a matter of major political importance.

Secretariat

As in the Canberra Convention, the draft mineral Convention also provides for the creation of a Secretariat to serve the various organs of the regime and to perform functions which they entrust to it. The Commission may appoint an Executive Secretary and authorize the recruitment of the corresponding staff.[177] This exemplifies a further major change in the attitude of States party to the Antarctic Treaty who were traditionally reluctant to create even a Secretariat under the 1959 Treaty, on the grounds that it represented a form of institutionalization. This unwillingness has been criticized on various occasions[178] but the trend within the resources regimes shows a clear departure from the early approach.

With regard to the Secretariat, a number of other useful functions have been proposed, particularly that it should serve as the depository for the data and information required to be provided under the regime and should maintain a public information system.[179] Other suggestions, however, go beyond the proper functions of the Secretariat and would entail taking on roles which belong to other organs. Such suggestions include proposals to the effect that the Secretariat should perform the functions of an 'Antarctic Environmental Protection Agency' or that it should address recommendations to the member countries on compliance with the objectives and principles of the regime.[180] The draft convention has provided for various measures concerning public information, in particular that the organs should maintain a public register of their decisions and reports,[181] facilitate the participation of observers and ensure that the points of view of relevant organizations are available.

Budgetary aspects of the regime

The budgetary aspects of the regime also have a number of institutional implications. Budgetary decisions will be adopted by the Commission by consensus and they will refer both to the activities of this and of other organs.[182] There has been a certain evolution of ideas concerning methods of funding the budget. It was initially thought that each member of the Commission would contribute on an equal basis to such funding.[183] Subsequently, however, a formula was worked out whereby funding would be ensured, in the first place, by the fees that were payable on submission of the relevant notifications or applications and by the levies to be paid by contractors, without prejudice to the taxes and charges to be determined in the management scheme; later this funding was to be contributed on an equal basis by the members of the Commission until such time as the budget could be funded entirely from fees and levies.[184]

This formula has been criticized on the grounds that it tends to give priority to mineral activities as a source of revenue which might diminish the significance to be accorded to environmental factors and other subjects that do not generate such financial resources.[185] This approach to funding the budget has some similarity with the approach of the Canberra Convention which provides that after the first five years criteria relating to production and direct contributions will be applied.[186]

Standard clauses have also been provided concerning audit and financial regulations as well as the sanction that right to participate in the decisions of the Commission will be lost if members are in arrears with their contributions for two consecutive years.[187]

Headquarters, legal personality, privileges and immunities

The requirements relating to headquarters, legal personality, privileges and immunities have followed the same structure as the equivalent provisions of the Canberra Convention.[188] The location of the headquarters will, of course, have to be determined when the time comes and there is no necessity for it to be mentioned in the text of the Convention, as was done in the case of the living resources regime. The legal personality of the Commission has been clearly established, as has such legal capacity in the territory of each party 'as may be necessary to perform its functions and achieve the objective of this regime'. On this basis, the Commission may enter into contracts, acquire movable and immovable property and sue or be sued through the courts, which are the normal attributes of legal capacity.[189] The question of privileges and immunities will have to be agreed with the host country, a situation which gave rise to certain difficulties in the case of the Canberra Convention.[190]

It is to be noted that in these two regimes it is laid down that it is the Commission which will have legal personality, legal capacity, privileges and immunities. Although the Commission is only one of the organs of the respective regime, the expression seems to be used in the sense of 'organization', and thus covers the other organs which will thus enjoy the benefits of those provisions that are applicable to them; it might be argued that the legal personality, privileges and immunities generally relate to the 'organization' which will be established by the Convention and which will be legally represented by the Commission, but it would certainly be preferable to make this clear in the text of the Convention itself.

8.7   Machinery for the settlement of disputes

Procedures for the settlement of disputes are another important part of the institutional scheme of the regime. Although none of the initial drafts contained provisions on this matter, in each case a chapter was envisaged on the subject, the content of which was to be developed in the course of the negotiations.[191] In this field, as in the case of the other institutions, the approaches have evolved within the framework of the Antarctic system.

The limited approach of the Antarctic Treaty

The 1959 Treaty, as a consequence of the unwillingness of its Parties to embrace any form of institutionalization, provided a system of a restrictive nature for settling disputes which corresponded to the loose type of co-operation prevailing at the time. Article XI of the Treaty envisages the case of disputes between two or more contracting Parties 'concerning the interpretation or application of the present Treaty'.[192] For this purpose there is provision, in the first place, for consultation between the Parties in order to select the means of solution of the dispute which may consist of negotiation, investigation, mediation, conciliation, arbitration or judicial settlement or other peaceful means. If the dispute is not resolved in this manner, the possibility of referring it to the International Court of Justice is envisaged but only on condition that this step is taken 'with the consent, in each case, of all parties to the dispute'.[193] In cases where no agreement is reached to refer the dispute to the Court, the obligation to seek a peaceful settlement procedure must still be fulfilled, a provision which probably had its origin in the unsuccessful attempt by the United Kingdom to take Argentina and Chile before the Court in 1955 concerning the disputed Antarctic territories.[194]

This provision concerning submission of the dispute to the International Court of Justice has raised a number of problems of interpretation. According to Auburn, since the subject of the dispute is the interpretation or application of the Treaty, it would not be restricted to the parties directly involved and any party might intervene in the matter; the consent of all of them would accordingly be required for purposes of recourse to the Court.[195] Although this situation is theoretically possible in regard to an eventual problem affecting all Contracting Parties, it does not appear to represent a commonly occurring case. Thus, the consent of the parties directly involved in the dispute will be sufficient for referral of the case to the Court. The interpretation mentioned above would seem to be somewhat far-fetched.

The second problem of interpretation is whether this consent is required in each case on an *ad hoc* basis or whether, for the countries that have accepted the compulsory jurisdiction of the Court, a general consent is sufficient. Although the text of the article refers to the fact that consent must be given in each case, in the final discussion on this article the United Kingdom and France interpreted its scope in the following way:

'. . . when a dispute is of such a nature that it falls within the acceptances of the compulsory jurisdiction of the Court previously put forward by the parties to the dispute, this paragraph cannot be interpreted in the sense that a further consent is required before a reference can be made';[196] such would be the case, according to this interpretation, if the Optional Clause of the States concerned covers reference of disputes concerning the interpretation or application of treaties to which it is a party. South Africa seems to have agreed with this interpretation since it mentioned that its acceptance of compulsory jurisdiction was subject to reservations, thus implicitly indicating that such acceptance was applicable.[197]

It must be noted that the question of the jurisdiction of the Court also raises the problem whether a third country that is not Party to the Treaty and has accepted the Court's jurisdiction could refer a dispute over Antarctic questions to be resolved by the Court with regard to another country that is a Party to the Treaty and has also accepted compulsory jurisdiction.[198] In any event, as the International Court of Justice ruled in the *South West Africa Cases,* the applicant must establish a 'legal right or interest (which is a different thing from a political interest)'.[199]

The restricted procedures in the Treaty for resolving disputes do not prevent the Parties from improving outside the Treaty the machinery that may exist for regulating their reciprocal relations on this matter. An example of this is the Peace and Friendship Treaty signed by Chile and Argentina on 29 November 1984 which puts an end to the dispute concerning the southern maritime boundary between the two countries.[200] Although the clauses concerning delimitation, navigation and other matters do not apply in the Antarctic, and cannot affect the rights or legal positions of the Parties on the continent or in its adjacent maritime spaces, there are a number of general provisions of the agreement which apply expressly to Antarctica. Among these are the provisions concerning peace and friendship, the non-use of force and the peaceful settlement of disputes.[201] The latter include a conciliation procedure and a compulsory arbitration procedure.[202] In this way the disputes that may arise in Antarctica between those two countries are covered by additional procedures whereby they may be resolved without prejudice to any procedures envisaged by the Antarctic system itself.

The first resources regimes, i.e. the Agreed Measures and the Seal Convention, following the same restrictive criterion, contained no machinery for resolving disputes. While the former are covered by the actual provisions of the Treaty on this subject, because they are incorporated in a recommendation adopted within the framework of the Treaty, the latter will be covered to the extent that the disputes are between countries which are, at the same time, Parties to the Antarctic Treaty. With regard to disputes that may arise with countries that are not Parties to the 1959 Treaty but which may be Parties to the Convention, or between such countries, there might be a vacuum in this connection. So far no country has acceded to the Convention without previously becoming a Party to the 1959 Treaty and for this reason the situation does not arise. This point will have to be considered if and when the Contracting Parties invite a country which finds itself in this situation to accede in accordance with the provisions of Article 12 of the Seals Convention.[203]

Initial innovations of the living resources regime
The regime for the conservation of living resources has already been faced with different requirements in this connection since it deals with a type of co-operation more closely directed towards the management of natural resources. Although Article XI of the 1959 Antarctic Treaty is closely followed, a special arbitration mechanism has been included also, in conjunction with the possibility of recourse to the International Court of Justice.[204] The procedure for constituting the arbitral tribunal is provided in the Annex to the Convention.[205] This arbitration procedure allows greater flexibility for disputes that may have a commercial scope or relate to the management of the resource, but even this approach has been criticized as being inadequate on the grounds of not having established compulsory procedures, possibly modelled on the Law of the Sea Conference approach in respect of dispute settlement.[206]

For countries that become Parties to the Law of the Sea Convention, the machinery of the Canberra Convention may be applied for resolving disputes concerning the interpretation or application of the Law of the Sea Convention, in the light of the provisions of Article 282 of that Convention, provided that the requirement of utilizing a procedure which leads to a binding decision is met.[207] In principle, the opposite case might also arise in which a dispute over the interpretation or application of the Canberra Convention, which is at the same time a problem of interpretation or application of the Law of the Sea Convention, is submitted by two countries party to the latter Convention, to the machinery for resolving disputes contained therein.[208]

The new requirements of the mineral regime
The nature of the Antarctic mineral regime has given rise to requirements in regard to the settlement of disputes that are entirely different from the traditional ones. Not only is this a regime in which State Parties have a major role to perform, but there will be also the active participation of the

institutions in matters and decisions of importance and, above all, the participation of private and public contractors and operators who have rights and obligations under this regime and its measures for implementation. The subjects who can intervene are closely similar to those under the Law of the Sea Convention sea-bed regime even though their relationships and powers are different. To this extent, the precedent of the system for the settlement of disputes designed for the latter regime may prove useful in the quest for appropriate solutions and in illustrating the problems that need to be dealt with.[209]

Disputes concerning the interpretation or application of the Convention
The first type of dispute that needs to be dealt with is one which may arise between Member States on questions of the interpretation or application of the Convention which establishes the regime. Given the importance of these matters for the management of the regime as a whole, they require a procedure for resolving disputes which is relatively institutionalized in order to ensure a measure of consistency in decisions. In the case of the deep sea-bed regime, following a difficult discussion on the alternatives to be envisaged three options were provided for settling this type of dispute: (i) submitting them to an *ad hoc* Chamber of the Law of the Sea Tribunal; (ii) submitting them to the Sea-Bed Disputes Chamber of that Tribunal; (iii) or submitting them to an *ad hoc* chamber of the Sea-Bed Disputes Chamber. The first option has been correctly described as being close to arbitration.[210]

In the case of the Antarctic regime, it will be necessary to provide machinery which embodies this greater degree of institutionalization and uniformity of interpretation. The traditionally provided recourse to the International Court of Justice, which might today also include a chamber of the Court, has certain limitations in this connection, although it might nevertheless be envisaged as an option. It would, in any case, be preferable to provide the regime with a tribunal of its own even if this were a relatively simple machinery. The use of the Law of the Sea Tribunal would be inappropriate for some kind of disputes since it would involve a confusion between the guiding criteria of each of the two regimes, which, as has been explained, are very different; nevertheless, some other disputes might be eventually submitted to this Tribunal. It is necessary, in any case, to keep in mind that solution through arbitration is not an adequate means of ensuring the required institutional basis and uniformity.

The States participating in the Antarctic mineral negotiations have shown some important reluctance to the idea of establishing a tribunal for the purpose of settling disputes or some other form of binding judicial settlement, being more inclined to the provision of an arbitral procedure and, in some cases, to empower the Commission with some functions in the field of dispute settlement, mainly in order to assist the parties in finding the appropriate means of settlement. The role of institutions in avoiding or minimizing disputes between member States will certainly be of a decisive importance.[211] Discussions have also taken place on whether arbitration should be optional or compulsory and on the alternative of compulsory conciliation. In any event, the arbitral tribunal or other institutions called to intervene in dispute settlement should have their competence clearly delimitated so as not to decide upon matters which might touch upon Article IV of the Antarctic Treaty or the responsibilities of Consultative Parties under the Antarctic Treaty System; given the political and legal importance of that Article and other functions of Consultative Parties it would be highly conflictive to have these issues subject to some form of judicial review which might upset the difficult balance of interests invoved.

Disputes concerning action taken by organs

A second type of dispute that may arise could be between the States Parties and the institutions of the regime, whether it is the Commission or the Regulatory Committees that are involved. In the case of the deep sea-bed, the Sea-Bed Disputes Chamber was provided with mandatory jurisdiction over all acts or omissions of the Authority that might be in contravention of the regime and of its rules and regulations, as well as for cases of excess of jurisdiction or abuse of power.[212] This recourse is open to States Parties, as it is also to contractors in the context of disputes concerning their contracts.[213] In the light of the complex problems relating to the distribution of competences within the framework of the sea-bed regime, a number of limitations have been established for this right of recourse which are intended to preserve the discretionary powers of the Authority.[214] In certain situations there also exists a recourse aimed at preventing the adoption of certain actions.[215]

The powers of the organs in the Antarctic regime are less than those of the Sea-Bed Authority but, as we have seen, they have an important regulatory, executive and administrative function. In the exercise of these powers, disputes may arise concerning the compatibility of certain decisions within the regime, concerning the competences of the organ to adopt specific measures or concerning problems of the abuse of power. For this reason it would be advisable that there should be a recourse similar to that which has been described and that it should be available, on an equal basis, to States and contractors. The tribunal could not have competence to declare an act null and void since that might give rise to difficult institutional conflicts but it would be available to rule on the inapplicability of the disputed measures to the case in question and to grant compensation and other means of redress for damage that may have been caused. It would also be necessary in this case to preserve the discretionary powers of the organs as regards, for example, the environmental assessments which will lead to a determination on whether the opening of an area is or is not an unacceptable risk for the environment. The concept of a recourse to prevent certain actions does not seem to be justified in the Antarctic case, since the powers of the organs are not as comprehensive as in the deep sea-bed regime and in the Antarctic case there is no body like an Assembly.

It would also be appropriate for recourse to be available to the institutions in regard to disputes involving States Parties since the latter have a number of important competences in the regime which may also give rise to disputes of this type. We may draw attention, in particular, to the competence of enforcement. To the extent that the rights of contractors may be affected, they should also be in a position to bring actions against States Parties. As we saw earlier, special tribunals have also been proposed for a number of matters such as the environment.[216]

Within the disputes that may concern action by the institutions there is also another situation that may be considered in the light of the precedent established by the sea-bed regime. The latter provided for the case of disputes relating to action by officials. An administrative tribunal is contemplated for the usual type of disciplinary measures[217] but, in the Antarctic case, this does not appear to be necessary although for these matters there could be a linkage to the administrative tribunal of some agreed international organization. The really important situation is that of disputes over violations of the prohibition to disclose information or industrial secrets for which, in the case of the deep sea-bed regime, a tribunal to try such cases is to be specified by the regulations of the Authority.[218] In the Antarctic case too, there may be officials who have access to confidential information concerning applications, inspections or other activities, and it would therefore be important to provide a mechanism of similar scope.

In the case of the deep sea-bed regime, certain actions of the machinery for the settlement of disputes have also been contemplated as a means of resolving institutional problems such as suspending a member for serious infringement of the provisions of the Law of the Sea Convention, a matter on which the determination of the Sea-Bed Disputes Chamber is envisaged.[219] This aspect does not arise to the same extent in the Antarctic context where participation in the regime is characterized by a co-operative approach. If violations of this nature were to occur it would be for the organs themselves to correct them on the basis of their powers of supervision and control over the process. In spite of the above, it must be borne in mind that one of the principal purposes of the machinery for resolving disputes is that of enabling the correct application of the regime, including ensuring compliance with its provisions and enforcement. To this end, provision might perhaps be made for a role of dispute settlement mechanisms in relation to specific problems of compliance and enforcement requiring independent determination, a step which would facilitate the work of the organs under this regime.

Disputes relating to contracts

The third and probably the most important category of disputes is that which refers to the exploration and exploitation contracts. This is the category for which the contractor will need to have direct and prompt access to the machinery for resolving disputes. Just as in the deep sea-bed regime under the Law of the Sea Convention, it will have to be provided that, in addition to the contractor, participation in the settlement procedure will be open to the sponsoring State by means of the submission of written or oral statements since the sponsoring State has functions relating to compliance with the regime and a measure of legal liability.[220] The same difficulty as in the sea-bed regime is also likely to arise concerning the disinclination of the socialist States to permit an individual to initiate legal action against a sovereign State. Paragraph 2 of Article 190 of the Law of the Sea Convention solved this problem by requiring that, in such cases, the respondent State might request that the sponsoring State should appear as the representative of the contractor or, on the contrary, that the respondent State should be represented by a juridical person of its own nationality. Thus the case will always, in formal terms, be one of State against State, or individual against individual.[221]

The interpretation or implementation of the contract and the acts or omissions of one party directed at the other party, or directly affecting his legitimate interests, are the key issues over which disputes may arise under the deep sea-bed regime.[222] Other disputes may concern the rejection of the contract, legal problems that arise during the negotiation, liability of the Authority, certain financial questions and other questions relating to the transfer of technology.[223] In view of the differences between this regime and that of the Antarctic, the machinery of the latter may be open to questions of interpretation and application and to matters concerning acts and omissions which directly affect the rights of the contractor. On other issues, such as the rejection of a contract, it is a matter within the discretionary powers of the regime, and there are yet other issues that relate to situations not envisaged in the Antarctic regime.

The Law of the Sea Convention sea-bed regime provided various procedures for resolving such disputes.[224] Some of them must be submitted to the exclusive jurisdiction of the Sea-Bed Disputes Chamber, because of their important institutional implications. For others, however, there is a choice of procedures owing to their more commercial nature. These include disputes concerning the interpretation or application of the contract. The procedural choices comprise an agreement to refer the matter to the Sea-Bed Disputes Chamber or, in the absence of an agreement, a unilateral recourse to that Chamber or submission of the matter to compulsory commercial arbitration in accordance with the UNCITRAL rules, or others which may be prescribed by the Authority. If, in the course of the arbitration procedure, a question of interpretation arises concerning Part XI of the Convention, the matter must be referred to the Sea-Bed Disputes Chamber and the arbitral award must be given in compliance with this latter decision. This referral procedure is inspired by Article 177 of the Treaty of Rome.[225]

These criteria are also relevant to the Antarctic case. Disputes which have an institutional content, such as those concerning acts or omissions, must normally be brought to the attention of the tribunal that has been suggested. Those relating to more commercial aspects may be submitted to arbitration for which purpose the pertinent rules must be defined. It would also be appropriate to provide for referral of questions of interpretation to the tribunal in order to ensure the principle of uniformity of the interpretation of the regime. Allowing a choice of procedures for specific disputes is also an advisable measure of flexibility.

The applicable law

We earlier had occasion to consider questions relating to the law applicable to the contract.[226] Such questions also relate to the law which will eventually be applicable by the suggested tribunal in the Antarctic regime. A first category of rules has its origins in international law, in relation to which the tribunal will apply the Convention which establishes the regime, and the rules and regulations promulgated by the organs, the clauses of the actual contract in relevant cases and other rules of international law compatible with the foregoing. In this context one may also note a close parallel with the sea-bed regime.[227] However, in the Antarctic case there also exists a second category of rules which may in certain cases be applicable. As we have indicated, the determination to be made in the management scheme concerning the law applicable to the contractor and his employees may include choice of a system of national law. In the case of a matter referred to the regime's machinery for the settlement of disputes, this domestic law may also be applied. To the extent that this determination of the national law simultaneously involves a determination of the national jurisdiction applicable for certain purposes, a conflict may arise concerning the competence of national courts and the machinery of the regime. In this connection it will be necessary to provide standards for resolving this situation and for drawing up the existing options. In the event of intervention by a national court, it would be appropriate also to consider the machinery for referral to a tribunal of the regime in the case of questions relating to the interpretation of the Convention.

In considering the sea-bed regime, a question of interpretation arose concerning whether the Sea-Bed Disputes Chamber can decide *ex aequo et bono* and, similarly, if this would be compatible with the intention of ensuring a uniform interpretation.[228] This consideration concerning compatibility is applicable, *mutatis mutandis,* to the Antarctic case. A decision *ex aequo et bono* does not seem to be appropriate for disputes which have a large institutional component or which refer to basic questions of interpretation. For other types of dispute, the arbitration procedure might provide adequate flexibility.

Special problems of international claims

The complex nature of the Antarctic regime raises certain other problems which it is necessary to bear in mind, mainly related to questions of nationality and the capacity of contractors to make international claims. The first question is whether a contractor may have recourse to the machinery for settlement of disputes involving his own sponsoring State. The reply would normally be in the negative, in view of the general rules of international law, unless such recourse were specifically provided for.[229] However, given the important functions which the sponsoring States have in the proposed Antarctic regime, including certain functions relating to the application of the regime, it may be necessary for the contractors to have this capacity for direct international action in cases where their rights are affected.

If this were so, the question would also arise as to whether it would be necessary previously to exhaust local remedies. Whether or not the national courts have exclusive competence to consider claims of this type, provision should be made, as we have seen, for referral to the tribunal of the regime for questions involving the interpretation of the Convention and other standards. The possibility of the recourse against the sponsoring State under the deep sea-bed regime is by no means clear but it would seem indirectly that this has not been envisaged in the light of the provision of Article 190, paragraph 1, concerning the notification of the sponsor and his right to participate in disputes in which an individual is a party.[230]

Another related problem arises concerning the requirements, with which both the applicant and the contractor must comply, relating to incorporation in the sponsoring State. Owing to the fact that they must have the nationality of the sponsoring State or be incorporated under its laws, when the question involves the local subsidiary of a foreign firm that has invested capital, the problem as to whether or not, in a situation in which the rights of the subsidiary are affected by the State of incorporation, the State with which the parent firm is related is entitled to intervene by submitting a claim.[231] The problem may be particularly complicated in the case of a joint venture which combines capital from various sources but which is formally incorporated under the national legislation of one State.

A comparable situation occurred with the incorporation requirements provided by the United Kingdom legislation in the oil sector. One author explains this in the following terms:

> Technically, the loss of any licence rights through, e.g., nationalization, would be a loss by a British company. The reality, of course, is otherwise. It is unclear whether the principle of nationality of claims affirmed in the *Barcelona Traction* case, whereby an international claim by a corporation can only be brought by the country of incorporation, would be applied in these circumstances. Would it be a fatal stumbling block to international litigation that the company which had sustained the loss was technically not, e.g., a United States or French company, but a United Kingdom company? And that therefore these Governments could not act on behalf of such company?[232]

From the point of view of the Antarctic regime, if what is required is the comprehensive protection of the investments and rights of the contractor, it is not only essential to provide for him to be protected against possible actions by the organs or other acts taken in the context of this regime, but also against other situations such as the one that has been described which takes place within the framework of the national law of a Member State. In situations of this latter type, the rules of the International Centre for the Settlement of Investment Disputes or other multilateral or bilateral agreements on the protection of investments may be relevant.[233]

A start has recently been made on consideration of the question of settling disputes relating to natural resources in the context of the global utilization of certain spaces and their resources[234] and in the context of interests of future generations in those resources.[235] This point of view, as far as the Antarctic is concerned, is more relevant to the problems of the external accommodation which will be considered in the chapters that follow.

From what has been explained in this and the preceding chapters concerning the internal accommodation within the Antarctic mineral regime, it can be seen that the institutional machinery envisaged has a key role to play in ensuring the necessary balance and the specific arrangements that will make that accommodation possible. The highly complex interests at stake in these negotiations are very difficult to reconcile unless this is done in the context of institutional arrangements where those interests can be merged in a common policy relating to the management of the regime and the administration of the resources in question.

However elaborate and sometimes intricate the institutional approach of this regime can be, it has so far succeeded in finding the right way to proceed in the search of the internal accommodation. No doubt many changes are desirable and many probably will be made in the institutional machinery that we have examined, particularly in so far as decision-making and relations between the several organs are concerned, but it is basically within this kind of arrangement that the final accommodation will take place. This fact alone is of the greatest importance for the successful outcome of the current negotiations.

In the search for appropriate solutions the negotiators have relied on many past experiences, both within the Antarctic Treaty system and in the broader framework of international law and its contribution to the development of institutional law. This has also been a useful approach to the success and progress of such negotiations since many precedents in this field have proven to be helpful to find the right solutions and overcome problems which otherwise might have constituted serious obstacles for the final outcome. This is not to say that there are no shortcomings in the draft articles that have been examined, but generally they do not affect the overall balanced result of the process and the fundamental role assigned to each institution. However, as we shall examine next, the issues of the external accommodation have meant a new challenge for the Antarctic mineral regime, particularly in terms of its institutional questions.

Chapter 8 Notes

1. See generally Chapter 1 supra.
2. On the Consultative meetings, see Truls Hanevold: 'The Antarctic Treaty Consultative Meetings – Form and Procedure', *Coop. and Confl,* 3/4, 1971, 183–199; F. M. Auburn: 'Consultative Status under the Antarctic Treaty', *I.C.L.Q.,* Vol. 28, 1979, 514–522; Alfred van der Essen: 'Les reunions consultatives du Traité sur l'Antarctique', *R.B.D.I.,* Vol. XV, 1980, 20–27; F. M. Auburn: *Antarctic Law and Politics,* 1982, Chapter 5; R. Tucker Scully: 'The Antarctic Treaty system: overview and analysis', in Lewis M. Alexander and Lynne Carter Hanson (eds.): *Antarctic Politics and Marine Resources: critical choices for the 1980's,* 1985, 3–11; R. Tucker Scully: 'The evolution of the Antarctic Treaty System – the institutional perspective', in US Polar Research Board: *Antarctic Treaty System, An Assessment,* 1986, 391–411; William F. Budd: 'The Antarctic Treaty as a Scientific Mechanism – Contributions of Antarctic scientific Research Post IGY', in US Polar Research Board, op. cit., 103–151.
3. Auburn, op. cit., note 2 supra, at 147; see also Peter J. Beck: 'Preparatory meetings for the Antarctic Treaty 1958–59', *Pol. Rec.,* Vol. 22, 1985, 653–664, at 661.
4. The procedure for the admission of Consultative Parties was established by the First Special Consultative Meeting, held in London 25–29 July 1977; for the final report of this meeting, see Chile: *Memoria del Ministerio de Relaciones Exteriores,* 1977, 1030–1032.
5. See Article IX, par. 2 of the Antarctic Treaty. The following countries have acceded to Consultative status under this article on the dates indicated: Poland, 17 September 1977; Federal Republic of Germany, 23 June 1981; Brazil and India, 12 September 1983; People's Republic of China and Uruguay, 7 October 1985.
6. For a listing of the exclusive powers of the Consultative Parties and a discussion of the 'special responsibility', see W. M. Bush: *Antarctica and International Law,* 1982, 84–86; for a discussion of the role of Consultative Parties in environmental protection and related issues, see also R. M. Laws: 'International stewardship of the Antarctic: problems, successes and future options', *Marine Pollution Bulletin,* UK, Vol. 16, N° 2, February 1985, 49–55.
7. Antarctic Treaty, Article IX, par. 4.
8. See Chapter 2 supra.
9. For a discussion of the institutional arrangements under the Antarctic Treaty and the 'double veto' concept in the decision-making procedures, see Gillian Triggs: 'The Antarctic Treaty Regime: a workable compromise or a "Purgatory of Ambiguity"?', *Case West R.J.I.L.,* Vol. 17, 1985, 195–228.
10. See the *Rules of Procedure* adopted on 10 July 1961, par. 23; text in Bush, op. cit., note 6 supra, at 116–118.
11. See for example Article XII of the Convention on the Conservation of Antarctic Marine Living Resources, which refers to consensus for decision-making in the Commission.
12. See generally Henry G. Schermess: *International Institutional Law,* 1980, particularly at 391–430.
13. Michel Fromont: 'L'abstention dans les votes au sein des organisations internationales', *A.F.D.I.,* 1961, 492–523.
14. Leland M. Goodrich, Edvard Hambro and Anne Patricia Simons: *Charter of the United Nations,* 1969, 215–231; Constantin A. Stavropoulos: 'The practice of voluntary abstentions by permanent members of the Security Council under Article 27, paragraph 3, of the Charter of the United Nations', *A.J.I.L.,* Vol. 61,

1967, 737–752; Sydney D. Bailey: *Voting in the Security Council,* 1969, 63–74; Sydney D. Bailey: *The procedure of the UN Security Council,* 1975.

15. Fernando Zegers: 'The Canberra Convention: objectives and political aspects of its negotiation', in Francisco Orrego Vicuña (ed.): *Antarctic Resources Policy,* 1983, 149–156, at 156.

16. Ibid., at 155, with particular reference to the practice of the Law of the Sea Conference; see also Giuseppe Barile: 'The way of negotiating at the Third United Nations Conference on the Law of the Sea', in C. L. Rozakis and C. A. Stephanou (eds): *The new Law of the Sea,* 1983, 21–31.

17. Edvard Hambro: 'Some notes on the future of the Antarctic Treaty Collaboration', *A.J.I.L.,* Vol. 68, 1974, 217–226, at 224.

18. Ernest B. Haas: 'Why collaborate? Issue-Linkage and international regimes', *World Politics,* Vol. 32, 1980, 357–405, at 358.

19. Oran R. Young: 'International regimes: problems of concept formation', *World Politics,* Vol. 32, 1980, 331–356, at 332.

20. Ibid., at 332–333; see also Ibid.: *Resource Management at the International level. The case of the North Pacific,* 1977, at 45.

21. Oran R. Young: *Compliance and Public Authority,* 1979, at 93.

22. R. Tucker Scully: 'Alternatives for co-operation and institutionalization in Antarctica: outlook for the 1990's', in Francisco Orrego Vicuña, op. cit., note 15 supra, 281–296, at 283.

23. Van der Essen, loc. cit., note 2 supra, at 20; translation by the author of this book.

24. Scully, loc. cit., note 22 supra, at 286.

25. See, for example, Article III and Article XIV of the Agreed Measures.

26. This is particularly the case of the designation of Specially Protected Areas, all of which have been approved by a Recommendation of the Consultative Meetings; see Annex B of the Agreed Measures and the reference to the pertinent recommendations in Bush, op. cit., note 6 supra, at 157–158.

27. See for example Article 2 and 4 and Article 3 of the Seal Convention.

28. Article 6, par. 1 (b) of the Seal Convention.

29. Article 6, par. 1 (c) (ii), and Article 6, par. 1 (a) of the Seal Convention.

30. Behring Fur Seals Arbitration: award of the tribunal, Paris, August 15, 1893, *A.J.I.L.,* Vol. 6, 1912, 233–241.

31. Douglas M. Johnston: *The International Law of Fisheries,* 1965; Albert W. Koers: *International regulation of marine fisheries,* 1973; J. E. Carroz: 'Institutional aspects of fishery management under the new regime of the oceans', *S.D.L.R.,* Vol. 21, 1984, 513–540.

32. Schermers, op. cit., note 12 supra; Goodrich et al., op. cit., note 14 supra; Inis L. Claude Jr.: *Swords into plowshares. The problems and progress of international organization,* 1971; D. W. Bowett: *The Law of international institutions,* 1982; Felipe H. Paolillo: 'Les structures institutionnelles du regime des fonds marins', in René-Jean Dupuy et Daniel Vignes: *Traité du Nouveau Droit de la Mer,* 1985, 603–684.

33. Convention on the Conservation of Antarctic Marine Living Resources, Articles VII to XVII.

34. Ibid., Article VII, par. 2 (a).

35. Ibid., Article VII, par. 2 (b).

36. Ibid., Article VII, par. 2 (c).

37. For a discussion of the case of the Netherlands and the Republic of Korea, see James N. Barnes: 'The emerging Convention on the Conservation of Antarctic Marine Living Resources: an attempt to meet the new realities of resource exploitation in the Southern Ocean', in Jonathan I. Charney (ed.): *The new nationalism and the use of common spaces,* 1982, 239–286, at 258.

38. Ibid., at 251, 262.

39. Japan, the United Kingdom and the United States were among the countries favouring a majority vote for decision-making; see Barnes, op. cit., note 37 supra, at 254.

40. Argentina, Chile, Poland and the USSR favoured consensus or unanimity; Barnes, op. cit., note 37 supra, at 254.

41. Convention on the Conservation of Antarctic Marine Living Resources, Article XII, par. 1, 2.

42. Zegers, loc. cit., note 15 supra, at 155. The 'Gentlemen's Agreement' which formed part of the Rules of Procedure of the Law of the Sea Conference provided that 'the Conference should make every effort to reach agreement on substantive matters by way of consensus; there should be no voting on such matters until all efforts at consensus have been exhausted' Doc. A/CONF. 62/L. 1, Appendix, *Official Docs.*, Vol. III, 1975, at 80; a veto or formal objection exercised by a State did not necessarily prevent the attainment of consensus, unless it were a so-called 'dominant States and groups of States', on which see Barile, loc. cit., note 16 supra, at 26–29; on the procedure of the Law of the Sea Conference, see also Helge Vindenes: 'Procedimientos y técnicas de negociación en la Tercera Conferencia de las Naciones Unidas sobre el Derecho del Mar y su incidencia en la busqueda de un acuerdo substancial sobre el tema', in CEPAL: *Economía de los Oceanos,* Vol. 1, 1978, 29–44. See also C. Wilfred Jenks: 'Unanimity, the veto, weighted voting, special and simple majorities and Consensus as modes of decision in international organisations', *Cambridge Essays in International Law,* Essays in honour of Lord McNair, 1965, 48–63.

43. Zegers, loc. cit., note 15 supra, at 155–156.

44. Ronald F. Frank: 'The Convention on the Conservation of Antarctic Marine Living Resources', *Ocean Dev. I.L.,* Vol. 13, 1983–1984, 291–345, at 310.

45. Objection procedures are contemplated, inter alia, by the North-East Atlantic Fisheries Convention, made in London, 24 January 1959, *UNTS,* 1964, Vol. 486, N° 7078, 157–182; the Convention on Northwest Atlantic Fisheries, made in Ottawa, 24 October 1978, which established the Northwest Atlantic Fisheries Organization, *Official Journal of the European Communities,* N° L 378, Vol. 21, 30 December 1978, 16–29; and the International Convention for the Regulation of Whaling. For comments on these procedures see Arild Underdal: *The politics of International Fisheries Management. The case of the Northeast Atlantic,* 1980, at 50–55; Koers, op. cit., note 31 supra, 119–169; and Albert W. Koers: 'The freedom of fishing in decline: the case of the North-East Atlantic', in Churchill, Simmonds and Welch: *New Directions in the Law of the Sea,* Vol. III, 1973, 19–35.

46. See the Rules of Procedure of the Scientific Committee, Rule 3; text in: *Report of the Second Meeting of the Scientific Committee,* Hobart, Australia, 1983, 43–49. The temporary rules of procedure had limited themselves to refer decision-making to the provisions of the Convention; see particularly Rule 15, text in ibid., at 39–42.

47. See Rule 3 of the Rules of Procedure of the Scientific Committee in conjunction with Article XVI of the Convention. While the first provision refers to 'all the views' expressed in the Committee, the latter refers to 'minority reports'; this last provision implies a decision taken by majority, and not necessarily by consensus as normally required by the Rules of Procedure.

48. Barnes, loc. cit., note 37 supra, at 267.

49. For the work of the institutions set up by the Convention, see *Report of the First Meeting of the Commission,* Hobart, 25 May–11 June 1982; *Report of the Second Meeting of the Commission,* Hobart, 29 August–9 September 1983; *Report of the Third Meeting of the Commission,* Hobart, 3–14 September 1984; *Report of the Fourth Meeting of the Commission,* Hobart, 2–13 September 1985, with

particular reference to conservation measures adopted on this occasion. See also: *Report of the First Meeting of the Scientific Committee,* Hobart, 7–11 June 1982; *Report of the Second Meeting of the Scientific Committee,* Hobart, 30 August–8 September 1983; *Report of the Third Meeting of the Scientific Committee,* Hobart, 3–13 September 1984; *Report of the Fourth Meeting of the Scientific Committee,* Hobart, 2–9 September 1985. See also Commission: *Basic Documents,* 1982; Commission: *Selected papers presented to the Scientific Committee of CCAMLR, 1982–1984,* Part 1, Part 2, 1985.

50. See Chapter 6 supra, Section 6.1.
51. See generally Barnes, loc. cit., note 37 supra; Frank, loc. cit., note 44 supra. See also Barbara Mitchell and Lee Kimball: 'Conflict over the cold continent', *For. Pol.* N° 35, Summer 1979, 124–141, at 136–138; see also generally, Barbara Mitchell and Richard Sandbrook: *The Management of the Southern Ocean,* International Institute for Environment and Development, 1980.
52. Hanevold, loc. cit., note 2 supra, at 199.
53. Scully, loc. cit., note 22 supra, at 295–296; see also Scully, works cit., note 2 supra.
54. C. D. Beeby: 'An overview of the problems which should be addressed in the preparation of a regime governing the mineral resources of Antarctica', in Francisco Orrego Vicuña, op. cit., note 15 supra, 191–198, at 195.
55. See generally Scully, loc. cit., note 22 supra and note 2 supra.
56. Scully, loc. cit., note 22 supra, at 295.
57. Ibid., at 295.
58. For the point of view of the concern of environmentalists on the institutions of the regime and other aspects, see generally Alastair Machin: 'Preferred futures: an environmental view', in *The Antarctic: preferred futures, constraints and choices,* New Zealand Institute of International Affairs, 1983, 69–74; also Alistair Graham: 'Environment hazards in the Antarctic', in Ibid., at 25–30.
59. Francisco Orrego Vicuña: 'The definition of a regime on Antarctic Mineral resources: basic options', in Ibid., op. cit., note 15 supra, 199–215, at 208–209.
60. Beeby, loc. cit., note 54 supra, at 194; see also generally the *1983 Draft Articles* and the *1984 Draft Articles.*
61. Paul Fauchille: *Traité de Droit International Public,* Tome I, Deuxieme Partie, Paris, 1925, at 659; see also Chapter 1 supra.
62. See, for example, Steven J. Burton: 'New stresses on the Antarctic Treaty: toward international legal institutions governing Antarctic resources', *Virg.L.R.,* Vol. 65, 1979, 421–512, at 485–490; Jonathan I. Charney: 'Future strategies for an Antarctic mineral resource regime – can the environment be protected?', in Charney, op. cit., note 37 supra, 206–238, at 225–226; Oscar Pinochet: 'Algunas reflexiones sobre el problema de la antártica en el año 2000', in Francisco Orrego Vicuña (ed.): *La Antártica y sus Recursos,* 1984, 355–367, at 361–363.
63. For a description and criticism of the US proposal of June 1982, see *E.C.O.,* Vol. XXII, N° 2, January 17–28, 1983, Wellington, New Zealand, at 2–3.
64. Reproduced from *E.C.O.* cit., note 63 supra, at 2.
65. *1983 Draft Articles,* Article XXIX, par. 1.
66. Graham, loc. cit., note 58 supra, at 28–29.
67. Ibid., at 28.
68. *1984 Draft Articles,* Article XX, par. 1; see also *E.C.O.,* Vol. XXVII, N° 2, Tokyo, May 22–31, 1984, at 6. See further *1986 Draft Articles,* Article 29, par. 1.
69. *1983 Draft Articles,* Article X, par. 2 (a).
70. Ibid., Article X, par. 2 (b).
71. Convention on the Conservation of Antarctic Marine Living Resources, Article VII, par. 2 (a).

72. *1984 Draft Articles,* Article X, par. 2 (a). On the question of participation in the regime see generally Chapter 9 infra.
73. *1984 Draft Articles,* Article X, par. 2 (b). See the *1986 Draft Articles,* Article 19, par. 2 (a), (b), where the situation of Consultative Parties is different depending on whether they had this status on signing the Convention or not.
74. See Section 8.1 of this Chapter for a comment on the fact that it is unlikely that once Consultative status has been recognized it will ever be withdrawn.
75. *1984 Draft Articles,* Article X, par. 2 (d). See also *1986 Draft Articles,* Article 19, par. 2 (c). The approach of Article X, par. 2 (b) of the *1983 Draft Articles,* was correspondingly changed, since membership was related there only to the condition of being 'engaged' in Antarctic mineral resource activities.
76. See, for example *E.C.O.,* Vol. XXIII, N° 1, Bonn, July 11–22, 1983 at 3.
77. *1983 Draft Articles,* Article X, par. 4. The *1984 Draft Articles* do not refer to the category of parties to the Antarctic Treaty; see Article X, par. 4; see also *1986 Draft Articles,* Article 19, par. 4. Under the later revision participation in the Mineral Convention presupposes participation in the Antarctic Treaty.
78. Chapter VIII of the *1983 Draft Articles,* refers to the final clauses, but these have not yet been elaborated; some aspects of the final clauses which are of interest for third States will be examined in Chapter 9 infra.
79. See generally Albert W. Koers: 'Participation of the European Economic Community in a new Law of the Sea Convention', *A.J.I.L.,* Vol. 73, 1979, 426–443, particularly at 433–435; Markus Ederer: 'Selective legal problems arising from the accession of the European Economic Community to the Law of the Sea Convention', Research paper, Ocean Law Seminar, University of Miami School of Law, Spring 1985, unpublished. See also Tullio Treves: 'The United Nations Law of the Sea Convention of 1982: prospects for Europe', in the Greenwich Forum IX: *Britain and the Sea,* 1984, 166–182, particularly at 176–180.
80. See the EEC Declaration concerning the Community competence in matters governed by the 1982 Convention on the Law of the Sea, made on 7 December 1984 with occasion of the signature of the Convention, *Bulletin of the European Communities,* Vol. 17, N° 12, 1984, at 108, 149. See also *Italy and the Law of the Sea Newsletter,* N° 13, January 1985, 6–10.
81. See the following Resolutions of the European Parliament: on the Conference on the Law of the Sea as it affects the European Community, *Official Journal,* No C 133, 6 June 1977, 50–52; on economic aspects of the exploitation of the sea-bed *Official Journal,* N° C 101, 4 May 1981, 65–68; on deep sea-bed mining and the marine environment, *Official Journal,* N° C 13, 17 January 1983, 32–33. See also the EEC report on the Conference on the Law of the Sea, *Bulletin,* N° 2, 1982, par. 2.2. 17, and N° 5, 1982, pars. 2.2. 23–30.
82. Written question N° 222/80 at the European Parliament on sea-bed mining legislation, *Official Journal,* N° C 198, 4 August 1980, 37–38; Written question N° 92/81 on sea-bed mining, *Official Journal,* N° C 147, 17 June 1981, 36.
83. See Question N° 64 by Mr. Johnson on Antarctic mineral negotiations, *Official Journal,* Debates of the European Parliament, N° 1–285, 1982–1983 session, Report of proceedings from 10 to 14 May 1982, at 156; Question N° 105 by Mr. Seligman on establishing a neutral zone in Antarctica to prevent conflicts in relation to minerals and discuss question at the United Nations, *Official Journal,* Debates of the European Parliament, N° 1–288, 1982–1983 session, Report of procedings from 13 to 17 September 1982, at 162. See also Question N° 66 by Mr. Schwartzenberg on dispute settlement procedures before the ICJ in relation to the Falkland Islands, *Official Journal,* Debates of the European Parliament, N° 1–285, 1982–1983 session, Report of proceedings from 10 to 14 May 1982, at 182.

84. See the reply by the President-in-Office of the Foreign Ministers to the Question N° 64 cit., note 83 supra, at 156.
85. *1983 Draft Articles,* Article XVI, par. 2 (a) (b); see the corresponding change in Article XVI, par. 2 (a) of the *1984 Draft Articles.*
86. *1983 Draft Articles,* Article XVI, par. 2 (c); *1984 Draft Articles,* Article XVI, par. 2 (b).
87. *1984 Draft Articles,* Article XVI, par. 3; the same approach was followed by the *1983 Draft Articles,* Article XVI, par. 3.
88. The *1983 Draft Articles* had foreseen in Article XVI, pars. 5 and 7, the establishment of a scientific and environmental subcommittee and a technical subcommittee; this approach has been simplified by the *1984 Draft Articles,* in the terms indicated, in Article XVI, pars. 6, 9; see also the *1986 Draft Articles,* Article 24, par. 9.
89. *1984 Draft Articles,* Article XVI, par. 7; see also *E.C.O.,* cit., note 68 supra, at 6; see further *1986 Draft Articles,* Article 24, par. 7.
90. See note 63 supra.
91. *1983 Draft Articles,* Article XX, par. 1 (a), (c) and (d).
92. Ibid., Article XX, par. 1 (b) and (e).
93. Graham, loc. cit., note 58 supra, at 28.
94. Rudiger Wolfrum: 'The use of Antarctic non-living resources: the search for a trustee?', in Rudiger Wolfrum (ed): *Antarctic Challenge,* 1984, 143–163, at 151; Ernst Jung: discussion at the Symposium, in ibid., at 177–178.
95. An author has commented that since small and big States are in opposition in Antarctica, a bloc behaviour could be expected, but this has not occurred until now because of the harmonious nature of the Antarctic model; see Gunnar Skagestad: 'Small States in international politics: a polar-political perspective', *Coop. and Confl.,* N° 2/3, 1974, 133–141, at 136.
96. See Chapter 7, section 7.4, supra.
97. *1984 Draft Articles,* Article XX, par. 3 (a), (b), (d).
98. Ibid., Article XX, par. 4.
99. Ibid., Article XX, par. 3 (e).
100. Ibid., Article XX, par. 3 (e).
101. Ibid., Article XX, par. 5.
102. Ibid., Article XX, par. 3 (c); note, however, that these two powers are no longer referred to as those having a 'basis of claim', but as those which 'prior to the entry into force of this regime, maintained the largest presence in Antarctica', an expression which might avoid the eventual territorial implications of the matter.
103. Ibid., Article XX, par. 3 (d), (e); par. 5.
104. These suggestions were raised informally during the negotiating session held in Rio de Janeiro, 26 February–12 March 1985.
105. See notes 39, 40 supra.
106. See notes 42, 43 supra.
107. *1983 Draft Articles,* Article XV.
108. Ibid., Article XXVI, par. 2.
109. Ibid., Article XIII, par. 1 (g).
110. Ibid., Article XIII, par. 1 (h).
111. Ibid., Article XIII, par. 1 (i).
112. Ibid., Article XXII, par. 3.
113. *1984 Draft Articles,* Article XV; *1986 Draft Articles,* Article 23.
114. 1982 Convention on the Law of the Sea, Article 161, par. 8.
115. Under the Chamber approach to decision-making that has been suggested as an alternative, a majority or qualified vote in each chamber of claimants and

non-claimants would be required. See Wolfrum, loc. cit., note 94 supra, at 158–159.

116. See, for example, the combination of consensus and majority proposed by Burton, loc. cit., note 62 supra, at 485–490.

117. *1983 Draft Articles,* Article XIX; see also *1984 Draft Articles,* Article XIX.

118. See notes 46 and 47 supra and associated text.

119. *1983 Draft Articles,* Article XVI, par. 6; the 1984 revision, however, changed this approach, requiring instead that the reports of the Committee reflect the views expressed by all the members of this body, a solution similar to that of the Rules of Procedure of the Scientific Committee established under the Canberra Convention; see *1984 Draft Articles,* Article XVIII, par. 3.

120. David M. Edwards and John A. Heap: 'Convention on the Conservation of Antarctic Marine Living Resources: a commentary', *Pol. Rec.,* Vol. 20, 1981, 353–362, at 356–357.

121. See note 48 supra and associated text.

122. See the *1983 Draft Articles,* Article XXVI, par. 2, and XXX; the *1984 Draft Articles* strengthened this institutional relationship, as can be seen from Articles XXVI, par. 2, and XXVIII, par. 8. See also *1986 Draft Articles,* Article 39, par. 1, and Article 43, par. 8.

123. *1984 Draft Articles,* Article XVIII, par. 1; *1986 Draft Articles,* Article 26, par. 1.

124. *1984 Draft Articles,* Article XXVI, par. 2; *1986 Draft Articles,* Article 39, par. 2.

125. *1984 Draft Articles,* Article XVI, par. 7; *1986 Draft Articles,* Article 24, par. 7.

126. See *E.C.O.* cit., note 68 supra, at 6.

127. *1983 Draft Articles,* Article XX, par. 3; *1984 Draft Articles,* Article XX (quarter); *1986 Draft Articles,* Article 32.

128. *1984 Draft Articles,* Article XXIX, par. 3; *1986 Draft Articles,* Article 44, par. 3.

129. *1984 Draft Articles,* Article XXXI, par. 1; *1986 Draft Articles,* Article 46, par. 1.

130. Francis Auburn: 'Antarctic Minerals and the Third World', *FRAM: The Journal of Polar Studies,* Winter 1984, 201–223, at 207–209.

131. Graham, loc. cit., note 58 supra, at 28.

132. See note 126 supra.

133. Graham, loc. cit., note 58 supra, at 28; but see also Christopher Beeby: 'A negotiator's view', in: *The Antarctic preferred futures, constraints and choices,* New Zealand Institute of International Affairs, 1983, 58–62.

134. See generally Chapter 5, 6 and 7 supra.

135. *1984 Draft Articles,* Article XIII, par. 1, Chapeau; *1986 Draft Articles,* Article 22, par. 1, Chapeau.

136. *1984 Draft Articles,* Article XIII, par. 1 (d); *1986 Draft Articles,* Article 22, par. 1 (d).

137. *1984 Draft Articles,* Article XIII, par. 1 (c); *1986 Draft Articles,* Article 22, par. 1 (c).

138. *1984 Draft Articles,* Article XIII, par. 1 (e), (f), (g), (i), (k), (l); see also generally *1986 Draft Articles,* Article 22, par. 1.

139. *1984 Draft Articles,* Article XIII, par. 1 (p). On the issue of revenue sharing see Chapter 10 infra. See also *1986 Draft Articles,* Article 22, par. 1 (e).

140. *1984 Draft Articles,* Article XIII, par. 1 (e), (f); *1986 Draft Articles,* Article 22, par. 1 (j).

141. *1984 Draft Articles,* Article XIII, par. 1 (i), (j). The *1986 Draft Articles,* Article 22, par. 1 (j) has entrusted the Commission with the task of deciding upon the distribution of funds.

142. On the question of financial arrangements see generally Chapter 6 supra.

143. *1984 Draft Articles,* Article XIII, par. 1 (a); see also the more emphatical language used by the same provision in the *1983 Draft Article.* In the *1986 Draft*

Articles, Article 22, par. 1 (a), the Commission has the function of deciding whether or not to identify an area for exploration, following the report by the Special Meeting of States Parties.

144. *1984 Draft Articles,* Article XIII, par. 1 (n). Under the *1986 Draft Articles,* Article 22, par. 1 (n), the Commission shall only review the management scheme in the cases provided for in Article 47, being the authorization for exploration and exploitation issued by the Regulatory Committee.

145. *1984 Draft Articles,* Article XIII, par. 1 (q); *1986 Draft Articles,* Article 22.

146. *1984 Draft Articles,* Article XIII, par. 1 (b); *1986 Draft Articles,* Article 22, par. 1 (b), (j).

147. *1984 Draft Articles,* Article XIII, par. 1 (m); *1986 Draft Articles,* Article 22, par. 1 (m).

148. *1984 Draft Articles,* Article XIII, par. 1 (o), (h); *1986 Draft Articles,* Article 22, par. 1 (o), (g).

149. *1984 Draft Articles,* Article XIII, par. 1 (r); *1986 Draft Articles,* Article 22, par. 1 (a).

150. See generally: 'Antarctic Minerals Regime', *E.C.O.,* cit., note 76 supra, at 15.

151. *E.C.O.,* cit., note 68 supra, at 6; see also Greenpeace International: *The future of the Antarctic,* Background for a second UN debate, October 22, 1984, at 16.

152. Graham, loc. cit., note 58 supra, at 29–30.

153. *1984 Draft Articles,* Article XVIII, par. 1, Chapeau; *1986 Draft Articles,* Article 26, par. 1, Chapeau.

154. *1983 Draft Articles,* Article XVIII, par. 1; see also *1984 Draft Articles,* Article XVIII, par. 1 (a), and *1986 Draft Articles,* Article 26, par. 1 (a).

155. *1984 Draft Articles,* Article XVIII, par. 1 (b), (c), (d), (e); see also generally *1986 Draft Articles,* Article 26, par. 1.

156. *1984 Draft Articles,* Article XVIII, par. 1 (e). In the *1986 Draft Articles* the Advisory Committee has the main function of advising the Commission about requests to identify an area, which will be done in application of the objectives and principles of the Convention, but there is no express reference to a determination about the request being an unacceptable risk to the environment (Article 26, par. 1 (f)).

157. *1984 Draft Articles,* Article XVIII, par. 1 (g); *1986 Draft Articles,* Article 26, par. 1 (h).

158. *1983 Draft Articles,* Article XVIII, par. 2 (a); *1984 Draft Articles,* Article XVIII, par. 1 (h); see also *1986 Draft Articles,* Article 26, par. 1 (i), which refers to the 'advice' to be given to the Regulatory Committee.

159. *1984 Draft Articles,* Article XVIII, par. 1 (j); *1986 Draft Articles,* Article 26, par. 1 (k) and Article 49.

160. *1984 Draft Articles,* Article XVIII, par. 1 (k); *1986 Draft Articles,* Article 26, par. 1 (l).

161. *1984 Draft Articles,* Article XX (ter.), par. 1 (a), (c), (d); *1986 Draft Articles,* Article 31.

162. *1984 Draft Articles,* Article XX (ter.), par. 1 (e); *1986 Draft Articles,* Article 31 (e).

163. See Chapter 5 supra.

164. *1984 Draft Articles,* Article XX (ter.), par. 1 (g); *1986 Draft Articles,* Article 31 (g).

165. *1984 Draft Articles,* Article XX (ter.), par. 1 (f); *1986 Draft Articles,* Article 31 (f), and 49.

166. See Chapter 7 supra.

167. *E.C.O.,* cit., note 76 supra, at 15; also *E.C.O.,* cit., note 68 supra, at 6.

168. See generally *E.C.O.,* cit., note 76 supra, at 1, 15.

169. Convention for the Conservation of Antarctic Seals, Article 6, par. 1 (b).
170. Convention for the Conservation of Antarctic Marine Living Resources, Article XIII, par. 2.
171. *1983 Draft Articles,* Article XI.
172. *1984 Draft Articles,* Article XI; *1986 Draft Articles,* Article 20.
173. *1983 Draft Articles,* Article XVII.
174. *1984 Draft Articles,* Article XVII; *1986 Draft Articles,* Article 25.
175. *1984 Draft Articles,* Article XX (bis), par. 1, and XXVI (bis), par. 1; *1986 Draft Articles,* Article 30, par. 1 and 41, par. 1.
176. *1984 Draft Articles,* Article XII, XVI, pars. 4, 5, 8, 9 and 10, XX (bis); see also *1986 Draft Articles,* Article 21, par. 1, 24, par. 5, 28, par. 4 and 30, par. 3.
177. *1984 Draft Articles,* Article XXI; *1986 Draft Articles,* Article 33.
178. See note 17 supra and associated text.
179. *E.C.O.,* Vol. XXVII, N° 3, Tokyo, May 22–31, 1984, at 4; see also Greenpeace, doc. cit., note 151 supra, at 17–18.
180. *E.C.O.,* cit., note 179 supra, at 4.
181. *1984 Draft Articles,* Article XIII, par. 3; *1986 Draft Articles,* Article 22, par. 3.
182. *1984 Draft Articles,* Article XXII, pars. 1, 3. *1986 Draft Articles,* Article 34, pars. 1, 3.
183. *1983 Draft Articles,* Article XXII, par. 2.
184. *1984 Draft Articles,* Article XXII, par. 2; *1986 Draft Articles,* Article 34, par. 2.
185. *E.C.O.,* Vol. XXVII, N° 1, Tokyo, May 22–31, 1984, at 2; Greenpeace, doc. cit., note 151 supra, at 21.
186. Convention for the Conservation of Antarctic Marine Living Resources, Article XIX, par. 3.
187. *1984 Draft Articles,* Article XXII, pars. 4, 6; *1986 Draft Articles,* Article 34, pars. 4, 6.
188. *1984 Draft Articles,* Article XII, pars. 5, 6, 7; see also the Convention for the Conservation of Antarctic Marine Living Resources, Article VIII. See also the corresponding provisions of the *1986 Draft Articles,* Article 21, pars. 5, 6, 7.
189. On the legal personality of international organizations see generally Schermers op. cit., note 12 supra, at 787–792, and Bowett, op. cit., note 32 supra, at 335–382, with particular reference to the law governing property, contracts and other activities at 365–377. Under the US Code, Title 22, Chapter 7, Subchapter XVIII, Section 288 (a), international organizations have the capacity to contract, to acquire and dispose of real and personal property and to institute legal proceedings 'to the extent consistent with the instrument creating them'. Under the UK International Organisations Act, 1950, Section 1 (2) (a), and 1968, Section 1 (a), international organisations have the 'legal capacities of a body corporate', a concept which has been broadly interpreted to include the capacity to contract, to acquire and dispose of movable and immovable property and to institute legal proceedings; on this point in relation to the UN see J. W. Bridge: 'The United Nations and English law', *I.C.L.Q.,* Vol. 18, 1969, 689–717, particularly at 705–706.
190. See the reports of the Commission cit., note 49 supra.
191. Both the 1983 and 1984 Draft Articles as well as the 1986 revision envisaged a Chapter 7 on dispute Settlement, the content of which was left blank with the purpose of allowing negotiations on the matter at a later point; such negotiations began in the Tokyo meeting of 1984.
192. Antarctic Treaty, Article XI, par. 1.
193. Ibid., Article XI, par. 2. For the broad role of the 1959 Antarctic Treaty as a mechanism for resolving conflicts, with particular reference to Article IV of such Treaty and the policy of self-restraint by the parties, see generally Arthur D.

Watts: 'The Antarctic Treaty as a conflict resolution mechanism', in U.S. Polar Research Board, op. cit., note 2 supra. 65–75.

194. International Court of Justice: Pleadings, *Antarctica Cases* (United Kingdom v. Argentina; United Kingdom v. Chile), applications instituting proceedings, 1955; the cases were removed from the Court's list by Orders of 16 March 1956 on the grounds of lack of jurisdiction, *Reports*, 1956, at 12–14 and 15–17. For a suggestion to submit the Falkland Islands dispute to the International Court of Justice, see also Question N° 66 at the European Parliament, cit., note 83 supra.

195. See Auburn, op. cit., note 2 supra, at 139.

196. Statements of the Contracting Parties made at the last meeting of the Plenary Committee of the 1959 Conference, on 30 November 1959, concerning particular articles of the Treaty; text in Chile: *Memoria del Ministerio de Relaciones Exteriores,* 1959, 698–704, translation in Bush, op. cit., note 6 supra, at 38–43; see in particular the British and French statements on Article XI, at 42.

197. Statements cit., note 196 supra, Statement by South Africa on Article XI, at 42.

198. On the question of validity of Antarctic claims and title to territory in international law and eventual disputes in this regard, see generally Gillian Triggs: 'Australian Sovereignty in Antarctica', *Mel. U.L.R.,* Vol. 13, 1981–1982, Part I, 123–158; Part II, 302–333.

199. International Court of Justice: *South West Africa Cases* (Ethiopia v. South Africa; Liberia v. South Africa), Second phase, Judgment of 18 July 1966, *Reports,* 1966, at 22; other references to legal right or interest are found at pages 18–23, 31–33, 37–40 and 51 of the judgement.

200. Treaty of Peace and Friendship between Chile and Argentina, signed on 29 November 1984, *ILM,* Vol. XXIV, 1985, 11–28.

201. Ibid., Article 15.

202. Ibid., Articles 1–6 and Annex N° 1.

203. Convention for the Conservation of Antarctic Seals, Article 12; this Article provides that the 'Convention shall be open for accession by any State which may be invited to accede to this Convention with the consent of all the Contracting Parties'.

204. Convention for the Conservation of Antarctic Marine Living Resources, Article XXV.

205. Ibid., Annex for an arbitral tribunal.

206. Barnes, loc. cit., note 37 supra, at 268.

207. Convention on the Law of the Sea, Article 282; this article provides the following: 'If the States Parties which are parties to a dispute concerning the interpretation or application of this Convention have agreed, through a general, regional or bilateral agreement or otherwise, that such dispute shall, at the request of any party to the dispute, be submitted to a procedure that entails a binding decision, that procedure shall apply in lieu of the procedures provided for in this Part, unless the parties to the dispute otherwise agree'.

208. See generally W. Riphagen: 'Dispute settlement in 1982 United Nations Convention on the Law of the Sea', in C. L. Rozakis and C. A. Stephanou (eds): *The New Law of the Sea,* 1983, 281–301; see also R. Ranjeva: 'Le reglement des differends', in Dupuy and Vignes, op. cit., note 32 supra, 1105–1167.

209. See generally Lucius C. Calflisch: 'The settlement of disputes relating to activities in the international sea-bed area', in Rozakis and Stephanou, op. cit., note 208 supra, 303–344.

210. Ibid., at 309.

211. For a discussion of this institutional role in relation to the Arctic and the proposal to establish an 'Arctic Resources Council', see generally Oran R. Young and Gail Osherenko: 'Arctic resource conflicts: sources and solutions', in William E.

Westermeyer and Kurt N. Shusterich: *United States Arctic Interests. The 1980's and 1990's,* 1984, 199–218.

212. Convention on the Law of the Sea, Article 187 (b).
213. Caflisch, loc. cit., note 209 supra, at 312–313.
214. Convention on the Law of the Sea, Article 189.
215. Ibid., Article 159, par. 10; this recourse is for requesting an advisory opinion from the Sea-Bed Disputes Chamber on the conformity with the Convention of a proposal before the Assembly on any matter.
216. See generally Chapters 5 and 6 supra.
217. Convention on the Law of the Sea, Article 168, par. 1.
218. Ibid., Article 168, par. 3.
219. Ibid., Article 185.
220. Ibid., Article 187 (c) in conjunction with Article 190, par. 1.
221. See Caflisch, loc. cit., note 209 supra, at 317–318.
222. Convention on the Law of the Sea, Article 187 (c).
223. Caflisch, loc. cit., note 209 supra, at 318–319.
224. Ibid., at 319–322.
225. Ibid., at 320.
226. See Chapter 5 supra.
227. Convention on the Law of the Sea, Annex III, Article 21.
228. Caflisch, loc. cit., note 209 supra, at 327–328.
229. On the questions of nationality in relation to the law of State responsibility, see generally Ian Brownlie: *Principles of Public International Law,* 1979, 480–495.
230. Convention on the Law of the Sea, Article 190, par. 1.
231. Rosalyn Higgins: 'The taking of property by the State: recent developments in international law', *Rec. Cours Ac. D.I,* 1982-III, 263–391, at 313–314.
232. Ibid., at 314.
233. See generally David M. Sassoon: 'Settlement of disputes governing law', in United Nations: *Negotiation and drafting of mining development agreements,* 1976, 209–217.
234. René-Jean Dupuy (ed.): *The settlement of disputes on the new natural resources,* Academie de Droit International de La Haye, Colloque 1982, 1983; L. F. E. Goldie: 'Reconciling values of distributive equity and management efficiency in the international commons', in Dupuy, op. cit., at 335–376.
235. Edith Brown Weiss: 'Conflicts between present and future generations over new natural resources', in Dupuy, op. cit., note 234 supra, at 177–195; see also Edith Brown Weiss: 'Conservation and Equity between generations', February 1983, prepared for the Festschrift in honour of Professor Louis B. Sohn, and by the same author: 'The Planetary Trust: Conservation and Intergenerational Equity', *Ecology Law Quarterly,* Vol. 11, 1984, 495–581.

Part III

Issues and options relating to the external accommodation

9

Participation of States other than the Consultative Parties in the Antarctic Treaty system

The Antarctic Treaty system has been based until now fundamentally on the activities of the Consultative Parties. This is not due to the fact that it is desired to make it an exclusive club, as some authors have described it,[1] but because all the States which historically have developed an interest in this continent have acquired the status of Consultative Party,[2] either because it was so recognized by the 1959 Treaty[3] or because the special admission procedure was used to admit them as such.[4]

The first programmes for the co-ordination of various types of international activity in Antarctica specified broad criteria for participation. The International Geophysical Year in 1957–1958 was a case in point.[5] Among the many countries which participated in it,[6] only twelve had a continuing interest in the Antarctic, shown by the maintenance of permanent bases in the continent and the carrying out of scientific research. It was from such interest and activities that the status of Consultative Party in the Antarctic Treaty originated and they have been the criterion generally adopted for the admission of new countries to this status.[7] Whenever a country has qualified in terms of conducting the pertinent activities in the Antarctic it has not failed to acquire the status of Consultative Party by means of the procedures for admission.

Interest in participating in Antarctic activities has been further stimulated by the new prospect of the possibility of utilization and management of natural resources which has been recently a subject of special attention within the Treaty system. Although such prospects are not of an immediate character and rather could only materialize at a distant date, at any rate in terms of mineral resources, in the view of the Antarctic Treaty parties it has become apparent that new measures are needed within the system to handle this new set of issues; at the same time these issues have become a new source of pressure on the part of those interested in the matter. These various aspects have come to be known as the 'external accommodation' of the system, a process which seeks to reconcile the various existing interests, both those inside and those outside the Antarctic Treaty System at present, through new mechanisms for participation. An examination of the problems concerning participation of the States parties to the Antarctic Treaty which do not have the status of Consultative Party, and of those states which can strictly be termed 'third states' in relation to the system, including the effect of the Antarctic Treaty on the latter and its relationship to customary international law, will be examined in this Chapter. In the following chapter, questions concerning links with international organizations and their participation in the Antarctic, together with proposals for new organizational models under the United Nations, will be discussed.

9.1   The need to balance the rights and obligations of signatory countries

A notable shortcoming of the 1959 Treaty is that while it established for the Consultative Parties a complete system of rights and obligations which together form a balanced and reciprocal whole,[8] on the other hand, for parties not possessing the status of Consultative Party the relationship between rights and duties lacks the natural balance. In fact, so much emphasis is placed on the obligations of non-Consultative Parties that there appears to be a general absence of special rights or, in other words, the rights which they do enjoy are no more than those generally possessed by third States. There is thus a lack of balance in this respect.[9] As long as the Antarctic Treaty system was chiefly concerned with questions of co-operation of a passive nature, such as freedom of scientific investigation and the duty not to interfere in such activities, or demilitarization or the prohibition of nuclear tests, the problem was not a particularly important one, since the rights of such parties and of third States were really the same. They were rights *erga omnes*.

However, the nature of the problem began to change when the need for a resources policy began to be felt. As scientific research began to be more closely related to the evaluation of Antarctica's resource potential, parties began to ask why scientific findings and consequent exchanges of information should be available only to the Consultative Parties and why an equal right to benefit from the results of research should not be extended to the other parties to the Treaty? What reason was there for not distributing the periodic reports on the activities of the Treaty to other parties, thus drawing their attention to the recommendations of the Treaty to which they, too, belonged? Similar questions might be asked as regards scientific reports, participation in the system's meetings or the sending of personnel on scientific expeditions undertaken by the Con- sultative Parties.

In response to such concerns, the delegation of Chile submitted a document to the Twelfth Consultative Meeting in 1983 entitled 'Opera- tion of the Antarctic Treaty', which dealt partly with the question of non-Consultative Parties and partly with that of third States and other matters connected with the 'external accommodation'.[10] It proposed that such parties should receive the Final Report and the Recommendations of the Consultative Parties, that they should have access to certain kinds of scientific information, and that they should be able to participate in the exchange of information provided for in Article III (i) of the Treaty and in the Antarctic activities of the Consultative Parties. More significantly, the document envisaged their right to participate as observers in the regular Consultative Meetings, a right which has begun to be exercised since that Consultative Meeting.[11] The Final Report of the Twelfth Consultative Meeting and Recommendation XII-6 contained various important provisions on this subject, which were further developed and improved at later Antarctic meetings.[12] As a result of these changes, non-Consultative Parties have today a standing invitation to attend regular Consultative Meetings and their preparatory meetings.

These first steps towards extending the participation of other parties represented an appropriate response to the original problem of lack of balance. The activity of these parties did in fact as a result gradually begin to increase. Encouragement of parties participating as observers in regular consultative meetings,[13] as well as the invitation to them to participate as observers in the special negotiations on mineral resources from 1985,[14] or even to take part as observers in meetings of the Commission of the Canberra Convention[15] – are all indications of a positive trend towards a greater degree of integration of all parties into the Antarctic system. A similar trend can be seen in proposals for their joint participation in Antarctic activities with the Consultative Parties and, generally, in the development of closer co-operation within the framework of the Treaty system.

As this process has gained momentum, however, new needs for coordination within the system have begun to make themselves felt, both as regards the non-Consultative Parties and, possibly, as regards third countries and international organizations. Certainly, methods of handling a growing volume of information and technical data, its processing and distribution, are today very different from those considered appropriate a quarter of a century ago. Although the Antarctic Treaty parties were in the past naturally reluctant to establish a permanent secretariat, in view of the implications in respect of fuller internationalization such a step might have,[16] the system cannot do without one much longer. Hambro clearly foresaw this need a decade ago[17] and the Chilean document referred to above raised the question again in more precise terms.[18] The establishment of a Secretariat *pro tempore* and of a data centre to handle the complex present-day Antarctic information system is an obvious necessity.

Such an institution would be particularly valuable for the mineral resources regime, especially for determining whether a particular activity falls within the category of scientific investigation or of prospecting, since, according to which is the case, it will be subject to a different set of rights and obligations. An assessment made by a specialized data centre would be crucial in deciding a question of that kind.[19] As was discussed in the previous chapter, it is proposed that a Secretariat be established as one of the organs of the mineral regime.

Moreover, the growing activity of the parties in the Antarctic continent has called for certain measures of co-ordination regarding the utilization of particular areas and facilities. Thus, for example, interest in making use of the Chilean Air Force's airfield and related facilities on King George Island has led to a great demand from other nations wishing to establish themselves in close proximity to the airbase and is leading to over-population and infrastructural difficulties.[20] Recommendation XIII-6 has called on governments whose stations have been established in the same vicinity to consult through their pertinent agencies in order to avoid operational logistic difficulties, safeguard scientific research activities and avoid adverse environmental effects.

Greater participation by the parties to the Antarctic Treaty within its framework or in special resources regimes such as the Seals Convention, the Canberra Convention or the emerging mineral convention, is not to be understood as in any way diminishing the role or responsibilities of Consultative Parties under those treaties or related arrangements. On the contrary, a mutually complementary role is beginning to evolve, which actually strengthens the system as a whole. This is a gradual development of a positive nature, in the writer's view, in contrast to unproductive confrontational and antagonistic attitudes sometimes adopted in the United Nations debate on the question of Antarctica.[21]

9.2   Accession clauses of the Antarctic Treaty and other instruments
Facilitation of participation by parties to the Antarctic Treaty and the other related treaty regimes is closely linked to the question of the

accession clauses of these instruments. Categorization of interests is also evolving, aimed at establishing different types of accession and participation. When the Antarctic Treaty was negotiated, only a general accession provision was apparently contemplated, whereby any country could participate in work under the Treaty without special qualifications. It was due to Chile's insistence that the special requirements for becoming a consultative party, which now figure in Article IX (2) of this instrument, were included.[22] Although the latter proposal may appear at first sight discriminatory, its aim was only to ensure that the countries undertaking the responsibility of managing the newly created Treaty system were those really engaged and interested in activities in the Antarctic; any country so doing would be entitled to become a Consultative Party and participate in the Consultative Meetings.

The general accession provision in Article XIII (1) of the Treaty establishes, in the first place, an unconditional criterion.[23] Any State Member of the United Nations may freely accede to the Treaty as, in fact, has happened with increasing frequency, but at the time same a second criterion of a restrictive character is provided, to the effect that other States not members of the United Nations may accede provided that they are invited to do so with the consent of all the Consultative Parties.[24] This latter provision gave rise to a difficult debate during the negotiation of the Treaty, it having been proposed that States that were Members of United Nations specialized agencies should also have unrestricted right of accession.[25] It is not clear whether this debate was related to the interest of a given country or countries in acceding or was only concerned with points of general policy in relation to the United Nations and the Specialized Agencies.[26] Japan, France, the Soviet Union and Australia supported the broader approach, while the United States let it be known that there was one country opposed to it, although the country was not identified.[27] Consequently, this solution was not approved and the article stayed as it was with the aboved-mentioned restriction. Further criticisms of this article were made in connection with the declarations of accession of the German Democratic Republic and Romania.[28] If the problem was in any way related to accession by the Federal Republic of Germany or the German Democratic Republic, this was settled when both countries acceded to the Treaty after being admitted to membership of the United Nations.[29]

The provisions for accession to the Agreed Measures are more simple, since technically they constitute only a Recommendation approved by the Consultative Parties. Once the latter have approved the Agreed Measures, any party to the Antarctic Treaty can accept these Measures and provide notification that it will consider itself bound by them.[30] This mechanism relates expressly to the terms of Recommendation III–IV, which states that Recommendations are considered to be 'a part of the overall structure of co-operation established by the Treaty'.[31]

The Convention for the Conservation of Antarctic Seals, as the first of the special treaty regimes established alongside the Antarctic Treaty, was particularly cautious concerning the need to maintain the Consultative Parties' strict control over the accession of new contracting parties to this instrument. In fact, its Article 12 provides that the Convention shall be open to accession by any State which has been invited to accede 'with the consent of all the Contracting Parties'.[32] As the latter consisted only of the Consultative Parties to the Antarctic Treaty, they have complete control of the process. Poland was invited to accede by means of this mechanism.[33]

The procedure for accession to the Convention on the Conservation of the Antarctic Marine Living Resources is simple for individual States and more complicated as regards the participation of regional economic organizations. The case of the latter will be considered in the next chapter. Pursuant to Article XXIX, paragraph 1 of this instrument, the Convention is open to accession by 'any State interested in research or harvesting activities in relation to the marine living resources to which this Convention applies'.[34] Acceding countries may become temporary members of the Commission by a special procedure provided for in paragraph 2 (d) of Article VII.[35] A distinction is thus maintained between the original signatory countries and those acceding subsequently, by placing greater responsibilities on the former than on the latter, in a way similar to the Antarctic Treaty. However, at the Diplomatic Conference which drew up the text of the Convention there were difficulties concerning the invitation to two States which were interested in participating, but which were rejected.[36]

Although the accession provisions of the mineral resources regime have not yet been formally drawn up, their close relationship with the question of participation in the institutions allows one to anticipate some of the situations which will arise in this connection. In the first place, as has been discussed, it is obvious that the Consultative Parties to the Antarctic Treaty will be original signatories to the new Convention, but the latter may, however, include some additional States invited to the diplomatic conference, as happened in the case of the Canberra Conference. Next, it is also obvious that parties to the Antarctic Treaty not having the status of a Consultative Party will also be able to accede to the new instrument. Other interested States may also be able to accede, possibly by agreeing to comply with specific obligations deriving from the Antarctic Treaty system, a procedure which was also adopted for the Canberra Convention.[37] The 1986 Draft Convention on mineral resources requires participation in the 1959 Antarctic Treaty for acceding to the new Convention.

It is of interest to envisage the situation which might arise with respect to Consultative Parties to the Antarctic Treaty which acquire this status subsequent to signing the convention on mineral resources. Will they retroactively become original signatories, or will they have to be treated in the same way as any other acceding country? Will their rights and obligations be the same as those of the former or the latter category? Just as a distinction is made between the original Consultative Parties and those subsequently acquiring this status in the Antarctic Treaty itself, so nothing prevents a similar differentiation in the new regime. Participation and membership in the Commission to be established by the minerals convention is in fact based on this distinction and other criteria, as we discussed in Chapter 8.

Beyond the formal legal provisions on accession, the mineral resources regime also provides an opportunity to facilitate substantive participation by other parties to the Antarctic Treaty, possibly by granting them more favourable treatment than that accorded to other categories of States which do not have this Antarctic connection.[38] Thus, for example, speedier access to the regime's operations, a broader institutional participation, including decision-making, preferential options in the joint ventures system or other modalities might be envisaged.[39] Treatment of this kind would demonstrate that the status of a party to the Antarctic Treaty is not without relevance to the system and that there may be ways of differentiating interested States which could act as a stimulus to those binding themselves more closely to the system.[40] The 1986 Draft Convention has included various provisions to this effect, as evidenced in particular by Article 7 of this instrument.

Hierarchical structure of the system and gradual expansion
The basic question concerning the participation of countries other than the Consultative Parties in the framework of the Antarctic Treaty and its complementary instruments is whether there is any justification for maintaining what one author has called '*une aristocracie conventionelle*'.[41] It should first be noted that a system of this type, in which Parties have different rights and obligations, is not new in the law of international organizations, especially if they are of a manifestly technical kind. On this point Depuy has rightly commented that:

This hierarchical system is unusual in that it is based, not on qualitative criteria, but on considerations of a quantitative nature: the actual importance of research carried out in the Antarctic. This is what gives the Treaty a character usually found in treaties dealing with technical matters or which set up specialised communities. And that is not surprising.[42]

Although the powers of the Consultative Parties are considerable when compared with the functions of other parties not possessing this status, it must also be kept in mind that these powers are not provided for or used in any way to establish rights which might benefit such Consultative Parties, but only to define obligations which Consultative Parties are bound to observe in their activities in Antarctica. In fact the Antarctic Treaty System has been described as one which does not confer rights but only imposes obligations.[43] If the countries active in the area were to proceed only in accordance with the general rules and principles of international law their freedom of action would be much greater than what is the case under the Antarctic Treaty and related arrangements, since the latter are generally quite restrictive in terms of obligations. In any event, the rights which have been developed under the Treaty System, such as freedom of scientific research, access to resources and other, are not restricted to Consultative Parties but available to any country acceding to the pertinent conventions or generally to the international community in some cases.

On the other hand, it must also be remembered that this is not a closed system and that progressive expansion is not ruled out, since it is possible for any State to gain Consultative Party status provided it shall meet the established requirements to this effect.[44] There is a special procedure for this, which has already been used on six occasions, at times with considerable flexibility.[45] Although there has been some discussion concerning whether Consultative Party status might be acquired automatically, without the need for a consultative meeting decision,[46] this idea has not met with acceptance. It should, however, be noted that in the case of the Canberra Convention a step has been taken towards forms of greater participation, since no special meeting will be required for the purpose of designating a new member of the Commission unless one is specifically requested.[47] In the mineral resources case, it would seem that some prior qualification would be justified in view of the extensive functions which the organs of the regime will have to perform.

While the system of 'graduation' in order to acquire Consultative Party status or its equivalent in any of the other Antarctic regimes must possess a reasonable degree of flexibility and openness, it must also be a controlled process, since otherwise we might end up with an admission procedure requiring virtually no real qualifications that would do serious harm to the Antarctic Treaty system in view of the sense of responsibility and prudence required for its operation. Thus, the expansion of the admission procedure must be truly gradual and respond to criteria that will not allow for the distortion of the purposes of this system.

Expansion of the norm-creating role

Another important aspect to be considered is the norm-creating function of the Antarctic Treaty system through the mechanism of its consultative meetings.[48] Originally, recommendations of the consultative meetings were basically addressed to the Parties participating in them, since they were in fact the only ones active in the Antarctic continent. However, as the activity of other parties expanded, the norm-creating role of the consultative meetings had to expand proportionately. Recommendation III–VII, as already mentioned, stated that these recommendations are 'a part of the overall structure of co-operation established by the Treaty' and urged both Consultative Parties and other parties to consider acceptance of these instruments and to be bound by them.[49] Such acceptance has been viewed as a positive qualification for Consultative Party status.[50]

The Agreed Measures already specifically provided for their acceptance by parties other than the Consultative Parties.[51] Subsequently, the norms contained in the more recent conventions were made applicable to all countries participating in those treaties as a matter of course. In this way, the Antarctic legal system, as developed through these treaties, began to take on a more complete and integrated shape.

One additional mechanism adopted in this process of legal development has been to insist on countries acceding to the new regimes recognizing specific responsibilities of the Consultative Parties or certain provisions of the Antarctic Treaty and other instruments. The Agreed Measures, the Convention for the Conservation of the Antarctic Seals and the Convention on the Conservation of Antarctic Marine Living Resources have specifically had recourse to this juridical linkage technique. As indicated earlier, this will also be the case with the mineral resource regime.

While the development of the Antarctic legal system in a more integrated manner has the advantage of providing a framework of greater coherence for the regulation of activities in Antarctica,[52] it has also been opened to criticism in so far as it consolidates and expands the role of Consultative Parties in the management of the Treaty system. This argument, as we shall examine in Chapter 10, has been repeatedly made during the United Nations debate on Antarctica. To the extent that the Treaty system could be kept as a closed mechanism, this argument would validly point to a serious legal weakness of such system; however, as we shall also see, the system has been gradually opening up, particularly in terms of participation in it, in recognition of the changing needs of the external accommodation.

9.3   Withdrawal and amendment provisions

The withdrawal provisions of the various instruments comprising the Antarctic system are also of interest insofar as they affect different types of participation. The Antarctic Treaty itself does not contain specific withdrawal provision, but links withdrawal with the amendment and revision procedures: once an amendment approved by all the Consultative Parties has entered into force, any other Contracting Party which fails to communicate its acceptance of this amendment within a period of two years 'shall be deemed to have withdrawn from the present Treaty'.[53] This provision seems somewhat disproportionate since, even a small amendment, if not accepted, may led to the exclusion of that Party from the entire Treaty.

A similar approach has been followed by the Convention on the Conservation of Antarctic Marine Living Resources which provides that if no notice of acceptance of an amendment that has entered into force has been received from a Contracting Party within a period of one year, such Party 'shall be deemed to have withdrawn from this Convention'; the entry into force of an amendment requires the acceptance of all the members of the Commission, so in fact this provision refers to parties which are not members of that organ.[54] During the negotiations of the Canberra Convention it was also proposed that only members of the Commission who are also Consultative Parties under the Antarctic Treaty should have the right to propose amendments, but such suggestions were not accepted in view of their restrictive character.[55]

The negotiations on the minerals regime have not yet been completed on this matter, but it is known that similar suggestions have been made concerning the approval of all members of the Commission for an amendment to enter into force, the clause that a Party shall be deemed to have withdrawn if no notice of acceptance of an amendment is received within a period of time, and the restriction of the right to propose amendments only to Consultative Parties. However, it is quite unlikely that the approach followed under the Canberra Convention might be changed in these other negotiations in favour of a more restricted mechanism. In any event, the amendments to the minerals Convention should not affect the provisions of management schemes in force before the date of the entry into force of any such amendment, since otherwise the stability of Antarctic contracts would be affected.

The amendments to the Seal Convention require the acceptance of all Contracting Parties for entry into force.[56] The Agreed Measures can be amended by the unanimous agreement of Consultative Parties, but the annexes can be more easily amended through a diplomatic procedure; the latter procedure allows for governments not to accept a given amendment and this does not entail an exclusion from the Agreed Measures.[57]

While exclusion from a Treaty might be justified in case of non-acceptance of a fundamental amendment, it does not seem to have any justification in situations where amendments do not have that character, a distinction that should hopefully be introduced at some point in the Antarctic Treaty system.

The 1959 Antarctic Treaty envisages a second situation relating amendment and withdrawal: if a review conference is convened after a period of thirty years, amendments then adopted will enter into force in accordance with the general rules of the Treaty.[58] If one of these amendments has not entered into force after two years, any Contracting Party 'may . . . give notice to the depositary government of its withdrawal from the present Treaty'.[59] Such withdrawal will in its turn take place two years after this notice has been given. It should be noted that in the second case there is no question of a mandatory withdrawal, but only an optional one, and, moreover, the provision applies to all the Contracting Parties and not merely to those not having Consultative Party status as in the first case mentioned.

The drafting of these provisions of the Antarctic Treaty gave rise to considerable difficulties. The fact that the approval of non-Consultative Parties was not required for the entry into force of amendments of the first type was apparently aimed at making a distinction between countries permanently carrying out activities in the Antarctic and those which did not do so, it being considered that the latter 'should not have the right of a veto of an amendment'.[60] Moreover, the thirty-year period before the convening of the review conference resulted from consideration of various other suggestions, Chile having proposed a five or ten years' moratorium on claims.[61] In any case, it seems that postponing revision for a lengthy period was a sensible decision. The idea of a review Conference for the minerals regime to be convened after a number of years has also been considered in the negotiations, but has not met with acceptance in view of the uncertainties it would create concerning the rights and obligations under the regime, a problem which was quite acute in the discussion of a review conference for Part XI of the Law of the Sea Convention.

Among the concluding statements of the delegations which negotiated the Antarctic Treaty one by Chile raises some interesting legal questions. It stated that it supported the formula contained in Article XII 'on the understanding that if any Contracting Party withdraws from the Treaty, its provisions will not be applicable to that Party from the time of this withdrawal and that with respect to the provisions of Article IV, the Parties will return to the previous *status quo*'.[62] While this attitude was obviously intended to safeguard the position of States with territorial claims, it is doubtful whether the effects of a treaty can simply be wiped out by the mere fact of a Party's withdrawal.

Under Article 70, 1 (b) of the Vienna Convention on the Law of Treaties, the termination of a Treaty 'does not affect any right, obligation or legal situation of the parties created through the execution of the treaty prior to its termination'.[63] Although this Convention was not in existence at the time of entry into force of the Antarctic Treaty, the provision mentioned obviously has some relevance to certain provisions of the Antarctic Treaty, particularly in terms of freedom of scientific research and peaceful uses, among other provisions which might be unaffected in the event of a withdrawal. This provision of the Vienna Convention might also be considered to reflect customary international law on the subject. In terms of the Harvard Research, 'the termination of a treaty puts an end to all executory obligations stipulated in the treaty; it does not affect the validity of rights acquired in consequence of the performance of obligations stipulated in the treaty', to what Lord McNair adds 'or the validity of rights acquired in the exercise of powers conferred by the treaty'.[64]

This discussion is of particular importance in view of the fact that a claimant country who withdraws from the Antarctic Treaty could invoke various activities it undertook whilst a party to support its title.[65] Although this would not be possible under Article IV of the Treaty, its terms could not be made applicable to a party that has withdrawn. The fact that other treaty parties might not recognize this claim, does not mean that it would be deprived of its effects under international law or that it could not be recognized by third states, even if this is quite unlikely. In practice many activities are undertaken in Antarctica with this very purpose in mind, both by claimants and non-claimants in support of their claimed rights. It does not appear, therefore, that the idea of simply reverting to the situation existing prior to the withdrawal may provide the best solution in some instances.

In the case of the minerals regime the withdrawal of a claimant State from the Convention could have serious implications concerning the mineral exploitation in the area claimed by that country; this might require some special consideration when dealing with the effects of withdrawal. Also, if it is required that accession to the minerals Convention presupposes to be a Party to the Antarctic Treaty, the withdrawal from the latter might entail also a withdrawal from the former.

Other complex issues will arise in relation to eventual withdrawal from the minerals Convention. Among other situations that can be envisaged, the sponsoring State might not be able to withdraw while the sponsored mineral activities are carried out in Antarctica, or if it does it should still be bound by the provisions on compliance, liability and other which it has concerning the contractor; like under the Canberra Convention, withdrawal should not affect financial obligations incurred into under the Convention;[66] nor should dispute settlement procedures under way be paralysed because of the withdrawal of a party.

It will, therefore, be necessary to provide for a period of time beyond the date of denunciation during which those obligations will continue to be enforceable. A number of treaties of economic co-operation and integration contain clauses of this kind;[67] the transfer of assets of the League of Nations to the United Nations[68] provides a further illustration of the discharge of obligations beyond the practical life of an organization, like the International Court of Justice Advisory Opinion on the International Status of South West Africa[69] illustrates the issues of legal succession of rights and obligations which do not terminate with the life of an organization.

The Agreed Measures do not contain withdrawal provisions, because they are in the form of a recommendation. Both the Convention for the Conservation of Antarctic Seals[70] and the Convention on the Conservation of Antarctic Marine Living Resources[71] contain formal withdrawal provisions. However, in the case of these Conventions, too, it is necessary to examine the effect of a withdrawal in the light both of the Vienna Convention and the juridical relationship between instruments of the Antarctic system.

9.4   Rights and obligations of third States

Consideration has been given so far to the situation of countries which, in one way or another, participate in the Antarctic Treaty or its associated regimes, although they may belong to different categories or participate in different ways. The most significant legal problem arises in the case of those countries which, from the point of view of the Treaty and the other instruments, are technically 'third parties'. Is it possible to sustain the view that rights and obligations derive for third countries from the Treaty or the instruments of the Antarctic system? This is the key question on which the opinions of authors have been markedly divided.[72]

The starting point for a reply is obviously the general rule of international law that treaties are only legally binding on the contracting parties.[73] This principle has not been questioned with respect to the Antarctic Treaty and the practice of the Treaty parties has been consistent with such principle.[74] However, other equally important criteria needs to be taken into account in the discussion of this crucial issue. In this connection, it must be remembered that the Treaty is conceived as being 'in the interest of all mankind',[75] particularly with respect to peaceful uses and freedom of scientific investigation, concepts which are influential from the point of view of establishing a norm of international custom.

The *stipulation pour autrui,* in so far as the creation of rights for third States under the Antarctic Treaty system is concerned, is a first point to be discussed in the light of the requirements of Article 36 of the Vienna Convention on the Law of Treaties. Freedom of scientific research is probably the paramount example of rights for third States established by the Antarctic Treaty, since any State can benefit from this stipulation and take advantage of it, as in fact has happened on several occasions. There is obviously no need in this case for an express assent on the part of a third State in order to invoke this right. The fact that Consultative Parties have indicated the wish that these activities be carried out in full observance of the appropriate recommendations and even encouraged interested States to become parties to the Treaty,[76] in no way affects the existence of the right.

Various other provisions on peaceful purposes and demilitarization, including the prohibition of nuclear explosions and disposal of radioactive waste, benefit third States and could be to some extent considered as establishing rights for them. Preservation of the environment and related measures are also important provisions in this connection. Under the resources regimes some benefits are also likely to emerge for third States.[77]

Some of these provisions can be viewed as giving rise to corresponding rules of customary international law, in view of a well-established practice which in some cases, like freedom of scientific research, was pre-existing to the Treaty, and in view of the international interest in the matter.[78] The absence of any objections and protests relating to the Treaty in general and to these provisions in particular is also a positive indication of the establishment of customary rules; although some aspects of the Antarctic co-operation have been questioned in the current United Nations debate, this criticism, as we shall examine in Chapter 10, has not touched the provisions mentioned which, on the contrary, have been generally re-affirmed in that debate.

The creation of obligations with respect to third States on the basis of a *stipulation pour autrui* is a more complicated question because, *inter alia,* the Vienna Convention requires an express acceptance of such an obligation in writing.[79] However, this is not necessarily so if the obligation is in turn established under customary international law, an aspect which we shall examine further below. On the other hand, the Vienna Convention is not necessarily a conclusive factor in this respect, as it was concluded after the Antarctic Treaty entered into force[80] and, in accordance with Article 4 of the Convention, cannot apply retroactively, although it can of course apply to some of the conventions dealing with Antarctic resources, namely that on living resources and eventually the minerals convention. It should also be noted that few Consultative Parties are parties to the Vienna Convention on the Law of Treaties.[81]

While the creation of such obligations is a difficult matter in international law, it cannot entirely be ruled out in the case of the Antarctic Treaty and related conventions. Besides the arguments related to customary law and to the potential existence of an 'objective regime', one might think, for example, of a situation in which a third State decided to carry out a nuclear explosion in the Antarctic, or dispose of radioactive waste, arguing that the prohibitions of the Treaty do not bind it and that no other prohibition is applicable either. Such an example is not too different from the arguments raised by the parties in the nuclear tests cases.[82]

Setting aside considerations of a political nature and the measures contemplated in Article X of the Treaty, which will be considered later, this could well be a case in which it could be argued that the third party concerned is subject to certain obligations deriving from the Treaty, even though they may not necessarily form part of customary international law nor be incurred under other existing treaties. It will always be necessary to examine in each case the complex network of treaties which may be relevant, including their relation to international custom, since, as was seen in connection with environmental policy, there is in existence an extensive corpus of interconnected obligations both under the Antarctic Treaty system and international environmental law which may throw light on the question.

The issue of nuclear tests and disposal of nuclear waste in Antarctica is a likely candidate for this type of treaty-created obligations, without prejudice to the argument that a rule of customary international law may also be in existence in this matter.

Obligations under the Antarctic Treaty system in the light of customary law

The argument that obligations are placed on third States by the Antarctic Treaty system is first and foremost based on the system's existing relationship with international custom.[83] On the one hand, the Antarctic Treaty incorporates pre-existing norms of international custom, such as protection of the freedom of the high seas, but this does not prevent that freedom from being subject to the rule of particular treaty regimes, as long as a reasonable regard for the freedom of others is observed.[84] However, the hypothesis which seems more relevant here is the converse one, namely, that some of the norms established by the Antarctic Treaty have been transformed into international custom and, as such, create general legal obligations.

A recent study summarizes the criteria adopted by the International Court of Justice in the North Sea Continental Shelf cases for determining the conditions whereby a treaty norm acquires the status of international custom in the following way: '(1) The presence of a "fundamentally norm-creating character such as could be regarded as forming the basis of a general rule of law"; (2) a "very widespread and representative participation in the convention", including "that of States whose interests were specifically affected"; (3) the extensiveness and virtual uniformity of state practice evidencing "a general recognition that a rule of law or legal obligation is involved"; and (4) the passage of some time, short though it may be'.[85]

While there is much discussion among writers of international law about the precise meaning and extent of each of the elements required for the formation of customary international law,[86] there is generally agreement in that treaties can create customary law or at any rate provide evidence of the existence of such custom as the case may be. [87] In Akehurst's view this role of treaties is only another means of evidencing State practice on the matter and will always need to be accompanied by *opinio juris* in order to achieve the legal result of custom formation.[88] This last requirement, according to the same author, can be found in the form of statements about customary law in the treaty itself or in the *travaux-pre-paratoires,* or in statements subsequent to the treaty; interestingly enough, if the treaty in any way affects the rights of third parties, the legal justification for such action cannot be found in the treaty itself but in the fact that in such event the contracting parties 'are in effect claiming that customary law permits them to take such action *vis-à-vis* other States, and, if other States do not protest against the conclusion or execution of such treaties, one is entitled to infer that there is a permissive rule of international law authorizing such action'.[89]

Do some of the norms of the Antarctic system comply with these criteria? Leaving aside political considerations, which always tend to introduce subjective criteria of an ideological nature, it may be accepted that the Antarctic system satisfies these requirements to some specific extent. In the first place, it should be noted that the basic norms of the Treaty, concerning peaceful use, non-militarization, freedom of scientific investigation, co-operation and the like, are indubitably of a 'fundamentally norm-creating character' such as may serve as a basis for the establishment of a general rule of law. This relates both to norms that create rights and to norms that can be regarded as establishing obligations, particularly in connection with the nuclear tests and relates issues mentioned above.

Some of these norms can be regarded as having been accepted in customary law prior to the date of the Antarctic Treaty,[90] in which case the Treaty will only provide evidence about such pre-existing rule or clarify its content and scope. Freedom of scientific research would again be a likely candidate in this regard. In other cases, however, the norms were clearly a creation of the Treaty, not only because some of the available *travaux-preparatoires* so indicate, but also because the conditions existing in Antarctica prior to the Treaty would have made impossible the emergence of such rule as pre-existing customary law; this is particularly the case of peaceful uses and non-militarization, objectives that were affected by the conflicts about sovereignty existing before 1959.[91]

It would probably be difficult to find evidence about *opinio juris* concerning these norms either in the Treaty or in the *travaux-preparatoires*, since this type of statement is not usually made at conferences which develop in a political context. However, this does not affect at all the establishment of a general rule of law nor its potential universal acceptance. *Opinio juris* might develop with time and even lead to the establishment of a norm of regional customary law.[92] The role of statements made subsequent to the Treaty plays an important function in this regard, and the United Nations debate that we shall examine in the next chapter has been particularly relevant in providing evidence about the large number of States that accept the general or basic norms of the 1959 Antarctic Treaty.

The second major criterion mentioned above refers to widespread and representative participation in the convention under consideration. This point has been a matter of criticism in relation to the Antarctic Treaty, it being argued that the parties to the Treaty are scarcely representative of the international community.[93] However, it should be noted that thirty-two parties to the 1959 Treaty is not a small number and that this number keeps increasing. Furthermore, the parties to the Treaty are representative of the principal types of legal, political and economic thought found in the world, and they include all those States 'whose interests were specially affected', a criteria which has also been taken into consideration by the decisions mentioned of the International Court of Justice. As we shall examine further below, the Antarctic Treaty system has also been regarded by some writers as a regional arrangement; from such point of view the number of parties to the Treaty should be compared, not with global organizations, but with other regional arrangements, in which case the number of Treaty parties becomes very significant. In any event, international law has never approached the question of the number of parties in relation to custom with a rigid or fixed criteria; the nature and circumstances of the convention will need to be taken into consideration.

The extensiveness and uniformity of State practice evidencing that a 'general recognition that a rule of law or legal obligation is involved'[94] is another element of custom formation which is found in the Antarctic Treaty system and practice. Firstly, it should be noted that among the Treaty parties the practice is very consistent with the basic rules of the Treaty, to the point that many norms and recommendations have been treated as binding despite their initially non-binding character or even before their entry into force.[95] Secondly, national legislation, treaties, diplomatic statements and other expressions of this practice have also been consistent with such rules. Of course, this is the normal effect of a Treaty and of obligations under it which are complied with by the parties and does not necessarily prove the existence of customary law; however, should the practice happen to be at variance with the rules we would then have a positive indication that customary law has not emerged from that legal process, which is not the case under the Treaty system.

The test that really matters is that concerning third States. Acquiescence on the part of third States in the basic norms of the Treaty has worked normally since 1959 and, as a consequence, no protest at all has ever been made about the Antarctic Treaty arrangements or related developments. This is an important evidence indeed about the existence of a general recognition of a rule of law. On this basis, a statement was made about acquiescence in the following terms:

> The International Community has given its tacit consent to the administration of Antarctica by the Consultative Parties for the past two decades and the work undertaken by them in connection with peaceful uses and disarmament, scientific research and conservation has been universally recognised.[96]

At a later point we shall examine the criticism made to the Antarctic Treaty in terms of restricted participation. It is quite true that the restricted participation which characterized until recently the Treaty system did not allow much choice to the international community, which is precisely the reason why this situation has been rapidly changing; but even so, the basic norms of the Treaty were never at issue nor have they been today. Similarly, the argument that many countries had not attained independence at the time of the entry into force of the Antarctic Treaty, what prevented them from protesting, is not different from the argument made in relation to international law and custom formation by writers and states who consider that consent is necessary to be bound by a rule of law;[97] however, in spite of this view, customary law has normally automatically bound new States.[98]

As we have mentioned earlier, the most important evidence about the widespread support that the basic norms of the Antarctic Treaty have received on the part of third States has been provided by the current United Nations debate on the question of Antarctica.[99] If there were any doubts on this point they have been today cleared. In this way, the reference contained in the preamble to the Antarctic Treaty to the interest of mankind and similar concepts, which implied the acceptance of the basic rules by the international community, has been confirmed in international practice. Even where it can be argued that a given rule is likely to form part of a regional custom relating to Antarctica, this custom can be founded on the broad recognition and acceptance of the Antarctic Treaty by the international community.[100]

The Antarctic Treaty parties have been very careful not to interfere with the rights of third States in Antarctica. An example of this is found in the fisheries agreements made by New Zealand with various countries; when these countries are parties to the Antarctic Treaty, like Japan and the USSR, reference is made to the Antarctic Treaty, but when they are not, like Korea, the reference is omitted.[101] As we shall see, a similar policy is followed under the Antarctic Treaty arrangements. In spite of this policy, the argument has been made that the Antarctic Treaty provisions collide with the rights and interests of mankind in the area. This argument, however, leads to the point made by Akehurst to the effect that if a Treaty in any way affects the rights of third parties this can only be based on customary law and if no protest has been made, as is the case in Antarctica, a permissive rule of international law can be inferred in connection with such action.[102]

In the opinion of other authors, however, the Antarctic Treaty system cannot have any effect in international custom as it is first and foremost a provisional arrangement.[103] Presumably this view is based on the fact that there is a possibility of a review conference after thirty years, although this does not necessarily mean that the arrangements can be termed provisional; the arrangements under Part XI of the Law of the Sea Convention have not been regarded as provisional because of the provisions on a review conference under that Part. Further, it has been argued that 'the silence of the community regarding that Treaty can hardly be understood as a form of acquiescence. Nor is it possible to say that there is any statute of limitation in respect of the options open to the rest of mankind'.[104] This question of options will be considered later. The United Nations debate mentioned above does not confirm this point of view, not only because prior acquiesence was reaffirmed by very specific and explicit statements but also because the discussion of options in no way contradicted the basic norms of the Antarctic Treaty.

The requirement concerning the passage of time for the establishment of a rule of customary law is something that international law approaches today with great flexibility.[105] The issue, more than time per se, seems to be the time that is necessary for the rule to become accepted by means of a practice which is uniform, widespread and unprotested. The qualifying norms of the Antarctic Treaty have certainly met this requirement during the quarter of a century that has passed since 1959.

The recognition of the Exclusive Economic Zone as an institution having become a part of customary law has taken place in a relatively short period of time, as was also the case of the continental shelf before it. The elusive approach followed by the International Court of Justice concerning fisheries and customary law in the *Fisheries Jurisdiction Case,*[106] was changed eleven years later, after an extensive development of State practice,[107] into a straightforward acceptance of the new concept in customary law as evidenced in the *Case concerning the continental shelf.*[108] Relative as all of it may be, it conveys an indication of the short-time requirements of international law today.

Relationship with special treaties and objective regimes
The interwoven relationship between a treaty and international custom is not, however, limited to the aspects just discussed. There exists also the concept that certain treaties which, because of their 'public law character' and because they contain provisions of a quasi-legislative kind, can come to have effects on third States.[109] In a well-known writing by Lord McNair, this situation is described in this way:

> When it is remembered that international society has at present no legislature, the treaty is the only instrument available for

doing many of the things which an individual State would do by means of its legislature; and the making of rules of law is not the only function of a legislature. It is therefore not surprising that from time to time groups of States should have assumed the responsibility of leadership and used the instrument of a treaty to make certain territorial or other arrrangements required, or which they consider to be required, in the interest of this or that particular part of the world . . . . Strictly speaking, a treaty of this kind (which may or may not contain an accession clause) binds at first the parties thereto and no other States. But it is undeniable that after a period of time, to which no fixed duration can be attributed, the mere lapse of time and the acquiescence of other States in the arrangement thus made have the effect of reinforcing the essential juridical element of the treaty and of converting what may at first have been a partly *de facto* situation into a *de jure* one.[110]

McNair gave a number of examples to illustrate this point, referring in particular to the Treaty of Vienna of 20 March 1815 establishing the permanent neutralization of Switzerland as forming 'part of the public law of Europe';[111] he also referred to the Convention on the Aaland Island of 30 March 1856.[112]

The issue of objective regimes was discussed extensively at the International Law Commission with occasion of its consideration of the Law of Treaties, with particular reference to the relationship between Treaties and third States, although it was also discussed at a later point as a separate problem. This discussion has been well documented and examined,[113] but it is, however, important to highlight some of the specific references made to the Antarctic Treaty in this context.

In his fifth report on the Law of Treaties, Sir Gerald Fitzmaurice mentioned the 1959 Antarctic Treaty as an example of a Treaty being effective *erga ommes*; while making clear that the Treaty does not purport to impose any obligation on non-parties, he also stated that it is difficult to believe that any non-party which became active in Antarctica would not 'consider itself, and be regarded, as bound to conform to the conditions of the user of Antarctica laid down by the Treaty, such as demilitarization of the area, prohibition of nuclear tests, provision for inspection of bases, etc. . . .'.[114] The rapporteur then discussed the effects of Article X of the Treaty as sanctions, a point which will be considered further below.[115]

Sir Humphery Waldock, in his third report on the Law of Treaties, specifically addressed the question of objective legal regimes that at the time was before the Commission as Article 63 of the draft; in this context, after giving the example of the Treaty of Vienna of 1815, the Aaland Islands Convention and other,[116] he commented that the 1959 Antarctic Treaty parties' 'intention to create an objective legal regime for Antarctica seems clear, both from the Preamble to the Treaty and from the objective formulation of the basic principles of the regime in articles 1 and 2'.[117] The variety of views existing on the matter was well illustrated during the debate of the Commission: some members tended to agree with Waldock's approach, as was the case of Verdross when referring to the Antarctic Treaty as the work of a group of States that 'had created a demilitarized regime which in principle was valid for all States if they did not protest against it';[118] other members, like de Luna, also referred to the Antarctic Treaty, but making the point that Article 63 of the draft 'did not confer a right or impose an obligation on a third State without its consent';[119] yet another member, namely Tunkin, reacted adversely to the idea of an objective regime recalling his participation in the Antarctic conference and stating that the 'intention had been to create a regime which could become universally accepted. But there had been no intention of imposing that regime; any attempt to do so would have been illegal'.[120] Other references to the Antarctic Treaty were given in the general reports of the work of the Commission.[121]

It is hardly surprising that the question of objective regimes did not meet with the agreement of the Commission, mainly on the grounds that it was considered in some opinion that the source of obligation for third countries was always international custom and not a particular treaty;[122] as a result of this debate the question was abandoned. However, this does not mean that objective regimes are non-existent. In fact the discussion on objective regimes was taken up again at the International Law Commission in the light of the succession of States in regard to treaties,[123] and Article 12 of the Vienna Convention on succession of States in respect of treaties refers to the special case of such regimes both in terms of obligations and of rights none of which are affected by the succession.[124] In this connection it is of interest to recall that Papua–New Guinea became a party to the Antarctic Treaty as the successor State to Australia.[125] Other recent academic discussions on objective regimes have involved the case of the EEC and other similar arrangements.[126]

To the extent that objective regimes are accepted in international law, as seems to be the case, that established by the Antarctic Treaty and related arrangements certainly qualifies in this category. The intention of the Treaty parties in this respect can be regarded today as well-established, even if during the negotiations of the Treaty the question might not have been entirely clear. From this point of view it is perhaps useful to introduce the distinction between binding obligations and legal consequences of a treaty;[127] while the 1959 Treaty parties might not have intended to create obligations for third States beyond some basic provisions, they certainly were aware that the Treaty would have generally legal consequences for such third States as has indeed happened.

On the other hand, third States have facilitated the consolidation of this legal effect of the Antarctic Treaty by means of their acquiescence and the lack of protest, in addition to the general duty of not to interfere with valid treaties. As was mentioned earlier, acquiescence has worked normally during the period since the Treaty came into force and the recent United Nations debate has not changed this legal process. However, there is still one issue pending. While it can be safely argued that the Antarctic Treaty qualifies and is accepted as an objective regime, is this also so for the resources regimes, such as the Seals and Living Resources Conventions and eventually the minerals regime?[128] It is still too early to know the answer to this question, although it can be noted, as we shall see in Chapter 10, that the recent debate has concentrated more on these resources regimes than in the case of the 1959 Treaty, with heavy emphasis on the minerals regime.

Although the view that the 1959 Treaty established an objective regime has been recently disputed,[129] the situation has been well summarized in the following manner:

> . . . the objective character of the situation established by the Treaty must be emphasized. In fact, as has often happened in history, an international body behaves in the same way as a governmental body and organizes the governing system of a region. For this system to be valid for non-signatories, those who have established it must still be in a position to enforce its compliance . . . . Neither the desire to see it receive wide recognition on the part of the global international community nor the contention that the General Assembly of the United Nations was the obvious body to provide such recognition prevent the regime established at Washington from being objectively valid *per se,* if only because of the effective role played by the twelve in the Antarctic . . . . Let us simply admit that it is a treaty establishing the governing system of a territory and, as such, enforceable *erga omnes.* Whether it is accepted, formally or tacitly, or not, by the rest of the international community, as things stand at present, no outside factor can, without their agreement, modify the special role of the twelve.[130]

As we shall examine in the following sections of this chapter the question is not posed so much in terms of enforcement of the Treaty provisions *vis-à-vis* third States, since this would pose difficult problems under the terms of Article X, particularly in the event of forceful enforcement and the issue of compatibility with the Charter of the United Nations; it is more a question of the development of co-operation under the Treaty system to meet the interests of third States potentially becoming involved in Antarctic activities. This does not exclude, of course, the adoption of the necessary action to prevent activities which could be regarded as unreasonable or disruptive of the objectives and principles of the Treaty.

Other perspectives tend to emphasize also the objective nature of the Antarctic Treaty. It has been viewed as in some respects resembling an international organization,[131] or as being a kind of regional arrangement such as those referred to in Article 52 and 54 of the Charter of the United Nations,[132] or even as a regional sub-system forming part of the general international system.[133]

9.5   Control over the activities of third parties: Article X of the Treaty and other provisions

The key provision of the Antarctic Treaty as regards control over the activities of the third parties is found in Article X: 'Each of the Contracting Parties undertakes to exert appropriate efforts, consistent with the charter of the United Nations, to the end that no one engages in any activity in Antarctica contrary to the principles or purposes of the present Treaty'.[134] The scope of this provision has given rise to very diverse interpretations. Moreover, the reference to 'each' of the Contracting Parties has been contrasted by one writer with the capacity for collective action which they might have in accordance with Article IX of the Treaty, implying that it could not refer to joint action.[135] However, the practice of the Treaty tends to contradict this interpretation.

The decisive criterion for interpretation of this article is whether the Consultative Parties can claim on the basis of this article some kind of legislative competence *erga omnes,* which could be invoked vis-à-vis third States, In Guyer's opinion, it is obvious that the article is not directed to the Contracting Parties of the Treaty, since they are bound anyhow to observe its provisions.[136] On this basis he concludes that 'this Article should be construed in the sense that if any third party should engage in activities contrary to the provisions of the Treaty, the Contracting Parties would have to consider jointly the action they would take'.[137] This author then concludes that, 'in a way one could say that the Treaty powers have generated a certain legislative right in reference to the region . . . .[138] In a more recent study, Guyer has reaffirmed this conclusion by stating that 'I continue to believe that the Treaty negotiators at Washington established an omni-comprehensive system of general application for the defence of the Antarctic region. It is for this reason that the Antarctic Treaty is a legislative agreement that covers non-signatories as well'.[139]

In this, as in other matters, the policy of the Consultative Parties has been to proceed with considerable 'restraint', seeking positive formulae for co-operation and not confrontation. A United States report on the provisions of the Treaty describes Article X as follows: 'In effect it pledges the Parties not only to refrain from giving assistance to persons or countries which might engage in non-peaceful activities or atomic tests in Antarctica, but to take active steps to discourage any such activity'.[140] The Treaty's original scope as regards peaceful uses has become broader to the extent that Antarctic activity has intensified. There have been numerous recommendations urging States, whether they are Consultative Parties or not, to accept their provisions. Some of these instruments have been specifically addressed to non-signatory countries, urging them in the same terms to follow the provisions.[141] This demonstrates that when third parties have been interested in carrying out activities in Antarctica, the attitude of the Consultative Parties has not been to discourage such activity, as one writer has suggested,[142] but to provide guidance as to how it could fit in with the general legislative framework of the Antarctic system. So far this approach has been always followed both by the Treaty Parties and by third States and is in a way further evidence of the existence of customary law in the matter and even a possible confirmation of an objective regime in Antarctica. The only incident that has taken place, as will be discussed further below, involved a private expedition and took place outside the Treaty area.

If there is no generally accepted principle of jurisdiction applicable to Antarctic activities,[143] then there cannot be one with respect to the activities of third States. However, solutions have been developed on a case-by-case basis, as they have among the Treaty Parties themselves. Therefore, the comment that 'it may thus be argued that the article recognizes the jurisdictional incompetence of the contracting parties to control foreign nationals generally including those of other contracting parties' is incorrect.[144] Nevertheless, as Bush also observes, it is easier for a claimant country to exercise jurisdiction over a third party than for a non-claimant country, which will encounter greater difficulties in justifying its jurisdiction in international law.[145] In practice, however, because of the fact of disputed claims, it will not be that easy for claimants to exercise such jurisdiction either.

Despite these difficulties, as we examined in Chapter 3, jurisdiction has been exercised occasionally by Consultative Parties over nationals of third States. This is particularly the case of foreign nationals, either of third States or of other Treaty parties, who participate in expeditions or activities carried out under the 'flag State jurisdiction' of a Consultative Party.[146] Jurisdiction over ships and aircraft, as well as increasing control over tourist activities, may lead to similar exercise of jurisdiction over third parties.[147]

Article X places special emphasis on respect for the principles and purposes of the Treaty in terms sufficiently broad to include its norm-creating aspects. It must be borne in mind that the recommendations under the Treaty form part of the process of development of the basic framework of the Treaty.[148] In general, the Consultative Parties have not adopted a policy of requiring the approval of the whole body of recommendations by the other Contracting Parties, since such a requirement is not even made of themselves. As Auburn observes they could hardly place such an obligation on third countries if it is not required of participants in the system.[149] Nevertheless, in order to acquire the status of Consultative Party, acceptance of the relevant recommendations of the system has usually been required.[150]

The foregoing arguments notwithstanding, many of the principles and purposes of the Treaty are of such a nature as to be considered 'self-executing' and, consequently, not requiring subsequent legislation for their implementation. One question which in this connection has been the subject of discussion regarding third parties is the possibility that some of them might decide to make a territorial claim.[151] While the Treaty remains in force the problem is more speculative than real, since all present trends reveal a tendency to depart from territorial claims and to concentrate on the resources regime.[152]

The Seventh Consultative Meeting had occasion to consider this question, with particular reference to the activities of third parties or their possible territorial claims. In this instance again, a positive attitude was adopted, it being considered advisable to hold intergovernmental consultations 'and to be ready to urge or invite as appropriate the state or states concerned to accede to the Treaty, pointing out the rights and benefits they would receive and also the responsibilities and obligations of Contracting Parties'.[153] Emphasis was placed on the region covered by the Treaty being considered 'a zone of peace' and special reference was made to Article IV of the Treaty.[154] A re-affirmation of this position is contained in Recommendation VIII-8 and other documents.[155] If a third party were to lay a claim to the area that has remained unclaimed, or to any other area of Antarctica, such action would be met by the criteria explained above, which involves in the first place the encouragement to accede to the Treaty and, hence, the application of Article IV of such Treaty. Moreover, as explained earlier, the unclaimed sector has never been excluded from the norm-creating activity of the Consultative Meetings under the Antarctic Treaty system.[156] On the other hand, Guyer's conclusion on this subject should also be taken into account: 'As all the historically interested parties are already in the region, one cannot see what basis for claims could be presented now by a country prior to its setting foot in the region'.[157]

The possibility that third States might dispose of radioactive waste in Antarctica and its adjacent seas has also been a matter of concern to the Consultative Parties, in view of the specific prohibition contained in Article V of the Treaty. Recommendation VIII-12 made specific reference to this subject,[158] as did a declaration made by Australia on the same occasion.[159] Although it has been maintained that the freedom of the high seas which is protected by the Treaty renders the prohibition in Article V inapplicable to that area,[160] such an interpretation is not justified in the light of the Treaty provisions nor in view of the ecological criteria which have been developed within the framework of the Treaty and of the Consultative Parties' special responsibility in this respect.[161] A number of international conventions might be applicable, for States parties to them, to Antarctic waters and other areas in this respect;[162] as explained in Chapter 6, the complex network of environmental conventions and related instruments needs always to be taken into account in respect of Antarctica.

It is also of interest to note that inspections under the Antarctic Treaty are not restricted to parties to this instrument. This inspection system, according to one commentator, was expressly designed for keeping an eye on the activities of third countries.[163]

Hitherto, the normal procedure adopted by the Consultative Parties has been to urge compliance by third countries with the relevant provisions and recommendations.[164] Article XI of the Agreed Measures refers expressly to the use of vessels of other nationalities, in which case an arrangement has to be sought to ensure observance of the measures by their crews.[165] The development of tourist activities, on the other hand, and of expeditions organized by non-signatory countries to the Treaty, has led to increased vigilance over observance of the measures by visitors and researchers. Various Recommendations have on several occasions referred to this subject or to particular aspects of it.[166]

Non-signatories have organized or sponsored both private and public expeditions. The view has been expressed that there is nothing in the Antarctic Treaty to prohibit private ventures and expeditions or aircraft flights, considering in this respect that Antarctica is an open continent.[167] Various private expeditions have in fact been organized by nationals or entities of States not parties to the 1959 Treaty. One sponsored by Italy in 1976, before this country signed the Treaty, met with obstacles on the part of the Argentine authorities in Buenos Aires, which prompted a discussion about the applicable rules of international law, the Antarctic Treaty and the meaning of Article X.[168] India undertook expeditions during the process of its accession to the Treaty.[169] It is also interesting to mention a project, which failed to materialize, for a European multinational expedition in which Austria, Belgium, the Federal Republic of Germany, France, Italy, the Netherlands, Norway, Sweden, Switzerland and the United Kingdom would have participated under the auspices of the Council of Europe.[170] The joint participation of party and non-party countries to the Treaty would have raised important jurisdictional and legal problems, particularly in terms of which State if any would have the expedition under its 'flag jurisdiction' or the role that an international organization, such as the Council of Europe, may have in this connection. Greenpeace organized a private expedition to the Ross Dependency in the Antarctic summer of 1985–1986 which failed and established a base near McMurdo in the southern summer of 1986–1987.

Criteria of the resources regimes

Identical or similar provisions to those of Article X of the Antarctic Treaty have been included in various other instruments of the system. Article X of the Agreed Measures reproduces the earlier article with much the same wording,[171] as does the Convention on the Conservation of Antarctic Marine Living Resources in its Article XXII, par. 1.[172] It is worthy of note that in the case of the latter Convention the Contracting Parties must notify the Commission of any activity contrary to the objective of the Convention.[173] In addition, the Commission is authorized to inform States not parties to the Convention about activities undertaken by their nationals or vessels which may affect the implementation of the objectives of the Convention.[174] By Recommendation IX-2, which pre-dates this Convention, governments not parties to the Antarctic Treaty were urged to comply with the provisional conservation measures.[175] As already mentioned, there have also been specific recommendations concerning the disposal of nuclear waste.[176]

The question of mineral resources is obviously the one which has caused the greatest concern in relation to the potential activities of third

States. Both Recommendations VII-6[177] and VIII-14[178] paraphrased Article X of the Antarctic Treaty, but with significant stress on the special responsibilities of the Consultative Parties. The Report of the Nansen Foundation also makes several references to Article X.[179] Recommendation XI-1 was not so explicit on the subject but, by referring to the need to maintain the Antarctic Treaty in its entirety and, specifically, to Recommendations VII-6 and VIII-14, it establishes an obvious link with Article X of the Antarctic Treaty.[180]

On the basis of these consistent statements of policy, the position is that any country will be able to participate in Antarctic mineral activities but, in this case, it will not be, strictly speaking, as a 'third country', but as one having acceded to the Convention in accordance with one of the mechanisms considered earlier on. The key principle is that no activity will be possible outside the regime and its norms.[181] This will apply of course as a legal obligation to the States parties to the Convention establishing the minerals regime. In so far as third States are concerned, in principle the creation of such an obligation would have to meet the requirements that we have examined of the Vienna Convention on the Law of Treaties, particularly in terms of the acceptance of obligations in writing; since the latter Convention is now in force it would certainly be applicable in this matter.[182] However, here again it would be important to keep State practice under examination because it could well happen that such norm could become a part of customary law; in any event it is also a norm which could eventually reveal the intention of establishing an objective regime in connection with the minerals regime. So as to ensure that the above mentioned principle is observed, similar concepts to those expressed in Article X of the Antarctic Treaty are repeated in the mineral regime and provision is made, as in the Convention on living resources, for relevant information to be sent to the Commission and for the latter to be enabled to draw to the attention of third States such activities of their nationals or vessels that may affect the implementation of the objectives or principles of the Convention.[183] It is worthy of note that, in this case, in addition to the collective responsibility placed on parties to the regime to prevent activities contrary to it, there is also an individual responsibility placed on them to adopt measures within their competence to ensure compliance with the regime and its norms;[184] although this individual responsibility is related primarily to nationals and other entities under the State jurisdiction, it could eventually reach nationals of third States, either directly or because of their participation in joint-ventures or other arrangements.

This situation raises the very important question of the validity of the moratorium on mining activities with respect to third parties. Are they obliged to respect recommendations in force for a moratorium on activities? This question gives rise to a strange mixture of juridical and metajuridical possibilities, which one writer has defined as follows:

> The position that non-Parties are obliged to respect such a moratorium must consequently rest on arguments that the Treaty regime has, by general international acceptance and recognition, become established as regional customary international law . . . . Nevertheless, other considerations, such as a lack of immediate interest in conducting Antarctic resource activities, a general habit of deference to the Treaty regime, and a political reluctance to incur possible adverse attitudes or actions by the Treaty Parties, are very likely to result in non-Parties respecting the moratorium.[185]

The gradual opening-up process

In accordance with the foregoing considerations, participation of third States in Antarctic mineral resources activities, in this writer's view, will be subject in principle to the provisions of the regime, and this means that they will in fact have to accede to the Convention establishing it and thus implicitly accept the basic rules of the Antarctic Treaty system as a whole. Otherwise we would have, like the situation of Part XI of the Law of the Sea Convention, competing regimes for the exploration and exploitation of mineral resources.

The parties to the Antarctic Treaty have approached this question in a positive way, seeking to facilitate various forms of participation. The general principle that the interests of mankind should not be prejudiced in Antarctica, the specific mechanisms for accession by third countries which have been described, including the joint ventures option and, especially, the potential extension of economic benefits to the international community, are all components of this developing policy of wider and more flexible participation.

While it is true that, from one point of view, these measures will by no means be sufficient to ensure control by the international community or by one of its organizations over the Antarctic development process,[186] the fact that the Consultative Parties cannot abandon or neglect their responsibilities in the region should not be forgotten. A gradual opening-up is possible, but renunciation cannot be expected. This opening-up process is already taking place in an orderly way. The number of new countries recently acceding to the Treaty,[187] the admission of new Consultative Parties,[188] the participation of observers in the mineral negotiations, the possibility of inviting several qualified international bodies as observers, the inclusion of non-governmental representatives in official delegations, parallel development in connection with the Convention of Living Resources, the active participation of various international organizations and other such measures, all point in the same opening-up direction.[189] Various other suggestions have been put forward for the improvement of the Antarctic system, particularly as regards its mechanisms for environmental protection.[190]

Although, obviously, the status of observer and access to information do not confer the same privileges as full participation, it represents a significant first step towards it, as it promotes reciprocal relationships and the development of new forms of co-operation, which are definitely being built on the basis of this principle of gradualism. In the case of several international organizations the status of observer has led to full membership in a short period of time, a case in point being that of the participation of European and other countries in the Inter-American Development Bank.

An important role in this opening-up process can be played by the adoption of a policy concerning availability and distribution of Antarctic information. Hitherto, regrettably this aspect of the Consultative Parties' activity has been neglected, resulting in unnecessary damage to the image of the Treaty system and the emerging minerals regime which could well have been avoided.[191] The view that the Antarctic Treaty system is an 'exclusive club' stems in large part from this lack of information. However, as has been already pointed out, since the adoption of Resolution XII-6, a start has been made on correcting this shortcoming. Wider circulation of the available reports and the fact that they are sent to the Secretary-General of the United Nations and may be drawn to the attention of certain specialized agencies, that they contain fuller information, and that some documents may be published if the delegations submitting them so decide, also make a useful contribution to the information process. This trend has been further strengthened by procedures for keeping an updated information about the Treaty system, including accurate records of the discussion at Consultative Meetings and follow-up action, and by the decision to make available the documents of early Consultative Meetings.[192]

To the extent that activity and interest in Antarctica have significantly increased, the need for coordination between Consultative Meetings and various other institutions has correspondingly become evident. Accordingly, Recommendation XIII-2 has decided that Special Consultative Meetings, such as the one dealing with mineral resources, or any other meeting held pursuant to a Recommendation, shall report through their chairman to the regular Consultative Meetings; such reports shall also be made by the Commission of the Living Resources Convention, SCAR and the Depositary government of the Seal Convention. In this manner, not only the coordination between the various components of the system will be improved, but the system as a whole will become more closely integrated under the general orientation of the Treaty Consultative Meetings. The Living Resources Commission and SCAR will be invited as observers to Consultative Meetings for the purpose of reporting, a development which is also entirely new within the system; this facilitates the participation of observers from other international organizations in the Treaty Consultative Meetings.[193]

Another recent development along the same lines of greater opening-up is the provision of assistance to countries interested in undertaking activities in Antarctica., The inclusion of scientists from other countries in national expeditions and the establishment of joint projects and scientific co-operation agreements can be of considerable help towards the gradual expansion of Antarctic activities. This is an aspect which will merit special attention with respect to developing countries and the development of the mineral resources regime. Brazil, the People's Republic of China and Uruguay have already benefited from various forms of assistance to their Antarctic operations by other Consultative Parties.

9.6   Limit to the policy of persuasion and legal capacity to take action against third parties

Success of the policy just outlined will depend to a large extent on how far it is capable of meeting with understanding on the part of third countries and of persuading them that it will be able to prevent actions or attitudes contrary to the aims and purposes of the Treaty and that these aims are themselves consistent with the interests of the international community as a whole and to its benefit. The same thought is also applicable to the various resources regimes.

The development of this policy has had an important evolution. The very general wording of Article X represents a first step in the direction of this accommodation. Subsequent recommendations have more clearly set out the rights and obligations deriving from being a Party to the Treaty and have urged accession to it. The Convention on Living Resources and the draft text on mineral resources contain still more specific obligations by providing that certain situations should be brought to the attention of the Commission and that the latter may take some form of action regarding third States in cases adversely affecting the implementation of the objectives of this instrument.[194] In addition, the conventional regimes already establish specific juridical links with particular articles of the Antarctic Treaty and other instruments, thereby creating a wide range of inter-connected legal obligations.

However, supposing that this policy of reaching an understanding and of persuasion were to fail and a third State decided in any case to undertake an activity contrary to the aims and purposes of the Treaty, or related instruments and conventions, what alternatives are available to the Treaty Parties or to the system as such? It will, of course, always be possible to exert a certain amount of economic pressure, particularly as regards infrastructural and logistic facilities. In addition, it will likewise be possible to envisage measures of a political nature, according to the particular case. The United States report on potential nuclear tests, mentioned further above, refers to the need to 'take active steps to discourage any such activity';[195] presumably they include political measures, such as diplomatic representations or action before specialized international organizations.

Nor, from a juridical point of view, does the Treaty system appear to lack tools for taking action. In the first place, if the action of the third State violates an obligation by which it is legally bound, either by international custom or by the combined effects of the system's instruments or the existence of an 'objective regime', there will be a clear case for requiring compliance and possibly for holding the State concerned responsible for any damage that occurs.

But even on the basis of a different hypothesis, the argument might follow a similar line. The Parties are empowered, individually under Article X and collectively under Article XI of the 1959 Treaty, to ensure implementation of the objectives and purposes of the Treaty. Faced with a failure to respect these principles, they could take the necessary action to redress the situation, provided such action is consistent with the Charter of the United Nations. In theory, a third State could become active in Antarctica without infringing the normative principles of the Treaty system and in such case action by the Treaty parties might be unwarranted; however, in practice this is very unlikely in view of the elaborate rules that have been developed under the Treaty and related conventions, which one way or the other are closely related to the basic principles. In any event, if all the basic rules are observed by a third State it would amount to a very specific recognition of their customary law character.

In his Fifth Report on the Law of Treaties Sir Gerald Fitzmaurice explained well the relationship between Article X of the Antarctic Treaty and the principle of effectiveness in international law; after quoting the Article, he wrote:

> At the root of such a position, as a causative element affecting the attitude of the third State, lies the existence of a simple if indirect sanction – the test of what it is practicable for it to do, except in co-operation with the parties – and this is itself but an offshoot of a principle fundamental to the 'imperfect' character of international law, as law lacking fully adequate means of central enforcement – the principle of effectiveness – of what can or cannot effectively be done by States acting individually.[196]

The very limited effectiveness of individual State action in Antarctica is the underlying reason for the success of international co-operation in the area, and explains why it would be extremely difficult for a third State to be active in Antarctica on its own, ignoring the existing process of co-operation, and doing so without breaking the basic principles of the Treaty system and the ensuing rules of conduct.

If the violation caused or likely to be caused by the attempted activity of a third State in Antarctica is of a serious nature, especially if it endangers the maintenance of international peace and security in the area, recourse to the United Nations is an option available to the Treaty Parties as one possible form of action to be taken under the 1959 Treaty; of course, that violation would have to affect simultaneously the pertinent articles of the Charter, particularly the purposes and principles set out in Articles 1 and 2. The fact that all the permanent members of the Security Council are Consultative Parties under the Antarctic Treaty would certainly facilitate this option.

The right of self-defence under Article 51 of the Charter has also been mentioned as another option available to the Treaty Parties;[197] the provisions of Chapter 8 of the Charter on regional arrangements could also be of interest to the extent that the Antarctic Treaty is viewed as a regional arrangement.[198] Since action in self-defence is not subject to the veto in the Security Council of the United Nations, Article 51 of the Charter has become increasingly important, unlike the rare findings that the Security Council has made under Article 39, which is subject to the veto.[199]

However, in this context the right of self-defence raises more questions than it provides answers. Firstly, the concept assumes that an armed attack occurs, and even if an anticipatory right of self-defence is recognized,[200] it is nonetheless related to the eventuality of such an armed attack. This is not a situation likely to happen in Antarctica as long as the Treaty is in force. In any event, there is also the question of what is self-defence as compared to collective security and community sanctions,[201] and the manner how the requirements of proportionality and reasonableness are to be met.[202] Secondly, there is the question of whether self-defence is related only with a threat to territorial integrity or political independence of a State, which are the basic interests reflected in Article 2, par. 4, of the Charter, or the concept can be invoked in other contexts.[203] This raises the issue of whether in Antarctica it could be invoked only by claimant States to protect their territorial integrity, or also by non-claimants to protect broader interests if this is admissible.

The latter question has already been discussed in connection with Antarctica. One writer has asked: 'Could the United States come to the aid of a claimant defending territorial sovereignty which it, the United States, did not recognize?'[204] Such a situation could well arise under the Inter-American Treaty of Reciprocal Assistance, which includes a part of the Antarctic;[205] if the mechanism of collective action under this Treaty is triggered, the American States parties to it are under the obligation to provide assistance, without any distinction being made between claimants, such as Argentina and Chile, or non-claimants, such as Brazil, Peru, Uruguay and the United States.[206]

It should be noted, however, that the concept of self-defence has been invoked from time to time to justify the adoption of measures related to natural resources and devoid of any military connotation; it was invoked, for example, by the American government against Britain in the *Behring Sea Arbitration,* and also invoked by a number of Latin American governments in connection with the claims to 200-mile offshore jurisdiction.[207] Similarly, the concepts of necessity, self-preservation and special interests of the coastal State have also been invoked in this other context.[208] It appears that in relation to Antarctica it has been discussed only in this economic dimension.

Normally the kind of violation which might be expected in Antarctica would not be so dramatic as to call for the intervention of the United Nations or the exercise of the right of self-defence or other similar concepts. It would most likely be a matter of non-compliance with the rules enacted under the System and ensuing environmental or similar harm. In a recent discussion of the question, one commentator asked in this regard: 'Imagine (*sic*) a party of a non-Treaty country would come and take the emperor penguins away . . . . What can we do about such a situation, how can we stop the slaughter, what are the legal provisions under the Treaty . . . ?'[209] This question received three different replies, which reveal the various responses possible. First, it was pointed out that it would be possible to 'exert political pressure on outsiders or, if adequately possible, even economic pressure'.[210] A second reply, which does not seem quite appropriate, stated that 'From the legal point of view you cannot do anything'.[211] The third reply, in what seems a more realistic vein, stated: 'But there are possibilities, and I have no doubt that at the very minimum there would be urgent action by the Consultative Parties to put a stop of (*sic*) any predatory action'.[212]

What specific actions can be taken under the Antarctic Treaty is a matter that will have to be considered by the pertinent meetings on a case by case basis, depending on the circumstances and facts of the eventual third-State activity which could result in given violations of the Treaty principles and related rules. Because this is and will always be a delicate political matter, whichever might be its legal justifications, it suggests the importance that if the Treaty parties ever face the need to consider action under Article X, they do so with the greatest restraint and prudence in order not to create a situation which might be controversial under basic principles of international law or the provisions of the U.N. Charter, as could happen with the eventuality of the use of force or similar measures. This prudent approach has until now been a very consistent practice under the Antarctic Treaty and on the part of third States, ensuring solutions that are in harmony with the needs of the external accommodation between the Treaty Parties and interested third States.

Conclusion

The creation of rights for third States under the Antarctic Treaty and related instruments is a relatively straightforward matter which can be easily reconciled with the provisions of the Vienna Convention on the Law of Treaties in the terms indicated. Different is the case of the creation of obligations for third States, a process that will require a very elaborate legal argument and evidence, either that the obligation is established under the Treaty itself or that it has become part of customary international law. The very special situation associated with the existence of an objective regime provides further ground for such an inquiry within the limits that we have discussed in connection with the application of this concept to Antarctica.

On this basis the Treaty parties will be able to take lawful action under Article X of the Treaty and equivalent provisions of the resources regimes if and when a third-State activity might incur in violation of such fundamental obligations. Many additional legal questions would be raised in such an eventuality, including the question of how such action relates to the United Nations Charter and meets the requirement of consistency with its provisions. In any event, such legal difficulties are not insurmountable and with the necessary restraint can lead to satisfactory solutions and enforcement of the pertinent measures decided upon.

As we have indicated, the problem is related not only to the attitude of the Treaty parties but also to that of third-States. The co-operative approach that has been followed until now has been very successful in the search for an accommodation of the interests involved. A confrontational attitude, on the contrary, would create additional tensions and make such accommodation more difficult. These are the fundamental options being discussed at present, with particular reference to the minerals regime, and which will be examined in Chapter 10.

Chapter 9 Notes

1. F. M. Auburn: *Antarctic Law and Politics,* 1982, at 147.
2. Roberto E. Guyer: 'Antarctica's role in international relations', in Francisco Orrego Vicuña (ed.): *Antarctic Resources Policy,* 1983, 267–279, at 275.
3. Antarctic Treaty, Article IX, par. 1.
4. Ibid., Article IX, par. 2. See also the Final Report of the First Special Antarctic Treaty Consultative Meeting, held in London, 25–29 July, 1977, text in W. M. Bush: *Antarctica and International Law,* 1982, 331–333. For the list of Consultative Parties admitted subsequently see Chapter 1 supra, note 113.
5. See generally Harold Bullis: *The political legacy of the International Geophysical Year,* US House of Representatives, Committee on Foreign Affairs, Subcommittee on National Security Policy and Scientific Developments, 1973.
6. Sixty-seven nations were represented in the work of the International Geophysical Year; see Bullis, op. cit., note 5 supra, at 8.
7. The requirement of 'conducting substantial scientific research' was introduced in the Treaty on the basis of a proposal by Chile made at the Antarctic Conference on 10 November 1959; see Oscar Pinochet de la Barra: 'La contribución de Chile al Tradado Antártico', in Francisco Orrego Vicuña, María Teresa Infante, and Pilar Armanet (eds): *Política Antártica de Chile,* 1985, 89–100, at 97–98.
8. For a list of the functions assigned to Consultative Parties, see Bush, op. cit., note 4 supra, at 84.
9. Francisco Orrego Vicuña: 'The definition of a regime on Antarctic mineral resources: basic options', in Ibid., op. cit., note 2 supra, 199–215, at 212–213.
10. Working document presented by the Delegation of Chile on the Operation of the Antarctic Treaty, ANT/XII/PREP/7, 11 April 1983; for comments on this proposal see Fernando Zegers: 'La Comunidad Internacional y la Antártica', in Orrego et al, op. cit., note 7 supra, 277–287.
11. See the Final Report of the Twelfth Antarctic Treaty Consultative Meeting, Canberra, 13–27 September 1983, par. 1 at 1; see also the Statement of Non-Consultative Parties included in Annex C of the report, at 122–123. For the work of the Twelfth Consultative Meeting, see 'International Legal Notes: Preparatory meeting in Canberra, April 1983, to the Twelfth Antarctic Treaty Consultative Meeting', *The Australian Law Journal,* Vol. 57, N° 7, July 1983, 428–429; and 'International Legal Notes: Twelfth Antarctic Treaty Consultative

Meeting, Canberra, 13–27 September 1983', Ibid., Vol. 58, N° 1, January 1984, 59–60.

12. Report cit., note 11 supra, pars. 32–46, at 13–18; see also Recommendation XII-6 on the 'Operation of the Antarctic Treaty System', at 41–44, and Recommendation XIII-15 (1985).

13. See notes 11 and 12 supra.

14. In May 1984 the non-consultative parties were invited to attend the meetings of the Fourth Special Consultative Meeting, where the mineral negotiations are conducted, beginning with the meeting held in Rio de Janeiro in February–March 1985; see generally Lee Kimball: *Report on Antarctica,* November 1, 1984, International Institute for Environment and Development, at 9–10.

15. Kimball, loc. cit., note 14 supra, at 6–7.

16. See Chapter 8 supra, section 8.1.

17. Edvard Hambro: 'Some notes on the future of the Antarctic Treaty collaboration', *A.J.I.L.,* Vol. 68, 1974, 217–226, at 224.

18. See note 10 supra.

19. See Chapter 5 supra.

20. For a technical description of the Chilean facilities, see Javier Lopetegui Torres: 'Infraestructura antártica y política de acceso al continente', in Orrego et al., op. cit., note 7 supra, 161–177, at 164–167. For the activities taking place in King George Island and the ensuing problems, see R. K. Headland and P. L. Keage: 'Activities on the King George Island Group, South Shetland Islands, Antarctica', *Pol. Rec.,* Vol. 22, N° 140, May 1985, 475–484; see also Marcia Poupin Berttoni: 'Poblamiento antártico', in Orrego et al., op. cit., note 7 supra, 115–118.

21. On the United Nations debate about Antarctica see generally Chapter 10 infra.

22. See note 7 supra.

23. Antarctic Treaty, Article XIII, par. 1.

24. Ibid.

25. Although the precise text of this proposal is not known, its general content can be established by means of various statements by delegations on Article XIII of the Treaty; see the Statements of the Contracting Parties made at the last meeting of the Plenary Committee of the 1959 Conference, on 30 November 1959, concerning Article XIII of the Treaty, in Chile: *Memoria del Ministerio de Relaciones Exteriores,* 1959, 698–704, translation in Bush, op. cit., note 4 supra, at 42–43.

26. For the relationship between the United Nations and the specialized agencies, see generally Jacques Dagory: 'Les rapports entre les institutions specialisees et l'organisation des Nations Unies', *RGDIP,* Vol. 73, 1969, 283–377. At the time of the preparation of the Antarctic Treaty the following countries were members of specialized agencies and not of the United Nations: Cameroun, Federal Republic of Germany, Holy See, Republic of Korea, Monaco, San Marino, Switzerland and Viet-Nam; the German Democratic Republic was not a member of the UN or of any specialized agency; see generally 'United Nations: membership of the United Nations and related agencies as of 31 March 1960', *Yearbook of the United Nations,* 1959, 536–537.

27. Statements by Japan, France, USSR, Australia and the United States in source cit., note 25 supra.

28. The text of the declaration of the German Democratic Republic is published in Bush, op. cit., note 4 supra, at 107; the instrument of accession was deposited on 19 November 1974. See also the Statement by the Council of State of Romania of 15 September 1971, text in Bush, op. cit., at 108.

29. The Federal Republic of Germany deposited its instrument of accession on 5 February 1979; for the diplomatic discussion about the application of the

Antarctic Treaty to Berlin, see Bush, op. cit., note 4 supra, at 107. For the accession of the German Democratic Republic, see note 28 supra.

30. Agreed Measures, Article XIII, par. 2.
31. See generally Chapter 2 supra.
32. Convention for the Conservation of Antarctic Seals, Article 12.
33. Bush, op. cit., note 4 supra, at 254–255.
34. Convention for the Conservation of Antarctic Marine Living Resources, Article XXIX, par. 1.
35. Ibid., Article VII, par. 2 (b), (d).
36. See Chapter 8 supra, note 37 and associated text.
37. See generally Chapter 8 supra.
38. See note 9 supra.
39. On participation in Joint Ventures, see Chapter 5 supra.
40. For the position of an acceding State in relation to the discussion about the Antarctic Treaty System, see Peter Bruckner: 'The Antarctic Treaty System from the perspective of a Non-Consultative Party to the Antarctic Treaty', in US Polar Research Board: *Workshop on the Antarctic Treaty System, An Assessment*, 1986, 315–335.
41. René–Jean Dupuy: 'Le Traité sur l'Antarctique', *An. Fr.D.I,* 1960, 111–132, at 118.
42. Ibid., at 119, translation by the author of this book.
43. Statement by the United Kingdom, UN General Assembly, First Committee, 52nd meeting, 29 November 1984, A/C.1/39/PV.52, 30 November 1984, 18–37, at 26–30.
44. See generally Francisco Orrego Vicuña: 'The Antarctic Treaty System: a viable alternative for the regulation of resource orientated activities', in Gillian Triggs (ed.): *The Antarctic Treaty Regime*, 1987, 65–76.
45. Poland, the Federal Republic of Germany, Brazil, India, the People's Republic of China and Uruguay have been admitted as Consultative Parties under this procedure; see generally Chapter 1 supra, note 113. Italy, Peru, Spain and Sweden have also suggested their interest in becoming Consultative Parties in the near future.
46. Brian Roberts: 'International cooperation for Antarctic Development: the test for the Antarctic Treaty', in Francisco Orrego Vicuña (ed.): *El desarrollo de la Antártica*, 1977, 336–356, at 349–352.
47. Convention for the Conservation of Antarctic Marine Living Resources, Article VII, par. 2 (d).
48. See generally Chapter 2 supra.
49. Recommendation III–VII, text in Bush, op. cit., note 4 supra, at 143.
50. Final report of the First Special Antarctic Treaty Consultative Meeting, cit., note 4 supra, Section I, par. 2.
51. Agreed Measures, Article XIII, par. 2.
52. See generally Chapter 5 supra.
53. Antarctic Treaty, Article XII, par. 1 (b).
54. Convention on the Conservation of Antarctic Marine Living Resources, Article XXX.
55. Bush, op. cit., note 4 supra, at 423.
56. Convention for the Conservation of Antarctic Seals, Article 8.
57. Agreed Measures, Article XIV, par. 1–6.
58. Antarctic Treaty, Article XII, par. 2 (b); see generally Finn Sollie: 'The duration of the Antarctic Treaty. An analysis of the amendment and revision procedures in a political perspective', Fridtjof Nansen Foundation, Study AA: P 108/ 2 (E), undated.

59. Antarctic Treaty, Article XII, par. 2 (c).
60. Statement by Mr. Herman Phleger before the US Senate Committee on Foreign Relations on the occasion of the ratification of the Antarctic Treaty, 14 June 1960; see Bush, op. cit., note 4 supra, at 104.
61. See Notes to Article XII, par. 2 of the Antarctic Treaty in Bush, op. cit., note 4 supra, at 105. A 5 or 10 year moratorium was suggested by Chile in 1948; see Bush, op. cit., Vol. II, at 383–384.
62. Statement by Chile on Article XII of the Antarctic Treaty, source cit., note 25 supra, at 42. This point was also raised, together with other insights into the negotiation of the Antarctic Treaty, during the parliamentary discussion in Chile concerning the approval of the Treaty; see 'Informe de la Comisión de Relaciones Exteriores del Senado sobre el Tratado Antártico', *Diario de Sesiones del Senado*, Sesión 32, 22 March 1961, at 1926–1933; the Senate discussion is in Sesión 33, 4 April 1961, at 1941–1992.
63. Convention on the Law of Treaties, Article 70, 1, (b); see also Francesco Capotorti: 'L'extinction et la suspension des traites', *Rec. Cours Ac.D.I.,* 1971-III, 417–587, particularly on Article 70, 1, (b) of the Vienna Convention, at 455–459.
64. Lord McNair: *The Law of Treaties,* 1961, at 532; the Harvard Research is cited as in McNair at 532.
65. On the question of title to Antarctic territory in international law, see generally Gillian Triggs: 'Australian sovereignty in Antarctica', *Mel.U.L.R.,* Vol. 13, 1981–1982, Part I, 123–158; Part II 302–333.
66. Convention on the Conservation of Antarctic Marine Living Resources, Article XXXI, par. 3.
67. See, for example, Article 64 of the Treaty establishing the Latin American Free Trade Association of 1960, under which obligations concerning trade and other matters continue in force for five years after withdrawal of a member; text in Inter-American Institute of International Legal Studies: *Instruments relating to the Economic Integration of Latin America,* 1968, 207–222.
68. Agreement concerning the execution of the transfer to the United Nations of certain assets of the League of Nations, 19 July 1946, *Yearbook of the United Nations,* 1946–1947, 269–271.
69. International Court of Justice: International Status of *South-West Africa,* Advisory opinion of July 11, 1950, *Reports,* 1950, particularly at 137, 159–160 and 172.
70. Convention for the Conservation of Antarctic Seals, Article 14.
71. Convention for the Conservation of Antarctic Marine Living Resources, Article XXXI.
72. For a recent discussion of the question of rights and obligations of third States under the Antarctic Treaty and related instruments, see generally Patricia Birnie: 'The Antarctic Regime and Third States', in Rudiger Wolfrum (ed.): *Antarctic Challenge II,* 1986, 239–262.
73. See generally Philippe Cahier: 'Le probleme des effets des traites a l'egard des etats tiers', *Rec. Cours Ac. D.I,* 1974-III, 589–735; A. McNair: *The Law of Treaties,* 1961, 309–342; Sir Ian Sinclair: *The Vienna Convention on the Law of Treaties,* 1984, 98–106; Luke T. Lee: 'The Law of the Sea Convention and Third States', *A.J.I.L.,* Vol. 77, 1983, 541–568. The discussion on the effect of treaties on third States was further enhanced by the provision of Article 2, par. 6, of the United Nations Charter to the extent that 'The organization shall ensure that states which are not Members of the United Nations act in accordance with these Principles so far as may be necessary for the maintenance of international peace and security'.

74. For the text of recommendations and other material of Antarctic Consultative Meetings concerning third-States, see generally Antarctic Treaty: *Handbook of the Antarctic Treaty System,* fourth edition, 1985, 6501–6503.
75. Antarctic Treaty, second preambular paragraph.
76. See the document cit., note 74 supra.
77. See generally Birnie, loc. cit., note 72 supra, at 250–251; this author makes also the interesting argument that some EEC members who are not parties to the Convention on the Conservation of Antarctic Marine Living Resources will benefit from EEC participation in the Commission of CCAMLR, at 250. For benefits related to the minerals regime, see Ibid., at 250–251, and Chapter 5 supra, with particular reference to joint-ventures.
78. For a discussion of the arguments in support of the conclusion that some basic principles of the Treaty are a part of customary law, and of the arguments against such conclusion, see Bush, op. cit., note 4 supra, at 102–103.
79. Vienna Convention on the Law of Treaties, Article 35.
80. The Vienna Convention on the Law of Treaties was signed on 23 May 1969 and entered into force on 27 January 1980; see generally M. J. Bowman and D. J. Harris: *Multilateral Treaties. Index and current status,* 1984, and *Supplement,* 1984.
81. The following Antarctic Treaty Consultative parties are parties to the Vienna Convention on the Law of Treaties: Argentina, Australia, Chile, Japan, New Zealand and the United Kingdom; Bowman and Harris, op. cit., note 80 supra, at 326. See also E. W. Vierdag: 'The law governing treaty relations between Parties to the Vienna Convention on the Law of Treaties and States not Party to the Convention', *A.J.I.L.,* Vol. 76, 1982, 779–801.
82. In the *Nuclear Tests Cases* decided by the International Court of Justice on 20 December 1974, *Reports,* 1974, the essential point of Australia's application was that French nuclear tests were 'not consistent with applicable rules of international law', at 256, while France disputed this argument as it did not consider itself bound by any rule of international law to terminate its tests, at 270; because the Court did not decide on the issue of legality, its judgement was criticized in the Joint Dissenting Opinion of Judges Onyeama, Dillard, Jimenez de Arechaga and Waldock, at 319–320; on the prohibition of nuclear tests in customary law see also the Memorial on Jurisdiction and Admissibility submitted by Australia, *Pleadings,* 1978, at 332–335, with particular reference to the freedom of the high seas at 337–343. On these cases see generally Brigitte Bollecker-Stern: 'L'Affaire des essais nucleaires francais devant la Cour Internationale de Justice', *An. Fr. D.I.,* Vol. XX, 1974, 299–333; Thomas M. Franck: 'World Made Law: the decision of the ICJ in the Nuclear Test Cases'. *A.J.I.L.,* Vol. 69, 1975, 612–620; R. St. J. Macdonald and Barbara Hough: 'The Nuclear Tests Case revisited', *G.Y.B.I.L.,* Vol. 20, 1977, 337–357.
83. See generally Bush, op. cit., note 4 supra, at 102–104.
84. See in particular Article 2 of the 1958 Convention on the High Seas; note, however, that this Convention entered into force on 30 September 1962, after the entry into force of the Antarctic Treaty. On the sources of the law of the sea, see generally Hugo Caminos: 'Les sources du Droit de la Mer', in René–Jean Dupuy and Daniel Vignes (eds): *Traité du Nouveau Droit de la Mer,* 1985, 27–121.
85. Lee, loc. cit., note 73 supra, at 561–562; see in particular the Judgment of the International Court of Justice in the *North Sea Continental Shelf Cases* of 20 February 1969, *Reports,* 1969, at 41–44.
86. See, for example, Michael Akehurst: 'Custom as a source of international law', *B.Y.B.I.L.,* Vol. 47, 1974–1975, 1–53; Maarten Bos: 'The identification of custom in international law', *G.Y.B.I.L.,* Vol. 25, 1982, 9–53.

87. See Akehurst, loc. cit., note 86 supra, at 42–52; and generally R. R. Baxter: 'Multilateral treaties as evidence of customary international law', *B.Y.B.I.L.*, Vol. 41, 1965–1966, 275–300.
88. Akehurst, loc. cit., note 86 supra, at 42–49.
89. Ibid., at 44.
90. Bush, op. cit., note 4 supra, at 102–103.
91. On the question of Antarctic conflict see generally Chapter 1 supra; see also Francisco Orrego Vicuña: 'Antarctic conflict and international cooperation', in US Polar Research Board, op. cit., note 40 supra, at 55–64.
92. Birnie, loc. cit., note 72 supra, at 252, and note 32 of such work.
93. See Chapter 10 infra.
94. See note 85 supra and associated text.
95. See Chapter 2 supra.
96. Speech by the Chairman of the Chilean delegation to the Second Special Antarctic Treaty Consultative Meeting, Ambassador Fernando Zegers, 27 February 1978; English translation in Bush, op. cit., note 4 supra, at 85.
97. For a discussion of this argument, see Akehurst, loc. cit., note 86 supra, at 27–28.
98. Ibid., at 27.
99. See generally Chapter 10 infra, with particular reference to the United Nations debate on the question of Antarctica and the views expressed by governments; see also the Report of the UN Secretary General on the Question of Antarctica, Part Two, *Views of States,* Vol. I to III, A/39/583, 2 November 1984; views of States on the issue have also been published in *Fram: The Journal of Polar Studies*; for statements by Mexico and Surinam, see the issue of Winter 1984, at 362–363.
100. This argument has been discussed specifically with regard to the issue of a moratorium on mineral activities; see Richard B. Bilder: 'The present legal and political situation in Antarctica', in Jonathan I. Charney (ed.): *The New Nationalism and the use of common spaces,* 1982, 167–205, at 186.
101. See the fisheries agreements between New Zealand and the USSR of 4 April 1978, *N.Z.T.S.,* 1978, 5; New Zealand and Japan of 1 September 1978, *N.Z.T.S.,* 1978, 12; and New Zealand and Korea of 16 March 1978, *N.Z.T.S.,* 1978, 4.
102. See note 89 supra and associated text.
103. Alvaro de Soto: 'Statement on Antarctic Resources and the Environment', *Earthscan Seminar,* Washington DC, 14 September 1979, at 4; see also Alvaro de Soto: 'Las Riquezas de la Antártica', *Política Internacional* (Yugoslavia), N° 726–7, 5–20 VII 1980, 38–41.
104. de Soto, Earthscan doc. cit., note 103 supra, at 4.
105. The requirement of a short period of time was already quite evident in the International Court of Justice judgment on the *North Sea Continental Shelf Cases,* cit., note 85 supra, at 3, 43; see also Akehurst, loc. cit., note 86 supra, at 15–16.
106. International Court of Justice: *Fisheries Jurisdiction Case,* Judgment of 25 July 1974, Reports, 1974, at 34; see also the Joint Separate Opinion of Judges Forster, Bengzon, Jimenez de Arechaga, Nagendra Singh and Ruda, at 46–52.
107. See generally FAO: *Coastal State requirements for foreign fishing,* Vol. 1, Legislative Study N° 21, Rev. 1, 1983.
108. International Court of Justice: *Case concerning the Continental Shelf* (Libyan Arab Jamahiriya v. Malta), Judgment of 3 June 1985, *Reports,* 1985, par. 34.
109. Lee, loc. cit., note 73 supra, at 564.
110. A. McNair, op. cit., note 73 supra, at 259; this citation is also included in Lee, loc. cit., note 73 supra, at 564, to illustrate the issue in relation to the discussions on the Law of the Sea Convention. See also the Separate Opinion of Judge McNair

on the Advisory Opinion of the I.C.J. on the International Status of South-West Africa of July 11, 1950, *Reports,* 1950, 146–163, in which he discusses the objective character of Article 22 of the Covenant of the League of Nations, at 153–155.

111. McNair, op. cit., note 73 supra, at 260.
112. Ibid., at 263.
113. See generally the comments of the International Law Commission on objective regimes created by treaty in *Y.B.I.L.C.,* 1964, Vol. II, 173–227, particularly at 184–185; also 1966, Vol. II, at 231. Article 63, par. 1 of the draft considered by the Commission in 1964 considered that a treaty established an objective regime when it appeared 'from its terms and from the circumstances of its conclusion that the intention of the parties is to create in the general interest general obligations and rights relating to a particular region, State, territory, locality, river, waterway, or to a particular area of sea, sea-bed, or air-space; provided that the parties include among their numbers any State having territorial competence with reference to the subject matter of the treaty, or that any such State has consented to the provision in question'. For decisions pertinent to the question of creation of such international regimes, see the *Wimbledon Case,* Permanent Court of International Justice, 1923, Ser. A/1, at 28; and *South-West Africa Case* (Preliminary Objections), International Court of Justice, *Reports,* 1962, at 329–331. See also Sinclair, op. cit., note 73 supra, at 104; Charles Rousseau: *Droit International Public,* 1977, Vol. III, at 217–230; and Birnie, loc. cit., note 72 supra, at 243–249.
114. Sir Gerald Fitzmaurice: 'Fifth Report on the Law of Treaties', 21 March 1960, *Y.B.I.L.C.,* 1960, Vol. II, 69–107, at 93–94.
115. Ibid., at 94.
116. Sir Humphrey Waldock: 'Third Report on the Law of Treaties', 3 March 1964, *Y.B.I.L.C.,* 1964, Vol. II, 5–65, at 26–34.
117. Ibid., at 30; see also the statement by Waldock at the 739th meeting of the Commission, 5 June 1964, *Y.B.I.L.C.,* 1964, Vol. 1, at 105; and Cahier, op. cit., note 73 supra, at 660–661.
118. Statement by Verdross, *Y.B.I.L.C.,* 1964, Vol. 1, at 99.
119. Statement by De Luna, ibid., at 99.
120. Statement by Tunkin, ibid., at 107.
121. See *Y.B.I.L.C.,* cit., note 113 supra; see also the question raised on objective regimes by Henkin, Pugh, Schachter and Smit: *International Law, Cases and Materials,* 1980, at 635.
122. See *Y.B.I.L.C.,* 1966, Vol. II, at 231.
123. Report of the International Law Commission, *Y.B.I.L.C.,* 1974, Vol. II, Part One, 157–331, at 204–206.
124. Article 12 of the Vienna Convention on succession of States in respect of Treaties reads: '2. A succession of States does not as such affect: (a) obligations relating to the use of any territory, or to restrictions upon its use, established by a treaty for the benefit of a group of States or of all States and considered as attaching to that territory; (b) rights established by a treaty for the benefit of a group of States or of all States and relating to the use of any territory, or to restrictions upon its use, and considered as attaching to that territory'. See also Sinclair, op. cit., note 73 supra, at 104–106.
125. See R. K. Headland: 'Antarctic Treaty; signatories and dates', *Pol. Rec.,* Vol. 22, Nº 139, January 1985, 438–439.
126. See generally the book review by Friedl Weiss on such discussion, *B.Y.B.I.L.,* Vol. 52, 1981, 281–286.

127. International Court of Justice: *South West Africa Cases,* Second Phase, Judgment of 18 July 1966, *Reports,* 1966, particularly at 34–35.
128. Birnie, loc. cit., note 72 supra, at 22.
129. Auburn, op. cit., note 1 supra, at 117–118.
130. Dupuy, loc. cit., note 41 supra, at 121–122; translation by the writer of this book.
131. Bilder writes in this regard: 'Indeed, while the Treaty does not in itself establish an international organization, the present Antarctic system and regime has come to resemble an international organization in a number of significant respects'; see Bilder, loc. cit., note 100 supra, at 174.
132. Fernando Zegers: 'The Antarctic System and the Utilization of Resources', *Univ. Mia. L. Rev,* Vol. 33, 1978, at 439.
133. Zegers, loc. cit., note 10 supra, at 286; see also the statement by R. Tucker Scully on the Antarctic system as a regional approach, in U.S. House of Representatives, Committee on Merchant Marine and Fisheries, Subcommittee on fisheries and wildlife conservation and the environment: *Hearing on Antarctic Marine Living Resources* (H.R. 3416), June 30, 1983, at 49.
134. Antarctic Treaty, Article X.
135. Auburn, op. cit., note 1 supra, at 118.
136. Roberto Guyer: 'Antarctic System', *Rec. Cours Ac.D.I,* 1973-II, 149–226, at 224.
137. Ibid., at 224.
138. Ibid., at 224–225.
139. Guyer, loc. cit., note 2 supra, at 278; the writer of this book has substituted the original expression 'legislators' for 'Treaty negotiators' in order to better reflect the Spanish meaning of this text.
140. United States report on provisions of the Antarctic Treaty, 4 February 1960, published in Department of State: *The Conference on Antarctica, 1959,* at 71–76, reproduced in Bush, op. cit., note 4 supra, at 111–112.
141. For the practice of the Antarctic System in relation to Article X of the Treaty, see the works cit., notes 74 and 83 supra.
142. Auburn, op. cit., note 1 supra, at 115.
143. See generally Chapter 3 supra.
144. Bush, op. cit., note 4 supra, at 100.
145. Ibid., at 79–80.
146. Ibid., at 80–81.
147. Ibid., at 80.
148. See generally Chapter 2 supra.
149. Auburn, op. cit., note 1 supra, at 120.
150. See note 50 supra.
151. Auburn, op. cit., note 1 supra, at 115–116.
152. See generally Chapter 1 supra.
153. Final Report of the Seventh Antarctic Treaty Consultative Meeting, Wellington, New Zealand, 30 October–1 November 1972, par. 16, text in Bush, op. cit., note 4 supra, at 266.
154. Report cit., note 153 supra, par. 17, text in Bush, op. cit., note 4 supra, at 266.
155. Recommendation VIII-8, par. 1; see also the reports of the IXth and Xth Consultative Meetings, in *Handbook 1985,* at 6502.
156. See generally Chapter 5 supra.
157. Guyer, loc. cit., note 136 supra, at 225.
158. Recommendation VIII-12; reference is also made to Article X in this recommendation. See also Boleslaw A. Boczek: 'The protection of the Antarctic ecosystem: a study in International Environmental Law', *Ocean Dev. I.L.,* Vol. 13, 1983–1984, 347–425, at 367.

159. Statement by the representative of Australia, Mr Keith Brennan, made on 12 June 1975; Final Report of the Eighth Antarctic Treaty Consultative Meeting, Oslo, 9–20 June 1975, Annex I, text in Bush, op. cit., note 4 supra, at 297.

160. Bush, op. cit., note 4 supra, at 67, 327; see also B. Vukas: 'L'utilisation pacifique de la mer, denuclearisation et desarmement', in Dupuy and Vignes, op. cit., note 84 supra, at 1079, 1088.

161. See in particular the history of the drafting of Article VI explained by Alfred Van der Essen: 'The application of the law of the sea to the Antarctic continent', in Orrego, op. cit., note 2 supra, at 233; see further Chapter 4 supra.

162. See, for example, the Statute of the International Atomic Energy Agency, of 26 October 1956, *U.N.T.S*, Vol. 276, 1957, 4–40, with particular reference to co-operation, safeguards and dispute settlement; see also the Convention on the prevention of marine pollution by dumping of wastes and other matter, London, 29 December 1972, in David C. Jackson (ed.): *World Shipping Laws*, Binder 3, VIII/10/ Conv., 1984 and also, as amended, in Nagendra Singh: *International Maritime Law Conventions,* 1983, Vol. 3, 2536–2545; and Convention on Civil Liability for oil pollution damage resulting from exploration for and exploitation of sea-bed mineral resources, London, 1 May 1977, in Jackson, op. cit., Binder 3, VIII/18/Conv., 1984. See also generally Boczek, loc. cit., note 158 supra, and Chapter 4 and 6 supra.

163. Bush, op. cit., note 4 supra, at 72; see also Truls Hanevold: 'Inspections in Antarctica', *Coop. and Confl,* 2, 1971, 103–114, at 107.

164. See notes 74 and 83 supra.

165. Agreed Measures, Article XI.

166. See, for example, Recommendation VIII-8; Final Report of the Ninth Antarctic Treaty Consultative Meeting, London, 19 September–7 October 1977, par. 14; and Final Report of the Tenth Antarctic Treaty Consultative Meeting, Washington, 17 September–5 October 1979, par. 15. See also Recommendation XIII-3 which reaffirms the need to maintain an awareness of the activities of tourists in Antarctica and exchange this information under the Treaty procedures; see further Liliana Nilo F.: 'Protección del ambiente antártico y expediciones no gubernamentales', *Boletin Antártico Chileno,* Vol. 4, N° 1, January–June 1984, 45–55.

167. See 'US and private ventures', *Antarctic,* Vol. 6, N° 4, December 1971, at 119.

168. See generally 'Italian expedition works off west coast of Antarctic Peninsula', *Antarctic,* Vol. 7, N° 9, March 1976, at 304–305; on the discussion with the Argentine authorities about Article X see Silvio Zavatti: 'La spedizione antarctica italiana e il diritto internazionale', *Il Polo,* Vol. 32, N° 2, Giugno 1976, 44–46. Italy signed the Antarctic Treaty on 18 March 1981. See also the Italian Law on the National Research Programme in Antarctica of 10 June 1985, *Official Journal,* N° 145, 21 June 1985.

169. On the interest of India in Antarctica and its ensuing expeditions, see K. Ahluwalia: 'The Antarctic Treaty: should India become a party to it?', *I.J.I.L.,* Vol. 1, 1960–1961, 473–483; Subash C. Jain: 'Antarctica: geopolitics and International law', *I.Y.B.I.A.,* 1974, 249–278; Deborah Shapley: 'India in Antarctica: international treaty still on ice', *Nature,* Vol. 301, N° 5899, 3 February 1983, at 362; K. S. Jayaraman: 'Expedition to Antarctica', *Indian and Foreign News,* 1 February 1982, 20–22; Peter J. Beck: 'Science – and politics – on ice. India in Antarctica', *Nature,* Vol. 306, 10 November 1983, 106–107; Joel Larus: 'India claims a role in Antarctica', *The Round Table,* N° 289, 1984, 45–56; S. Z. Qasim and H. P. Rajan: 'The Antarctic Treaty System from the perspective of a new member', in US Polar Research Board, op. cit., note 40 supra, 345–374.

170. Gaston de Gerlache de Gomery: 'A proposed European Antarctic Expedition', *Ant.J.U.S.,* Vol. VIII, N° 1, January–February 1973, 15, 28.
171. Agreed Measures, Article X; see also Recommendation 1-VIII, par. (iii).
172. Convention on the Conservation of Antarctic Marine Living Resources, Article XXII, par. 1.
173. Ibid., Article XXII, par. 2.
174. Ibid., Article X, par. 1.
175. Recommendation IX-2, Part II, par. 1 (c).
176. See note 158 supra.
177. Recommendation VII-6, preambular par. 2.
178. Recommendation VIII-14, preambular par. 4.
179. Report of the meeting of experts organized by the Fridtjof Nansen Foundation, 30 May–10 June 1973; report of the working group on legal and political questions, par. 3 (8), 23.
180. Recommendation XI-1, preambular par. 8, and par. 5 (b).
181. *1984 Draft Articles,* Article III (bis); *1986 Draft Articles,* Article 3.
182. See notes 80 and 81 supra.
183. *1983 Draft Articles,* Article VI, XIV; *1984 Draft Articles,* Articles VI, XIV; *1986 Draft Articles,* Article 9.
184. *1984 Draft Articles,* Article VI, par. 1; *1986 Draft Articles,* Article 8.
185. Bilder, loc. cit., note 100 supra, at 188.
186. See generally Chapter 10 infra.
187. Four countries acceded to the Treaty in 1984: Hungary (27 January 1984), Sweden (24 April 1984), Finland (15 May 1984), and Cuba (16 August 1984); the total number of contracting parties was of 32 at the end of 1985; see generally Headland, loc. cit., note 125 supra.
188. See note 45 supra.
189. For a summary of these developments, see generally Kimball, loc. cit., note 14 supra; see also the reports by Kimball published on 5 July and 8 November 1985.
190. Recommendation XII-6 and doc. cit., note 10 supra; see also Recommendation XIII-4 on improvement of the procedures for waste disposal, XIII-5 on additional protective arrangements in relation to man's impact on the Antarctic environment, and XIII-8 on management plans for various Sites of Special Scientific Interest and Specially Protected Areas. The Thirteenth Consultative Meeting also discussed the environmental impact assessment of scientific and logistic activities in Antarctica.
191. Orrego, loc. cit., note 9 supra, at 212–213.
192. Recommendation XIII-1; as a result of these new measures the documents from the first three Consultative Meetings will no longer be treated as confidential, and those of Meetings IV to VII will be dealt with at the XIV Consultative Meeting in 1987; see generally Kimball, Report of November 8, 1985, cit., note 189 supra, at 5.
193. Recommendation XIII-2, and Kimball, Report of November 8, 1985, cit., note 189 supra, at 5.
194. See note 183 supra.
195. See note 140 supra.
196. Fitzmaurice, report cit., note 114 supra, at 94.
197. See Guyer, loc. cit., note 136 supra, at 224.
199. See notes 132 and 133 supra.
199. Rosalyn Higgins: *The development of international law through the political organs of the United Nations,* 1963, at 198; see also Leland M. Goodrich, Edvard Hambro and Anne Patricia Simmons: *Charter of the United Nations,* 1969, at 342–353.

200. Higgins, op. cit., note 199 supra, at 199.
201. Ibid., at 209.
202. Ibid., at 205.
203. For a discussion of the various justifications claimed for the use of force, especially with regard to the vital interests of the State, see ibid., at 197–222. The traditional right of self-defence has generally been interpreted in a flexible manner, not restricting its meaning to the case of an armed attack; for the view of authors see Whiteman, *Digest of International Law,* Vol. 5, 971–991.
204. Auburn, op. cit., note 1 supra, at 118.
205. See Chapter 1 supra, note 57 and associated text.
206. See in particular Articles 3 and 6 of the Inter-American Treaty of Reciprocal Assistance of 2 September 1947, and the Protocol of Amendments of 26 July 1975; for texts and comments, see F. V. García-Amador: *The Inter-American System,* 1983, Vol. 1, Part II, 261–395.
207. See Winston Conrad Extavour: *The Exclusive Economic Zone,* 1981, at 93–94, with particular reference to Latin American claims; a reference to the *Behring Sea Arbitration* is made at 93, note 117 of such work.
208. Ibid., at 93–95, and 118–121.
209. Comments by Professor G. Hempel, in Rudiger Wolfrum (ed.): *Antarctic Challenge,* 1984, at 124; the text marked (*sic*) should read 'Imagine *that* . . .'.
210. Comments by Dr. R. Illing, in Wolfrum, op. cit., note 207 supra, at 124.
211. Comments by Professor R. Lagoni, in Wolfrum, op. cit., note 207 supra, at 124.
212. Comments by Mr R. Wyndham, in Wolfrum, op. cit., note 207 supra, at 125; the text marked (*sic*) should read '. . . put a stop *to* . . .'. See also Guyer, as cited in note 197 supra, who justifies the adoption of measures by the Treaty Parties to ensure that the objectives of the Treaty are complied with by third States.

10

The Antarctic Treaty system and the international community

10.1 First proposals for internationalization

The academic and diplomatic debate which has been going on throughout the present century about the legal status of Antarctica and the possible forms of international co-operation therein, has been generally dominated by proposals for various forms of internationalization of the continent or for the establishment of some sort of linkage with the international community in a broad sense.[1] The ideas expressed by Fauchille in 1925 concerning the participation of all States in the exploitation of the wealth of Antarctica[2] have been a recurrent theme in this debate.

The wide range of proposals put forward before the Antarctic Treaty was concluded may be classified into three main categories. The first refers to the establishment of international machinery for the organization of co-operation in Antarctica which would, in general, be restricted to the countries directly concerned. This type of proposal implies a limited degree of internationalization, but not to such a generalized extent as in other schemes. Proposals for the establishment of a Permanent International Commission for Antarctica[3] and those aimed at ensuring the internationalization or demilitarization of the continent[4] fall within this category.

A second category of proposals envisaged forms of internationalization based on functional criteria, implying co-operation in specific spheres of activity. Jenk's proposal for the establishment of common international services for Antarctica comes within this category.[5] In each of the specialized subjects in this proposal the provision of particular functions could be undertaken by appropriate international organizations. Thus, for example, aviation would come within the scope of the International Civil Aviation Organization (ICAO), meteorological aspects would be dealt with by the World Meteorological Organization (WMO) and scientific matters by the United Nations Educational, Scientific and Cultural Organization (UNESCO). This would not preclude the participation of organizations such as the United Nations, as it was also proposed that the latter, or some other specialized organization, might hold the title to the mineral resources of Antarctica and be able to grant licences or concessions.[6] Some of the alternatives for co-operation proposed by Jessup and Taubenfeld were also based on functional criteria and envisaged the participation of United Nations specialized agencies or other international organizations of co-operation.[7]

However, the idea which has had the greatest attraction for writers – and this constitutes the third main category of proposals for an Antarctic regime – is one for a general internationalization of Antarctica within the purview of the United Nations, or the creation of a special organization. A great many proposals of this kind were made during the years immediately following the creation of the United Nations, as that was a period when the world organization enjoyed great prestige and many hopes for new forms of internationalization were based on it.

Many commentators who have studied alternatives to the Antarctic regime have contemplated a direct or indirect role for the United Nations, or similar approaches. A role for the United Nations without prejudice to possible decisions of the International Court of Justice in sovereignty disputes, was one of the solutions contemplated by Gidel.[8] Jessup and Taubenfeld looked into the alternative of renunciation of all claims to sovereignty in favour of a supranational body, either of restricted membership or representative of the interests of 'all nations and peoples'. In the latter case, they suggested a United Nations agency, a body established under the Trusteeship Council or the General Assembly, or an entirely new entity.[9] Similar solutions were contemplated for outer space, based on the Antarctic model.[10]

Other similar proposals which were considered were for a dependency of the international public domain and delegated trusteeship;[11] complete internationalization, possibly under the United Nations;[12] the creation of a 'United Nations Territory', administered by a subsidiary body of the General Assembly and even having a United Nations Force available to forestall military incidents;[13] or the development of a significant indirect role of the world organization.[14]

Several initiatives by political or intellectual leaders of various countries with an interest in Antarctica adopted the same line of approach. As we examined in Chapter 1, Lord Shackleton proposed in 1949 that 'the Antarctic should be administered internationally, and the United Nations should be the body to do it . . . ultimately the Antarctic should become United Nations territory'.[15] A few years later he reiterated that Antarctica 'should come under the direct authority of the United Nations'.[16] Ideas about the neutralization of Antarctica were discussed in the House of Lords in 1959,[17] as they have been raised again more recently in a different context in the European Parliament.[18] In a noteworthy debate in the House of Lords in 1960, Lord Shackleton pressed for the complete internationalization of Antarctica, modelled on the International Atomic Energy Agency; the statements at the time of Lord Denning and Lord McNair on the subject indicate a certain degree of support for an undertaking of this kind.[19]

The subject was also discussed on several occasions in the House of Commons where, in 1956, the question was raised as to whether the United Nations might perhaps accept the cession of sovereignty rights in its favour. The Government replied in the negative on the grounds that such a proposal 'is not in keeping with the principles of the Charter as it stands, nor is there any provision in the Charter for it'.[20] Two years later, similar questions were again raised on the occasion of Prime Minister Macmillan's statements on the possible tenor of an Antarctic agreement.[21] Although these statements have occasionally been interpreted as favouring a generalized internationalization of Antarctica, in fact they were aimed more at the type of Antarctic regime that was established in 1959, with particular emphasis on neutralization and demilitarization.[22] The debate helped to make this aim clear and with respect to the proposed system's relationship with the United Nations it was stated that it 'would be one of the principal questions to be settled'.[23]

The Prime Minister of New Zealand, Sir Walter Nash, had from 1956 onwards been making various suggestions for the internationalization of Antarctica. They were outlined by that country's representative at the 1959 Antarctic conference in the following terms:

> . . . my Prime Minister has put forward the view that the establishment of a completely international regime for Antarctica would require countries to forego their national claims. In Mr. Nash's view it is only on this basis that a fully effective administration of the whole of Antarctica could be achieved . . . . Such an international regime could prepare for the eventual use of the resources of Antarctica in a regulated and orderly manner. New Zealand would . . . envisage the establishment of an organic relationship between such an Antarctic regime and the United Nations in the belief that joint international action in Antarctica could provide a practical demonstration of the principles for which the United Nations stands.[24]

Although this proposal comes closer to a generalized internationalization of Antarctica,[25] at the same time it could be understood in a more restricted way since the scheme would have organic links with the United Nations but would possess its own separate regime. In this sense a regime such as the one adopted in 1959 was totally acceptable from such a point of view.

Trusteeship proposals and India's initiatives
At the same time as the foregoing developments were taking place, various formal proposals were made with the aim of securing possible forms of United Nations intervention in the Antarctic question. The first of these was a series of petitions presented to the United Nations Trusteeship Council in 1947, requesting 'the international control and administration of the polar regions' by that Council.[26] By its resolution 22 (11) of 11 December 1947, the Council decided not to take action on the matter.[27]

In 1948, the United States put forward a complex plan for the international administration of Antarctica.[28] This administration would be undertaken by seven nations claiming sovereignty and by the United States, which would advance its own claim. At the same time, a United Nations trust territory would be established under the supervision of those eight countries.[29] The trusteeship suggestion was endorsed by New Zealand,[30] but it met with general resistance from other claimant countries which were unwilling to see United Nations intervention in the question.[31] Subsequently, the United States inclined towards a condominium.[32] Although none of these initiatives met with acceptance, the consequent diplomatic debate had a considerable influence on the proposals which shortly afterwards were incorporated in the 1959 Treaty.[33]

A more comprehensive proposal was put forward by India in 1956 at first entitled 'The question of Antarctica' and later 'The peaceful utilization of Antarctica' – a suggestive change.[34] The main substance of this initiative was that the General Assembly 'should call upon all States to agree to and affirm the peaceful utilization of Antarctica for the general welfare'.[35] Some academic commentaries of the period suggested the establishment of a body to study the question or that it be referred to the International Law Commission.[36] Likewise, the initiative gave rise to various complementary activities on the part of the United Nations Secretariat.[37]

The Indian proposal met with strong opposition on the part of those countries that had advanced claims to Antarctic territory or were otherwise active in that continent, in so far as the proposal involved some form of general internationalization; such reactions resulted in an intense diplomatic activity, particularly by Chile,[38] and in discussions of the initiative by public opinion.[39] Considerations of sovereignty and of non-interference in the internal affairs of States were invoked in this connection. At the same time, there were expressions of willingness to study ways of avoiding friction between friendly countries, by means of 'direct agreements between States with legitimate interests in the region, outside the framework of the international organizations'.[40] As a result of the general opposition which India's initiative enountered, it was withdrawn on 14 November 1956.[41] However it was destined to be reissued in 1958, again as 'The question of Antarctica', but again without success.[42] The explanatory memorandum pointed that 'this subject is of great importance to the international community as a whole and not merely for certain countries', adding that the peaceful purposes 'can be achieved without any nation renouncing such rights as it may claim in Antarctica, or claims of sovereignty or other rights consistent with the Charter'.[43] The Indian proposals were very much present in the background of the negotiations leading to the Antarctic Treaty and were discussed during the 1959 Antarctic Conference in relation to the links that the Treaty could have with the United Nations.[44]

10.2   Relationship between the Antarctic Treaty system and the international community

The discussion of the various proposals for the internationalization of Antarctica outlined above shows that when the Antarctic Treaty was being negotiated in 1959 the countries involved were fully aware of international interest in the arrangements to be made for that continent. For this reason, the Treaty contains various clauses reflecting the relationship which it was sought to establish with the international community.

The second preambular paragraph of the Treaty is particularly important in this respect, since it recognizes that the principle of peaceful use and absence of discord 'is in the interest of all mankind'.[45] As the Antarctic Treaty system evolved towards the formulation of a resources policy, this concept was also made applicable to the various kinds of resources to be regulated. The preamble to the Canberrra Convention includes it with respect to the waters surrounding the Antarctic continent.[46] Similarly, several of the recommendations on the minerals regime refer to this concept,[47] which also appears in the drafts for a convention on the subject.[48] The argument that some of the provisions of the Treaty form part of international custom is also supported by this preambular provision.[49]

The last preambular paragraph states that the Antarctic Treaty 'will further the purposes and principles embodied in the Charter of the United Nations'.[50] The establishment of a link with the United Nations is also contained in Article X, with respect to the activity of third countries, and in Article XIII, as regards the conditions for accession to the Treaty. At one stage in the negotiations provision was made for any acceding country to be able to participate in the machinery for the administration of the Treaty, which would have meant a policy of open participation in decision-making by all Members of the United Nations acceding to the Treaty. Subsequently, however, the qualifying criterion for becoming a Consultative Party was introduced.[51] The link which Article XI establishes with the International Court of Justice also forms part of the relationship with the United Nations.[52]

Nor was co-operation with international organizations overlooked by the authors of the Treaty. Provision for such co-operation is made in Article III, concerning international scientific co-operation, expressed as the establishment of 'co-operative working relations with those Specialized Agencies of the United Nations and other international organizations having a scientific or technical interest in Antarctica'.[53] The reference to international organizations having a scientific or technical interest in Antarctic issues is the essential feature of such co-operation and clearly distinguishes such organizations from others whose aims are rather of a political nature. It is therefore not important that such organizations be of a specialized type or related to general international co-operation, but that the bodies concerned should carry on their activities as part of this scientific or technical interest. As a Chilean diplomatic document of the time indicated, co-operation with the specialized agencies of the United Nations was possible in so far as it did not affect sovereign rights[54] or, in the words of one writer, provided that it did not involve any form of internationalization.[55]

This aspect of the question constitutes an important point of divergence between the way the Consultative Parties envisage the type of co-operation to be engaged in and the view of it held by other countries or some international organizations. While the Consultative Parties only admit co-operation of a scientific or technical nature, the others have at times viewed such co-operation as a model for internationalization, whose different variants will be examined later. A United Kingdom proposal made in 1964, at the Third Consultative Meeting, aimed at clarifying the relationship between the Antarctic system and international organizations, met with no response.[56] The view of the Consultative Parties on the question of co-operation with international organizations has, however, begun to change as a result of the debate at the United Nations and the evolution of the Treaty system; a more active participation of international organizations in Antarctic programmes is an emerging trend in this matter, as we shall examine below.

The practice of the Antarctic Treaty system shows that there has been extensive scientific and technical co-operation with international organizations.[57] The role played by SCAR in promoting and co-ordinating such co-operation has been especially important.[58] Organizations which have participated in Antarctic programmes or activities include, among others, the World Meteorological Organization (WMO), the International Tele-communications Union (ITU), the Food and Agriculture Organization (FAO), the Intergovernmntal Oceanographic Commission (IOC), the International Civil Aviation Organization (ICAO) and the International Council of Scientific Unions (ICSU) – the latter being a non-governmental organization. The International Whaling Commission is also of importance in this field of activity.[59]

The extensive network of international linkages thus being developed in connection with the Antarctic can be compared in a way with the development of international co-operation on a gradual basis in other areas of the world. The example of the International Council for the Exploration of the Sea (ICES)[60] and its relations with various organizations, such as the Oslo and Paris Commissions,[61] or fisheries arrangements, such as the North-East Atlantic Fisheries Convention[62] and the Northwest Atlantic Fisheries Organization,[63] is one of interest in this regard; the fact that ICES provides independent scientific research to some of these bodies and secretarial services to others, is also a point of interest in relation to the needs of Antarctic co-operation that are emerging. The network of Antarctic international co-operation being formed to some extent supports the arguments mentioned in Chapter 9 about the existence of an objective regime for this continent.

International co-operation in the resources regimes
Although Article III of the Treaty is limited to international co-operation of a scientific nature, the substance of this co-operation has expanded in proportion to the evolution of the Antarctic Treaty system itself, especially with the development of its resources policy. Article 5, paragraph 6, of the Convention for the Conservation of Antarctic Seals provided, for example, for SCAR's co-operation with FAO in evaluating resources and gathering other information. On the question of oil pollution, SCAR may consult with 'other appropriate international organizations', which presumably includes the International Maritime Organization (IMO).[64] The Scientific Committee on Problems of the Environment (SCOPE), a subsidiary body of ICSU, is another non-governmental organization

which has participated in Antarctic programmes connected with its speciality.[65]

The Convention on the Conservation of Antarctic Marine Living Resources, in its Article XXIII, has provided for a more complete system of international co-operation. This includes co-operation with the Consultative Parties within the Antarctic Treaty system and, outside it, with FAO and other United Nations specialized agencies. In the same way, co-operation is envisaged with other intergovernmental and non-governmental organizations, with special reference to SCAR, the Scientific Committee for Oceanic Research and the International Whaling Commission. Co-operation agreements may be concluded and observers exchanged with all these organizations.[66] It should be noted, however, that some organizations have adopted a cautious policy with regard to participation in resources activities. SCAR's Constitution states in this respect that it will abstain 'from involvement in political and juridical matters, including the formulation of management measures for exploitable resources, except where SCAR accepts an invitation to advise on a problem'.[67]

The fact that the Canberra Convention has set up an international organization within the Antarctic system makes it easier for it to establish different kinds of relations and co-operation with other bodies. The participation of the European Economic Community in this Convention is an interesting case, since, as we examined in Chapter 4, the Community has a competence of its own in relation to fisheries and the management of the living resources of the sea and other questions of jurisdiction.[68] From this point of view the EEC could not be described as a specialized organization of a scientific or technical character, nor its relationship with the Commission established under the Canberra Convention is one of mere co-operation; it is fundamentally a political organization which as such enjoys special rights of participation under this Convention.[69]

The mineral resources regime shows a similar tendency to that of the Canberra Convention. Recommendation XI-1 stated that the regime must 'include provisions for co-operative arrangements between the regime and other relevant international organizations',[70] without prejudice to the fact that at the same time it must safeguard the special responsibility of the Consultative Parties in environmental matters, 'taking into account responsibilities which may be exercised in the area by other international organizations'.[71] This last situation is related to the need for co-ordination within the Antarctic Treaty system, particularly when different regimes and their organizations will be functioning at the same time; it is also related to the exercise of competence in the area of the regime that might correspond to other organizations of a world or regional character.

The draft texts for the minerals regime envisage various kinds of linkage with international organizations. In the first place, co-operation within the Antarctic Treaty system is seen as essential and provision is made for the Commission to co-operate with the Consultative Parties, with the Commission established under the Canberra Convention and with SCAR, thus ensuring co-ordination between the different regimes. Next, there is provision for co-operation with other international organizations, the United Nations and its specialized agencies and other relevant organizations.[72] It may be noted that in this case the criterion used in the Antarctic Treaty is modified, since the latter refers only to the specialized agencies of the United Nations whereas the minerals regime adds co-operation with the United Nations as an organization in its own right; however, this does not imply an intention of changing the nature of co-operation, which must still be of a scientific or technical kind, as specified in the Antarctic Treaty, subject to the evolution that is taking place in the matter.

On the other hand, the minerals regime drafts do make indirect reference to the very special case of the Seabed Authority or other entities competent in the field, stating that the Commission 'shall, as appropriate, seek to develop a co-operative working relationship with any international organization which may have competence in respect of mineral resources in areas adjacent to those covered by this regime'.[73] This relationship will be discussed later. The Commission will also be able to conclude agreements with all the organizations mentioned.[74]

In addition to these types of co-operation, the regime also establishes certain criteria for participation by international organizations. Relevant organizations designated by the Commission will be able to have observer status with this body, as will certain categories of States.[75] They will also be entitled to the same status in the Advisory Committee.[76] These criteria are indications of the trend towards broader participation in Antarctic activities and regimes, including participation by international organizations. Through this broader participation it is hoped to establish a closer relationship with States and international organizations which make up the international community.

Improvement of the machinery for co-operation
The relationship with international organizations and their greater participation in the Antarctic Treaty system in general were also discussed at the Twelfth and Thirteenth Consultative Meetings. Recommendation

XII-6 on the operation of the system provided, along with measures to benefit states, for a much closer relationship with international organizations.[77] These measures include the decision to send the Final Report and recommendations of each meeting to the Secretary General of the United Nations and to draw the attention of specialized agencies of the United Nations or other organizations having a scientific or technical interest to those parts of the Report and to other documents which may be of relevance to their interest in Antarctica. These measures are to be taken in implementation of Article III, paragraph 2, of the Treaty, which means that the scientific and technical aspect of co-operation will continue to be paramount. Consideration was also given to the possibility that these organizations might participate in consultative meetings as observers, the conclusion being that a decision would be taken during the preparatory work for each meeting if such participation was considered appropriate in the light of the subjects to be discussed.[78]

Other measures to improve the system's operation which have been considered include a study of joint research projects between the Consultative Parties and international organizations and the convening of meetings for the exchange of relevant information.[79] It has also been suggested that a representative of the Antarctic Treaty system might take part as an observer in meetings of the United Nations agencies and other organizations, including regional ones.[80] Although the latter suggestion stems from the view that the Treaty system resembles in some respect an international organization, an aspect that was discussed in Chapter 2, such representation poses a number of legal issues; however broadly an international organization can be defined, it usually will have organs of some kind and an international personality that will allow its functioning as a legal entity, elements that are not given in relation to the Antarctic Treaty as such but that do exist in the case of the Convention on the Conservation of Antarctic Marine Living Resources and that will be provided for in the minerals convention. Could there be such representation of the Treaty without permanent organs and in the absence of international personality? In a strict legal analysis the answer to this question would probably be negative; however, to the extent that the system becomes institutionalized, including the role performed by the Consultative Meetings, it comes closer to the requirements of international law in this matter. An indication of this trend is that Consultative Parties and Treaty parties have begun to work at international organizations of which they are members through a common spokesman.

A different question deserving consideration concerns participation by non-governmental organizations in the Antarctic Treaty system. The

Antarctic Treaty system has a long tradition in this respect, due to its already close relationship with SCAR. Occasionally, other organizations have participated in Antarctic programmes. As already mentioned, the Scientific Committee on Problems of the Environment (SCOPE) itself a subsidiary body of the International Council of Scientific Unions (ICSU), affords an example.[81] This tradition has been exemplified in several of the resources regimes, which provide for a role for SCAR.[82]

The minerals regime is no exception, since it provides for the establishment of co-operative relations with SCAR and with the International Union for the Conservation of Nature.[83] Consideration has also been given to the possibility of non-governmental organizations designated by the Commission being included among the international organizations having observer status with the Advisory Committee.[84]

Non-governmental organizations have naturally expressed an interest in attaining a broader participation in the system activities.[85] The trend among the Treaty parties has been in general to establish some criteria for making a determination about those non-governmental organizations that should be accepted as observers to meetings, with the purpose of avoiding that too many such organizations might be represented as has happened in the experience of some international organizations.[86] This trend is very evident in the case of the Commission for the Conservation of Antarctic Marine Living Resources, which has accepted as observers the International Union for the Conservation of Nature and Natural Resources (IUCN), SCAR and the Scientific Committee on Oceanic Research (SCOR), the last two organizations having been named in Article XXIII of the Convention and IUCN being the parent organization; all of them have met in the view of the Parties the criteria established by that article to the extent of being a non-governmental organization which could contribute to the work of the Commission and the Scientific Committee.[87] The requests made by the Antarctic and Southern Ocean Coalition (ASOC) and Greenpeace International have met with greater difficulty as to the determination of whether they qualify under the criteria established by the Convention; and active correspondence has been exchanged between the Executive Secretary of the Commission and these organizations, which have been required to 'state unequivocally that they support the principles and objectives as set out in Article II' of the Convention.[88]

It would thus appear that in the case of this Commission the criterion for selection of observers is the ability of the requesting entity to contribute to the work of that organ and of the Scientific Committee, a requirement that is measured by the support of the principles and objectives of the Convention. It is very probable that a similar trend will become at its time evident in the case of the minerals convention.

The issue underlying this discussion is of course the different view that Consultative Parties and some non-governmental organizations have as to the way in which Antarctic affairs should be managed. While the former will wish to keep the Antarctic process under their control, some of the latter have questioned the present arrangements and argued for a different policy. This explains the insistence of Consultative Parties on the scientific and technical requirements of the co-operation and the view of such non-governmental organizations in having a broader policy-oriented role within the system.

The increased activity within the Treaty system has led to the recognition of the need to have a greater co-ordination between its meetings and institutions. Under Recommendation XIII-2 a regular overview of the system will take place in each Consultative Meeting, with particular reference to the relationships among the components of the system. To this effect, the Chairmen of Special Consultative Meetings and of other meetings held pursuant to a Recommendation, as well as the Chairman of the Commission for the Conservation of Antarctic Marine Living Resources and the President of SCAR, shall report to the Consultative Meetings about the activities of those meetings or organizations; pending the establishment of a Commission under the Seals Convention, the reporting on this other field shall be done by the Government of the United Kingdom as the Depositary Government of this Convention. The Consultative Parties will keep in this manner a central role in the overview of the system as a whole.

10.3 The model for general internationalization

When various models for the organization of Antarctic activities were considered in Chapter 7, with their varying approaches to the question of jurisdiction, mention was made of another central approach to the question, namely, the model for generalized internationalization. According to this view, the basic competences of the Antarctic Treaty system would be transferred to the international community, in accordance with the various ways suggested or, as one writer puts it, 'an international regime for Antarctica would bring the entire international community into the Antarctic decision-making process'.[89]

International debate about a new direction of this kind has recently gained in intensity, as various writers anticipated that such a trend would be an inevitable consequence of the present features of the Antarctic system.[90] This important discussion has influenced the development of the Antarctic Treaty system and the resources regimes, particularly in terms of broadening participation in Antarctic activities and strengthening international co-operation related thereto and giving a certain sense of urgency to the internal and external accommodation.[91] As one writer has stated, although the Antarctic Treaty does not provide a precise model for co-operation in economic exploitation, yet it does not 'preclude such co-operation',[92] and thus opens up possibilities for an accommodation. In this spirit, Recommendation XI-1 emphasized that the minerals regime 'should not prejudice the interests of all mankind in Antarctica',[93] thus maintaining the parallel with the interest of mankind expressed in the 1959 Treaty.

Many different forms for this internationalization have been proposed, although the majority are limited to general aspects. Thus, for example, there have been suggestions for a new Antarctic Treaty to be drawn up by the General Assembly of the United Nations, the establishment of a trusteeship under the Charter, or the incorporation of all or part of the area to which the Treaty applies into the Sea-bed Authority.[94] The international trusteeship model has recently been advocated once again by various writers.[95] A supposed similarity to colonialism and the need to reduce global inequalities have also been invoked as reasons why Antarctica should form part of the 'global commons'.[96] 'Global sharing' and its implications for the North–South conflict have also been analysed as part of the discussion of internationalization models.[97]

Influence of the Conference on the Law of the Sea

Perhaps no model has aroused so much interest in this connection as the sea-bed regime and the negotiations thereon at the Third UN Conference on the Law of the Sea.[98] Many writers on the Antarctic minerals regime have drawn parallels between it and the sea-bed situation as an organizational model;[99] some of these writers have placed special emphasis on the concept of the common heritage of mankind and the possible intervention of the International Sea-bed Authority, an aspect which will be examined further below.

The parallel with the Conference on the Law of the Sea has also been extended to various other situations. Thus, it has been proposed that the Antarctic continental margin should become a United Nations trust territory, whose administration could be delegated to individual countries, groups of countries, such as the members of the Antarctic Treaty, or an international body like the Sea-bed Authority.[100] Another view is that many chapters of the 1982 Convention might be applicable to Antarctica.[101] The Antarctic and sea-bed situations have been seen as competing regimes, particularly with regard to the different policy adopted in each case by the United States.[102] Resolution III of the Conference, which refers to some aspects of colonial domination, has also been considered relevant to the case of Antarctica.[103]

Nevertheless, as Charney observes of these comparisons, this type of universal participation in the Antarctic minerals regime would give rise to numerous conflicts, and the more the regime was identified with the sea-bed situation, the greater would be the difficulties in reaching an agreement.[104] It is argued that in a proposal of this type, 'it is most probable that the negotiators would set as their goal the establishment of a comprehensive international organization to manage the Antarctic mineral resources similar to the proposed International Sea-bed Authority'.[105] It has been further argued that the interests of the claimant countries, of those interested in the exploitation of resources and of environmental groups would not be adequately safeguarded in such an approach and that would render the necessary accommodation and consequent agreement much more difficult to achieve.[106]

Models based on environmental concerns
Another category of proposals for types of internationalization of Antarctica is due to concern for the environment on the part of organizations, governments and writers. Some proposals call for Antarctica to be included in universal or generalized environmental protection regimes.[107] In others, instead, concern for the environment is shown by suggestions for improving the resources regimes adopted within the Antarctic Treaty system.[108] Some of these initiatives have made important contributions to the discussion of Antarctica issues.

One proposal which has received a certain amount of support from non-governmental organizations and other media seeks the establishment of Antarctica as a 'world park', which would mean that economic activities and, especially, mineral resources exploitation, would be permanently prohibited.[109] The Second World Conference on National Parks, held at Grand Teton in the United States in 1972, recommended the adoption of such a concept under the auspices of the United Nations, a recommendation that was reiterated at Bali in 1982.[110] Various non-governmental organizations have welcomed this idea,[111] as have several well-known naturalists and explorers.[112]

A proposal of this type was officially endorsed by New Zealand in 1975 and formed the basis of the initiative on the mineral exploration regime which the New Zealand Government submitted to the Special Meeting in Paris in 1976.[113] Although the declaration proposed at that time was to be brought to the attention of the United Nations, it was conceived as a measure to be adopted within the Antarctic Treaty system. A scheme for a world-wide conservation system which would include Antarctica,[114] and the renunciation of all claims to sovereignty in favour of the United Nations with the consequent establishment of an Antarctic park, have been the subjects of recurrent discussion in New Zealand.[115]

A variant of the 'world park' idea is the establishment of Antarctica as a special natural and historical conservation area. To that end, there have been suggestions that Antarctica should be placed under the protection of the 1972 UNESCO Convention on the Protection of the World Cultural and Natural Heritage,[116] or turned into a 'world preserve',[117] or subject to an extensive system of declarations of protected areas.[118] A bill for the creation of an 'Antarctic Historic and Natural Preserve' was submitted to the United States House of Representatives.[119] The proposal to establish an 'Antarctic environmental protection agency' in the mineral resources regime has a certain similarity with all these suggestions.[120]

The establishment of a permanent or lengthy moratorium on mineral activities, which these proposals would involve, seems most unlikely to be accepted. While the concept of an Antarctic park would certainly satisfy the environmental interest that has been expressed in connection with Antarctica, it would mean setting aside the interest that has also been expressed in the distribution of economic benefits. On the other hand, these proposals are clearly irreconcilable with interest in exploitation, which is one of the factors which any regime will have to take into account and which has the support of several important countries, both claimant and non-claimant. In addition, although national claims could be maintained in this kind of scheme,[121] not all the claimant countries would consider that their interests were adequately protected. Such proposals, therefore, can have only a limited influence on the process of accommodation.

It is interesting to note that some proposals have also been made for the internationalization of the Arctic.[122] They place considerable emphasis on environmental considerations, some maintaining the concept of the 'common heritage of all'[123] and others the converse goal of avoiding any form of intervention by the United Nations in the forms of co-operation to be undertaken in that other region.[124]

Proposals submitted to United Nations specialized agencies
The model of generalized internationalization of Antarctica has also been put forward from time to time at meetings of the United Nations and some of its specialized agencies. Since India's initiatives of 1956 and 1958, the

subject has been raised on several occasions at the General Assembly or its affiliated bodies. When Ceylon proposed, in 1971, that the Indian Ocean should be declared a Zone of Peace, that country referred to the 'principle that areas not assimilated to national jurisdiction constitute an international domain that should be subject to international regulation and international responsibility', and mentioned the sea-bed, outer space and Antarctica as examples.[125] In the debate on the subject the Argentine representative specifically objected to the reference to Antarctica.[126] An annex on the natural resources of Antarctica was included in an information document prepared by the Secretariat for the Committee on Natural Resources of the Economic and Social Council (ECOSOC) in 1971.[127] Although only a matter of technical information, its inclusion was indicative of the body's interest in beginning to discuss a subject considered of importance within the field of natural resources.

At the ECOSOC session held at Geneva in the summer of 1975, the observer for Sri Lanka raised the question of information about Antarctica's natural resources in the context of the debate on coastal development and uses of the seas.[128] Although that body did not take any action on the matter and none of its members sponsored it, subsequently the Secretariat prepared a document on 'Marine Resources in Antarctica', but it was not circulated because of the opposition of the Consultative Parties.[129] The latter apparently feared that the initiative was part of a plan to set up a special committee of the General Assembly on Antarctica as a first stage in a similar process to the one which had been adopted with respect to the sea-bed. In the context of this initiative mention was also made by an author of the interest of other countries in the internationalization of Antarctica.[130]

FAO also began to show interest in the subject in connection with world fisheries questions. Its 1975 Conference 'noted the competence of the signatories of the Antarctic Treaty for all matters concerning the ecosystem of Antarctica, particularly its equilibrium and preservation, and the adoption of measures for the preservation of the Antarctic environment and its natural resources by the contracting parties over the last decade'.[131] This important recognition of the competence of the Antarctic Treaty Parties did not in fact prevent an agreement being reached that FAO should keep itself informed on the subject and should co-ordinate its activities with the Treaty action in that area. One delegation asked for clarification of the relations between the Organization and member countries of the Antarctic Treaty.[132]

FOA's first intention seems to have been to establish its competence in connection with the living resources of Antarctica, as opposed to that of the Consultative Parties, as can be inferred from the discussion held at the eleventh session of the Committee on Fisheries in 1977.[133] A note from Argentina quoted at that meeting maintained that 'these pertinent programmes of study should be unanimously approved by the consultative parties when they refer to marine zones south of 60° S latitude'.[134] Other delegations were of the opinion that this zone 'should be shared by the whole international community and it is particularly of interest to the developing countries'.[135] One non-signatory country to the Treaty, however, recognized that the international community had benefited by the measures adopted within the framework of the Treaty.[136] Subsequently, this FAO programme adopted a definitely technical approach, having produced documents of interest[137] and, on this basis, more straightforward co-operation with the Consultative Parties became possible, as reflected today in the framework of the Canberra Convention. At the same time, the Organization began to accord priority to its programme on the development of the Exclusive Economic Zone and its interest in Antarctica diminished proportionately.[138]

The United Nations Environment Programme (UNEP) also showed an interest in the Antarctic question in 1975. The programme proposed by the Organization's Executive Director contained a section on Antarctica, aimed at preparing for the 'extension' of the 1959 Treaty, with particular attention to the environmental and resources problems of the continent.[139] To that end, it was proposed to hold consultations with the governments involved and with other interested governments, to convene a group of experts to prepare exploration and exploitation criteria, to consult a group of legal experts who might draft the new articles for the Treaty and to discuss with the governments their inclusion in the proposed extension.[140] Other UNEP documents referred to Antarctica as an 'international commons'[141] and to the need for a moratorium on the development of its resources.[142]

On this basis, the Executive Director sent a cable to the Chairman of the Eighth Consultative Meeting in an attempt to start UNEP's proposed consultation procedure.[143] As, however, it was obvious that the Organization's aim was to intervene in the management of Antarctic policy, the Consultative Parties replied by approving Recommendation VIII-13,[144] which summarizes the environmental protection measures carried out by the Treaty system and further states: 'Recognizing that prime responsibility for Antarctic matters, including protection of the Antarctic environment, lies with the States active in the area which are parties to the Antarctic Treaty'.[145] The initiative of UNEP was considered by the Consultative Parties as departing from the scientific and technical interest which under the Antarctic Treaty governs co-operation with international organizations in the light of Article III and the practice thereon, an aspect which we have discussed earlier. UNEP has not since had a role in the discussion of Antarctic issues, in spite of the fact that many such issues are related to environmental matters; one of UNEP's programmes, however, has indirectly shown an interest in this field by means of publications on Antarctic affairs.[146]

The United Nations Institute for Training and Research (UNITAR) has also referred to the question of Antarctica on one occasion by listing it among the international commons.[147]

Proposals submitted to the United Nations General Assembly

It does not seem to be a matter of chance that most of these proposals were made in 1975 in various international forums and other media. In that year the Conference on the Law of the Sea began the search for an agreement on the sea-bed regime and other issues what could have prompted various initiatives on the question of Antarctica by interested governments, international officials and non-governmental organizations, possibly with a view to discuss its internationalization in a manner similar to that underway at the time for the sea-bed. It is known that, at that Conference, several attempts were made to include Antarctica in the sea-bed negotiations, but they were unsuccessful due to definite but informally expressed objections on the part of the Consultative Parties.[148] In other matters discussed by the Conference, however, it became quite apparent that Antarctica was considered as a very specific question; such was in particular the case of the various formulae considered for the outer limit of the continental shelf, which were also applied in relation to Antarctica and so illustrated by a map published by the Conference Secretariat.[149]

The President of that Conference, speaking as Sri Lanka's representative at the 1975 United Nations General Assembly, supported the internationalization policy, maintaining that Antarctica provided an opportunity for a new form of co-operation 'on the part of the international community for the common good of all rather than for the benefit of a few', and referring especially to 'the principle of equitable sharing of the world's resources'.[150] The pressure which was obviously building up within the United Nations led to a study in the Australian Senate of the available alternatives, with particular reference to the question of the dependent territories.[151]

However, it was not until the conclusion of the Conference on the Law of the Sea that the United Nations General Assembly decided to give specific consideration to the subject of Antarctica.[152] The Seventh Conference of Heads of State or Government of the Non-Aligned Movement, held at New Delhi from 7 to 12 March 1983, approved a paragraph in its final declaration which stressed the importance of Antarctica in world terms and agreed that 'the exploration of the area and the exploitation of its resources shall be carried out for the benefit of all mankind'.[153] At the same time, it requested the United Nations General Assembly to produce a comprehensive report on the subject. Malaysia had been pressing for such a declaration for some time, as Sri Lanka had done previously, but these initiatives had met with opposition from Argentina, the only Consultative Party belonging to the Non-Aligned Movement. It seems that on this occasion Argentina got the approach proposed by Malaysia considerably toned down.[154] Shortly afterwards, the Prime Minister of Antigua and Barbuda referred to the parties to the Antarctic Treaty as wishing to 'appropriate for themselves the world's bounty'.[155]

Formal inclusion of the subject in the Agenda of the General Assembly was requested in 1983 by the representatives of Antigua and Barbuda and Malaysia, the request being accompanied by a short explanatory memorandum whose basic aim was to ensure 'a more positive and wider international concert through a truly universal framework of international co-operation through the United Nations, to ensure that activities carried out in Antarctica are for the benefit and in the interest of mankind as a whole'.[156] This proposal prompted a collective response by the Consultative Parties, which pointed to the achievements of the Antarctic Treaty system and warned of the risk that a revision of the 1959 Treaty would determine that Antarctica 'became an area of international conflict and discord'.[157] For these and other reasons, they expressed serious reservations with regard to this initiative.[158] These two basic positions confronted each other during the debate on the question of Antarctica that began in 1983 at the thirty-eighth session of the General Assembly and is still ongoing;[159] the terms of the debate will be examined further below.[160]

General Assembly Resolution 38/77, adopted by consensus after a difficult compromise, requested the Secretary General to prepare a 'comprehensive, factual, and objective study on all aspects of Antarctica'.[161] These terms of reference were aimed at excluding both questions of an ideological nature and adoption of political positions from the analysis, thus avoiding a pre-judgement of the Antarctic Treaty system.[162] The study by the Secretary-General kept to this mandate and provided basically descriptive information about the Antarctic regime and the area's natural resources.[163] But, inevitably, the replies of governments to the request for their comments and the debate at the General Assembly clearly revealed the politico–ideological component of the question.

The difference of views became still more evident during the debate that took place at the United Nations General Assembly in 1985 and related developments. The Council of Ministers and the twenty-first summit meeting of the Organization of African Unity had adopted a Declaration on Antarctica stating that the area should be declared the common heritage of mankind and calling on all members to take appropriate steps to this end at the United Nations General Assembly.[164] The Declaration on Antarctica adopted by the Ministerial Conference of the Non-Aligned countries, held in Luanda, 4–7 September 1985, took, however, a more moderate line by reaffirming the Ministers' 'conviction that in the interest of all mankind, Antarctica should continue forever to be used exclusively for peaceful purposes, should not become the scene or object of international discord and should be accessible to all nations', and at the same time it called for the UN General Assembly to remain seized of the question of Antarctica.[165]

The discussions of the fortieth session of the General Assembly on Antarctica in 1985 could not, for the first time, reach a consensus resolution on the matter. While a number of States not party to the Antarctic Treaty favoured the declaration of Antarctica as the common heritage of mankind and the establishment of an *ad hoc* Committee of the General Assembly to consider the matter, the 1959 Treaty parties tended to keep the discussion as a point of information for the General Assembly about Antarctic activities and resisted any substantive involvement of this or other UN bodies.[166] These views were reflected in a draft resolution circulated informally by Malaysia, which contained a preambular reference to the resources of Antarctica as the common heritage of mankind and an operative paragraph establishing the *ad hoc* Committee, a draft which was not finally introduced; the view of the Treaty parties were reflected in a draft resolution introduced by Australia and later withdrawn, which requested a supplementary study of the Secretary-General on the availability of information to the United Nations and the involvement of specialized agencies and intergovernmental organizations in the Antarctic Treaty system.[167] Although this latter aspect represented an interesting opening of the Treaty system to discuss UN involvement in Antarctic activities, also referring to other international organizations, it was not sufficient to off-set the pressure for more profound measures relating to the Antarctic issues.

As a result of these divergent views the General Assembly adopted three resolutions on the question of Antarctica. The first requested the

Secretary-General to update and expand the study on Antarctica by including the availability of information to the United Nations on Antarctic activities, the involvement of specialized agencies and inter-governmental organizations in the Treaty system 'and the significance of the United Nations Convention on the Law of the Sea in the Southern Ocean'.[168] The second Resolution referred specifically to the minerals regime, recalling the benefit of mankind as a whole and affirming that the exploitation of Antarctic resources 'should ensure the maintenance of international peace and security in Antarctica, the protection of its environment, the non-appropriation and conservation of its resources and the international management and equitable sharing of the benefits of such exploitation'; the Resolution also invited the Consultative Parties to inform the Secretary General about the minerals negotiations and requested the latter to report on the matter to the General Assembly.[169] The third Resolution urged Consultative parties to exclude South Africa from participation in Consultative Meetings in view of the *apartheid* policies of that government.[170]

In addition to the problem that these resolutions were not adopted by consensus, the debate also saw for the first time the rupture of the consensus among the 1959 Treaty parties in general and the Consultative Parties in particular, which in some cases voted differently.[171]

In examining the relationship between the Antarctic Treaty system and the international community in a long-term perspective, the fact that the United Nations, after many abortive attempts, finally decided to take up the subject is of obvious significance. As Beck has observed, 'so, finally, the traditional isolation of the Antarctic Treaty system from international politics has come under threat . . . the challenge from outside cannot be ignored, and inevitably the forthcoming moves at the UN will pose the severest challenge yet to the survival and relative exclusivity of the Antarctic club'.[172] Once that first step had become a reality, the conflict between the different positions has been directed towards ensuring that the debate will favour their respective points of view. Those favouring internationalization are now in the process of seeking the establishment of the *ad hoc* Committee of the General Assembly mentioned to continue consideration of the subject[173] and, as happened with the sea-bed question, to prepare for a conference which would draw up the desired new regime.[174] The Antarctic Treaty Parties, on the other hand, have tried to hold up that procedural step until negotiation of the mineral regime is completed and the Antarctic Treaty system thus consolidated, seeking in this way to avoid the potential risk to their interests of general internationalization.[175] All of the above is, of course, closely connected with the discussion of the merits of the problem, which will now be considered.

10.4   Criticism of the Antarctic Treaty system and the trend towards change

The arguments in favour of the model based on general internationalization advocated in the United Nations debate and other discussions on Antarctica have concentrated on four central issues: participation in the Antarctic Treaty system; the secretive nature of the system; the question of accountability to the international community; and the principle of the common heritage of mankind.[176]

Problems related to participation in the Antarctic Treaty system

The difficulties and problems related to participation in the Treaty system have been clearly recognized as a serious question for the purpose of the external accommodation.[177] Criticism on this account relates partly to the 1959 Treaty itself, in that it establishes a distinction between the Consultative Parties and the other Treaty parties by giving the power of decision-making and control of the system only to the former;[178] the concept of a 'two-tier system' was seen as being undemocratic in the debate at the United Nations, especially as regards access to decision-making.[179] But this criticism also relies on the argument that the Antarctic Treaty parties constitute a self-designated group which has taken control of the continent since 1959 and is not representative of the international community.[180]

Various suggestions for overcoming these difficulties were made during the debate. Some called for widening the decision-making machinery of the system,[181] while others sought to increase the representation of the international community.[182] Co-operation with international organizations such as FAO and UNEP has also been suggested;[183] Resolution 156A of 1985, mentioned above, specifically requested the Secretary-General to enlarge his study on Antarctica so as to deal with the question of involvement of specialized agencies and international organizations in the Treaty system, thus evidencing the priority accorded to this aspect of a broader participation policy. The ASOC proposal for the creation of an 'Antarctic Environmental Protection Agency' was also endorsed in the UN debate.[184]

In Chapter 9 we discussed the various measures adopted within the Treaty system so as to increase participation in its activities, which represent the Consultative Parties' position on the question, and which were explained as such by various delegations at the United Nations.[185]

The gradual increase in the number of Consultative Parties, the enlargement of the number of Treaty Parties, the establishment of the status of observer, wider access to the resources regimes and the discussion which has begun on the operation of the Treaty system, provide some indication of the developments which have taken place in this direction. This evolution is particularly noteworthy in the case of the minerals regime. However, in the opinion of the Consultative Parties, the process must be a gradual one whereby countries acquiring the necessary experience step by step gain admission, including access to Consultative Party status and the decision-making arrangements. There have also been expressions of interest in providing assistance through joint programmes and other forms of co-operation to countries wishing to acquire the necessary Antarctic experience. Although in the view of the Treaty Parties these measures are sufficient to refute the accusation that the Treaty system is an exclusive club,[186] other countries interested in the question of Antarctica still regard the role of Consultative Parties as a negative feature of the system.

One particularly sensitive aspect of the debate concerned the participation of South Africa in the Antarctic Treaty system and the criticisms of the policy of *apartheid*. There were many calls for the exclusion of that country from the Antarctic Treaty system,[187] and Resolution 156C of 1985 on the Question of Antarctica urged the Consultative Parties to exclude the South African government from participation in their meetings.[188]

None of the other Consultative Parties either supports or approves of the policy of *apartheid,* but that does not mean that the possibility of excluding South Africa from the Treaty system can be entertained. Apart from considerations of international law, which raise serious doubts about the legality of such an exclusion,[189] it would represent a political measure which could be detrimental to the functioning and stability of the Treaty system. It might even introduce elements of discord and confrontation into the Treaty area, and this is precisely what it is intended to avoid. The Antarctic Treaty meetings have never provided a political forum for dealing with problems of this kind and in the view of the Treaty parties must not do so in the future; it is interesting to note, however, that no Consultative Meetings have taken place in South Africa.

The Consultative Parties have sometimes been accused of setting up an 'international *apartheid*' in respect of the Antarctic Treaty system[190] or of practising colonialism in the Antarctic continent,[191] points of view which can only be regarded as lacking any serious foundation.[192]

Availability of information on the system's activities

The second type of argument in favour of the general internationalization model relates to the 'secret' nature of the system, which is seen as a deliberate attempt to keep the international community out of the Antarctic activities and decision making.[193] This criticism has been particularly strong in relation to the minerals negotiations; Resolution 156B on the question of minerals adopted in 1985, after stating that States not parties to the Antarctic Treaty 'are not privy' to the negotiations on the Antarctic minerals regime, invites the Consultative Parties to inform the Secretary-General about the matter and requests the latter to report to the General Assembly; a similar concern was expressed in Resolution A/C. 1/41/2. 86 of 18 November 1986.

While the criticism on the lack of available information on Antarctic activities is to a large extent well-founded, it should also be noticed that the fact that the deliberations of the Consultative Parties have hitherto been conducted largely in private does not mean that it is a situation to which the term 'secret' can be strictly applied. Privacy has meant that the debates have not been published, but that does not mean secrecy, as can be evidenced by the fact that governments, organizations or writers desirous of obtaining information about them have had the possibility of doing do.[194]

Of more importance is the consideration that the aim of this privacy was not to exclude the international community, but to create an atmosphere for negotiation which would enable the different positions of the Consultative Parties to be reconciled without provoking governmental or public opinion repercussions in their own countries. If every Antarctic problem had been discussed in public the 1959 Treaty would not have been agreed upon and there would have been even less progress towards the stage at which the Treaty system finds itself today. Moreover, it is noteworthy and significant that the same procedure had eventually to be adopted at other international negotiations such as the Conference on the Law of the Sea, where every compromise reached resulted from private and informal negotiations, without publicity of any kind.[195]

The Consultative Parties have, however, accepted the criticism that the privacy might have been excessive, especially with regard to the circulation of documents and reports. The measures adopted to remedy this deficiency of the Treaty system by starting to make information more widely available – a process which will certainly continue – were outlined and considered in Chapter 9.

The issue of accountability of the Treaty system before the United Nations
Arguments have also been advanced to the effect that the Antarctic Treaty system should be 'accountable' to some other international organization, with particular reference to the United Nations. This view has been expressed in negative terms, such as that 'the Consultative Parties are not, and do not regard themselves as accountable to the international community',[196] or that their decisions 'are not subject to review or even to discussion by any other body ("unaccountable")'.[197] This argument to some extent resembles the initial proposals to organize the Antarctic regime in the form of a trust territory or similar arrangements, with the trustees being subject to accountability about their work and decisions.[198]

This discussion is closely connected with the question of whether there exists a 'right' of the Consultative Parties to regulate activities in Antarctica. While the existence of this right has been questioned in the current debate about Antarctica,[199] it should be noted that the right which the Consultative Parties may exercise is not different from the normal rights which all States have under international law to organize their activities in given areas or matters in a lawful manner. If this right is not recognized, there is the implicit affirmation that the right appertains to someone else, being the international community generally suggested for this purpose.[200] The argument of accountability supposes that the United Nations has a better right or title in the matter, on which its superiority is founded, but this aspect, it is submitted, is arguable in international law and the law governing Antarctic activities.

A further legal problem is that the question of accountability entails to some extent the power to revise international treaties, a power which cannot be explicitly found in the Charter of the United Nations[201] after the problems that arose under Article 19 of the Covenant of the League of Nations.[202] The implications of this problem for the principle *Pacta Sunt Servanda* were clearly stated at the UN debate in the following terms: 'States that are not parties to a binding treaty ought not to be able, through the United Nations, to call into question the obligations of States parties to the treaty'.[203]

The discussion about the issues of accountability does not preclude, of course, the development of many forms of co-operation between the Antarctic Treaty system, the United Nations and other international organizations, a process which, as we have examined, is well under way.

Another related issue is the criticism that has been made to the Treaty system because of its 'comprehensive' nature and the fact that it has been developed to cover all activities in Antarctica, thus exceeding the more limited purposes of the 1959 Treaty.[204] Why this is so is because all the activities taking place in Antarctica are closely bound together by their very nature and all of them have an effect on the values protected by the 1959 Treaty.[205] As we shall examine later, there have been suggestions for 'decoupling' the resource regimes, with particular reference to the minerals regime, from the Antarctic Treaty system.

Application of the concept of the common heritage of mankind to Antarctica

The central theme of the international debate on Antarctica has been the possible application of the principle of the common heritage of mankind, which its proponents consider should govern a model of total internationalization of that continent. The arguments just considered about participation, problems of secretiveness, accountability and others, ultimately led up to the question of whether this principle is applicable to Antarctica, and consequently, whether it can serve as a basis for generalized internationalization.[206] This point involves the assessment of complex juridical and political considerations.

The application of the concept of the common heritage of mankind to the sea-bed regime gave rise to considerable discussion of the place of this principle in international law.[207] According to one point of view, it is an established principle which can extend much beyond the specific regime into which it was incorporated.[208] Its application to outer space, radio frequencies and, generally speaking, to any area which may be considered to be a common space, is cited as an example.[209] Hence, it is argued that it can also be applied to Antarctica, on the basis that there has not been and cannot be any effective recognition of claims to sovereignty nor any clear definition of national title to its resources.[210] This approach would also result in avoiding an alleged national or Treaty party appropriation of Antarctic resources.

From another point of view, however, the concept can have no autonomous existence independent of the regime incorporating it and is not sufficiently specific as to be legally accepted as a principle of international law, chiefly because its content is too vague.[211] This position occasionally tends to question the principle even in the context of the sea-bed regime[212] and, consequently, rejects its application to any other domain.

Neither of these positions, however, would appear to be realistic. The concept of the common heritage of mankind may reasonably be considered as having been clearly established in the ambit of the sea-bed regime and to be sufficiently specific as to have a legal identity in that regime. There have also been suggestions that it should be recognized as a norm of *jus cogens,* with specific reference to the sea-bed regime.[213] Other regimes could then adopt the concept if that was the wish of the contracting parties.

But to maintain on this basis that it is a general principle of international law is to go much further. There is no evidence that the concept has been transformed into a norm of international custom apart from the status which the sea-bed regime could eventually attain in customary law. The hypothesis that the concept has been established as a norm of *jus cogens* applies only to the sea-bed and not to other aspects of international law;[214] because of this reason the clause contained in Article 311, paragraph 6, of the Law of the Sea Convention, to the extent that the parties to this Convention shall not be party to any agreement in derogation of the principle of the common heritage of mankind, applies only to the question of the sea-bed and has no relationship at all with the situation of the Antarctic.[215] It could even be argued that the situation is rather the converse: some selected provisions of the 1959 Antarctic Treaty, having been transformed into rules of customary law in the light of what we examined in Chapter 9, could be likely candidates to qualify as rules of *jus cogens* to the extent that the concept is accepted in international law.

As regards the specific case of Antarctica, the proposal that this continent should be regarded as part of the principle of the common heritage of mankind has been explained by an author as resting on the following grounds:

> First, writers have argued that traditional theories of territorial acquisition are redolent of a past colonial era inappropriate to modern times, and, therefore, should not be applied to Antarctica. Second, it is argued that the Antarctic Treaty and subsequent practices of the Parties confirm the existence of common rights of access and exploitation throughout the Antarctic. Thirdly, it is argued that the common heritage concept, developed in relation to outer space and the resources of the deep sea-bed, has crystallized into a principle of customary international law which applies to all 'new' spaces or territories, including Antarctica.[216]

The first argument is more of a political than of a legal nature; in any event, as we examined in Chapter 1, sovereignty became established in Antarctica in a lawful manner under international law. The second argument is in general correct in so far as the access to Antarctic activities is concerned; however, that does not mean that there are no rules governing such activities, since, as we examined in Chapter 9, the Antarctic Treaty and related arrangements have been, or can be applied to third States under certain conditions.[217]

As Triggs comments the more important argument is that related to the comparison of Antarctica with the situation of the deep sea-bed and outer space.[218] Firstly, it should be observed that the fact that the concept of the common heritage might have been accepted for the sea-bed or outer space in no way signifies its consequent applicability to Antarctica. The converse argument is more valid, since it was the 1959 Antarctic Treaty which served as a model and source of inspiration for the outer space[219] and sea-bed regimes.[220] Secondly, the legal status of Antarctica is entirely different from that of the other areas mentioned[221] for the reasons that will be examined next.

The first substantial difference is that, as Lagoni has noted, 'in the case of the sea-bed and ocean floor, it was doubtful whether the area could be subjected to sovereign rights of States at all, whereas in the case of Antarctica there was never any serious doubt that the territory could principally be subjected to the sovereignty of States; only the validity of the existing claims are in dispute'.[222] The possibility of establishing territorial sovereignty in Antarctica is thus a fact which cannot be ignored in any arrangement.[223]

The second substantial difference is that the Antarctic continent and its adjacent maritime areas are subject to a legal regime established by the 1959 Treaty and the other instruments constituting the Treaty system, which was not the case with the other areas referred to,[224] or the applicable regimes were only of a very general nature, such as the high seas regime in relation to the sea-bed. This Antarctic regime can certainly be improved, but its participating countries would be unlikely to accept an alternative regime which disregarded their existing interests in Antarctica or which, in their view, failed to offer more effective protection of the environment or control of future exploitation, since any fundamental change in the existing Treaty system might plunge Antarctica into an undesirable state of instability.

The argument that Antarctica and other areas mentioned are incapable of supporting human life and that a common regime is justified on this account, which has also been put forward,[225] is not a convincing legal argument either, since the fact is that man has maintained a sustained activity in the continent for a considerable number of years[226] and, as was established in Chapter 1, in the case of remote territories with hostile environment only a modest amount of activity is necessary to establish claims based on occupation. Whether sufficient level of activity has been carried out to found the various national claims has, however, never been put to the test of submission to any international tribunal and the sector principle remains a disputed basis of claims to exercise sovereignty. In any event, the fundamental contention of the current debate is not so much the validity of claims but whether the regime governing Antarctic activities should be that of the present Treaty system or an entirely different one.

In the light of this debate, the Treaty parties have rejected the common heritage approach to Antarctica. As Ralph Harry has observed, 'the concept of a common heritage in the Antarctic has not been adopted as a rule of international law',[227] or in the writing of another author, 'even if Antarctica is considered part of the common heritage of mankind this conclusion would not necessarily mean that sovereignty claims are invalid or that exploitation of Antarctic resources – either by the unilateral action of claimant states, or under the Treaty regime – is now prohibited . . . . If claims to territorial sovereignty in Antarctica have already been perfected, nothing in the notion of a common heritage as a matter of law could supplant or displace those titles'.[228] But here again the issue is not so much related to titles but to the nature of the regime being proposed as an alternative to the present one.

So long as the Treaty Parties, as being the countries directly involved in Antarctica, do not accept an Antarctic regime which specifically incorporates the concept of the common heritage of mankind, this concept will not be established as a rule of international law in this context. Further below we shall discuss the issue of potential parallel regimes, which have also been characteristic of the deep sea-bed situation.

Content of the common heritage concept and the Antarctic case
The debate about the applicability to Antarctica of the concept of the common heritage of mankind that we have examined has been of a somewhat general nature.[229] However, there have been several, generally recent, attempts to outline a regime embodying this concept, including as a consequence more detailed proposals.

There is general agreement among commentators on the main aspects which the common heritage concept should cover. Paolillo lists prohibition of appropriation, the establishment of an international regime and the benefit of mankind.[230] Another writer invokes several common principles of the law of 'common spaces', referring particularly to common sovereignty over physical space, common rights of access, common rights to resources, common rights in the adoption of decisions, common rights and obligations for the protection of the environment and peaceful use, freedom of scientific investigation and the duty of 'information sharing'.[231] From these and other proposals, the essential components of the concept can be identified as the non-appropriation of the area, activities exclusively for peaceful purposes, establishment of an internationally administered regime, rational use of resources and equitable participation in benefits.[232] It is interesting to note in this connection that the 1985 UN General Assembly Resolution 156B on the question of minerals while having refrained from utilizing the expression 'common heritage of mankind' has in fact listed the basic components of the concept, in the following terms: 'Affirms that any exploitation of the resources of Antarctica should ensure the maintenance of international peace and security in Antarctica, the protection of its environment, the non-appropriation and conservation of its resources and the international management and equitable sharing of the benefits of such exploitation'.[233]

One view is that the present Antarctic Treaty system cannot satisfy these requirements and should be replaced by another system based on the following principles: (1) universality; (2) 'a holistic approach to issues', whereby the Antarctic question would be dealt with in the same way as other subjects in contemporary international law; (3) 'decision-making by consensus-oriented rules'; (4) 'sharing' and integration; (5) co-operation; and (6) 'non-reciprocal conduct', which would emphasize the distribution of benefits to those most in need.[234] Following the same line of thought, Luard finds it difficult to accept any solution of the minerals question based on the Antarctic Treaty as it would maintain its exclusive character, its mineral resources would appear only to benefit the industrialized countries and it would continue 'to be based on questionable legal fundations'.[235] Another analysis of the matter concludes that the influence of the concept of the common heritage of mankind in Antarctica is scarcely perceptible in the present system since, although it meets the requirements of peaceful use, scientific co-operation and a certain degree of international administration, it departs from the main attributes of the concept by its exclusive character and by the fact that it is subject to sovereignty claims.[236]

One of the main tendencies of this position is to identify the Antarctic situation with regimes devised for what are usually called 'global commons'.[237] This perspective has been to some extent endorsed by one Treaty party: the Constitutional Assembly of Peru has declared that this country sponsors an international regime for Antarctica which can ensure 'the rational and equitable exploitation of the resources of that continent in the benefit of all mankind';[238] that government has also stated that it shall seek the establishment of a permanent and broad regime for Antarctica.[239]

Apart from the differences which have been indicated before, it should be noted that forms of joint exploitation are not infrequent in international law without necessarily being considered to form part of global regimes. Brownlie has examined various forms of joint exploitation under bilateral treaties, such as the situation of single geological structures foreseen in Article 4 of the 1965 Anglo–Norwegian Treaty; the Joint Fisheries Zones established in the 1975 Japan–China Agreement in the Yellow Sea and East China Sea; the joint development of continental shelf resources contemplated in the 1974 Sudan–Saudi Arabia Agreement on the Red Sea and in the 1974 Japan–Korea Agreement; or the Saudi Arabia–Kuwaiti Neutral Zone of 1922.[240] The same author has also referred in this context to the Svalbard Treaty and the Antarctic Treaty.[241]

A different view is that most of the basic components of the common heritage of mankind concept are present in the Antarctic Treaty system.[242] Its use exclusively for peaceful purposes is beyond doubt. Moreover, the component of non-appropriation of the area is also present to a certain extent, since all claims to sovereignty are subject to Article IV of the Antarctic Treaty. While this article does not exclude earlier claims, it subordinates them to the needs of mutual co-operation and, in addition, prohibits any new claims. The same line has been followed in the various resources regimes and there is every indication that it will be continued as long as no change is made in the 1959 Treaty and its system of co-operation. In practice, the system operates as if the region were subject to non-appropriation.

The evolution of the institutional aspects of the Antarctic Treaty system also leads to some form of international administration of the area. Although this form of administration is very limited under the Consultative Meetings approach of the Treaty, the fact that the operation of the system is now under review is indicative of a trend towards greater institutionalization. The same trend is apparent in the Canberra Convention and in the mineral negotiations. The rational use of resources on a long-term basis, with due attention to the protection of the environment, is one important aim of the resources regimes that are in force or under discussion, thus coinciding also on this point with some of the elements or concerns of the concept of the common heritage of mankind. The concept of an equitable international participation in benefits is at a more rudimentary stage in the Antarctic Treaty system. International access to the results of scientific investigation has been indicated as a first stage in such participation,[243] but there is no doubt that the chief problem concerns the resources policy. The proposed mineral resources convention has recognized the need for such participation by including among the functions of the Commission that it should 'establish measures to ensure participation by the international community in possible benefits derived from the regime'.[244] Several commentators have realized that this is one of the key questions for the external accommodation of this regime.[245]

So far there has been little detailed discussion of how participation in benefits could be put into practice. Earlier we examined proposals for a common fund and other similar suggestions;[246] in this context there was a suggestion that claimants should have access to benefits on a preferential basis, but that this preferential treatment would decrease with time.[247] The participation of the different interest groups in the distribution of benefits would have to be suitably balanced so as to avoid otherwise inevitable conflicts.[248] During the discussion at the United Nations there was a suggestion that a central fund to be administered by the World Bank should be established, which could provide grants and loans.[249]

After examining all these elements and proposals, one writer concludes: 'On the whole, one can conclude that the Antarctic regime meets the criteria of the common heritage of mankind. However, this concordance is not always perfect: some conditions are better complied with than others'.[250] As will be seen, several of the suggestions for modifying the Antarctic Treaty system seek to bring it into line with other international regimes in which the concept of the common heritage has been incorporated. They all reveal the conflict between preservation of the Antarctic Treaty system's identity and its assimilation to other regimes of international management of resources,[251] which is also the basic issue under discussion at the United Nations.

10.5 Proposals for new forms of organization for the Antarctic Treaty system

The intense international political debate about the Antarctic question[252] has resulted in several proposals being made for the replacement of the present Antarctic Treaty system by other models based on the general principles of the concept of the common heritage of mankind.

The long-standing interest in establishing some kind of institutional link or affiliation between the Antarctic Treaty system and the United Nations has continued to find expression in various of these proposals. The idea of creating an international organization for Antarctica under the aegis of the United Nations has been suggested as the ideal,[253] but for this approach to materialize it would probably require the support of the

Antarctic Treaty Consultative Parties, a support which in view of the existing interests in the region is not at the time forthcoming.[254] The concept of Antarctica as a United Nations 'territory' has also been recently suggested.[255] Some analyses of the subject have even doubted the effectiveness of the Antarctic treaty's provisions on peaceful use and demilitarization, on the grounds that questions concerning 'property rights' might lead to the use of force and that therefore the common heritage concept and general internationalization of Antarctica are still justified.[256] This view, however, met with no response in the recent United Nations debate, where those provisions were generally supported.[257]

The most marked tendency is to advocate changes of a functional kind, which differ from the all-embracing models of international control. Following this line of thought, Tinker has suggested that a *rapprochement* between the Antarctic Treaty system and the international community could take the form of revenue sharing and the inclusion in the system of 'half a dozen representative Third World powers' as Consultative Parties.[258] Pinto originally proposed establishing a committee of the General Assembly to reconcile the interests of the international community with those of member countries of the Antarctic Treaty, such a committee to be composed of the latter and fifteen other countries chosen on a geographical basis.[259] A variation on this proposal is the inclusion as Consultative Parties of fifteen additional countries chosen according to a different criterion, but which would be basically geographical; meanwhile, appropriate studies and discussions would continue under United Nations auspices and, as a first step, the unclaimed sector of the Antarctic continent would be placed under United Nations jurisdiction.[260]

As an alternative to complete internationalization, which many developing countries favour, Luard has suggested maintaining the Antarctic Treaty for all its existing purposes and establishing a separate system for the administration of resources, especially the mineral resources.[261] The latter system would have a much more international character and wider participation, and might be administered by a council of some thirty countries which would include the traditional Antarctic countries and others representing special interests.[262] This suggestion to decouple the minerals regime from the Treaty system seeks to reconcile preservation of the advantages of the latter with the need for an external accommodation as regards the resources regimes.[263]

The United Nations debate has largely followed the line of the proposals for general internationalization. Although some countries have postulated a complete replacement of the Antarctic Treaty system,[264] the majority have recognized the advantages of the aims and purposes of the 1959 Treaty[265] while seeking at the same time to widen or restructure the resources regimes.[266] This represents a more realistic and constructive attitude than merely negative or destructive criticism.

Some of the other models suggested are based on regional considerations. Thus, there have been proposals that Antarctica should be declared the common heritage of the States of the southern hemisphere;[267] alternatively, attention has been drawn to the interest of Latin American countries in sharing in the area claimed by Chile and Argentina.[268] Another suggestion has included both the Arctic and the Antarctic in the common heritage of mankind.[269] The concept of Antarctica as a regional arrangement under the United Nations,[270] or as a sub-system within the general international system[271] which we have commented on earlier, also represents a regional approach to the question.

The Sea-bed Authority model

Within the context of the influence exercised by the Conference on the Law of the Sea on general internationalization proposals for Antarctica, the specific case of the Sea-bed Authority has been the source of inspiration for several initiatives for complete or partial application of the common heritage of mankind concept to this continent and its adjacent seas. The sea-bed model has been suggested as a basis for a new Antarctic regime in general[272] or for the adaptation of some of its principles to the Antarctic situation.[273] It has also been considered from an economic viewpoint,[274] as it has been seen as an alternative which could be adopted in place of current negotiations on mineral exploitation.[275]

Some proposals have outlined more detailed schemes. One has proposed an 'Antarctic common space regime', in which sovereignty rights over all Antarctic areas 'shall be vested in the international community as a whole', and would be administered by an Assembly, a Council of thirty members and a Secretariat.[276] The institutional structure of the Sea-bed Authority has also been advocated in other suggestions,[277] as has been the parallel system of exploitation, production controls and the transfer of technology.[278]

Although a general scheme of this kind is most unlikely to be implemented, for the reasons mentioned earlier in connection with the proposals for general internationalization, some initiatives of a more limited or partial character have been taken into consideration. This is the case, in particular, as regards the area to which the minerals regime should be applicable, which as has been examined, has been defined in such a way as not to include the area of the deep sea-bed, which might come under the competence of the Sea-bed Authority.[279] This decision was taken specifically to facilitate the external accommodation and to avoid friction, although at least one commentator has maintained that the regime could cover the whole area south of the parallel of 60° S latitude.[280]

Brennan has based his approach to the external accommodation on the argument that the concept of the common heritage of mankind can be applied with more justification to the Antarctic deep sea-bed.[281] Although he realistically accepts that the idea of the Authority's jurisdiction over the resources of the Antarctic continental margin would meet with resistance in the Antarctic system, the Authority might be granted 'the right to participate in decisions on access to all areas of the Antarctic continental margin'.[282] The distribution of benefits should, in his opinion, be done through the Authority, as a necessary part of the external accommodation.[283]

The various proposals for linking the Sea-bed Authority with the Antarctic Treaty system, or specifically with the minerals regime, raise the question of the attitude which might be adopted by the Consultative Parties that have not become parties to the Law of the Sea Convention because of objections to the regime established under Part XI and that, in consequence, shall not participate in the Sea-bed Authority.[284] The existence of such objections should not necessarily result in an obstacle for establishing the appropriate links between the institutions to be established under the minerals Convention and the Sea-bed Authority. From a legal point of view, this situation would not be entirely different from that created by the EEC participation in the Canberra Convention, since the political reluctance of some Consultative Parties to recognize the EEC has not prevented the appropriate participation in that Convention; similarly, the objections mentioned have not been an obstacle for the participation of the EEC in the Law of the Sea Convention.

10.6   The future of the Antarctic Treaty system

To the extent that the United Nations debate on Antarctica continues to unfold there shall no doubt be a great number of proposals put forward on the specific arrangements suggested for a new Antarctic Treaty system based on the approach of general internationalization. The relevant question seems to be, however, where will all this discussion lead to. Will it lead to the replacement of the present Treaty system by a model of organization inspired in the common heritage of mankind; or will the present Treaty system acquire additional strength and attraction through the process of increased participation, availability of information and greater opening-up already under way; or could it still result in the development of parallel and competitive Antarctic arrangements?

An author has concluded that the evolution of the Antarctic question will be characterized by the following central points; the number of Consultative parties will continue to increase; the Third World will make greater efforts to obtain future benefits; the mineral resources convention will be concluded; the calls for an alternative regime will become numerous; and changes are unlikely to take place as long as the Consultative Parties maintain their cohesiveness.[285] This view seems to be confirmed by the current debate on the matter since, on the one hand, it has resulted in a greatly increased awareness of the importance of activities conducted in the continent and its adjacent seas as well as of the regimes under which these activities are organized,[286] and, on the other hand, it has led to a clearer understanding of the concerns of the international community at large. At the same time, the limitations of both the model based on general internationalization and that resting on the concept of exclusive national sovereignty have become apparent in the course of this debate.

Limitations of the general internationalization model
The limitations of this model[287] stem, in the first place, from the difficulties inherent in establishing an international organization of a universal character, a task which is of course of great complexity.[288] But more serious perhaps is the problem that a model of this type has not proved acceptable to all the relevant interests which must be taken into account for attaining a satisfactory accommodation that can ensure the viability of the proposed regime and secure the co-operation of the States most concerned.

Besides the conflicts that would inevitably arise with the position of those countries claiming sovereignty in Antarctica,[289] the general internationalization model has also been resisted by those countries interested in the development of resources, mostly on the grounds that such model might not be sufficiently effective and economically viable to justify the potential investments.[290] The difficulties over this point which occurred in connection with the deep sea-bed regime have become more acute in the case of Antarctica since, while the negotiations within the Antarctic Treaty system have been extremely pragmatic, some of the discussions at the United Nations have made use of the rhetoric of confrontation, which is not conducive to a solution.

Some authors have also questioned whether the interest in environmental protection can be adequately safeguarded in a universal regime of the type proposed,[291] pointing out in this connection that the deep sea-bed regime is not a good example of environmental concern;[292] it has been further noted that the very concept of the common heritage of mankind is characterized by the pursuit of development.[293]

For all the foregoing reasons, the universal alternative has come to be regarded as a 'poor choice'[294] or as 'only the second best solution'.[295] It follows that it is highly improbable that the countries participating in the Antarctic Treaty system, and particularly the Consultative Parties, might support a universalist formula – and without their support it will be neither juridically nor politically viable.[296]

The concern for the external accommodation that has become evident in the negotiations and work of the parties to the Antarctic Treaty is of course closely connected with the purpose of satisfying to some extent the interests of the international community.[297] The fact that some of the criticism of the Treaty system is justified and that corrective measures are required does not mean, however, that there is any justification for replacing or radically changing the Treaty system. There has been an active evolution and development of the latter in response to the new needs and changing circumstances, but this is a gradual process. A closer relationship between the Antarctic Treaty system and the international community will undoubtedly continue to be developed on the basis, not of confrontation, but of search for solutions acceptable to the legitimate interests which must be taken into account.

It is in the light of these considerations that the question of the eventual establishment of an Antarctic parallel system under the United Nations can be examined.[298] The situation in the case of the Antarctic would be entirely different from that which has occurred in relation to the competing deep sea-bed regimes established under the Law of the Sea Convention and under the arrangements made among those countries which do not accept the approach of that Convention. The first difference is that the Antarctic Treaty system has been long established and the competing regime would be newly created, while in the case of the Law of the Sea both competing regimes have emerged at the same time; although the negotiations relating to the Antarctic minerals regime have not yet concluded, they are very much part of the evolution of the Treaty system as a whole.

A second important difference is that the Antarctic Treaty system has the participation of all the States active in the Antarctic or potentially interested in becoming active, while in the Law of the Sea situation the States most concerned with deep sea-bed mining have opted for different regimes, some joining the general regime and some other joining the special arrangements referred to.

The fundamental difference, however, lies perhaps in the argument that three-quarters of the world population, that is three billion of the world's four billion people, are represented in the Antarctic Treaty system;[299] any alternative regime would have great difficulty in justifying the claim to the representation of mankind in relation to Antarctica.

In view of these reasons a UN sponsored parallel system would probably not be viable and might even lack the necessary legitimacy; from a legal point of view it could even be regarded as a violation of the duty of States not to interfere with valid treaties.

Limitations of the model of exclusive sovereignty
Just as the recent discussion of general internationalization proposals has revealed their limitations, so also the evolution of the Antarctic Treaty system which has taken place has shown that the model of exclusive national sovereignty and similar approaches is of limited value. As matters stand at present, it can reasonably be assumed that the Antarctic Treaty system will not be organized exclusively on the basis of national sovereignty, although the existence and influence of claims to sovereignty will continue to be one of the legitimate interests of which any arrangement will have to take account.[300] Only in the case of the breakdown of the Antarctic Treaty would this model again come to the fore, after a period of crisis and conflict which would lead to the destruction of all the positive values so laboriously fostered to date.

The reason why the role of State sovereignty is limited is not because of the political arguments recently put forward and which we have examined earlier, but because it is an organizational model that does not adequately safeguard all the interests concerned; in fact some of the interests associated with the exploitation of resources, the environment and, above all, the international community, cannot be readily accommodated in a framework of exclusive national sovereignty. It is this complex conjunction of interests which determines the need to seek alternative models, as the Antarctic Treaty itself and the resources regimes have done.

The political criticism of the Antarctic Treaty system and its legal foundations[301] can well be understood as a part of the debate currently being held at the United Nations and other bodies, but a different conclusion will certainly emerge in an analysis from the point of view of international law or even from the point of view of the characteristic of the present international political system.[302] In fact, as we have examined before, the absence of protest in relation to the Treaty system has led to forms of acquiescence on the part of the States not parties to the Antarctic Treaty and related instruments, giving in turn place to what Brownlie describes as 'opposable situations';[303] furthermore, rules of customary law have also emerged from the Antarctic Treaty.[304]

Reappraisal of the Antarctic system of co-operation

In view of the limitations of the universal and exclusive sovereignty models, the only viable alternative is for the Antarctic continent to have a system of international co-operation of its own adapted to its specific circumstances and needs. Just such a system was the one established by the 1959 Treaty, which has evolved through its successive complementary regimes. National sovereignty claims are integrated within this system in a pragmatic way, so as to make them compatible with the requirements of international co-operation. They are not eliminated, but acquire a functional meaning which allows for that integration.

In the same way, this special type of co-operation does not exclude the interest of the international community, which has gradually begun to be integrated with it in the ways described. This latter type of integration has been more recent, not because the system was a closed one, but because the international interest which justifies it was not actively expressed earlier.

The central role played in the administration of this system of co-operation by the Consultative Parties, is a most important one and without it the system would probably have been unable to achieve the balance which characterizes it. Although their role has also been subject to recent criticism,[305] a number of countries are aspiring to acquire the status of Consultative Parties within the Treaty system; as we have noted earlier, the number of Consultative Parties has expanded and will continue to expand as other countries become qualified for inclusion. Various forms of assistance and training can also be offered to those countries interested in gaining Antarctic experience. However, the criteria for attaining the status of Consultative Party must be exacting in the future in order to ensure that the system is not diverted from its purposes;[306] only truly qualified States should be admitted.

The system of Antarctic co-operation has been in a way strengthened as a result of the United Nations debate since, on the one hand, the countries participating in it have come to appreciate that its merits are greater than might have been supposed and, on the other hand, its deficiencies have been more closely perceived, thus leading to the improvement process which has been described. As a result, the advantages of Antarctic co-operation have been assessed at their true value when compared with the difficulties and limitations inherent in the other alternatives examined.[307]

Importance of the minerals regime and evolution of the Antarctic Treaty system

Referring to the negotiation of the mineral resources regime and the political pressures which have arisen in the international community, Triggs notes that 'it may be that the possibility of mineral exploitation brings these threads together in such a way that states can no longer exercise exclusive territorial sovereignty in Antarctica'.[308] The minerals regime undoubtedly represents the greatest challenge which the Antarctic Treaty system has so far had to face since it must not only arrive at a formula which reconciles claims to sovereignty with the necessary international co-operation in this field but must also heed the legitimate demands of the international community. It is this difficult task which the internal and external accommodation process has been carrying out.

The internal accommodation has been so far outstandingly successful in convincing the Consultative Parties of the need for pragmatic and imaginative formulae which do not prejudice their respective positions. This has meant that each has made concessions so as to enable the basic interests of all to be met.

The process of external accommodation has proved more difficult than anticipated. One of the major aims of the minerals regime has been to ease the way for this accommodation by providing for specific ways of broader participation, availability of information, the sharing of benefits and other measures. Nevertheless, some of the demands made at the United Nations have gone much beyond the minerals regime and have sought to replace the Antarctic Treaty system as a whole by other models of universal extent.

In spite of these difficulties, the minerals regime will still take the interests of the international community into account, since this has been the general rule in the Antarctic Treaty system. In addition the system's development clearly points to greater integration in the general international system through a gradual process of linkage and interaction. To the extent that the Treaty system continues to evolve towards a greater degree of institutionalization and even towards the establishment of a formal international organization, the process of internal and external accommodation and international linkage will be correspondingly facilitated.

The view that the Antarctic Treaty or its related system will be abruptly replaced by another model does not therefore appear to be a realistic one. The option offered by the Treaty of a revision conference in 1991, thirty years after the Treaty's entry into force, does not seem at present to be as eminent a reality as was once envisaged.[309]

Chapter 10 Notes

1. See generally M. W. Mouton: 'The International regime of the Polar regions', *Rec. Cours Ac. D.I.*, 1962-III, 169–284; L. F. E. Goldie: 'International relations in Antarctica', *Aust. Q.*, Vol. XXX, 1958, 7–29; Juan Carlos Puig: *La Antartida Argentina ante el derecho*, 1960. See also generally Chapter 1 supra.

2. Paul Fauchille: *Traité de Droit International Public*, Tome 1, deuxieme partie, 1925, 651–663.

3. J. Daniel: 'Conflict of sovereignties in the Antarctic', *Y.B.W.A.*, Vol. 3, 1949, 241–272.

4. Robert D. Hayton: 'Polar problems and international law', Notes and Comments, *A.J.I.L.*, Vol. 52, 1958, 746–765; particular reference to the announcement on internationalization and demilitarization of the Antarctic made by Prime Minister Macmillan during his visit to Australia, on 11 February 1958, is made at 755.

5. C. Wilfred Jenks: *The Common Law of Mankind*, 1958, Chapter 8, 'An international regime for Antarctica?', 366–381; see also the contribution by the same author on this subject to *Int.Af.*, Vol. 32, 1956, 414–426; see further G. C. L. Bertram: *Antarctica today and tomorrow*, University of Otago, Dunedin, 1957, particularly at 25–30.

6. Jenks, op. cit., note 5 supra, at 376–378.

7. Philip C. Jessup and Howard J. Taubenfeld: *Controls for outer space and the Antarctic analogy*, 1959, 95–110; see also Jessup: 'Sovereignty in Antarctica', *A.J.I.L.*, Vol. 41, 1947, 117–119; and Taubenfeld: 'A Treaty for Antarctica', *Int.Conc*, N° 531, January 1961, 245–322.

8. Gilbert Gidel: *Aspects juridiques de la lutte pour l'Antarctique*, Paris, 1948.

9. Jessup and Taubenfeld, op. cit., note 7 supra, at 180.

10. Ibid., at 265–282; see also Jessup and Taubenfeld: 'Outer Space, Antarctica, and the United Nations', *I.O.*, Vol. XIII, 1959, 363–379.

11. René–Jean Dupuy: 'Le Statut de l'Antarctique', *An. Fr.D.I.*, Vol. IV, 1958, 196–229.

12. Walter Sullivan: 'Antarctica in a two-power world', *For.Af.*, Vol. 36, 1957–1958, 154–166, at 164.

13. Robert D. Hayton: Remarks of the chairman of the panel on 'Legal problems and the political situation in the Polar Areas', *Proc.A.S.I.L.*, 1958, 135–136, 171–174.

14. Robert D. Hayton: 'The Nations and Antarctica', *O.Z.F.O.R.*, Vol. X, 1959–1960, 368–412, at 410.

15. Edward Shackleton: 'The New Continent', *United Nations World*, Vol. 1, N° 10, July 1949, 380–382, at 382.

16. Ibid.: 'Antarctica: the case for permanent international control – a possible solution', *World Affairs*, N° 243, May–June 1958, 23–25, at 24.

17. United Kingdom, House of Lords: Statement by Lord Shackleton on neutralization of Antarctica, *Hansard*, House of Lords, Vol. 216, N° 70, 4 May 1959, 42–43; see also the reply by Earl Attlee, at 54.

18. European Parliament: Question N° 105 by Mr Seligman on establishing a neutral zone in Antarctica to prevent conflicts in relation to minerals and discuss the issue at the United Nations, *Official Journal of the European Communities*, Debates of the European Parliament, N° 1–288, 1982–1983 session, Report of proceedings from 13 to 17 September 1982, p. 162.

19. United Kingdom, House of Lords: *official report,* Parliamentary debates (Hansard), Vol. 221, N° 40, 18 February 1960, 158–169, particularly at 167–168; for the statements of Lord Denning and Lord McNair, see ibid., at 178–183.

20. United Kingdom, House of Commons: Question of United Nations and Antarctica, Hansard, 13 June 1956; reply by Mr Nutting.
21. Ibid.: Questions on the Prime Minister's statement on international control of Antarctica, Hansard, 18 February 1958; also reported in *The Times* of 19 February 1958.
22. For comments on the initiative of Prime Minister Macmillan, see Hayton, loc. cit., note 4 supra, at 755.
23. United Kingdom, House of Commons: Questions on international control of Antarctica, related to statement by Prime Minister, Hansard, 19 February 1958; reply by Mr Ormsby-Gore.
24. A. D. McInthosh: Statement at the Antarctic Conference, Washington, 1959, as reproduced in John Hill: *New Zealand and Antarctica,* 1983, at 30.
25. For comments on the proposal by Prime Minister Nash, see Barbara Mitchell: *Frozen Stakes, The future of Antarctic minerals,* 1983, at 93.
26. John Kish: *The Law of International spaces,* 1973, at 76.
27. United Nations Trusteeship Council: Petition on polar internationalization, *Yearbook of the United Nations,* 1947–1948, at 769; see also UN Trusteeship Council, Official Records, Second session, first part, Vol. 2, 1947, 62–65; the petitions are contained in Doc. T/Pet. General/15, 2 June 1947; Doc. T/Pet. General/16, 30 August 1947; Doc. T/Pet. General/18, 13 September 1947; reproduced in official Records cit., Supplement, 218–224.
28. Philip W. Quigg: *A Pole Apart, the emerging issue of Antarctica,* 1983, 133–136.
29. The Text of the 1948 American plan is published in *Foreign Relations of the United States,* 1948, Vol. 1, Part 2, USGPO, 1976, at 977–987.
30. Hill, op. cit., note 24 supra, at 22.
31. For the Argentine, British and Chilean reaction, see Quigg, op. cit., note 28 supra, at 134, 136.
32. Ibid., at 134.
33. For the Chilean proposals on moratorium of claims and other arrangements in Antarctica in 1948 and following years, see W. M. Bush: *Antarctica and International Law,* Vol. II, 1982, at 383–384.
34. United Nations General Assembly: Letter dated 17 February 1956 addressed to the Secretary General by the Permanent Representative of India on *The Question of Antarctica,* Doc. A/3118, 21 February 1956, add. 1, 13 September 1956; add. 2, 17 October 1956.
35. See Explanatory Memorandum on *The Peaceful Utilization of Antarctica,* UN Doc. A/3118, Add. 2, 17 October 1956.
36. 'Issues before the Eleventh General Assembly: Antarctica', *Int.Conc.,* N° 510, November 1956, 135–143, at 142–143.
37. See for example United Nations Library: *Antarctica. A selected bibliography,* New York, 1956.
38. For the diplomatic documents and material, see Bush, op. cit., note 33 supra, Vol. 1, at 502–507.
39. See for example, Ramón Cañas Montalva: 'La Antartica y las proposiciones de la India ante las Naciones Unidas', Editorial, *Revista Geográfica de Chile 'Terra Australis',* N° 14, 1956–1957, 3–4.
40. Chilean memorandum on the Indian proposal on Antarctica of 4th October 1956, reproduced in Bush, op. cit., note 33 supra, Vol. 1, at 502–504.
41. Bush, op. cit., note 33 supra, Vol. 1, at 506.
42. United Nations General Assembly: Letter dated 15 July 1958 from the Permanent Representative of India, addressed to the Secretary General, on *The Question of Antarctica,* Doc. A/3852, 15 July 1958.

43. Explanatory Memorandum of India, Doc. A/3852, 15 July 1958, at 3. After examining the proposals of India of 1956 and 1958 and other initiatives, an Indian author concludes that 'The Antarctica, therefore, should be controlled by the United Nations in conformity with the wider community expectations'; see Subash C. Jain: 'Antarctica: geopolitics and International Law', *I.Y.B.I.A.*, 1974, 249–278, at 278.

44. See generally Peter J. Beck: 'Preparatory meetings for the Antarctic Treaty 1958-59', *Pol. Rec.*, Vol. 22, 1985, 653–664.

45. Antarctic Treaty, second preambular paragraph.

46. Convention on the Conservation of Antarctic Marine Living Resources, ninth preambular paragraph.

47. Recommendation IX-1, par. 4 (IV); Recommendation XI-1, par. 5 (d); see also Recommendation VIII-13, par. 1 (a).

48. See, for example, *1984 Draft Articles*, Preamble, par. (c).

49. Bush, op. cit., note 33 supra, Vol. 1, at 103.

50. Antarctic Treaty, lst preambular paragraph. The contribution of the Antarctic Treaty to the purposes and principles of the Charter has been recognized by various United Nations studies, particularly in the field of disarmament; see for example UN Department of Political and Security Council Affairs: *The United Nations and disarmament, 1945–1970*, 1970, particularly at 137; UN General Assembly: *Introduction to the report of the Secretary General on the work of the Organization*, Official Records, 27th. session, Doc. Supplement N° IA (A/8701/Add. 1), August 1972, at 3; see also Pilar Armanet: 'La Antártica y el desarme', in Francisco Orrego Vicuña et al. (eds): *Política Antártica de Chile*, 1985, 289–294. The United Nations debate on the Question of Antarctica, which is discussed in this Chapter, reveals a similar trend of opinion.

51. See Chapter 9 supra, notes 7, 22 and associated texts.

52. See Chapter 8 supra.

53. Antarctic Treaty, Article III, par. 2.

54. Diplomatic note dated 14 May 1958 from the Chilean Minister of Foreign Affairs to the United States Chargé d'Affaires in Santiago, reproduced in Bush, op. cit., note 33 supra, Vol. II, at 417–419, par. 4 (4).

55. Bush, op. cit., note 33 supra, Vol. 1, at 55–56.

56. Jeffrey D. Myhre: *The Antarctic Treaty Consultative Meetings, 1961–1968*, Ph.D. Thesis, London School of Economics, 1983, as cited by Peter J. Beck; 'The United Nations and Antarctica', *Pol.Rec.*, Vol. 22, N° 137, May 1984, 137–144, at 142.

57. Richard Woolcott: 'The interaction between the Antarctic Treaty System and the United Nations System, in US Polar Research Board: *Workshop on the Antarctic Treaty System, An Assessment*, 1986, 375–390.

58. See generally James H. Zumberge: 'The Antarctic Treaty as a scientific mechanism – SCAR and the Antarctic Treaty System', in US Polar Research Board, op. cit., note 57 supra, 153–168.

59. On the current activities of international organizations in Antarctica, see Lee Kimball: *Report on Antarctica*, International Institute for Environment and Development, 1 November, 1984; 5 July, 1985; 8 November, 1985. See also the account given by the *Report of the Secretary General* on the Question of Antarctica UN Doc. A/41/722, 7 November 1986, Section II.

60. International Council for the Exploration of the Sea: *General information by the Secretary General*, December 1981, mimeo; A. E. J. Went: *Seventy Years Agrowing. A history of the International Council for the Exploration of the Sea, 1902–1972*, 1972; B. B. Parrish: 'The future role of ICES in the light of changes in fisheries jurisdiction', *Marine Policy*, Vol. 3, 1979, 232–238; Hans

Tambs-Lyche: 'Le Conseil International pour l'exploration de la mer (CIEM) et la formulation d'avis scientifiques', *An.Fr.D.I.,* Vol. XXVI, 1980, 728–740. Reports of ICES are circulated and noted at the meetings of the Commission for the Conservation of Antarctic Marine Living Resources; see for example *Report of the Fourth Meeting of the Commission,* Hobart, 2–13 September 1985, at 16, par. 47.

61. See generally *The Oslo and Paris Commissions: history and progress 1974–1984,* The Secretariat, 1984; Convention for the prevention of marine pollution by dumping from ships and aircraft, Oslo, 15 February 1972; Convention for the prevention of marine pollution from land-based sources, Paris, 4 June 1974; Agreement for co-operation in dealing with pollution of the North Sea by Oil, Bonn, 9 June 1969; Agreement for co-operation in dealing with pollution of the North Sea by Oil and other harmful substances, Bonn, 1983; see also *Prevention of Marine Pollution in the North–East Atlantic region. The work of the Oslo and Paris Commissions and the Bonn Agreement,* May 1982.

62. North–East Atlantic Fisheries Convention, 24 January 1959, *U.N.T.S.,* 1964, Vol. 486, N° 7078, 157–182.

63. Convention of Future multilateral co-operation in the Northwest Atlantic Fisheries, Ottawa, 24th October 1978, *Official Journal of the European Communities,* N° L 378, Vol. 21, 30 December 1978, 16–29.

64. Recommendation X-7 on 'oil contamination of the Antarctic Marine Environment', par. 3. Other organizations or programmes thereof could also eventually qualify under this provision; see, for example, United Nations Environment Programme: 'Achievements and planned development of UNEP's Regional Seas Programme and comparable programmes sponsored by other bodies', *UNEP Regional Seas Reports and Studies,* N° 1, 1982; see also UNEP: 'Prospects for global ocean pollution monitoring, *UNEP Regional Seas Reports and Studies,* N° 47, 1984.

65. Bush, op. cit., note 33 supra, Vol. 1, at 56.

66. The International Whaling Commission and the Commission for the Conservation of Antarctic Marine Living Resources exchange observers to their meetings on regular basis; for the IWC observers' reports see the following documents: IWC/34/11D (1981, Statement at preparatory meetings), IWC/35/21 (Report on co-operation), IWC/36/11A (Second meeting of CCAMLR, 1983), IWC/37/11A (Third meeting of CCAMLR,1984), Chairman's Report of the 33rd (1982), 34th (1983) and 35th (1984) meetings of IWC. See also the Fourth Report of the CCAMLR cit., note 60 supra, par. 47, at 16. See also Patricia Birnie: *International Regulation of Whaling,* 1985, with particular reference to the Seals Convention at 383–390, and the Convention on the Conservation of Antarctic Marine Living Resources at 522–532, 577–581.

67. SCAR: *Constitution, procedures and structure,* 1958, par. 3 of guidelines for the conduct of SCAR Affairs, reproduced in Bush, op. cit., note 33 supra, Vol. 1, at 6.

68. On the EEC Common Fisheries Policy and its relevance for Antarctica, see Chapter 4 supra, notes 239, 240 and 241 and associated texts.

69. Tullio Treves: 'The United Nations Law of the Sea Convention of 1982: prospects for Europe', in The Greenwich Forum IX: *Britain and the Sea,* 1984, 166–182; see also Jeannette Irigoin: 'La participación de las organizaciones internacionales en la Convención sobre la Conservación de los Recursos vivos marinos de la Antártica y en la Convención sobre el Derecho del Mar', in Francisco Orrego Vicuña (ed.): *La Zona Económica Exclusiva. Una perspectiva latinoamericana,* 1982, 170–182; Daniel Vignes: 'La Convention sur la Conservation de la faune et de la flore marine de l'Antarctique', *An. Fr.D.I.,* 1980, 741–772.

70. Recommendation XI-1, par. 7 III.

71. Ibid., par. 7 V.
72. *1983 Draft Articles,* Article XXXVI, par. 1; the same approach, with minor modifications, was followed by the *1984 Draft Articles,* Article XXXVI, par. 1, 2. See also *1986 Draft Articles,* Article 52.
73. *1984 Draft Articles,* Article XXXVI, par. 3; an identical provision was contained in the *1983 Draft Articles,* Article XXXVI, par. 2. See also *1986 Draft Articles,* Article 52, par. 3.
74. *1984 Draft Articles,* Article XXXVI, par. 4; *1986 Draft Articles,* Article 52, par. 4.
75. *1984 Draft Articles,* Article X, par. 4 (b); *1986 Draft Articles,* Article 19, par. 4.
76. *1984 Draft Articles,* Article XVI, par. 3; *1986 Draft Articles,* Article 24, par. 3.
77. Recommendation XII-6; particular reference to international organizations is made in the last preambular paragraph as an indication of the importance attributed to the subject.
78. Antarctic Treaty, Report of the Twelfth Consultative Meeting, Canberra 13–27 September 1983, par. 42; for the discussions of the Thirteenth Consultative Meeting on this point, see Kimball, report cit. (8 November, 1985), note 59 supra, at 5.
79. Chile: Working document on the Operation of the Antarctic Treaty, Doc. ANT/XII/Prep./7, 11 April 1983, 3–4.
80. Ibid., at 4.
81. See note 65 supra and associated text.
82. See the Convention for the Conservation of Antarctic Seals, Article 5; and the Convention on the Conservation of Antarctic Marine Living Resources, Article XXIII.
83. *1984 Draft Articles,* Article XXXVI, par. 2 (b); *1986 Draft Articles,* Article 52, par. 2 (b).
84. *1984 Draft Articles,* Article XVI, par. 3; *1986 Draft Articles,* Article 24, par. 3.
85. See for example the document prepared by Greenpeace International and the Antarctic and Southern Ocean Coalition (ASOC), 'Non-paper on the role of NGOS', ANT 84/IV SCM/5 (NGO 4), 28 May 1984; see also ASOC: 'The role of NGO's', 1 October 1985, ASOC Paper N° 2, ANT SCM/7; ASOC: 'Background on ASOC', 1 October 1985, ASOC Paper N°1, ANT SCM/7; James Barnes: 'Non-Governmental organizations. Increasing the global perspective', *Marine Policy,* Vol. 8, 1984, 171–184; Greenpeace International: *The future of the Antarctic-Background for a second UN debate,* 22 October 1984.
86. Because of the difficulties experienced by the International Whaling Commission in this matter, Article 2 (b) of the Rules of Procedure (1985) provides, among other requirements, that organizations wishing to be represented by observers should have offices in more than three countries, and that the Commission shall levy a registration fee and may define other conditions. Rules of conduct for observers have also been issued by the Commission. See also the Chairman's report of the 36th meeting (1985), at 23–24.
87. Convention on the Conservation of Antarctic Marine Living Resources, Article XXIII, par. 3.
88. Report of the Third Meeting of the Commission of CCAMLR (1984), at 15; for the correspondence between the Executive Secretary and non-governmental organizations and the discussion about their participation as observers, see the Report of the Third Meeting cit., at 13–15, and Report of the Fourth Meeting of the Commission (1985), at 16–17. See also a reference to the matter in UN Report cit., note 59 supra, p. 12, par. 19.
89. William E. Westermeyer: *The Politics of Mineral resource development in Antarctica,* 1984, at 83.

90. See, for example, John Lawrence Hargrove: 'Environmental problems of Antarctic Resource Management: legal and institutional aspects', *American Society of International Law,* 1976, unpublished paper, at 15; Alvaro de Soto: 'Comments at the Seminar on Antarctic resources and the environment', *Earthscan,* Washington D.C., 14 September 1979, mimeo, at 10; Keith Brennan: 'Criteria for access to the resources of Antarctica: alternatives, procedures and experience applicable', in Francisco Orrego Vicuña (ed.): *Antarctic Resources Policy,* 1983, 217–227, at 225–226.

91. Francisco Orrego Vicuña: *El futuro de la Antártica,* Instituto de Estudios Internacionales de la Universidad de Chile, Serie de Publicaciones Especiales, N° 48, 1980, at 10.

92. Gunnar Skagestad: 'The frozen frontier: models for international co-operation', *Coop. and conflict,* 3, 1975, 167–187, at 174.

93. Recommendation XI-1, par. 5 (d).

94. Frank C. Alexander Jr: 'A recommended approach to the Antarctic resource problem', *Univ.Mia. L. Rev.,* Vol. 33, 1978, 371–423, at 409. For other suggestions as to universal action and UN involvement see also Jonathan I. Charney: 'Future strategies for an Antarctic mineral resource regime – can the environment be protected?, in Jonathan I. Charney (ed.): *The new nationalism and the use of common spaces,* 1982, 206–238, at 218; see also Jonathan I. Charney: 'Remarks on the development of Antarctica', *Proc. ASIL,* 1979, 268–271.

95. Edvard Hambro: 'Some notes on the future of the Antarctic Treaty collaboration', *A.J.I.L.,* Vol. 68, 1974, 217–226, at 225; see also Christopher C. Joyner: 'Antarctica and the Law of the Sea: rethinking the current legal dilemmas', *San. D.L.R.,* Vol. 18, 1980–1981, 415–442, at 438–439.

96. M. J. Peterson: 'Antarctica: the last great land rush on earth', *I.O.,* Vol. 34, 1980, 377–403, at 398–399.

97. Steven J. Burton: 'New stresses on the Antarctic Treaty: toward international legal institutions governing Antarctic resources', *Virg. L.R.,* Vol. 65, 1979, 421–512, at 497–510.

98. See, for example, Lee Kimball: 'Implications of the arrangements made for deep sea mining for other joint exploitations', *C.J.W.B.,* Vol. 15, 1980, 52–61. On the sea-bed regime see generally, E. D. Brown: *Sea-Bed energy and mineral resources and the Law of the Sea,* Vol. 1–3, 1984–1985.

99. See, for example, Hambro, loc. cit., note 95 supra, at 225; Joyner, loc. cit., note 95 supra, at 439–442; Rainer Lagoni: 'Antarctica's mineral resources in international law', *Z.A.O.R.V.,* Vol. 39, 1979, 1–37, at 32–33. This comparison with the Law of the Sea Conference has been criticized by other authors: Roland Rich: 'A minerals regime for Antarctica', *I.C.L.Q.,* Vol. 31, 1982, 709–725, at 712–715; Rudiger Wolfrum: 'The use of Antarctic non-living resources: the search for a trustee?, in Rudiger Wolfrum (ed.): *Antarctic Challenge,* 1984, 143–163, at 145; Gilbert Guillaume: 'Oil as a special resource, problems and experiences', in Francisco Orrego Vicuña (ed.), op. cit., note 90 supra, 185–190, at 189–190.

100. J. Michel Marcoux: 'Natural resource jurisdiction on the Antarctic continental margin', *Virg. J.I.L.,* Vol. 11, 1971, 374–404, at 402; see also Anthony Bergin: 'Frozen assets – resource problems and Antarctica', Dyason House Papers: *Australia, Asia and the World,* September 1979, 7–12.

101. Christopher C. Joyner: 'Antarctica and Law of the Sea: new resources vs. legal dilemmas', *Oceans,* September 1982, 1211–1215.

102. James E. Caroll: 'Of icebergs, oil wells, and Treaties: hydrocarbon exploitation offshore Antarctica', *Stan.J.I.L.,* Vol. 19, 1983, 207–227.

103. Gregory P. Wilson: 'Antarctica, the Southern Ocean, and the Law of the Sea', *J.A.G. Jour.,* Vol. 30, 1978, 47–85, at 76, with reference to the first drafts of such resolution.

104. Charney, loc. cit., note 94 supra, at 218–219.

105. Ibid., at 219; see also Brian Roberts: 'International cooperation for Antarctic development: the test for the Antarctic Treaty', in Francisco Orrego Vicuña (ed.): *El Desarrollo de la Antártica,* 1977, 336–356, at 353.

106. Charney, loc. cit., note 94 supra, at 219–221.

107. Edith Brown Weiss et al: 'Protection of the global heritage', Panel discussion, *Proc. A.S.I.L.,* April 1981, 32–55; see also Gerard S. Schatz: 'The polar regions and human welfare: regimes for environmental protection', in Edmund A. Schofield (ed.): *Earthcare: global protection of natural areas,* 1978, 465–478.

108. See, for example, Barbara Mitchell and Richard Sandbrook: 'Statement on behalf of the International Institute for Environment and Development on Antarctic Living Marine Resources negotiations', in United States Senate: *Antarctic Living Marine Resources Negotiations,* Hearing, 1978, 39–45; International Union for the Conservation of Nature: 'Background statement and action plan for Antarctica and the Southern Ocean', 1981; World Wildlife Fund News: *The question of krill,* N° 24, July–August 1983; International Union for Conservation of Nature and Natural resources – 1981 General Assembly Resolution, in James N. Barnes: *Let's Save Antarctica!,* 1982, at 61–63; IUCN et al.: *World Conservation Strategy, objectives for Antarctica,* 1980, in Barnes, op. cit., at 65; National Wildlife federation: *Resolution N° 2 on Antarctica,* undated, mimeo.

109. Barbara Mitchell: *Frozen Stakes. The Future of Antarctic minerals,* 1983, at 81–86; Geoff Mosley: 'The natural option: the case for an Antarctic world park', in Stuart Harris (ed.): *Australia's Antarctic Policy Options,* A.N.U., 1984, 307–327.

110. Mitchell, op. cit., note 109 supra, at 82–83. For the text of the recommendation of the Second World Conference on National Parks, see Barnes, op. cit., note 108 supra, appendix 6, at 59; for the text of the 1982 Bali Resolution see U.S. House of Representatives, Committee on Merchant Marine and Fisheries, Subcommittee on Fisheries and Wildlife conservation and the environment: Hearing on *Antarctic Marine Living Resources* (H.R. 3416), June 30, 1983, at 182.

111. See the Resolution of non-governmental organizations concerning Antarctica and the Southern Ocean, adopted in Nairobi, 1982; text in Barnes, op. cit., note 108 supra, appendix J, at 64. The 1986 private expedition of Greenpeace to Antarctica was organized with the purpose of supporting the world park concept for this continent; see Stephen Taylor: 'Greenpeace Antarctic crusade', London Observer Service, *El Mercurio,* Santiago, Chile, 7 January 1986, at 2.

112. Sir Peter Scott: 'Foreword', in Barnes, op. cit., note 108 supra, at 3; Jacques-Ives Cousteau: 'Foreword', in K. D. Suter: *World Law and the last wilderness,* 1980, at 8.

113. John Hill: *New Zealand and Antarctica,* 1983, at 58; Barbara Mitchell: 'Resources in Antarctica. Potential for conflict', *Marine Policy,* Vol. 1, 1977, 91–101. Chile also supported this approach when the first discussions on the minerals regime took place at the Consultative Meetings.

114. See, for example, Auckland District Law Society: 'How strong is New Zealand's claim to the Ross Dependency?, *N.Z.L.J.,* 1980, N° 4, 76–77.

115. Laurie Barber and Michael Selby: 'The search for an alternative strategy: New

Zealand and the Antarctic', *The Round Table,* N° 288, 1983, 466–472, particularly at 471–472. For the concept of Treaty nations as 'park rangers', see W. F. Budd: 'The Antarctic Treaty as a scientific mechanism – contributions of Antarctic scientific research (Post IGY)', in US Polar Research op. cit., note 57 supra, 103–151.

116. K. D. Suter, op. cit., note 112 supra, at 56–68; Ibid.: 'The Antarctic: a crisis for the 1980's?', *Journal of the Royal United Services Institute,* March 1981, 39–44, at 44; Ibid.: 'The Antarctic: a public policy problem for Australia in the 1980's', in R. A. Herr, R. Hall, B. W. Davis (eds): *Issues in Australia's Marine and Antarctic Policies,* University of Tasmania, 1982, 101–137, at 134–135.

117. Sierra Club, *Resolution on Antarctica,* undated.

118. National Audubon Society, *Statement on Antarctica,* undated.

119. US House of Representatives: *H.R. 4311,* 5 June 1979, 96th Congress, 1st Session.

120. Greenpeace International: 'An Antarctic environmental protection Agency', *Antarctica briefing,* N° 3. 16 April 1984; also N° 6, 12 October 1984. For a critical view of this proposal see R. M. Laws: 'International stewardship of the Antarctic: problems, successes and future options', *Marine Pollution Bulletin* (U.K.), Vol. 16, N° 2, February 1985, 49–55.

121. Mitchell, op. cit., note 109 supra, at 83–85.

122. Brian Meredith: 'A Plan for the Arctic. Mr Trudeau's international regime', *The Round Table,* N° 60, N° 238, April 1970, 177–182; Elizabeth Young: 'The Arctic – in need of an international regime', *Marine Policy,* Vol. 5, 1981, 154–156. See also generally William E. Westermeyer and Kurt M. Shusterich: *United States Arctic interests. The 1980's and 1990's,* 1984.

123. Joan E. Moore: 'The polar regions and the law of the sea', Notes, *Case W.R.J.I.L.,* Vol. 8, 1976, 204–219, at 215–216.

124. Lincoln P. Bloomfield: 'The Arctic: last unmanaged frontier', *For Af.,* Fall 1981, 87–105, at 104.

125. UN General Assembly, Twenty-sixth session: *Declaration of the Indian Ocean as a zone of peace,* Letter dated 1 October 1971 from the Permanent Representative of Ceylon, Doc. A/8492, 1 October 1971. The permanent representative of Ceylon at the time was Mr H. Shirley Amerasinghe.

126. Statement by Ambassador Carlos Ortiz de Rozas (Argentina), First Committee, 1827th. Meeting, UN General Assembly Official Record, 22 September–17 December 1971, Vol. I, at 12.

127. UN Economic and Social Council, Committee on Natural Resources: *Natural resources information and documentation,* Note by the Secretary-General, Doc. E./C.7/5, 25 January 1971.

128. UN Economic and Social Council: request of information on Antarctica by Sri Lanka, Doc. E/AC.24/SR.555–581, session 563, 14 July 1975, at 72–73.

129. UN: *Marine resources in Antarctica,* Doc. EC/RSL/cl, 8 February 1977, not distributed.

130. For a reference to Algeria, Guinea and Libya, see Ursula Wassermann: 'The Antarctic Treaty and Natural Resources', *J.W.T.L.,* Vol. 12, 1978, 174–179, at 179.

131. FAO, *Report of the Conference,* Eighteenth session, Rome, 8–27 November 1975, Doc. C 75/REP, at 39.

132. Ibid., at 38–40.

133. See generally FAO, Committee on Fisheries, 11th session, 19–26 April 1977, on the 'Review of the state of exploitation of the world fish resources: living resources of the Southern Ocean', Verbatim of discussion, 21–22 April 1977; see

particularly the statements by Argentina and Chile, at 3–10, and 14–20, respectively.

134. Statement by Argentina cit., note 133 supra, citing notes from that government to UNDP and FAO of 1976, at 6–7.
135. Statement by Senegal, source cit., note 133 supra, at 12; see also the statements by Guinea, at 25, and Sri Lanka, at 37.
136. Statement by Uruguay, source cit., note 133 supra, at 40–41. Uruguay became a signatory of the Treaty on 11 January 1980.
137. See the following technical documents: FAO, Committee on Fisheries: *Review of the state of exploitation of the world fish resources: living resources of the Southern Ocean,* Doc. COFI/77/5, Sup. 2, March 1977; FAO/UNDP: *Los Mares australes: los recursos vivos de los mares australes,* Doc. GLO/SO/77/1, 1979; FAO/UNDP: *Los mares australes: la recolección del krill,* Doc. GLO/SO/77/2, 1979; FAO/UNDP: *Los mares australes: la utilización del krill,* Doc. GLO/SO/77/3, 1979; FAO: *Global research, Southern Ocean Fisheries Survey Programme,* Doc. UNDP DP/GLO/Final Report/5, 24 May 1979.
138. On the FAO programme on the Exclusive Economic Zone see generally Tony Loftas: 'FAO's EEZ Programme', *Marine Policy,* Vol. 5, 1981, 229–239; Kenneth C. Lucas and Tony Loftas: 'FAO's EEZ Program: helping to build the fisheries of the future', *Ocean Year-book,* 3, 1982, 38–76.
139. United Nations Environment Programme: *The proposed programme,* Note by the Executive Director, Doc. UNEP/GC/31, 11 February, 1975.
140. Ibid., at 58.
141. UNEP, Doc. GC/44, 20 February 1975, at 3.
142. UNEP, Doc. GC/30, 4 February 1975, at 19.
143. For an account of this initiative see Mitchell, op. cit., note 109 supra, at 73.
144. See the comments by Bush, op. cit., note 33 supra, Vol. 1, at 328.
145. Recommendation VIII-13, first preambular paragraph.
146. See, for example, the article published in *The Siren,* a publication of UNEP's Regional Seas Programme, cit., Chapter 3 supra, note 192.
147. UNITAR, Doc. A/36/143, September 1981, and General Assembly Resolution 36/107, 10 December 1981. For comments on this study see Angel Ernesto Molinari: 'Antartida Argentina, una esperanza en peligro', *Geopolítica,* Vol. X, Nº 30, 1984, 51–53, at 52; Miryam O. Colacrai de Trevisan: 'La cuestión antártica en el ámbito de las Naciones Unidas', *Revista Argentina de Estudios Estratégicos,* Vol. 1, Nº 2 October–December 1984, 36–45, at 41–42. See also generally ibid., 'El ingreso de la Antártida a la escena mundial', *Rivista di Studi Politici Internazionali,* Vol. 50, July–September 1983, 386–396.
148. A tacit agreement to the effect that Antarctic would be left out of the Law of the Sea Conference has also been reported; see Mitchell, op. cit., note 109 supra, at 42.
149. See Doc. A/CONF.62/C.2/L.98 and Add. 1–3, 18 April 1978. The map published by the Secretariat illustrating the outer limit of the continental shelf according to the various formulae proposed, including the case of Antarctica, had at first the following explanation: 'Maps illustrating proposed limits of national jurisdiction over the continental shelf'. One Antarctic Treaty Consultative Party, not recognizing claims to national sovereignty or jurisdiction, objected informally to this wording because it could have implied that there was a recognition of national jurisdiction over the Antarctic continental shelf. The explanation was changed to read 'Maps illustrating various formulae for the definition of the continental shelf'. In view of this objection, the document has followed an approach similar to that of Article IV of the Antarctic Treaty by stating: 'The study, including the maps, has no legal implications, and should not be interpreted as prejudicing the

position of any delegation or State as regards the applicability of the various formulae to specific areas or in any other way'.

150. United Nations General Assembly: Statement by Mr H. Shirley Amerasinghe (Sri Lanka), Doc. A/PV. 2380, 8 October 1975, at 13–16.

151. Australia: Report of the Senate standing committee on Foreign Affairs and Defence on United Nations involvement with Australia's territories, 1976; see Bush, op. cit., note 33 supra, Vol. 1, at 504. See also the Australian parliamentary question on the revision of the Antarctic Treaty and related developments, of 29 February 1984, *A.F.A.R.*, Vol. 55, March 1984, 247–248.

152. Both Malaysia and Tanzania made statements concerning Antarctica during the signing ceremonies of the Law of the Sea Convention in Montego Bay, Jamaica, December 1982. Malaysia also addressed the issue in a speech made by its Prime Minister to the UN General Assembly on 29 September 1982. For accounts on these initiatives, see Peter J. Beck: 'Antarctica: a case for the UN?', *The World Today,* April 1984, 165–172, at 169–170; Mitchell, op. cit., note 109 supra, at 42–43.

153. Final communiqué of the seventh meeting of Heads of State or Government of the Non-Aligned Movement, New Delhi, 7–12 March 1983, Section on Antarctica, UN Doc. A/38/132, Section III, pars. 122, 123; the text is also published in *Environmental Policy and Law,* Vol. 11, 1983, at 54. See also the Communiqué adopted by the Meeting of Ministers and Head of Delegation of the Non-Aligned countries to the thirty-eighth session of the UN General Assembly, October 4–7, 1983, Doc. A/38/495, S/16035, 12 October 1983, pars. 87, 88.

154. See Beck, loc. cit., note 152 supra, at 170, comparing the Malaysian statement at the U.N. of 1982 with the Declaration of the Non-Aligned in 1983, the latter being more general and less critical of the 1959 Treaty, with particular reference to the role played by Argentina in this change of approach.

155. Address by the Hon. Lester Bird, outgoing chairman of the organization of Eastern Caribbean States at the meeting of the Authority in Dominica, 26 May 1983, Ministry of Foreign Affairs, Antigua and Barbuda, mimeo. On this and related developments in the Caribbean, see Mitchell, op. cit., note 109 supra, at 43–44.

156. UN General Assembly: *Request for the inclusion of a supplementary item: Antarctica,* Letter dated 11 August 1983 from the representatives of Antigua and Barbuda and Malaysia, Doc. A/38/193, 9 August 1983.

157. UN General Assembly: *Peaceful settlement of disputes between States,* Letter dated 19 September 1983 from the Permanent Representative of Australia on behalf of the Consultative Parties to the Antarctic Treaty, Doc. A/38/439, 21 September 1983; see also: *Question of Antarctica,* Letter dated 5 October 1983 from the Permanent representative of Australia, Doc. A/38/439, Rev. 1, 10 October 1983.

158. Reservations have also been expressed by means of various published articles on the UN initiative; see, for example, Y. Deporov 'Antarctica: a zone of peace and cooperation', *International Affairs* (USSR), N° 11, 1983, 29–37, at 37; Fernando Zegers: '*La comunidad internacional y la antártica*', in Francisco Orrego Vicuña, María Teresa Infante, Pilar Armanet (eds): *Política Antártica de Chile,* 1985, 277–287, at 285–287, R. Tucker Scully: Statement before the Subcommittee on Fisheries and Wildlife Conservation and the environment, Committee on Merchant Marine and Fisheries, U.S. House of Representatives, *Hearings on Antarctic Marine Living Resources* (H.R. 3416), June 30, 1983, at 51–52; Rainer Lagoni: 'Die Vereinten Nationen und die Antarktis', *Europa-Archiv,* Vol. 39, 1984, 473–482, with particular reference to the legal problems of UN competence in the matter in view of existing territorial claims.

159. On the 1983 debate see UN General Assembly: official records of the thirty-eighth session, First Committee, 42nd–46th meeting, 28–30 November 1983, Docs. A/C. 1/38/PV. 42–46, 29 December 1983–7 January 1984; on the 1984 debate see UN General Assembly: official records of the thirty-ninth session, First Committee, 50th meeting, 52nd–55th meeting, 28–30 November 1984, Docs. A/C. 1/39/PV. 50, 52–55, 30 November–3 December 1984; on the 1985 debate see UN General Assembly: official records of the fortieth sessions, First Committee, 48th–54th meeting, 25–29 November 1985, Docs. A/C. 1/40/PV. 48–54, 29 November–4 December 1985.

160. For accounts and discussion of the UN debate and related developments see generally K. S. R. Menon: 'The Scramble for Antarctica', *South,* April 1982, 11–13; Peter J. Beck: 'Antarctica's Indian Summer', *Contemporary Review,* Vol. 243, Nº 1415, December 1983, 297–299; ibid., loc. cit., note 152 supra; ibid.: 'The United Nations and Antarctica', *Pol.Rec.,* Vol. 22, Nº 137, May 1984, 137–144; ibid.: 'Antarctica at the UN', *B.A.S. Club Newsletter,* Nº 15, Spring 1984, 27–28; ibid.: 'Antarctica since the Falklands conflict: the continent's emerging role in international politics', British International Studies Association Conference, University of Durham, December 1984; ibid.: 'The United Nations' Study on Antarctica, 1984', *Pol.Rec.,* Vol. 22, Nº 140, May 1985, 499–504; Lee Kimball 'Antarctica: summary and comment on background and recent developments', International Institute for Environment and Development, April 6, 1984; ibid., Reports cit., note 59 supra; ibid.: 'Unfreezing international cooperation in Antarctica', *The Christian Science Monitor,* August 1, 1983; Zain-Azraai: 'The Antarctic Treaty System from the perspective of a State not party to the system', in US Polar Research Board, op. cit., note 57 supra, 305–313; Lagoni, loc. cit., note 158 supra. See also Philip W. Quigg: *Antarctica, the Continuing experiment,* Foreign Policy Association, Headline Series, Nº 273, March–April 1985.

161. UN General Assembly: Resolution 38/77, 15 December 1983; see also the following related documents: Draft resolution, A/C1/38/L.80, 28 November 1983; amendment by Sierra Leone on behalf of the African Group, on the question of the participation of South Africa, tabled and later withdrawn, A/C.1/38/L.84, 30 November 1983 an issue which was to become very contentious later in the debate; Report of the First Committee, A/38/646, 12 December 1983; adoption by the General Assembly, A/38/PV.97, 20 December 1983. See also UN Department of Public Information, Press Release, GA/PS/2437, 30 November 1983.

162. See also UN General Assembly: Resolution 39/152 on the Question of Antarctica, adopted by consensus on 17 December 1984; the terms of this resolution are virtually identical to those of Resolution 38/77, with the exception of minor changes; see also the draft resolution in Doc. A/C.1/39/L. 83, 30 November 1984.

163. United Nations. *Question of Antarctica, Report of the Secretary General,* Doc. A/39/583, Part I, 31 October 1984. For the Views of States see Part II, Vol. I, 28 October 1984; Vol. II, 2 November 1984. Vol. III, 9 November 1984. (Hereinafter cited as *Views of States.*)

164. Organization of African Unity, 42nd Assembly of the Council of Ministers, Addis-Ababa, 10–17 July 1985, Declaration on Antarctica; 21st Summit Meeting, Addis Ababa, 18–20 July 1985, Declaration on Antarctica.

165. Ministerial Conference of the Non-Aligned countries, Final Communiqué, Luanda, 4–7 September 1985, Declaration on Antarctica. See also the Political Declaration of the Eighth Conference of Heads of State or Government of

Non-Aligned countries, Harare, 1–6 September 1986; and the decision of the Council of Ministers of the League of Arab States, Tunis, 17–18 September 1986.

166. For a summary of the UN General Assembly general debate on Antarctica see Kimball, report of 8 November 1985 cit., note 59 supra, at 8.

167. Australia: draft resolution on the Question of Antarctica, A/C.1/40/L.84, 27 November 1985.

168. Resolution on the Question of Antarctica, A/Res/40/156A, 27 November 1985. This Resolution was carried by 80 votes in favour, none against, 9 abstentions, 35 countries not participating in the vote, 33 absent. The updated report was issued by the UN Secretary General on 7 November 1986, as cited in note 59 supra.

169. Resolution on the Question of Antarctica, A/Res/40/156B, 27 November 1985. This Resolution was carried by 78 votes in favour, none against, 10 abstentions, 35 countries not participating in the vote, 34 absent. See also the Resolutions contained in documents A/C.1/41/L.86 and L.87, both of 18 November 1986, on the Question of Antarctica, the latter requesting a moratorium on minerals negotiations.

170. Resolution on the Question of Antarctica, A/Res/40/156C, 27 November 1985. This Resolution was carried by 81 votes in favour, none against, 9 abstentions, 36 countries not participating in the vote, 31 absent.

171. The Consultative Parties to the Antarctic Treaty decided not to participate in the vote of the resolutions adopted in 1985; however, China abstained in Resolutions 156A and 156B, and together with India voted in favour of Resolution 156C. The non-consultative parties to the 1959 Treaty in general also did not participate in the votes, a policy also followed by some other countries; however, Peru and Romania voted in favour of 156A, Peru abstained and Romania was in favour of 156B, and both countries voted in favour of 156C. For the voting record in the First Committee see the *Report* of the Committee, Doc. A/40/996, 9 December 1985. A similar decision of non-participation was adopted by all the treaty parties in 1986 at the forty-first session of the UN General Assembly, with only two countries casting an abstention vote.

172. Beck, loc. cit., note 152 supra, at 172.

173. See generally Zain-Azraai, loc. cit., note 160 supra.

174. See, for example, the statement by Pakistan, UN Doc. A/C.1/39/PV.54, 30 November 1984, at 21; *Views of States:* Pakistan, UN. Doc. A/39/583, Part II, Vol. III, 9 November 1984, at 35.

175. On the policy and arguments of the Consultative Parties see generally Beck, loc. cit., note 160 supra *(Pol.Rec. 1985.)*.

176. See generally the studies cit., note 160 supra; see also Zain Azraai: 'Antarctica: the claims of "expertise" v. "interest"', in Gillian Triggs (ed.): *The Antarctic Treaty Regime*, 1987, 211–217; and ibid.: 'The future of the Antarctic Treaty System. The Malaysian Perspective', in Lewis M. Alexander and Lynne Carter Hanson (eds): *Antarctic Politics and Marine Resources: critical choices for the 1980's*, 1985, 232–237.

177. C. D. Beeby: 'An overview of the problems which should be addressed in the preparation of a regime governing the mineral resources of Antarctica', in Francisco Orrego Vicuña, op. cit., note 90 supra, 191–198, at 196–198; Francisco Orrego Vicuña: 'The definition of a regime on Antarctic mineral resources: basic options', in ibid., op. cit., 199–215, at 209–212; Keith Brennan: 'Criteria for access to the resources of Antarctica: alternatives, procedure and experience applicable', in Francisco Orrego Vicuña, op. cit., 217–227, at 225–227; see also C. D. Beeby: 'Towards an Antarctic mineral resources regime', *N.Z.I.R.*, Vol. VII, N° 3, May–June 1982, 4–6.

178. See generally Chapter IX supra; see also Peter Bruckner: 'The Antarctic Treaty System from the perspective of a Non-Consultative Party to the Antarctic Treaty', in US Polar Research Board, op. cit., note 57 supra, 315–335.

179. See, for example, Statement by Malaysia, UN Doc. A/C.1/38/PV.42, 29 December 1983, at 16.

180. See, for example, Statement by Ghana, UN Doc. A/C.1/38/PV.43, 29 December 1983, at 21.

181. See, for example, *Views of States:* Antigua and Barbuda, country which suggested that the supreme decision-making body should be made out of existing Contracting Parties as permanent members and representatives of regions as non-permanent members; UN Doc. A/39/583, Part II, Vol. I, 29 October 1984, at 3.

182. See, for example, *Views of States:* Kenya, which advocates that the Antarctic regime should be representative in character and should encompass the whole membership of the United Nations; UN Doc. A/39/583, Part II, Vol. II, 2 November 1984, at 106.

183. See *Views of States:* Malaysia, UN Doc. A/39/583, Part II, Vol. II, 2 November 1984, at 108.

184. *Views of States:* Ghana, UN Doc. A/39/583, Part II, Vol. II, 2 November 1984, at 83.

185. See, for example, *Views of States:* Australia, UN Doc. A/39/583, Part II, Vol. I, 29 October 1984, at 86–91; *Views of States:* Chile, UN Doc. A/39/583, Part II, Vol. II, 2 November 1984, at 20–21, 28–33; Statement by the United Kingdom, UN Doc. A/C.1/39/PV.52, 30 November 1984, at 18–37; *Views of States:* New Zealand, UN Doc. A/39/583, Part II, Vol. III, 9 November 1984, at 15. For a reply to the various criticisms to the Treaty System, see also generally Statement by Australia, UN Doc. A/C.1/40/PV.48, 29 November 1985, and Statement by the United Kingdom, UN Doc. A/C.1/40/PV.53, 4 December 1985.

186. See Francisco Orrego Vicuña: 'The Antarctic Treaty System: a viable alternative for the regulation of resource orientated activities', in Triggs, op. cit., note 176 supra, 65–76; see also Rolf Trolle Andersen: 'The Antarctic scene, legal and political facts', in British Institute, op. cit., at 11–12 (draft version).

187. See, for example, Statement by Sierra Leone, UN Doc. A/C.1/38/PV.42, 29 December 1983, at 37; Statement by Sri Lanka, UN Doc. A/C.1/39/PV.50, 30 November 1984, at 43–45; *Views of States:* Bangladesh, UN Doc. A/39/583, Part II, Vol. I, 29 October 1984, at 92.

188. See Resolution 156C cit., note 170 supra; see also Resolution A/C.1/41/L.88, cit., note 170 supra; for earlier efforts in this direction see the drafts cit., note 161 supra.

189. See the statement by Japan to the extent that since the Antarctic Treaty does not envisage that a Party may be deprived of its status on account of a particular policy, it is not appropriate for the UN General Assembly to make a request to that effect. UN Doc. A/C.1/40/PV.51, 4 December 1985, at 35.

190. Alvaro de Soto: Statement at the Earthscan seminar on Antarctic resources and the environment, Washington DC, 14 September 1979, at 13.

191. Statement by Ghana, UN Doc. A/C.1/38/PV.43, 29 December 1983, at 20.

192. For a reply to the various criticisms made to the Antarctic Treaty System, see generally *Views of States:* Australia, Doc. cit., note 185 supra, at 86–91.

193. See, for example, Statement by Indonesia, UN Doc. A/C.1/38/PV.43, 29 December 1983, at 6.

194. See generally Orrego, loc. cit., note 186 supra.

195. Ibid., at 70–71.

196. *Views of States:* Malaysia, UN Doc. A/39/583, Part II, Vol. II, 2 November 1984, at 110.
197. Zain Azraai, loc. cit., note 160 supra, at 305; see also Zain Azraai, loc. cit., note 176 supra, at 3.
198. For a discussion about the role of a trustee in the Antarctic context, see generally Rudiger Wolfrum, loc. cit., note 99 supra, and the Comment by Christopher Pinto in Wolfrum, op. cit., note 99 supra, at 164–165.
199. Zain Azraai, loc. cit., note 160 supra, at 183.
200. See Orrego, loc. cit., note 186 supra, at 72–73.
201. Ian Brownlie: *Principles of Public International Law,* 1979, at 622.
202. Orrego, loc. cit., note 186 supra, at 73.
203. Statement by the United Kingdom, UN Doc. A/C.1/39/PV.52, 30 November 1984, at 33–35. For a summary of the UK statement see also United Kingdom Materials on International Law, *B.Y.B.I.L.,* Vol. 54, 1983, 490–495.
204. Zain Azraai, loc. cit., note 160 supra, at 180–181.
205. Orrego, loc. cit., note 186 supra, at 71.
206. In the course of the UN discussion on Antarctica numerous references were made to the concept of the common heritage of mankind. For references supporting the application of such concept to Antarctica see, for example, Statement by the Philippines, UN Doc. A/C.38/PV.44, 30 December 1983, at 7; Statement by Pakistan, UN Doc. A/C.1/39/PV.54, 3 December 1984, at 18; *Views of States:* Egypt, UN Doc. A/39/583, Part II, Vol. II, 2 November 1984, at 46. For references opposing this application see, for example, *Views of States:* Argentina UN Doc. A/39/583, Part II, Vol. I, 29 October 1984, at 25; *Views of States:* Brazil, Ibid., Vol. II, 2 November 1984, at 12;*Views of States:* German Democratic Republic, Ibid., Vol. II, 2 November 1984, at 71. See also generally Stephen A. Zorn: 'Antarctic minerals, A common heritage approach', *Resources Policy,* Vol. 10, N° 1, March 1984, 2–18.
207. See generally Seyom Brown, Nina W. Cornell, Larry L. Fabian, Edith Brown Weiss: *Regimes for the Ocean, Outer Space, and Weather,* 1977; Garrett Hardin and John Baden (eds.): *Managing the Commons,* 1977; Bradley Larschan and Bonnie C. Brennan: 'The common heritage of mankind principle in international law', *C.J.T.L.,* Vol. 21, 1982–1983, 305–337; René-Jean Dupey: 'La notion de patrimoine commun de l'humanité appliqué aux fonds marins', in *Droit et libertés a la fin du XXe siecle,* Etude offertes a Claude-Albert Colliard, 1984, 197–205 (English version in C. L. Rozakis and C. A. Stephanou (eds): *The New Law of the Sea,* 1983, 199–208); René-Jean Dupuy: 'La Zone, patrimoine commun de l'humanité', in René-Jean Dupuy and Daniel Vignes (eds): *Traité du Nouveau Droit de la Mer,* 1985, 499–505; Arvid Pardo and Carl Q. Christol: 'The common interest: tension between the whole and the parts', in R. St. J. MacDonald and Douglas M. Johnston: *The Structure and Process of International Law,* 1983, 643–660; Rudiger Wolfrum: 'The principle of the common heritage of mankind', *Z.A.O.R.V.,* 1983, 43/2, 312–337; Roderick Ogley: *Internationalizing the sea-bed,* 1984; Felipe Paolillo: 'Naturaleza jurídica del principio del patrimonio común de la humanidad', *Anuario Hispano Luso Americano de Derecho Internacional,* N° 7, 1984, 353–377; Alexandre-Charles Kiss: 'La notion de patrimoine commun de l'humanité, *Rec. Cours. Ac. D.I.,* 1982-II, 99–256.
208. For discussion of this argument, see Paolillo, loc. cit., note 207 supra, at 377. This is generally the underlying thought of the argument supporting the application of the principle to Antarctica, as evidenced by the UN debate, for which see note 206 supra.
209. Mitchell, op. cit., note 109 supra, at 91–97.
210. See note 206 supra.

211. For a discussion of this view in the context of the work of the UN General Assembly and State practice, see Paolillo, loc. cit., note 207 supra, at 358–367.

212. James L. Malone: 'Freedom and opportunity: the foundation for a dynamic national oceans policy', address to the Eighteenth Annual Meeting of the Law of the Sea Institute, in Robert B. Krueger and Stefan A. Riesenfeld: *The Developing Order of the Oceans,* 1985, 85–94, at 86.

213. UN Law of the Sea Conference: Chile: draft article on *Jus Cogens,* Doc. FC/14, 20 August 1979.

214. Orrego, loc. cit., note 186 supra, at 74; see also S. Muller: 'The impact of UNCLOS III on the Antarctic regime', in Rudiger Wolfrum, op. cit., note 99 supra, at 171.

215. Article 311, par. 6, of the Convention on the Law of the Sea provides: 'The States Parties to this Convention agree that there can be no amendments to the basic principle relating to the common heritage of mankind set forth in article 136 and that they shall not be party to any agreement in derogation thereof'.

216. Gillian Triggs: 'The Antarctic Treaty Regime: a workable compromise or a "Purgatory of Ambiguity"?', Case *W.R.J.I.L.,* Vol. 17, 1985, 195–228, at 217–218 (footnotes omitted).

217. Ibid., at 218.

218. Ibid., at 218.

219. See generally O. J. Lissitzyn: 'The American position in outer space and Antarctica', Editorial comment, *A.J.I.L.,* Vol. 53, 1959, 126–131, an author who considered that the comparison between Antarctica and outer space is not convincing on the grounds of the existence of claims and other aspects; Thomas R. Adams: 'The Outer Space Treaty: an interpretation in light of the no-sovereignty provision', Comment, *Har. I.L.J.,* Vol. 9, 1968, 140–157; Myres S. McDougal, Harold D. Lasswell, Ivan A. Vlasic, Joseph C. Smith: 'The enjoyment and acquisition of resources in outer space', *University of Pennsylvania Law Review,* Vol. 111, 1963, 521–636, particularly at 588–589; S. Houston Lay and Howard J. Taubenfeld: *The law relating to activities of man in space,* 1970, 59–62; H. Gerald Staub: 'The Antarctic Treaty as precedent to the outer space treaty', in *Proceedings of the seventeenth colloquium on the Law of Outer Space,* International Institute of Space Law, October 1–4, 1974, 1975, 282–287; Imre Anthony Csabafi: *The concept of State Jurisdiction in International Space Law,* 1971; Richard B. Bilder: 'Emerging legal problems of the deep seas and polar regions', in R. B. Lillich and J. N. Moore (eds): *U.S. Naval War College International Law Studies,* Vol. 61, 1980, 504–519, at 512. See also generally Nicolas Mateesco Matte: 'The Law of the Sea and Outer Space: a comparative survey of specific issues', *Ocean Yearbook,* 3, 1982, 13–37.

220. Francisco Orrego Vicuña: *Los Fondos Marinos y Oceánicos,* 1976, at 256, with reference to the United Nations debate on the sea-bed and the influence of the Antarctic Treaty.

221. Ibid., loc. cit., note 186 supra, at 74; see also General Statement by Australia, UN Doc. A/C.1/40/PV.48, 29 November 1985.

222. Rainer Lagoni: 'Antarctica's mineral resources in international law', *Z.A.O.R.V.,* Vol. 39, 1979, 1–37, at 34.

223. Ralph L. Harry: 'The Antarctic regime and the Law of the Sea Convention: an Australian view', *Virg.J.I.L.,* Vol. 21, 1981, 727–744, at 735–736; Roland Rich: 'A minerals regime for Antarctica', *I.C.L.Q.,* Vol. 31, 1982, 709–725, at 712–719; Luz O'Shea: 'El patrimonio común de la humanidad y la Antártica', research paper, Institute of International Studies of the University of Chile, graduate programme, 17 August 1983; Orrego, loc. cit., note 186 supra, at 65–66. Most of the authors agree, however, that sovereignty will not be the single

controlling factor of activities in Antarctica and that co-operation is an essential component of such arrangements. See also in relation to sovereignty and co-operation Shirley Oakes Butler: 'Owning Antarctica: co-operation and jurisdiction at the South Pole', *J. Int. Af.,* Vol. 31, 1977, 35–51; Rudy J. Cerone: 'Survival of the Antarctic Treaty: economic self-interest v. enlightened international cooperation', *Bost.Coll. I.C.L.R.,* Vol. 2, 1978–1979, 115–129.

224. Lagoni, loc. cit., note 222 supra, at 34; Gillian Triggs: 'The Antarctic Treaty system: some jurisdictional problems', in ibid. (ed.), op. cit., note 176 supra, 88–109, at 98–105. For the summary of the arguments of the Treaty Parties at the UN debate on this matter, see also Lee Kimball, report cit., note 160 supra (6 April 1984), at 7. See also, however, UN Report cit., note 59 supra, where the argument is made that maritime areas subject to national jurisdiction and the regime applicable beyond is unclear in Antarctica at pars. 145, 151.

225. See generally 'Thaw in international law? Rights in Antarctica under the Law of Common Spaces', *Y.L.J.,* Vol. 87, 1977–1978, 804–859, particularly at 818–820, 847.

226. O'Shea, loc. cit., note 223 supra, at 17–22; Rich, loc. cit., note 223 supra, at 713–714.

227. Harry, loc. cit., note 223 supra, at 736; see also Gillian Triggs: 'Australian sovereignty in Antarctica: traditional principles of territorial acquisition versus a "common heritage" ', in Stuart Harris (ed.): *Australia's Antarctic Policy Options,* A.N.U., 1984, 29–66, at 57; Triggs, loc. cit., note 224 supra, 104.

228. Triggs, loc. cit., note 216 supra, at 224–225; ibid., loc. cit., note 227 supra, at 58.

229. For other general aspects of the discussion, see also 'Antarctica – a continent of international harmony?', *A.F.A.R.,* February 1980, 4–12; Hervé Coutau-Bégarie: 'L'Antarctique, dernière terre à prendre', *Defense Nationale,* December 1984, 85–98; UK Foreign and Commonwealth Office: 'Antarctic Treaty: 25th. Anniversary', background brief, November 1984; Barbara Mitchell: 'The Southern Ocean in the 1980's', *Ocean Yearbook,* 3, 1982, 349–385; ibid.: 'The Antarctic Treaty: victim of its own success?', in Alexander and Hanson, op. cit., note 176 supra, 13–21; Karla Bell: 'Antarctica: getting into hot water', *Chain Reaction* Supplement, undated, 21–28; Michael Donoghue: 'The last gold rush', *La Sirena* (UNEP's Regional Seas Programme), N° 26, December 1984, 11–20; Mairuth Sarsfield: 'Cuál es el futuro del Tratado de la Antártida?', *La Sirena* cit., 26–30.

230. Paolillo, loc. cit., note 207 supra, at 370–375.

231. Loc. cit., note 225 supra, at 829–833.

232. See generally the works cited in note 207 supra, and in particular Kiss, loc. cit., note 207 supra, at 135; Larschan and Brennan, loc. cit., note 207 supra, at 305; Statement by Malaysia, UN Doc. A/C.1/38/PV.42, 29 December 1983, at 20; *Views of States:* Pakistan, UN Doc. A/39/583, Part II, Vol. III, 9 November 1984, at 35; *Views of States:* Zambia, UN Doc. cit., at 138.

233. Resolution 156B cit., note 169 supra, par. 1. See also Resolution A/C.1/41/L.87, 18 November 1986, par. 1.

234. Christopher Pinto: 'Comment', in Wolfrum, op. cit., note 99 supra, 164–168, at 166–167. For a reply to some earlier views of Pinto, see Finn Sollie: 'The political problems of Antarctica', Fridtjof Nansen Foundation, 1977; see also generally ibid.: 'Polar politics: old games in new territories, or new patterns in political development?', *International Journal,* Vol. 39, 1984, 695–720.

235. Evan Luard: 'Who owns the Antarctic?', *For. Af.,* Summer 1984, 1175–1193, at 1186. The main criticism to the legal foundation of an Antarctic mineral regime based on the Treaty system is, according to Luard's view, that 'critics could point

out that even the Treaty itself does not make any provision for mineral exploitation. Nor does it put forward any claim to control over the resources of the area', ibid., at 1186–1187. See, however, the legal foundation explained in Chapter 2 supra.

236. Larschan and Brennan, loc. cit., note 207 supra, at 332–334.

237. See generally Magnus Wijkman: 'Managing the global commons', *O.I.,* Vol. 36, 1982, 511–536; Pardo and Christol, loc. cit., note 207 supra; Nicholas de B. Katzenbach: 'Sharable and strategic resources: outer space, polar areas, and the oceans' *Proc. A.S.I.L.,* 1959, 206–212; R. N. Bing: *Role of the developing states in the formulation of international controls for unoccupied regions: outer space, the ocean floor, and Antarctica,* Ph.D.Thesis, Tufts University, 1972; Lee Kimball, loc. cit., note 98 supra; Mary Victoria White: 'The Common heritage of mankind: an assessment', *Case W.R.J.I.L.,* Vol. 14, 1982, 509–542; Keith D. Suter: 'The Antarctic: a public policy problem for Australia in the 1980's', in R. A. Herr, R. Hall and B. W. Davis (eds): *Issues in Australia's marine and Antarctic policies,* 1982, 101–137; Eleonore Schlaich: 'Mineral resource policy in the Antarctic: common heritage of mankind or area of "frozen" economic nationalism?', Essay, MSc degree, international relations, London School of Economics and Political Science, 1984, unpublished.

238. Perú: *Declaration of the Constitutional Assembly on Antarctica,* 3 May 1979; text in Edgardo Mercado Jarrin et al.: *El Perú y la Antártica,* 1984, at 257.

239. Perú: note of accession to the Antarctic Treaty, 10 April 1981, and particularly see the Press Communiqué of 11 April 1981; texts in Mercado, op. cit., note 238 supra, at 259–261; see also the Peruvian statement as an observer to the XII Antarctic Treaty Consultative Meeting, 13–27 September 1983, in *Revista Peruana de Derecho Internacional,* Vol. XXXV, July–September 1983, 46–49. On the Peruvian policies in relation to Antarctica, see generally Gonzalo Fernandez Puyó: 'Evaluación del proceso antártico sudamericano', *Revista Peruana* cit., Vol. XXXII, July–September 1980, 45–54; ibid.: 'El Perú y el proceso antártico', *Revista Peruana,* cit., Vol. XXXV, July–September 1983, 15–28 (also published in Mercado, op. cit., note 238 supra, 147–162); ibid.: 'Interés internacional por la antártica', *Revista de la Academia Diplomática del Perú,* Nº 23, January–December 1984, 73–84; Alberto Ruiz Eldredge: 'Regimen internacional de la antártica y principios esenciales para la administración internacional de dicho continente', in Mercado, op. cit., note 238 supra, 163–184; Juan Miguel Bákula: 'La Antártica y el Derecho del Mar', in Mercado, op. cit., note 238 supra, 225–248; Enrique Bernales, José de la Puente, Manuel Ulloa, Andrés Townsend: 'El Nuevo Derecho del Mar, la Antártica y el Perú frente a la Cuenca del Pacífico', in Centro Peruano de Estudios Internacionales: *Perú: Perspectivas de política exterior,* 1985, 58–78.

240. Ian Brownlie: 'Legal status of natural resources in international law', *Rec.Cours Ac. D.I.,* 1979-I, 245–317, at 289–292.

241. Ibid., at 292–293.

242. Kiss, loc. cit., note 207 supra, at 142–144.

243. Ibid., at 144.

244. *1984 Draft Articles,* Article XIII, par. 1 (p); the *1986 Draft Articles* link the disposition of funds more closely with the promotion of research, Article 22, par. 1 (j).

245. Beeby, loc. cit., note 177 supra, at 197–198; Orrego, loc. cit., note 177 supra, at 210; Brennan, loc. cit., note 177 supra, at 224–225.

246. See generally Chapter 6 supra, section 6.2. See also Antarctic and Southern Ocean Coalition: *The Antarctic Fund,* February 26, 1985.

247. Frank Pollone: 'Resource exploitation: the threat to the legal regime of Antarctica', *Conn. L. Rev.*, Vol. 10, 1978, 401–417, at 414; (also published in *Manitoba Law Journal*, Vol. 7, 1976, 597–610).

248. It has been suggested that funds could be used to finance schemes that would enable developing countries to undertake research in Antarctica and for transfer of technology in exploitation; see Luard, loc. cit., note 235 supra, at 1192. It has also been suggested that the entire international community benefit might be allocated to a single purpose, such as the UN High Commissioner for Refugees; see Francis Auburn: 'The Antarctic minerals regime: sovereignty, exploration, institutions and environment', in Harris, op. cit., note 227 supra, 271–300, at 289.

249. *Views of States:* Antigua and Barbuda, UN Doc. A/39/583, Part II, Vol. I, 29 October 1984, at 3–4.

250. Kiss, loc. cit., note 207 supra, at 144–145. Translation from French by the author of this book.

251. Orrego, loc. cit., note 186 supra, at 157–158.

252. For additional comments on the trends emerging from the current debate, see Ernest Friedrich Jung: 'Die Antarktis in der internationalen politik', *Aussenpolitik,* Vol. 35, 1984, 80–86; F. M. Auburn: 'Antarctic minerals and the Third World'. *FRAM, The Journal of Polar Studies,* Winter 1984, 201–223. See also Oscar Pinochet de la Barra: 'Algunas reflexiones sobre el problema de la antártica en el año 2000', in Francisco Orrego Vicuña (ed.): *La Antártica y sus recursos,* 1983, 355–367; Vicente Palermo: 'El futuro del continente antártico', *Geopolítica,* Buenos Aires, Vol. VI, N° 18, June 1980, 45–55; Jorge A. Fraga: 'Antártica 1991. El factor económico', *Geopolítica,* Vol. X, N° 30, 1984, 47–50.

253. Konstantin Theile: *Possibilities for an internationalization of Antarctica,* Thesis (in German), St Gallen, 20 April 1977. See also, for example, Statement by Ghana, UN Doc. A/C.1/38/PV.43, 29 December 1983, at 23. For a summary of the UN debate on this and other points, see also note 160 supra.

254. Orrego, loc. cit., note 186 supra, at 75.

255. Statement by Sierra Leone, UN Doc. A/C.1/38/PV.42, 29 December 1983, at 35. See also note 15 supra and associated text.

256. Jozef Goldblat: 'The arms-control experiment in the Antarctic', *SIPRI Yearbook,* 1973, 477–486; ibid.: 'Troubles in the Antarctic?', *Bulletin of Peace Proposals,* 1973, N° 3, 286–288.

257. See, for example, Statement by the Philippines, UN Doc. A/C.1/38/PV.44, 30 December 1983, at 6; Statement by Trinidad and Tobago, UN Doc. A/C.1/39/PV.53, 30 November 1984, at 26. See also Robert Guyer: 'Antarctica's role in international relations', in Francisco Orrego Vicuña, op. cit., note 90 supra, 267–279, at 274; Francisco Orrego Vicuña: 'Antarctic conflict and international cooperation', in US Polar Research Board, op. cit., note 57 supra, 55–64. For a reference to the status of the basic principles of the Antarctic Treaty in customary law, see the Statement by Italy, UN Doc. A/C.1/40/PV.49, 29 November 1985, at 2; and see further Chapter 9 supra.

258. Jon Tinker: 'Antarctica: towards a new internationalism', *New Scientist,* Vol. 83, N° 1172, 13 September 1979, 799–801, at 801. For a discussion of trends in relation to the internationalization of Antarctica, see also Barbara Mitchell and Jon Tinker: *Antarctica and its resources,* International Institute for Environment and Development, 1980; Barbara Mitchell: 'Antarctica: a special case?', *New Scientist,* Vol. 73, N° 1034, 13 January 1977, 64–66; Barbara Mitchell: 'Attention on Antarctica', *New Scientist,* 22 September 1977, reprinted in the U.S. Senate: *Hearing on Exploitation of Antarctic Resources,* 1978, at 68; Barbara Mitchell: 'La Antártica, ¿Bien común?', *Mazingira,* N° 2, 1977, 70–78.

259. M. C. W. Pinto: 'The International Community and Antarctica', *Univ.Mia.L.Rev.,* Vol. 33, 1978, 475–487, at 484.
260. Pinto, loc. cit., note 234 supra, at 168.
261. Luard, loc. cit., note 235 supra, at 1188–1192.
262. Ibid., at 1191.
263. See also J. R. Rowland: 'Whither Antarctica?, Alternative strategies', in Triggs, op. cit., note 176 supra, 218–226.
264. See, for example, Statement by the Libyan Arab Jamahiriya, UN Doc. A/C.1/38/PV.44, 30 December 1983, at 16; Statement by Pakistan, UN Doc. A/C.1/39/PV.54, 3 December 1984, at 21.
265. See, for example, Statement by Oman, UN Doc. A/C.1/38/PV.55, 3 December 1984, at 2; Statement by Yugoslavia, UN.Doc. A/C.1/38/PV.45, 6 December 1983, at 16; *Views of States:* Mexico, UN Doc. A/39/583, Part II, Vol. II, 2 November 1984, at 112.
266. For proposals suggesting institutional arrangements that would include representatives of regions in the decision-making process of Antarctica, see, for example, *Views of States:* Antigua and Barbuda, UN Doc. A/39/583, Part II, Vol. I, 29 October 1984, at 3; *Views of States:* Bangladesh, UN Doc. cit., at 92.
267. Herber Arbuet, Roberto Puceiro, Belter Garé: *Antártica: continente de los más, para los menos,* Montevideo, 1979, at 115; also Heber Arbuet: 'Estatuto jurídico y situación político-jurídica de la Antártica', Comité Jurídico Interamericano, *Sexto Curso de Derecho Internacional,* 1979, 453–480, at 479.
268. Luard, loc. cit., note 235 supra, at 1190. For a discussion of the interest of Latin American states see generally Carlos J. Moneta: 'Antarctica, Latin America, and the International system in the 1980's. Toward a New Antarctic Order?', *J.I.A.S.W.A.,* Vol. 23, 1981, 29–68; Edward S. Milenky and Steven I. Schwab: 'Latin America and Antarctica' *Current History,* Vol. 82, Nº 481, February 1983, 52–53, 89–90.
269. Donat Pharand: 'L'Artique et l'Antarctique: patrimoine commun de l'humanité?', *Annals of Air and Space Law,* Vol. VII, 1982, 415–430.
270. Fernando Zegers: 'The Antarctic System and the utilization of resources', *Univ.Mia.L.Rev.,* Vol. 33, 1978, 426–473, at 439.
271. Ibid.: 'La Comunidad Internacional y la Antártica', in Francisco Orrego Vicuña, op. cit., note 50 supra, 277–287, at 286. See also R. Tucker Scully, Statement cit., note 158 supra, at 49–50.
272. See loc. cit., note 225 supra, at 844–848.
273. De Soto, loc. cit., note 190 supra, at 9–10.
274. Kurt Michael Shusterich: *Resource management and the oceans. The Political Economy of Sea-bed Mining,* 1982, particularly Chapter 6 on 'Precedents for other global commons', at 161–193.
275. See generally Carroll, loc. cit., note 102 supra.
276. Edward Honnold: 'Draft provisions of a new international convention on Antarctica', *Yale Studies in World Public order,* Vol. 4, 1977, 123–153, at 131; this article is a development of that cited in note 225 supra.
277. Mitchell, op. cit., note 109 supra, at 93–94.
278. For a discussion of these aspects see Westermeyer, op. cit., note 89 supra, at 88–89.
279. See Chapter 5 supra.
280. Frida M. Pfirter de Armas: *La situación jurídica de la antártica y el nuevo derecho del mar,* Facultad de Derecho y Ciencias Sociales del Rosario, Argentina, 1982, at 15–18. But see also the view that the jurisdiction of the Sea-bed Authority extends South of 60° S. to include the Antarctic Continent, *Views of States:* Philippines, UN Doc. A/39/583, Part II, Vol. III, 9 November 1984, at 45.

281. Brennan, loc. cit., note 177 supra, at 221–222.
282. Ibid., at 222.
283. Ibid., at 224. For the point of view that the Sea-bed Authority should have a role in the regulatory and revenue-sharing agencies of the Antarctic minerals regime see Ramesh Thakur and Hyam Gold: 'The Antarctic Treaty regime: exclusive preserve or common heritage?' *Foreign Affairs Reports* (New Delhi), Vol. 32, N° 11–12, Nov.–Dec. 1983, 169–186, at 185; a different view, however, is put forward by Beeby, loc. cit., note 177 supra, at 197.
284. Gilbert Guillaume: 'Oil as a special resource: problems and experiences', in Francisco Orrego Vicuña, op. cit., note 177 supra, 185–190, at 189–190.
285. Kurt M. Shusterich: 'The Antarctic Treaty System: history, substance, and speculation', *International Journal,* Vol. 39, 1984, 800–827, at 825–827; see also Quigg, op. cit., note 160 supra, 47–52.
286. W. F. Budd, loc. cit., note 115 supra, at 141; see also Christopher D. Beeby: 'The Antarctic Treaty System as a resource management mechanism – Non-living resources', in US Polar Research Board, op. cit., note 57 supra, 269–284.
287. See generally Orrego, loc. cit., note 186 supra, at 73–75.
288. Lagoni, loc. cit., note 222 supra, at 34–35.
289. Charney, loc. cit., note 94 supra, at 220; Pinto, loc. cit., note 234 supra, at 168. On the question of conflict, see generally Francisco Orrego Vicuña, loc. cit., note 257 supra; see also Bo Johnson Theutenberg: *The evolution of the Law of the Sea,* 1984, at 83.
290. Charney, loc. cit., note 94 supra, at 220.
291. See, for example, ibid., at 219; see also Lagoni, loc. cit., note 222 supra, at 35.
292. Charney, loc. cit., note 94 supra, at 219.
293. *Views of States:* Australia, UN Doc. A/39/583, Part II, Vol. I, 29 October 1984, at 90.
294. Charney, loc. cit., note 94 supra, at 221.
295. Lagoni, loc. cit., note 222 supra, at 35.
296. On the need of the support of Consultative Parties for any new arrangement, see Quigg, op. cit., note 160 supra, at 51.
297. See generally Barry Jones: 'Antarctic dilemma', *A.F.A.R.,* Vol. 55, 1984, 183–185.
298. For a reference to the threat of a UN parallel system, see Quigg, op. cit., note 160 supra, at 51.
299. Ibid., at 47.
300. Orrego, loc. cit., note 186 supra, at 65–66.
301. For this type of criticism see Zain-Azraai, loc. cit., note 160 supra, at 307–308; see also the Statement by Malaysia, UN Doc. A/C.1/40/PV.48, 29 November 1985, at 2–10.
302. See generally Guyer, loc. cit., note 257 supra, at 274–279.
303. Brownlie: *Principles of Public International Law,* 1979, at 637.
304. See generally Chapter 9 supra.
305. Zain-Azraai, loc. cit., note 176 supra, at 213–214; see also generally Bruckner, loc. cit., note 178 supra.
306. Francisco Orrego Vicuña: 'The application of the Law of the Sea and the Exclusive Economic Zone to the Antarctic continent', in ibid., op. cit., note 90 supra, 243–251, at 250.
307. Beeby, loc. cit., note 286 supra, at 281–283; see also generally Richard Woolcot: 'The future of the Antarctic Treaty System. One Consultative Party outlook', in Alexander and Hanson, op. cit., note 176 supra, 225–232; and 'Message from the President of the United States on the commemoration of the 25th anniversary of

the Antarctic Treaty', 1 December 1984, *Ant. J.U.S.,* Vol. XIX, N° 4, December 1984, 12–13.

308. Triggs, loc. cit., note 227 supra, at 60.
309. On the importance of 1991 for a review of the Treaty, see Orrego, loc. cit., note 91 supra, at 12–13; also Jones, loc. cit., note 297 supra, at 185.

11

Conclusions

A trend clearly emerging from the evolution of the Antarctic Treaty System and its historical background is the strengthening of the process of international co-operation in Antarctica. While the development of this process has been characterized by a slow pace during the first twenty-five years since the 1959 Treaty came into force, there has been a recent acceleration of that pace and it can only be expected that further and quicker developments will take place in the near future.

Co-operation in the Antarctic has gained, firstly, in intensity. The rather simple approach of the 1959 Antarctic Treaty and early recommendations has given place to more elaborate mechanisms in recent recommendations and, above all, in the conventions that have come to supplement the initial framework of co-operation. Greater availability of instruments and procedures has accompanied this aspect of the unfolding process of co-operation, for which purpose the Treaty system has relied on some elements of flexibility arising from the Law of Treaties and from the practice of international organizations relating to the approval, entry into force and legal effects of resolutions and other instruments. This process has also gained in extension, as can be measured by the growing number of subjects covered by various forms of co-operation and by the larger number of States acceding to the Treaty system and related instruments or becoming engaged in active work in the Antarctic. A major turning point within this evolution has been the incorporation of resource-orientated policies in the Treaty system and the negotiation of the pertinent arrangements for addressing the issues associated with this new phase of the co-operation in Antarctica.

The evolution that has taken place has had profound legal effects on the Treaty system and on the approach of participating States towards co-operation in the area. The antagonism once existing between sovereignty claims and the resulting reluctance to advance in any form of international co-operation in Antarctica, have gradually been modified by more favourable attitudes towards achieving a common understanding in relation to the activities undertaken in that continent and the Southern Ocean. Sovereignty and international co-operation in Antarctica are no longer irreconcilable concepts, but, on the contrary, have become mutually complementary in the terms that have been indicated. Because of the peculiar geographical and legal situation of Antarctica, the interaction between international law and the applicable domestic legal orders has been more intensive than is normally the case with other experiences of international co-operation.

An important consequence of the changing attitudes toward the Treaty system has been that jurisdiction by States in the area is no longer conceived in terms of a conflictive or mutually exclusive relationship between the paramount principles of jurisdiction based on nationality or on territorial sovereignty. Pragmatic formulae have been devised for reconciling the different interests existing in this respect and achieving what in fact amounts to forms of concurrent jurisdiction. This has in no way precluded the principle of nationality being more readily used in this context than other principles. The fact that the 1959 Antarctic Treaty did not attempt to settle once and for all the problem of jurisdiction in the area was considered to be a serious weakness; however, this has been, on the contrary, one of its achievements, since it has allowed for the development of pragmatic solutions of the problems at issue at different points in time, following in a sense the changes that are simultaneously taking place in international law on this very point.

The changes that have been introduced into the Law of the Sea in the light of the 1982 United Nations Convention and related developments in customary law have posed additional challenges in relation to the claims of jurisdiction and its exercise in the Southern Ocean. The different legal views held by claimant and non-claimant countries in this context have also been reconciled by means of very pragmatic negotiations on the matter. National claims to an Exclusive Economic Zone and the Continental Shelf in Antarctica have been few and always made with great restraint; for their part, the resource regimes in force have taken special care not to prejudge this or any other position, as is also the case with the minerals regime under negotiation. As a result of this process the parties to the 1959 Treaty and related conventions have turned to the exercise of various forms of joint jurisdiction under the Law of the Sea within the framework of the resource regimes, an approach which has greatly facilitated the accommodation of differing legal views and, above all, provides the legal setting for the relationship between the Treaty system and the international Law of the Sea.

The negotiations on the minerals regime have been the most difficult yet undertaken by the Treaty parties. The essence of the problem has been how to devise a mechanism that might prove to be acceptable both to claimant and non-claimant countries, while at the same time ensuring efficiency in the development of resources, legal stability and environmental safeguards. The diversity of interests that needs to be taken into consideration accounts for the enormous obstacles that have to be surmounted in order to achieve an arrangement satisfactory to all. In the first place, the fact that mineral resources are so closely linked to the concepts of sovereignty and territorial jurisdiction has meant that the current negotiations have had to address issues far more complicated than those that were raised in relation to fisheries. Secondly, because of the limited number of precedents in international law for arrangements to organize mineral activities under forms of international co-operation and administration, the current negotiations have been led to devise unique approaches and solutions in international law in order to meet the requirements of a successful internal and external accommodation of interests.

The area of application of the regime has been agreed upon with due regard both to the practice that has evolved under the Antarctic Treaty system and to the rules resulting from the new Law of the Sea. The regime will thus apply to the whole continental and insular areas under the Antarctic Treaty, including the non-claimed area, and to the Antarctic continental shelf, but excluding the deep sea-bed. The precise definition of the area poses a number of interesting legal questions in relation to the Law of the Sea and again raised the issue of the joint jurisdiction of the parties to the regime.

The rules relating to prospecting, exploration and development that have been envisaged in the negotiation texts have in general followed what is the normal practice of mining legislation throughout the world, adapted to the special conditions of Antarctica. However, specific criticism has been levelled at some of the proposed articles, particularly inasmuch as prospecting would not require prior authorization and the transition from exploration to development would not necessarily be subject to a detailed review by the institutions of the regime. In general, criticism has been founded on concern about the environmental implications of mining activities in Antarctica, which has led to the inclusion in the regime of detailed environmental standards and other safeguards.

Financial arrangements, anti-monopoly mechanisms and scientific research policy in connection with minerals have also been the subject of discussion in the context of these negotiations. The question of distribution of benefits will be a particularly difficult one to resolve. Although some clauses of the draft articles reflect the concern felt about these matters, the respective issues will in due course need to be addressed by the Treaty parties in detail. The precedent of the deep sea-bed negotiations at the Third United Nations Conference on the Law of the Sea has had some influence on these and other questions arising in the Antarctic mineral negotiations, but in the latter case they have been purged of the negative ideological connotations they often had in the former.

The difficult problem of the criteria for access to the mineral resources of Antarctica has been settled by means of the specific rules mentioned above in relation to prospecting, exploration and development, as well as other applicable mechanisms of the proposed regime. While access is open to all participating States on fairly broad bases, the specific activities of exploration and development of resources will require an authorization granted under the regime; the decision as to granting this authorization will take into consideration the environmental issues that such activities might raise. Again in this matter the regime has sought solutions unprecedented in international law.

A most important legal problem connected with these negotiations has been the specific rules that will govern contracts in the context of the mineral regime. The need to ensure the stability of contracts has been a paramount consideration in this respect. While at an early point in the negotiations consideration was given to the establishment of a kind of licensing arrangement, subsequently a contractual relationship was envisaged in order to better reflect the legal nature of the arrangement. In any event, contracts will be subject to a specific regulatory function of the institutions of the regime. The management scheme will contain most of the applicable rules to this effect and will be incorporated in each contract. Contracts will be governed by the rules laid down in the convention and other instruments enacted under its authority, as well as by other applicable rules of international law; national law will also apply to the extent specified in each management scheme. Here there will be a case of internationalized contracts with the exceptions that might be agreed upon in certain respects.

Another important legal question has related to the entities that might qualify as contractors under the regime. Broadly conceived options have been envisaged in this regard, including a flexible regime for the participation of joint ventures. The link with the sponsoring States poses a number of legal issues that will need to be considered in due course under the regime.

A fundamental problem that has divided opinions in the negotiations has been the question of who shall have the final authority for the approval of contracts and the granting of authorizations to undertake mineral activities in the area. This problem lies at the heart of the interests of both claimant and non-claimant countries as well as of other interests. Various theoretical models, ranging from nationalistic options based on the territorial authority of the State to fully internationalized regimes attributing authority to existing or *ad hoc* international organizations, have been proposed by authors and governments. However, none of them seems to meet the variety of views that needs to be taken into account in order to reach a satisfactory solution.

The draft articles emerging from the negotiations have adopted a strongly pragmatic approach in this matter, devising solutions geared to achieving the desired internal accommodation among the participants. To this end, a careful and balanced distribution of competences has been proposed within the regime. The various interests mentioned can thus obtain recognition of some elements representing their views, while at the same time accepting to some extent the views of others.

In order to achieve this balanced distribution of competences, the institutional arrangements being discussed have proved to be crucial. A central Commission and Advisory Committee would ensure representation of all the relevant interests while retaining some basic decision-making powers, particularly in terms of opening given areas to exploration; these powers, in turn, will be interlinked with a Special Meeting of States Parties which will ensure the broader representation of participating States; more restricted Regulatory Committees would also be established to deal with specific conditions and authorizations relating to contracts and mineral activities. The composition and procedures for decision-making of the Regulatory Committees, including the question of veto and chamber voting, have been a most difficult question in the negotiations. It is through these very specific arrangements that the distribution of competences is taking place, including those which may be retained by claimant States. The procedures for the settlement of disputes are still in an early stage of negotiation; various options are suggested to this effect in the book, taking into account the experience of the negotiations at the Law of the Sea Conference.

These various institutional arrangements are the most elaborate yet discussed within the Antarctic Treaty system, involving stronger institutional functions than those of a very elementary character that were envisaged by the 1959 Treaty, or the machinery set up under other conventions dealing with Antarctic resources. The institutional evolution that is taking place within the Treaty system is indicative of the changing attitude of participating States towards co-operation in Antarctica. To some extent the Treaty system is evolving towards the establishment of an international organization.

The issues and options relating to external accommodation are also of particular importance for the achievement of a satisfactory minerals regime and for the relationship between the Treaty system as a whole and the interests of third States and international organizations in Antarctic affairs. Participation in the Treaty system and its activities has been expanded in the past few years in order to meet these interests in part, a trend which is likely to continue as long as other States qualify for this purpose; a similar opening-up can be observed in relation to the activities of international organizations relevant to Antarctica. Greater availability and dissemination of information is also part of the new approach to the operation of the Treaty system, thus to some extent invalidating the criticism that it is restricted and secretive.

The situation of third States in relation to the Treaty system poses particularly difficult legal issues. Third States enjoy a variety of rights under the 1959 Antarctic Treaty and the conventional regimes, an aspect which is not difficult to reconcile with the 1969 Vienna Convention on the Law of Treaties; some of the pertinent norms of the Antarctic Treaty meet the requirement of international law as to having become rules of customary law. The possibility of the eventual existence of obligations for third States under these arrangements is more difficult to ascertain. However, to the extent that customary rules have emerged they will have a binding effect on third States. Of particular interest in this context is the question of whether the Antarctic Treaty qualifies as an objective regime and what are the implications of such types of regime in international law. Although the question was not clearly answered in the context of the work of the International Law Commission concerning the Law of Treaties, in the light of the meaningful discussions that took place on the matter it can be concluded that the 1959 Treaty qualifies under this concept. A further complicating factor is of course that even though the Antarctic Treaty may have a close relationship with customary law and objective regimes, this is not necessarily the position of the conventional resource regimes, nor will necessarily be that of the minerals regime. In any event, the Treaty Parties can take lawful action under Article X of the 1959 Treaty or similar provisions of the associated conventions should third States undertake activities in Antarctica in violation of the basic obligations and principles applicable in that respect.

The most delicate issue affecting the external accommodation of the Treaty system in general and the minerals regime in particular consists of the differing views existing as to the model that should govern Antarctic co-operation or mineral activities. While the Treaty Parties have in general opted for a model of limited internationalization, which will satisfactorily accommodate sovereignty claims and other legal standings, a number of countries have called for the adoption of forms of full internationalization in connection either with the Treaty system as a whole or more specifically with the minerals regime. In fact, discussion on this issue is not entirely new, since there were initiatives relating to internationalization at the very early stages of activities in Antarctica and subsequently in various other instances, such as the negotiation of the 1959 Treaty, the first discussions that took place on the matter at the United Nations and other bodies, or, to a limited extent, on the occasion of the work of the Law of the Sea Conference.

The latter conference has been very influential in providing a model for the internationalization of the deep sea-bed under the concept of the common heritage of mankind. During the current United Nations debate on the question of Antarctica this concept has been repeatedly invoked, as it has also been invoked by numerous authors. However, its application to Antarctica is a different proposition from that of the deep sea-bed, in part because of the existence of claims of sovereignty in the area and in part because there is a specific legal regime governing co-operation in Antarctica; on this and other legal grounds the application of the concept in question to Antarctica has not been accepted by the Treaty parties, particularly those having the status of Consultative Parties. Although there are many possibilities for fruitful co-operation between the Treaty system, the United Nations and other international organizations, these prospects have been so far limited as a consequence of the debate on the applicable model. In the context of the evolution of the Treaty system and the new approach towards the operation of that system, a number of steps have been taken in order to further co-operation with international organizations and disseminate the appropriate information.

It is very unlikely that the present Antarctic Treaty system might be replaced by an entirely new and different arrangement, not even as the 1991 date foreseen by the Treaty for an eventual review approaches. As long as the Consultative and other Treaty Parties keep their commitment to the model of Antarctic co-operation actually in application such radical departures will not be feasible. This is not to say that the Treaty system will be kept unchanged, since the evolution actually under way, including the trend towards greater participation in its meetings and institutions, will continue at a rapid pace.

Both the model based on exclusive sovereignty and that proposed for a general or full internationalization have proved their limitations in the course of the evolution of the Treaty system. These limitations are basically related to the same cause, i.e. that neither is capable of meeting the various interests at work in Antarctica and providing an adequate legal basis for their accommodation. The only viable alternative, then, is the development of a system of co-operation adapted to the specific needs and circumstances of Antarctica, such as the one that has been evolving since 1959. The successful conclusion of the negotiations on a minerals regime will be a most important step in this evolution, in part because it will provide a new and dynamic framework for Antarctic co-operation in that respect and in part because it will also contribute an important precedent to the new dimensions that international law is acquiring in the organization of resource development and other forms of modern international co-operation.

APPENDIX 1

The Antarctic Treaty

Done at Washington, 1 December 1959

The Governments of Argentina, Australia, Belgium, Chile, the French Republic, Japan, New Zealand, Norway, the Union of South Africa, the Union of Soviet Socialist Republics, the United Kingdom of Great Britain and Northern Ireland, and the United States of America;

Recognizing that it is in the interest of all mankind that Antarctica shall continue forever to be used exclusively for peaceful purposes and shall not become the scene or object of international discord;

Acknowledging the substantial contributions to scientific knowledge resulting from international co-operation in scientific investigation in Antarctica;

Convinced that the establishment of a firm foundation for the continuation and development of such co-operation on the basis of freedom of scientific investigation in Antarctica as applied during the International Geophysical Year accords with the interests of science and the progress of all mankind;

Convinced also that a treaty ensuring the use of Antarctica for peaceful purposes only and the continuance of international harmony in Antarctica will further the purposes and principles embodied in the Charter of the United Nations;

Have agreed as follows:

Article I

1. Antarctica shall be used for peaceful purposes only. There shall be prohibited, *inter alia,* any measures of a military nature, such as the establishment of military bases and fortifications, the carrying out of military manoeuvres, as well as the testing of any type of weapons.

2. The present Treaty shall not prevent the use of military personnel or equipment for scientific research or for any other peaceful purpose.

Article II
Freedom of scientific investigation in Antarctica and co-operation toward that end, as applied during the International Geophysical Year, shall continue, subject to the provisions of the present Treaty.

Article III
1. In order to promote international co-operation in scientific investigation in Antarctica, as provided for in Article II of the present Treaty, the Contracting Parties agree that, to the greatest extent feasible and practicable:
   a. information regarding plans for scientific programmes in Antarctica shall be exchanged to permit maximum economy and efficiency of operations;
   b. scientific personnel shall be exchanged in Antarctica between expeditions and stations;
   c. scientific observations and results from Antarctica shall be exchanged and made freely available.
2. In implementing this Article, every encouragement shall be given to the establishment of co-operative working relations with those Specialized Agencies of the United Nations and other international organizations having a scientific or technical interest in Antarctica.

Article IV
1. Nothing contained in the present Treaty shall be interpreted as:
   a. a renunciation by any Contracting Party of previously asserted rights of or claims to territorial sovereignty in Antarctica;
   b. a renunciation or diminution by any Contracting Party of any basis of claim to territorial sovereignty in Antarctica which it may have whether as a result of its activities or those of its nationals in Antarctica, or otherwise;
   c. prejudicing the position of any Contracting Party as regards its recognition or non-recognition of any other State's right of or claim or basis of claim to territorial sovereignty in Antarctica.
2. No acts or activities taking place while the present Treaty is in force shall constitute a basis for asserting, supporting or denying a claim to territorial sovereignty in Antarctica or create any rights of sovereignty in Antarctica. No new claim, or enlargement of an existing claim, to territorial sovereignty in Antarctica shall be asserted while the present Treaty is in force.

Article V
1. Any nuclear explosions in Antarctica and the disposal there of radioactive waste material shall be prohibited.
2. In the event of the conclusion of international agreements concerning the use of nuclear energy, including nuclear explosions and the disposal of radioactive waste material, to which all of the Contracting Parties whose representatives are entitled to participate in the meetings provided for under Article IX are parties, the rules established under such agreements shall apply in Antarctica.

Article VI

The provisions of the present Treaty shall apply to the area south of 60° South Latitude, including all ice shelves, but nothing in the present Treaty shall prejudice or in any way affect the rights, or the exercise of the rights, of any State under international law with regard to the high seas within that area.

Article VII

1. In order to promote the objectives and ensure the observance of the provisions of the present Treaty, each Contracting Party whose representatives are entitled to participate in the meetings referred to in Article IX of the Treaty shall have the right to designate observers to carry out any inspection provided for by the present Article. Observers shall be nationals of the Contracting Parties which designate them. The names of observers shall be communicated to every other Contracting Party having the right to designate observers, and like notice shall be given of the termination of their appointment.

2. Each observer designated in accordance with the provisions of paragraph 1 of this Article shall have complete freedom of access at any time to any or all areas of Antarctica.

3. All areas of Antarctica, including all stations, installations and equipment within those areas, and all ships and aircraft at points of discharging or embarking cargoes or personnel in Antarctica, shall be open at all time to inspection by any observers designated in accordance with paragraph 1 of this Article.

4. Aerial observation may be carried out at any time over any or all areas of Antarctica by any of the Contracting Parties having the right to designate observers.

5. Each Contracting Party shall, at the time when the present Treaty enters into force for it, inform the other Contracting Parties, and thereafter shall give them notice in advance, of

    a. all expeditions to and within Antarctica, on the part of its ships or nationals, and all expeditions to Antarctica organized in or proceeding from its territory;

    b. all stations in Antarctica occupied by its nationals; and

    c. any military personnel or equipment intended to be introduced by it into Antarctica subject to the conditions prescribed in paragraph 2 of Article I of the present Treaty.

Article VIII

1. In order to facilitate the exercise of their functions under the present Treaty, and without prejudice to the respective positions of the Contracting Parties relating to jurisdiction over all other persons in Antarctica, observers designated under paragraph 1 of Article VII and scientific personnel exchanged under subparagraph 1 (b) of Article III of the Treaty, and members of the staffs accompanying any such persons, shall be subject only to the jurisdiction of the Contracting Party of which they are nationals in respect of all acts or omissions occurring while they are in Antarctica for the purpose of exercising their functions.

2. Without prejudice to the provisions of paragraph 1 of this Article, and pending the adoption of measures in pursuance of subparagraph 1 (e) of Article IX, the Contracting Parties concerned in any case of dispute with regard to the exercise of jurisdiction in Antarctica shall immediately consult together with a view to reaching a mutually acceptable solution.

Article IX

1. Representatives of the Contracting Parties named in the preamble to the present Treaty shall meet at the City of Canberra within two months after the date of entry into force of the Treaty, and thereafter at suitable intervals and places, for the purpose of exchanging information, consulting together on matters of common interest pertaining to Antarctica, and formulating and considering, and recommending to their Governments, measures in furtherance of the principles and objectives of the Treaty, including measures regarding:

    a. use of Antarctica for peaceful purposes only;

    b. facilitation of scientific research in Antarctica;

    c. facilitation of international scientific co-operation in Antarctica;

    d. facilitation of the exercise of the rights of inspection provided for in Article VII of the Treaty;

    e. questions relating to the exercise of jurisdiction in Antarctica;

    f. preservation and conservation of living resources in Antarctica.

2. Each Contracting Party which has become a party to the present Treaty by accession under Article XIII shall be entitled to appoint representatives to participate in the meetings referred to in paragraph 1 of the present Article, during such time as that Contracting Party demonstrates its interest in Antarctica by conducting substantial scientific research activity there, such as the establishment of a scientific station or the despatch of a scientific expedition.

3. Reports from the observers referred to in Article VII of the present Treaty shall be transmitted to the representatives of the Contracting Parties participating in the meetings referred to in paragraph 1 of the present Article.

4. The measures referred to in paragraph 1 of this Article shall become effective when approved by all the Contracting Parties whose representatives were entitled to participate in the meetings held to consider those measures.

5. Any or all of the rights established in the present Treaty may be exercised as from the date of entry into force of the Treaty whether or not any measures facilitating the exercise of such rights have been proposed, considered or approved as provided in this Article.

Article X

Each of the Contracting Parties undertakes to exert appropriate efforts, consistent with the Charter of the United Nations, to the end that no one engages in any activity in Antarctica contrary to the principles or purposes of the present Treaty.

Article XI

1. If any dispute arises between two or more of the Contracting Parties concerning the interpretation or application of the present Treaty, those Contracting Parties shall consult among themselves with a view to having the dispute resolved by negotiation, inquiry, mediation, conciliation, arbitration, judicial settlement or other peaceful means of their own choice.

2. Any dispute of this character not so resolved shall, with the consent, in each case, of all parties to the dispute, be referred to the International Court of Justice for settlement; but failure to reach agreement on reference to the International Court shall not absolve parties to the dispute from the responsibility of continuing to seek to resolve it by any of the various peaceful means referred to in paragraph 1 of this Article.

Article XII

1a. The present Treaty may be modified or amended at any time by unanimous agreement of the Contracting Parties whose representatives are entitled to participate in the meetings provided for under Article IX. Any such modification or amendment shall enter into force when the depositary Government has received notice from all such Contracting Parties that they have ratified it.

b. Such modification or amendment shall thereafter enter into force as to any other Contracting Party when notice of ratification by it has been received by the depositary Government. Any such Contracting Party from which no notice of ratification is received within a period of two years from the date of entry into force of the modification or amendment in accordance with the provisions of subparagraph 1 (a) of this Article shall be deemed to have withdrawn from the present Treaty on the date of the expiration of such period.

2a. If after the expiration of thirty years from the date of entry into force of the present Treaty, any of the Contracting Parties whose representatives are entitled to participate in the meetings provided for under Article IX so requests by a communication addressed to the depositary Government, a Conference of all the Contracting Parties shall be held as soon as practicable to review the operation of the Treaty.

b. Any modification or amendment to the present Treaty which is approved at such a Conference by a majority of the Contracting Parties there represented, including a majority of those whose representatives are entitled to participate in the meetings provided for under Article IX, shall be communicated by the depositary Government to all the Contracting Parties immediately after the termination of the Conference and shall enter into force in accordance with the provisions of paragraph 1 of the present Article.

c. If any such modification or amendment has not entered into force in accordance with the provisions of subparagraph 1 (a) of this Article within a period of two years after the date of its communication to all the Contracting Parties, any Contracting Party may at any time after the expiration of that period give notice to the depositary Government of its withdrawal from the present

Treaty; and such withdrawal shall take effect two years after the receipt of the notice by the depositary Government.

Article XIII
1. The present Treaty shall be subject to ratification by the signatory States. It shall be open for accession by any State which is a Member of the United Nations, or by any other State which may be invited to accede to the Treaty with the consent of all the Contracting Parties whose representatives are entitled to participate in the meetings provided for under Article IX of the Treaty.
2. Ratification of or accession to the present Treaty shall be effected by each State in accordance with its constitutional processes.
3. Instruments of ratification and instruments of accession shall be deposited with the Government of the United States of America, hereby designated as the depositary Government.
4. The depositary Government shall inform all signatory and acceding States of the date of each deposit of an instrument of ratification or accession, and the date of entry into force of the Treaty and of any modification or amendment thereto.
5. Upon the deposit of instruments of ratification by all the signatory States, the present Treaty shall enter into force for those States and for States which have deposited instruments of accession. Thereafter the Treaty shall enter into force for any acceding State upon the deposit of its instrument of accession.
6. The present Treaty shall be registered by the depositary Government pursuant to Article 102 of the Charter of the United Nations.

Article XIV
The present Treaty, done in the English, French, Russian, and Spanish languages, each version being equally authentic, shall be deposited in the archives of the Government of the United States of America, which shall transmit duly certified copies thereof to the Governments of the signatory and acceding States.

IN WITNESS WHEREOF, the undersigned Plenipotentiaries, duly authorized, have signed the present Treaty.
DONE at Washington this first day of December one thousand nine hundred and fifty-nine.

APPENDIX 2

Signatures and ratifications by the Antarctic
Treaty Parties of major international
conventions relevant to the Antarctic Treaty
system

Antarctic Treaty Consultative Parties	Antarctic Treaty 1959[1]	Seals Conv. 1972[1]	CCAMLR 1980[1]	Territ. Sea Conv. 1958[2]	Conv. on Cont. Shelf 1958[2]	High Seas Conv. 1958[2]	Conv. on Fish 1958[2]	Op. Prot. 1958[2]	Law of the Sea Conv. 1982[3]
Argentina (original)	23 June 61	7 Mar. 78	28 Apr. 82	S	S	S	S		5 Oct. 84
Australia (original)	23 June 61	5 Oct. 72 (sig.)	6 May 81	R	R	R	R	R	10 Dec. 82
Belgium (original)	26 July 60	9 Feb. 78	22 Feb. 84	R		R	R	R	5 Dec. 84
Chile (original)	23 June 61	7 Feb. 80	22 July 81		S	S			10 Dec. 82
France (original)	16 Sep. 60	19 Feb. 75	16 Sep. 82	R	R	R	R	R	10 Dec. 82
Japan (original)	4 Aug. 60	28 Aug. 80	26 May 81	R		R	S		7 Feb. 83
New Zealand (original)	1 Nov. 60	9 June 72 (sig.)	8 Mar. 82	S	R	S	S	R	10 Dec. 82
Norway (original)	24 Aug. 60	10 Dec. 73	6 Dec. 83		R				10 Dec. 82
South Africa (original)	21 June 60	15 Aug. 72	23 July 81	R	R	R	R		5 Dec. 84
United Kingdom (original)	31 May 60	10 Sep. 74	31 Aug. 81	R	R	R	R	R	
United States (original)	18 Aug. 60	28 Dec. 76	18 Feb. 82	R	R	R	R	S	
USSR (original)	2 Nov. 60	8 Feb. 78	26 May 81	R	R	R			10 Dec. 82
Poland (17 Sep. 77)	8 June 61		24 Mar. 84		R	R		S	10 Dec. 82
Federal Republic of Germany (23 June 81)	5 Feb. 79		23 Apr. 82		S	S		R	
Brazil (12 Sep. 83)	16 May 75		28 Jan. 86					S	10 Dec. 82
India (12 Sep. 83)	19 Aug. 83		17 June 85						10 Dec. 82
China (7 Oct. 85)	8 June 83								10 Dec. 82
Uruguay (7 Oct. 85)	11 Jan. 80		22 Mar. 85	S	S	S	S	R	10 Dec. 82

534

OTHER PARTIES

Country									
Czechoslovakia	14 June 62		R	R	R				10 Dec. 82
Denmark	20 May 65		R	R	R	R	R		10 Dec. 82
Netherlands	30 Mar. 67		R	R	R	R	R		10 Dec. 82
Romania	15 Sep. 71		R	R	R				10 Dec. 82
GDR	19 Nov. 74	30 Mar. 82	R	R					10 Dec. 82
Bulgaria	11 Sep. 78			R	R				10 Dec. 82
Papua New Guinea (succession)	16 Mar. 81				R				10 Dec. 82
Italy	18 Mar. 81		R		R				7 Dec. 84
Peru	10 Apr. 81		S	S	S				
Spain	31 Mar. 82	9 Apr. 82	R	R	R	R			4 Dec. 84
Hungary	27 Jan. 84			R	R				10 Dec. 82
Sweden	24 Apr. 84	7 June 84	R		R		R		10 Dec. 82
Finland	15 May 84		R		R	S	R		10 Dec. 82
Cuba	16 Aug. 84		S		S	S	R		10 Dec. 82
(EEC)	21 Apr. 82								
Korea	29 Mar. 85								7 Dec. 84

[1]*Source:* Handbook of the Antarctic Treaty System, October 1985; dates given are for ratification or accession, or succession, except where it is indicated that is the date of signature (sig.) Dates are also given for those parties which have become Consultative Parties. C.C.A.M.L.R. dates have been supplemented with information from the Scott Polar Research Institute.

[2]*Source:* John King Gamble Jr.: *Global Marine Attributes*, 1974. No dates given for these conventions. R = Ratification. S = Signature.

[3]*Source:* United Nations: *Law of the Sea Bulletin*, N° 6, October 1985. Status of this Convention as of 30 September 1985. Dates given are for signature of the Convention.

Antarctic Treaty Consultative Parties	Solas 74[4]	Solas Prot. 78[5]	Marpol Prot. 78[6]	Intervention 69[7]	Interv. Prot. 73[8]
Argentina	5 Dec. 79	24 Feb. 82			
Australia	17 Aug. 83	17 Aug. 83		7 Nov. 83	7 Nov. 83
Belgium	24 Sep. 79	24 Sep. 79	6 Mar. 84	21 Oct. 71	9 Sep. 82
Chile	28 Mar. 80				
France	25 May 77	21 Dec. 79	25 Sep. 81	10 May 72	
Japan	15 May 80	15 May 80	9 June 83	6 Apr. 71	
New Zealand				26 Mar. 75	
Norway	15 Feb. 77	25 Mar. 81	15 Jul. 80	12 Jul. 72	15 Jul. 80
South Africa	23 May 80	11 Jan. 82	28 Nov. 84		
United Kingdom	7 Oct. 77	5 Nov. 79	22 May 80	12 Jan. 71	5 Nov. 79
United States	7 Sep. 78	12 Aug. 80	12 Aug. 80	21 Feb. 74	7 Sep. 78
USSR	9 Jan. 80	12 May 81	3 Nov. 83	30 Dec. 74	30 Dec. 82
Poland	15 Mar. 84	15 Mar. 84		1 June 76	10 Jul. 81
Federal Rep. of Germany	26 Mar. 79	6 June 80	21 Jan. 82	7 May 75	
Brazil	22 May 80				
India	16 June 76				
China	7 Jan. 80	17 Dec. 82		1 Jul. 83	
Uruguay	30 Apr. 79	30 Apr. 79	30 Apr. 79		

OTHER PARTIES

Czechoslovakia	18 Aug. 80	2 June 83	2 Jul. 84		9 May 83
Denmark	8 Mar. 78	27 Nov. 80	27 Nov. 80	18 Dec. 70	10 Sep. 80
Netherlands	10 Jul. 78	8 Jul. 80	30 June 83	19 Sep. 75	
Romania	24 May 79				
GDR	15 Mar. 79	28 Apr. 83	25 Apr. 84	21 Dec. 78	
Bulgaria	2 Nov. 83	2 Nov. 83	12 Dec. 84	2 Nov. 83	
Papua New Guinea	12 Nov. 80			12 Mar. 80	
Italy	11 June 80	1 Oct. 82	1 Oct. 82	27 Feb. 79	1 Oct. 82
Peru	4 Dec. 79	16 Jul. 82	25 Apr. 80		
Spain	5 Sep. 78	30 Apr. 80	6 Jul. 84	8 Nov. 73	
Hungary	9 Jan. 80	3 Feb. 82			
Sweden	7 July 78	21 Dec. 79	9 June 80	8 Feb. 73	28 June 76
Finland	21 Nov. 80	30 Apr. 81	20 Sep. 83	6 Sep. 76	
Cuba				5 May 76	

[4] The source for this and following conventions is I.M.O.: *Status of Multilateral Conventions*, as at 31 Dec. 84. Dates are for ratification or accession except where otherwise indicated. SOLAS is the International Convention for the Safety of Life at Sea, 1974, as amended.

[5] Protocol of 1978 relating to the International Convention for the Safety of Life at Sea, 1974, as amended.

[6] Protocol of 1978 relating to the International Convention for the prevention of pollution from ships, 1973.

[7] International Convention relating to intervention on high seas is cases of oil pollution casualties, 1969.

[8] Protocol relating to intervention on the high seas in cases of pollution by substances other than oil, 1973.

Antarctic Treaty Consultative Parties	CLC 69[9]	CLC Prot. 76[10]	CLC Prot. 84[11]	Fund. 71[12]	Fund. Prot. 76[13]	Fund. Prot. 84[14]	SFV 77[15]	LDC 72[16]	78 Amend.[17]
Argentina	7 Nov. 83	7 Nov. 83					7 Dec. 83	11 Sep. 79	
Australia	12 Jan. 77								
Belgium	2 Aug. 77						14 Sep. 82		
Chile								4 Aug. 77	
France	17 Mar. 75	7 Nov. 80		11 May 78	7 Nov. 80		15 Feb. 79	3 Feb. 77	1 Oct. 79
Japan	3 June 76			7 July 76				15 Oct. 80	15 Oct. 80
New Zealand	27 Apr. 76							30 Apr. 75	
Norway	21 Mar. 75			21 Mar. 75	17 Jul. 78		13 Nov. 79	4 Apr. 74	
South Africa	17 Mar. 76							7 Aug. 78	
United Kingdom	17 Mar. 75	17 Jul. 78		2 Apr. 76	31 Jan. 80		22 May 80	17 Nov. 75	21 Mar. 80
United States		31 Jan. 80	(Signatory)			(Signatory)		29 Apr. 74	24 Oct. 80
USSR	24 June 75							30 Dec. 75	
Poland	18 Nov. 76							23 Jan. 79	
Federal Rep. of Germany	20 May 75	28 Aug. 80		30 Dec. 76	28 Aug. 80		18 Nov. 83	8 Nov. 77	
Brazil	17 Dec. 76							26 Jul. 82	
India									
China	30 Jan. 80								
Uruguay									

OTHER PARTIES

	[9]	[10]	[11]	[12]	[13]	[14]	[15]	[16]	[17]
Czechoslovakia									
Denmark	2 Apr. 75	3 June 81		2 Apr. 75	3 June 81			23 Oct. 74	12 June 79
Netherlands	9 Sep. 75	3 Aug. 82		3 Aug. 82	1 Nov. 82			2 Dec. 77	20 Sep. 79
Romania									
GDR	13 Mar. 78			29 Aug. 79				20 Aug. 76	
Bulgaria									
Papua New Guinea	12 Mar. 80			10 Mar. 80					
Italy	27 Feb. 79	3 June 83		15 Dec. 83	21 Sep. 83			30 Apr. 84	30 Apr. 84
Peru	8 Dec. 75	22 Oct. 81		16 July 82					
Spain	8 Oct. 81			12 Dec. 79	5 Apr. 82			31 Jul. 74	
Hungary								5 Feb. 76	
Sweden	17 Mar. 75	7 Jul. 78		17 Mar. 75	7 Jul. 78			21 Feb. 74	16 May 80
Finland	10 Oct. 80	8 Jan. 81		10 Oct. 80	8 Jan. 81			3 May 79	
Cuba								1 Dec. 79	

[9] International Convention of Civil Liability for Oil Pollution Damage, 1969.

[10] Protocol of 1976 to the International Convention on Civil Liability for Oil Pollution Damage.

[11] Protocol of 1984 to amend the International Convention on Civil Liability for Oil Pollution Damage.

[12] International Convention on the Establishment of an International Fund for Compensation for Oil Pollution Damage, 1971.

[13] Protocol of 1976 to the International Convention on the Establishment of an International Fund for Compensation for Oil Pollution Damage.

[14] Protocol of 1984 to amend the International Convention on the Establishment of an International Fund for Compensation for Oil Pollution Damage.

[15] Torremolinos International Convention for the Safety of Fishing Vessels, 1977.

[16] Convention on the Prevention of Marine Pollution by Dumping of Wastes and other Matter, 1972, as amended.

[17] 1978 (Disputes) Amendment to the Convention cit., note 16 supra.

Table of Cases

Alcoa (United States v. Aluminum Co. of America et al.), 148 F. 2d. 416, 1945.
Aminoil (Government of Kuwait v. American Independent Oil Company – Aminoil), 24
    March 1982, International Law Reports, Vol. 66, 519–627.
Antarctica Cases (United Kingdom v. Argentina; United Kingdom v. Chile), International
    Court of Justice, Applications instituting proceedings, 1955; orders of 16 March
    1956, *Reports* 1956, 12–14, 15–17.
Aramco (Saudi Arabia v. Arabian American Oil Company – Aramco), 23 August 1958,
    International Law Reports, Vol. 27, 117–233.
BP v. Libya (BP Exploration Company (Libya) Limited v. Government of the Libyan Arab
    Republic), 10 October 1973, 1 August 1974, International Law Reports, Vol. 53,
    297–388.
Beattie (Martin John Beattie et al Plaintiffs, v. US, Defendant), United States District
    Court, District of Columbia, 25 June 1984, 592 F. Supp. 780 (1984); US Court of
    Appeals DC, 31 December 1984, 756 F. 2d.
Behring Fur Seals Arbitration: award of the tribunal of arbitration constituted under the
    treaty concluded at Washington, 29 February 1892, between the United States of
    America and Her Majesty the Queen of the United Kingdom of Great Britain and
    Ireland, Paris, 15 August 1893, American Journal of International Law, Vol. 6,
    1912, 233–241.
Case Concerning the Continental Shelf (Libyan Arab Jamahiriya/Malta), Judgement of 3
    June 1985, International Court of Justice, Reports, 1985.
Clipperton (Affaire de L'ile de Clipperton, Mexique–France), Sentence du 28 Janvier 1931,
    United Nations, Reports of International Arbitral Awards, Vol. II, 1105–1111.
Eastern Greenland (Legal Status of Eastern Greenland), Judgement of 5 April 1933,
    Permanent Court of International Justice, Series A/B, Judgements, orders and
    advisory opinions, No. 53, 21–147.
Fisheries Jurisdiction Case (UK v. Iceland), Judgement of 25 July 1974, International Court
    of Justice, Reports, 1974.
Flegenheimer Claim, 20 September 1958, Italian–United States Conciliation Commission,
    International Law Reports, Vol. 25, 1958–I, 91–167.
International Status of South-West Africa, Advisory Opinion of 11 July 1950, International
    Court of Justice, Reports, 1950.
Island of Palmas Case (Netherlands–USA), Award of 4 April 1928, United Nations,
    Reports of International Arbitral Awards, Vol. II, 829–871.
Joyce v. Director of Public Prosecutions, House of Lords, 1946, The Law Reports, 1946,
    347–382.

Kawakita v. United States, United States Supreme Court, 1952, 343 US 717, 96L ed. 1249.

Kramer (Cornelis Kramer and others) Joined cases 3, 4, and 6/76, European Court of Justice, Judgement of 14 July 1976, Reports, 1976, 2, 1279–1328.

Laker Airways (British Airways Board v. Laker Airways Ltd. and others), 1983 3 ALL ER 375.

Laker Airways v. Sabena, KLM, 731 F. 2d. 909 (1984).

Liamco v. Libya (Libyan American Oil Company (LIAMCO) v. Government of the Libyan Arab Republic), 12 April 1977, International Law Reports, Vol. 62, 141–219.

Lotus (The Case of the SS 'Lotus'), Collection of Judgements, Permanent Court of International Justice, Serie A, No. 10, 1927.

Mannington Mills Inc. v. Congoleum Corporation, Third Circuit, United States Court of Appeals, 3 April 1979, 595 F. 2d. 1287 (1979).

Martin (Larry R. *Martin*, Petitioner v. Commissioner of Internal Revenue, Respondent), Tax Court of the United States, Reports, Vol. 50, 15 April 1968, 59–62. See also American Journal of International Law, Vol. 63, 1969, Judicial Decisions, 141–142 (Summary of case).

Minquiers and Ecrehos (France–United Kingdom), Judgement of 17 November 1953, International Court of Justice, Reports of Judgements, advisory opinions and orders, 1953, 47–109.

Murphyores Incorporated Pty. Ltd. and Another v. the Commonwealth of Australia and others, The Australian Law Journal Reports, Vol. 50, 1976, 570–580.

North Sea Continental Shelf Cases (FRG v. Denmark; FRG v, Netherlands), Judgements of 20 February 1969, International Court of Justice, Reports, 1969.

Nottebohm (Liechtenstein v. Guatemala), Second phase, Judgement of 6 April 1955, International Court of Justice, Reports of Judgements, Advisory opinions and orders, 1955.

Nuclear Tests Cases (Australia v. France) (New Zealand v. France), Judgements of 20 December 1974, International Court of Justice, Reports, 1974.

Reparation for Injuries suffered in the service of the United Nations, Advisory opinion, International Court of Justice, Reports, 1949, 174.

South West Africa Cases (Ethiopia v. South Africa; Liberia v. South Africa), Second phase, Judgement of 18 July 1966, International Court of Justice, Reports, 1966.

Texaco v. Libya (Texaco Overseas Petroleum Company and California Asiatic Oil Company v. The Government of the Libyan Arab Republic), 27 November 1975, 19 January 1977, International Law Reports, Vol. 53, 389–511.

Timberlane Lumber Co. v. Bank of America, 549 F. 2d. 597 (1976).

Trail Smelter Case (United States, Canada), Awards of April 16, 1938; 11 March 1941, United Nations, Reports of International Arbitral Awards, Vol. III, 1949, 1905–1982.

Transports routiers, Cour de Justice des Communautés Européennes, Arret sur l'Affaire 22–70, 'Accord européen sur les transports routiers', Commission contre Conseil, 31 Mars 1971, *Recueil de la Jurisprudence de la Cour*, vol. 17, 1971, 263–296.

Van Dam, (Criminal proceedings v. Firma J, van Dam en Zonen and others), European Court of Justice, Joined Cases 185 to 204/78, Judgement of 3 July 1979, Reports, 1979, 2, 2345–2371.

Table of Statutes and National Legislation

Collections of Laws, other legislation and reference material

Bush, W. M.: *Antarctica and International Law.* A collection of Inter-State and National Documents, 1982, Vol. I, II.

Terence **Daintith** and Geoffrey **Willoughby**: *United Kingdom Oil and Gas Law*, 1984.

del Valle Stark: Disposiciones legales relativas a la Antártica o Territorio Chileno Antártico, 1900–1980, in *Revista de Legislación y Documentación en Derecho y Ciencias Sociales*, Santiago, Chile, Año II, No. 2, Abril 1980, 7–14.

Other legislation and references

Australia: Antarctic Treaty Act 1960.

Australia: Territory of Heard Island and McDonald Islands: *Environmental Protection and Management Ordinance 1984.*

Australia: Territory of Heard Island and McDonald Islands: *Migratory Birds Ordinance 1980, Migratory Birds (Amendment) Ordinance 1985.*

Chile: Register of Antarctic Property, Punta Arenas, 1961, pg. 1, No. 1, 9 March 1961.

Chile: Law No. 17170, 8 August 1969, on a regime in bond for the supply of Antarctic Stations, *Official Journal*, 20 August 1969; see also Decree No. 1731, 31 July 1970, on regulations of Law No. 17170, *Official Journal*, 7 September 1970.

Chile: Decreto Supremo No. 191 sobre aprobación de la Convención sobre Conservación de Focas Antárticas, 21 Febrero 1980, *Diario Oficial*, 24 de Abril de 1980.

Chile: Law No. 18392, 10 January 1985, on preferential customs and tax regime south of the Strait of Magellan, *Official Journal*, 14 January 1985; see also Resolution No. 1057, 25 April 1985, on regulations of Law No. 18392, *Official Journal*, 30 April 1985.

Italy: Law on the National Research Programme in Antarctica, 10 June 1985, *Official Journal*, No. 145, 21 June 1985.

New Zealand: Antarctica Act 1960.

New Zealand Territorial Sea and Exclusive Economic Zone Act 1977.

Norway: Act of 17 July 1925 relating to Spitzbergen, in: Willy Ostreng: *Politics in High Latitudes. The Svalbard Archipelago*, 1977, 105–108.

Norway: The Mining Code (the Mining Regulations) for Spitzbergen, Royal Decree of 7 August 1925, as amended by Royal Decree of 11 June 1975, in: Willy Ostreng: *Politics in High Latitudes. The Svalbard Archipelago*, 1977, 108–116.

Norway: Norwegian sovereignty in the Antarctic, Proclamation of January 14, 1939, *American Journal of International Law,* Vol. 34, 1940, Supplement, 83–85.

Norway: Law No. 91 of 17 December 1976, on the Economic Zone and Royal Decree of same date.

Perú: Comisión Nacional de Asuntos Antárticos, Decreto Supremo No. 009-83-RE, 11 de Julio de 1983, in *Revista Peruana de Derecho Internacional*, Vol. XXXV, Julio-Setiembre 1983, 63–65.

South Africa: South African Citizens in Antarctica Act, 1962.

United Kingdom: International organizations (Immunities and Privileges) Act, 1950, Law Reports, *Statutes*, 1950, 14 & 15 Geo. 6, 213. Also: The International Organizations Act 1968. Section 1(a): 'Confer on the organization the legal capacities of a body corporate'. Halsbury's Statutes of England, Third edition, Vol. 6, 1052.

United Kingdom: Oil in Navigable Waters Act 1955.

United Kingdom. Legislation on Antarctica:
- The Antarctic Treaty Order in Council, 1961 (Falkland Islands), S.I. 1961, No. 570;
- The British Antarctic Territory Order in Council, 1962 (South Atlantic Territories), S.I. 1962, No. 400;
- The Antarctic Treaty Order in Council, 1962 (South Atlantic Territories), S.I. 1962, No. 401;
- Instructions to our High Commissioner for the British Antarctic Territory, The Queen in Council, 26 Feb. 1962;
- Antarctic Treaty Act 1967 (Agreed Measures);
- The Antarctic Treaty (Specially Protected Area) order 1969, S.I. 1969, No. 854.

United Kingdom: British Fishery Limits Act 1976.

United Kingdom: Protection of Trading Interests Act 1980, Public General Acts and Measures of 1980, Part I, Chapter 11, 243–249.

United States: Antarctic Conservation Act of 1978, Public Law 95-541, 95th Congress, *International Legal Materials*, Vol. 18, 1979, 131–136; see also US HR 7749.

United States: 'Antarctic Marine Living Resources Convention Act', Public Law 98-623, 8 November 1984, Title III, *U.S. Code Annotated*, Title 16, Chapter 44 A, Sections 2431–2444, 573–585.

United States Code: international organizations privileges and immunities, Title 22, Chapter 7, Subchapter XVIII, Section 288a.

Table of Treaties

Collected Treaties and reference works

Bowman, M. J., **Harris,** D. J.: *Multilateral Treaties-Index and Current Status*, 1984 (Supplement, 1984).

Bush, W. M.: *Antarctica and International Law.* A Collection of Inter-State and National Documents, 1982, Vol. I–Vol. II.

Inter-American Institute of International Legal Studies: *Instruments relating to the Economic Integration of Latin America*, 1968.

International Maritime Organization: Status of multilateral conventions and instruments in respect of which the I.M.O. or its Secretary-General performs depositary or other functions, 31 December 1984.

Lyster, Simon: *International Wildlife Law*, 1985.

Additional Treaties and references

Agreement concerning the execution of the transfer to the United Nations of certain assets of the League of Nations, signed on 19 July 1946, *Yearbook of the United Nations*, 1946–47, 269–271.

Antarctic Treaty. Signed at Washington on 1 December, 1959, official sources:
 – *United Nations Treaty Series*, Vol. 402, 1961, No. 5778, 71–102.
 – *United Kingdom Treaty Series*, No. 97 (1961), Cmnd. 1535.

Argentina–Chile: Treaty of Peace and Friendship of 29 November 1984 and related documents, *International Legal Materials*, Vol. XXIV, No. 1, January 1985, 3–31.

Australia–France: Agreement on Maritime Delimitation, signed at Melbourne on 4 January 1982, entry into force on 10 January 1983, *Australian Treaty Series*, 1983, No. 3.

Charter of the United Nations, 1945.

Conference on Antarctica: Final Act, Washington D.C. October 15–December 1 1959, *A.J.I.L.*, Vol. 54, 1960, Official Documents, 476–483.

Conference on Conservation of Antarctic Marine Living Resources, Canberra, 7–20 May 1980, Final Act, Text of the Convention, *International Legal Materials*, Vol. XIX, 1980, 837–859.

Convention on Civil Liability for oil pollution damage resulting from exploration for and exploitation of seabed mineral resources, London, 1 May 1977, Sir David C. Jackson (ed.): *World Shipping Laws*, Binder 3, VIII/18/Conv., 1984.

Convention on Consular Relations, Vienna, 24 April 1963, 21 *U.S.T.* 77, 596 *U.N.T.S.* 261.

Convention on Future multilateral cooperation in the Northwest Atlantic Fisheries, Ottawa, 24 October 1978, *Official Journal of the European Communities*, No. L 378, Vol. 21, 30 December 1978, 16–29.

Convention on the Law of Treaties, Vienna, 23 May 1969, *A.J.I.L.*, Vol. 63, 1969, 875.
Convention on long-range transboundary air pollution, Geneva, 13 November 1979, *International Legal Materials*, Vol. 18, 1979, 1442–1455.
Convention on the prevention of marine pollution by dumping of wastes and other matter, London, 29 December 1972, in David C. Jackson (ed.): *World Shipping Laws*, Binder 3, VIII/10/Conv., 1984.
Convention on succession of States in respect of Treaties, Vienna, 23 August 1978, *International Legal Materials*, Vol. 17, 1978, 1488–1517.
Convention on the Territorial Sea and the Contiguous Zone, 1958.
Convention on the Continental Shelf, 1958.
Convention on the High Seas, 1958.
Convention on Fishing and the Conservation of the Living Resources of the High Seas, 1958.
Inter-American Treaty of Reciprocal Assistance, 2 September 1947, 21 U.N.T.S., 77.
Inter-American Treaty of Reciprocal Assistance: Final Act of the Conference for the amendment of, San José, Costa Rica, 26 July 1975 (Declarations by Chile and Statements by Argentina, US), *International Legal Materials*, Vol. XIV, 1975, 1117–1132.
International Convention for the Regulation of Whaling, 1946, *Schedule*, as amended to June 1984, January 1985.
Memorandum of understanding on Port State control in implementing agreements on maritime safety and protection of the marine environment, Paris, 26 January 1982, in David C. Jackson (ed.): *World Shipping Laws*, International Conventions, VIII-Marine Pollution, VIII/23/Conv. Oceana, May 1984.
New Zealand–Korea: Agreement on Fisheries of 16 March 1978, *N.Z.T.S.*, 1974, 4.
New Zealand–Japan: Agreement on Fisheries of 1 September 1978, *N.Z.T.S.*, 1978, 12.
New Zealand–USSR: Agreement on Fisheries of 4 April 1978, *N.Z.T.S.*, 1978, 5.
New Zealand–United States: Agreement with memorandum of understandings concerning US operations in Antarctica, signed at Washington on 24 December 1958; *United States Treaties and other international agreements*, Vol. 9, 1958, 1502–1509.
North-East Atlantic Fisheries Convention, London, 24 January 1959, *United Nations Treaty Series*, 1964, Vol. 486, 157–182, No. 7078.
Optional Protocol of Signature Concerning the Compulsory Settlement of Disputes, 1958.
Oslo and Paris Commissions:
 – Convention for the prevention of marine pollution by dumping from ships and aircraft, Oslo, 15 February 1972;
 – Convention for the prevention of marine pollution from land-based sources, Paris, 4 June 1974;
 – Agreement for co-operation in dealing with pollution of the North Sea by oil, Bonn, 9 June 1969;
 – Agreement for co-operation in dealing with pollution of the North Sea by oil and other harmful substances, Bonn, 1983.
Permanent Commission of the South Pacific: Convenio para protección del medio marino y la zona costera del Pacífico Sudeste, Lima, 12 November 1981; see also
 – Acuerdo sobre la cooperación regional para el combate contra la contaminación del Pacífico Sudeste por hidrocarburos y otras sustancias nocivas en caso de emergencia (Lima, 12 November 1981);
 – Protocolo complementario del Acuerdo (Quito, 22 July 1983), United Nations, 1984.
South Pacific Nuclear Free Zone Treaty, 6 August 1985, *Law of the Sea Bulletin*, No. 6, October 1985, 24–39.
Statute of the International Atomic Energy Agency, 26 October 1956, *U.N.T.S.*, Vol. 276, 1957, 4–40.
Treaty banning nuclear weapon tests in the atmosphere, in outer space and under water, Moscow, 5 August 1963, *U.N.T.S.*, Vol. 480, 1963, 44–99.

Treaty concerning the archipelago of Spitsbergen, signed at Paris, 9 February 1920, *League of Nations Treaty Series*, Vol. 2, 1920, No. 1, 8–19 (No. 41); see also *A.J.I.L.*, Supplement, Vol. 18, 1924, official Documents, 199–208; Status of ratifications, in Clive Parry, Charity Hopkins (compilators): *An Index of British Treaties, 1101–1968*, HMSO, 1970, Vol. 2, 605–606.

Treaty on Principles governing the activities of States in the exploration and use of outer space, including the moon and other celestial bodies, 1967, 610 *U.N.T.S.*, 205.

United Nations Convention on the Law of the Sea, 10 December 1982; Status of signature and ratification as at 31 December 1984, in *Multilateral Treaties Deposited with the Secretary General*, Status as at 31 December 1984, United Nations, 1985, 671–672.

Bibliography

1. Documents of the Antarctic Treaty System

Collected Documents

Antarctic Treaty: Handbook of Measures in furtherance of the principles and objectives of the Antarctic Treaty, second edition, September 1979; third edition, April 1983; *Handbook of the Antarctic Treaty System*, fourth edition, 1985.

Bush, W. M.: *Antarctica and International Law*, 2 Vol., 1982.

Documents and reports

Antarctic Treaty: Recommendations of the First Antarctic Treaty Consultative Meeting, Canberra, 10–24 July 1961, HMSO, Cmnd. 2822, 1–18; see also U.S. Treaties and other international agreements, Vol. 13, Part 2, 1962, 1349–1356.

Antarctic Treaty: Recommendations of the Second Antarctic Treaty Consultative Meeting, Buenos Aires, 18–28 July, 1962, HMSO, Cmnd. 2822, 19–22; see also U.S. Treaties and other international agreements, Vol. 14, Part I, 1963, 99–103.

Antarctic Treaty: Recommendations of the Third Antarctic Treaty Consultative Meeting, Brussels, 2–13 June 1964, HMSO, Cmnd. 2822, 23–34; see also United States Treaties and other international agreements, Vol. 17, Part 1, 1966, 991–1003.

Antarctic Treaty: Recommendations of the Fourth Consultative Meeting, Santiago, 3–18 November, 1966, HMSO, Cmnd. 3404.

Antarctic Treaty: Recommendations of the Fifth Consultative Meeting, Paris, 18–29 November, 1968, HMSO, Cmnd. 3993; see also Extracts from the Final Report, 10.

Antarctic Treaty: Recommendations of the Sixth Consultative Meeting, Tokyo, 19–31 October, 1970, HMSO, Cmnd. 4698; see also Extracts from the final report, 16.

Antarctic Treaty: Recommendations of the Seventh Consultative Meeting, Wellington, 30 October–10 November, 1972, HMSO, Cmnd. 5502; see also Extracts from the final report, 14–17.

Antarctic Treaty: Recommendations of the Eighth Consultative Meeting, Oslo, 9–20 June, 1975, HMSO, Cmnd. 6786; see also Extracts from the final report, 35–37; see further *Report of the Eighth Consultative Meeting*, Oslo, 1975.

Antarctic Treaty: Report of the Ninth Consultative Meeting, London, 19 September–7 October, 1977, Foreign and Commonwealth Office, 1977.

Antarctic Treaty: Recommendations of the Tenth Consultative Meeting, Washington, 17 September–5 October 1979, HMSO, Cmnd. 8652, 7–28; see also Extracts from the final report, 29–31; see further *Report of the Tenth Consultative Meeting*, Washington, 1979.

Antarctic Treaty: Recommendations of the Eleventh Consultative Meeting, Buenos Aires, 23 June–7 July 1981, HMSO, Cmnd. 8652, 41–46; see also Extracts from the final report, 47–50.

Antarctic Treaty: Report of the Twelfth Consultative Meeting, Canberra, 13–27 September 1983, Australian Government Publishing Service, 1984.

Antarctic Treaty: Preparatory meeting in Canberra, April 1983, to the Twelfth Antarctic Treaty Consultative Meeting, International Legal Notes, *The Australian Law Journal*, Vol. 57, No. 7, July 1983, 428–429.

Antarctic Treaty: Twelfth Antarctic Treaty Consultative Meeting, Canberra, 13–27 September 1983, International Legal Notes, *The Australian Law Journal*, Vol. 58, No. 1, January 1984, 59–60.

Antarctic Treaty: Reports of the Thirteenth Consultative Meeting, Brussels, 7–18 October 1985.

Antarctic Treaty: Informe final de la primera reunión consultiva especial, Chile, Memoria del Ministerio de Relaciones Exteriores, 1977, 1030–1032.

Antarctic Treaty: Final Report of the Second Special Antarctic Treaty Consultative Meeting, Canberra 27 February–16 March 1978/Buenos Aires, 17–28 July 1978/Canberra 5–6 May 1980, HMSO, Cmnd. 8652, 4–6.

Antarctic Treaty: Final report of the Third Special Antarctic Treaty Consultative Meeting, Buenos Aires, 3 March 1981, HMSO, Cmnd. 8652, 39–40.

Antarctic Treaty: Approval of measures relating to the furtherance of the principles and objectives of the Antarctic Treaty, as notified to the Government of the United States of America, HMSO, Cmnd. 8652, 52.

Antarctic Treaty: Special Preparatory Meeting on Antarctic Mineral Resources, Paris, 28 June 1976, RPS-10, Document presented by the US Delegation, in: US Senate, Committee on Foreign Relations, Subcommittee on Arms Control, Oceans, and International Environment, *Hearing on Exploitation of Antarctic Resources*, 95th Congress, 2nd Session, 1978, 109–117.

Antarctic Treaty: Report of the group of experts on mineral exploration and exploitation, ANT/IX/51, Rev. 1, 29 September 1977, Ninth Consultative Meeting, London, 1977; reprinted in US Senate: Hearing on Exploitation of Antarctic Resources, 1978, 118–148; see also Annex 5 of the Report of the Ninth Consultative Meeting, Foreign and Commonwealth Office, 1977.

Antarctic Treaty: Report of the Group of Ecological, Technological and other related experts on Mineral Exploration and Exploitation in Antarctica, Washington D.C., June 29, 1979, HMSO, Cmnd. 8652, 32–38.

Antarctic Treaty: Report of the Working group on the question of Antarctic Mineral Resources. Legal and political aspects, Final Report of the Tenth Consultative Meeting, Annex 5, in Jonathan I. Charney (ed.): *The new nationalism and the use of common spaces*, 1982, 304–312.

Antarctic Treaty: 1983 Draft Articles on the Antarctic Mineral Resources Regime and Personal Report by the Chairman on the meeting on Antarctic Mineral Resources (Wellington, New Zealand, 17–18 January 1983), *Environmental Policy and Law*, Vol. 11, 1983, 47–52; see also ECO, Vol. XXIII, No. 1, July 11–22, 1983, Bonn, 5–13.

Antarctic Treaty: 1984 Draft Articles on the Antarctic Mineral Resources Regime, 29 March 1984, in Greenpeace International: *The future of the Antarctic*, Background for a second UN debate, 22 October 1984, Appendix 8.

Antarctic Treaty: 1986 Draft Convention on the Antarctic Mineral Resources Regime, 19 September 1986.

Antarctic Treaty: 1987 Draft Convention on the Antarctic Mineral Resources Regime, 2 April 1987.

Convention for the Conservation of Antarctic Marine Living Resources, Commission, *Basic Documents*, 1982.

Convention for the Conservation of Antarctic Marine Living Resources, Commission, *Report of the First Meeting*, Hobart, Australia, 25 May–11 June 1982, 1982.

Convention for the Conservation of Antarctic Marine Living Resources, Commission, *Report of the Second Meeting*, Hobart, Australia, 29 August–9 September 1983, 1983.

Convention for the Conservation of Antarctic Marine Living Resources, Commission, *Report of the Third Meeting*, Hobart, Australia, 3 September–14 September 1984, 1984.

Convention for the Conservation of Antarctic Marine Living Resources, Commission, *Report of the Fourth Meeting*, Hobart, Australia, 2–13 September 1985.

Convention for the Conservation of Antarctic Marine Living Resources, Commission, *Selected papers presented to the Scientific Committee*, 1982–1984, Part 1, Part 2, 1985.

Convention for the Conservation of Antarctic Marine Living Resources, Scientific Committee, *Report of the First Meeting*, Hobart, Australia, 7–11 June, 1982, 1982.

Convention for the Conservation of Antarctic Marine Living Resources, Scientific Committee, *Report of the Second Meeting*, Hobart, Australia, 30 August–8 September 1983, 1983.

Convention for the Conservation of Antarctic Marine Living Resources, Scientific Committee, *Report of the Third Meeting*, Hobart, Australia, 3–13 September 1984, 1984.

Convention for the Conservation of Antarctic Marine Living Resources, Scientific Committee, *Report of the Fourth Meeting*, Hobart, Australia, 2–9 September 1985.

Convention for the Conservation of Antarctic Marine Living Resources, Commission: *Report of Members' Activities*, 1984/85.

SCAR: Wildlife conservation laws relating to the Antarctic and Subantarctic, Prepared by M. W. Holdgate and B. B. Roberts, July 1961, Mimeo.

SCAR: Mineral occurrences and mineral exploration in the Antarctic, Report of the Working Group on Geology, 1976.

SCAR: Antarctic Resources-Effects of Mineral Exploration. Initial response by SCAR, dated May 1976, to Antarctic Treaty Recommendation VIII-14, *SCAR Bulletin*, No. 57, September 1977, 209–214.

SCAR: A Preliminary Assessment of the Environmental Impact of Mineral Exploration/Exploitation in Antarctica, Group of Specialists on the Environmental Impact Assessment of Mineral Exploration/Exploitation in Antarctica (EAMREA), August 1977.

SCAR: Group of Specialists on Antarctic Environmental Implications of Possible Mineral Exploration and Exploitation (AIMEE), Report No. 1, University of Nebraska-Lincoln, 26–29 May 1981.

SCAR: Group of Specialists on Antarctic Environmental Implications of Possible Mineral Exploration and Exploitation (AIMEE), Report No. 2, The University of Texas at Dallas, September 30–October 2, 1982.

SCAR: 'Conservation areas in the Antarctic', March 1985.

2. Documents of international organizations and international meetings

EEC: Regulation No. 1496/68 of the Council, 27 September 1968, on the definition of the customs territory of the Community, HMSO, 1969.

EEC: Council Regulation No. 101/76, 19 January 1976, *Official Journal of the European Communities*, Vol. 19, No. L20, 28 January 1976, 19–22.

EEC: Report on the Conference on the Law of the Sea, *Bulletin*, No. 2, 1982, par. 2.2.17.

EEC: Report on the Conference on the Law of the Sea, *Bulletin*, No. 5, 1982, pars. 2.2.23–30.

EEC: Declaration concerning the competence of the EEC in matters governed by the 1982 Convention on the Law of the Sea, made on 7 December 1984 on signing the Convention, *Italy and the Law of the Sea Newsletter*, No. 13, January 1985, 6–10; *Bulletin* of the European Communities, Vol. 17, No. 12, 1984, 108–149.

European Parliament: Resolution on the Conference on the Law of the Sea as it affects the European Community, *Official Journal of the European Communities*, No. C133, 6 June 1977, 50–52.

European Parliament: Written question No. 222/80 on seabed mining legislation and answer by the Commission, *Official Journal of the European Communities*, No. C198, 4 August 1980, 37–38.

European Parliament: Resolution on economic aspects of the exploitation of the seabed, *Official Journal of the European Communities*, No. C101, 4 May 1981, 65–68.

European Parliament: Written question No. 92/81 on seabed mining and answer by the Commission, *Official Journal of the European Communities*, No. C147, 17 June 1981, 36.

European Parliament: Question No. 64 by Mr Johnson on Antarctic minerals negotiations, *Official Journal of the European Communities*, Debates of the European Parliament, No. 1–285, 1982–1983 Session, Report of proceedings from 10 to 14 May 1982, p. 156.

European Parliament: Question No. 66 by Mr Schwartzenberg on dispute settlement procedures before the ICJ for the Falkland islands, *Official Journal of the European Communities*, Debates of the European Parliament, No. 1–285, 1982–1983 Session, Report of proceedings from 10 to 14 May 1982, p. 182.

European Parliament: Question No. 105 by Mr Seligman on establishing neutral zone in Antarctica to prevent conflicts at the UN, *Official Journal of the European Communities*, Debates of the European Parliament, No. 1–288, 1982–1983 Session, Report of proceedings from 13 to 17 September 1982, p. 162.

European Parliament: Resolution on deep seabed mining and the marine environment, *Official Journal of the European Communities*, No. C13, 17 January 1983, 32–33.

FAO: *Report of the Conference*, Eighteenth Session, Rome, 8–27 November 1975, C75/REP, 38–40.

FAO: Committee on Fisheries, *Review of the State of Exploitation of the World Fish Resources: Living Resources of the Southern Ocean*, COFI/77/5, Sup. 2, March 1977, Eleventh Session, Rome 19–26 April 1977.

FAO: Committee on Fisheries, 11th Session, 19–26 April 1977, *Review of the State of Exploitation of the World Fish Resources: Living Resources of the Southern Ocean*, Verbatim of discussion, 21–22 April.

FAO/P.N.U.D.: *Los Mares Australes: los recursos vivos de los mares australes*, GLO/SO/77/1, 1979.

FAO/P.N.U.D.: *Los Mares Australes: la recolección del krill*, GLO/SO/77/2, 1979.

FAO/P.N.U.D.: *Los Mares Australes: la utilización del krill*, GLO/SO/77/3, 1979.

FAO: Global research. Southern Ocean Fisheries Survey Programme, Doc. UNDP DP/GLO/Final Report/5, 24 May 1979; also GLO/75/006.

FAO: Coastal State requirements for foreign fishing, Vol. 1, Legislative Study No. 21, Rev. 1, 1983.

International Council for the Exploration of the Sea: General Information by the Secretary General, December 1981, Mimeo.

International Whaling Commission: Chairman's report of the Thirty-Fourth Annual Meeting, Brighton, 19–24 July 1982.

International Whaling Commission: Reports of observers on meetings of CCAMLR and related material, IWC/34/11D (1981, Statement at Preparatory meeting, Resolution on cooperation, observers' report); IWC/35/21 (Report on cooperation); IWC/36/11A (Second meeting of CCAMLR-1983); IWC/37/11A (Third meeting of CCAMLR-1984); Chairman's report of the 33rd meeting of IWC (1982); Chairman's report of the 34th meeting of IWC (1983); Chairman's report of the 35th meeting of IWC (1984).

International Whaling Commission: Rules of Procedure and Financial Regulations, June 1984.

International Whaling Commission: Rules of conduct for observers and related material; also Chairman's report of the 36th meeting (1985), 23–24; Rules of Procedure (1985), article 2(b).

Organization of African Unity: Council of Ministers, 42nd Assembly; Declaration on Antarctica; Addis Ababa, 10–17 July 1985.

Organization of African Unity: 21st Summit Meeting; Declaration on Antarctica; Addis Ababa, 18–20 July 1985.

Oslo and Paris Commissions: Prevention of Marine Pollution in the North-East Atlantic region. The work of the Oslo and Paris Commissions and the Bonn Agreement, May 1982.

Oslo and Paris Commissions: History and progress, 1974–1984, The Secretariat, 1984.

Societé des Nations: Actes de la Conference pour la codification du droit international, La Haye, 13 Mars-12 Avril 1930, Vol. I, Seances plenieres, Appendice II, Rapport de la sous-commission No. II: 'Ligne de Base'.

United Nations: membership of the United Nations and related agencies, as of 31 March 1960, *Yearbook of the United Nations*, 1959, 536–537.

United Nations: The United Nations and disarmament, 1945–1970, Department of Political and Security Council Affairs, 1970.

United Nations: Introduction to the report of the Secretary General on the work of the organization, General Assembly, *Official Records*, Twenty-seventh session, Supplement No. 1A (A/8701/Add.1), August 1972.

United Nations: Marine Resources in Antarctica, Doc. EC/RSL/c1, 8 February 1977.

United Nations: Question of Antarctica, Report of the Secretary General, Doc. A/39/583 (Part I), 31 October 1984; (Part II) Vol. I, 29 October 1984; (Part II) Vol. II, 2 November 1984; (Part II) Vol. III, 9 November 1984.

United Nations Conference on the Human Environment, Stockholm, 5–16 June 1972, *Report*, New York, 1973, Action Plan for the human environment.

United Nations: Department of Public Information, Press Release: 'First Committee proposes comprehensive study on all aspects of Antarctica be undertaken by Secretary General', GA/PS/2437, 30 Nov. 1983.

United Nations Economic and Social Council: Natural resources information and documentation. General Issues, Note by the Secretary General, Doc. E/C.7/5, 25 January 1971.

United Nations Economic and Social Council: request of information on Antarctica by Sri Lanka, Doc. E/AC.24/SR.555–581/ Session 563, 14 July 1979, 72–73.

United Nations Environment Programme: The proposed programme, Doc. UNEP/GC/31, 11 February 1975; Doc. UNEP/GC/30, 4 February 1975; Doc. UNEP/GC/44, 20 February 1975.

United Nations Environment Programme: Achievements and planned development of UNEP's Regional Seas Programme and comparable programmes sponsored by other bodies, UNEP Regional Seas Reports and Studies No. 1, UNEP 1982.

United Nations Environment Programme: Prospects for global ocean pollution monitoring, UNEP Regional Seas Reports and Studies No. 47, UNEP 1984.

United Nations General Assembly: the question of Antarctica, proposals by India, Doc. A/3118, 21 Feb. 1956; Add. 1, 13 Sep. 1956; Add. 2, 17 Oct. 1956; Doc. A/3882, 15 July 1958.

United Nations General Assembly: Resolution 2574 (XXIV), 1833rd plenary meeting, 15 December 1969, Moratorium Resolution, text in Lay, Churchill and Nordquist: *New Directions in the Law of the Sea*, Vol. II, 737.

United Nations General Assembly: Declaration of the Indian Ocean as a Zone of Peace, Doc. A/8492, 1 Oct. 1971.

United Nations General Assembly: Statement by Argentina, Twenty-sixth session, First Committee, 1827th Meeting, *UNGAOR*, Verbatim record of meetings, First Committee, 22 Sep–17 Dec. 1971, Vol. 1, p. 12.

United Nations General Assembly: Statement by Mr Amerasinghe, Sri Lanka, Doc. A/PV. 2380, 8 October 1975.

United Nations General Assembly: Request for the inclusion of a supplementary item: Antarctica, Letter dated 11 August 1983 from the representatives of Antigua and Barbuda and Malaysia, A/38/193, 9 August 1983.

United Nations General Assembly: Letter dated 10 October 1983 from the Permanent Representative of India, Communiqué adopted by the Meeting of Ministers and Heads of Delegation of the Non-Aligned countries to the thirty-eighth session of the General Assembly, October 4–7, 1983, Doc. A/38/495; S/16035, 12 October 1983.

United Nations General Assembly: Peaceful settlement of disputes between States, Letter dated 19 September 1983 from the Permanent representative of Australia, A/38/439, 21 September 1983; Question of Antarctica, Letter dated 5 October 1983 from the Permanent Representative of Australia, A/38/439, Rev. 1, 10 October 1983.

United Nations General Assembly: Resolution 38/77, 15 Dec. 1983; A/C.1/38/L.80, 28 Nov. 1983 (Draft resolution); A/C.1/38/L.84, 30 Nov. 1983 (Sierra Leone on behalf of the African Group: Amendment on South Africa, withdrawn); A/38/646, 12 Dec. 1983, Report of the First Committee; A/38/PV. 97, 20 Dec. 1983 (adoption of Resolution).

United Nations General Assembly: Official Records of the Thirty-eighth session, First Committee, 42nd meeting, 28 Nov. 1983, A/C.1/38/PV.42, 29 Dec. 83; 43rd meeting, 29 Nov. 1983, A/C.1/38/PV.43, 29 Dec. 83; 44th meeting, 29 Nov. 1983, A/C.1/38/PV.44, 30 Dec. 83; 45th meeting, 30 Nov. 1983, A/C.1/38/PV.45, 7 Jan. 84; 46th meeting, 30 Nov. 1983, A/C.1/38/PV.46, 6 Jan. 84.

United Nations General Assembly: Cuestión de la Antártida, Proyecto de Resolución, Malasia, Doc. A/C.1/39/L.83, 30 de Noviembre de 1984.

United Nations General Assembly: Resolution 39/152, *Question of Antarctica*, 17 Dec. 1984.

United Nations General Assembly: Official Records of the Thirty-ninth session, First Committee, 50th meeting, 28 November 1984, A/C.1/39/PV.50, 30 Nov. 84; 52nd meeting, 29 November 1984, A/C.1/39/PV.52, 30 Nov. 84; 53rd meeting, 29 November 1984, A/C.1/39/PV.53, 30 Nov. 84; 54th meeting, 30 November 1984, A/C.1/39/PV.54, 3 Dec. 84; 55th meeting, 30 November 1984, A/C.1/39/PV.55, 3 Dec. 84.

United Nations General Assembly: Resolutions of the Fortieth Session on Antarctica, 1985, General Resolution on Antarctica, A/C.1/40/L.82, 27 Nov. 85, A/Res/40/156A; Resolution on Antarctic minerals, A/C.1/40/L.83, 27 Nov. 85, A/Res/40/156B; Draft consensus resolution on Antarctic (Australia), withdrawn A/C.1/40/L.84, 27 Nov. 85; Resolution on South Africa, A/C.1/40/L.85, 27 Nov. 85, A/Res/40/156C; Report of the First Committee, A/40/996, 9 December 1985.

United Nations General Assembly: Official Records of the Fortieth session, First Committee, 48th meeting, 25 Nov. 1985, A/C.1/40/PV.48, 29 Nov. 85; 49th meeting, 26 Nov.

1985, A/C.1/40/PV.49, 29 Nov. 85; 50th meeting, 26 Nov. 1985, A/C.1/40/PV.50, 2 Dec. 85; 51st meeting, 27 Nov. 1985, A/C.1/40/PV.51, 4 Dec. 85; 52nd meeting, 27 Nov. 1985, A/C.1/40/PV.52, 4 Dec. 85; 53rd meeting, 29 Nov. 1985, A/C.1/40/PV.53, 4 Dec. 85; 54th meeting, 29 Nov. 1985, A/C.1/40/PV.54, 4 Dec. 85.

United Nations, International Law Commission: Regime of the Territorial Sea, Doc. A/CN.4/53, 4 Avril 1952, Rapport par J. P. A. Francois, *Yearbook of the International Law Commission*, 1952, Vol. II, 25–43.

United Nations, International Law Commission: Debate on treaties providing for objective regimes (art. 63 of draft), 738th–740th meeting, 1964, *Yearbook of the International Law Commission*, 1964, Vol. I, 96–109.

United Nations, International Law Commission: Report to the General Assembly, Doc. A/5809, Sixteenth session, 11 May–24 July 1964, *Yearbook of the International Law Commission*, 1964, Vol. II, 173–227.

United Nations, International Law Commission: Report to the General Assembly, Doc. A/9610/Rev.1, Twenty-sixth session, 6 May–26 July 1974, *Yearbook of the International Law Commission*, 1974, Vol. II, Part one, 157–331.

United Nations Library: *Antarctica. A Selected Bibliography*, New York, 1956.

United Nations, Third Conference on the Law of the Sea: Preliminary study illustrating various formulae for the definition of the continental shelf, Doc. A/CONF.62/C.2/L.98, and Add.1–3, 18 April 1978.

United Nations Trusteeship Council: Official Records, Second Session, First Part, Vol. 2, 1947, Discussion on petitions to internationalize polar regions, 62–65; Supplement: Doc. T/Pet. General/15, 2 June 1947; Doc. T/Pet. General/16, 30 Aug. 1947; Doc. T/Pet. General/18, 13 Sept. 1947; 218–224.

United Nations Trusteeship Council: Petition on polar internationalization, *Yearbook of the United Nations*, 1947–48, p. 769.

Documents of international meetings

Imperial Conference, 1926, HMSO, Cmnd. 2768, 1926.

Imperial Conference, 1930, HMSO, Cmnd. 3717, 1930.

Imperial Conference, 1937, HMSO, Cmnd. 5482, 1937.

Non-Aligned nations: Meeting of Heads of State or Government, New Delhi, 7–12 March 1983 (paragraphs on Antarctica), *Environmental Policy and Law*, Vol. 11, 1983, 54.

Non-Aligned countries, Ministerial Conference: Declaration on Antarctica, *Final Communiqué*, Luanda, 4–7 September 1985.

3. Government Documents and Parliamentary Material

Collected Documents

Bush, W. M.: *Antarctica and International Law*, 2 Vol., 1982.

Government Documents

Argentina, Comisión Nacional del Antártico: *Soberanía Argentina en la Antártida*, Buenos Aires, 1947.

Australia: 'The value of the Antarctic Treaty System', *Australian Foreign Affairs Record*, Vol. 55, 1984, 905–910.

Australia: 'Challenge to the Antarctic Treaty within the United Nations', *Australian Foreign Affairs Record*, Vol. 56, 1985, 27–28.

Australia: 'Antarctic minerals regime', *Australian Foreign Affairs Record*, Vol. 56, 1985, 29–30.

554   *Bibliography*

Brazil, Ramiro Saraiva *Guerreiro*: 'Discurso por ocasiao da abertura da Reuniao sobre Recursos Minerais da Antártida', Rio de Janeiro, 26 fevreiro 1985, *Resenha de politica exterior do Brasil*, No. 44, Janeiro-marco 1985, 19–21.

Chile: Declaración del Ministerio de Relaciones Exteriores sobre Ensayos Nucleares en la Antártica, 1 Dic. 1959, *Memoria del Ministerio de Relaciones Exteriores*, 1959, 704–705.

Chile: Participación de Chile en la Conferencia Antártica de Washington, *Memoria del Ministerio de Relaciones Exteriores*, 1959, 684–704.

Chile: Statement at the Conference on the Conservation of Antarctic Seals, concerning the Convention for the Conservation of Antarctic Seals, February 11, 1972, *International Legal Materials*, Vol. XI, 1972, 417.

Chile: Informe de la Dirección Jurídica del Ministerio de Relaciones Exteriores sobre Ratificación de la Convención Internacional sobre la Caza de la Ballena, No. 136, 18 Octubre 1978, *Memoria del Ministerio de Relaciones Exteriores*, 1978, 388–391.

Chile: Informe de la Dirección Jurídica del Ministerio de Relaciones Exteriores sobre la Convención para la Conservación de la Focas Antárticas, No. 157, 11 de Noviembre de 1978, *Memoria del Ministerio de Relaciones Exteriores*, 1978, 394–395.

Chile: 'Informe de la Asesoría Jurídica del Ministerio de Relaciones Exteriores sobre posibles reclamaciones antárticas de Brasil', No. 90, 1971, in Hugo Llanos: *Teoría y Práctica del Derecho Internacional Público*, II, 1980, 174–181.

Mexico and Antarctica: Letter by the Mexican Ambassador to the United States on Mexico's position, *FRAM: The Journal of Polar Studies*, Winter 1984, 362.

Perú: Nota de adhesión al Tratado Antártico, 10 de Abril de 1981, Comunicado de prensa, 11 de April de 1981; in Edgardo Mercado Jarrín et al: *El Perú y la Antártida*, 1984, 259–261.

Perú: Exposición del representante del Perú a la XII reunión Consultiva del Tratado Antártico (13–27 de Setiembre de 1983) *Revista Peruana de Derecho Internacional*, Vol. XXXV, Julio-Setiembre 1983, 46–49.

Suriname and Antarctica: Letter by the Suriname Ambassador to the United States on Suriname's position, *FRAM: The Journal of Polar Studies*, Winter 1984, 363.

United Kingdom: Speech of welcome by Mr Anthony Kershaw on the occasion of the opening of the Conference on the Conservation of Antarctic Seals, 3 February 1972, UK Foreign and Commonwealth Office: *Report of the Conference on the Conservation of Antarctic Seals*, London, 3–11 February 1972, 5–6.

United Kingdom, Materials on International Law 1983: Antarctic Treaty, *British Year Book of International Law*, Vol. 54, 1983, 488–495.

United Kingdom, Foreign and Commonwealth Office: *Antarctic Treaty*: 25th Anniversary, Background brief, November 1984.

United States Government: Antarctica, Paper prepared by the Policy Planning Staff and Draft agreement prepared by the Department of State, June 9, 1948, *Foreign Relations of the United States*, 1948, Vol. 1, Part 2, USGPO, 1976, 977–987.

United States: Report of United States observers on inspection of Antarctic Stations, 1963–64 Austral summer season, *International Legal Materials*, Vol. III, 1964, 650–661.

United States: United States policy and international cooperation in Antarctica, Message from the President of the United States, 88th Congress, 2nd Session, House Document No. 358, 1964.

United States: Statement concerning the Convention for the Conservation of Antarctic Seals, February 11, 1972, *International Legal Materials*, Vol. XI, 1972, 417.

United States, Message from the President of the United States on the Commemoration of the 25th Anniversary of the Antarctic Treaty, December 1, 1984, in: *Antarctic Journal of the United States*, Vol. XIX, No. 4, December 1984, 12–13.

United States, C.I.A.: *U.S. Antarctic Inspection,* 1983, Map. 1984.

United States, Department of Justice: *Guidelines for International Operations,* 1977; Comments and discussion: *Proceedings of the American Society of International Law,* 1977, Panel on International Restrictive Business Practices?, 213–224.

United States, Department of State: *The Conference on Antarctica,* 1960.

United States, Department of State: Statement concerning the United States Decision to conduct an Antarctic inspection, Dept. of State Press Release No. 469, Sept. 13, 1963, *American Journal of International Law,* Vol. 58, 1964, 166–167.

United States, Department of State: Statements by US representatives at the Eighth Consultative Meeting on the question of Antarctic Mineral resources, *American Journal of International Law,* Vol. 70, 1976, 113–115; *Digest of US Practice in International Law,* 1975, 104–107.

United States, Department of State: Letter to Australian Embassy not recognizing sovereignty over the Antarctic Continental shelf, *Digest of US Practice in International Law,* 1975, 110–111.

United States, Department of State: *Legal status of Areas South of 60° South latitude,* in: *United States Senate: US Antarctic Policy,* Hearing, 1975, 18–20; also in *American Journal of International Law,* Vol. 70, 1976, 115–117; *Digest of US Practice in International Law,* 1975, 107-110.

United States, Department of State: *Environmental impact statement on the Convention for the Conservation of Antarctic Seals,* August 8, 1974.

United States, Department of State: *Final Environmental Impact Statement on the Negotiation of a Regime for Conservation of Antarctic Marine Living Resources,* June 1978, in: *United States Senate: Antarctic Living Marine Resources Negotiations,* Hearing, 1978, 45–76.

United States, Department of State: *Final Environmental Impact Statement on the negotiation of an international regime for Antarctic mineral resources,* 1982.

United States, Department of State: International regime for Antarctic mineral resources, proposed negotiation, *US Federal Register,* Nov. 8, 1982, Vol. 47, No. 216, 50598–50599.

United States, National Science Foundation: *U.S. Antarctic Program final environmental impact statement,* June 1980 (reprinted October 1984).

United States: Office of the White House Press Secretary, Press release of May 1, 1965; in: *United States Senate: US Antarctic Policy,* Hearing, 1975, 28–29.

United States: Office of the White House Press Secretary, Press release of October 13, 1970; in: *United States Senate: US Antarctic Policy,* Hearing, 1975, 30.

Parliamentary Documents

Australia: Parliamentary question about Antarctica of 29 February 1984, *Australian Foreign Affairs Record,* Vol. 55, March 1984, 247–248.

Chile: Informe de la Comisión de Relaciones Exteriores del Senado sobre el Tratado Antártico, *Diario de Sesiones del Senado,* Sesión 32, 22 de marzo de 1961, 1926–1933; Discusión del Senado: Sesión 33, 4 de Abril de 1961, 1941–1992.

Chile: La Antártida en el Parlamento Chileno, 1900–1973 (María Teresa Alfaro y Ximena Valenzuela), *Revista de Legislación y Documentacíon en Derecho y Ciencias Sociales,* Santiago, Chile, Año II, No. 2, Abril 1980, 15–23.

Perú: Declaración de la Asamblea Constituyente del Perú sobre la Antártica, 3 de Mayo de 1979, in: Edgardo Mercado Jarrín et al: *El Perú y la Antártica,* 1984, 257.

United Kingdom, House of Commons: Question on United Nations and Antarctica, Hansard, 13 June 1956.

United Kingdom, House of Commons: Questions on the Prime Minister's statement on international control of Antarctica, Hansard, 18 February 1958; also reported in *The Times,* 19 Feb. 1958.

United Kingdom, House of Commons: Questions on international control of Antarctica, related to statement by Prime Minister, Hansard, 19 February 1958.

United Kingdom, House of Commons: *Official Report*, Parliamentary Debates (Hansard), Vol. 737, No. 109, Friday, 2 December 1966, 892–899, Antarctic Treaty Bill (Agreed Measures).

United Kingdom, House of Commons: *Official Report*, Parliamentary Debates, Standing Committee C, *Antarctic Treaty Bill* (Agreed Measures), Wednesday 22 March 1967.

United Kingdom, House of Commons: *Official Report*, Parliamentary Debates (Hansard), Vol. 744, No. 179, Friday 14 April 1967, 1589–1574, Antarctic Treaty Bill (Agreed Measures).

United Kingdom, House of Lords: Statement by Lord Shackleton on neutralization of Antarctica, Hansard, House of Lords, Vol. 216, No. 70, 4 May 1959, Col. 42–43, 54 (Reply by Earl Attlee).

United Kingdom, House of Lords: *Official Report*, Parliamentary Debates (Hansard), Vol. 221, No. 40, Thursday 18 February 1960, 158–191 (The Antarctic Treaty).

United Kingdom, House of Lords: Statement by Baroness Phillips on the Antarctic Treaty, Parliamentary Debates (Hansard), House of Lords, Official Report, Vol. 282, No. 144, 1 May 1967, Cols. 761–765.

United Kingdom, House of Lords: *Official Report*, Parliamentary Debates (Hansard), Vol. 282, No. 144, Monday 1 May 1967, 738–766, Antarctic Treaty Bill (Agreed Measures).

United Kingdom, House of Lords: *Official Report*, Parliamentary Debates (Hansard), Vol. 285, No. 184, Monday 24 July 1967, 622–626, Antarctic Treaty Bill (Agreed Measures).

United Kingdom, House of Lords: Debate on the Falklands and the Antarctic, House of Lords, *Official Report*, Parliamentary Debates (Hansard), Vol. 462, No. 77, Monday 22 April 1985, Cols. 904–953.

United States, House of Representatives, *H.J. Res. 184*, 85th Congress, 1st session, January 23, 1957 (Joint Resolution declaring the right of sovereignty).

United States, House of Representatives: *Antarctica legislation – 1961, Hearings* before the Subcommittee on Territorial and Insular Affairs of the Committee on Interior and Insular Affairs, 87th Congress, 1st session 1961, U.S. Government Printing Office, 1962.

United States, House of Representatives, Committee on Interior and Insular Affairs, Subcommittee on Territorial and Insular Affairs, *Hearings on Antarctica Report 1965*, 89th Congress, 1st session, 1965.

United States, House of Representatives, Committee on Science and Technology, Subcommittee on Energy research, development and demonstration, *Polar Energy Resources Potential*, Report prepared by the Congressional Research Service, 94th Congress, 2nd Session, 1976.

United States, House of Representatives, Committee on the Judiciary, Subcommittee on Immigration, Citizenship, and international law, *Hearing on Extraterritorial Criminal Jurisdiction* (H.R. 763, 6148, 7842), July 21, 1977, USGPO, 1977, Serial No. 16.

United States, House of Representatives, Committee on Merchant Marine and Fisheries, Subcommittee on Fisheries and Wildlife Conservation and the Environment, *Antarctic Fauna and Flora Conservation*, Hearing on H.R. 7749 (Bill to implement Agreed Measures), 95th Congress. 1st session, 1977, USGPO, 1978, 245–369.

United States, House of Representatives: H.R. 4311, a Bill to authorize a plan for an Antarctic Historic and Natural Preserve, 96th Congress, 1st Session, June 5, 1979.

United States, House of Representatives, Committee on Merchant Marine and Fisheries, Subcommittee on Fisheries and Wildlife conservation and the environment,

Hearing on Antarctic Marine Living Resources (H.R. 3416), June 30, 1983, USGPO, 1983, Serial No. 98-24.

United States, Senate: *US Antarctic Policy*, Hearing before the Subcommittee on Oceans and International Environment of the Committee on Foreign Relations, 94th Congress, 1st Session, US Government Printing Office, 1975.

United States, Senate: *Antarctic Living Marine Resources Negotiations*, Hearing before the National Ocean Policy Study of the Committee on Commerce, Science and Transportation, 95th Congress, 2nd Session, 14 June 1978, US Government Printing Office, 1978.

United States, Senate, Committee on Foreign Relations, Subcommittee on Arms Control, Oceans and international environment, *Hearing on Exploitation of Antarctic Resources*, 95th Congress, 2nd Session, 1978.

United States, Senate, Committee on Foreign Relations, *Hearing on the Antarctic Treaty*, 86th Congress, 2nd Session, 14 June 1960, USGPO, 1960.

4. Books and theses on international law and related subjects

Ago, Roberto: Il requisito dell'effettività dell'occupazione in diritto internazionale, 1934.

Asamoah, Obed Y.: The legal significance of the Declarations of the General Assembly of the United Nations, 1966.

Bailey, Sydney D.: The procedure of the UN Security Council, 1975.

Bailey, Sydney D.: Voting in the Security Council, 1969.

Bentham, R. W. (ed.): Recent developments in United Kingdom Petroleum Law, University of Dundee, Centre for Petroleum and Mineral Law Studies, 1984.

Bishop, R. W. Jr: International Law Cases and Materials, 1962.

Bowett, D. W.: The Law of International Institutions, 1982.

Brierly, J. L.: The Law of Nations, Sixth edition, 1963.

Brown, E. D.: Sea-bed energy and mineral resources and the Law of the Sea, Vol. 1, 1984.

Brown, Roland and **Faber,** Mike: *Some policy and legal issues affecting mining legislation and agreements in African Commonwealth countries*, Commonwealth Secretariat, 1977.

Brown, Seyom, **Cornell,** Nina W., **Fabian,** Larry L., **Weiss,** Edith Brown: Regimes for the Ocean, Outer Space, and Weather, Brookings Institution, 1977.

Brownlie, Ian: System of the Law of Nations. State Responsibility, Part I, 1983.

Brownlie, Ian: Principles of Public International Law (Third edition), 1979.

Buzan, Barry: Seabed politics, 1976.

Cameron, Peter D.: Property rights and Sovereign rights. The Case of North Sea Oil, 1983.

Churchill, R. R.: The common fisheries policy of the European Economic Community: a legal analysis, PhD Thesis, UWIST, 1984 (2 vol.).

Churchill, R. R. and **Lowe,** A. V.: The Law of the Sea, 1983.

Claude, Inis L. Jr: Swords into plowshares. The problems and progress of international organization, 1971.

Colombos, C. John: The International Law of the Sea, 1967.

Csabafi, Imre Anthony: The Concept of State Jurisdiction in International Space Law, 1971.

De Visscher, Charles: Problèmes de Confins en Droit International Public, 1969.

Daintith, Terence and **Willoughby,** Geoffrey: United Kingdom Oil and Gas Law, 1984.

Daintith, Terence (ed.): The legal character of petroleum licences: a comparative study, University of Dundee, Centre for Petroleum and Mineral, Law Studies and Energy and Natural Resources Committee of the International Bar Association, 1981.

Di Qual, Lino: Les effets des Resolutions des Nations Unies, 1967.

Dupuy, René-Jean (ed.): The settlement of disputes on the new natural resources, Academie Droit International de La Haye, Colloque 1982, 1983.

Dupuy, René-Jean et **Vignes,** Daniel: Traité du Nouveau Droit de la Mer, 1985.

Extavour, Winston Conrad: The Exclusive Economic Zone, 1981.
Fauchille, Paul: Traité du Droit International Public, Tome 1er, Deuxieme partie, 1925.
Fenwick, Charles G.: International Law, Fourth edition, 1965.
Ferencz, Benjamin: An international criminal court. A step towards world peace, 2 vol.,
    1980.
Friedmann, Wolfgang G., **Kalmanoff,** George (eds): Joint International Business
    Ventures, 1961.
Friedmann, Wolfgang: The Changing Structure of International Law, 1964.
García-Amador, F. V.: The Inter-American System, 1983.
Gilson, Bernard: The conceptual system of sovereign equality, 1984.
Goebel, Julius: The struggle for the Falkland Islands. A study in legal and diplomatic
    history, 1927.
Goodrich, Leland M., **Hambro,** Edward and **Simons,** Anne Patricia: Charter of the United
    Nations, 1969.
Grattan, C. Hartley: the United States and the Southern Pacific, 1961.
Gray, Louis H.: Spitsbergen and Bear Island, Washington, Government Printing Office,
    1919.
Greig, D. W.: International Law, 1976.
Hackworth, G. H.: Digest of International Law, Vol. 1, 1940.
Hall, William Edward: A treatise on International Law, Eighth edition, 1924.
Hardin, Garrett, **Baden,** John (eds): Managing the Commons, 1977.
Hart, H. L. A.: The Concept of Law, 1970.
Higgins, Rosalyn: The development of international law through the political organs of the
    United Nations, 1963.
Hyde, Charles Cheney: International Law chiefly as interpreted and applied by the United
    States, Vol. 1, 1947.
Jaenicke, Gunther, **Schanze,** Erich, **Hauser,** Wolfgang: A Joint Venture agreement for
    seabed mining, 1981.
Jenks, C. Wilfred: The Common Law of Mankind, 1958.
Jennings, R. Y.: The Acquisition of Territory in International Law, 1963.
Jessup, Philip C.: A modern Law of Nations, 1949.
Johnston, Douglas M.: The International Law of Fisheries, 1965.
Johnston, Douglas M. (ed.): Arctic Ocean Issues in the 1980s, Law of the Sea Institute,
    University of Hawaii, 1982.
Kelsen, Hans: Principles of International Law, second edition, 1966.
Kelsen, Hans: General Theory of Law and State, 1949.
Kirby, Glenn S.: Economic rent and leasing policy choices for petroleum development in
    northern Canada, Dissertation, Diploma in Polar Studies, Scott Polar Research
    Institute, Cambridge, 1975–1976.
Kish, John: The Law of International Spaces, 1973.
Koers, Albert W.: International regulation of marine fisheries, 1973.
Lay, Houston and **Taubenfeld,** Howard J.: The law relating to activities of man in space,
    1970.
Lindley, A. V.: The acquisition and government of Backward Territory in International
    Law, 1926.
Lowe, A. V.: Extraterritorial Jurisdiction, an annotated collection of legal materials, 1983.
Monaco, Riccardo: Lezioni di organizzazione internazionale, Vol. II, 1968.
Morton, Desmond Nicholas: Present political attitudes towards non-renewable resource
    development in selected northern areas, Thesis, Diploma in Polar Studies, Scott
    Polar Research Institute, Cambridge, 1980.
McNair, Lord: The Law of Treaties, 1961.
Oda, Shigeru: International law of the resources of the sea, 1979.
Ogley, Roderick: Internationalizing the Seabed, 1984.
Oppenheim, L.: International Law, A Treatise, Vol. I, Eighth Edition, 1962.

Orrego Vicuña, Francisco (ed.): The Exclusive Economic Zone. A Latin American perspective, 1984.

Ostreng, Willy: Politics in High Latitudes: The Svalbard Archipelago, 1977.

Papadakis, N.: The international legal regime of artificial islands, 1977.

Perl, Perl: The Falkland Islands Dispute in International Law and Politics. A documentary sourcebook, 1983.

Pharand, Donat: The Law of the Sea of the Arctic, 1973.

Post, Alexandra M.: Deepsea Mining and the Law of the Sea, 1983.

Remiro Brotons, Antonio: Derecho Internacional Público, 1. – Principios fundamentales, 1983.

Rousseau, Charles: Droit International Public, Tome I, 1970.

Rousseau, Charles: Droit International Public, Tome III, 1977.

Schermers, Harry G.: International Institutional Law, 1980.

Schwebel, Stephen M. (ed.): The effectiveness of international decisions, 1971.

Shusterich, Kurt Michael: Resource Management and the oceans. *The Political Economy of Deep Seabed Mining,* 1982.

Sinclair, Sir Ian: The Vienna Convention on the Law of Treaties, Second edition, 1984.

Singh, Nagendra: International Maritime Law Conventions, Vol. 3, 1983.

Smith, David N., **Wells,** Louis T. Jr: Negotiating Third World Mineral Agreements, 1975.

Underdal, Arild: The Politics of International Fisheries Management. The Case of the Northeast Atlantic, 1980.

United Nations: Legal and institutional arrangements in minerals development, 1982.

United Nations: Negotiation and drafting of mining development agreements, 1976.

Verzijl, J. H. W.: International Law in Historical Perspective, Vol. III, IV, 1970, 1971.

Went, A. E. J.: Seventy Years Agrowing. A history of the International Council for the Exploration of the Sea 1902–1972, 1972.

Westermeyer, William E., **Shusterich,** Kurt M.: United States Arctic interests, The 1980s and 1990s, 1984.

Whiteman, Marjorie M.: Digest of International Law, Vol. 2, 1963.

Young, Oran R.: Compliance and Public Authority, 1979.

Young, Oran: Resource Management at the International Level. The case of the North Pacific, 1977.

5. Articles, pamphlets, contributions to books and other material on international law and related subjects

Adams, Thomas R.: 'The Outer Space Treaty: an interpretation in light of the No-Sovereignty Provision', *Harvard International Law Journal,* Vol. 9, 1968, 140–157.

Akehurst, Michael: 'Custom as a source of international law', *British Yearbook of International Law,* Vol. 47, 1974–1975, 1–53.

Akinsanya, Adeoye: 'The "Pueblo" Affair and international law', *Indian Journal of International Law,* Vol. 15, 1975, 485–500.

Allot, Philip: 'Power sharing in the Law of the Sea', *American Journal of International Law,* Vol. 77, 1983, 1–30.

American Law Institute: Restatement of the Law (Second), Foreign Relations Law of the United States, 1965; see also Restatement of the Law, Foreign Relations Law of the United States (Revised), Tentative Draft No. 2, March 27, 1981.

Asante, Samuel K. B.: 'Restructuring transnational mineral agreements', *American Journal of International Law,* Vol. 73, 1979, 335–371.

Asante, Samuel and **Stockmayer,** Albrecht: 'Evolution of development contracts: the issue of effective control', in United Nations: *Legal and institutional arrangements in minerals development,* 1982, 53–67.

Archer, Clive and **Scrivener,** David: 'Frozen frontiers and resource wrangles: conflict and cooperation in Northern waters', *International Affairs*, Vol. 51, No. 1, Winter 1982/83, 59–76.

Aubry, Lloyd W., Jr: 'Criminal jurisdiction over Arctic ice islands: United States v. Escamilla', *UCLA-Alaska Law Review*, Vol. 4, 1974–1975, 419–440.

Auburn, F. M.: 'International Law and Sea-Ice Jurisdiction in the Arctic Ocean', *The International and Comparative Law Quarterly*, Vol. 22, 1973, 552–557.

Ausland, John C.: 'Spitsbergen: Who's in control?', *United States Naval Institute Proceedings*, Vol. 104/11/909, November 1978, 63–70.

Bassiouni, M. Cherif: 'Theories of jurisdiction and their application in extradition law and practice', *California Western International Law Journal*, Vol. 4–5, 1973–1975, 1–61.

Baxter, R. R.: 'Multilateral treaties as evidence of customary international law', *British Yearbook of International Law*, Vol. 41, 1965–1966, 275–300.

Beauchamp, Ken: 'International legal issues in Arctic waters', in *Canadian Arctic Resources Committee*, 1984, 53–79.

Beesley, J. A.: 'Rights and Responsibilities of Arctic Coastal States: The Canadian View', *Journal of Maritime Law and Commerce*, Vol. 3, 1971–1972, 1–12.

Bennouna, Mohamed: 'Le Droit International relatif aux matiéres premiéres', *Recueil des Cours de l'Academie de Droit International*, 1982-IV, 103–191.

Bentham, R. W.: 'The oil industry and problems of extraterritoriality', in R. W. Bentham (ed.): *Recent developments in United Kingdom Petroleum Law*, University of Dundee, Centre for Petroleum and Mineral Law Studies, 1984, 50–71.

Bergsager, Egil: 'Oil and Gas in the USSR', *Noroil*, August 1984 (Reprint).

Bergsager, Egil: 'Arctic Experiences', Introductory talk at O.N.S. Advanced Projects Conference, 15–17 November 1983, Stavanger, NDP-Contribution No. 15, Oljedirektoratet, March 1984.

Bernhardt, J. Peter A.: 'Spitsbergen: Jurisdictional friction over unexploited oil reserves', *California Western International Law Journal*, Vol. 4, 1973, 61–120.

Bindschedler, Rudolf L.: 'La délimitation des compétences des Nations Unies', *Recueil des Cours de l'Academie de Droit International*, 1963-I, 307–424.

Birnie, Patricia: 'Developments in the law for prevention of marine pollution from petroleum during 1983–1984', in R. W. Bentham (ed.): *Recent developments in United Kingdom Petroleum Law*, University of Dundee, Centre for Petroleum and Mineral Law Studies, 1984, 72–127.

Bloomfield, Lincoln P.: 'The Arctic: last unmanaged frontier', *Foreign Affairs*, Fall 1981, 87–105.

Boczek, Boleslaw: 'The Arctic Ocean: an international legal profile', *International Studies Notes*, Vol. 11, No. 3, 1985, 10–15.

Bollecker-Stern, Brigitte: 'L'Affaire des essais nucléaires francais devant la Cour Internationale de Justice', *Annuaire Francais de Droit International*, Vol. XX, 1974, 299–333.

Bollecker-Stern, Brigitte: 'L'Arbitrage dans l'affaire du Canal de Beagle entre l'Argentine et le Chili', *Revue General de Droit International Public*, 1979, 7–52.

Bos, Maarten: 'The identification of custom in international law', *German Yearbook of International Law*, Vol. 25, 1982, 9–53.

Bowett, D. W.: 'Jurisdiction: Changing Patterns of Authority over Activities and Resources', in: R. St. J. MacDonald and Douglas M. Johnston: *The Structure and Process of International Law: Essays in Legal Philosophy Doctrine and Theory*, 1983, 555–580.

Bridge, J. W.: 'The United Nations and English law', *International and Comparative Law Quarterly*, Vol. 18, 1969, 689–717.

Brown, E. D.: 'Pollution from seabed mining: legal safeguards', *Environmental Policy and Law*, Vol. 10, 1983, 122–134.

Brown, Roland: 'Choice of law provisions in concession and related contracts', in Roland Brown and Mike Faber: *Some policy and legal issues affecting mining legislation and agreements in African Commonwealth countries*, Commonwealth Secretariat, 1977, 82–107.

Brown, Roland: 'The legislative framework', in Roland Brown and Mike Faber: *Some policy and legal issues affecting mining legislation and agreements in African Commonwealth countries*, Commonwealth Secretariat, 1977, 1–29.

Brownlie, Ian: 'Legal status of natural resources in international law', *Recueil des Cours de l'Academie de Droit International*, Vol. 162, 1979-I, 245–317.

Buzan, Barry: 'Negotiating by consensus: developments in technique at the United Nations Conference on the Law of the Sea', *American Journal of International Law*, Vol. 75, 1981, 324–348.

Caflisch, Lucius C.: 'The settlement of disputes relating to activities in the international seabed area', in C. L. Rozakis and C. A. Stephanou (eds): *The New Law of the Sea*, 1983, 303–344.

Cahier, Philippe: 'Le problème des effets des traités a l'égard des états tiers', *Recueil des Cours de l'Academie de Droit International*, 1974-III, 589–735.

Caminos, H.: 'Les sources du Droit de la Mer', in René-Jean Dupuy et Daniel Vignes: *Traité du Nouveau Droit de la Mer*, 1985, 27–121.

Capotorti, Francesco: 'L'extinction et la suspension des traités', *Recueil des Cours de l'Academie de Droit International*, 1971, Vol. III, 417–587.

Carlson, Cynthia E.: 'The international regulation of small cetaceans', *San Diego Law Review*, Vol. 21, 1984, 577–623.

Carroz, J. E.: 'Institutional aspects of fishery management under the new regime of the oceans', *San Diego Law Review*, Vol. 21, 1984, 513–540.

Castañeda, Jorge: 'Valeur juridique des résolutions des Nations Unies', *Recueil des Cours de l'Academie de Droit International*, 1970-I, 205–331.

Cates, Melissa B.: 'Offshore oil platforms which pollute the marine environment: a proposal for an international treaty imposing strict liability', *San Diego Law Review*, Vol. 21, 1984, 691–708.

Charney, Jonathan I.: 'Transnational corporations and developing public international law', *Duke Law Journal*, Vol., 1983, 748–788.

Christie, G. C.: 'What constitutes a taking of property under international law?', *British Yearbook of International Law*, Vol. 38, 1962, 307–338.

Colson, David A.: 'Political and Boundary issues affecting energy resources', Comments, *18th Annual Conference of the Law of the Sea Institute*, September 26, 1984.

Comisión Chilena del Cobre: 'Contribución al estudio de la concesión minera en el derecho comparado', 1981.

Cooper, John C.: 'Airspace rights over the Arctic', *Air Affairs*, Vol. 3, No. 3, 1950, 516–540.

Cot, Jean-Pierre: 'La conduite subsèquente des parties a un traité', *Revue Generale de Droit International Public*, Tome LXX, 1966, 632–666.

Crommelin, Michael: 'The legal character of petroleum production licences in Australia', in: Terence Daintith (ed.): *The Legal Character of Petroleum licences: a comparative study*, Centre for Petroleum and Mineral Law Studies, University of Dundee, 1981, 60–100.

Cruickshank, David A.: 'Arctic Ice and International Law: The Escamilla Case', *Western Ontario Law Review*, Vol. 10, 1971, 178–194.

Curtis, Clifton E.: 'Recent developments under special environmental conventions', *18th Annual Conference of the Law of the Sea Institute*, San Francisco, 24 September 1984.

Dagory, Jacques: 'Les rapports entre les institutions spécialisées et l'organisation des Nations Unies', *Revue Generale de Droit International Public*, Vol. 73, 1969, 283–377.

Daillier, Patrick: 'Les Communautés Européennes et le Droit de la Mer', *Revue Generale de Droit International Public*, Vol. LXXXIII, 1979, 417–473.

Daintith, Terence: 'The petroleum production licence in the United Kingdom', in Terence Daintith (ed.): *The legal character of petroleum licences: a comparative study*, 1981, 200–225.

Daintith, Terence: 'Petroleum Licences: A Comparative Introduction', in Terence Daintith (ed.): *The legal character of petroleum licences: a comparative study*, 1981, 1–34.

Dalhousie Ocean Studies Programme: 'Conservation and Management of the Marine Environment. Responsibilities and required initiatives in accordance with the 1982 U.N. Convention on the Law of the Sea', 1984.

Dell, Edmund: 'Interdependence and the judges: civil aviation and antitrust', *International Affairs*, Vol. 61, 1985, 355–373.

Dolzer, Rudolf: 'New foundations of the law of expropriation of alien property', *American Journal of International Law*, Vol. 75, 1981, 553–589.

Dugger, John A.: 'Arctic Oil and Gas: policy perspectives', in William E. Westermeyer, Kurt M. Shusterich: *United States Arctic interests. The 1980s and 1990s*, 1984, 19–38.

Dupuy, P. M. et **Rémond–Gouilloud,** M.: 'La préservation du milieu marin', in René-Jean Dupuy et Daniel Vignes: *Traité du Nouveau Droit de la Mer*, 1985, 979–1045.

Dupuy, René-Jean: 'The notion of common heritage of mankind applied to the seabed', in C. L. Rozakis and C. A. Stephanou (eds): *The New Law of the Sea*, 1983, 199–208.

Dupuy, René-Jean: 'La notion de patrimoine commun de l'humanité appliquée aux fond marins', in *Droit et libertés a la fin du XXe siecle*, Etudes offertes a Claude-Albert Colliard, 1984, 197–205.

Dupuy, René-Jean: 'La Zone, patrimoine commun de l'humanité', in René-Jean Dupuy et Daniel Vignes: *Traité du Nouveau Droit de la Mer*, 1985, 499–505.

Dutheil de la Rochere, Jacqueline: 'L'Affaire du Canal de Beagle', *Annuaire Francais de Droit International*, 1977, 408–435.

Ederer, Markus: 'Selective legal problems arising from the accession of the European Economic Community to the Law of the Sea Convention', Research Paper, Ocean Law Seminar, School of Law, University of Miami, Spring 1985.

Eigen, Peter: 'Default, termination and surrender', in United Nations: *Negotiation and drafting of mining development agreements*, 1976, 155–172.

El-Kosheri, Ahmed Sadek: 'Le regime juridique créé par les accords de participation dans le domaine pétrolier', *Recueil des Cours de l'Academie de Droit International*, 1975-IV, 219–393.

Engel, Uggi: 'The legal character of the Danish sole concession', in: Terence Daintith (ed.): *The legal character of petroleum licences: a comparative study*, Centre for Petroleum and Mineral Law Studies, University of Dundee, 1981, 163–175.

European Economic Community: 'Watch on the fishing grounds', Europe 1984, No. 11, November 1984, 3–5.

Faber, Mike: 'The Fiscal Regime', in Roland Brown and Mike Faber: *Some policy and legal issues affecting mining legislation and agreements in African Commonwealth countries*, Secretariat, 1977, 30–81.

Faber, Michael: 'Some old and new devices in mineral royalties and taxation', in United Nations: *Legal and institutional arrangements in minerals development*, 1982, 104–122.

Fahrney, Richard L. II: 'Status of an Island's Continental Shelf Jurisdiction: A case study of the Falkland Islands', *Journal of Maritime Law and Commerce*, Vol. 10, 1978–1979, 539–553.

Finch, Stephan B. Jr: 'Pueblo and Mayaguez: a legal analysis', *Case Western Reserve Journal of International Law*, Vol. 9, 1977, 79–116.

Fitzmaurice, Gerald: 'The Law and Procedure of the International Court of Justice, 1951–1954: points of substantive law, Part II', *British Yearbook of International Law*, 1955–1956, 20–96.

Fitzmaurice, Sir Gerald: 'The General Principles of International Law considered from the standpoint of the rule of law', *Recueil des Cours de l'Academie de Droit International*, Vol. 92, 1957-II, 1–227.

Fitzmaurice, Sir Gerald: 'Fifth report on the Law of Treaties', Doc. A/CN.4/130, 21 March 1960, *Yearbook of the International Law Commission*, 1960, Vol. II, 69–107.

Fleischer, Carl August: 'Le regime d'exploitation du Spitsberg', *Annuaire Francais de Droit International*, 1978, 275–300.

Fleischer, Carl August: 'The Northern waters and the new maritime zones', *German Yearbook of International Law*, Vol. 22, 1979, 100–118.

Franck, Thomas M.: 'World Made Law: the decision of the ICJ in the Nuclear Test Cases', *American Journal of International Law*, Vol. 69, 1975, 612–620.

Fromont, Michael: 'L'abstention dans les votes au sein des organisations internationales', *Annuaire Francais de Droit International*, 1961, 492–523.

Friedman, Alan E.: 'The Economics of the common pool: property rights in exhaustible resources', *UCLA Law Review*, Vol. 18, 1971, 855–887.

Friedrichs, Jorge Walter: 'Granting of rights, work obligations, waiver, stages of the agreement and time limits', in United Nations: *Negotiation and drafting of mining development agreements*, 1976, 173–183.

García-Amador, F. V.: 'The proposed new International Economic Order: a new approach to the law governing nationalization and compensation', *Lawyer of the Americas*, Vol. 12, 1980, 1–58.

García-Amador, F. V.: 'Current attempts to revise international law – a comparative analysis', *American Journal of International Law*, Vol. 77, No. 2, April 1983, 286–295.

Garret, John Norton: 'Conventional hydrocarbons in the United States Arctic: an industry appraisal', in William E. Westermeyer, Kurt M. Shusterich: *United States Arctic interests, The 1980s and 1990s*, 1984, 39–58.

Goldie, L. F. E.: 'Liability for damage and the progressive development of international law', *International and Comparative Law Quarterly*, Vol. 14, 1965, 1189–1264.

Goldie, L. F. E.: 'A General International Law Doctrine for Seabed Regimes', *The International Lawyer*, Vol. 7, 1973, 796–824.

Goldie, L. F. E.: 'Reconciling values of distributive equity and management efficiency in the international commons', in René-Jean Dupuy (ed.): *The settlement of disputes on the new natural resources, Academie de Droit International de La Haye*, Colloque 1982, 1983, 335–376.

Goldie, L. F. E.: 'Title and use (and usufruct) – An ancient distinction too oft forgot', *American Journal of International Law*, Vol. 79, 1985, 689–714.

Haas, Ernst B.: 'Why Collaborate? Issue-Linkage and International Regimes', *World Politics*, Vol. 32, No. 3, April 1980, 357–405.

Handl, Gunther: 'The principle of "equitable use" as applied to internationally shared natural resources: its role in resolving potential international disputes over transfrontier pollution', *Revue Belge de Droit International*, Vol. XIV, 1978–1979, 40–64.

Hargrove, John Lawrence and **Kellner,** Nancy J.: 'The international legal regime of the Arctic', in Ira Dyer and Chryssostomos Chryssostomidis: *Arctic Technology and Policy*, 1984, 47–60.

Harrison, Rowland J.: 'The legal character of petroleum production licences in Canada', in Terence Daintith (ed.): *The Legal Character of Petroleum licences: a comparative study,* Centre for Petroleum and Mineral Law Studies, University of Dundee, 1981, 101–162.

Harvard Research in International Law: 'Jurisdiction with respect to crime', *Supplement to the American Journal of International Law*, Vol. 29, 1935, 435–651.

Head, Ivan L.: 'Canadian claims to territorial sovereignty in the Arctic regions', *McGill Law Journal*, Vol. 9, No. 3, 1963, 200–226.

Hegelson, G. J. F. van: 'The argument for an interim arrangement', *Marine Policy*, Vol. 5, 1981, 260–264.

Henkin, Louis: 'Arctic Anti-Pollution: Does Canada make – or break – International Law?', *American Journal of International Law*, Vol. 65, 1971, 131–136.

Higgins, Rosalyn: 'The International Law Perspective', in Terence Daintith (ed.): *The legal character of petroleum licences: a comparative study*, 1981, 35–59.

Higgins, Rosalyn: 'Ten years of state involvement in the offshore petroleum industry – The U.K. experience', Reprint from *Cambridge II Seminar Proceedings*.

Higgins, Rosalyn: 'The taking of property by the State: recent developments in international law', *Recueil des Cours de l'Academie de Droit International*, Vol. 176, 1982-III, 263–391.

Higgins, Rosalyn: 'The legal bases of jurisdiction', in Cecil J. Olmstead: *Extra-territorial application of laws and responses thereto*, 1984, 3–14.

Himmelreich, David M.: 'The Beagle Channel Affair: A Failure in Judicial Persuasion', *Vanderbilt Journal of Transnational Law*, Vol. 12, 1979, 971–998.

Institut de Droit International: 'Resolution on Contracts concluded by International organizations with private persons', *Annuaire de l'Institut de Droit International*, Vol. 57-II, 1977, 333–337.

Institut de Droit International: 'Resolution on Multinational Enterprises', *Annuaire de l'Institut de Droit International*, Vol. 57-II, 1977, 339–343.

Institut de Droit International: 'Resolution on the proper law of the contract in agreements between a State and a foreign person', *Annuaire de l'Institut de Droit International*, Vol. 58-II, 1979, 193–195.

Institut de Droit International: 'Le droit applicable aux entreprises internationales communes. Projet définitif de resolution', *Annuaire de l'Institut de Droit International*, Vol. 60-I, 1983, 103–106.

James, Alan: 'Sovereignty: ground rule or gibberish?', *Review of International Studies*, Vol. 10, 1984, 1–18.

Jenks, C. Wilfred: 'An International Regime for Antarctica?', *International Affairs*, Vol. 32, 1956, 414–426.

Jenks, C. Wilfred: 'Unanimity, the veto, weighted voting, special and simple majorities and Consensus as modes of decision in international organisations', *Cambridge Essays in International Law*, Essays in honour of Lord McNair, 1965, 48–63.

Jessup, Philip C.: 'The Palmas Island Arbitration', *American Journal of International Law*, Vol. 22, 1928, 735–752.

Jessup, Philip C.: 'Sovereignty in Antarctica', *American Journal of International Law*, Vol. 41, 1947, 117–119.

Jessup, Philip C.: 'Jurisdiction', in Richard B. Lillich and John Norton Moore (eds): *Role of International Law and an evolving ocean law*, U.S. Naval War College, International Law Studies, Vol. 61, 1980, 303–318.

Jiménez de Aréchaga, Eduardo: 'State responsibility for the nationalization of foreign owned property', *New York University Journal of International Law and Politics*, Vol. 11, 1978, 179–195.

Jonathan, Gerard Cohen: 'Les Iles Falkland (Malouines)', *Annuaire Francais de Droit International*, Vol. XVIII, 1972, 235–262.

Joseph, James: 'The management of highly migratory species', *Marine Policy*, Vol. 1, 1977, 275–288.

Kaczynski, Vladimir: 'Distant water fisheries and the 200 mile Economic Zone', *Law of the Sea Institute, Occasional Paper No. 34*, 1984.

Kaeckenbeeck, Georges: 'La protection internationale des droits Acquis', *Recueil des Cours de l'Academie de Droit International*, Vol. 59, 1937-I, 317–419.

Kahn-Freund, O.: 'Delictual liability and the conflict of laws', *Recueil des Cours de l'Academie de Droit International*, Vol. 124, 1968-II, 1–166.

Kemper, Ría: 'The concept of permanent sovereignty and its impact on mineral contracts', in United Nations: *Legal and institutional arrangements in minerals development*, 1982, 29–36.

Kestenbaum, Lionel: 'Antitrust's "Extraterritorial" Jurisdiction: a progress report on the balancing of Interests Test', *Stanford Journal of International Law*, Vol. 18, 1982, 311–346.

Kimball, Lee: 'Implications of the Arrangements Made for Deep Sea Mining for other joint exploitations', *Columbia Journal of World Business*, Vol. 15, No. 4, Winter 1980, 52–61.

Kindt, John Warren, **Perriot,** Todd Jay: 'Ice-covered areas: The competing interests of conservation and resource exploitation', *San Diego Law Review*, Vol. 21, 1984, 941–983.

Kiss, Alexandre-Charles: 'La notion de patrimoine commun de l'humanité', *Recueil des Cours de l'Academie de Droit International*, 1982-II, 99–256.

Koers, Albert W.: 'The freedom of fishing in decline: the case of the North-East Atlantic', in Robin Churchill, K. R. Simmonds, Jane Welch: *New Directions in the Law of the Sea*, Vol. III, 1973, 19–35.

Koers, Albert W.: 'The external authority of the EEC in regard to marine fisheries', *Common Market Law Review*, Vol. 14, 1977, 269–301.

Koers, Albert W.: 'Participation of the European Economic Community in a new law of the sea convention', *American Journal of International Law*, Vol. 73, 1979, 426–443.

Koers, Albert W.: 'The fisheries policy', in Commission of the European Communities: *Thirty Years of Community Law*, 1983, 467–475.

Kokkini-Iatridou, D. and **de Waart,** P. J. I. M.: 'Foreign investments in developing countries – legal personality of multinationals in international law', *Netherlands Yearbook of International Law*, Vol. XIV, 1983, 87–131.

Krem, Alexander J.: 'Financing ocean mineral developments: feasible under what terms?', *Eighteenth Annual Conference of the Law of the Sea Institute*, San Francisco, Sept. 24–27, 1984.

Lagoni, Rainer: 'Oil and Gas deposits across national frontiers', *American Journal of International Law*, Vol. 73, 1979, 215–243.

Lakhtine, W.: 'Rights over the Arctic', *American Journal of International Law*, Vol. 24, 1930, 703–717.

Lansing, Robert: 'A unique international problem', *American Journal of International Law*, Vol. 11, 1917, 763–771.

Larschan, Bradley and **Brennan,** Bonnie C.: 'The Common Heritage of Mankind Principle in International Law', *Columbia Journal of Transnational Law*, Vol. 21, 1982–1983, 305–337.

Lee, Luke T.: 'The Law of the Sea Convention and Third States', *American Journal of International Law*, Vol. 77, 1983, 541–568.

Legoux, Pierre Ch. A.: 'Depletion Allowance', in United Nations: *Negotiation and drafting of mining development agreements*, 1976, 34–42.

Lipton, C. J.: 'Forms of agreement', in United Nations: *Negotiation and drafting of mining development agreements*, 1976, 92–102.

Loftas, Tony: 'FAO's EEZ Programme', *Marine Policy*, Vol. 5, 1981, 229–239.

Lowe, A. V.: 'Blocking extraterritorial jurisdiction: the British protection of trading interests act, 1980', *American Journal of International Law*, Vol. 75, 1981, 257–282.

Lucas, Kenneth C. and **Loftas,** Tony: 'FAO's EEZ Program: helping to build the fisheries of the future', *Ocean Yearbook* 3, 1982, 38–76.

Macdonald, R. St. J. and **Hough,** Barbara: 'The Nuclear Tests Case revisited', *German Yearbook of International Law*, Vol. 20, 1977, 337–357.

Maier, Harold G.: 'Interest balancing and Extraterritorial Jurisdiction', *The American Journal of Comparative Law*, Vol. 31, 1983, 579–597.

Marshall, David W. I.: 'The Canadian Experience', in *The Antarctic: preferred futures, constraints and choices*, New Zealand Institute of International Affairs, 1983, 41–49.

Marshall, J. A.: 'UK Petroleum Taxation: where we stand in 1984 – a look back and a look ahead', in R. W. Bentham (ed.): *Recent Developments in United Kingdom Petroleum Law*, University of Dundee, Centre for Petroleum and Mineral Law Studies, 1984, 1–21.

Mateesco Matte, Nicolas: 'The Law of the Sea and Outer Space: a comparative survey of specific issues', *Ocean Yearbook* 3, 1982, 13–37.

Meessen, Karl M.: 'Antitrust jurisdiction under customary international law', *American Journal of International Law*, Vol. 78, 1984, 783–810.

Meredith, Brian: 'A plan for the Arctic. Mr Trudeau's international regime', *The Round Table*, Vol. 60, No. 238, April 1970, 177–182.

Mikesell, Raymond F.: 'Financial Considerations in Negotiating Mining Development Agreements', in United Nations: *Negotiation and drafting of mining development agreements*, 1976, 7–20.

Miller, David Hunter: 'Political rights in the Arctic', *Foreign Affairs*, Vol. IV, 1925–1926, 47–60.

Morin, Jacques-Yvan: 'Le progrés technique, la pollution et l'evolution récente du droit de la mer au Canada, particuliérment à l'égard de l'Arctique', *Canadian Yearbook of International Law*, Vol. VIII, 1970, 158–248.

Morris, Michael A.: 'The 1984 Argentine–Chilean Pact of Peace and Friendship', *Oceanus*, Vol. 28, 1985, 93–96.

McDougal, Myres S., **Lasswell,** Harold D., **Vlasic,** Ivan A. and **Smith,** Joseph C.: 'The enjoyment and acquisition of resources in outer space', *University of Pennsylvania Law Review*, Vol. 111, 1963, 521–636.

McDowell, Eleanor C.: 'Contemporary practice of the United States relating to international law: SS Mayaguez incident', *American Journal of International Law*, Vol. 69, 1975, 875–879.

McLoughlin, Donald: 'Social considerations and environmental protection', in United Nations: *Negotiation and drafting of mining development agreements*, 1976, 43–54.

McKitterick, T. E. M.: 'The validity of territorial and other claims in polar regions', *Journal of Comparative Legislation and International Law*, Vol. XXI, 1939, 89–97.

McNair, A.: 'Separate Opinion on the Advisory Opinion of the International Status of South-West Africa of July 11, 1950', *Reports*, 1950, 146–163.

McRae, D. M., **Goundrey,** D. J.: 'Environmental jurisdiction in arctic waters: the extent of Article 234', *University of British Columbia Law Review*, Vol. 16, 1982, 197–228.

Nielsen, Fred K.: 'The solution of the Spitsbergen question', *American Journal of International Law*, Vol. 14, 1920, 232–235.

Nigrelli, Vincent J.: 'Ocean Mineral Revenue Sharing', *Ocean Development and International Law*, Vol. 5, 1978, 153–180.

O'Connell, D. P.: 'The Condominium of the New Hebrides', *The British Yearbook of International Law*, 43, 1968–1969, 71–145.

Onorato, William T.: 'Apportionment of an international common petroleum deposit', *International and Comparative Law Quarterly*, Vol. 17, 1968, 85–102.

Orrego Vicuña, Francisco: 'The Law of the Sea experience and the corpus of international law: effects and interrelationship', in Robert B. Krueger and Stefan A. Riesenfeld: *The Developing Order of the Oceans*, 1985, 5–22.

Orrego Vicuña, Francisco: 'Le regime de l'exploration et de l'exploitation des fonds marins', in René-Jean Dupuy et Daniel Vignes: *Traité du Nouveau Droit de la Mer*, 1985, 551–601.

Ostreng, Willy: 'Regional delimitation arrangements in Arctic seas. Cases of precedence?', *Eighteenth Annual Conference of the Law of the Sea Institute*, San Francisco, September 24–27, 1984.

Ostreng, Willy: 'Soviet-Norwegian relations in the Arctic', *International Journal*, Vol. 39, 1984, 866–887.

Oxman, Bernard H.: L'accord entre le Brésil et les Etats-Unis concernant la pêche a la crevette', *Annuaire Francais de Droit International*, Vol. XVIII, 1972, 785–803.

Oxman, Bernard H.: 'La Troisieme Conference des Nations Unies sur la Droit de la Mer', in René-Jean Dupuy et Daniel Vignes: *Traité du Nouveau Droit de la Mer*, 1985, 143–216.

Paolillo, Felipe: 'Naturaleza jurídica del principio del patrimonio común de la humanidad', *Anuario Hispano-Luso-Americano de Derecho Internacional*, No. 7, 1984, 353–377.

Paolillo, Felipe H: 'Les structures institutionnelles du regime des fonds marins', in René-Jean Dupuy et Daniel Vignes: *Traité du Nouveau Droit de la Mer*, 1985, 603–684.

Pardo, Arvid and **Christol,** Carl Q.: 'The Common Interest: Tension between the whole and the parts', in R. St. J. MacDonald and Douglas M. Johnston: *The Structure and Process of International Law: Essays in Legal Philosophy Doctrine and Theory*, 1983, 643–660.

Parrish, B. B.: 'The future role of ICES in the light of changes in fisheries jurisdiction', *Marine Policy*, Vol. 3, 1979, 232–238.

Partridge, Ben: 'The White Shelf: A Study of Arctic Ice Jurisdiction', *United States Naval Institute Proceedings*, Vol. 87, No. 9, September 1961, 51–57.

Peyroux, Evelyne: 'Les reglementations internationales de protection des phoques', *Revue Generale de Droit International Public*, 1976, 104–129.

Pharand, Donat: 'State jurisdiction over Ice Island T-3: The Escamilla Case', *Arctic*, Vol. 24, 1971, 83–89.

Pharand, Donat: 'The Continental Shelf redefinition, with special reference to the Arctic', *McGill Law Journal*, Vol. 18, No. 4, 1972, 536–559.

Pharand, Donat: 'The Arctic Waters in Relation to Canada', in R. St. J. Macdonald, Gerald L. Morris, Douglas M. Johnston: *Canadian Perspectives on International Law and organization*, 1974, 434–448.

Pharand, Donat: 'The legal status of the arctic regions', *Recueil des Cours de l'Academie de Droit International*, 1979-II, 53–115.

Pharand, Donat: 'The legal régime of the Arctic: some outstanding issues', *International Journal*, Vol. 39, 1984, 742–799.

Pontecorvo, Giulio: 'Reflections on the Economics of the Common Heritage of Mankind: The Organization of the Deep-Sea Mining Industry and the expected benefits from resource exploitation', *Ocean Development and International Law*, Vol. 2, 1974, 203–216.

Pulvenis, J. F.: 'Le plateau continental, définition et régime', in R. J. Dupuy et Daniel Vignes: *Traité du Nouveau Droit de la Mer*, 1985, 275–336.

Rama-Montaldo, Manuel: 'International legal personality and implied powers of international organizations', *The British Yearbook of International Law*, 1970, 111–155.

Ranjeva, R.: 'Le reglement des differends', in René-Jean Dupuy et Daniel Vignes: *Traité du Nouveau Droit de la Mer*, 1985, 1105–1167.

Rein, John A.: 'The legal character of petroleum production licences in Norway', in Terence Daintith (ed.): *The legal character of petroleum licences: a comparative study*, 1981, 185–199.

Riphagen, W.: 'Dispute settlement in the 1982 United Nations Convention on the Law of the Sea', in C. L. Rozakis and C. A. Stephanou (eds): *The New Law of the Sea*, 1983, 281–301.

Rolland, Louis: 'Alaska: Maison de jeu établie sur les glaces au delá de la limite des eaux territoriales', *Revue Generale de Droit International Public*, Vol. XI, 1904, 340–345.

Ross Tolmie, J.: 'Canadian mineral landholding system, royalties, rentals and taxation', in United Nations: *Negotiation and drafting of mining development agreements*, 1976, 55–80.

Rouhani, Fuad: 'Assignment and renegotiation', in United Nations: *Negotiation and drafting of mining development agreements*, 1976, 21–33.

Rousseau, Charles: 'Chronique des Faits Internationaux. Canada: Réaffirmation de la souveraineté canadienne sur les regions arctiques/conséquences en ce qui concerne les espaces maritimes/nature juridique et condition internationale de l'Ocean Arctique', *Revue Generale de Droit International Public*, 1970, 120–126.

Rousseau, Charles: 'Chronique des Faits Internationaux. Canada et Etats-Unis: Franchissement du passage nord-ouest par le petrolier brise-glace americain *Manhattan*/Probléme de "exercise du passage innocent dans l'Arctique" ', *Revue Generale de Droit International Public*, 1970, 130–137.

Sassoon, David M.: 'Settlement of disputes governing law', in United Nations: *Negotiation and drafting of mining development agreements*, 1976, 209–217.

Scarff, James E.: 'The international management of Whales, Dolphins, and Porpoises: an interdisciplinary assessment', *Ecology Law Quarterly*, Vol. 6, 1977, 326–427 (Part One), 574–638 (Part Two).

Schanze, Erich and others: 'Mining Agreements in Developing Countries', *Journal of World Trade Law*, Vol. 12, 1978, 135–173.

Schoenborn, W.: 'La Nature juridique du territoire', *Recueil des Cours de l'Academie de Droit International*, Vol. 30, 1929-V, 81–189.

Schwarzenberger, Georg: 'Title to territory: response to a challenge', *American Journal of International Law*, Vol. 51, 1957, 308–324.

Scott, James Brown: 'Arctic Exploration and International Law', *American Journal of International Law*, Vol. 3, 1909, 928–941.

Seyersted. Finn: 'United Nations Forces: some legal problems', *British Yearbook of International Law*, 1961, 351–475.

Shusterich, Kurt M.: 'International Jurisdictional issues in the Arctic Ocean', *Ocean Development and International Law*, Vol. 14, No. 3, 1984, 235–272.

Shusterich, Kurt M.: 'International Jurisdictional issues in the Arctic Ocean', in William E. Westermeyer, Kurt M. Shusterich: *United States Arctic Interests. The 1980s and 1990s*, 1984, 240–267.

Silverstein, Edward M.: 'United States Jurisdiction: crimes committed on Ice Islands', *Boston University Law Review*, Vol. 51, 1971, 77–89.

Simsarian, James: 'The acquisition of legal title to terra nullius', *Political Science Quarterly*, Vol. 53, 1938, 111–128.

Smith, David N.: 'Conduct of operations and development goals', in United Nations: *Negotiation and drafting of mining development agreements*, 1976, 139–154.

Smith, David N. and **Wells,** Louis T. Jr: 'Mineral agreements in developing countries: structures and substance', *American Journal of International Law*, Vol. 69, 1975, 560–590.

Smith, Robert W.: 'National claims and the geography of the Arctic', *Eighteenth Annual Conference of the Law of the Sea Institute*, San Francisco, September 24–27, 1984.

Sohn, Louis B.: 'Implications of the Law of the Sea Convention regarding the protection and preservation of the marine environment', *Eighteenth Annual Conference of the Law of the Sea Institute*, San Francisco, 24 September 1984.

Sollie, Finn: 'Norway's Continental Shelf and the Boundary Question on the Seabed', *Cooperation and Conflict*, 2/34, 1974, 101–113.

Stavropoulos, Constantin A.: 'The practice of voluntary abstentions by permanent members of the Security Council under Article 27, paragraph 3, of the Charter of the United Nations', *American Journal of International Law*, Vol. 61, 1967, 737–752.

Suratgar, David: 'International project finance and security for lenders', in United Nations: *Legal and institutional arrangements in minerals development*, 1982, 144–157.

Suy, Erik: 'Reflexions sur la distinction entre la souveraineté et la competence territoriale', *Internationale Festschrift fur Alfred Verdross*, 1971, 493–508.

Svarlien, Oscar: 'The legal status of the Arctic'. *Proceedings of the American Society of International Law*, 1958, 136–144.

Svarlien, Oscar: 'The sector principle in law and practice', *Polar Record*, Vol. 10, 1960–1961, 248–263.

Swan Sik, Ko: 'The concept of acquired rights in international law: a survey', *Netherlands International Law Review*, Vol. 24, 1977, 120–142.

Tambs-Lycre, Hans: 'Le Conseil International pour l'exploration de la mer (CIEM) et la formulation d'avis scientifiques', *Annuaire Francais de Droit International*, Vol. XXVI, 1980, 728–740.

Thylstrup, Asper: 'The legal character of petroleum licences in Greenland and the Faroe Islands', in Terence Daintith (ed.): *The legal character of petroleum licences: a comparative study*, Centre for Petroleum and Mineral Law Studies, University of Dundee, 1981, 176–184.

Traavik, Kim and **Ostreng,** Willy: 'The Arctic Ocean and the Law of the Sea', *Cooperation and Conflict*, 2/3, 1974, 53–67.

Treves, Tullio: 'The EEC and the Law of the Sea: How close to one voice?', *Ocean Development and International Law Journal*, Vol. 12, 1982–1983, 173–189.

Treves, Tullio: 'The United Nations Law of the Sea Convention of 1982: prospects for Europe', The Greenwich Forum IX: *Britain and the Sea*, 1984, 166–182.

Valenzuela, Mario: 'IMO: public international law and regulation', in D. M. Johnston and N. Q. Letalik (eds): *The Law of the Sea and Ocean Industry: new opportunities and restraints*, Law of the Sea Institute, 1984, 141–151.

Vierdag, E. W.: 'The law governing treaty relations between Parties to the Vienna Convention on the Law of Treaties and States not Party to the Convention', *American Journal of International Law*, Vol. 76, 1982, 779–801.

Vignes, Daniel: 'The problem of access to the European Economic Community's Fishing Zone as the cornerstone for the adoption of a common fisheries policy', in C. L. Rozakis and C. A. Stephanou (eds): *The New Law of the Sea*, 1983, 83–96.

Vindenes, Helge: 'Procedimiento y técnicas de negociación en la Tercera Conferencia de las Naciones Unidas sobre el Derecho del Mar y su incidencia en la búsqueda de un acuerdo substancial sobre el tema', in CEPAL: *Economía de los Océanos*, Vol. 1, 1978, 29–44.

van der Heydte, F. A. F.: 'Discovery, symbolic annexation and virtual effectiveness in international law', *American Journal of International Law*, Vol. 29, 1935, 448–471.

von Mehren, Robert B. and **Kourides,** P. Nicholas: 'International arbitration between states and foreign private parties: the Libyan nationalization cases', *American Journal of International Law*, Vol. 75, 1981, 476–552.

Vukas, B.: L'utilisation pacifique de la mer, dénucléarisation et désarmement', in
René-Jean Dupuy et Daniel Vignes: *Traité du Nouveau Droit de la Mer*, 1985,
1047–1093.

Walde, Thomas: 'Contract stability: adoptation and conflict resolution', in United Nations:
Legal and institutional arrangements in minerals development, 1982, 163–175.

Waldock, Sir Humphrey: 'Third report on the Law of Treaties', Doc. A/CN.4/167 and Add.
1-3. 3 March 1964 and subsequent dates, *Yearbook of the International Law
Commission*, 1964, Vol. II, 5–65.

Walser, Christian H.: 'Resource projects and the political risk', in United Nations: *Legal
and institutional arrangements in minerals development*, 1982, 133–143.

Ward, Robert E.: 'The *Mayaguez:* The right of innocent passage and the legality of
reprisal', *San Diego Law Review*, Vol. 13, 1975–1976, 765–778.

Waultrin, René: 'Le question de la souveraineté des terres arctiques', *Revue Generale de
Droit International Public*, Tome XV, 1908, 78–125 (1st Part), 185–209 (2nd
part), 401–423 (3rd part).

Waultrin, René: 'Le probleme de la souveraineté des poles', *Revue Generale de Droit
International Public*, Vol. XVI, 1909, 649–660.

Waultrin, René: 'La Mer Blanche est-elle une mer libre? L'affaire de l'*Onward Ho*', Revue
Generale de Droit International Public, Tome XVIII, 1911, 94–99.

Weiss, Edith Brown et al: 'Protection of the Global Heritage', Panel discussion,
Proceedings of the American Society of International Law, April 1981, 32–55.

Weiss, Edith Brown: 'Conflicts between present and future generations over new natural
resources', in René-Jean Dupuy (ed.): *The Settlement of Disputes on the new
natural resources*, Academie de Droit International de La Haye, Colloque, 1982,
1983, 177–195.

Weiss, Edith Brown: 'Conservation and Equity between generations', Prepared for
publication in Festschrift in honour of Professor Louis B. Sohn, February 1983.

Weiss, Edith Brown: 'The Planetary Trust: Conservation and Intergenerational Equity',
Ecology Law Quarterly, Vol. 11, 1984, 495–581.

Weiss, Friedl: 'Book review of "Die volkerrechtliche Beschrankung der
Vertragsschlussfahigkeit von Staaten" (by Rudolf Geiger-Schriften zum
Volkerrecht, Vol. 24, 1979), and of "Statusvertrage im Volkerrecht.
Rechtsfragen territorialer Sonderregime" (by Eckart Klein, 1980)', *British
Yearbook of International Law*, Vol. 52, 1981, 281–286.

Westermeyer, William E: 'The growing significance of the Arctic: opportunities for
transnational cooperation', *International Studies Notes*, Vol. 11, No. 3, 1985, 5–9.

Weston, Burns H.: 'Constructive Takings' under international law: a modest foray into the
problem of "creeping expropriation" ', *Virginia Journal of International Law*,
Vol. 16, 1975, 103–175.

Weston, Burns H.: 'The Charter of economic rights and duties of States and the deprivation
of foreign-owned wealth', *American Journal of International Law*, Vol. 75, 1981,
437–475.

White, Mary Victoria: 'The Common Heritage of Mankind: an assessment', *Case Western
Reserve Journal of International Law*, Vol. 14, No. 3, 1982, 509–542.

Wijkman, Magnus: 'Managing the global commons', *International Organization*, Vol. 36,
No. 3, Summer 1982, 511–536.

Wildhaber, Luzius: 'Sovereignty and International Law', in R. St. J. Macdonald and
Douglas M. Johnston: *The Structure and Process of International Law: Essays in
Legal Philosophy Doctrine and Theory*, 1983, 425–452.

Wilkes, Daniel: 'Law for special environments: ice islands and questions raised by the T-3
case', *Polar Record*, Vol. 16, No. 100, 1972, 23–27.

Wilkes, Daniel: 'Law for special environments: jurisdiction over polar activities', *Polar
Record*, Vol. 16, No. 104, 1973, 701–705.

Wilson, George G.: 'Jurisdiction and polar areas', in *International law situations with solutions and notes*, USGPO, 1939, 69–131.

Wolfrum, Rudiger: 'The Principles of the Common Heritage of Mankind', *Zeitschrift fur auslandisches offentliches Recht und Volkerrecht*, 1983, 43/2, 312–337.

Wood, Philip: 'Commercial bank project finance agreements', Commonwealth Law Students' Conference, *British Institute of International and Comparative Law*, March 1984.

Young, Elizabeth: 'The Arctic – In need of an international regime', *Marine Policy*, Vol. 5, 1981, 154–156.

Young, Oran R.: 'International Regimes: problems of concept formation', *World Politics*, Vol. 32, No. 3, April 1980, 331–356.

Young, Oran R. and **Osherenko,** Gail: 'Arctic resource conflicts: sources and solutions', in William E. Westermeyer, Kurt M. Shusterich: *United States Arctic Interests. The 1980s and 1990s*, 1984, 199–218.

Zorn, Stephen: 'The security of mineral supplies: impacts on developing countries', in United Nations: *Legal and institutional arrangements in minerals development*, 1982, 123–131.

6. Books and special publications on Antarctica

Acuña de Mones Ruiz, Primavera: Antártida Argentina, Islas oceánicas, mar argentino, Buenos Aires, 1948.

Alexander, Lewis M. and **Hanson,** Lynne Carter (eds): Antarctic Politics and Marine Resources: critical choices for the 1980s, 1985.

Arbuet, Herber, **Puceiro,** Roberto y **Garré,** Belter: Antártica Continente de los más, para los menos, Fundación de Cultura Universitaria, Montevideo, 1979.

Armitage, Albert B.: Two years in the Antarctic, 1905 (edition of 1984).

Auburn, F. M.: The Ross Dependency, 1972.

Auburn, F. M.: Antarctic Law and Politics, 1982.

Azambuja, Péricles: Antártica, historia e geopolítica, 1982.

Barnes, James N.: Let's Save Antarctica!, 1982.

Barreda Laos, Felipe: La Antártica Sudamericana ante el Derecho Internacional, Buenos Aires, 1948.

Battaglini, G.: I Diritti degli Stati nelle Zone Polari, 1974.

Battaglini, Giovanni: La Condizione dell' Antartide nel Diritto Internazionale, 1971.

Berkowitz, Ethan Avram: Interests on Ice relations on target: the effect of economic and political attractions on national interests and international relations in the Antarctic, Thesis, B.A., Harvard College, March 1983.

Berraz Montyn, Carlos: La soberanía argentina en tierras antárticas, Universidad Nacional del Litoral, Facultad de Ciencias Jurídicas y Sociales, Santa Fé, 1948.

Bertram, G. C. L.: Antarctica today and tomorrow, University of Otago, Dunedin, 1957.

Bertram, Colin: Arctic and Antarctic. A prospect of the Polar Regions, 1957.

Bing, R. N.: Role of the Developing States in the formulation of International Controls for unoccupied regions: Outer Space, the Ocean Floor, and Antarctica, Ph.D. Thesis, Tufts University, 1972.

Birnie, Patricia: International Regulation of Whaling, 2 Vol., 1985.

Bonner, W. N. and **Walton,** D. W. H.: Key environments: Antarctica, 1985.

Braun Menéndez, Armando: Pequeña historia antártica, 1974.

Brewster, Barney: Antarctica: wilderness at risk, Friends of the Earth, Wellington, 1982.

Bull, H. J.: The cruise of the 'Antarctic', 1896 (edition of 1984).

Bush, W. M.: Antarctica and International Law, 2 Vol., 1982.

CIA: Polar Regions Atlas, 1978.

Cameron, Ian: Exploring Antarctica, 1984.

Casellas, Alberto: Antártida, un malabarismo político, Instituto de Publicaciones Navales, Buenos Aires, 1981.
Charney, Jonathan I. (ed.): The new nationalism and the use of common spaces, 1982.
Christie, F. W. Hunter: The Antarctic problem. An historical and political study, 1951.
Cordovez Madariaga, Enrique: La Antártida Sudamericana, Santiago, 1945.
Crawford, Leslie: Uruguay atlanticense y los derechos a la Antártida, 1974.
Curtze Sancho, Joaquín E.: Soberanía Marítima Nacional en la Antártida chilena, Tesis, Universidad de Chile, Escuela de Derecho, Valparaíso, 1957.
Da Costa, J. F.: Souveraineté sur l'Antarctique, 1958.
Deacon, George. The Antarctic circumpolar ocean, 1984.
De Wit, Maarten J.: Minerals and Mining in Antarctica, 1985.
Drewry, D. J.: Antarctica: Glaciological and Geophysical Folio, Scott Polar Research Institute, 1983.
Dumbar, M. J.: Ecological Development in Polar Regions. A Study in evolution, 1968.
Eyzaguirre, Jaime: La soberanía de Chile en las tierras australes, Santiago, 1958.
Ferrer Vieyra, Enrique: Las islas Malvinas y el derecho internacional, Depalma, 1984.
Ferrer Vieyra, Enrique: An annotated legal chronology of the Malvinas (Falkland) Islands Controversy, Córdoba, 1985.
Follegati, Renzo G.: The Exploitation of the Antarctic oil and its environmental and legal implications, Master of Marine Affairs Major Paper, University of Rhode Island, 1982.
Fox, Robert: Antarctica and the South Atlantic, Discovery, Development and Dispute, 1985.
Fraga, Jorge A.: La Argentina y el atlántico sur, 1983.
Fuchs, Sir Vivian: Of Ice and Men, 1982.
Gidel, Gilbert: Aspects juridiques de la lutte pour l'Antarctique, Academie de Marine, Paris, 1948.
Golitsyn, V. V.: Antarctica: the international law regime, 1983.
Harris, Stuart (ed.): Australia's Antarctic Policy options. Centre for Resource and Environmental Studies, Australian National University, 1984.
Hayes, J. Gordon: Antarctica. A Treatise on the Southern Continent, 1928.
Hayton, Robert D.: National Interests in Antarctica. An annotated bibliography, United States Antarctic Projects Officer, 1959.
Headland, Robert: The Island of South Georgia, 1984.
Herr, R. A., **Hall,** R. and **Davis,** B. W. (eds): Issues in Australia's Marine and Antarctic Policies, University of Tasmania, 1982.
Hill, John: New Zealand and Antarctica, Commission for the Environment, May 1983.
Hill, Norman: Claims to territory in international law and relations, 1945.
Holdgate, M. W. and **Tinker,** Jon: Oil and other minerals in the Antarctic, 1979.
Honnymill, Eleanor: The Challenge of Antarctica, 1984.
Huneeus Gana, Antonio: Antártida, Santiago, 1948.
Husseiny, A. A. (ed.): Iceberg utilization, 1978.
Institute of Polar Studies, Ohio State University: A framework for assessing environmental impacts of possible Antarctic mineral development, Part I, II, January 1977, U.S. Department of Commerce – National Technical Information Service.
International Institute for Environment and Development: Antarctica, a continent in transition, Information package, 1983.
Jessup, Philip C. and **Taubenfeld,** Howard J.: Controls for Outer Space and the Antarctic Analogy, 1959.
Karlqvist, Anders (ed.): Sweden and Antarctica, 1985.
Keage, P. L.: 'Antarctic protected areas: future options', University of Tasmania, *Environmental Studies Occasional Paper* 19, 1986.
Laws, R. M. (ed.): Antarctic Ecology, 2 Vol. 1984.

Lewis, Richard S. and **Smith,** Philip M.: Frozen Future, 1973.
Logan, H. F. M.: Cold Commitment: The Development of New Zealand's Territorial Role in Antarctica, Thesis, Master of Arts in History, University of Canterbury, Christchurch, New Zealand, 1979.
Lonergan, Stephen J.: The legal status of the Antarctic airspace, Institute of Air and Space Law, McGill University, Thesis, January 1972.
Lovering, J. F. and **Prescott,** J. R. V.: Last of lands . . . Antarctica, 1979.
Mercado Jarrín, Edgardo et al.: El Perú y la Antártida, 1984.
Milia, F. A. et al.: La Atlantártida. Un espacio geopolítico, 1978.
Mitchell, Barbara and **Sandbrook,** Richard: The management of the Southern Ocean, International Institute for Environment and Development, 1980.
Mitchell, Barbara: Frozen Stakes. The Future of Antarctic Minerals, International Institute for Environment and Development, 1983.
Mitchell, Barbara and **Tinker,** Jon: Antarctica and its resources, International Institute for Environment and Development, 1980.
Murdock, W. G. Burn: From Edinburgh to the Antarctic, 1894 (edition of 1984).
Myhre, Jeffrey D.: The Antarctic Treaty System: Politics, Law, and Diplomacy, 1986.
McEwan, David: The future political and economic development of the Antarctic, Dissertation, Diploma in Polar Studies, Scott Polar Research Institute, Cambridge, 1978.
McDevitt Jr, James: The geopolitical and geostrategic importance of the Antarctic regions, Dissertation, Master of Arts, Institute of International Law and Relations, Catholic University of America, 1966.
Oerding, James B.: The frozen friction point. A geopolitical analysis of sovereignty in the Antarctic peninsula. M.A. Thesis, Department of Geography, University of Florida, 1977.
Orrego Vicuña, Francisco and **Salinas Araya,** Augusto (eds): El Desarrollo de la Antártica, 1977.
Orrego Vicuña, Francisco, **Infante,** María Teresa, **Armanet,** Pilar (eds): Política Antártica de Chile, 1985.
Orrego Vicuña, Francisco (ed.): Antarctic Resources Policy. Scientific, legal and political issues, 1983.
Pacific Circle Consortium: International relations in Antarctica, Canberra, Curriculum Development Centre, Undated.
Pacific Circle Consortium: The Geology and Mineral Resources of Antarctica, Canberra, Curriculum Development Centre, Undated.
Parker, B. C. (ed.): Conservation problems in Antarctica, 1972.
Parker, Bruce C. (ed.): Environmental Impact in Antarctica, Biology Department, Virginia Polytechnic Institute and State University, Blacksburg, Virginia, 1978.
Pinochet de la Barra, Oscar: La Antártica Chilena, Third edition, 1955.
Pinochet de la Barra, Oscar: Chilean Sovereignty in Antarctica, 1955.
Pinto Coelho, Aristides: Nos confins dos três mares . . . a Antártida, 1983.
Plott, B. M.: The Development of United States Antarctic Policy, Ph.D. Thesis, Fletcher School of Law and Diplomacy, 1969.
Puig, Juan Carlos: La Antártida Argentina ante el Derecho, Buenos Aires, 1960.
Quigg, Philip W.: A Pole Apart. The emerging issue of Antarctica, 1983.
Quigg, Philip W.: Antarctica, the continuing experiment, Foreign Policy Association, Headline Series, No. 273, March/April, 1985.
Sahurie, Emilio: 'Antarctica and Contemporary International Law. A Policy Perspective, Ph.D. Thesis, Yale Law School, 1985.
Schatz, Gerald S. (ed.): Science, technology, and Sovereignty in the Polar Regions, 1974.
Scilingo, Adolfo: El Tratado Antártico, 1963.
Shackleton, E.: Falkland Islands Economic Study 1982, HMSO, 1982, Cmnd. 8653.

Shackleton, Sir Ernest: South, 1919.
Shapley, Deborah: The Seventh Continent. Antarctica in a Resource Age, 1985.
Slevich, S.: The ice continent today and tomorrow, 1968.
Slevich, S. B.: Antarctica in the modern world, 1985.
Smedal, Gustav: Acquisition of Sovereignty over polar areas, Oslo, 1931.
Smith, Olaf M.: Le Statut Juridique des Terres Polaires, 1934.
Sugden, David: Arctic and Antarctic. A modern geographical synthesis, 1982.
Sullivan, Walter: Quest for a Continent, 1957.
Sullivan, Walter: Assault on the Unknown. The International Geophysical Year, 1961.
Thatcher, Diane G.: Australia and Antarctica, Thesis, History Department, University of
    Queensland, 1961.
Theile, Konstantin: Possibilities for an internationalization of Antarctica (in German),
    Thesis, St. Gallen, 20 April 1977.
Theutenberg, Bo Johnson: The Evolution of the Law of the Sea. A study of resources and
    strategy with special regard to the Polar Areas, 1984.
Triggs, Gillian (ed.): The Antarctic Treaty Regime, 1987.
U.S. Polar Research Board: Antarctic Treaty System, An Assessment, 1986.
Vila Labra, Oscar: Chilenos en la Antártica, Santiago, 1947, segunda edición.
Vila Labra, Oscar: Historia y Geografía de la Antártica chilena, Santiago, 1948. Segunda
    edición.
Wall, Patrick: The Southern Oceans and the security of the free world, 1977.
Westermeyer, William E.: The Politics of Mineral Resource Development in Antarctica.
    Alternative Regimes for the Future, 1984.
Wolfrum, Rudiger (ed.): Antarctic Challenge, 1984.
Zumberge, J. H. (ed.): Possible environmental effects of Mineral Exploration and
    Exploitation in Antarctica, S.C.A.R., 1979.

7. Articles, Pamphlets, Contributions to books and other material on Antarctica and Related Matters

Ahluwalia, K.: 'The Antarctic Treaty: should India become a party to it?', *Indian Journal
    of International Law*, Vol. 1, 1960–1961, 473–483.
Alegría Amar, Marcelino: 'Aspectos geográficos y políticos de la Antártida', in Edgardo
    Mercado Jarrín et al.: *El Perú y la Antártida*, 1984, 1–24.
Alexander, Frank C. Jr.: 'A Recommended Approach to the Antarctic Resource Problem',
    University of Miami Law Review, Vol. 33, 1978, 371–423.
Alley, Roderic: 'New Zealand and Antarctica', *International Journal*, Vol. 39, 1984,
    911–931.
Almond, Harry H., Jr: 'Demilitarization and arms control: Antarctica', *Case Western
    Reserve Journal of International Law*, Vol. 17, 1985, 229–284.
Alverson, Dayton L.: 'Tug-of-War for the Antarctic Krill', *Ocean Development and
    International Law*, Vol. 8, 1980, 171–182.
American Geographical Society: 'Antarctic Maps and Surveys. 1900–1964', *Antarctic Map
    Folio Series*, Folio 3, 1965.
American Geographical Society: 'Terrestrial life of Antarctica', *Antarctic Map Folio Series*,
    Folio 5.
American Geographical Society: 'Glaciers of the Antarctic', *Antarctic Map Folio Series*,
    Folio 7, 1967.
American Geographical Society: 'Geologic maps of Antarctica', *Antarctic Map Folio Series*,
    Folio 12, 1969, 1970.
American Geographical Society: 'Circumpolar characteristics of Antarctic Waters',
    Antarctic Map Folio Series, Folio 13, 1970.

American Geographical Society: 'Birds of the Antarctic and Subantarctic', *Antarctic Map Folio Series*, Folio 14, 1971.

American Geographical Society: 'Coastal and Deep-water Benthic Fishes of the Antarctic', *Antarctic Map Folio Series*, Folio 15, 1971.

American Geographical Society: 'Marine sediments of the Southern Oceans', *Antarctic Map Folio Series*, Folio 17, 1973.

American Geographical Society: 'Antarctic Mammals', *Antarctic Map Folio Series*, Folio 18, 1974.

American Geographical Society: 'History of Antarctic Exploration and Scientific Investigation', *Antarctic Map Folio Series*, Folio 19, 1975.

Anderson, David: 'The Conservation of Wildlife under the Antarctic Treaty', *Polar Record*, Vol. 14, No. 88, 1968, 25–32.

Anderson, Ian: 'Oil and geological chaos found off Antarctica', *New Scientist*, Vol. 106, No. 1452, 18 April 1985, 9.

Antarctic and Southern Ocean Coalition: 'Protected areas in the Antarctic', Workshop, Washington D.C., 23 January 1984.

Antarctic and Southern Ocean Coalition: 'Report on the Antarctic Minerals Meeting (Washington D.C. 18–27 January 1984), 6 February 1984.

Antarctic and Southern Ocean Coalition: 'An indefinite moratorium on all Antarctic minerals activities', 21 January 1985.

Antarctic and Southern Ocean Coalition: 'Background paper on the French airfield at Pointe Geologie, Antarctica', 1 March 1985.

Antarctic and Southern Ocean Coalition: 'The Antarctic Fund', 26 February 1985.

Antarctic and Southern Ocean Coalition: 'Impacts of seismic testing', 1 October 1985, A.S.O.C. Paper No. 3, ANT SCM/7.

Antarctic and Southern Ocean Coalition: 'The role of NGOS', 1 October 1985, A.S.O.C. Paper No. 2, ANT SCM/7.

Antarctic and Southern Ocean Coalition: 'Background on A.S.O.C.', A.S.O.C. Paper No. 1, ANT SCM/7, 1 October 1985.

Antarctic and Southern Ocean Coalition: 'The World Park Option for Antarctica', A.S.O.C. Paper No. 4, ANT SCM/8, 21 April 1986.

Antarctica and the question of the exploitation of its resources, *Australian Foreign Affairs Record*, December 1977, 604–611.

Antarctica briefing: 'An Antarctic environmental protection agency', No. 3, 16 April 1984; No. 6, 12 October 1984.

Antarctica briefing: 'Status of Antarctic Minerals negotiations', No. 1, 3 April 1984.

Antarctica briefing: 'Protected areas in the Antarctic', No. 4, 23 April 1984.

Antarctica briefing: 'A non-commercial approach to Antarctic minerals', No. 2, 9 April 1984.

Antarctic Treaty Workshop, *Antarctic Journal of the United States*, Vol. XX, No. 2, June 1985, 10–11.

Antezana, T., **Ray, K.** y **Morales,** C.: 'Ecosistema antártico: naturaleza, impacto y conservación', in: Orrego, Infante and Armanet: *Política Antártica de Chile*, 1985, 181–189.

Antonsen, P.: 'Natural resources in Antarctica', *Internasjonal Politikk*, Oct.–Dec. 1974, No. 4, 801–816 (In Norwegian).

Arbuet Vignali, Heber: 'Estatuto jurídico y situación político-jurídica de la Antártica', Comité Juríidico Interamericano, Sexto Curso de Derecho Internacional, 1979, 453–480.

Arduino, Norberto: 'Antártica Argentina: su situación actual', *Revista Argentina de Relaciones Internacionales*, 1978, No. 11, 42–55.

Argentine proposals for polar air route, *Antarctic*, Vol. 8, No. 10, June 1979, 367–368.

Armanet, Pilar: 'La política de los Estados Unidos en la Antártica', Cono Sur, FLACSO, Santiago, Vol. III, No. 2, Junio-Julio 1984, 10–11; also in *Revista Peruana de Derecho Internacional*, Vol. XXXV, Julio-Setiembre 1983, 41–45.

Armanet, Pilar: 'La Antártica y el desarme', in Orrego et al. (eds): *Política Antártica de Chile*, 1985, 289–294.

Asbroeck, Jean Van: 'L'actualité des questions antarctiques et la Belgique', *Bulletin de la Societé Royale de Geographie d'Anvers*, Tome LXI, 1946–1947, 42–58.

Auburn, F. M.: 'The Ross Dependency – An Undeclared Condominium', *Auckland University Law Review*, Vol. 1, No. 3, 1970, 89–106.

Auburn, F. M.: 'The White Desert', *The International and Comparative Law Quarterly*, Vol. 19, 1970, 229–256.

Auburn, F. M.: 'A sometime world of men: legal rights in the Ross Dependency', *American Journal of International Law*, Vol. 65, 1971, 578–582.

Auburn, F. M.: 'Problems in Polar Criminal Law', *Antarctic*, Vol. 7, No. 1, March 1974, 27–29.

Auburn, F. M.: 'Offshore oil and gas in Antarctica', *German Yearbook of International Law*, Vol. 20, 1977, 139–173.

Auburn, F. M.: 'United States Antarctic Policy', *Marine Technology Society Journal*, Vol. 12, No. 1, 1978, 31–36.

Auburn, F. M.: 'Legal implications of petroleum resources of the Antarctic Continental Shelf', *Ocean Yearbook* 1, 1978, 500–515.

Auburn, F. M.: 'Consultative Status under the Antarctic Treaty', *The International and Comparative Law Quarterly*, Vol. 28, 1979, 514–522.

Auburn, F. M.: 'The Antarctic Environment', *The Yearbook of World Affairs*, 1981, 248–265.

Auburn, F. M.: 'The Falkland Islands Dispute and Antarctica', *Marine Policy Reports*, Vol. 5, No. 3, December 1982, 1–4.

Auburn, F. M.: 'Antarctic Minerals and the Third World', *FRAM: The Journal of Polar Studies*, Winter 1984, 201–223.

Auburn, Francis: 'The Antarctic minerals regime: sovereignty, exploration, institutions and environment', in Stuart Harris (ed.): *Australia's Antarctic Policy Options*, A.N.U., 1984, 271–300.

Auckland District Law Society: 'How strong is New Zealand's claim to the Ross Dependency?', *New Zealand Law Journal*, 1980, 4, 76–77.

National **Audubon** Society: 'Statement on Antarctica', undated.

Australia: 'Antarctica – A continent of international harmony?', *Australian Foreign Affairs Record*, February 1980, 4–12.

Azambuja, Pericles: 'Brasil y su derecho a la Antártida', **Geosur**, Año II, No. 23, Julio 1981, 36–40.

Bákula, Juan Miguel: 'La Antártida y el Derecho del Mar', *Revista de la Academia Diplomática del Perú*, No. 23, January–December 1984, 85–103; also in: Edgardo Mercado Jarrín et al.: *El Perú y la Antártida*, 1984, 225–248.

Balch, Thomas Willing: 'The Arctic and Antarctic region and the Law of Nations', *American Journal of International Law*, Vol. 4, 1910, 265–275.

Baldwin, Gordon Brewster: 'The Dependence of Science on Law and Government – The International Geophysical Year – A case study', *Wisconsin Law Review*, Vol. 1964, 1964, 78–118.

Bankes, N. D.: 'Environmental protection in Antarctica: a comment on the Convention on the Conservation of Antarctic Marine Living Resources', *The Canadian Yearbook of International Law*, Vol. 19, 1981, 303–319.

Barber, Laurie: 'Keeping New Zealand's back door closed', *New Zealand International Review*, Vol. VII, No. 3, May–June 1982, 13–14.

Barber, Laurie and **Selby,** Michael: 'The search for an alternative strategy: New Zealand and the Antarctic', *The Round Table. The Commonwealth Journal of International Affairs,* No. 288, 1983, 466–472.

Barnes, James N.: 'The emerging Antarctic living resources convention', *Proceedings of the American Society of International Law,* 1979, 272–292.

Barnes, James N., **Jackson,** Thomas C. and **Rich,** Bruce: 'An introduction to Southern Ocean Conservation issues', *The Oceanic Society,* 1980.

Barnes, James N.: 'The emerging convention on the Conservation of Antarctic Marine Living Resources: an attempt to meet the new realities of resource exploitation in the Southern Ocean', in Jonathan I. Charney (ed.): *The new nationalism and the use of common spaces,* 1982, 239–286.

Barnes, James: 'Non-Governmental organizations. Increasing the global perspective', *Marine Policy,* Vol. 8, April 1984, 171–184.

Barnes, James N.: 'Environmental protection and the future of the Antarctic: new approaches and perspectives are necessary', in Gillian Triggs (ed.): *The Antarctic Treaty Regime,* 1987, 150–158.

Barrera Valdebenito, Humberto: 'Los asuntos antárticos y la participación de algunas instituciones chilenas', *Boletín Antártico Chileno,* Vol. III, No. 2, Julio-Diciembre 1983, 16–26.

Barrie, G. N.: 'The Antarctic Treaty: example of law and its sociological infrastructure', *The Comparative and International Law Journal of Southern Africa,* Vol. VIII, 1975, 212–224.

Basset, P. G.: 'Australia's maritime boundaries', *Australian Foreign Affairs Record,* Vol. 55, March 1984, 186–191.

Beck, Peter J.: 'Cooperative confrontation in the Falkland Islands Dispute. The Anglo-Argentine search for a way forward, 1968–1981', *Journal of Inter-American Studies and World Affairs,* Vol. 24, No. 1, February 1982, 37–58.

Beck, Peter J.: 'Argentine postmarks in the South Orkneys', *Polar Post,* Vol. 14, No. 2, June 1982, 49.

Beck, Peter J.: "Britain and Antarctica', Memorandum No. 119/82-83/FM, *House of Commons, Foreign Affairs Committee,* Session 1982–83, Falkland Islands, Minutes of Evidence, Monday 13 Dec. 1982, 109–113.

Beck, Peter J.: 'The results of research into the history of the Anglo-Argentine dispute over the sovereignty of the Falkland Islands', Memorandum 120/82-83/FM, *House of Commons, Foreign Affairs Committee,* Session 1982–83, Falkland Islands, Minutes of Evidence, Monday 13 Dec. 1982, 114–117.

Beck, Peter J.: 'Antarctica's Indian Summer', *Contemporary Review,* Vol. 243, No. 1415, Dec. 1983, 297–299.

Beck, Peter J.: 'The Anglo-Argentine dispute over title to the Falkland Islands: changing British perceptions on sovereignty since 1910', *Millennium, Journal of International Studies,* Vol. 12, No. 1, 1983, 6.

Beck, Peter J.: 'Britain's Antarctic Dimension', *International Affairs,* Vol. 59, No. 3, Summer 1983, 429–444.

Beck, Peter J.: 'Science – and politics – on ice. India in Antarctica', *Nature,* Vol. 306, 10 Nov. 1983, 106–107.

Beck, Peter J.: 'British Antarctic Policy in the early 20th century', *Polar Record,* Vol. 21, No. 134, 1983, 475–483.

Beck, Peter J.: 'Securing the dominant 'Place in the Wan Antarctic Sun' for the British Empire: the policy of extending British control over Antarctica', *Australian Journal of Politics and History,* Vol. 29, No. 3, 1983–1984, 448–461.

Beck, Peter J.: 'Britain and Antarctica: the historical perspective', *The Journal of Polar Studies,* Vol. 1, No. 1, 1984, 66–82.

Beck, Peter J.: 'Britain's role in the Antarctic: some recent changes in organization', *Polar Record*, Vol. 22, No. 136, January 1984, 85–87.

Beck, Peter J.: 'Britain's Falklands Future. The need to look back', *The Round Table*, 1984, No. 290, 139–152.

Beck, Peter J.: 'Antarctica: a case for the UN?', *The World Today*, April 1984, 165–172.

Beck, Peter J.: 'The United Nations and Antarctica', *Polar Record*, Vol. 22, No. 137, May 1984, 137–144.

Beck, Peter J.: 'Antarctica at the U.N.', *BAS Club Newsletter*, No. 15, Spring 1984, 27–28.

Beck, Peter J.: 'The United Nations' Study on Antarctica, 1984', *Polar Record*, Vol. 22, No. 140, May 1985, 499–504.

Beck, Peter J.: 'Preparatory meetings for the Antarctic Treaty 1958–59', *Polar Record*, Vol. 22, 1985, 653–664.

Beck, Peter J.: 'Antarctica since the Falklands conflict: the continent's emerging role in international politics', *British International Studies Association Conference*, University of Durham, December 1984.

Beck, Peter J.: 'Antarctica at the United Nations, 1985: The end of consensus?', *Polar Record*, Vol. 23, No. 143, May 1986, 159–166.

Beeby, Christopher: 'The Antarctic Treaty', New Zealand Institute of International Affairs, 1972.

Beeby, C. D.: 'Towards an Antarctic mineral resources regime', *New Zealand International Review*, Vol. VII, No. 3, May/June 1982, 4–6.

Beeby, Christopher: 'A negotiator's view', in *The Antarctic: preferred futures, constraints and choices*, New Zealand Institute of International Affairs, 1983, 58–62.

Beeby, C. D.: 'An overview of the problems which should be addressed in the preparation of a regime governing the mineral resources of Antarctica', in Francisco Orrego Vicuña (ed.): *Antarctic Resources Policy*, 1983, 191–198.

Beeby, C. D.: 'The Antarctic Treaty system and a minerals regime', *New Zealand Foreign Affairs Review*, Vol. 35, 1985, 18–26.

Beeby, Christopher D.: 'The Antarctic Treaty System as a resource management mechanism – Non-living resources', in U.S. Polar Research Board: *Antarctic Treaty System, An Assessment*, 1986, 269–284.

Behrendt, John C. (ed.): 'Petroleum and Mineral Resources of Antarctica', *Geological Survey Circular 909*, 1983.

Behrendt, John C.: 'Are there petroleum resources in Antarctica?', in Lewis M. Alexander, Lynne Carter Hanson (eds): *Antarctic Politics and Marine Resources: critical choices for the 1980s*, 1985, 191–202.

Bell, Karla: 'Antarctica: getting into hot water', *Chain Reaction supplement*, undated, 21–28.

Bengtson, John L.: 'Review of Information regarding the Conservation of Living Resources of the Antarctic Marine Ecosystem', Final Report to the U.S. Marine Mammal Commission, July 1978, in United States Senate: *Antarctic Living Marine Resources Negotiations. Hearing 1978*, 87–234.

Benninghoff, W. S. and **Bonner,** W. N.: 'Man's impact on the Antarctic environment: a procedure for evaluating impacts from scientific and logistic activities', *SCAR*, 1985.

Bentley, Charles R.: 'International Science Programs in Antarctica', in Lewis M. Alexander, Lynne Carter Hanson (eds): *Antarctic Politics and Marine Resources: critical choice for the 1980's*, 1985, 45–54.

Benuzzi, Felice: 'Il Trattato sull'Antartide', *Rivista di Studi Politici Internazionali*, Vol. XLVII, No. 2, 1980, 224–236.

Bergin, Anthony: 'Frozen assets – Resource problems and Antarctica', *Dyason House Papers*, Melbourne, Vol. 6, No. 1, September 1979, 7–12.

Bergin, Anthony: 'Recent developments in Australia's Antarctic policy', *Marine Policy*, Vol. 9, 1985, 180–191.

Bergsager, Egil: 'Basic conditions for the exploration and exploitation of mineral resources in Antarctica: options and precedents', in Francisco Orrego Vicuña (ed.): *Antarctic Resources Policy*, 1983, 167–183.

Berguño Barnes, Jorge: 'Chile y el descubrimiento de la Antártica', in Chile, Ministerio de Relaciones Exteriores, *Anales de la Diplomacia*, 1984, 274–279.

Berguño, Jorge: 'Criterios de aceptabilidad en un régimen para los minerales antárticos', in Orrego et al. (eds): *Política Antártica de Chile*, 1985, 249–274.

Bernales, Enrique, **de la Puente,** José, **Ulloa,** Manuel, **Townsend,** Andrés: 'El Nuevo Derecho del Mar, la Antártida y el Perú frente a la Cuenca del Pacífico', in: *Perú: Perspectivas de Política Exterior*, Centro Peruano de Estudios Internacionales, 1985, 58–78.

Bernhardt, J. Peter A.: 'Sovereignty in Antarctica', *California Western International Law Journal*, Vol. 5, No. 2, Spring 1975, 297–349; also in U.S. Senate: *U.S. Antarctic Policy*, Hearing, 1975, 85–112.

Bertram, G. C. L.: 'Antarctic Prospect', *International Affairs*, Vol. 33, 1957, 143–153.

Bertram, Colin and **Stephenson,** Alfred: 'Archipelago to peninsula', *The Geographical Journal*, Vol. 151, 1985, 155–167.

Bertrand, Gerard A.: 'Antarctica. Conflict or compromise?', *Frontiers*, Vol. 43, No. 1, Autumn 1978, 9–12.

Bilder, Richard B.: 'Control of Criminal Conduct in Antarctica', *Virginia Law Review*, Vol. LII, 1966, 231–285.

Bilder, Richard B. et al.: 'Development of Antarctica', *Proceedings of the American Society of International Law*, April 1979, 264–294.

Bilder, Richard B.: 'Emerging legal problems of the deep seas and polar regions', in R. B. Lillich and J. N. Moore (eds): *U.S. Naval War College, International Law Studies*, Vol. 61, 1980, 504–519.

Bilder, Richard B.: 'The present legal and political situation in Antarctica', in Jonathan I. Charney (ed.): *The new nationalism and the use of common spaces*, 1982, 167–205.

Birch, W. F.: 'Antarctica: sovereignty and stewardship', *New Zealand Foreign Affairs Review*, July–December 1979, 35–39.

Bird, Lester: 'Address by Honourable Lester Bird at meeting of the Authority of OECS', Dominica, May 26, 1983.

Birnie, Patricia: 'The Antarctic Regime and Third States', in Rudiger Wolfrum (ed.): *Antarctic Challenge II*, 1986, 239–262.

Bishop, William W. Jr: 'International Law problems of acquisition and transportation of Antarctic icebergs', in A. A. Husseiny (ed.): *Iceberg Utilization*, 1978, 586–596.

Blij, Harm J. de: 'A regional geography of Antarctica and the Southern Ocean', *University of Miami Law Review*, Vol. 33, 1978, 299–314.

Boczek, Boleslaw Adam: 'The Protection of the Antarctic ecosystem: a study in International Environmental Law', *Ocean Development and International Law*, Vol. 13, 1983–1984, 347–425.

Boczek, Boleslaw A.: 'The Soviet Union and the Antarctic Regime', *American Journal of International Law*, Vol. 78, 1984, 834–858.

Bonnemains, Jacky: 'Antarctique: les avions dénicheurs', *La Sirena* (UNEP's Regional Seas Programme), No. 26, December 1984, 21–26.

Bonner, W. N.: 'Conservation and the Antarctic', in R. M. Laws (ed.): *Antarctic Ecology*, Vol. 2, 1984, 821–850.

Bonner, W. Nigel: 'The future of Antarctic resources', *The Geographical Journal*, Vol. 152, No. 2, July 1986, 248–255.

Brennan, Keith: 'Recent international developments regarding Antarctica', in R. A. Herr, R. Hall, B. W. Davis (eds): *Issues in Australia's Marine and Antarctic Policies*, Public Policy Monograph, University of Tasmania, 1982, 91–99.

Brennan, Keith: 'Criteria for access to the resources of Antarctica: alternatives, procedure and experience applicable', in Francisco Orrego Vicuña (ed.): *Antarctic Resources Policy*, 1983, 217–227.

Brennan, Keith: 'International Constraints', in *The Antarctic: Preferred futures, constraints and choices*, New Zealand Institute of International Affairs, 1983, 12–24.

British Antarctic Survey: 'Metallic Mineral Resources of Antarctica', Memorandum by the British Antarctic Survey, in House of Lords select committee on the European Communities: *Strategic minerals with minutes of evidence*, Session 1981–1982, 20th report (217), HMSO, 267–274.

Brook, John: 'Australia's policies towards Antarctica', in Stuart Harris (ed.): *Australia's Antarctic Policy Options*, A.N.U., 1984, 255–264.

Brown, Hugh A.: 'Antarctica Disaster', *Fate Magazine*, May 1956, 28–34.

Brown, R. N. Rudmose: 'Political Claims in the Antarctic', *World Affairs*, October 1947, 393–401.

Brown, William Y.: 'The Conservation of Antarctic Marine Living Resources', *Environmental Conservation*, Vol. 10, No. 3, Autumn 1983, 187–196.

Brown, William Y., **Manheim,** Bruce S.: Conservation of Antarctic Marine Living Resources: the environmental perspective', in Lewis M. Alexander, Lynne Carter Hanson (eds): *Antarctic Politics and Marine Resources: critical choices for the 1980s*, 1985, 123–129.

Bruckner, Peter: 'The Antarctic Treaty System from the perspective of a Non-Consultative Party to the Antarctic Treaty', in U.S. Polar Research Board: *Antarctic Treaty System. An Assessment*, 1986, 315–335.

Bruno Bologna, Alfredo: 'La Antártida: aspectos políticos y jurídicos de la explotación de los recursos naturales', in Asociación Argentina de Derecho Internacional: *El Derecho Internacional en los Congresos Ordinarios*, Córdoba, Argentina, 1981, 275–314.

Budd, W. A.: 'Scientific research in Antarctica and Australia's effort', in Stuart Harris (ed.): *Australia's Antarctic Policy Options*, A.N.U., 1984, 217–247.

Budd, William F.: 'The Antarctic Treaty as a Scientific Mechanism (Post-IGY) – Contributions of Antarctic Scientific Research', in U.S. Polar Research Board: *Antarctic Treaty System, An Assessment*, 1986, 103–151.

Burton, Steven J.: 'Legal/Political aspects of Antarctic iceberg utilization', in A. A. Husseiny (ed.): *Iceberg Utilization*, 1978, 604–615.

Burton, Steven J.: 'New Stresses on the Antarctic Treaty: Toward International Legal Institutions governing Antarctic Resources', *Virginia Law Review*, Vol. 65, 1979, 421–512.

Butterworth, D. S.: 'Antarctic marine ecosystem management', *Polar Record*, Vol. 23, No. 142, 1986, 37–47.

C.I.A.: 'Antarctic Treaty and Territorial Claims', A reference aid (Map), April 1982.

C.I.A.: 'Antarctica: Research Stations and Territorial Claims', Map, 1984.

Cabezas Bello, Roberto: 'El desarrollo de la explotación del krill antártico', in Francisco Orrego Vicuña (ed.): *El Desarrollo de la Antártica*, 1977, 169–181.

Cabezas Bello, Roberto: 'Alternativas de política para la utilización de los recursos vivos marinos antárticos', in Orrego et al. (eds): *Política Antártica de Chile*, 1985, 237–248.

Cabezas Bello, Roberto: 'Estrategia nacional para el desarrollo de la pesquería del krill antártico', Seminario *Chile y la Pesquería del Krill*, Instituto de Fomento Pesquero, 1985.

Cameron, P. J.: 'The petroleum potential of Antarctica and its continental margin', *Australian Petroleum Exploration Association Journal*, Vol. 21, No. 1, 1981, 99–111.

Cano I., Percy R.: 'Aspectos técnicos, científicos y de recursos naturales sobre la Antártida', in Edgardo Mercado Jarrín et al.: *El Perú y la Antártida*, 1984, 25–62.

Cañas Montalva, Ramón: 'La Antártica y las proposiciones de la India ante la NU', Editorial, *Revista Geográfica de Chile, 'Terra Australis'*, No. 14, 1956–1957, 3–4.

Cañas Montalva, Ramón: 'Chile: el país más austral de la tierra', *Geosur*, Año II, No. 23, Julio 1981, 22–35.

Candioti, Alberto M.: 'Nuestra Antártida no es tierra conquistada ni anexada. El Tratado Antártico no debe ratificarse', Buenos Aires, 1960.

Candioti, Alberto M.: 'El Tratado Antártico y nuestras fuerzas armadas', Buenos Aires, 1960.

Candioti, Alberto M.: 'El Tratado Antártico y el Derecho Público Argentino', Buenos Aires, 1961.

Carl, Beverly May: 'International Law – Claims to Sovereignty Antarctica' (Comments), *Southern California Law Review*, Vol. 28, 1954–1955, 386–400.

Carrol, James F.: 'Of icebergs, oil wells, and treaties: hydrocarbon exploitation offshore Antarctica', *Stanford Journal of International Law*, Vol. XIX, Issue 1, Spring 1983, 207–227.

Castles, A. C.: 'The International Status of the Australian Antarctic Territory', in D. P. O'Connell (ed.): *International Law in Australia*, 1965, 341–367.

Cerone, Rudy J.: 'Survival of the Antarctic Treaty: economic self-interest v. Enlightened International Cooperation', *Boston College International and Comparative Law Review*, Vol. 2, 1978–1979, 115–129.

Chamoux, Jean Pierre: 'Some international implications of iceberg transfer', in A. A. Husseiny (ed.): *Iceberg Utilization*, 1978, 597–603.

Charney, Jonathan I.: 'Development of Antarctica', Remarks, *Proceedings of the American Society of International Law*, 1979, 268–271; other remarks by Richard B. Bilder (265–266); Giulio Pontecorvo (266–267); John Dugger (267–268); John D. Negroponte (271).

Charney, Jonathan I.: 'Future strategies for an Antarctic Mineral Resource Regime – Can the environment be protected?', in Jonathan I. Charney (ed.): *The new Nationalism and the use of common spaces*, 1982, 206–238.

Charteris, A. H.: 'Australasian claims in Antarctica', *Journal of Comparative Legislation and International Law*, Vol. XI, 1929, 226–232.

Cheever, Daniel S.: 'Antarctica and the Exclusive Economic Zone', *International Studies Association*, Mexico City, April 1983.

Child, John: 'Geopolitical thinking in Latin America', *Latin American Research Review*, Vol. XIV, 1979, 89–111.

Child, Jack: 'South American Geopolitical thinking and Antarctica', *International Studies Notes*, Vol. 11, No. 3, 1985, 23–28.

Chile, Instituto de Fomento Pesquero: 'Chile y la pesquería del krill', Seminario, 1985.

Chingotto, Mario Raúl: 'El Mar y los intereses argentinos', Buenos Aires, 1982.

Chittleborough, Graham: 'Nature, extent and management of Antarctic living resources', in Stuart Harris (ed.): *Australia's Antarctic Policy Options*, A.N.U., 1984, 135–163.

Chopra, Sudhir K.: 'Antarctica in the United Nations: Rethinking the problems and prospects', Paper delivered at the *Annual Meeting of the American Society of International Law*, April 11, 1986.

Clark, Margaret: 'Antarctica: a wilderness compromised', *International Studies Notes*, Vol. 11, No. 3, 1985, 29–33.

Clark, M. R. and **Dingwall,** P. R.: 'Conservation of islands in the Southern Ocean: a review of the protected areas of Insulantarctica', Document prepared for the *IUCN Commission on National Parks and Protected Areas*, February 1985.

Clemons, John A.: 'Recent developments in the Law of the Sea 1983–1984', *San Diego Law Review*, Vol. 22, 1985, 801–838.

Colacrai de Trevisan, Miryam: 'A 20 años de la puesta en vigencia del Tratado Antártico', *Revista de Derecho Internacional y Ciencias Diplomáticas*, Rosario, 1981, No. 50–51, 31–40.

Colacrai de Trevisan, Miryam: 'El ingreso de la Antártida a la escena mundial', *Rivista di Studi Politici Internazionali*, Vol. 50, No. 3, July–Sep. 1983, 386–396.

Colacrai de Trevisan, Miryam O.: 'La cuestión antártica en el ámbito de las Naciones Unidas', *Revista Argentina de Estudios Estratégicos*, Año 1, No. 2, Oct.–Diciembre 1984, 36–45.

Colson, David A.: 'The Antarctic Treaty System: the mineral issue', *Law and Policy in International Business*, Vol. 12, 1980, 841–902.

Comisión Chilena del Cobre: 'Los recursos minerales de la Antártica y los posibles efectos ambientales de su exploración y explotación', Santiago, 1982.

Conant, Melvin A.: 'Polar strategic concerns', *Oceanus*, Vol. 28, 1985, 62–66.

Convention on the Conservation of Antarctic Marine Living Resources: 'Preparatory Meeting at Hobart, 10th–24th September, 1981, to give effect to the Convention of 1980 on the Conservation of Antarctic Marine Living Resources', International Legal Notes, *The Australian Law Journal*, Vol. 56, No. 1, January 1982, 49–50.

Convention on the Conservation of Antarctic Marine Living Resources: 'Third Meeting of the Commission for the Conservation of Antarctic Marine Living Resources, Hobart, September 1984', International Legal Notes, *The Australian Law Journal*, Vol. 58, 1984, 740–741.

Cosslett, Clare: 'United States Criminal Jurisdiction in Antarctica: how old is the ice?', Note, *Brooklyn Journal of International Law*, Vol. 9, No. 1, Winter 1983, 67–69.

Couratier, Josyane: 'The regime for the conservation of Antarctica's living resources', in Francisco Orrego Vicuña (ed.): *Antarctic Resources Policy*, 1983, 139–148.

Coutau-Bègarie, Hervé: 'L'Antarctique, derniere terre à prendre', *Defense Nationale*, Decembre 1984, 85–98.

Croasdale, K. R.: 'Arctic offshore technology and its relevance to the Antarctic', in U.S. Polar Research Board: *Antarctic Treaty System, An Assessment*, 1986, 245–263.

Cuevas Farren, Gustavo: 'Possibilidades estratégicas da Antártica', *Politica e Estrategia*, Vol. 2, No. 1, Jan–Mar. 1984, 201–209.

da Costa, J. F.: 'A Teoría dos setores polares', *Boletim da Sociedade Brasileira de Direito Internacional*, Ano 7, Nos. 13–14, Janeiro-Dezembro 1951, 87–128.

da Costa, Joao Frank: 'Antartida: o problema político', *Revista Brasileira de Política Internacional*, Vol. 4, 1961, No. 15, 85–102.

Daniel, J.: 'Conflict of sovereignties in the Antarctic', *The Year Book of World Affairs*, Vol. 3, 1949, 241–272.

Daniels, Paul C.: 'The Antarctic Treaty', *Science and Public Affairs*, Vol. XXVI, No. 10, December 1970, 11–15.

Dater, Henry M.: 'Organizational developments in the United States Antarctic Program. 1954–1965', *Antarctic Journal of the United States*, Vol. 1, No. 1, January–February 1966, 21–32.

Dater, Henry M.: 'The Antarctic Treaty in Action. 1961–1971', *Antarctic Journal of the United States*, Vol. VI, No. 3, May–June 1971, 67–72.

Davis, Bruce: 'Australia and Antarctica: aspects of policy process', in Stuart Harris (ed): *Australia's Antarctic Policy Options*, A.N.U., 1984, 339–354.

del Aguila, Jorge: 'Posibilidades de la primera expedición peruana a la antártida', in Edgardo Mercado Jarrín et al.: *El Perú y la Antártida*, 1984, 185–194.

Deporov, Y.: 'Antarctica: a zone of peace and cooperation', *International Affairs* (USSR), No. 11, 1983, 29–37.

Dollot, René: 'Le droit international des espaces polaires', *Recueil des Cours de l'Academie de Droit International*, Vol. 75, 1949-II, 115–200.

Donoghue, Michael: 'The last gold rush', *La Sirena* (UNEP's Regional Seas Programme), No. 26, December 1984, 11–20.

Drewry, D. J.: 'The Antarctic physical environment', in Gillian Triggs (ed.): *The Antarctic Treaty Regime*, 1987, 6–27.

Dugger, John A.: 'Exploiting Antarctic Mineral Resources – Technology, Economics and the Environment', *University of Miami Law Review*, Vol. 33, 1978, 315–339.

Dupuy, René-Jean: 'Le Statut de l'Antarctique', *Annuaire Francais de Droit International*, IV, 1958, 196–229.

Dupuy, René-Jean: 'Le Traité sur l'Antarctique', *Annuaire Francais de Droit International*, 1960, 111–132.

ECO, Vol. XXIII, No. 1–5, Bonn, July 11–22, 1983; Vol. XXVI, No. 1–3, Washington, January 18–27, 1984; Vol. XXVII, No. 1–3, Tokyo, May 22–31, 1984; Vol. XXIX, No. 1–3, Hobart, 3–14 September 1984; Vol. XXXIII, No. 2, Paris, 23 September–4 October, 1985.

ECO: 'Dump the US proposal', Vol. XXII, No. 2, January 17–28, 1983, Wellington, New Zealand, 2–3.

Eagleton, Clyde: 'International Law and Aerial discovery at the South Pole', *Air Law Review*, Vol. 1, No. 1, January 1930, 125–127.

Earthscan: 'The future of Antarctica', Earthscan press briefing document No. 5, 1977, reprinted in U.S. Senate: *Hearing on Exploitation of Antarctic Resources*, 1978, 189–224.

Economides, Costas P.: 'Le statut international de l'Antarctique', rèsultant du traité du 1 Décembre 1959', *Revue Hellénique de Droit International*, Vol. 15, 1962, 76–86.

Edwards, David M. and **Heap,** John A. 'Convention on the Conservation of Antarctic Marine Living Resources: a commentary', *Polar Record*, Vol. 20, 1981, 353–362.

Eilers, Stephan: 'Antarctica adjourned'? The U.N. deliberations on Antarctica', *The International Lawyer*, Vol. 19, 1985, 1309–1318.

Epperson, Curt: 'International legal issues regarding towing of icebergs and environmental effects of iceberg exploitation', in John King Gamble Jr (ed): *Law of the Sea: Neglected Issues*, 1979, 209–239.

Escudero Guzmán, Julio: 'El Decreto Antártico de 1940', in Chile, Ministerio de Relaciones Exteriores, *Anales de la Diplomacia*, 1984, 279–281.

Fedorov, Ye. K.: 'Antarctica: Experimental proving ground for peaceful coexistence and International Collaboration', *Science and Public Affairs*, Vol. XXVI, No. 10, December 1970, 22–28.

Fernández Puyó, Gonzalo: 'Evaluación del proceso antártico sudamericano', *Revista Peruana de Derecho Internacional*, Vol. XXXII, Julio-Sep. 1980, 45–54.

Fernández Puyó, Gonzalo: 'El Perú y el proceso antártico', *Revista Peruana de Derecho Internacional*, Vol. XXXV, Julio-Setiembre 1983, 15–28; also in Edgardo Mercado Jarrín et al.: *El Perú y la Antártida*, 1984, 147–162.

Fernández Puyó, Gonzalo: 'Interés internacional por la Antártida', *Revista de la Academia Diplomática del Perú*, No. 23, January–December 1984, 73–84.

Ferrer Vieyra, Enrique (ed.): 'Antártida Argentina', *Seminario de Derecho Internacional, Instituto Argentino de Estudios Internacionales*, Buenos Aires, 1960.

Ferrer Vieyra, Enrique: 'Problemática Jurídica de la Antártida Argentina', Conferencia pronunciada el 28 de Abril de 1981 en el Departamento de Ciencia Política de la

Facultad de Derecho y Ciencias Sociales, Universidad Nacional de Córdoba, Argentina, Mimeo; also in Enrique Ferrer Vieyra: *Las Islas Malvinas y el Derecho Internacional*, 1984, 264–286.

Fleming, W. L. S.: 'Contemporary international interest in the Antarctic', *International Affairs*, Vol. XXIII, 1947, 546–557.

Fourcade, Néstor H.: 'Algunas consideraciones sobre los recursos no renovables del antártico', in F. A. Milia et al.: *La Atlantártida. Un espacio geopolítico*, 1978, 217–224.

Fraga, Jorge A.: 'El futuro incierto político-económico de la Antártida', in F. A. Milia et al.: *La Atlantártida. Un espacio geopolítico*, 1978, 225–235.

Fraga, Jorge A.: 'Introducción a la Geopolítica Antártida', in *El Mar y la Antártida en la Geopolítica Argentina*, Colección Estrategia, Instituto de Publicaciones Navales, Buenos Aires, 1980, 211–261.

Fraga, Jorge A.: 'Antártida 1991. El factor económico', *Geopolítica*, Vol. X, No. 30, 1984, 47–50.

Francis, Henry S. Jr: 'The Antarctic Treaty – a reality before its time', in Lewis M. Alexander, Lynne Carter Hanson (eds): *Antarctic Politics and Marine Resources: critical choices for the 1980s*, 1985, 87–98.

Frank, Ronald F.: 'The Convention on the Conservation of Antarctic Marine Living Resources', *Ocean Development and International Law*, Vol. 13, 1983–1984, 291–345.

Fridtjof Nansen Foundation: 'Antarctic resources', *Report from the meeting of experts at Polhøgda*, May 30–June 10, 1973; in: United States Senate: *U.S. Antarctic Policy*, Hearing 1975, 68–85.

Fuchs, V. E.: 'Antarctica: its history and development', in Francisco Orrego Vicuña (ed.): *Antarctic Resources Policy*, 1983, 13–19.

Gajardo Villarroel, Enrique: 'Apuntes para un libro sobre la Historia Diplomática del Tratado Antártico y la participación chilena en su elaboración', Instituto Antártico Chileno, *Revista de Difusión* , No. 10, 1977, 41–74.

Gajardo Villarroel, Enrique: 'Chile, el Tratado Antártico y su sistema', *Boletín Antártico Chileno*, Vol. III, No. 2, Julio-Diciembre 1983, 7–15.

Gajardo Villarroel, Enrique: 'Antecedentes de la negociación diplomática previa al Tratado de 1959 y la posición de Chile', in Orrego et al. (eds): *Política Antártica de Chile*, 1985, 81–87.

Gallardo, Víctor Ariel: 'El impacto ambiental del posible desarrollo de los recursos mineros antárticos', in Orrego et al. (eds): *Política Antártica de Chile*, 1985, 191–222.

Gamboa, Fernando: 'Hacia una redefinición de nuestra soberanía antártica', *El Mercurio*, 7 de Junio, 1986, A2.

Garret, John Norton: 'The economics of Antarctic oil', in Lewis M. Alexander, Lynne Carter Hanson (eds): *Antarctic Politics and Marine Resources: critical choices for the 1980s*, 1985, 185–190.

Gerlache de Gomery, Gastón de: 'A proposed European Antarctic Expedition', *Antarctic Journal of the United States*, Vol. III, No. 1, January–February 1973, 15, 28.

German raiders in the Antarctic during the second world war, *Polar Record*, Vol. 6, No. 43, January 1952, 399–403.

Gjelsvik, Tore: 'The work of SCAR for conservation of nature in the Antarctic', in Francisco Orrego Vicuña (ed.): *El Desarrollo de la Antártida*, 1977, 328–334.

Gjelsvik, Tore: 'The mineral resources of Antarctica: progress in their identification', in Francisco Orrego Vicuña (ed.): *Antarctic Resources Policy*, 1983, 61–76.

Gjelsvik, Tore: 'Scientific Research and Cooperation in Antarctica', in Rudiger Wolfrum (ed.): *Antarctic Challenge*, 1984, 41–51.

Glassner, Martin Ira: 'The view from the near North-South American view Antarctica and the Southern Ocean geopolitically', *Political Geography Quarterly*, Vol. 4, 1985, 329–342.

Goldblat, Jozef: 'Troubles in the Antarctic?', *Bulletin of Peace Proposals*, 1973, 3, 286–288.

Goldblat, Jozef: 'The arms-control experiment in the Antarctic', *SIPRI Yearbook*, 1973, 477–486.

Goldie, L. F. E.: 'International relations in Antarctica', *The Australian Quarterly*, Vol. XXX, No. 1, March 1958, 7–29.

Gonzáles-Ferrán, Oscar: 'El Continente antártico. Sus recursos no renovables', in Francisco Orrego Vicuña (ed.): *El Desarrollo de la Antártica*, 1977, 228–251.

Gonzáles-Ferrán, Oscar: 'Geologic data and its impact on the discussion on a regime for mineral resources', in Francisco Orrego Vicuña (ed.): *Antarctic Resources Policy*, 1983, 159–166.

Gould, Laurence M.: 'Antarctic in World Affairs', *Foreign Policy Association*, Headline Series, No. 128, March–April 1958.

Gould, Laurence M.: 'The Polar Regions in their relation to human affairs', *The American Geographical Society*, 1958.

Gould, Laurence M.: 'Emergence of Antarctica: The Mythical Land', *Science and Public Affairs*, Vol. XXVI, No. 10, December 1970, 5–10.

Graham, Alistair: 'Environment hazards in the Antarctic', in *The Antarctic: preferred futures, constraints and choices*, New Zealand Institute of International Affairs, 1983, 25–30.

Graham, Gerald F.: 'Ice in international law', *Thesaurus Acroasium*, Vol. VII, 1977, 489–495.

Greenpeace International: 'The future of Antarctic. Background for a second UN debate', October 22, 1984.

Greenpeace International: 'Legal aspects concerning the French airstrip construction programme', *ATCM* 13/NGO/2, April 22, 1985.

Greig, D. W.: 'Territorial sovereignty and the status of Antarctica', *Australian Outlook*, 32, 1978, 2, 117–129.

Greño Velasco, José Enrique: 'La adhesión de Brasil al Tratado Antártico', *Revista de Política Internacional*, No. 146, Julio-Agosto 1976, 71–89.

Guglialmelli, Juan E.: 'El área meridional del Atlántico suroccidental, la geopolítica de Chile y el laudo del Beagle', *Estrategia*, No. 48, Setiembre-Octubre 1977, 5–18.

Guillaume, Gilbert: 'Oil as a special resource: problems and experiences', in Francisco Orrego Vicuña (ed.): *Antarctic Resources Policy*, 1983, 185–190.

Gulland, John A.: 'The Antarctic Treaty System as a resource management mechanism – Living Resources', in U.S. Polar Research Board: *Antarctic Treaty System, An Assessment*, 1986, 221–234.

Guyer, Roberto E.: 'The Antarctic System', *Recueil des Cours de l'Academie de Droit International*, 1973-II, Vol. 139, 149–226.

Guyer, Roberto E.: 'Antarctica's role in international relations', in Francisco Orrego Vicuña (ed.): *Antarctic Resources Policy*, 1983, 267–279.

Hambro, Edvard: 'Some notes on the future of the Antarctic Treaty Collaboration', *American Journal of International Law*, Vol. 68, 1974, 217–226.

Hambro, Edvard: 'A Noble experiment', *Norseman*, No. 1, 1975, 7–10.

Hammond, Katherine A. Green: 'Environmental aspects of potential petroleum exploration and exploitation in Antarctica: forecasting and evaluating risks', *Final Report to the U.S. Marine Mammal Commission*, February 1982.

Hanessian, John Jr: 'Antarctica: current national interests and legal realities', *Proceedings of the American Society of International Law*, 1958, 145–164.

Hanessian, John Jr: 'The Antarctic Treaty', American Universities Field Staff, *Reports Service*, Polar Area Series, Vol. 1, No. 2, July 6, 1960.

Hanessian, John: 'The Antarctic Treaty 1959', *The International and Comparative Law Quarterly*, Vol. 9, 1960, 436–480.

Hanessian, John Jr: 'National Activities and interests in Antarctica', American Universities Field Staff, Reports Service, Part I: *The Why of Antarctica*, Polar Area Series, Vol. II, No. 5, Sep. 1962; Part II: *The Claimant Nations*, Polar Area Series, Vol. II, No. 6, Sep. 1962: Part III: *The Nonclaimant Nations*, Polar Area Series, Vol. II, No. 7, Sep. 1962.

Hanessian, John Jr: 'National Interests in Antarctica', in Trevor Hatherton (ed.): *Antarctica*, 1965, 3–53.

Hanevold, Truls: 'Inspections in Antarctica', *Cooperation and Conflict*, 2, 1971, 103–114.

Hanevold, Truls: 'The Antarctic Treaty Consultative Meetings – Form and Procedure', *Cooperation and Conflict*, 3/4, 1971, 183–199.

Hargrove, John Lawrence: 'Environmental problems of Antarctic Resource Management: legal and institutional aspects', Unpublished paper, *American Journal of International Law*, 1976.

Harris, Stuart: 'A review of Australia's Antarctic Policy Options', in Stuart Harris (ed.); *Australia's Antarctic Policy Options*, 1984, 1–28.

Harris, Ralph L.: 'The Antarctic Regime and the Law of the Sea Convention: an Australian view', *Virginia Journal of International Law*, Vol. 21, 1981, 727–744.

Hatherton, Trevor: 'Antarctica prior to the Antarctic Treaty – an historical perspective', in U.S. Polar Research Board: *Antarctic Treaty System, An Assessment*, 1986, 15–32.

Hayden, Bill: 'Keeping tension out of the last continent', *Australian Foreign Affairs Record*, Vol. 56, 1985, 25–27.

Hayes, Dennis E.: 'An overview of the geological history of Antarctica with regard to mineral resource potential', in Lewis M. Alexander, Lynne Carter Hanson (eds): *Antarctic Politics and Marine Resources: critical choices for the 1980s*, 1985, 173–184.

Hayton, Robert D.: 'Chile, Argentina and Great Britain in the Antarctic', *Inter-American Juridical Yearbook*, 1955–1957, 119–125.

Hayton, Robert D.: 'The "American" Antarctic', *American Journal of International Law*, Vol. 50, 1956, 583–610.

Hayton, Robert D.: 'Polar problems and international law', Notes and Comments, *American Journal of International Law*, Vol. 52, 1958, 746–765.

Hayton, Robert D.: 'Remarks of the chairman of panel on "Legal Problems and the Political Situation in the Polar Areas" ', *Proceedings of the American Society of International Law*, 1958, 135–136, 171–174.

Hayton, Robert D.: 'The Nations and Antarctica', *Osterreichische Zeitschrift fur offentliches Recht*, Vol. X, 1959–1960, 368–412.

Hayton, Robert D.: 'The Antarctic settlement of 1959', *American Journal of International Law*, Vol. 54, 1960, 349–371.

Headland, R. K.: 'Antarctic Treaty: signatures and dates', *Polar Record*, Vol. 22, No. 139, January 1985, 438–439; as corrected, *Polar Record*, Vol. 22, No. 140, May 1985, 559.

Headland, R. K. and **Keage,** P. L.: 'Activities on the King George Island Group, South Shetland Islands, Antarctica', *Polar Record*, Vol. 22, No. 140, May 1985, 475–484.

Heap, J. A.: 'Cooperation in the Antarctic: a quarter of a century's experience', in Francisco Orrego Vicuña (ed.): *Antarctic Resources Policy*, 1983, 103–108.

Heap, John A. and **Holdgate,** Martin W.: 'The Antarctic Treaty System as an environmental mechanism – an approach to environmental issues', in U.S. Polar Research Board: *Antarctic Treaty System, An Assessment*, 1986, 195–210.

Heimsoeth, Harold: 'Antarctic Mineral Resources', *Environmental Policy and Law*, Vol. 11, No. 3, November 1983, 59–61.
Heron, David Winston: 'Antarctic claims', *Foreign Affairs*, Vol. 32, 1953–1954, 661–667.
Herrera Rosas, José: 'Importancia geoestratégica de la antártida', in Edgardo Mercado Jarrín et al.: *El Perú y la Antártida*, 1984, 87–106.
Hofman, Robert I.: 'The Convention on the Conservation of Antarctic Marine Living Resources', in Lewis M. Alexander, Lynne Carter Hanson (eds): *Antarctic Politics and Marine Resources: critical choices for the 1980s*, 1985, 113–122.
Holdgate, M. W.: 'The Antarctic ecosystem', *Philosophical Transactions of the Royal Society of London*, B, Vol. 252, 1967, 363–383.
Holdgate, M. W.: 'Terrestrial ecosystems in the Antarctic', *Philosophical Transactions of the Royal Society of London*, B, Vol. 279, 1977, 5–25.
Holdgate, M. W.: 'Environmental factors in the development of Antarctica', in Francisco Orrego Vicuña (ed.): *Antarctic Resources Policy*, 1983, 77–101.
Holdgate, M. W.: 'The use and abuse of polar environmental resources', *Polar Record*, Vol. 136, January 1984, 25–49.
Holdgate, M. W.: 'Regulated development and conservation of Antarctic resources', in Gillian Triggs (ed.): *The Antarctic Treaty Regime*, 1987, 128–142.
Holdgate, M. W.: 'International workshop on the Antarctic Treaty System, 7–13 January 1985', *Polar Record*, Vol. 22, No. 140, May 1985, 538–539.
Honnold, Edward: 'Draft provisions of a new international convention on Antarctica', *Yale Studies in World Public Order*, Vol. 4, No. 1, 1977, 123–153.
Hook, Elizabeth K.: 'Criminal Jurisdiction in Antarctica', *University of Miami Law Review*, Vol. 33, 1978, 489–514.
Hyde, Charles Cheney: 'Acquisition of sovereignty over polar areas', *Iowa Law Review*, Vol. XIX, 1933–34, 286–294.
Ihl C., Pablo: 'Relato sobre la antártica y la polinesia sur oriental según la obre "Narratio de Terra Australis Incognita", editada en Sevilla, en 1610', *Revista Geográfica de Chile. 'Terra Australis'*, Año V, No. 7, Septiembre 1952, 11–14.
Infante, María Teresa: 'The continental shelf of Antarctica: legal implications for a regime on mineral resources', in Francisco Orrego Vicuña (ed.): *Antarctic Resources Policy*, 1983, 253–264.
Infante, María Teresa: 'Los recursos minerales antárticos y su régimen', in Orrego et al. (eds): *Política Antártica de Chile*, 1985, 225–236.
International Legal Notes: 'Convention on the Conservation of Antarctic Marine Living Resources, signed at Canberra, 20th May 1980', *The Australian Law Journal*, Vol. 54, 1980, 432–434.
International Union for Conservation of Nature and Natural Resources: 'Conservation and development of Antarctic ecosystems', Paper submitted to the United Nations Political Affairs Division for consideration at the General Assembly debate on Antarctica, 1984.
International Union for the Conservation of Nature: 'Background statement and action plan for Antarctica and the Southern Ocean', 1981.
Irigoin Barrenne, Jeannette: 'La participación de las organizaciones internacionales en la Convención sobre la Conservación de los Recursos vivos marinos de la antártica y en la Convención sobre el Derecho del Mar', in Francisco Orrego Vicuña (ed.): *La Zona Económica Exclusiva. Una perspectica latinoamericana*, Instituto de Estudios Internacionales de la Universidad de Chile, 1982, 170–182.
Issues before the eleventh General Assembly: 'Antarctica', *International Conciliation*, No. 510, November 1956, 135–143.
Italian Expedition worked off west coast of Antarctic Peninsula, *Antarctic*, Vol. 7, No. 9, March 1976, 304–305.

Jain, Subash C.: 'Antarctica: Geopolitics and International Law', *The Indian Year Book of International Affairs*, 1974, 249–278.

Jayaraman, K. S.: 'Expedition to Antarctica', *Indian and Foreign Review*, 1 February 1982, 20–22.

Jessup, Phillip C. and **Taubenfeld,** Howard J.: 'Outer Space Antarctica, and the United Nations', *International Organization*, Vol. XIII, 1959, 363–379.

Johnson, Eric W.: 'Quick, before it melts: toward a resolution of the jurisdictional morass in Antarctica', *Cornell International Law Journal*, Vol. 10, No. 1, December 1976, 173–198.

Jones, Barry: 'Antarctica dilemma', *Australian Foreign Affairs Record*, Vol. 55, March 1984, 183–185.

Jones, P.: 'Whose oil resources? The question of Antarctic sovereignty', Note, *Geography*, No. 272, Vol. 61, Part 3, July 1976, 167–168.

Joyner, Christopher C.: 'Antarctica and the Law of the Sea: Rethinking the Current Legal Dilemmas', *San Diego Law Review*, Vol. 18, 1980–1981, 415–442.

Joyner, Christopher C.: 'The Exclusive Economic Zone and Antarctica', *Virginia Journal of International Law*, Vol. 21, 1981, 691–725.

Joyner, Christopher C.: 'Antarctica and the Law of the Sea: New Resources vs. Legal dilemmas', in *Oceans 82 Conference Record*, Marine Technology Society, Washington D.C., Sep. 20–22, 1982, 1211–1215.

Joyner, Christopher C.: 'Antarctica and the Law of the Sea: an Introductory overview', *Ocean Development and International Law*, Vol. 13, 1983–1984, 277–289.

Joyner, Christopher C.: 'Anglo-Argentine rivalry after the Falkland/Malvinas war: laws, geopolitics, and the Antarctic connection', *Lawyer of the Americas*, Vol. 15, No. 3, Winter 1984, 467–502.

Joyner, Christopher C.: 'Oceanic pollution and the Southern Ocean: rethinking the international legal implications for Antarctica', *Natural Resources Journal*, Vol. 24, No. 1, January 1984, 1–40.

Joyner, Christopher C.: 'Security issues and the Law of the Sea: the Antarctic', *International Studies Association*, Atlanta, March 1984.

Joyner, Christopher C.: 'The Southern Ocean and Marine Pollution: problems and prospects', *Case Western Reserve Journal of International Law*, Vol. 17, 1985, 165–194.

Joyner, Christopher C.: 'Security issues and the Law of the Sea: The Southern Ocean', *Ocean Development and International Law*, Vol. 15, 1985, 171–195.

Joyner, Christopher C.: 'Polar politics in the 1980s: some preliminary thoughts on polar contrasts and geopolitical considerations', *International Studies Notes*, Vol. 11, No. 3, 1985, 1–4.

Jung, Ernst Friedrich: 'Die Antarktis in der internationalen Politik', *Aussenpolitik*, Vol. 35, No. 1, 1984, 80–86.

Kaczynski, Vladimir M.: 'Economic aspects of Antarctic fisheries', in Lewis M. Alexander, Lynne Carter Hanson (eds): *Antarctic Politics and Marine Resources: critical choices for the 1980s*, 1985, 141–158.

Katzenbach, Nicholas de B.: 'Sharable and strategic resources: Outer Space, Polar Areas, and the Oceans', *Proceedings of the American Society of International Law*, 1959, 206–212.

Kemp, Geoffrey: 'The new strategic map', *Survival*, Vol. XIX, No. 2, March/April 1977, 50–59.

Kesteven, G. L.: 'The Southern Ocean', *Ocean Yearbook*, 1, 1978, 467–499.

Keys, J. R.: 'Antarctic Marine Environments and offshore oil', *Commission for the Environment*, Wellington, New Zealand, 1984.

Khlestov, O., **Golitsyn,** V.: 'The Antarctic: Arena of Peaceful Cooperation', *International Affairs* (USSR), August 1978, 61–66.

Kimball, Lee: 'La carrera por la pesca antártica está en marcha', in C. J. Moneta et al.: *Geopolítica y política del poder en el Atlántico Sur*, 1983, 195–223.

Kimball, Lee: 'Unfreezing international cooperation in Antarctica', *The Christian Science Monitor*, August 1, 1983; reprinted in International Institute for Environment and Development: *Antarctica, a continent in transition*, 1983.

Kimball, Lee: 'Antarctica: Summary and Comment on Background and Recent Developments', International Institute for Environment and Development, April 6, 1984.

Kimball, Lee: 'Environmental issues in the Antarctic minerals negotiations', in Lewis M. Alexander, Lynne Carter Hanson (eds): *Antarctic Politics and Marine Resources: critical choices for the 1980s*, 1985, 204–214.

Kimball, Lee: 'The future of the Antarctic Treaty System. Environmental community suggestions', in Lewis M. Alexander, Lynne Carter Hanson (eds): *Antarctic Politics and Marine Resources: critical choices for the 1980s*, 1985, 237–247.

Kimball, Lee: 'Report on Antarctica', International Institute for Environment and Development, November 1, 1984; July 5, 1985; November 8, 1985.

Kimball, Lee: 'Whither Antarctica?', *International Studies Notes*, Vol. 11, No. 3, 1985, 16–22.

Knox, George: 'Antarctic resources: implications for the Antarctic Treaty and New Zealand', *New Zealand International Review*, July/August 1976, 18–22.

Knox, George: 'The Southern Ocean: an ecosystem under threat', *New Zealand International Review*, Vol. VII, No. 3, May/June 1982, 15–18.

Knox, George A.: 'The living resources of the Southern Ocean: a scientific overview', in Francisco Orrego Vicuña (ed.): *Antarctic Resources Policy*, 1983, 21–60.

Knox, George A.: 'The key role of krill in the ecosystem of the Southern Ocean with special reference to the Convention on the Conservation of Antarctic Marine Living Resources', *Ocean Management*, Vol. 9, 1984, 113–156.

Koch, Michael: 'The Antarctic Challenge: conflicting interests, cooperation, environmental protection, and economic development', Report of a symposium at the Christian-Albrechts University of Kiel, June 21–24, 1983, *Journal of Maritime Law and Commerce*, Vol. 15, No. 1, January 1984, 117–126.

Korotkenich, E. S. and **Dubrovin,** L. I.: 'Two decades of Soviet research in the Antarctic', in *The Antarctic Committee Reports*, No. 17, 1984, 1–18.

Koyanec, Giovanni: 'La situazione giuridica dell'Antartide', *La Communitá Internazionale*, Vol. 15, 1960, 21–48.

Lagoni, Rainer: 'Die vereinten Nationen und die Antarktis', *Europa Archiv*, Vol. 39, 1984, 473–482.

Lagoni, Rainer: 'Antarctica's Mineral Resources in International Law', *Zeitschrift fur Auslandisches offentliches Recht und Volkerrecht*, Band 39, 1979, 1–37.

Lagoni, Rainer: 'Antarctica: German activities and problems of jurisdiction over marine areas', *German Yearbook of International Law*, Vol. 23, 1980, 392–400.

Lagoni, Rainer: 'Convention on the Conservation of Marine Living Resources: a model for the use of a common good?', in Rudiger Wolfrum (ed.): *Antarctic Challenge*, 1984, 93–108.

Larson, David L.: 'Security issues and the Law of the Sea: a general framework', *Ocean Development and International Law*, Vol. 15, 1985, 99–146.

Larus, Joel: 'India claims a role in Antarctica', *The Round Table*, No. 289, 1984, 45–56.

Law, Phillip: 'Possibilities for Exploitation of Antarctic Resources', in Francisco Orrego Vicuña (ed.): *El Desarrollo de la Antártica*, 1977, 24–37.

Laws, R. M.: 'International stewardship of the Antarctic: problems, successes and future options', *Marine Pollution Bulletin* (UK), Vol. 16, No. 2, February 1985, 49–55.

Laws, R. M.: 'Scientific opportunities in the Antarctic', in Gillian Triggs (ed.): *The Antarctic Treaty Regime*, 1987, 28–48.

Laws, Richard M.: 'The Ecology of the Southern Ocean', *American Scientist*, Jan.–February 1985, 26–40.

Lewis, Richard S.: 'Antarctic research and the relevance of science', *Science and Public Affairs*, Vol. XXVI, No. 10, December 1970, 2–4.

Lillie, Harry R.: 'The Antarctic in World Affairs', *Canadian Geographical Journal*, Vol. 36, 1948, 283–294.

Lissitzyn, O. J.: 'The American position in outer space and Antarctica', Editorial comment, *American Journal of International Law*, Vol. 53, 1959, 126–131.

Llano, George A.: 'Ecology of the Southern Ocean Region', *University of Miami Law Review*, Vol. 33, 1978, 357–369.

Logan, Hugh: 'Antarctica: why are we there?', *New Zealand International Review*, Vol. VII, No. 3, May/June 1982, 9–11.

Lopetegui Torres, Javier: 'Infraestructura antártica y política de acceso al continente', in Orrego et al. (eds): *Política Antártica de Chile*, 1985, 161–177.

Luard, Evan: 'Who owns the Antarctic?', *Foreign Affairs*, Summer 1984, 1174–1193.

Lundquist, Thomas R.: 'The Iceberg cometh?: International Law relating to Antarctic Iceberg exploitation', *Natural Resources Journal*, Vol. 17, January 1977, No. 1, 1–41.

Machowski, Jacek: 'The Status of Antarctica in the light of international law', National Center for scientific, technical and economic information. Warsaw, Poland, 1977 (translated from Polish).

Mac-Kechnie, Russell W. Jr: 'Sovereignty in Antarctica: the Anglo-Argentine dispute', Comment, *Syracuse Journal of International Law and Commerce*, Vol. 5, No. 1, Summer 1977, 119–148.

Macedo, de Soares Guimaraes L. F.: 'The Antarctic Treaty System from the perspective of a New Consultative Party', in U.S. Polar Research Board: *Antarctic Treaty System, An assessment*, 1986, 337–344.

MacKenzie, William H., **Rootes,** Rebecca S.: 'Implementing the Convention on Conservation of Antarctic Marine Living Resources: the legislative process', in Lewis M. Alexander, Lynne Carter Hanson (eds): *Antarctic Politics and Marine Resources: critical choices for the 1980s*, 1985, 129–141.

Machin, Alastair: 'Preferred futures: an environmental view', in *The Antarctic: preferred futures, constraints and choices*, New Zealand Institute of International Affairs, 1983, 69–74.

Macknis, Joseph: 'United States Policy in Antarctica', *Marine Policy Reports*, University of Delaware, Vol. 2, No. 2, May 1979.

Maddox, John: 'Antarctic mining regime at risk', *Nature*, Vol. 307, No. 5947, January 1984, 105–106.

Mahon, The Hon. Peter: 'The Antarctica air disaster – the role of the black box', Speech, *Law Institute Journal*, Vol. 56, No. 12, December 1982, 1069–1071.

Manzoni, Marcello: 'Rapporto Informativo sulle risorse minerarie ed energetiche dell'Antartide', Istituto di Geologia Marina, *Rapporto Tecnico*, No. 16, Bologna, 1981.

Maquieira, Cristián: 'Antarctica prior to the Antarctic Treaty: a political and legal perspective', in U.S. Polar Research Board: *Antarctic Treaty System, An Assessment*, 1986, 49–54.

Marcoux, J. Michel: 'Natural resource jurisdiction on the Antarctic continental margin', *Virginia Journal of International Law*, Vol. 11, 1971, 374–404.

Martin, Laura H.: 'Sovereignty in Antarctica', *Journal of Geography*, Vol. 29, No. 3, 1930, 112–120.

Martínez Moreno, Raúl: 'Soberanía Antártica Argentina', Tucumán, 1951.

Meira Mattos, Carlos de: 'O hemisferio sul e o equilibrio do poder', *Politica e Estrategia*, Vol. 2, No. 1, Jan–Mar. 1984, 115–121.

Menon, K. S. R.: 'The Scramble for Antarctica', *South*, April 1982, 11–13.

Mercado Jarrín, Edgardo: 'La Antártida: intereses geopolíticos', in Ibid.: *El Perú y la Antártida*, 1984, 107–146.

Milenky, Edward S. and **Schwab,** Steven I.: 'Latin America and Antarctica', *Current History*, Vol. 82, No. 481, February 1983, 52–53, 89–90.

Miles, P. and **Wright,** N. J. R.: 'An outline of mineral extraction in the Arctic', *Polar Record*, Vol. 19, 1978, 11–38.

Mitchell, Barbara: 'Resources in Antarctica. Potential for conflict', *Marine Policy*, Vol. 1, 1977, 91–101.

Mitchell, Barbara: 'Antarctic riches – for whom?', Forum, *Mazingira*, August 1977, 71–77; also reprinted in U.S. Senate: *Hearing on Exploitation of Antarctic resources*, 1978, 70–76.

Mitchell, Barbara: 'La Antártida, Bien común?', *Mazingira*, No. 2, 1977, 70–78.

Mitchell, Barbara: 'Antarctic enlightenment?', *New Scientist*, 20 October 1977, 130; also reprinted in U.S. Senate: *Hearing on Exploitation of Antarctic Resources*, 1978, 69.

Mitchell, Barbara: 'Attention on Antarctica', *New Scientist*, 22 September 1977, 714; reprinted in U.S. Senate: *Hearing on Exploitation of Antarctic Resources*, 1978, 68.

Mitchell, Barbara: 'Antarctica: a special case?', *New Scientist*, Vol. 73, No. 1034, 13 January 1977, 64–66; reprinted in U.S. Senate: *Hearing on Exploitation of Antarctic Resources*, 1978, 65–67; also published in *Environment*, 22, Jan.–Feb. 1980, 12–20.

Mitchell, Barbara: 'Cracks in the Ice', *The Wilson Quarterly*, Autumn 1981, 69–84.

Mitchell, Barbara: 'The Southern Ocean in the 1980s', *Ocean Yearbook*, 3, 1982, 349–385.

Mitchell, Barbara: 'The Management of Antarctic Mineral Resources', International Institute for Environment and Development, 1982.

Mitchell, Barbara: 'The Antarctic Treaty: victim of its own success?', in Lewis M. Alexander, Lynne Carter Hanson (eds): *Antarctic Politics and Marine Resources: critical choices for the 1980s*, 1985, 13–21.

Mitchell, Barbara and **Kimball,** Lee: 'Conflict over the cold continent', *Foreign Policy*, No. 35, Summer 1979, 124–141.

Mitchell, Barbara and **Sandbrook,** Richard: 'Statement on behalf of the International Institute for Environment and Development on Antarctic Living Marine Resources Negotiations', in United States Senate: *Antarctic Living Marine Resources Negotiations*, Hearing 1978, 39–45.

Molinari, Angel Ernesto: 'Antártida argentina, una esperanza en peligro', *Geopolítica*, Año X, No. 30, 1984, 51–53.

Moncayo, Guillermo R.: 'La situación jurídica de la Antártida', *Estrategia*, No. 43/44, Nov.-Dic. 1976/Enero–Feb. 1977, 47–59.

Moneta, Carlos J.: 'América Latina y el Sistema Internacional en la década del ochenta: Hacia un nuevo orden antártico?', *Estudios Internacionales*, No. 52, Oct.–Dic. 1980, 481–526.

Moneta, Carlos J.: 'Antártida, América Latina e o sistema internacional na decada de oteinta: Para una nove orden Antártica?', *Revista Brasileira de Politica Internacional*, 89–92, 129–174.

Moneta, Carlos J.: 'Antarctica, Latin America, and the International System in the 1980s. Toward a New Antarctic Order?', *Journal of Interamerican Studies and World Affairs*, Vol. 23, No. 1, February 1981, 29–68.

Moore, Joan E.: 'The Polar regions and the law of the Sea', Note, *Case Western Reserve Journal of International Law*, Vol. 8, 1976, 204–219.

Moro, Rubén Oscar: 'Geopolítica transpolar', *Geopolítica*, No. 9/10, 7–12.

Mosley, Geoff: 'The natural option: the case for Antarctic World park', in Stuart Harris (ed.): *Australia's Antarctic Policy Options*, A.N.U., 1984, 307–327.

Mouton, M. W.: 'The International Regime of the Polar Regions', *Recueil des Cours de l'Academie de Droit International*, 1962-III, Vol. 107, 169–284.

Movchan, A. P.: 'The Legal Status of Antarctica: an International Problem', *Soviet Yearbook of International Law*, 1959, 342–356 (Russian text); 356–359 (English summary).

Muller, Scharnhorst: 'The Impact of UNCLOS III on the Antarctic Regime', Comment, in Rudiger Wolfrum (ed.): *Antarctic Challenge*, 1984, 169–176.

McElroy, James: 'Krill – still an enigma', Viewpoint, *Marine Policy*, Vol. 6, No. 3, July 1982; reprinted in International Institute for Environment and Development: *Antarctica, a continent in transition*, 1983.

McElroy, James K.: 'Antarctic fisheries. History and prospects', *Marine Policy*, Vol. 8, 1984, 239–258.

Nagata, Takesi: 'The Advancement of scientific research as the basis of Antarctic development', in Francisco Orrego Vicuña (ed.): *El desarrollo de la Antártica*, 1977, 70–131.

Nagata, Takesi: 'The implementation of the Convention on the Conservation of Antarctic Marine Living Resources: needs and problems', in Francisco Orrego Vicuña (ed.): *Antarctic Resources Policy*, 1983, 119–137.

National Wildlife Federation: 'Ranger Rick', Special issue on Antarctica, February 1984.

New Zealand: 'The Antarctic Treaty', *New Zealand Foreign Affairs Review*, June 1972, 19–35.

New Zealand Institute of International Affairs: 'Seminar on the Antarctic: preferred futures, constraints and choices. Victoria University of Wellington, 17–18 June 1983', Report of the proceedings, *New Zealand International Review*, Vol. VIII, No. 5, Sept.–Oct. 1983, 2–5.

Nicholson, I. E.: 'Address to a conference on Antarctic Mineral resources organized by the Australian Mining and Petroleum Association', Sydney, 20 March 1985, Mimeo.

Nilo F., Liliana: 'Protección del ambiente antártico y expediciones no gubernamentales', *Boletín Antártico Chileno*, Vol. 4, No. 1, Enero–Junio 1984, 45–55.

Núñez, Liliana: 'El Territorio Chileno Antártico', *Memorandum preparado para el Ministerio de Relaciones Exteriores*, Mimeo, 1959.

Odishaw, Hugh: 'The International Geophysical Year and World Politics', *Journal of International Affairs*, Vol. 13, 1959, 47–56.

Operti, Patricia A.: 'Pretensiones chilenas en Antártida'. *Revista de Derecho Internacional y Ciencias Diplomáticas*, Vol. XXIX, No. 50–51, 1981, 89–96.

Orheim, Olav: 'Norwegian Antarctic research. Past and Present', in Francisco Orrego Vicuña (ed.): *El Desarrollo de la Antártica*, 1977, 154–160.

Orrego Vicuña, Francisco et **Infante,** María Teresa: 'Le Droit de la Mer dans l'Antarctique', *Revue Generale de Droit International Public*, 1980, 340–350.

Orrego Vicuña, Francisco: 'El Futuro de la Antártica', Instituto de Estudios Internacionales de la Universidad de Chile, *Serie de Publicaciones Especiales*, No. 48, 1980.

Orrego Vicuña, Francisco: 'La proyección extracontinental de Chile. Interpretación de la política marítima, antártica y del Pacífico', Discurso de incorporación a la Academia de Ciencias Sociales del Instituto de Chile, 27 de Julio de 1983, in *Diplomacia*, Publicación de la Academia Diplomática de Chile, No. 29, 1983, 33–48; also in in Francisco Orrego Vicuña et al. (ed.): *Política Antártica de Chile*, 1985, 15–34.

Orrego Vicuña, Francisco: 'Antarctic Resources Policy: An Introduction', in Francisco Orrego Vicuña (ed.): *Antarctic Resources Policy*, 1983, 1–10.

Orrego Vicuña, Francisco: 'The application of the law of the sea and the Exclusive Economic Zone to the Antarctic continent', in Francisco Orrego Vicuña (ed.): *Antarctic Resources Policy*, 1983, 243–251.

Orrego Vicuña, Francisco: 'The definition of a regime on Antarctic mineral resources: basic options', in Francisco Orrego Vicuña (ed.): *Antarctic Resources Policy*, 1983, 199–215.

Orrego Vicuña, Francisco: 'The Antarctic Treaty System: a viable alternative for the regulation of resource orientated activities', in Gillian Triggs (ed.): *The Antarctic Treaty Regime*, 1987, 65–76.

Orrego Vicuña, Francisco: 'Antarctic conflict and international cooperation', in U.S. Polar Research Board: *Antarctic Treaty System, An Assessment* 1986, 55–64.

O'Shea, Luz: 'El Patrimonio común de la humanidad y la Antártica', Research paper, Institute of International Studies of the University of Chile, graduate program, 17 August 1983.

Oxman, Bernard H.: 'The Antarctic Regime: An Introduction', *University of Miami Law Review*, Vol. 33, 1978, 285–297.

Palermo, Vicente A.: 'Latinoamérica puede más: geopolítica del atlántico sur', in F. A. Milia et al.: *La Atlantártida. Un Espacio Geopolítico*, 1978, 163–194.

Palermo, Vicente: 'El continente antártico en el contexto internacional contemporáneo', *Geopolítica*, Año III, Abril–Agosto 1978, No. 5, 35–46.

Palermo, Vicente: 'El futuro del continente antártico', *Geopolítica*, Buenos Aires, Año VI, No. 18, Junio 1980, 45–55.

Palermo, Vicente: 'La Argentina y la Antártida', *Geosur*, Año II, No. 23, Julio 1981, 3–21.

Pallone, Frank: 'Resource exploitation: the threat to the legal regime of Antarctica', *Connecticut Law Review*, Vol. 10, 1978, 401–417; also published in *Manitoba Law Journal*, Vol. 7, 1976, 597–610.

Parfond, P.: 'La Terre Adélie et le droit international', *La Revue Maritime*, n.s., Tome 50, Juin 1950, 741–752.

Peel, David A.: 'Antarctic ice: the frozen time capsule', *New Scientist*, 1983, Vol. 98, No. 1358, 477–483.

Peterson, M. J.: 'Antarctica: the last great land rush on earth', *International Organization*, Vol. 34, 1980, 377–403.

Peterson, M. J.: 'Antarctic implications of the new Law of the Sea', *Ocean Development and International Law*, Vol. 16, 1986, 137–181.

Pfirter de Armas, Frida M.: 'La situación jurídica de la Antártida y el nuevo derecho del mar', *Facultad de Derecho y Ciencias Sociales del Rosario*, 1982.

Pharand, Donat: 'L'Arctique et l'Antarctique: patrimoine commun de l'humanité?', *Annals of Air and Space Law*, Vol. VIII, 1982, 415–430.

Pincheira, Guido: 'La investigación científica como fundamento de una política nacional antártica', in Orrego et al. (eds): *Política Antártica de Chile*, 1985, 121–130.

Pinochet de la Barra, Oscar: 'Bases para el desarrollo económico de la Antártica en una perspectiva político-jurídica', in Francisco Orrego Vicuña (ed.): *El Desarrollo de la Antártica*, 1977, 357–366.

Pinochet de la Barra, Oscar: 'Evolución político-jurídica del problema antártico', *Estudios Internacionales*, Vol. XIV, No. 55, Julio–Sep. 1981, 380–393.

Pinochet de la Barra, Oscar: 'Algunas reflexiones sobre el problema de la Antártica en el año 2.000', in Francisco Orrego Vicuña (ed.): *La Antártica y sus recursos*, 1983, 355–367.

Pinochet de la Barra, Oscar: 'Antecedentes históricos de la política internacional de Chile en la Antártica: negociaciones Chileno-Argentinas de 1906, 1907 y 1908', in Orrego et al. (eds): *Política Antártica de Chile*, 1985, 67–80.

Pinochet de la Barra, Oscar: 'La contribución de Chile al Tratado Antártico', in Orrego et al. (eds): *Política Antártica de Chile*, 1985, 89–100.

Pinto, M. C. W.: 'The International Community and Antarctica', *University of Miami Law Review*, Vol. 33, 1978, 475–487.

Pontecorvo, Giulio: 'The Economics of the resources of Antarctica', in Jonathan I. Charney (ed.): *The new nationalism and the use of common spaces*, 1982, 155–166.

Potter, Neal: 'Natural Resource Potentials of the Antarctic', *The American Geographical Society*, 1969.

Potter, Neal: 'Economic potentials of the Antarctic', *Antarctic Journal of the United States*, Vol. IV, No. 3, May–June 1969, 61–72.

Potter, Neal: 'The Antarctic: any economic future?', *Science and Public Affairs*, Vol. XXVI, No. 10, December 1970, 94–99.

Poupin Berttoni, Marcia: 'Poblamiento antártico', in Orrego et al. (eds): *Política Antártica de Chile*, 1985, 115–118.

Powell, D. L.: 'Scientific and economic considerations relating to the conservation of marine living resources in Antarctica', in Francisco Orrego Vicuña (ed.): *Antarctic Resources Policy*, 1983, 111–118.

Prescott, J. R. V.: 'Actual and potential political boundaries in the Antarctic region', *The Globe, Journal of the Australian Map Circle*, No. 21, 1984, 12–26.

Prescott, J. R. V.: 'Boundaries in Antarctica', in Stuart Harris (ed.): *Australia's Antarctic Policy Options*, A.N.U., 1984, 83–111.

Ptitsyn, V.: 'The legal regime in Antarctic waters and questions regarding the exploitation of marine resources', *Morskoy Flot*, 1965, No. 3, 17–18 (translation from Russian).

Purver, Ron: 'Security and arms control at the poles', *International Journal*, Vol. 39, 1984, 888–910.

Qasim, S. Z. and **Rajan,** H. P.: 'The Antarctic Treaty System from the perspective of a new member', in U.S. Polar Research Board: *Antarctic Treaty System, An Assessment*, 1986, 345–374.

Quilty, Patrick: 'Mineral resources of the Australian Antarctic Territory', in Stuart Harris (ed.): *Australia's Antarctic Policy Options*, A.N.U., 1984, 165–203.

Ramacciotti de Cubas, Beatriz: 'Recursos naturales antárticos: problemas y posibilidades', *Revista Peruana de Derecho Internacional*, Vol. XXXV, Julio–Setiembre 1983, 29–40.

Ramacciotti de Cubas, Beatriz: 'Algunas consideraciones sobre la explotación de los recursos naturales de la Antártica y la protección del medio ambiente', in Edgardo Mercado Jarrín et al.: *El Perú y la Antártida*, 1984, 63–86.

Ramalhete, Clovis: 'A Antartica e o Brasil', *Revista de Informacao Legislativa do Senado Federal*, 1975, Vol. 12, No. 48, 41–56.

Ramírez, Lucía: 'El SCAR y el desarrollo de la cooperación en materia científica', in Orrego et al. (eds): *Política Antártica de Chile*, 1985, 131–146.

Ratiner, Leigh: 'Statement at press briefing Seminar on the Future of Antarctica', *Earthscan*, 25 July 1977.

Reeves, J. S.: 'George V Land', Editorial Comment, *American Journal of International Law*, Vol. 28, 1934, 117–119.

Reeves, J. S.: 'Antarctic Sectors', Editorial Comment, *American Journal of International Law*, Vol. 33, 1939, 519–521.

Reich, R. J.: 'Tourism in the Antarctic: its present impact and future development', *Dissertation*, Diploma in Polar Studies, Scott Polar Research Institute, Cambridge, 1979.

Retamal, Eugenio: 'Algunos aspectos de la ingeniería antártica', in Orrego et al. (eds): *Política Antártica de Chile*, 1985, 147–159.

Reynolds, John M.: 'On the history of the economic use of natural ice', *Iceberg Research*, 1983, No. 3, 3–4.

Ribeiro de Bakker, Mucio P.: 'O Brasil na antártica', *Política e Estrategia*, Vol. 2, No. 1, Jan–Mar. 1984, 172–200.

Rich, Roland: 'A minerals regime for Antarctica', *International and Comparative Law Quarterly*, Vol. 31, 1982, 709–725.

Richardson, Ivor L. M.: 'New Zealand's claims in the Antarctic', *New Zealand Law Journal*, Vol. XXXIII, February 19, 1957, No. 3, 38–42.

Riesco, Ricardo: 'Chile y sus perspectivas geográficas frente al Pacífico y la Antártica', *Revista de Geografía Norte Grande*, No. 7, 1980, 49–56.

Riesco J., Ricardo: 'Geopolítica austral y antártica', *El Mercurio*, Santiago, Chile, 29 de mayo de 1984; *Boletín Antártico Chileno*, Vol. 4, No. 2, Julio–Diciembre 1984, 14–17.

Riesco, Ricardo: 'La geografía antártica como base de nuevas orientaciones políticas', in Orrego et al. (eds): *Política Antártica de Chile*, 1985, 103–114.

Riesco, Ricardo: 'Perspectiva geopolítica del diferendo austral', *Boletín Antártico Chileno*, Vol. 5, No. 2, Jul.–Dic. 1985, 9–11.

Roberts, Brian: 'Chronological list of Antarctic expeditions', *Polar Record*, Vol. 9, 1958, 97–134/191–239.

Roberts, Brian: 'International cooperation for Antarctic development: the test for the Antarctic Treaty', in Francisco Orrego Vicuña (ed.): *El Desarrollo de la Antártica*, 1977, 336–356; also published in *Polar Record*, Vol. 19, 1978, 107–120.

Roberts, Brian B.: 'Conservation in the Antarctic', *Phil. Trans. Royal Society, London*, B. 279, 1977, 97–104.

Roberts, Nigel: 'New Zealand interest in Antarctica', *New Zealand International Review*, Vol. VIII, No. 5, Sep.–Oct. 1983, 6–12.

Rodas, Joao Grandino: 'Brasil adere ao Tratado da Antártida', *Revista da Faculdade de Direito*, Universidade de Sao Paulo, 1976, No. 71, 151–161.

Rodríguez, Bernardo N.: 'Soberanía argentina en la Antártida', in F. A. Milia et al.: *La Atlantártida. Un espacio geopolítico*, 1978, 195–216.

Rodríguez, Juan Carlos: 'La República Argentina y las adquisiciones territoriales en el continente antártico', Buenos Aires, 1941.

Romero, Pedro: 'Presencia de Chile en la Antártica', in Orrego et al. (eds): *Política Antártica de Chile*, 1985, 35–50.

Romero Julio, Pedro: 'Síntesis de la historia antártica de Chile', Instituto de investigaciones del Patrimonio Territorial de Chile, Universidad de Santiago, *Colección 'Terra Nostra'*, No. 6, 1985.

Romero Julio, Pedro: 'La Investigación Científica Antártica', *Instituto Antártico Chileno*, 1986.

Roots, E. F.: 'Resource development in polar regions: comments on technology', in Francisco Orrego Vicuña (ed.): *Antarctic Resources Policy*, 1983, 297–315.

Roots, E. Fred: 'The role of science in the Antarctic Treaty System', in U.S. Polar Research Board: *Antarctic Treaty System, An Assessment*, 1986, 169–184.

Rose, Julia: 'Antarctic Condominium: building a new legal order for commercial interests', *Marine Technology Society Journal*, Vol. 10, No. 1, January 1976, 19–27.

Rowland, J. R.: 'Whither Antarctica? Alternative strategies', in Gillian Triggs (ed.): *The Antarctic Treaty Regime*, 1987, 218–226.

Ruiz Eldredge, Alberto: 'Régimen internacional de la Antártida y principios esenciales para la administración internacional de dicho continente', in Edgardo Mercado Jarrín et al.: *El Perú y la Antártida*, 1984, 163–184.

Rutford, Robert H.: 'Summary of Science in Antarctica prior to and including the I.G.Y.', in U.S. Polar Research Board: *Antarctic Treaty System, An Assessment*, 1986, 87–101.

Rutford, Robert H.: 'United States Antarctic Program', in Lewis M. Alexander, Lynne Carter Hanson (eds): *Antarctic Politics and Marine Resources: critical choices for the 1980s*, 1985, 55–64.

Rybakov, Yuri M.: 'Juridical nature of the 1959 Treaty System', in U.S. Polar Research Board: *Antarctic Treaty System, An Assessment*, 1986, 33–45.

Sabaté Lichtschein, Domingo: 'La cuestión de la soberanía estatal y del dominio privado en la antártida', Santa Fé, Argentina, 1960.

Sahrhage, Dietrich: 'Present Knowledge of living marine resources in the Antarctic, possibilities for their exploitation and scientific perspectives', in Rudiger Wolfrum (ed.): *Antarctic Challenge*, 1984, 67–88.

Sahrhage, Dietrich: 'Fisheries overview', in Lewis M. Alexander, Lynne Carter Hanson (eds): *Antarctic Politics and Marine Resources: critical choices for the 1980s*, 1985, 101–112.

Sanderson, T. J. O.: 'Offshore oil development in polar regions', *New Zealand Antarctic Record*, Vol. 5, No. 1, 1983, 30–44.

Sarsfield, Mairuth: 'Cuál es el futuro del Tratado de la Antártida?', *La Sirena* (UNEP's Regional Seas Programme), No. 26, December 1984, 26–30.

Savin, O. G.: 'Marine living resources of the Antarctic regions: experience with conventional regulation of conservation and use', *Soviet Yearbook of International Law*, 1981, 187–200.

Schatz, Gerald S.: 'Transnational Science and Technology in the absence of defined sovereignty: developments in the Polar Regions and in legally similar situations', in Gerald S. Schatz (ed.): *Science, Technology, and Sovereignty in the Polar Regions*, 1974, 1–13.

Schatz, Gerald S.: 'The polar regions and human welfare: regimes for Environmental Protection', in Edmund A. Schofield: *Earthcare: global protection of natural areas*, 1978, 465–478.

Scheihing Navarro, Rubén: 'Importancia de la Antártica', *Revista de Marina*, 1985/3, 354–377.

Schlaich, Eleonore: 'Mineral resource policy in the Antarctica: common heritage of mankind or area of "frozen" economic nationalism?', Essay, MSc degree, International Relations, London School of Economics and Political Science, 1984, unpublished.

Schroff, G. W.: 'Antarctica: politics and resources', Royal College of Defence Studies, *Seaford House Papers*, 1982, 99–125.

Schwob, William S., **Tollerton,** Harry M.: 'A new focus on Antarctica', *United States Naval Institute Proceedings*, Vol. 105/12/922, December 1979, 42–45.

Scully, R. Tucker: 'The Marine Living Resources of the Southern Ocean', *University of Miami Law Review*, Vol. 33, 1978, 341–356.

Scully, R. Tucker: 'Alternatives for cooperation and institutionalization in Antarctica: outlook for the 1990s', in Francisco Orrego Vicuña (ed.): *Antarctic Resources Policy*, 1983, 281–296.

Scully, R. Tucker: 'The Antarctic Treaty System: overview and analysis', in Lewis M. Alexander, Lynne Carter Hanson (eds): *Antarctic Politics and Marine Resources: critical choices for the 1980s*, 1985, 3–11.

Scully, R. Tucker: 'The evolution of the Antarctic Treaty System – the institutional perspective', in U.S. Polar Research Board: *Antarctic Treaty System, An Assessment*, 1986, 391–411.

Sebenius, James K.: 'Financial aspects of Antarctic Mineral regimes', Appendix to Barbara Mitchell: *The Management of Antarctic Mineral Resources*, International Institute for Environment and Development, January 1982.

Shackleton, Edward: 'The New Continent', *United Nations World*, Vol. 1, No. 10, July 1949, 380–382.

Shackleton, Edward: 'Antarctica: the case for permanent international control – A possible solution', *World Affairs*, No. 243, May–June 1958, 23–25.

Shackleton, Lord: 'The Falkland Islands and Antarctica', *Proceedings of the Royal Institution*, Vol. 56, 1984, 147–160.

Shapley, Deborah: 'Antarctica: World Hunger for oil spurs security council review', *Science*, Vol. 184, May 17, 1974, 776–779; also in United States Senate: *U.S. Antarctic Policy*, Hearing 1975, 31–33.

Shapley, Deborah: 'India in Antarctica: international treaty still on ice', *Nature*, Vol. 301, No. 5899, 3 February 1983, 362.

Shapley, Deborah: 'Antarctica: up for grabs', *Science*, November 1982; reprinted in International Institute for Environment and Development: *Antarctica, a continent in transition*, 1983.

Shapley, Deborah: 'Pax Antarctica', *Bulletin of the Atomic Scientists*, June–July 1984, Vol. 40, No. 6, 30–33.

Shusterich, Kurt M.: 'The Antarctic Treaty System: history, substance, and speculation', *International Journal*, Vol. 39, 1984, 800–827.

Sierra Club: 'Summary of Meeting on Environmental Policy Considerations in the Antarctic region', 15 June 1976.

Sierra Club: 'Resolution on Antarctica', undated.

Simsarian, James: 'Inspection experience under the Antarctic Treaty and the International Atomic Energy Agency', *American Journal of International Law*, Vol. 60, 1966, 502–510.

Simmonds, K. R.: 'The Antarctic Treaty, 1959', *Journal du Droit International*, 1960, No. 3, 668–701.

Skagestad, Gunnar: 'Small States in International Politics: a Polar–Political Perspective', *Cooperation and Conflict*, 2/3, 1974, 133–141.

Skagestad, Gunnar: 'The Frozen Frontier: Models for International Cooperation', *Cooperation and Conflict*, 3, 1975, 167–187.

Skagestad, Gunnar and **Traavik,** Kim: 'New Problems – Old Solutions', *Cooperation and Conflict*, 2/3, 1974, 39–51.

Slevich, S. B.: 'Basic problems of Antarctica Exploitation', Joint Publications Research Service, Arlington, Virginia, 6 June 1974 (translation from Russian).

Slevich, S. B.: 'Economic geography of the southern ocean', *Polar Geography and Geology*, Vol. 8, January–March 1984, 54–62.

Smith, Philip M. and **Dana,** John B.: 'Airbus: an international air transportation system for Antarctica', *Antarctic Journal of the United States*, Vol. VIII, 1973, 16–19.

Smith, Philip M.: 'International cooperation in Antarctica. The Next Decade', *Science and Public Affairs*, Vol. XXVI, No. 10, December 1970, 29–32.

Sollie, Finn: 'Arctic and Antarctic. Current problems in the Polar Regions', *Cooperation and Conflict*, 2, 1969, 124–144.

Sollie, Finn: 'The political experiment in Antarctica', *Science and Public Affairs*, Vol. XXVI, No. 10, December 1970, 16–21.

Sollie, Finn: 'The New Development in the Polar Regions', *Cooperation and Conflict*, 2/3, 1974, 23–37.

Sollie, Finn et al.: 'The Challenge of New Territories', Oslo, 1974; also published in *Cooperation and Conflict*, 2/3, 1974.

Sollie, Finn: 'The political problems of Antarctica', *Fridtjof Nansen Foundation*, 1977.

Sollie, Finn: 'Trends and prospects for regimes for living and mineral resources in the Antarctic', in John King Gamble Jr: *Law of the Sea: Neglected Issues*, 1979, 193–208.

Sollie, Finn: 'The legal status of the Antarctic', SCAR: *Biological Investigations of Marine Antarctic Systems and Stocks*, Vol. II, February 1981, 1–7.

Sollie, Finn: 'Jurisdictional problems in relation to Antarctic mineral resources in political perspective', in Francisco Orrego Vicuña (ed.): *Antarctic Resources Policy*, 1983, 317–335.

Sollie, Finn: 'The Development of the Antarctic Treaty System: Trends and Issues', in Rudiger Wolfrum (ed.): *Antarctic Challenge*, 1984, 17–37.

Sollie, Finn: 'Polar politics: old games in new territories, or new patterns in political development?', *International Journal*, Vol. 39, 1984, 695–720.

Sollie, Finn: 'The duration of the Antarctic Treaty. An analysis of the amendment and revision procedures in a political perspective', *Fridtjof Nansen Foundation*, Study AA: P108/2 (E), undated.

Soto, Alvaro de: 'Statement at Earthscan Seminar on Antarctic Resources and the Environment', Washington D.C., 14 September 1979.

Soto, Alvaro de: 'Las riquezas de la Antártida', *Política Internacional* (Yugoslavia), No. 726-7, 5–20 VII, 1980, 38–41.

Spencer, Cisca: 'The evolution of Antarctic interest', in Stuart Harris (ed.): *Australia's Antarctic Policy Options*, A.N.U., 1984, 113–129.

Splettstoesser, John F.: 'Mining in Antarctica: Survey of Mineral resources and possible exploitation methods', *Third International Conference on Port and Ocean Engineering under Arctic Conditions*, 11–15 August 1975, Vol. II, 1137–1155, University of Alaska.

Splettstoesser, John F.: 'Offshore development for oil and gas in Antarctica', *Fourth International Conference on Port and Ocean Engineering under Arctic Conditions*, Memorial University of New Foundland, St. John's, Newfoundland, Canada, Sep. 26–30, 1977, Vol. II, 811–820.

Splettstoesser, John F.: 'Underground technology for offshore hydrocarbon development in Antarctica', *Fifth International Conference on Port and Ocean Engineering under Arctic Conditions*, Norwegian Institute of Technology, 1979, Vol. 3, 233–245.

Splettstoesser, John F.: 'Antarctic geology and mineral resources', *Geology Today*, Mar–Apr. 1985, 41–45.

Staub, H. Gerald: 'The Antarctic Treaty as precedent to the outer space treaty', *Proceedings of the seventeenth Colloquium on the Law of Outer Space*, International Institute of Space Law, Oct. 1–4, 1974, Amsterdam, 1975, 282–287.

Stone, Jeffrey E.: 'Convention on the Conservation of Antarctic Marine Living Resources', Notes on recent development, *Harvard International Law Journal*, Vol. 22, 1981, 195–200.

Sullivan, Walter: 'Antarctica in a two-power world', *Foreign Affairs*, Vol. 36, 1957–1958, 154–166.

Sullivan, Walter: 'The International Geophysical Year', *International Conciliation*, No. 521, January 1959, 259–336.

Suter, K. D.: 'World Law and the last wilderness', 1980 (Friends of the Earth, Sydney).

Suter, Keith D.: 'The Antarctic: a crisis for the 1980s?', *Journal of the Royal United Services Institute*, March 1981, 39–44.

Suter, Keith D.: 'The Antarctic: A public policy problem for Australia in the 1980s', in R. A. Herr, R. Hall, B. W. Davis (eds): *Issues in Australia's Marine and Antarctic Policies*, Public Policy Monograph, Univ. of Tasmania, 1982, 101–137.

Swithinbank, Charles: 'The Antarctic connection', in *The Geography of the Falkland Islands, Geographical Journal*, 1983, Vol. 149, pt. 1, 8–9.

Symmons, C. R.: 'Who owns the Falkland Island Dependencies in International Law? An analysis of certain recent British and Argentinian official statements', *International and Comparative Law Quarterly*, Vol. 33, Part 3, July 1984, 726–736.

Taijudo, Kamae: 'Japan and the problems of sovereignty over the polar regions', *The Japanese Annual of International Law*, No. 3, 1959, 12–17.

Talboys, B. E.: 'New Zealand and the Antarctic Treaty', Address by the Minister of Foreign Affairs to the New Zealand Antarctic Society, 26 April 1978, *New Zealand Foreign Affairs Review*, July–Sep. 1978, 29–35.

Taubenfeld, Howard J.: 'A treaty for Antarctica', *International Conciliation*, No. 531, January 1961, 245–322.

Taylor, Stephen: 'Cruzada Antártica de Greenpeace', London Observer Service, *El Mercurio*, Santiago, Chile, 7 January 1986, p. A2.

Tessensohn, Franz: 'Present knowledge of non-living resource in the Antarctic, possibilities for their exploitation and Scientific Perspectives', in Rudiger Wolfrum (ed.): *Antarctic Challenge*, 1984, 189–210.

Tetra Tech: 'The Antarctic krill resource: prospects for commercial exploitation', Final Report, February 1978, in United States Senate: *Antarctic Living Marine Resources Negotiations*, Hearing, 1978, 237–379.

Thakur, Ramesh and **Gold,** Hyam: 'The Antarctic Treaty regime: exclusive preserve or common heritage?', *Foreign Affairs Reports* (New Delhi), Vol. 32, No. 11-12, Nov.–Dec. 1983, 169–186.

'Thaw in International Law? Rights in Antarctica under the Law of Common Spaces', *The Yale Law Journal*, Vol. 87, 1977–1978, 804–859.

'The Antarctic: preferred futures, constraints and choices', *Proceedings of a seminar held by the New Zealand Institute of International Affairs*, Wellington, 17–18 June 1983, New Zealand Institute of International Affairs, 1983.

'The growing riches of Antarctica', *New Scientist*, Vol. 90, No. 1256, 4 June 1981, 621.

Theutenberg, Bo Johnson: 'The evolution of the Law of the Sea with special regard to the polar areas', in René-Jean Dupuy (ed.): *The settlement of disputes on the new natural resources*, Academie de Droit International, Colloque, 1982, 1983, 377–424.

Thomson, R. B.: 'United States and New Zealand Cooperation in Environmental Protection', *Antarctic Journal of the United States*, Vol. VI, No. 3, May–June 1971, 59–62.

Thomson, R. B.: 'Transport and tourism in Antarctic development', in Francisco Orrego Vicuña (ed.): *El Desarrollo de la Antártica*, 1977, 290–294.

Thomson, R. B.: 'The development of living resources of Antarctic Krill, in Francisco Orrego Vicuña (ed.): *El Desarrollo de la Antártica*, 1977, 182–185.

Thomson, R. B.: 'Antarctic mineral resources: possibilities and problems', *New Zealand International Review*, Vol. VII, No. 3, May/June 1982, 7–8.

Thomson, R. B.: 'New Zealand and Antarctic environmental protection', New Zealand Antarctic Record, Vol. 5, No. 1, 1983, 46–51.

Thomson, Michael and **Swithinbank,** Charles: 'The prospects for Antarctic minerals', *New Scientist*, 1 Apr. 1985, No. 1467, 31–35.

Tinker, Jon: 'Antarctica: towards a new internationalism', *New Scientist*, Vol. 83, No. 1172, 13 September 1979, 799–801.

Tinker, Jon: 'Cold war over Antarctic wealth', *New Scientist*, Vol. 83, No. 1173, 20 September 1979, 867–868.

Tolstikov, E. I.: 'Antarctica is continent of peace', in *The Antarctic Committee Reports*, No. 17, 1984, 19–27.

Toma, Peter A.: 'Soviet attitude towards the acquisition of territorial sovereignty in the Antarctic', *American Journal of International Law*, Vol. 50, 1956, 611–626.

Toro Alvarez, Carlos de: 'Vinculación histórica del territorio continental y la Antártica', in Orrego et al. (eds): *Política Antártica de Chile*, 1985, 51–65.

Traavik, Kim: 'Antarctica and the International Seabed regime', *Internasjonal Politikk*, Oct.–Dec. 1974, No. 4, 783–800 (Norwegian).

Triggs, Gillian: 'Australian Sovereignty in Antarctica', *Melbourne University Law Review*, Vol. 13, 1981–1982, 123–158 (Part I); 302–333 (Part II).

Triggs, Gillian: 'Australian Sovereignty in Antarctica: traditional principles of territorial acquisition versus a "common heritage" ', in Stuart Harris (ed.): *Australia's Antarctic Policy Options*, A.N.U., 1984, 29–66.

Triggs, Gillian: 'The Antarctic Treaty system: some jurisdictional problems', in ibid. (ed.): *The Antarctic Treaty Regime*, 1987, 88–109.

Triggs, Gillian: 'The Antarctic Treaty Regime: a workable compromise or a "Purgatory of Ambiguity" '?, *Case Western Reserve Journal of International Law*, Vol. 17, 1985, 195–228.

Trolle Andersen, Rolf: 'The Antarctic Scene: legal and political facts', in Gillian Triggs (ed.): *The Antarctic Treaty Regime*, 1987, 57–64.

Tunkin, G. I.: 'An example of International Co-operation', *International Affairs* (USSR), 1960, 2, 42–45.

Turner, Mort D.: 'Antarctica Mineral Resources', *Frontiers*, Vol. 43, No. 1, Autumn 1978, 27–29.

U.K. Liberal Party, Foreign Affairs Panel: 'The Falkland Islands. A secure and peaceful future', August 1984.

'U.S. and private ventures', *Antarctic*, Vol. 6, No. 4, December 1971, 119.

U.S. House of Representatives. Committee on Foreign Affairs, Subcommittee on National Security Policy and Scientific Development: *The Political Legacy of the International Geophysical Year*, Prepared by Harold Bullis, Nov. 1973.

Valenzuela, Juan Guillermo: 'La política antártica chilena y las bases de una estructura administrativa', in Orrego et al. (eds): *Política Antártica de Chile*, 1985, 297–305.

Van der Essen, Alfred: 'Le probleme politico-juridique de l'Antarctique et le Traité de Washington du 1er décembre 1959', *Annales de Droit et de Sciences Politiques*, Tome XX, No. 3, 1960, 227–252.

Van der Essen, Alfred: 'L'Antarctique et le Droit de la Mer', *Revue Iranienne de Relations Internationales*, No. 5–6, 1975–1976, 89–98.

Van der Essen, Alfred: 'Les reunions consulatives du traité sur l'Antarctique', *Revue Belge de Droit International*, Vol. XV, 1980, 20–27.

Van der Essen, Alfred: 'The application of the law of the sea to the Antarctic continent', in Francisco Orrego Vicuña (ed.): *Antarctic Resources Policy*, 1983, 231–242.

Van der Essen, A.: 'Les regions arctiques et antarctiques', in René-Jean Dupuy et Daniel Vignes: *Traité de Nouveau Droit de la Mer*, 1985, 463–496.

Van der Essen, Philippe: 'L'economie des regions polaires, realisations et perspectives', *Chronique de Politique Etrangere*, Vol. XXV, 1972, 391–545.

Vedovato, Giuseppe: 'L'Antartide oggi', *Rivista di Studi Politici internazionali*, Vol. XLVII, No. 2, 1980, 215–223.

Vidas, Davor: 'The legal status of Antarctica with special reference to the Antarctic sea-bed and its subsoil', in Budislav Vukas (ed.): *Essays on the New Law of the Sea*, 1985, 504–536.

Vignes, Daniel: 'La Convention sur la Conservation de la faune et de la flore marines de l'Antarctique', *Annuaire Francais de Droit International*, 1980, 741–772.

Villacres M., **Jorge** W.: 'Los Derechos del Ecuador en la Antártida', Instituto de Diplomacia, 1979, Mimeo.

Vittone, José Carlos: 'La soberanía argentina en el continente antártico', Buenos Aires, 1944.

Voelckel, Michel: 'L'Inspection en Antarctique', in Georges Fischer et Daniel Vignes (eds.): *L'Inspection Internationale*, Bruxelles 1976, 223–246.

Wadhams, Peter: 'The resource potential of Antarctic icebergs', *Iceberg Research*, No. 10, April 1985, 9–23.

Waldock, C. H. M.: 'Disputed Sovereignty in the Falkland Islands Dependencies', *The British Year Book of International Law*, 1948, 311–353.

Wall, E. H.: 'The Polar regions and International Law, Editorial Notes, *The International Law Quarterly*, Vol. 1, 1947, 54–58.

Walton, D. W. H.: 'The first south Georgia leases: Compañía Argentina de Pesca and the South Georgia Exploring Company Limited', *Polar Record*, Vol. 21, No. 132, 1982, 231–240.

Washburn, A. L.: 'Focus on Polar Research', *Science, Reprint Series*, 8 August 1980, Vol. 209, 643–652.

Wassermann, Ursula: 'The Antarctic Treaty and Natural Resources', *Journal of World Trade Law*, Vol. 12, 1978, 174–179.

Watts, A. D.: 'Antarctic mineral resources: negotiations for a mineral resources regime', in Gillian Triggs (ed.): *The Antarctic Treaty Regime*, 1987, 164–175.

Watts, Arthur D.: 'The Antarctic Treaty as a conflict resolution mechanism', in U.S. Polar Research Board: *Antarctic Treaty System, An Assessment*, 1986, 65–75.

Westermeyer, William: 'Resource allocation in Antarctica. A review', *Marine Policy*, Vol. 6, 1982, 303–325.

Westermeyer, William E.: 'Alternative regimes for future mineral resource development in Antarctica', *Ocean Management*, Vol. 8, 1982–1983, 197–232.

Westermeyer, William E.: 'Energy from the polar regions', *International Journal*, Vol. 39, 1984, 721–741.

National **Wildlife** Federation: 'Resolution No. 2 on Antarctica', undated.

World **Wildlife** Fund News: 'The Question of krill', *World Wildlife Fund News*, No. 24, July/August 1983; reprinted in International Institute for Environment and Development: *Antarctica, a continent in transition*, 1983.

Wilson, Gregory P.: 'Antarctica, The Southern Ocean, and the Law of the Sea', *The JAG Journal*, Vol. 30, 1978, 47–85.

Wilson, Robert E.: 'National interests and claims in the Antarctic', *Arctic*, Vol. 17, 1964, 15–32.

Wolfrum, Rudiger: 'The use of Antarctic Non-Living Resources: The Search for a Trustee?, in Ibid. (ed.): *Antarctic Challenge*, 1984, 143–163.

Wolk, S.: 'The Basis of Soviet claims in the Antarctic', *Bulletin of the Institute for the Study of the USSR*, Vol. 5, April 1958, No. 4, 43–48.

Woolcott, Richard: 'The Interaction between the Antarctic Treaty System and the United Nations System', in U.S. Polar Research Board: *Antarctic Treaty System, An Assessment*, 1986, 375–390; also published in *Australian Foreign Affairs Record*, No. 56, Jan. 1985, 17.

Woolcott, Richard: 'The future of the Antarctic Treaty System. One Consultative Party Outlook', in Lewis M. Alexander, Lynne Carter Hanson (eds): *Antarctic Politics and Marine Resources: critical choices for the 1980s*, 1985, 225–232.

Wright, N. A. and **Williams,** P. L.: 'Mineral Resources of Antarctica', U.S. Geological Survey, Circular 705, 1974, in United States Senate: *U.S. Antarctic Policy*, Hearing 1975, 35–67.

Wyndham, R. H.: 'The Antarctic', in Coral Bell (ed.): *Agenda for the eighties*, A.N.U., 1980, 179–196.

Young, Allan: 'Antarctic resource jurisdiction and the Law of the Sea: a question of compromise', *Brooklyn Journal of International Law*, Vol. XI, 1985, 45–78.

Zain-Azraii: 'Antarctica: the claims of "expertise" vs. "interest"', in Gillian Triggs (ed.): *The Antarctic Treaty Regime*, 1987, 211–217.

Zain-Azraii, Datuk: 'The future of the Antarctic Treaty System. The Malaysian Perspective', in Lewis M. Alexander, Lynne Carter Hanson (eds): *Antarctic Politics and Marine Resources: critical choices for the 1980s*, 1985, 232–237.

Zain-Azraii: The Antarctic Treaty System from the perspective of a State not party to the system', in U.S. Polar Research Board: *Antarctic Treaty System, An Assessment*, 1986, 305–313.

Zamora Lazo, Arnoldo: 'Proyección peruana a la Antártida', *Geosur*, Año II, No. 23, Julio 1981, 41–43.

Zavatti, Silvio: 'La spedizione antartica italiana e il diritto internazionale', *Il Polo*, Vol. 32, No. 2, Giugno 1976, 44–46.

Zegers, Fernando: 'The Antarctic System and the Utilization of Resources', *University of Miami Law Review*, Vol. 33, 1978, 426–473.

Zegers, Fernando: 'The Canberra Convention: objectives and political aspects of its negotiation', in Francisco Orrego Vicuña (ed.): *Antarctic Resources Policy*, 1983, 149–156.

Zegers, Fernando: 'La Comunidad internacional y la antártida', in Orrego et al. (eds): *Política Antártica de Chile*, 1985, 277–287.

Zorn, Stephen A.: 'Antarctic minerals. A common heritage approach', *Resources Policy*, Vol. 10, No. 1, March 1984, 2–18.

Zuccaro, Emil A.: 'Iceberg appropriation and the Antarctic's Gordian Knot', Comment, *California Western International Law Journal*, Vol. 9, 1979, 405–429.

Zumberge, James H.: 'Potential mineral resources availability and possible environment problems in Antarctica', in Jonathan I. Charney (ed.): *The new nationalism and the use of common spaces*, 1982, 115–154.

Zumberge, James H.: 'The Antarctic Treaty as a scientific mechanism – SCAR and the Antarctic Treaty System', in U.S. Polar Research Board: *Antarctic Treaty System, An Assessment*, 1986, 153–168.

Index

Wherever the word *Treaty* is used in this index without qualification, it is to be understood as referring to the Antarctic Treaty of 1959.

A page number in italic refers to a diagram or a map.